# PRINCIPLES OF MACROECONOMICS
## EDITION 3

**FRED M. GOTTHEIL**
UNIVERSITY OF ILLINOIS

SOUTH-WESTERN
THOMSON LEARNING

Australia · Canada · Mexico · Singapore · Spain · United Kingdom · United States

*To my wife, Diane*

*To my children, Lisa and Joshua,
who grew up together, not just as
sister and brother, but as best friends.*

Vice President/Publisher: Jack W. Calhoun
Acquisitions Editor: Michael Worls
Senior Marketing Manager: Lisa L. Lysne
Developmental Editor: Andrew J. McGuire
Production Editor: Elizabeth A. Shipp
Media Technology Editor: Vicky True
Media Developmental Editor: Peggy Buskey
Media Production Editor: John Barans
Manufacturing Coordinator: Sandee Milewski
Internal Design: Michael H. Stratton
Cover Design: Michael H. Stratton
Cover Images: © PhotoDisc, Inc.
Production House: Lachina Publishing Services, Inc.
Printer: QuebecorWorld-Taunton, MA

Copyright © 2002 by South-Western, a division of Thomson Learning.
The Thomson Learning logo is a registered trademark used herein under license.

All Rights Reserved. No part of this work covered by the copyright hereon may be reproduced or used in any form or by any means—graphic, electronic, or mechanical, including photocopying, recording, taping, or information storage and retrieval systems—without the written permission of the publisher.

Printed in the United States of America
1 2 3 4 5 04 03 02 01

**Library of Congress Cataloging-in-Publication Data**

Gottheil, Fred M.
    Principles of macroeconomics / Fred M. Gottheil.—3rd ed.
       p.  cm.
    Includes index.
    ISBN 0-324-10677-7
    1. Macroeconomics.   I. Title.

HB172.5.G68 2002
339—dc21
2001020826

For more information contact South-Western, 5101 Madison Road, Cincinnati, Ohio, 45227 or find us on the Internet at http://www.swcollege.com

For permission to use material from this text or product, contact us by
- telephone: 1-800-730-2214
- fax: 1-800-730-2215
- web: http://www.thomsonrights.com

# BRIEF CONTENTS

## PART 1 — THE BASICS OF ECONOMIC ANALYSIS — 1

1. INTRODUCTION — 2
2. PRODUCTION POSSIBILITIES AND OPPORTUNITY COSTS — 24
3. DEMAND AND SUPPLY — 44

## PART 2 — EMPLOYMENT, INFLATION, AND FISCAL POLICY — 73

4. AGGREGATE DEMAND AND AGGREGATE SUPPLY — 75
5. GROSS DOMESTIC PRODUCT ACCOUNTING — 100
6. CONSUMPTION AND INVESTMENT — 122
7. EQUILIBRIUM NATIONAL INCOME — 147
8. FISCAL POLICY: COPING WITH INFLATION AND UNEMPLOYMENT — 171
9. LONG-RUN ECONOMIC GROWTH AND BUSINESS CYCLES — 196

## PART 3 — MONEY, BANKING, AND MONETARY POLICY — 221

10. MONEY — 223
11. MONEY CREATION AND THE BANKING SYSTEM — 245
12. THE FEDERAL RESERVE SYSTEM AND MONETARY POLICY — 266

## PART 4 — GOVERNMENT AND THE MACROECONOMY — 297

13. CAN GOVERNMENT REALLY STABILIZE THE ECONOMY? — 287
14. GOVERNMENT SPENDING — 327
15. FINANCING GOVERNMENT: TAXES AND DEBT — 346

## PART 5 — THE WORLD ECONOMY — 369

16. INTERNATIONAL TRADE — 371
17. EXCHANGE RATES, BALANCE OF PAYMENTS, AND INTERNATIONAL DEBT — 400
18. THE ECONOMIC PROBLEMS OF LESS-DEVELOPED ECONOMIES — 425

PRACTICE TEST ANSWER KEY — AK-1
GLOSSARY — G-1
INDEX — I-1
PHOTO CREDITS — PC-1

# CONTENTS

## PART 1 — THE BASICS OF ECONOMIC ANALYSIS    1

### 1  INTRODUCTION  2

No One Ever Made an Ounce of Earth  3
*Are We Running Out of Natural Resources?  3
Renewable and Nonrenewable Natural Resources  3*
**Historical Perspective: Coal . . . Then (1865) and Now (2000)  4**  *How Do You Satisfy Insatiable Wants?  5*  **Theoretical Perspective: If Not the Depletion of Coal, Then Perhaps Oil  5**  *Scarcity Forces Us to Make Choices  6*

What Is Economics?  6
*Economics Is Part of Social Science  6  Using Economic Models  7  Ceteris Paribus  8  The Circular Flow Model of Goods and Money  8  Microeconomics and Macroeconomics  10*  **Theoretical Perspective: The Link Between the Circular Flow Model and Adam Smith's Views on Self-Interest, Public Interest, and the Invisible Hand  11**  *Positive and Normative Economics  12*

What Do Economists Know?  12

*Chapter Review  13    Key Terms  14    Questions  14
Practice Problem  15*  **Economic Consultants: Economic Research and Analysis by Students for Professionals  15**  *Practice Test  16*

Appendix
On Reading Graphs  17

The Only Thing We Have to Fear Is Fear Itself  17
*A Graphic Language  17  Know Your Point of Reference  17  Measuring Distances on Graphs  18  Graphing Relationships  18  Connecting Points to Form Curves  19*

The Slope of a Curve  20
*U-Shaped and Hill-Shaped Curves  22  Vertical and Horizontal Curves  22  Measuring the Slope of a Point on a Curve  23*

*Key Terms  23*

### 2  PRODUCTION POSSIBILITIES AND OPPORTUNITY COSTS  24

Factors of Production  25
*Labor  25    Capital  25    Land  26
Entrepreneurship  26*

Robinson Crusoe's Production Possibilities  26
*Opportunity Cost  27    The Law of Increasing Costs  28*
**Applied Perspective: Did You Ever Find a Penny on a Sidewalk?  29    Theoretical Perspective: Guns and Butter  30**    *Once Rich, It's Easy to Get Richer  32  Once Poor, It's Easy to Stay Poor  32*

The Productive Power of Advanced Technology  33
*The Indestructible Nature of Ideas  34*

Possibilities, Impossibilities, and Less Than Possibilities  34
**Historical Perspective: The Destruction and Reconstruction of Rotterdam  35**

Production Possibilities and Economic Specialization  36
*Specialization on the Island  37    International Specialization  37    The Principle of Comparative Advantage  37*

The Universality of the Production Possibilities Model  39

*Chapter Review  39    Key Terms  40    Questions  40
Practice Problems  41    What's Wrong with This Graph?  42*  **Economic Consultants: Economic Research and Analysis by Students for Professionals  42**    *Practice Test  43*

### 3  DEMAND AND SUPPLY  44

Measuring Consumer Willingness  45

Measuring Consumer Demand  45
*Measuring Individual Demand  45    Measuring Market Demand  46*

Measuring Supply  47
*Market-Day Supply  47*

Determining Equilibrium Price  48
*Suppose the Price Is $8  48    Suppose the Price Is $4  49
Price Always Tends Toward Equilibrium  50*

Market-Day, Short-Run, and Long-Run Supply  50

**Theoretical Perspective: How Long Does It Take to Get to the Long Run?  52**

Changes in Demand  53
*Changes in Income  54    Changes in Taste  54*  **Interdisciplinary Perspective: Whether It's Love or Wisdom, the Answer Is Fish  55**  *Changes in the Prices of Other Goods  55    Changes in Expectations About Future Prices  56    Changes in Population Size  56    A Change in Demand or a Change in Quantity Demanded?  56*

Changes in Supply  57
*Changes in Technology  57    Changes in Resource Prices  58    Changes in the Prices of Other Goods  58    Changes in the Number of Suppliers  58*

Why the Price of an Orange Is 30 Cents at the Supermarket  58

Postscript: Price as a Rationing Mechanism  60

*Chapter Review  62    Key Terms  63    Questions  63    Practice Problems  64    What's Wrong with This Graph?  65*  **Economic Consultants: Economic Research and Analysis by Students for Professionals  65**  *Practice Test  66*

Appendix
On Reading Graphs  67

How Much Is That Doggie in the Window?  67

The Case of the Guide Dog  67

From Dogs to Human Beings  69
*The Market for Organ Transplants  69*

Scalping Tickets at a Yankee Game  71
*Questions  72    Practice Problems  72*

---

**PART 2    EMPLOYMENT, INFLATION, AND FISCAL POLICY    73**

**4    AGGREGATE DEMAND AND AGGREGATE SUPPLY  75**

Why Recession? Why Prosperity?  76
*The Business Cycle  76    Economic Growth  77*

Measuring the National Economy  77
**Interdisciplinary Perspective: The Phenomenon of Cyclical Activity  78**  *Adjusting for Prices  79    From Nominal to Real GDP  80*  **Applied Perspective: What's in the CPI Basket?  81**

Deriving Equilibrium GDP in the Aggregate Demand and Supply Model  82
*Explaining Aggregate Supply  83    Explaining Aggregate Demand  85*  **Global Perspective: Economic Success? Depends on What You Measure  86**  *Shifts in the Aggregate Demand and Aggregate Supply Curves  87*

Macroeconomic Equilibrium  89
**Applied Perspective: "If Winter Comes, Can Spring Be Far Behind?"  90**

Equilibrium, Inflation, and Unemployment  91
*The Depression of the 1930s  91    Demand-Pull Inflation: The Vietnam War  92    Cost-Push Inflation: The OPEC Legacy  93    The Recession and Economic Stagnation of the Early 1990s  93*

Can We Avoid Unemployment and Inflation?  94

*Chapter Review  96    Key Terms  96    Questions  96    Practice Problems  97    What's Wrong with This Graph?  98*  **Economic Consultants: Economic Research and Analysis by Students for Professionals  98**  *Practice Test  99*

**5    GROSS DOMESTIC PRODUCT ACCOUNTING  100**

Two Approaches to Calculating GDP  101

The Expenditure Approach  101
*Counting Final Goods and Services  101    The Four Expenditure Categories of GDP  103*  **Historical Perspective: The Wealth of Nations  105
Theoretical Perspective: An Expanded Circular Flow  106**

The Income Approach  108
*Compensation of Employees  109    Interest  109    Corporate Profit  109    Rent  110    Proprietors' Income  110*

Bringing GDP and National Income into Accord  110
*From GDP to GNP  110*  **Global Perspective: Is the 2000 Composition of GDP for the United States Unique?  111**  *From GDP to NDP  112    From NDP to National Income  113    GDP, GNP, NNP, and National Income for 2000  113*

Personal Income and Personal Disposable Income  113

How Comprehensive Is GDP?  114
*Value of Housework  114    The Underground Economy  115    Leisure  115*  **Applied Perspective:**

*Underground Economy Doing Thriving Business 116* Quality of Goods and Services 117 Costs of Environmental Damage 117

Chapter Review 118    Key Terms 118    Questions 119    Practice Problems 119    **Economic Consultants: Economic Research and Analysis by Students for Professionals 120**    Practice Test 121

## 6   CONSUMPTION AND INVESTMENT 122

What Determines Consumption Spending? 123
*Keynes's Absolute Income Hypothesis 123    Duesenberry's Relative Income Hypothesis 125    **Historical Perspective: John Maynard Keynes: A New Macroeconomics 127**    Friedman's Permanent Income Hypothesis 128    Modigliani's Life-Cycle Hypothesis 130    Autonomous Consumption Spending 130    Shifts in the Consumption Curve 130    **Theoretical Perspective: The Long and Short of It: The Consumption Function in the United States 132***

The Consumption Equation 133

What Determines the Level of Saving? 134
***Historical Perspective: Propensity to Save 136***

The Investment Function 137

What Determines Investment? 137
*Determinants of Investment 138    The Volatile Nature of Investment 140*

Combining Consumption Spending and Investment Spending 140

Chapter Review 141    Key Terms 142    Questions 142    Practice Problems 143    What's Wrong with This Graph? 144    **Economic Consultants: Economic Research and Analysis by Students for Professionals 145**    Practice Test 146

## 7   EQUILIBRIUM NATIONAL INCOME 147

Interaction Between Consumers and Producers 148

The Economy Moves Toward Equilibrium 149
*How Consumers and Producers Behave When Y = $900 Billion 149    **Applied Perspective: Interview with the Author's Brother, Irving Gottheil, CEO of the Artistic Hat Company, Montreal, Canada 150**    How Consumers and Producers Behave When Y = $700 Billion 151    How Consumers and Producers Behave When Y = $800 Billion 152*

Equilibrium National Income 153

Changes in Investment Change National Income Equilibrium 155

*Y = $950 Billion: The New Equilibrium 156    **Interdisciplinary Perspective: A Fractured Version of the Exodus Story 157**    An Alternative Method of Calculating Equilibrium 158*

The Income Multiplier 158
*Deriving the Multiplier 158    What If MPC = 0.90? 160    **Global Perspective: How the Income Multiplier Intensifies the Impact of Aggregate Expenditure Shifts Within Different Economies 161**    The Income Multiplier Works in Either Direction 162    Aggregate Expenditure and Aggregate Demand 162*

The Paradox of Thrift 164
**Applied Perspective: GM's Money Machine 165**

Chapter Review 166    Key Terms 167    Questions 167    Practice Problems 168    What's Wrong with This Graph? 169    **Economic Consultants: Economic Research and Analysis by Students for Professionals 169**    Practice Test 170

## 8   FISCAL POLICY: COPING WITH INFLATION AND UNEMPLOYMENT 171

Equilibrium and Full Employment 172
*Identifying Unemployment 172    **Interdisciplinary Perspective: From John Steinbeck's Cannery Row 174**    Calculating an Economy's Rate of Unemployment 174    The Bureau of Labor Statistics Definition of Unemployment 175    The Natural Rate of Unemployment 175    Full-Employment Level 176*

Understanding Inflation 177
*Winners and Losers from Inflation 178    **Historical Perspective: Inflation and Hyperinflation 179***

Living in a World of Inflation and Unemployment 180
*Identifying the Recessionary Gap 181    Identifying the Inflationary Gap 181*

Closing Recessionary and Inflationary Gaps 182
***Historical Perspective: J.M. Keynes and Say's Law 183***    Enter Government 184    Government Spending Is Not Problem-Free 184    **Applied Perspective: The Record on Deficit Budgets Undermines the Idea That They Are Strictly Tools of Countercyclical Fiscal Policy 185**    Closing the Inflationary Gap 185*

Making Fiscal Policy 186
*Choosing the Tax Option 186    Full Employment, Zero Inflation, and a Balanced Budget 186    The Balanced Budget Multiplier 188    Balancing the Budget at $80 Billion 188    How to Get to Full-Employment National Income and Balance the Budget 188    Just a Spoonful*

*of Deficit Makes the Medicine Go Down 189   How Mixed Is the Mixed Economy? 189   Creating Surplus Budgets 190   Are Fiscal Policy Options Really That Straightforward? 190*

*Chapter Review 191   Key Terms 192 Questions 192   Practice Problems 192 What's Wrong with This Graph? 193* **Economic Consultants: Economic Research and Analysis by Students for Professionals 194** *Practice Test 195*

## 9 LONG-RUN ECONOMIC GROWTH AND BUSINESS CYCLES 196

Long-Run Economic Growth 197
*Creating the Environment for Long-Run Growth 197*   **Interdisciplinary Perspective: Political Uncertainty Hampers Quebec's Long-Run Economic Growth 199**   *What Causes Economic Growth? 200   A Simple Model of Economic Growth 200*   **Theoretical Perspective: A View From the Past: Zero Long-Run Economic Growth 203**   *U.S. Economic Growth: 1947–2000 204*   **Global Perspective: I've Got to Admit It's Getting Better, a Little Better All the Time 205**

The Business Cycle 206

Traditional Theories of the Business Cycle 207
*External Theories of Cycles 207*   **Applied Perspective: You Got the Dates? We Got the Growth Rates 208**   *Internal Cycles 210*

Real Business Cycle Theory 212

Countercyclical Fiscal Policy 213
**Interdisciplinary Perspective: Congressional Phase of an Administrative Lag 214**

*Chapter Review 216   Key Terms 216   Questions 216 Practice Problems 217   What's Wrong with This Graph? 218*   **Economic Consultants: Economic Research and Analysis by Students for Professionals 219**   *Practice Test 220*

---

## PART 3   MONEY, BANKING, AND MONETARY POLICY   221

## 10 MONEY 223

The Invention of Money 224
*Gold as Money 225   Gold-Backed Paper as Money 225*   **Historical Perspective: Fluffy Rabbits and Gresham's Law 226**   *Fiat, or Paper, Money 227*

Money in a Modern Economy 227
*Money and Liquidity 227   The Liquidity Character of Our Money Supply 228*   **Applied Perspective: Have You Written a Check Lately? 229**   *Money and "Near" Money 230   What Isn't Money? 230*   **Historical Perspective: Explaining the Impressive Growth of M2 Money 231**   *Adding Up Our Money Supply 231*

The Quantity Theory of Money 232
*The Velocity of Money 232*   **Applied Perspective: Money Challenge Quiz 234**   *The Classical View 235*   **Interdisciplinary Perspective: Velocity of Another Kind 236**   *Monetarism: A Modification of the Classical View 237   The Keynesian View 237*

The Demand for Money 238
*The Classical View 238   The Keynesian View 238*

*Chapter Review 241   Key Terms 241   Questions 241 What's Wrong with This Graph? 242*   **Economic Consultants: Economic Research and Analysis by Students for Professionals 243**   *Practice Test 244*

## 11 MONEY CREATION AND THE BANKING SYSTEM 245

How Banks Create Money 246
*Attracting Depositors 247   Making Loans 247*   **Theoretical Perspective: Virtual Banks Raise Regulatory Challenges 248**   *The Interaction of Deposits and Loans 249*

Reversing the Money Creation Process 252
**Interdisciplinary Perspective: If William Shakespeare Ran the Fed 253**

Why Banks Sometimes Fail 254
**Theoretical Perspective: Federal Deposit Insurance and Moral Hazard 255**

Safeguarding the System 255
*The Federal Deposit Insurance Corporation 256 Bank Audits and Examinations 256   Still, Banks Do Go Under 256*   **Global Perspective: Deposit Insurance, Assurance-Dépôts, Tutela Dei Depositi, Protección Al Ahorro Bancario, Etc., Etc. 258**

Controlling the Financial Institutions That Control the Money Supply 260

*Chapter Review 261   Key Terms 262   Questions 262 Practice Problems 263*   **Economic Consultants: Economic Research and Analysis by Students for Professionals 264**   *Practice Test 265*

## 12 THE FEDERAL RESERVE SYSTEM AND MONETARY POLICY 266

A Glimpse at History 267
*Continental Notes 268 The Chartering of State Banks 267 The First Bank of the United States 268 The Second Bank of the United States 268 The National Bank Act 269 The Knickerbocker Trust Disaster 270*

The Federal Reserve System 270
*Who Owns the Fed? 270 The Fed's Purpose and Organization 272 The Fed as Money Printer 273 The Fed as the Bankers' Bank 274* **Global Perspective: Check Out the Central Banks 276**

Controlling the Money Supply 278
*Changing the Legal Reserve Requirement 279 Changing the Discount Rate 279* **Applied Perspective: How the Interest Rate on Government Securities Is Determined 280** *Engaging in Open Market Operations 282*

Controlling the Interest Rate: The Fed's Alternative Target Option 284
*Choosing the Money Supply Option 285 Choosing the Interest Rate Option 285* **Applied Perspective: The U.S. Banking System in a Nutshell 286** *Is There Really a Preferred Target Option? 287 What the Fed Ended Up Choosing 287 Ancillary Tools Available to the Fed 287* **Applied Perspective: The Honorable Martha Seger: Ex-Fed Governor Tells It Like It Is 288**

The Fed's Countercyclical Monetary Policy 290
**Interdisciplinary Perspective: Politics at the Fed? 291** *The Fed and the Government Don't Always Agree 292*

*Chapter Review 293 Key Terms 294 Questions 294* **Economic Consultants: Economic Research and Analysis by Students for Professionals 295** *Practice Test 296*

---

## PART 4 GOVERNMENT AND THE MACROECONOMY 297

## 13 CAN GOVERNMENT REALLY STABILIZE THE ECONOMY? 298

The Nature of Economic Advice 299

Why Does the Economy Generate Inflation and Unemployment? 299

The Classical School 300
*Why Unemployment? 300 Why Inflation? 301*

The Keynesian School 302
*Why Unemployment? 304 Why Inflation? 304 The Economics of Fine-Tuning 305*

The Neo-Keynesian School 305
*Phillips Curve Trade-Offs 305 The Phillips Curve and Countercyclical Policy 308 The Humphrey-Hawkins Act of 1978 308 Long-Run Phillips Curves 309*

The Rational Expectations School 311
**Theoretical Perspective: The Power of an Idea: The 6 Percent Natural Rate of Unemployment 312** *Anticipation of Fiscal Policy Undermines the Policy 313* **Applied Perspective: Does the Phillips Curve Really Exist? 314** *Anticipation of Monetary Policy Undermines the Policy 315 A New Wrinkle to the Phillips Curve 315*

Supply-Side Economics 316 **Theoretical Perspective: An Exchange Between a Keynesian and a Rational Expectations (New Classical) Economist 317** *Lower Tax Rates 317 Less Government Regulation 318* **Global Perspective: NAIRU Estimates for OECD Economies 319** *Less Government Spending 319*

Is There a Macro Consensus? 320

Automatic Stabilizers 321
*Unemployment Insurance 321 Personal and Corporate Income Taxes 321*

*Chapter Review 322 Key Terms 323 Questions 323 What's Wrong with This Graph? 324* **Economic Consultants: Economic Research and Analysis by Students for Professionals 325** *Practice Test 326*

## 14 GOVERNMENT SPENDING 327

Government Spending and Public Goods 328

Government Spending and Merit Goods 329

Government Spending and Transfer Payments 329
**Global Perspective: Government Spending on the Arts 330**

Government Spending and the Public Debt 331

How Much Does Government Spend? 331
*Security 331 Education 333 Transportation, Natural Resources, and Space 333 Agriculture and Public Assistance 334* **Applied Perspective: Welfare Reform and Low-Skilled Employment 336** *Social Insurance 337* **Applied Perspective: Are the Social Security and Medicare Systems in Jeopardy? 338** *Interest 340*

Is the Level of Government Spending Too
High? 340
*The Growth of Government Spending 340   Government
Spending in Other Economies 341*

Government Spending and Resource Allocation 342

*Chapter Review 342   Key Terms 343   Questions 343
Economic Consultants: Economic Research and
Analysis by Students for Professionals 344
Practice Test 345*

## 15  FINANCING GOVERNMENT: TAXES AND DEBT 346

Opportunity Costs and Taxes 347

Commandeering Resources 347

The Tax System 348

There's More Than One Way to Levy Taxes 348
*The Poll (or Head) Tax 348   The Income Tax 348
The Corporate Income Tax 349   **Applied Perspective: Are We Really Paying High Taxes? 350**
The Property Tax 350   Excise Taxes 351*

The Social Security Tax 351

Actually, Everything Is Taxable! 352

The U.S. Tax Structure 352

Federal, State, and Local Tax Revenues 353
***Interdisciplinary Perspective: Don't Mess with the
IRS: Al Capone's Ultimate Mistake 354***

Taxes, Spending, and Deficits 355

Financing Government Spending Through
Debt 355
*Treasury Bonds, Bills, and Notes 356*

Tracking Government Debt 356
*Looking at Ratios, Not Dollars 357*

Does Debt Endanger Future Generations? 358
***Global Perspective: Hatred of Tax Collection Is
the Way of the World 359***   *Are There No Problems
with Incurring Debt? 361   External Debt Is a Different
Matter 362*

Are Deficits and Debt Inevitable? 363
*The Tax Reforms of 1981 and 1986 363   Congressional
Attempts to Reduce the Deficit 364   The Clinton Era 364*

*Chapter Review 365   Key Terms 365   Questions 366
Economic Consultants: Economic Research and
Analysis by Students for Professionals 367
Practice Test 368*

## PART 5   THE WORLD ECONOMY                                  369

## 16  INTERNATIONAL TRADE 371

Intrastate Trade 372
*Illinois Corn for Illinois Oil 372   Oklahoma Corn for
Oklahoma Oil 373*

Interstate Trade 373
*The Case for Geographic Specialization 373   Nobody
Loses? 375*

International Trade 375

Absolute and Comparative Advantage 376
*Comparative Advantage 376   How Much Is Gained
from Free Trade Depends on Price 377*

Calculating Terms of Trade 378
*The Dilemma of the Less-Developed Countries 378
Looking at Real-World Numbers 379*

Who Trades with Whom? Tracking International
Trade 380
*The Major Leagues 381*

Who Does the United States Trade With? 381
***Interdisciplinary Perspective: Trade and
Culture 382***

Do We Need Protection Against Free Trade? 383

*The National Security Argument 384   The Infant
Industries Argument 384   The Cheap Foreign
Labor Argument 385   The Diversity-of-Industry
Argument 385   The Antidumping Argument 385
The Retaliation Argument 386*

The Economics of Trade Protection 386
*Tariffs 386   Quotas 387   Other Nontariff Barriers 388*

Negotiating Tariff Structures 389
*GATT 389   GATT Concessions to Less-Developed
Countries 389   **Global Perspective: How
Much Do Barriers to Imports Cost Japanese
Consumers? 390**   Customs Unions 391   Free
Trade Areas 392   The North American Free Trade
Agreement 392*

Tracking Tariffs Since 1860 392
***Applied Perspective: Is NAFTA Worker
Friendly? 394***

*Chapter Review 395   Key Terms 396   Questions 396
Practice Problems 397   What's Wrong with This
Graph? 397   Economic Consultants: Economic
Research and Analysis by Students for Professionals 398   Practice Test 399*

## 17 EXCHANGE RATES, BALANCE OF PAYMENTS, AND INTERNATIONAL DEBT 400

The Money Tower of Babel 401

The Foreign Exchange Market: The Buying and Selling of Currencies 401
*The Demand Curve for Yaps 401 The Supply Curve of Yaps 402 Shifts in the Demand Curve for Yaps 402 Shifts in the Supply Curve of Yaps 403*

Floating Exchange Rates 404
*Depreciation and Appreciation 404* **Applied Perspective: Tourists at the Mall 405** *Arbitrage Creates Mutually Consistent Exchange Rates 406 Problems with Floating Exchange Rates 406 Fixing Exchange Rates 406* **Global Perspective: Brazil and the IMF 408** *What If the Government Runs Out of Foreign Exchange Reserves? 409*

Balance of Payments 409
*Balance on Current Account 410 Balance on Capital Account 413*

What Is a Balance of Payments Problem? 413
**Global Perspective: The Euro 414** *Do Trade Imbalances Always Create Problems? 415*

How Deficits on Current Account Develop 415
*The Trouble with Being Popular 415 The High Cost of High Interest Rates 416 The High Cost of Budgetary Deficits 416 The High Cost of Low Productivity 416*

International Debt 416

Will It All Work Out Right in the Long Run? 417
**Applied Perspective: Forgiving the International Debt of LDCs 418**

*Chapter Review 419 Key Terms 420 Questions 421 Practice Problems 421 What's Wrong with This Graph? 423* **Economic Consultants: Economic Research and Analysis by Students for Professionals 423** *Practice Test 424*

## 18 THE ECONOMIC PROBLEMS OF LESS-DEVELOPED ECONOMIES 425

Confronting National Poverty 426
*The Language of National Poverty 426 There Are Important Differences Among the Less-Developed Economies 426*

LCD Per Capita Incomes 427

Other Indicators of the LCDs' Lack of Economic Well-Being 429

Economic Dualism 430
**Applied Perspective: China's Population Policy: One Couple, One Child 431**

The Absence of Basic Prerequisites 433
*Political Instability 433 Nonscientific Perceptions 433 The Absence of Infrastructure 434* **Global Perspective: Internet and Infrastructure 435**

Pursuing Strategies of Development 436
*The Big Push 437 The Unbalanced Development Strategy 438* **Applied Perspective: The Road to Better Farming 440**

Foreign Direct Investment 441
*Images from the Colonial Past 441*

Foreign Economic Aid 442
**Global Perspective: Food for Peace 443**

*Chapter Review 444 Key Terms 445 Questions 445 What's Wrong with This Graph? 446* **Economic Consultants: Economic Research and Analysis by Students for Professionals 446** *Practice Test 447*

PHOTO CREDITS PC-1
PRACTICE TEST ANSWER KEY AK-1
GLOSSARY G-1
INDEX I-1

**University of Illinois
at Urbana-Champaign**

Department of Economics
Box 111
330 Commerce Building (West)
1206 South Sixth Street
Champaign, IL 61820

217-333-0120

Dear Student,

Economics is a part of your daily life, a part of how you make everyday decisions, a part of the way you think about and understand the world around you. Curious? If you are, this textbook is for you. There are no endless lists of facts here, no dry and obscure examples. Instead, you'll find stories, conversations, explanations, and powerful ideas. These are the tools and techniques that effectively teach economics.

Economics must be real, even personal. To truly understand economics—not just learn economic concepts and terminology, but understand the essence of economic thinking—you must relate on an emotional level to what you are learning. You must absorb the ideas in this book through your head, your heart, and your innards. Feel the ideas in your bones and relate them to what you know best—your life. Only then will you understand and remember economics, and only with this accomplishment will you enjoy your course in economics.

Over the next several weeks you will find that economics and economists have something important to say about how the world works. And with hard work, at the end of this journey you will be able to meaningfully join the conversation.

To help you along the way, I have included numerous learning aids in each chapter. Some features demonstrate the relevancy of what you are reading, some teach you how economic concepts apply to a variety of situations, some alert you to particularly important material, and some test your understanding of the principles presented in the chapter. In addition, you'll find that there are many additional print and technology resources available to enhance your learning experience. Look over the next few pages to become familiar with all of these aids. And enjoy! Economics is an exciting, inspiring, and relevant subject.

*Fred Gottheil*

# FEATURES YOU'LL FIND IN EACH CHAPTER

**PART OPENERS** "Economics Chat" Part Openers capture real-life student conversations about economics. "Economics Chat" helps demonstrate why the chapters that follow are important to you.

**LEARNING OBJECTIVES** Each chapter opens with "Learning Objectives" that introduce the key principles raised in the chapter. "Learning Objectives" do not highlight everything in the chapter, only the most important principles.

**CHECK YOUR UNDERSTANDING** "Check Your Understanding" features raise questions at key junctures in the text, questions you should be able to answer if you understand the material. For help, arrows point to the portion of the text that contains the explanation.

**INTERACTIVE EXAMPLES** "Your Turn" features provide an example of a concept discussed in the text, and then ask you to go to the Gottheil Web site to create and post an example of your own, as well as to see what examples other students have come up with.

**APPLICATIONS** "Perspective" boxed features show you how the economic principles introduced in the chapter relate to real-world events in many different contexts. You'll find 5 types of "Perspectives" in the book: historical, global, interdisciplinary, applied (business and daily life examples), and theoretical. Most "Perspectives" include a question for further consideration and Internet addresses for further exploration.

**KEY GRAPHS** All exhibits illustrate key graphical concepts in a clear, efficient manner. "Key Graphs" icons highlight those exhibits that demonstrate crucial principles.

**MARGIN DEFINITIONS** Margin Definitions define important vocabulary introduced in the chapter.

**ON THE NET** "On the Net" margin notes show you where to find and how to use the best economic resources on the Internet. You'll be surprised what information lies at your fingertips.

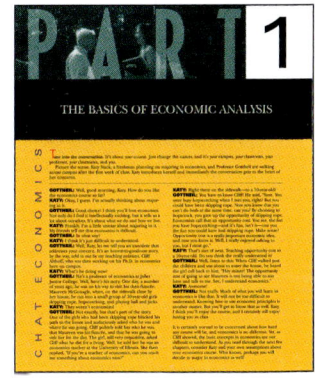

The Bureau of Labor Statistics provides recent and historical data on labor productivity.
http://stats.bls.gov/eag.table.html

> "I just wanted to comment on the structure and innovation that you have brought to learning. It has actually given me . . . a major reason to change my major to economics. This way of learning is the most interactive next to actually attending class."
>
> Justin—*Student, San Diego State University*

# END-OF-CHAPTER MATERIAL

**ECONOMIC CONSULTANTS ACTIVITIES**
"Economic Consultants" features place you in the role of the economist! "Economic Consultants" is a hypothetical economic research and analysis firm run by students for professionals. In your role, you need to prepare a report for a client that applies the fundamental economic issues you have learned in the chapter to his or her particular situation. Useful Internet addresses are included with these activities to help you with your research and analysis.

**CHAPTER REVIEW & KEY TERMS** Chapters end with a Chapter Review (a brief recounting of the principles covered in the chapter with explanation) and Key Terms (a list of the important vocabulary introduced in the chapter).

**QUESTIONS & PRACTICE PROBLEMS** Questions test your understanding of the qualitative concepts covered in the chapter. Practice Problems test your ability with quantitative and graphing techniques.

**WHAT'S WRONG WITH THIS GRAPH?** After the questions, a "What's Wrong with This Graph?" feature presents one of the chapter's key graphs with an error for you to correct. This activity tests your ability to read and understand graphs.

**PRACTICE TEST** To wrap up the chapter, a Practice Test presents 8–10 multiple choice problems, like those typically found on exams, addressing the key principles in the chapter. Answers are found in an appendix at the end of the textbook.

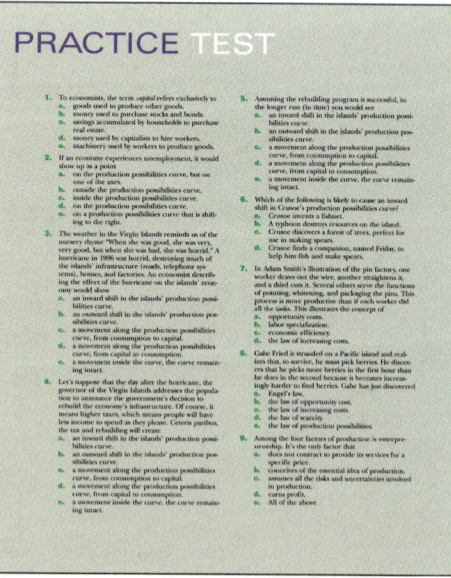

> "Good read. Excellent references to real events help me to understand application of the concepts described."
>
> Richard—*Student*
> *Oakland Community College*

> "Doing these Economic Consultants exercises has definitely helped me grasp the concepts after reading the chapters. Putting things into practice always helps."
>
> Becky—*Student*
> *San Diego State University*

# ADDITIONAL RESOURCES FOR STUDENTS

*The following list of additional print, multimedia, and online resources available with this text is designed to help you in your economics class:*

## Print, Multimedia, and Online Ancillary Products:

**STUDY GUIDE: TOOLS FOR SUCCESS IN ECONOMICS**
The Study Guide, available in a comprehensive version or in macroeconomics and microeconomics versions, explains, reviews, and tests the important principles introduced in every chapter. Featured sections include Chapter in a Nutshell, Concept Check, Am I on the Right Track?, Graphing Tutorials and Graphing Pitfalls, True/False Questions, Multiple Choice Questions, Fill-in-the-Blank Questions, and Discussion Questions.

**A sample chapter of the Study Guide is available in the Learning Resources section of the Gottheil Web site http://gottheil.swcollege.com**

**INFOTRAC COLLEGE EDITION**
If you bought a new copy of the InfoTrac College Edition of this text, don't forget to take advantage of your subscription. With InfoTrac College Edition, you can receive anytime, anywhere, online access to a database of full-text articles from hundreds of scholarly and popular periodicals. You can use its fast and easy search tools to find what you're looking for among the tens of thousands of articles—updated daily and dating back as far as four years—all in this single Web site. It's a great way to locate resources for papers and projects without having to travel to the library.

**To log on and get started, visit http://www.infotrac-college.com**

**THE WALL STREET JOURNAL EDITION**
If you bought a new copy of the special *Wall Street Journal* Edition of the Gottheil textbook, a 10-week subscription to both *The Wall Street Journal* Print and Interactive versions was included with your purchase. Be sure to take advantage of all *The Wall Street Journal* has to offer by activating your subscription to this authoritative publication that is synonymous with the latest word on business, economics, and public policy. It provides an excellent resource for you to observe economic concepts in action, in the real world, every day—and helps you prepare long-term for your successful economics/business career.

**To activate your subscription, visit http://wsj.swcollege.com**

 ### PERSONAL WEBTUTOR
This Web-based study guide reviews critical text material chapter by chapter. Concepts are reinforced through extensive exercises, problems, cases, flashcards, self-tests, and other tools. If an access certificate for Personal WebTutor™ did not come bundled with your textbook, you can preview and purchase the product directly online for subscription periods of 1 month or 4 months.

**For more details, visit http://pwt.swcollege.com**

 ### SMARTHINKING
Live online tutoring—get the help you need when you need it. Thomson Learning and Smarthinking have partnered to bring you the best academic assistance the Web has to offer. Purchasers of the Gottheil textbook are eligible for 1 free hour of online tutoring, as well as unlimited access to valuable online study resources. You can choose to get help in your subject, or in any subject Smarthinking covers: accounting, economics, mathematics, statistics, and psychology. Or get help with your writing through the online writing lab.

**To sign up, visit http://www.smarthinking.com/thomsonfreehour.html**

### ECONOMICS ALIVE! CD-ROMS
These interactive multimedia study aids for economics are the high-tech, high-fun way to study economics. Through a combination of animated presentations, interactive graphing exercises, and simulations, the core principles of economics come to life and are driven home in an upbeat and entertaining way.

Macroeconomics Alive! CD-ROM
ISBN: 0-538-86850-3

Microeconomics Alive! CD-ROM
ISBN: 0-538-84650-X

**For more details, visit the Economics Alive! Web site http://econalive.swcollege.com**

# TEXT-SUPPORTING WEB SITES:

**SOUTH-WESTERN'S ECONOMICS RESOURCE CENTER**

A unique, rich, and robust online resource for economics students, **http://economics.swcollege.com** provides customer service and product information, learning tips and tools, information about careers in economics, access to all of South-Western's text-supporting Web sites, and other cutting-edge educational resources, such as our highly regarded EconNews, EconDebate, EconData, and EconLinks online features.

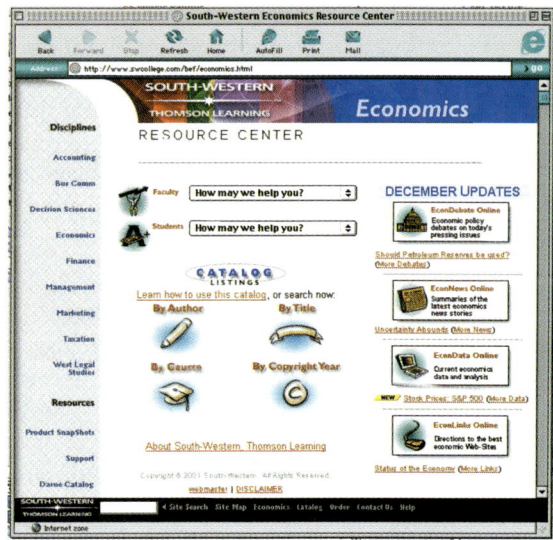

**GOTTHEIL SUPPORT WEB SITE**

The Gottheil Web site (**http://gottheil.swcollege.com**) provides you with open access to online study guide updates to the text, online quizzes with immediate student feedback, the opportunity to communicate with the author, direct links to all the Internet addresses and activities mentioned in the text, downloadable learning support tools, and much more.

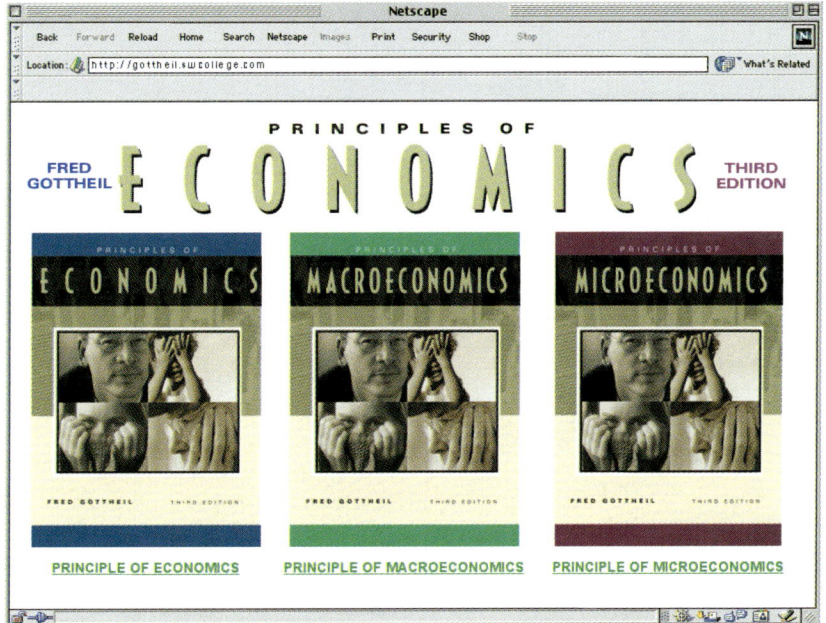

*"The Internet access and the online quizzes are wonderful. It helps me to know what of the chapter I understood and what I need to re-read and study better. Thank you so much for this wonderful tool."*

Jamie—*Student*
*Hope College*

**GOTTHEIL XTRA! CD-ROM**

Gottheil Xtra! CD-ROM, packaged with every new text, provides you with complimentary access to the robust set of additional online learning tools found at the site. If you don't have the CD, you can purchase access to the online version at **http://gottheil.swcollege.com**. Here is a tour through some of the study support features you will find there:

**The Graphing Workshop**

For most students, graphing is one of the most difficult aspects of the Principles course. The Graphing Workshop is your one-stop learning resource for help in mastering the language of graphs. You'll explore important economic concepts through a unique learning system made up of tutorials, interactive tools, and exercises that teach you how to interpret, reproduce, and explain graphs:

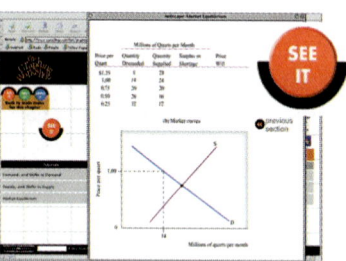

**SEE IT!** Animated graphing tutorials provide step-by-step graphical presentations and audio explanations.

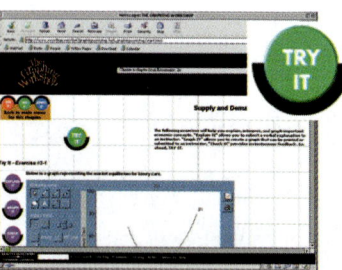

**TRY IT!** Interactive graphing exercises have you practice manipulating and interpreting graphs with GraphIt—a hands-on Java graphing tool. You can check your work online.

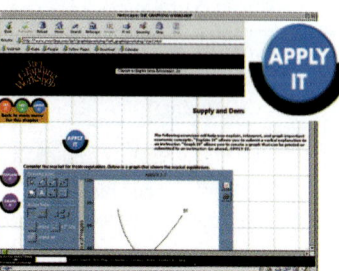

**APPLY IT!** Interactive graphing assignments challenge you to apply what you have learned by creating your own graph from scratch to analyze a specific scenario. You can print out and/or e-mail answers to your instructor for grading.

## Video Lecture and Applications

Via streaming video, difficult concepts from each chapter are explained and illustrated by the text author. These video clips can be extremely helpful review and clarification tools if you had trouble understanding an in-class lecture or if you are more of a visual learner who sometimes has difficulty grasping concepts as they are presented in the text. In addition, CNN video segments bring the "real world" right to your desktop. The accompanying CNN video exercises help to illustrate how economics is an important part of your daily life.

## Additional Self-Testing Opportunities

In addition to the open-access chapter-by-chapter quizzes found at the Gottheil Product Support Web site, Gottheil Xtra offers you an opportunity to practice for midterms and finals by taking online quizzes that span multiple chapters.

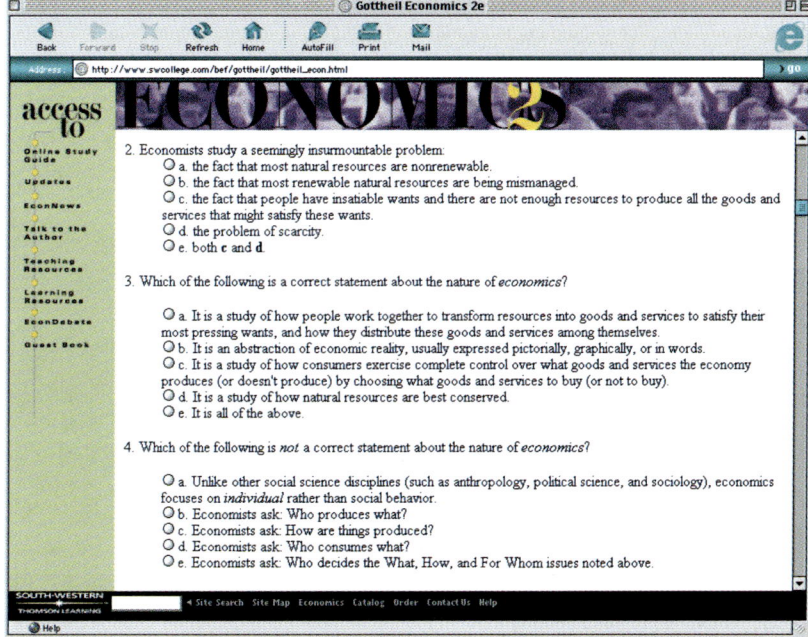

# TO THE INSTRUCTOR

At the end of fall semester a few years ago, I told my class of 1,000 Economics 101 students that I wanted to see how much of the course they would be able to recall 4 months after the final exam. I asked them to take a post-final exam in early April, covering the same material. A few hundred showed up to take the April exam. The results were instructive, and perhaps not too surprising.

These were very bright students. The scholastic entrance requirements to the University of Illinois are quite high. During the semester, they were able to handle the math and graphs without difficulty. Yet, when it came to the April exam—only 4 months after the final—there was much confusion explaining, and even more graphing, market equilibrium, national income determination, and other basic ideas.

If I ever thought that the analysis offered in lectures and in the textbook is what students really ingest during the semester, that thought was very quickly dispelled.

Why is the half-life of what we teach so short? Are we trying to teach too much? Is our basic principles course getting away from being an analysis of basic principles? Have we forgotten that there is an opportunity cost every time we add material to a course or textbook? Are our textbooks more plumbers' manuals on technique than analyses of a social science subject? What do we want our students to know?

## A Book Written for the Student

I wrote this textbook with the above questions in mind. It is written for the student, not for the professor. These are 2 very different readers. To my surprise, I found it difficult to keep the focus on the student who comes to the material without prior knowledge. It was much easier to write to the professor. Most of my rewriting had to do with correcting the focus. Much of the differences in style, content, and depth of analysis between my text and the others on the market reflect this focus. My preference was to sacrifice the number of topics for depth and to present the basics in as nonthreatening a style as possible. I tried always to keep the analysis within reach of students. Make it real, even personal. Allow them to enjoy the subject matter, not just to think about the coming exam.

We absorb ideas in many ways: through our heads, our hearts, and our innards. An idea that emotionally stirs you has staying power. If you can feel it in your bones, it becomes more than an intellectual exercise. I kept that in mind in every chapter and in every paragraph written. The style is intentionally conversational, but the discussion is always serious. If the story is really understood, it will be remembered. Economists have something to say. That's what my textbook is about.

- **Cutting the Distance Between the Student and the Material**

Think of it also as distance cutting, that is, cutting the distance between the professor, the textbook, and the student. Too often, the relationship between them turns out to be adversarial. The student sees the professor and the textbook as "endangering," as "obstacles that have to be overcome." How many times have you heard a student ask: "What chapters *do I have to* read for the exam?" Not: "What chapters will *help me understand* the material you covered in class?" Nothing subtle about the difference in character and tone, is there? And you've experienced the difference, haven't you?

So have I. And it's the reason for this textbook. *I try to put the professor, the textbook, and the student on the same side.* It's important to keep in mind that we're not just teaching economics, we're teaching students. Of course the subject matter is economics, but the focus of the economics must be the student.

This textbook makes the student the centerpiece of the analysis. It *talks* to the student. The economics is built on a foundation of stories and scenarios that makes sense to the student because the stories and scenarios are part of the student's life, or at least familiar to him or her. This personal identity and familiarity help internalize the economics for the student. As you know, one simple "ah ha" from a student reading a paragraph is worth a million paragraphs committed to memory. That's what I mean by distance cutting.

How do I achieve that? One way is to build the text's narrative on questions. There is hardly a page or paragraph in the text where a question concerning the analysis doesn't precede it. Why questions? Because I think the best way to understand an idea or a concept is to put the idea or concept in the form of a question and then answer it. That's built-in dialogue. That's conversational. That's learning. There is nothing passive about the student's involvement in this text. I make it virtually impossible for the student not to participate.

- **The Focus Is on the Basics**

I love the marvelous story about a young boy who goes to the library in search of material on penguins for a school essay. The librarian recommends a book. He takes it to the reading table but, after 10 minutes, returns it to the librarian. "What's wrong with the book?" she asks. "It tells me more about penguins than I really want to know," he replies.

Perhaps one reason students have trouble mastering the principles of economics at the introductory level is that we try to give them too much information. That's not what a principles course or text should be about. That's not what this text is about. A principles text should be about basic principles. The tough decision I had to make writing the textbook was not what to include but what to leave out. I chose to

> "The main strength of the text is the conversational tone... Fred's personality and many years' experience come shining through... for the student. He shows them in many different ways how economic concepts apply to their lives and to the lives of those around them."
>
> Peggy Crane
> *Southwestern College*

> "When students are complimenting the book, they almost always like the way the author seems to be a real person talking to them."
>
> Cliff Althoff
> *Joliet JC*

sacrifice exciting new ideas and scores of recent research outcomes to keep the discussion basic. As you know, so much time can be spent on new developments that we end up with too little time on the fundamentals.

- **An Interdisciplinary Emphasis**

It is one thing to say that economics is part of the social sciences; it is quite another to make the text reflect that emphasis. This third edition strengthens the emphasis that was already a hallmark of the earlier editions. How is it done? I doubled the perspective boxes in each chapter (from 2 to 4) and differentiated them by focus. The perspectives are organized into 5 specific categories: *global perspectives* that take the student beyond our national borders; *interdisciplinary perspectives* that show how economics is rooted in or linked to our philosophical, psychological, cultural, social, political, and literary worlds; *historical perspectives* that provide historical economic thought content to the narrative; *applied perspectives* that offer real-world illustrations of a specific theoretical idea; and, finally, the *theoretical perspectives* that elaborate on new ways of thinking about economic problems. Many texts concentrate on the applied and theoretical, with some attention given to the historical. I think I do that well and better than most. But I honestly believe that no text can challenge mine in bringing philosophical, psychological, cultural, political, and literary content into the analysis. *It is another way of showing the students that economics matters in their lives.*

# CONTENT INNOVATIONS

- **Macroeconomics Coverage**

Macroeconomics remains a contentious field of study. A key issue—although certainly not the only one—is, What do we do about Keynesian analysis? The ideological battle lines are tightly drawn on this issue, and, often, the student ends up the casualty. Why? Because there's an intense anti-Keynesian point of view in some texts—particularly among those parading as "new and improved"—that sometimes borders on anti-Keynesian hysteria. These texts have become so thin on the analysis of national income determination—no Keynesian cross, of course—that they include, as part of their macroeconomic coverage, their microeconomic chapter on elasticity. If you're looking for such a text here, you're looking in the wrong place.

This text employs 3 basic models: aggregate demand and aggregate supply, the Keynesian cross, and variations on the Phillips curve. In each of the theory chapters, the policy issues are never out of reach. Students already have a fair idea of what the macro issues are. Almost every media source comments daily on inflation, the Fed, budgets, unemployment, business cycles, and economic growth. Students know that economics affects their lives, and they come into the course with strong interest. Our job is to link their lives to the body of economic thought we offer. I typically discuss policy before theory. This is an attempt to make students appreciate why we get involved with theory in the first place.

# THE SUPPORT PACKAGE

## For the Instructor

### INSTRUCTOR'S MANUAL
The Instructor's Manual, written by the text author, provides ideas on how to approach each chapter, tips on how to present the chapter's material, and alternative illustrations that can be used to explain points of theory and policy. It also discusses how to turn student questions into teaching opportunities. In each chapter of the manual, the corresponding text chapter outline and its key terms are included for easy reference. The manual also provides detailed answers to the many questions that appear at the end of each chapter in the text.

### TEST BANK
With the author's assistance, John Stoll of University of Wisconsin–Green Bay and Margaret Landman of Bridgewater State College have revised and rewritten the Test Bank. The Test Bank has been thoroughly edited, with numerous new questions added to each chapter.

### EXAMVIEW TESTING SOFTWARE
ExamView—Computerized Testing Software contains all of the questions in the printed Test Bank. ExamView is an easy-to-use test creation software compatible with both Microsoft Windows and Macintosh. Instructors can add or edit questions, instructions, and answers and select questions by previewing them on the screen, selecting them randomly, or selecting them by number. Instructors can also create and administer quizzes online, whether over the Internet, a local-area network (LAN), or a wide-area network (WAN).

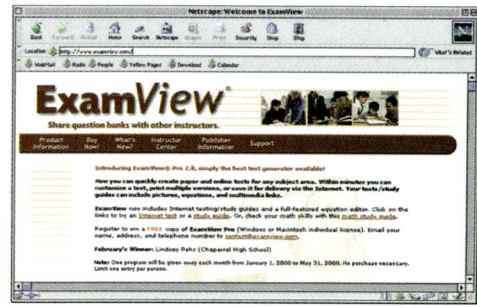

### TRANSPARENCY ACETATES
A set of approximately 200 full-color transparency acetates has been created from the key graphs and diagrams in the text.

### POWERPOINT SLIDES
A comprehensive set of PowerPoint slides is available to accompany each chapter in the text and includes most of the graphs and diagrams in the book as well as detailed lecture material.

### CNN VIDEO
Professors can bring the real world into the classroom by using the *CNN Principles of Economics Video Updates*. This video provides current stories of economic interest. The video is produced by Turner Learning, Inc., using the resources of CNN, the world's first 24-hour, all-news network.

### INSTRUCTOR'S RESOURCE CD-ROM
Get quick access to all instructor ancillaries from your desktop. This easy-to-use CD lets you review, edit, and copy exactly what you need in the format you want.

# For the Student

### STUDY GUIDE: TOOLS FOR SUCCESS IN ECONOMICS

The Study Guide, available in a comprehensive version or in macroeconomics and microeconomics versions, explains, reviews, and tests the important principles introduced in every chapter. Featured sections include Chapter in a Nutshell, Concept Check, Am I on the Right Track?, Graphing Tutorials and Graphing Pitfalls, True/False Questions, Multiple Choice Questions, Fill-in-the-Blank Questions, and Discussion Questions.

### GOTTHEIL XTRA! CD-ROM

Gottheil Xtra! CD-ROM, packaged with every new text, provides you with complimentary access to the robust set of additional online learning tools found at the site. Some of the powerful study support features found on this CD include The Graphing Workshop, a unique learning system made up of tutorials, interactive tools, and exercises that teach students how to interpret, reproduce, and explain graphs; video lecture and application segments; and extensive self-testing opportunities. Students who do not buy a new text/CD package can purchase access to the site online.

### THE WALL STREET JOURNAL EDITION

*The Wall Street Journal* is synonymous with the latest word on business, economics, and public policy. *Principles of Economics* makes it easy for students to apply economic concepts to this authoritative publication, and for you to bring the most up-to-date, real-world events into your classroom. For a nominal additional cost, *Principles of Economics* can be packaged with a card entitling students to a 10-week subscription to both the print and interactive versions of *The Wall Street Journal*. Instructors who have at least seven students activate their subscriptions will automatically receive their own free subscription. Contact your South-Western/Thomson Learning sales representative for package pricing and ordering information.

### INFOTRAC COLLEGE EDITION

With InfoTrac College Edition, your students can receive anytime, anywhere, online access to a database of full-text articles from hundreds of scholarly and popular periodicals such as *Newsweek, Fortune, American Economist,* and the *Quarterly Journal of Economics*. Students can use its fast and easy search tools to find what they're looking for among the tens of thousands of articles—updated daily and dating back as far as 4 years—all in this single Web site. It's a great way to expose students to online research techniques, while being secure in the knowledge that the content they find is academically based and reliable. An InfoTrac College Edition subscription card can be packaged free with new copies of the Gottheil text. Contact your South-Western/Thomson Learning sales representative for package pricing and ordering information, or, for more information on InfoTrac College Edition, visit **http://www.swcollege.com/infotrac/infotrac.html**

### PERSONAL WEBTUTOR

This Web-based study guide reviews critical text material chapter by chapter. Concepts are reinforced through extensive exercises, problems, cases, flashcards, self-tests, and other tools. Access certificates for Personal WebTutor™ can be bundled with the textbook, or students can preview and purchase the product directly online (**http://pwt.swcollege.com**) for subscription periods of 1 month or 4 months.

### SMARTHINKING

Live online tutoring—students can get the help they need when they need it. Thomson Learning and Smarthinking have partnered to bring students the best academic assistance the Web has to offer. Students purchasing the Gottheil textbook are eligible for one free hour of online tutoring, as well as unlimited access to valuable online study resources. They can choose to get help in their subject, or in any subject Smarthinking covers: accounting, economics, mathematics, statistics, and psychology. Or they can get help with their writing through the online writing lab.

For more information, visit http://www.smarthinking.com/thomsonfreehour.html

### ECONOMICS ALIVE! CD-ROMS

These interactive multimedia study aids for economics are the high-tech, high-fun way to study economics. Through a combination of animated presentations, interactive graphing exercises, and simulations, the core principles of economics come to life and are driven home in an upbeat and entertaining way.

Macroeconomics Alive! CD-ROM, ISBN: 0-538-86850-3
Microeconomics Alive! CD-ROM, ISBN: 0-538-84650-X

Ask your Thomson Learning sales representative for more details, or visit the Economics Alive! Web site http://econalive.swcollege.com

### THE NEW YORK TIMES GUIDE TO ECONOMICS
by Bernard F. Sigler, Cheryl Jennings, and Jamie Murphy
More than just a printed collection of articles, this Guide provides access, via password, to an online collection of the most current and relevant *New York Times* articles that are continually posted as news breaks. Also included are articles from *CyberTimes*, the online technology section of *The New York Times* on the Web. Correlation guides for many South-Western economics texts are available on the South-Western/*New York Times* Web site at **http://nytimes.swcollege.com**
ISBN: 0-324-04159-4

### THE TOBACCO WARS
*The Tobacco Wars*, by Walter Adams (Michigan State University) and James W. Brock (Miami University of Ohio) presents the economic theory surrounding the tobacco litigation as a creative dialogue between many key players in the debate—including tobacco industry executives, consumers, attorneys, economists, health care professionals, historians, and political activists. Their fictional conversations illustrate the real-life issues, controversies, and points of view currently at play, giving readers a balanced and provocative framework to reach their own conclusions. The text provides a unique way to illustrate microeconomic principles, such as:
- Consumer behavior
- Industrial organization and public policy
- Antitrust policy
- Externalities, social costs, and market imperfections

ISBN: 0-324-01296-9

# FOR STUDENTS AND INSTRUCTORS

### GOTTHEIL ECONOMICS WEB SITE
(http://gottheil.swcollege.com)
The Gottheil Web site provides open access to an online study guide (with chapter review, quizzing, and more), updates to the text, the opportunity to communicate with the author, direct links to all the Internet addresses and activities mentioned in the text, and other teaching and learning resources.

### SOUTH-WESTERN ECONOMICS RESOURCE CENTER
A unique, rich, and robust online resource for economics instructors and students, **http://economics.swcollege.com** provides customer service and product information, teaching and learning tips and tools, information about careers in economics, access to all of our text-supporting Web sites, and other cutting-edge educational resources such as our highly regarded EconNews, EconDebate, EconData, and EconLinks online features.

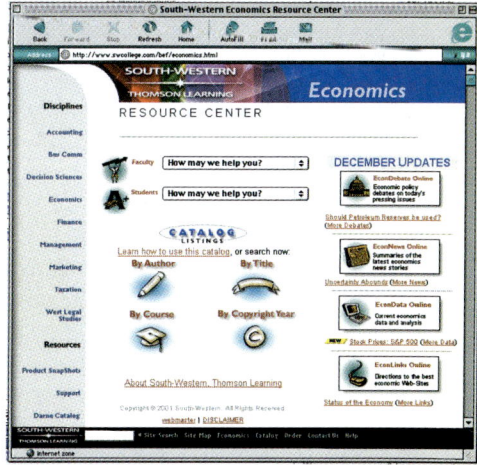

### WEBTUTOR ON WEBCT AND ON BLACKBOARD
*WebTutor™ on Web CT* or *WebTutor on Blackboard* complements *Principles of Economics, 3e* by providing interactive reinforcement that helps students grasp complex concepts. WebTutor's online teaching and learning environment brings together content management, assessment, communication, and collaboration capabilities for enhancing in-class instruction or delivering distance learning. For more information and a demo of what WebTutor can do for your classes, visit
**http://webtutor.swcollege.com**

### PRINCIPLES OF MACROECONOMICS TELECOURSE
### PRINCIPLES OF MICROECONOMICS TELECOURSE

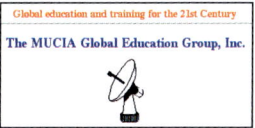

Produced by MUCIA Global Education Network, this series of 56 one-half hour lectures by Fred Gottheil provides a complete introduction to the principles of economics.
To learn more about this full distance learning package, contact MUCIA at **http://www.muciaglobal.edu**

# FAREWELL

*News-Gazette* file photo

Friday, May 12, 1989
*The Champaign-Urbana News-Gazette Weekend*

"His eyes would light up and he'd talk fast and you couldn't help being excited about the band or record he'd discovered, too."

**P. Gregory Springer**

Part of being young is the feeling of being indestructible. Josh Gottheil, who died last month after a two-year battle against leukemia, probably understood that he wouldn't live forever. But he never stopped working to bring the music he loved to the world around him. Rock and roll would carry on.

The punk movement—simultaneously cynical and realist and suicidal and idealistic—tried in a frenzy to wipe out the commercialism and mass media hallucination which blurred life's realities, even unpleasant ones like death. There were bands named Dead Kennedys, Dead Milkmen, the prototype Dead Boys, and Gottheil's local band, Dead Relatives.

When he was only a sophomore in high school, Gottheil became a drummer for the short-lived band, but he was no angry punk. He heard the message in the music and he set out, ambitious at a tender age, to deliver it to the community.

At 17, he already had promoted dozens of concerts for teens in community centers and church foundations. He was the least pushy music promoter I ever met, enticing me to see at least one political rock and folk concert through his complete, quiet reticence.

It was the music that spoke to and through him.

At one concert he arranged, I watched Billy Bragg and Michelle Shocked get their introductions to the area. And I saw Josh, standing by the door at Mabel's, anxious to see that the message and the feeling came across.

His bands rarely disappointed.

Among the many other national bands he brought to Champaign's clubs were Living Colour, They Might Be Giants, Soul Asylum, Throwing Muses, Jane's Addiction, Dead Milkmen, Hüsker Dü, Let's Active, Timbuk 3, Ministry, and the Pixies.

"The scene wouldn't be what it was today without Josh," said Chris Corpora, an area rock promoter of Trashcan Productions. "He didn't look the part and he risked his own money. About four years ago he started teen nights when there was a lull in the scene. I don't want to deify him, but he had an incredible will, poise, and the wherewithal to get contracts signed and do things he probably shouldn't have been able to do. When I was 15, I couldn't even read a contract."

Even in the hard-core punk scene, Josh maintained a romantic side, often bringing roses for the girls in his favorite bands, notably Throwing Muses and the Pixies.

"He was always in love with every girl in a band," said Katy Stack, one of many people who considered Josh a best friend.

"He made friends with the Pixies and we flew to California to see them play in San Francisco," Stack said. "They invited him on stage to sing."

For a couple of summers, he worked at the desk at Crystal Lake Pool, announcing the adult swim and checking in bags. After high school, he took some college classes in philosophy and math at Parkland and at the UI, where his father, Fred, is a professor of economics. When he got sick, "it didn't look like he needed to go to college," according to Stack. "He was real busy doing all the music and he always had a lot of money. He was the only 16-year-old that had $2,000 in his checking account."

Another friend, Shara Gingold, actually wrote a book about her crush on Josh.

"He was two years older. The book is called 'I Love You, Josh. Do You Even Know I Exist?'," said Gingold, who lives in Urbana. "I think that it was [the fact that] he was very understanding and caring. We'd meet to play tennis and then we'd just sit and hit the tennis ball against the wall and talk about everything."

Last year, his health started to improve. He gained weight. He was working at Record Swap, surrounding himself in music during the day for the concerts he promoted at night. He had teamed with Chicago promoter Tony Polous, established a limited partnership called Concert One Productions, rented an office in Chicago's Mercantile Building, and developed the financing for big arena shows.

"Josh was destined to be huge," said Polous from the Chicago office. "He was the most effective, easy-going person I ever met. It's not hard to master being pushy and strong. Josh mastered being effective in an unassuming way.

"When he had to go back to the hospital, he never let on how sick he was. Every day I'd call him and he'd ask about what this manager was doing or that agent and he'd make decisions. We never really talked about his health. I never thought he was going to die. I think about him every day."

Despite his illness, Josh moved to Chicago last fall to be immersed in the music business.

"It was a chance, a break, an exciting thing to do. The world was his to conquer," said Fred Gottheil from his UI office. "I remember going up to visit and spend the night. The wind was howling, but he was so proud of the apartment. He was designing tickets on his computer, telling me [about] all the bands he had booked, his new ideas, bubbling with enthusiasm for the possibilities. The move was exhilarating for him. He called home quite frequently, but [Chicago] was where he had to be."

Said former Champaign-Urbana DJ Charlie "The Quaker" Edwards, who shared the Chicago apartment, "He had a real vitality, youth, and infectiousness. His eyes would light up and he'd talk fast and you couldn't help being excited about the band or record he'd discovered, too. Even though there was almost 20 years age difference between us, we'd listen to albums and talk about the bands and share a mutual excitement.

"He was a really good, serious businessman. Much better than I could have been, always dealing with five shows at once. He really loved it, too. He just loved the music."

"Definitely, there are people who are into [punk] because it is a fad," Gottheil said three years ago. "But for the people who really believe in it, it won't die for them."

Josh Gottheil died April 4 at Barnes Hospital in St. Louis, three months short of his 20th birthday. There was a turn-away crowd for his funeral on April 7 at the Sinai Temple in Champaign. Because he did so much to bring a new attitude about music in this area, one of the bands he helped find national prominence, Throwing Muses, has donated its performance at a benefit concert this Sunday at Mabel's, with proceeds going to the Josh Gottheil Memorial Fund for Lymphoma Research.

# AUTHOR

Fred M. Gottheil is a professor of economics at the University of Illinois in Urbana-Champaign. He came to Illinois in 1960, planning to spend one year before returning to his native Canada. But he fell in love with the campus, the community, and the Midwest, and he has been at Illinois ever since. He earned his undergraduate degree at McGill University in Montreal, Canada, and his Ph.D. at Duke University. His primary teaching is the principles of economics, and, on occasion, he has taught the history of economic thought, Marxian economics, and the economics of the Middle East. He is the author of *Marx's Economic Predictions* and numerous articles that have appeared in scholarly journals, among them the *American Economic Review,* the *Canadian Journal of Economics,* the *Journal of Post-Keynesian Economics,* and the *Middle East Review.* He has also contributed articles to several edited books on the Middle East. Although he enjoys research, his labor of love is teaching the principles course. His classes have been as large as 1,800 students. He has won the department's annual excellence-in-teaching award in economics 12 times during the past dozen years and, along with his college and university-wide teaching awards, holds the distinction of having won the most teaching awards on the Urbana campus. Aside from his research and publications as a professor of economics, Professor Gottheil is also on the university's medical faculty, co-teaching the College of Medicine's course on medicine and society. As well, he is director of the University of Illinois's Center for Economic Education. In this capacity, he organizes and team-teaches minicourses and workshops on the principles of economics. He was a White House consultant on the Middle East during the Carter administration and offered expert testimony to several congressional committees. Professor Gottheil was a visiting professor at Northwestern University and at the Hebrew University in Jerusalem, Israel. He has lectured at many universities in the United States, Canada, and abroad, including universities in Syria, Egypt, Israel, and Jordan.

# ACKNOWLEDGMENTS

I am grateful to many people for help and encouragement throughout the development of this textbook. Many came to the project in a strictly professional capacity; most ended up as good friends. I owe them more than they believe is their due. At the beginning, George Lobell was enthusiastic about the idea of the textbook and believed that it would make a difference in the profession. He read many chapters, stayed in close touch, and still does. I thank this textbook for introducing me to George. David Wishart was a dear friend before we started the project, and working together on this textbook added another dimension to our friendship. Jack Calhoun, South-Western's editor-in-chief, sold me on the idea of the team concept of publishing. It was Andy McGuire, the developmental editor at South-Western, who saw this third edition to completion. He also carefully managed and helped improve the comprehensive supplements package that accompanies this book. Lisa Lysne has contributed her insight and deftly handled the marketing campaign. Finally, Mike Stratton, Libby Shipp and the staff at Lachina Publishing Services played major roles in translating my word-processed drafts and rough sketches into the pleasing book you hold in your hands.

During this book's long gestation period, I have benefited from the comments and suggestions of many reviewers. My heartfelt thanks go to the following economists. This book is much improved because of their efforts.

Carl J. Austermiller,
*Oakland Community College*

Michael Bodnar,
*Stark Technical College*

John Booth,
*Stetson University*

David Bunting,
*Eastern Washington University*

Tom Cate,
*Northern Kentucky University*

Robert Catlett,
*Emporia State University*

Christopher Colburn,
*Old Dominion University*

James Cover,
*University of Alabama, Tuscaloosa*

Jerry Crawford,
*Arkansas State*

Jane Crouch,
*Pittsburgh State University*

Susan Davis,
*SUNY College at Buffalo*

Daniel Fagan,
*Daniel Webster College*

Abdollah Ferdowsi,
*Ferris State University*

Eric Fisher,
*Ohio State University*

Carol Hogan,
*University of Michigan, Dearborn*

William Holmes,
*Temple University*

Paul Huszer,
*Colorado State University*

Bruce K. Johnson,
*Centre College*

Patrick Kelso,
*West Texas State University*

Alan Kessler,
*Providence College*

Joseph Kotaska,
*Monroe Community College*

Robert Litro,
*Mattatuck Community College*

Lawrence Mack,
*North Dakota State University*

Joseph Maddalena,
*St. Thomas Aquinas College*

John Makrogianis,
*Middlesex Community Collage*

Gabriel Manrique,
*Winona State University*

John Marsh,
*Montana State University*

G. H. Mattersdorff,
*Lewis and Clark College*

xxxi

John Merrifield,
*University of Texas—San Antonio*

James McBearty,
*University of Arizona*

Henry McCarl,
*University of Alabama, Birmingham*

James McLain,
*University of New Orleans*

Lon Mishler,
*North Wisconsin Technical College*

Norma Morgan,
*Curry College*

Allan Olsen,
*Elgin Community College*

Peter Pedroni,
*Indiana University*

Mitchell Redlo,
*Monroe Community College*

Terry Riddle,
*Central Virginia Community College*

Paul Rothstein,
*University of Washington at St. Louis*

Richard Schiming,
*Mankato State University*

Jerry Sidwell,
*Eastern Illinois University*

Phillip Smith,
*DeKalb College*

Philip Sprunger,
*Lycoming College*

William Stull,
*Temple University*

Tapan Thoy,
*Eastern Connecticut State University*

Doug Wakeman,
*Meredith College*

Jim Watson,
*Jefferson College*

Larry Wolfenbarger,
*Georgia College*

Finally, I want to thank Peter Schran, my colleague and close friend at Illinois, whose advice always made sense although it sometimes took me a while to appreciate it.

*Fred Gottheil*
*University of Illinois*

# PART 1

## THE BASICS OF ECONOMIC ANALYSIS

**CHAT ECONOMICS**

**T**une into the conversation. It's about *your* course. Just change the names, and it's *your* campus, *your* classroom, *your* professor, *your* classmates, and *you*.

Picture the scene. Katy Stack, a freshman planning on majoring in economics, and Professor Gottheil are walking across campus after the first week of class. Katy introduces herself and immediately the conversation gets to the heart of her concerns.

**GOTTHEIL:** Well, good morning, Katy. How do you like the economics course so far?
**KATY:** Okay, I guess. I'm actually thinking about majoring in it.
**GOTTHEIL:** Good choice! I think you'll love economics. Not only do I find it intellectually exciting, but it tells us a lot about ourselves. It's about what we do and how we live.
**KATY:** Frankly, I'm a little uneasy about majoring in it. My friends tell me that economics is difficult.
**GOTTHEIL:** In what way?
**KATY:** I think it's just difficult to understand.
**GOTTHEIL:** Well, Katy, let me tell you an anecdote that addresses your concern. It's an honest-to-goodness story, by the way, told to me by my teaching assistant, Cliff Althoff, who was then working on his Ph.D. in economics here on campus.
**KATY:** What's he doing now?
**GOTTHEIL:** He's a professor of economics at Joliet Junior College. Well, here's his story. One day, a number of years ago, he was on his way to visit his then-fiancée, Maureen McGonagle, when, on the sidewalk close by her house, he ran into a small group of 10-year-old girls skipping rope, hopscotching, and playing ball and jacks.
**KATY:** They weren't economists!
**GOTTHEIL:** Not exactly, but that's part of the story. One of the girls who had been skipping rope blocked his path to the house and audaciously asked who he was and where he was going. Cliff politely told her who he was, that Maureen was his fiancée, and that he was going to visit her for the day. The girl, still very inquisitive, asked Cliff what he did for a living. Well, he told her he was an economics teacher at the University of Illinois. She then replied, "If you're a teacher of economics, can you teach me something about economics now?"

**KATY:** Right there on the sidewalk—to a 10-year-old?
**GOTTHEIL:** You have to know Cliff! He said, "Sure. You were busy hopscotching when I met you, right? But you could have been skipping rope. Now you know that you can't do both at the same time, can you? By choosing to hopscotch, you gave up the opportunity of skipping rope. Economists call that an opportunity cost. You see, the fun you have hopscotching—and it's fun, isn't it—cost you the fun you could have had skipping rope. Make sense? Opportunity cost is a really important economic idea, and now you know it. Well, I really enjoyed talking to you, but I must go."
**KATY:** That's sort of neat. Teaching opportunity cost to a 10-year-old. Do you think she really understood it?
**GOTTHEIL:** Well, listen to this: When Cliff walked past the children and was about to enter the house, he heard the girl call back to him, "Hey mister! The opportunity cost of going to see Maureen is not being able to stay here and talk to me. See, I understand economics."
**KATY:** Awesome!
**GOTTHEIL:** Not really. Much of what you will learn in economics is like that. It will not be too difficult to understand. Knowing how to use economic principles is another matter. But you'll get to know that as well. Katy, I think you'll enjoy the course, and I certainly will enjoy having you in class.

It is certainly normal to be concerned about how hard any course will be, and economics is no different. Yet, as Cliff showed, the basic concepts in economics are not difficult to understand. As you read through the next few chapters, consider Katy and your own assumptions about your economics course. Who knows, perhaps you will decide to major in economics as well!

# CHAPTER 1

## INTRODUCTION

"In the beginning God created the heaven and the earth" is about as familiar a sentence as any written. The Bible tells us that in the five days that followed the creation of heaven and earth, God separated darkness from light and water from dry land, and brought forth a multiplicity of living plants and creatures to inhabit the newly created land, waters, and skies. And on the sixth day, God created people:

> So God created man in his own image, in the image of God created he him; male and female created he them. And God blessed them, and God said unto them, Be fruitful, and multiply, and replenish the earth, and subdue it: and have dominion over the fish of the sea, and over the fowl of the air, and over every living thing that moveth upon the earth.
>
> And God said, Behold, I have given you every herb bearing seed, which is upon the face of all the earth, and every tree, in the which is the fruit of a tree yielding seed; to you it shall be for meat. And to every beast of the earth, and to every fowl of the air, and to every thing that creepeth upon the earth, wherein there is life, I have given every green herb for meat: and it was so.

**THIS CHAPTER INTRODUCES YOU TO THE ECONOMIC PRINCIPLES ASSOCIATED WITH:**

- THE EARTH'S RENEWABLE AND NONRENEWABLE RESOURCES
- THE CONCEPT OF INSATIABLE WANTS
- THE CONCEPTS OF SCARCITY AND CHOICE
- THE VALUE OF ECONOMIC MODEL BUILDING
- MICROECONOMIC AND MACROECONOMIC ANALYSIS
- POSITIVE AND NORMATIVE ECONOMICS

## NO ONE EVER MADE AN OUNCE OF EARTH

What's the lesson we are supposed to draw from this creation narrative? To an economist, the first chapter of Genesis is both a powerful and humbling account of how our **natural resources** came into being. The message is clear. It doesn't even require particular religious conviction. After all, when you think about it, who ever made an ounce of earth? Who ever created a lump of coal or a nugget of gold? It seems that they have always been here for our use. Nobody ever added to nature's bounty.

Although the scientific interpretation of our resource availability differs dramatically from the biblical one, the message is similar. Natural resources have always been here. Physicists express this idea of prior existence and the continuance of matter in the first law of thermodynamics—the conservation principle—which asserts that energy can be neither created nor destroyed.

Economists, too, accept as fact that every resource on the face of this earth is a gift of nature. Resources were here before men and women arrived on the scene. Every ounce of iron, tungsten, nickel, petroleum, copper, zinc, asbestos, gypsum, and the many other metals, minerals, and energy sources, including those yet undiscovered, were here long before we learned how to make cement, gasoline, steel, plastics, and aspirin.

The nutrients attached to every grain of soil were already imbedded in the soil before people even began to think about working the land. The herds of goats, the schools of sea bass, the flocks of geese, the reindeer and rabbits, the forests and grasses, and all our other food resources were there for the taking.

And, of course, we took! We learned how to extract natural resources from the earth, how to fish them out of the waters, and how to harvest them from the lands. Most exciting of all, we learned the tricks of transforming resources from their original states into new ones. We transform iron ore into steel, crude petroleum into plastic, trees into furniture, rays of the sun into energy, coal into nylon, sand into glass, limestone into cement, bauxite into aluminum, and water flow into electricity. We are continually discovering newer techniques for transformation. And we have been doing this for a long, long time.

### Are We Running Out of Natural Resources?

We live in a finite world. No matter how seemingly bountiful the quantity of our natural resources may be or how carefully we try to conserve them, if we keep using them, they eventually are going to run out. It just seems reasonable. Or does it?

### Renewable and Nonrenewable Natural Resources

Many natural resources are renewable. Consider, for example, our supply of forests, sea and land animals, water, and grasses. Are not these resources self-renewing? But with rapidly growing human populations, overuse of productive lands can turn them into deserts, and overharvesting of fish and land animals can destroy these living resources. Properly managed conservation, on the other hand, can not only protect these natural resources but even increase their supply.

Admittedly, our metal and mineral resources are not self-renewing. Gold nuggets don't breed. Because the earth contains finite space, its mineral resources exist only in finite quantities. You do not have to be a rocket scientist to figure out that mining one ton of copper ore depletes that resource by one ton. In fact, we have been depleting our copper supply ever since King Solomon began mining copper in the Negev desert. However, before we work our way down to the last ton of copper, it

**Natural resources**
The lands, water, metals, minerals, animals, and other gifts of nature that are available for producing goods and services.

**CHECK YOUR UNDERSTANDING**

Can you describe the finite character of the earth's resources?

**CHECK YOUR UNDERSTANDING**

What distinguishes renewable from nonrenewable resources?

is very possible that we will have already abandoned it as a usable resource. In other words, even though copper may not be a renewable resource, we may be well advised to treat it as one.

Does this mean, then, that we will never run out of any natural resource? No such luck. It just means that our knowledge of a resource's relative scarcity, particularly when we consider its availability in the not-too-distant future, is less than exact.

Thousands of years ago, flint was a primary resource used in the production of tools and weapons. Do you know anyone today concerned about our flint supply? We still produce tools and weapons, but we have moved to other technologies that use very different resources. Is copper's future, then, mirrored in flint's past? If so, we may someday regret having conserved our copper supply. We might end up with mountains of unused, useless copper.

Should we conserve the world's oil supply or instead go full speed ahead, using up as much of it as we need to satisfy our current demands? After all, in a genera-

## HISTORICAL PERSPECTIVE

### COAL . . . THEN (1865) AND NOW (2000)

**In 1865, the celebrated economist Stanley Jevons wrote a very sobering book,** *The Coal Question.* **Jevons set out to prove that England's economic progress and power were on the verge of collapse.** The reason? The energy source that powered England's economic growth—coal—was being rapidly depleted. No alternative energy source seemed likely. Jevons estimated that England's commercially available coal supply would run out in one hundred years. He warned:

> . . . I must point out the painful fact that such a rate of [economic] growth will before long render our consumption of coal comparable with the total supply. In the increasing depth and difficulty of coal mining we shall meet that vague but inevitable boundary that will stop our progress. . . . A farm, however far pushed, will under proper cultivation continue to yield for ever a constant crop. But in a mine there is no reproduction, and the produce once pushed to the utmost will soon begin to sink to zero. (pp. 154–155)

Has England run out of coal? England's coal problem in 2000, ironically, seems to be too much coal! The *Economic Bulletin*, a bimonthly summary of the Nottinghamshire economy, reported in its March/April 2000 issue: "RJB Mining, Britain's biggest coal producer, announced a 130 million pound sterling pre tax loss for 1999. RJB said that without government aid it would be forced to close Ellington colliery [coal mine] in Northumbria and Clipstone in Nottinghamshire, with a loss of 450 jobs. Only 17 deep mines are left in the UK, 13 of them owned by RJB Mining, and nearly half are in trouble after a glut of coal on the world market sent prices plummeting."

It's not a new story. A decade earlier, the House of Commons energy committee published a report that outlined the bleak future facing the coal industry, despite the fact that productivity in the industry is relatively high. Britain, the committee report stated, still has three centuries' worth of coal at the present rate of consumption. Can you imagine Jevons reading the committee's report? He would be flabbergasted!

#### MORE ON THE NET

Learn more about Stanley Jevons (http://www.cpm.ll.ehime-u.ac.jp/AkamacHomePage/Akamac_E-text_Links/Jevons.html). What problems does England face today with coal? Visit the United Kingdom Parliament (http://www.parliament.uk/).

tion or two our energy technologies may have already switched to solar and nuclear power, or to some yet unknown technology. What then do we do with oceans of unused, unwanted oil?

## How Do You Satisfy Insatiable Wants?

Suppose we had an infinite supply of natural resources. We would still have an insurmountable economic problem. There simply are not enough hours in a day to allow us to transform those resources into all the goods and services we want. That is, the problem ultimately may not be the limited quantity of resources available to us, but rather our limitless, or insatiable, wants.

Let's go back to the biblical story to illustrate the point. Adam and Eve were happy in the Garden of Eden, not because the garden had so much but because they wanted so little. Their problem was eating the fruit from the Tree of Knowledge: One bite and they suddenly realized they had no clothes, no air

# THEORETICAL PERSPECTIVE

### IF NOT THE DEPLETION OF COAL, THEN PERHAPS OIL

In the 1970s, economists and government people looking at the soaring price of oil panicked. What did they see as the cause for rising oil prices? You guessed it! Listen to President Jimmy Carter:

> It is obvious to anyone that looks at it [the oil crisis] that we've got a problem that's serious now. It's going to get more serious in the future. We're going to have less oil. Those are the facts. They are unpleasant facts. (May 25, 1979)

Sound familiar? Perhaps President Carter should have read Stanley Jevons's 1865 book *The Coal Question*. He might have found some reason to be more optimistic about our future and less reason to assert his fears about oil supplies as "unpleasant facts."

In July 2000, the Energy Information Administration (EIA) of the U.S. Department of Energy reported that "data continues to confirm no shortage of crude oil in the open market." And that's no surprise. Why not? Because if we were really running out of oil, we would spend a great deal of time looking for it, wouldn't we? We would be drilling and drilling, using as many drilling rigs as we could employ. But look at the drilling rig data. In June 2000, the U.S. weekly rig count was 878. Since 1940, the highest weekly rig count was 4,530, recorded in December 1981. The lowest rig count was recorded in April 1999. The 878 rigs in operation tend to confirm the EIA report that nobody is really worried about crude oil supply.

#### MORE ON THE NET

Visit the U.S. Department of Energy (http://www.energy.gov/) and the White House (http://www.whitehouse.gov/). What about oil concerns the federal government?

IT'S A LONG, LONG HAUL. BUT DON'T WORRY. THERE'S PLENTY OF OIL IN THE PIPELINE AND OCEANS MORE WHERE THAT CAME FROM.

conditioning, no videocassettes, no quartz watches, no phones, and no Buick. It was a quick trip from the state of ignorant bliss to paradise lost. Their wants became insatiable.

We inherited their genes. Our tastes for goods and services are virtually limitless. There is always something else we want. And once these wants are satisfied, our minds are just as capable of conceiving new wants as they are of conceiving ways of satisfying them. In this respect, we differ from lions and tigers who, after a kill, are prepared to rest until hungry again. Instead, we are perpetually in a state of hunger. Even if we had a never-ending supply of the natural resources required to satisfy our limitless wants, it would take more than 24 hours a day to transform them into all the goods and services we want.

## Scarcity Forces Us to Make Choices

If we can't have everything we want today, what do we do? We are forced to make choices. We must choose to produce some goods and services and not others. Sometimes this kind of choosing can be visibly painful. Have you ever watched children in Toys "R" Us with a gift certificate in hand? It can take them all day before they make a choice. And instead of bubbling with excitement over the toy they bought, they usually appear frustrated over not being able to walk away with everything!

Life is like that. **Scarcity** governs us. Because we cannot have everything all at once, we are forever forced to make choices. We can use our resources to satisfy only some of our wants, leaving many others unsatisfied.

**CHECK YOUR UNDERSTANDING**

Why does scarcity force people to make choices?

**Scarcity**
The perpetual state of insufficiency of resources to satisfy people's unlimited wants.

# WHAT IS ECONOMICS?

What has **economics** to do with Genesis 1, Adam and Eve, the first law of thermodynamics, scarcities of resources, and infinite wants? Everything! *Economics is the study of how we work together to transform scarce resources into goods and services to satisfy the most pressing of our infinite wants, and how we distribute these goods and services among ourselves.*

The study of economics focuses on four central issues. Who produces what? How? Who consumes what? And who decides? Taken together, these issues form the analysis of how an economy works.

## Economics Is Part of Social Science

It is sometimes difficult to separate the study of economics from the study of the other social sciences, such as sociology, anthropology, political science, and psychology. All the social science disciplines, including economics, examine individual and social behavior. While economics concentrates on those aspects of behavior that affect the way we, as individuals and as a society, produce and consume goods and services, our production and consumption are not done in a social vacuum.

What we consume, what we produce, how we produce, and how we go about exchanging resources and products among ourselves is determined, in part, by the character of our political system, by the customs and traditions of our society, and by the set of social institutions and ethical standards we have established.

Our political and economic rights and freedoms stem from the same root. Our right to vote at the ballot box, for example, is not unrelated to **consumer sovereignty** in the marketplace—that is, our freedom to buy or not buy the goods and services offered. This right to choose what we want dictates what producers will ultimately

**Economics**
The study of how people work together to transform resources into goods and services to satisfy their most pressing wants, and how they distribute these goods and services among themselves.

**Consumer sovereignty**
The ability of consumers to exercise complete control over what goods and services the economy produces (or doesn't produce) by choosing what goods and services to buy (or not buy).

produce, just as our right to choose our political leaders dictates what kind of government policies we ultimately get.

We grow up in a society whose value system, sometimes described as the Protestant ethic, implants in us a belief in the importance of personal frugality, honest labor, and enterprise. To many of us, any alternative value system is considered deviant or antisocial. In this respect, our ethical standards establish the boundaries of permissible economic behavior. We are also taught from childhood to accept a broad set of social responsibilities, many requiring us to share part of our income, through taxes, with people who are less fortunate than us. These accepted social values and responsibilities contribute to the way we select and meet our economic goals and the role we expect our government to play in the economy.

The contributions that economics as a social science discipline makes to the other social sciences are also fundamental. For example, it is difficult to appreciate what federal, state, and local governments do without understanding the economic circumstances underlying their actions. After all, government budgets are economic documents. Taxes and government spending are economic tools used by the political system to meet economic as well as political and social objectives. Political debates on issues such as the national debt, budget deficits, and the welfare system require an understanding of economics.

It is difficult, as well, for sociologists to study the role of the family in society without at the same time studying how the family behaves as an economic unit. To some extent, even when and whom we marry, the number of children we have, and interpersonal relationships within the family are governed by economics.

## Using Economic Models

Our real economic world is incredibly complex. Millions of people, making independent economic decisions every day, affect not only their own lives but the lives of everyone around them. In many cases, they influence even the lives of people great distances away. It is one thing to appreciate the fact that we are all mutually interrelating, but quite another to untangle these relationships to draw specific one-to-one, cause-and-effect economic correspondences. It's an imposing intellectual challenge, but economists have been working at it with at least modest success, and in some cases, quite remarkable results.

How do economists start? By abstracting from reality. The purpose of such abstraction is to reduce the complexity of the world we live in to more simplified, manageable dimensions. That is essentially what the economists' models do. The models capture the essence of an economic reality. They try to simplify it without distorting its truth.

In a way, when economists build economic models, they are like children playing house. In both cases, it is essentially reduction and imitation. In child's play, many of the household activities are ignored and many of the real problems are overlooked. However, the central figures are there, the accuracy of their behavior is uncanny, and the issues basic to most households are reflected in the children's mimicry of adult conversation.

Most **economic model** builders insist that while their models exclude many economic activities of the real world, overlook the complexities of how people really behave, and ignore many pressing issues that people confront every day, what they portray in their models is nevertheless the quintessence of how the real economy works.

**Economic model**
An abstraction of an economic reality. It can be expressed pictorially, graphically, algebraically, or in words.

**Ceteris paribus**
The Latin phrase meaning "everything else being equal."

And that's the point of economic analysis. Economists are not really interested in pure intellectual exercise. Their interest is not the economic model per se but the real world of economics. Their models are designed to serve only as vehicles to a fuller comprehension of what really goes on.

## Ceteris Paribus

One of the most important aids economists use in model building is the assumption of **ceteris paribus,** which translated means "holding constant" or "controlling for the influence of other factors." Ceteris paribus allows economists to develop one-to-one, cause-and-effect relationships in isolation, that is, removed from other potentially influential factors. For example, when the price of filet mignon decreases, economists assert that the quantity of filet mignon demanded increases. But this one-to-one, cause-and-effect relationship between price and quantity demanded holds only if everything else going on in the economy is ignored. If the prices of other foods fall at the same time, then it is questionable whether more filet mignon would be demanded when its price falls. After all, people may be more attracted to the other price-reduced foods than they are to the lower-priced filet.

Or suppose people lost their jobs on the very day the filet prices were cut. Chances are fewer filets would be demanded. When you're out of work, filet mignon at any price is probably out of mind.

How then can economists make definitive statements about any economic relationship when so many economic events, all potentially influencing each other, may be occurring at the same time? They do so by assuming ceteris paribus. It focuses the analysis. That one-to-one, cause-and-effect relationship between price and quantity demanded, however limited by the exclusion of other considerations, is still highly insightful and turns out to be of critical importance to our understanding of price determination.

Ceteris paribus is not confined to economic analysis. When the surgeon general of the United States asserts that smoking causes lung cancer, isn't there a ceteris paribus assumption lurking in the background? After all, the smoking–cancer relationship ignores a host of other factors that may explain the cancer. Consider the science of meteorology. When the weather forecast is rain, isn't there a ceteris paribus assumption made as well? Weather fronts can and often do change direction.

## The Circular Flow Model of Goods and Money

**Circular flow model**
A model of how the economy's resources, money, goods, and services flow between households and firms through resource and product markets.

**Household**
An economic unit of one or more persons, living under one roof, that has a source of income and uses it in whatever way it deems fit.

**Firm**
An economic unit that produces goods and services in the expectation of selling them to households, other firms, or government.

Let's look now at an honest-to-goodness economic model. Perhaps the simplest model illustrating how an economy works is the **circular flow model** of money, goods, and services shown in Exhibit 1.

In this model, people are both consumers and producers. They live in **households,** where they consume the goods and services they buy on the product market, and they supply their resources—land, labor, capital, and entrepreneurship—on the resource market to **firms** that use the resources to produce the goods and services that appear on the product market.

In the upper half, the purple arrow depicts the direction of the flow of goods and services from firms, through the product market, to households. Households pay for them with money earned in the resource market. The green arrow depicts the flow of money from households, through the product market, to the firms.

Let's look at households now in their capacity as money earners. They earn money—wages, interest, rent, and profit—by selling or leasing their resources—labor, capital, land, and entrepreneurship—to firms. The yellow arrow in the bot-

**THE CIRCULAR FLOW MODEL**

Households supply resources—land, labor, capital, and entrepreneurship—to firms through the resource market in return for money payments—rent, wages, interest, and profit. Firms use the resources to produce goods and services that they supply on the product market. There, households buy those goods and services with the incomes received from the resources they supplied.

tom half depicts the resource flow from households, through the resource market, to firms. Firms transform those resources into goods and services that eventually appear on the product market. The money firms earn selling goods and services pays for the resources they buy. The green arrow depicts the pay-for-resources flow of money from firms, through the resource market, to the households. As you see, for every flow of goods, services, and resources there is a counterflow of money.

How would *you* fit into the circular flow model of Exhibit 1? Suppose you have a summer job making cotton candy at a neighborhood water slide. The job pays $200 weekly. The yellow arrow represents your labor flow to the water slide firm, while the bottom-half green arrow represents the $200 you receive from the firm.

Now let's look at your activity in the upper half of the circular flow model. Using the $200 you earn at the slide—which is now your household income—you go to the product market to buy $200 of goods and services that firms have produced for sale on the market. (Among the goods available is cotton candy.) The purple arrow represents a $200 flow of goods and services to you, while the upper-half green arrow represents the flow of money from you to firms for the goods and services.

Is the circular flow model an accurate reflection of our economic reality? Not really. Where in Exhibit 1's portrayal of that circular flow are the banks? Where is government? Doesn't government, too, consume goods and services? Where are the unemployed? They consume some of the economy's goods and services, but if they are unemployed, they aren't providing resources. Where, then, do they get the money? How does the model account for retired people? They no longer work, but they continue to consume. Where in the model do we find the economy's exports and imports? Where are savings and investments?

Nowhere! The circular flow model of Exhibit 1 isn't designed as a complete picture of our economic reality. In fact, it ignores a host of major economic institutions and activities.

But these omissions are far from being shortcomings of the model; in fact, they illustrate the model's strength. The model is designed to reflect one basic fact about how the economy works: It shows how money, goods, and services flow between households and firms through resource and product markets.

Most of the economic models analyzed in this text are no more complicated than this circular flow model. Some, like Exhibit 1, are portrayed pictorially, others graphically, and still others take the form of simple algebraic expressions. For example, economists build models of a firm to illustrate how market prices are determined. Other economic models are designed to show how unemployment and inflation arise. Models also illustrate why some nations grow faster than others and why some do not grow at all. Most of these models are expressed graphically. The one thing all of these models have in common is the use of abstraction—that is, the use economists make of simplifying assumptions to distill the essence out of the complicated economic realities they study.

## Microeconomics and Macroeconomics

Economists who look at the real world and create simple models to illustrate what they see do not necessarily look at the same things, nor do they ask the same kinds of questions. **Microeconomics,** for example, looks at the behavior of individual households and firms. It asks, Why do firms produce what they do? How do they price their goods and services? How do markets work? What distinguishes competitive from noncompetitive markets? How are resource prices such as wage rates, interest rates, and rents determined? How do firms make profits? What determines people's demands for goods and services?

As these questions suggest, the focus of microeconomic analysis is on the individual. Microeconomists study individuals as consumers and producers. The economy is regarded as a composite of interacting individual economic units. To understand how the economy functions, then, requires an understanding of how each of these individual units behaves and interacts.

**Macroeconomics,** on the other hand, tries to explain a different set of facts about the economy. It focuses attention on the behavior of the economy as a whole. To macroeconomists, the economy is more than simply a collection of its individual parts. It has character. It has its own vitality and history. It has an identifiable substance. The macroeconomic unit of analysis, then, is the economy.

The macroeconomic questions concern not the behavior and activities of individual households, firms, or markets, but the behavior and activity of the economy itself. They ask, for example, Why do national economies grow? Why do some grow faster than others? What determines a nation's savings, its investments, or its consumption? Why does it experience inflation? Why does it generate unacceptable

*Can you think of any people or institutions in your life that do not fit into the circular flow model? Go to the Interactive Study Center at http://gottheil.swcollege.com and click on the "Your Turn" button to submit your example. Student submissions will be posted to the Web site, and perhaps we will use some in future additions of the book!*

**CHECK YOUR UNDERSTANDING**

What are some advantages and limitations of the circular flow model?

**Microeconomics**
A subarea of economics that analyzes individuals as consumers and producers, and specific firms and industries. It focuses especially on the market behavior of firms and households.

Read a copy of today's newspaper, such as *USA Today* (http://www.usatoday.com/). Can you find articles that address microeconomic and macroeconomic issues?

**Macroeconomics**
A subarea of economics that analyzes the behavior of the economy as a whole.

**Invisible hand**
Adam Smith's concept of the market, which, as if it were a hand, guides firms that seek only to satisfy their own self-interest to produce precisely those goods and services that consumers want.

## THEORETICAL PERSPECTIVE

### THE LINK BETWEEN THE CIRCULAR FLOW MODEL AND ADAM SMITH'S VIEWS ON SELF-INTEREST, PUBLIC INTEREST, AND THE INVISIBLE HAND

In 1776, the Scottish moral philosopher and economist Adam Smith, in his *Wealth of Nations*, perhaps the most celebrated book ever written on economics, had this to say about why we end up having precisely the kinds of food we enjoy at our dinner table: "It is not from the benevolence of the butcher, the brewer, or the baker that we expect our dinner, but from their regard to their own self interest." That's a mighty statement! Smith assures us that there's no need to thank the butcher, the baker, nor anyone else who provides us with the goods we consume. These goods are provided only because producers hope to gain by providing them. Concern for your welfare? Don't be silly! But there's no reason to fret about self-centered motivation because working for their own self-interest works to your advantage. Smith explains: "Every individual generally neither intends to promote the public interest, nor knows how much he is promoting it. He intends only his own gain. And he is in this led by an **invisible hand** to promote an end, which was no part of his intention. By pursuing his own interest he frequently promotes that of society more effectually than when he really intends to promote it." In other words, greed can end up promoting munificence. The invisible hand Smith refers to is nothing more (or less) than the market. Anchored in consumer sovereignty, the product market guides producers to produce precisely those goods that consumers want and in this way transforms producers' private interest into our public interest.

LOOK, IF THIS ISN'T FRESH, WOULD I SELL IT TO YOU AND RISK LOSING A GOOD CUSTOMER?

How does invisible hand fit into the circular flow model? Unlike the ring on your finger that has no beginning or end, the circular flow of resources, goods, and services begins somewhere. Its starting point is the household.

Why the household? Because that's where consumer sovereignty resides. What you choose to consume dictates what firms will ultimately produce. Feel the power? You really have it! If firms fail to produce precisely what you want, they simply won't be around very long. For example, if consumers want four-cylinder cars and General Motors ignores consumer preferences by manufacturing eight-cylinder cars, those eight-cylinder monsters will remain clogged in the product market of the circular flow model, never making it through the clockwise flow in Exhibit 1 from the product market to the households. And if those cars don't end up in households, the money that General Motors expects to receive from selling those cars—the counterclockwise flow of dollars from households to firms—never materializes.

But General Motors does produce four-cylinder cars precisely because your wishes are its command. For the same reason, other firms produce the tens of thousands of other goods and services we demand from the market daily. Firms produce these goods and services not to please us, but because they are interested in pleasing themselves. That is to say, we get the goods we want because firms pursue their own self-interest.

Even though no one actually tells firms in the circular flow model what to produce, the right goods get produced in the right quantities because firms keep their antennae fixed on the product market. That's where consumer sovereignty, originating in the households, is expressed.

Study the circular flow model again. You may not see it, but an invisible hand guides the firms to produce only those goods consumers want. This invisible hand is nothing more (or less) than the combination of consumer sovereignty and firms' self-interest operating on the product market.

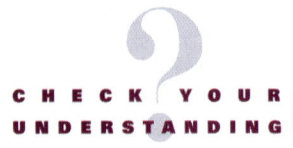

**CHECK YOUR UNDERSTANDING**

What's the difference between positive and normative economics?

**Positive economics**
A subset of economics that analyzes the way the economy actually operates.

**Normative economics**
A subset of economics founded on value judgments and leading to assertions of what ought to be.

unemployment? Why does it fluctuate from periods of economic prosperity to periods of economic recession?

## Positive and Normative Economics

It is one thing for economists to explain why our economy grows at 2.6 percent per year and quite another to advocate that it ought to grow faster. It is one thing to explain why the price of corn is $2.10 per bushel and another to advocate that it ought to be higher. It is one thing to explain what happens when firms in certain industries merge and another to advocate that they ought to merge.

You see the differences, don't you? One is a statement of fact (the economy grows at 2.6 percent per year), while the other passes judgment (it ought to grow faster). Economists are typically very careful about differentiating between analysis of *what is* and *what ought to be*. These are not mutually exclusive, but they are different. Economists refer to *what is* analysis as **positive economics** and *what ought to be* analysis as **normative economics.**

There's nothing inherently wrong with advocacy, although these *oughts* are heavily laden with personal and social values. For example, should we have a minimum wage? Should we subsidize farmers? Should we protect our steel industry? Should we tax the rich more than the poor? Should we disallow mergers? Should we regulate bank loans? Should we monitor industrial pollution? Should we control population size?

These are serious economic issues. There is nothing improper about economists applying their own values to economic issues, as long as we know where their value judgments start and their economic analysis ends. It is sometimes difficult to separate the two. Economists, at times, unintentionally disguise advocacy in the language of positive economics. The simple cause-and-effect analysis of positive economics is sometimes taken one step further to advocate policy. For example, analyses of market structures are not always separated from the economists' general view that perfect competition is the most socially desirable market form. Most economists share that view, and some will even argue that their analysis of market structures leads inexorably to that view. Their *analysis* of markets may be positive economics, but their *judgment* that competitive markets are more desirable is normative.

## WHAT DO ECONOMISTS KNOW?

Does it matter much what policies economists advocate? It matters very much. The White House, for example, has its own Council of Economic Advisers. Congress and the Federal Reserve System have their own cadres of economists. Many corporations, banks, and labor unions have economists on their payrolls. Economists are everywhere in the media, explaining and advising. Still, what do they know?

We listen attentively each morning to the weather forecast, although few of us fully trust what we hear. We know from experience that if the meteorologist predicts sunny skies, we take an umbrella along for insurance. Meteorologists seem to be forever explaining why yesterday's forecast turned out to be inaccurate. Sometimes we feel that they do not know much more about the weather than we do. But, in fact, they do.

The problem is not their forecast, but our reading of it. We expect too much. The forecast is sunny skies *if* the highs and lows behave properly. Remember ceteris paribus? The forecast depends on the fronts moving into our weather region as

The Council of Economic Advisers (http://www.whitehouse.gov/WH/EOP/CEA/html/) and the Bank of America (http://www.bankofamerica.com/) are two examples of organizations that hire economists to predict how the economy will behave.

expected. If they don't, all bets are off. How can meteorologists be held accountable for totally unpredictable changes?

In this respect, economic forecasting is similar to meteorological forecasting. Economic analysis is typically conditioned on the assumption of ceteris paribus, that is, that everything else remains unchanged, but it usually doesn't. The economists' world is one of uncertainty, and economists cannot take into account unforeseen future events that come to bear on their analyses. Explaining why previous economic forecasts were inaccurate doesn't build confidence. Instead, people think twice about whether economists really know more about the economy than anybody else. They do.

In the past fifty years, there has been a continuing, dramatic enrichment of our economic knowledge. New and more sophisticated models have been developed to represent our changing world. Also, the growth of economic data along with the ability to apply modern statistical methods to test models have created a branch of economics called **econometrics.** Econometricians are busy expanding these new and exciting areas of quantitative economic research.

In macroeconomics, for example, we now know more about what determines the levels of national income and employment than ever before. Knowing more doesn't necessarily resolve controversy, however. For example, there is no consensus among economists concerning the role government should play in our economy. Much of the debate is founded upon different readings of the same data.

In microeconomics, quantitative research on international trade, tax incidence, and market and investment behavior is adding more information to an already rich literature. New theories about uncertainty have given economists new insights into microeconomic questions.

Economists can rightfully claim to have covered an impressive intellectual distance in a very short period of time. Economists really do have something to say, but they realize that they must forever be on guard against claiming too much. As in medical research, the more we know, the more complex are the questions we can ask. Today, the task of the economist is no less difficult than fifty years ago, and the problems encountered no easier. The results of our economic research tell us just a little bit more about ourselves and are well worth the effort.

**Econometrics**
The use of statistics to quantify and test economic models.

Take a look at econometricians in practice. Visit the econometrics group at the University of Illinois (http://www.econ.uiuc.edu/) and the econometrics laboratory at the University of California, Berkeley (http://elsa.berkeley.edu/eml/).

# CHAPTER REVIEW

1. Natural resources are gifts of nature. Our supplies of them are basically finite, fixed by what the earth makes available. Some natural resources are renewable, such as our forests and livestock. Others are nonrenewable, such as our supplies of copper and iron ore.

2. Our wants of goods and services seem to be unlimited and forever expanding. We are able to conjure up new wants just as readily as we have learned how to satisfy others.

3. The problem of economic scarcity is defined by these facts: Our natural resources are limited, while our wants are unlimited. This universal scarcity forces us to make choices concerning which of our unlimited wants we will satisfy and which ones we will not.

4. Economics is the study of how we deal with scarcity. We define economics as the study of how we work together to transform resources into goods and services to satisfy our most pressing wants, and how we distribute these goods and services among ourselves.

5. Economics is an integral part of the social sciences discipline, which includes sociology,

6. Economists use models to describe economic behavior. These models are abstractions of the real world, based on simplifying assumptions about that world, which allow us to focus on basic economic relationships in the model. By understanding cause-and-effect relationships in the model, economists believe they can better understand how the real world works.
7. Microeconomics explains economic relationships at the level of the individual consumer, firm, or industry, addressing such questions as what determines people's demand for goods, why some prices increase while others decrease, and why some people earn higher incomes than others.
8. Macroeconomics considers the economic behavior of an entire economy, addressing such questions as what determines national economic growth and why unemployment and inflation occur.
9. Positive economic statements are statements of fact. For example, "When the price of popcorn increases, the quantity demanded of popcorn decreases." Normative economic statements are statements expressing value judgments. For example, "The price of popcorn is too high."

# KEY TERMS

Natural resources
Scarcity
Economics
Consumer sovereignty
Economic model
Ceteris paribus
Circular flow model
Household
Firm
Invisible hand
Microeconomics
Macroeconomics
Positive economics
Normative economics
Econometrics

# QUESTIONS

1. Does scarcity *always* require us to make choices? Why or why not?
2. Is the idea of insatiable wants unreasonable? Can you imagine a situation in which you have everything you want? What about everything you *need*?
3. What is the difference between renewable and nonrenewable resources?
4. Do you think we should be conserving our oil resources for future generations? After all, there is only so much oil on earth. List the main arguments you can make in favor of conservation. List arguments opposed to conservation.
5. What do you think would happen to our idea of the basic economic problem if we discovered a natural resource that could reproduce itself any number of times and could be transformed by labor into any good or service? Before answering, make sure you understand what the basic economic problem is.
6. What is economics? Why is economics considered one of the social sciences? What are some of the other social sciences? What do social scientists study?
7. What does *ceteris paribus* mean? Why is the concept useful to economists? Cite an example.
8. What defines an economic model? In what way is the circular flow model a simplification of reality? Why would economists want to simplify reality?
9. What is the difference between resource markets and product markets? Cite examples.
10. Consider these two statements: "Fifteen percent of our people live below the poverty line" and "Too many people live below the poverty line." Can you distinguish the positive economic statement from the normative economic statement? Compose two additional examples of each.

11. Suppose you look through the catalog of advanced economic courses and find two that particularly appeal to you: Economics 306, the study of the health care industry, and Economics 359, the study of why economies grow. Which would you take to satisfy the college's requirement for a microeconomics course?
12. Suppose your economics professor predicted that the rate of inflation would be 5 percent by the time you took the first economics exam. Instead, the inflation rate was twice the predicted rate. Would you categorically dismiss the professor as a poor predictor and, perhaps worse, an unknowledgeable economist? Why or why not?
13. Identify where each of the following belongs (upper or lower half, flowing in which direction) in the circular flow model in Exhibit 1: automobiles, automobile workers, your purchase of a new automobile, and a $100 rebate payment you receive from General Motors.
14. Consumer sovereignty is an integral part of a democratic society. Why?

# PRACTICE PROBLEM

1. Construct a circular flow, and fill in the missing value.

| | |
|---|---|
| **CONSUMER SPENDING FOR GOODS AND SERVICES** | **$57** |
| WAGES | |
| INTEREST | $ 6 |
| RENT | $ 4 |
| PROFIT | $ 7 |

# ECONOMIC CONSULTANTS

## ECONOMIC RESEARCH AND ANALYSIS BY STUDENTS FOR PROFESSIONALS

Computer Sell! is a retailer of computers and software. The owners of Computer Sell! are worried that they do not understand the economics of the computer industry or the economic events that affect this industry.

The owners of Computer Sell! have approached Economic Consultants for advice. Prepare a report for Computer Sell! that addresses the following issues:

1. In general, what resources are available?
2. What sources of economic news and analysis, if any, are available for the national economy? For the regional economy where you currently are?
3. What economic resources for the computer industry, if any, are available on the Internet?

You may find the following resources helpful as you prepare this report for Computer Sell!:

- **Yahoo!** (http://www.yahoo.com), **Excite** (http://www.excite.com/), and **Lycos** (http://www.lycos.com/)—These popular search engines and directories enable you to get a quick grasp of what is available on the Internet for certain topics, such as economics.
- **Resources for Economists on the Internet** (http://rfe.wustl.edu/EconFAQ.html) and **WebEc** (http://www.helsinki.fi/WebEc/WebEc.html)—Resources for Economists and WebEc are directories that focus exclusively on economic materials on the Internet.
- **ZDNet** (http://www.zdnet.com/) and **News.Com** (http://www.news.com/)—ZDNet and News.Com, sponsored by CNET, provide news coverage of the technology industry.

# PRACTICE TEST

1. Which of the following is not microeconomic subject matter?
   a. The price of bananas
   b. The quantity of bananas produced for the banana market
   c. The cost of producing a fire truck for the fire department of Cincinnati
   d. The cost of producing a fire truck for the fire department of London, England
   e. The national economy's annual rate of growth

2. JULIE: My corn harvest this year is very poor.
   DANA: Don't worry. Price increases will compensate for the fall in quantity supplied.
   KIM: Climate affects crop yields. Some years are good, others are bad.
   LISA: The government ought to guarantee that our incomes will not fall.
   In this conversation, the normative statement is made by
   a. Julie.
   b. Dana.
   c. Kim.
   d. Lisa.
   e. There are no normative statements.

3. Consider the following and decide which, if any, economy is without scarcity.
   a. The pre–Civil War U.S. economy, where most people were farmers
   b. A mythical economy where everyone is a billionaire
   c. Any economy where there is full employment of resources
   d. Any economy where income is distributed equally among its people
   e. None of the above

4. In our economy, people have the freedom to buy or not buy the goods offered in the marketplace, and this freedom to choose what they want to buy dictates what producers will ultimately produce. The key term defining this condition is
   a. economic power of choice.
   b. consumer sovereignty.
   c. ultimate producer sovereignty.
   d. political economy.
   e. positive economics.

5. Economic models
   a. are designed to explain all aspects of the economy.
   b. never employ assumptions that cannot be tested.
   c. abstract from reality to reduce the complexity of the world we live in to more simplified, manageable dimensions.
   d. provide detailed statistical analysis of the economy.
   e. are more useful in macroeconomic applications than in microeconomic ones.

6. In the circular flow model,
   a. households supply resources to firms through the resource market.
   b. households buy goods and services in the product market.
   c. money flows from firms to households through the resource market.
   d. All of the above
   e. None of the above

7. Apply the idea of a nonrenewable resource to best describe one of the following as nonrenewable:
   a. Eggs used in baking a cake
   b. Corn used to feed hogs
   c. Copper tubing used in residential construction
   d. Hot water used in commercial laundries
   e. Lumber used in industrial construction

8. Which of the following is not one of the four central questions that the study of economics is supposed to answer?
   a. Who produces what?
   b. How are goods produced?
   c. Who consumes what?
   d. When are goods produced?
   e. Who decides what goods to produce?

9. Ceteris paribus is a tool used by economists to
   a. develop one-to-one, cause-and-effect economic relationships.
   b. link resources to goods and services.
   c. promote consumer sovereignty.
   d. distinguish microeconomics from macroeconomics.
   e. perform modern statistical testing of economic data.

10. Econometrics
    a. links positive to normative economics.
    b. applies modern statistical methods to test models.
    c. is an appropriate use of economic models.
    d. is real-world economics as distinguished from economic models.
    e. is the use of ceteris paribus in real-world situations.

# APPENDIX
## ON READING GRAPHS

## THE ONLY THING WE HAVE TO FEAR IS FEAR ITSELF

It's happened a zillion times: Students buy their economics textbooks, flip through the pages, spot the dozens of equations and graphs, and fear, before they start, that it's going to be a losing battle. But it hardly ever is, and certainly not because of the graphs or mathematics. There simply isn't enough information in those graphs or equations to confuse or exasperate.

If you can shake the trauma of the graphic and mathematical form of expression, you will do just fine. As President Franklin D. Roosevelt said during his 1933 inaugural speech, "The only thing we have to fear is fear itself!"

### A Graphic Language

Graphs and mathematics are simplified languages. Most of what appears in graphics or mathematics can be described in written form—in fact, most ideas are best expressed that way. In *some* circumstances, however, the written exposition becomes so convoluted that graphs and equations can present the idea more clearly.

Suppose, for example, that the simple arithmetic statement

$$(4)(6) + (8/2) - 12 = 16$$

were written as 12 subtracted from the product of 4 multiplied by 6 plus the quotient of 8 divided by 2 equals 16. You lose track of the calculations, don't you? The equation form is easier to read. Graphs are like that, too. They are pictorial representations of ideas that could be expressed otherwise, but not with the same degree of clarity.

### Know Your Point of Reference

When you read a map, you typically measure out where you want to go from where you are. The where-you-are position is always your point of reference, putting everything else in place.

If you're sitting in St. Louis, Missouri, then Kansas City, Kansas, is 257 miles due west. If you're searching for Louisville, Kentucky, it's 256 miles due east. Kansas City and Louisville are west and east only because you're looking at them from St. Louis. People in Tallahassee, Florida, see Atlanta as due north, but viewed from St. Louis, Atlanta is southeast. In map reading, everything is measured from a point of reference.

Graphs are read the same way. If you can read a map, you can read a graph. Look at Exhibit A1.

*The graph's point of reference is called the* **origin.** Using our map example, the origin is the graph's St. Louis. Everything on the graph is measured from it. Points can be viewed as lying to the east of the origin, or to the west, or north, or south. More

**Origin**
A graph's point of reference.

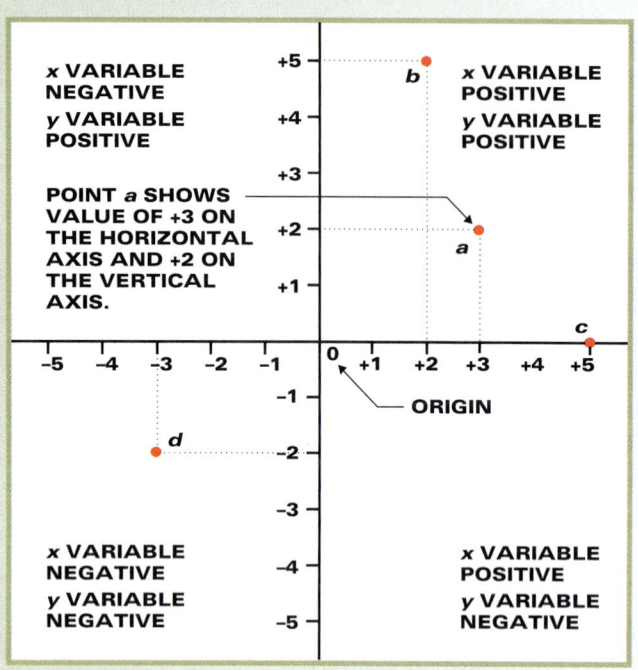

precise readings describe the points as "north by northwest" or "east by southeast." You can see them in your mind's eye.

Note that Exhibit A1 is divided into four quadrants (or parts). The vertical ($y$) axis—running north and south through the origin—and the horizontal ($x$) axis—running east and west through the origin—are its dividers.

## Measuring Distances on Graphs

Have you ever seen a NASA space shot countdown? As you know, its point of reference is blastoff. Typically, NASA starts counting before ignition. If you're watching on TV, you'll see the digital readout register $-10$ seconds, then $-9$, then $-8$, counting down to 0. At 0, ignition occurs and the count continues from 0 to $+1$ seconds, then $+2$, and so on. The time scale is a continuum, with 0 separating the minuses from the pluses.

Graph scaling is also on a continuum. In Exhibit A1, the vertical scale north of the origin (which is 0) and the horizontal scale east of the origin (which is 0) measure positive values. For example, point $a$, located at $(+3, +2)$, reads $+3$ units away from the origin horizontally and $+2$ units away from the origin vertically. It marks the intersection of $+3$ and $+2$. Point $b$, located at $(+2, +5)$, reads $+2$ units away from the origin horizontally and $+5$ units away from the origin vertically. Look at point $c$ $(+5, 0)$. It is $+5$ units away from the origin horizontally and at 0 on the vertical scale.

The vertical scale south of the origin and the horizontal scale west of the origin measure negative values. For example, point $d$, located at $(-3, -2)$, reads $-3$ units away from 0 horizontally and $-2$ units away from the origin vertically. As you see, every point in every quadrant has its own specific numerical bearings.

## Graphing Relationships

It's generally true that the more you study, the higher your grade. Suppose somebody who is less convinced than you about the relationship between effort and reward insists on evidence. What can you do to make the point? If logic doesn't work, perhaps a test will. For example, you could experiment with Economics 101 and over the course of the semester, compare your exam scores with the number of hours spent studying for them.

The underlying assumption in such a relationship is that exam scores *depend* on the number of hours of study. By varying the hours studied, you vary the scores obtained. Hours studied is described as the **independent variable** in the relationship, exam scores as the **dependent variable.**

Typically, economists work with relationships that express dependence. For example, the quantity of fish people are willing to buy depends on the price of fish. The price of fish is the independent variable, and the quantity people are willing to buy is the dependent one. The amount of money people spend consuming goods and services depends on their income—again a link between a dependent variable and an independent one. Another such dependent relationship is the number of hours people are willing to work and the wage rate offered.

Suppose you find that with 0 hours of study, you fail miserably, scoring 20 out of a possible 100. With 2 hours per week of study, you score 50. With 5 hours per week, you raise your grade to 70. With 7 hours per week, your grade improves to 80. With 10 hours per week, you top the class with the highest score, 85.

If you experimented with Biology 101 exams, the effort-and-reward relationship would still be positive, but the specific payoffs might be different. For example, with 0 hours, you still fail, this time scoring only 12 out of a possible 100. With 2 hours per week, you score only 35. With 5 hours, you get considerably better, scoring 55; with 7 hours, you score 70; and with 10 hours a week studying biology, you score 75.

That's convincing evidence that increased hours of study produce higher grades, but the written presentation can get confusing, particularly when the number of exams and courses increases. The written form is not always the clearest way to express observations.

Perhaps a clearer presentation of the evidence could be made by converting the information into table form. Look, for example, at the table in Exhibit A2.

Is it any clearer? The information is the same; it's just displayed differently. It is easier to see that the more time spent on study, the higher the score, and comparisons between economics and biology are more readily observed.

**Independent variable**
A variable whose value influences the value of another variable.

**Dependent variable**
A variable whose value depends on the value of another variable.

Look how the same information is transcribed into graphic form. Exhibit A2, panel *a*, records the same information as the table.

As you see, in panel *a*, hours of study are measured along the horizontal axis. Exam scores are measured along the vertical axis. Both variables in our example are positive. Therefore, the corresponding points in the table—such as 5 hours of study and an exam score of 70 in economics—locate in the upper-right quadrant of the graph. Both graphs in Exhibit A2 show that quadrant.

## Connecting Points to Form Curves

The table and graphs in panel *a*, Exhibit A2, are abbreviated

**TEST SCORES FOR ECONOMICS 101 AND BIOLOGY 101**

NUMBER OF HOURS SPENT STUDYING AND TEST SCORES FOR ECONOMICS 101 AND BIOLOGY 101

| HOURS | ECONOMICS 101 SCORES | BIOLOGY 101 SCORES |
|---|---|---|
| 0 | 20 | 12 |
| 2 | 50 | 35 |
| 5 | 70 | 55 |
| 7 | 80 | 70 |
| 10 | 85 | 75 |

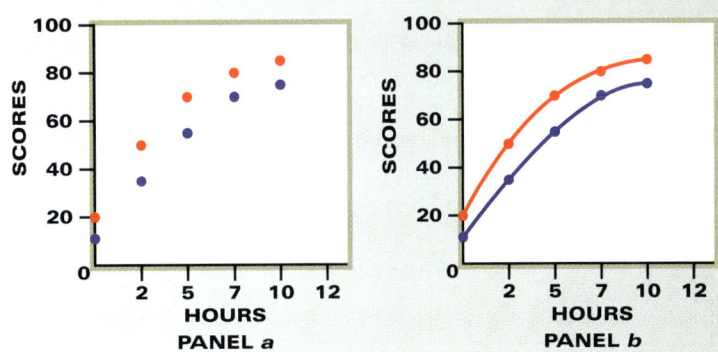

displays of evidence. They record only ten pieces of data. The experiment could have been expanded to record an exam score for every hour of study, or even every minute instead of every five hours. That is, if the intervals between the points in panel *a* could be filled in to create a *continuous* series of data points connecting study hours and exam scores (unrealistic, of course, because nobody could take that many exams in one semester), such a completed series would trace a continuous curve on the graph, which is what we see in panel *b*.

But is it necessary to ascertain every point to create a curve? Suppose you want to graph the relationship between income and saving. And suppose the table accompanying Exhibit A3 presents the relevant data.

Note that the data set starts with $40,000 of income. If the graph were to plot *every* income value from $0 at the origin to, say, $43,000 in units of $1,000, 43 units would be marked off on the horizontal axis, but only the last 4 of the 43 units would bear any data. The graph becomes dominated then by empty, dataless space. And to keep the graph within the bounds of the page, it may even be necessary to make each income unit represent $2,000. By doing so, it becomes even more difficult to read on the vertical axis the increases in saving that are associated with the $1,000 increases in income.

Breaking the axes—as shown in Exhibit A3—cuts out the empty, dataless space. The break, introduced after the first units on both the vertical and horizontal axes, allows the graphmaker to magnify the data, making it easier for the reader to focus on the relevant part of the graph. The 40th unit of income follows the break on the horizontal axis, and the 80th unit of saving—each unit representing $1,000 of saving—follows the first unit on the vertical axis. The resulting graph maps out a clear picture of the saving curve.

### EXHIBIT A3

#### INCOME AND SAVING

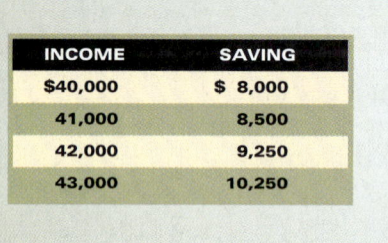

| INCOME | SAVING |
|---|---|
| $40,000 | $ 8,000 |
| 41,000 | 8,500 |
| 42,000 | 9,250 |
| 43,000 | 10,250 |

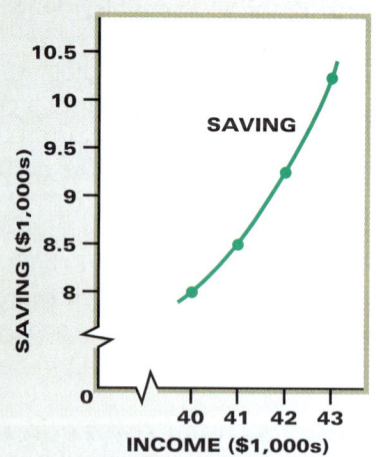

## THE SLOPE OF A CURVE

Consider the law of demand: As the price of a good falls, the quantity of the good demanded increases. The table and graph in panel *a*, Exhibit A4, depict such a relationship between the price of fish and quantity demanded. (The law of demand will be studied more closely in Chapter 3.)

Panel *a*, Exhibit A4, connects the discrete data given in the accompanying table to form a solid curve that, as you see, is in the form of a straight line.

The **slope of a curve** measures the ratio of change in the value on the vertical axis to the corresponding change in value on the horizontal axis between two points:

$$\text{slope} = \frac{\text{rise}}{\text{run}} = \frac{\text{change in the value on vertical axis}}{\text{change in the value on horizontal axis}}$$

**Slope of a curve**
The ratio of the change in the variable measured on the vertical axis to the corresponding change in the variable measured on the horizontal axis, between two points.

Downward-sloping curves—sloping from northwest to southeast—are considered *negatively sloped;* that is, a positive (negative) change in the independent variable is associated with a negative (positive) change in the dependent variable. Upward-sloping curves—sloping from southwest to northeast—are *positively sloped;* that is, a positive (negative) change in the independent variable is associated with a positive (negative) change in the dependent variable.

Look again at Exhibit A4, panel *a*. Every $1 change in price generates a 1-unit change in quantity demanded. For example, when price falls from $10 to $9 (−$1), the quantity demanded increases from 1 to 2 fish (+1). The slope of the curve, within the $10 to $9 price range, then, is

$$-1/+1 = -1$$

The slope is negative. Note that any other price change within any other price range in this example still generates a negative slope of −1. When price increases from $3 to $4 (+$1), the quantity demanded decreases from 7 fish to 6 (−1). The slope +1/−1 remains −1. *Any curve with a constant slope is a straight line.* That's precisely what we see in panel *a*.

Panel *b* represents a typical supply curve. It depicts the willingness of the fishing industry to supply varying quantities of fish at varying prices. The curve slopes upward, indicating that higher prices induce greater quantities supplied. Unlike the demand curve in panel *a*, the supply curve here is not a straight line. It is less steep at low price ranges than at higher ones. Let's calculate the slopes within different price ranges. When price increases from $2 to $3 (+$1), the quantity supplied increases from 3 to 5 fish (+2). The slope of the curve, within the $2 to $3 price range, then, is

$$+1/+2 = +0.5$$

But when the price rises from $3 to $4 (+$1), the quantity supplied increases only from 5 fish to 6 (+1). The slope of the curve within the $3 to $4 price range is

$$+1/+1 = +1$$

There's nothing peculiar or complicated about any curve on any graph or the measurement of its slope. The slope of the curve is only a

## PRICE AND QUANTITIES DEMANDED AND SUPPLIED OF FISH

### PRICE AND QUANTITY DEMANDED OF FISH

| PRICE | QUANTITY DEMANDED |
|-------|-------------------|
| 10    | 1                 |
| 9     | 2                 |
| 8     | 3                 |
| 7     | 4                 |
| 6     | 5                 |
| 5     | 6                 |
| 4     | 7                 |
| 3     | 8                 |
| 2     | 9                 |
| 1     | 10                |

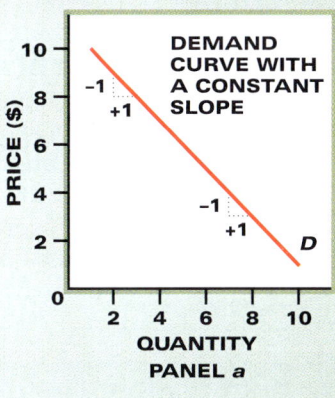

PANEL *a*

### PRICE AND QUANTITY SUPPLIED OF FISH

| PRICE | QUANTITY SUPPLIED |
|-------|-------------------|
| 5     | 6.5               |
| 4     | 6                 |
| 3     | 5                 |
| 2     | 3                 |
| 1     | 0                 |

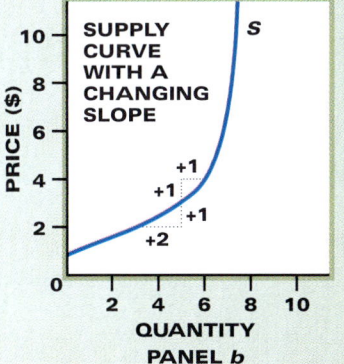

PANEL *b*

numerical way of expressing the curve's shape. The numerical value signals the strength of the relationship between changes in the variables measured on the vertical and horizontal axes.

## U-Shaped and Hill-Shaped Curves

Some curves that are part of the economists' bag of tools contain both positive- and negative-sloping segments. Look, for example, at Exhibit A5, panels *a* and *b*.

The U-shaped curve in panel *a* shows the relationship between the average cost of producing a good and the quantity of goods produced. Typically, the average cost falls as more units are produced—that's the downward-sloping part of the curve. Beyond some point, however—100 units in panel *a*—average cost begins to increase with production, which is the upward-sloping part of the curve.

From 0 to 100 units, the slope of the curve, although changing, is always negative. Beyond 100 units, it becomes positive. There's nothing complicated about reading the graph if you consider each point on the curve, one at a time. *Every point on that U-shaped average cost curve represents a specific quantitative relationship between average cost and level of production.* Nothing more!

The hill-shaped curve in panel *b* is much the same. It shows the relationship between the total utility or benefit derived from consuming a good and the quantity of goods consumed. The basic idea is that for some goods—water, for instance—the more consumed, the greater the total enjoyment, but only up to a point. Beyond that point—100 units in panel *b*—the more water, the lower the total enjoyment. Who, for example, enjoys a flood? From 0 to 100 units, the slope of this curve is positive, but it becomes negative thereafter.

## Vertical and Horizontal Curves

Economists also work with relationships that, when graphed, trace out as perfectly vertical or horizontal curves. These are represented in Exhibit A6, panels *a* and *b*.

Consider the circumstance where a fisherman returns home after a day's work with 100 fish. Suppose he is willing to supply those fish at whatever price the fish will fetch. After all, a day-old fish isn't something to prize. If the price is $10 per fish, he is willing to sell all 100. If the price is only $9, he is still willing to sell all of them. If the price is $100 per fish, he *still* will supply only 100 fish, because the day's work is done and there are no more fish available. The supply curve, shown in panel *a*, is a vertical line to denote a supply of 100 fish, whatever the price. Its slope is everywhere infinite. That is, when price changes from $10 to $9 (−$1), quantity doesn't change (0). The slope, then, is −1/0. That's infinity.

What about the perfectly horizontal curve? Suppose you are selling tomatoes in an outdoor market, competing against hundreds of other tomato growers. Suppose also that the price is $0.50 per

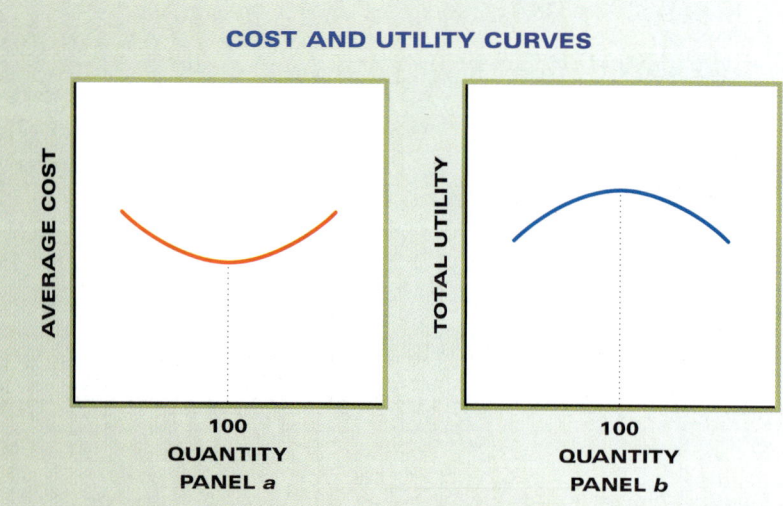

COST AND UTILITY CURVES

pound, and you can sell as much as you want at that price. If you were to raise your price by just one penny, or even less, you couldn't sell any tomatoes at all. What a difference a fraction of a penny makes! After all, why would anyone buy your tomatoes when they can buy all they want from your competitors at $0.50?

How would you graph the demand curve you face? It would be a straight horizontal curve, as shown in panel *b*. At $0.50 you could sell 10, 20, or 200 tomatoes. At just an infinitesimally small increase—approaching 0—in price, you sell 0 tomatoes. The slope, then, is 0 divided by any number, which is 0.

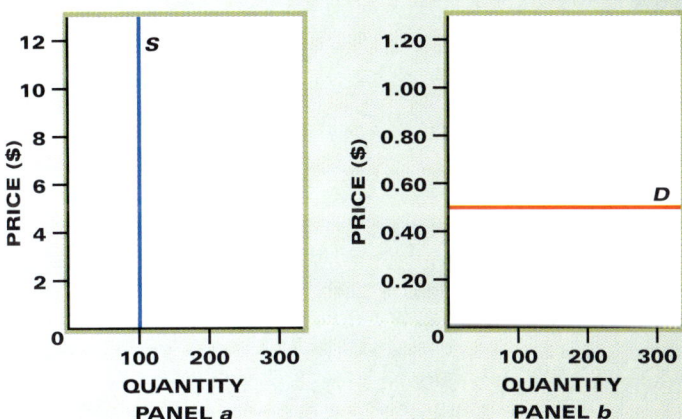

**VERTICAL SUPPLY CURVE AND HORIZONTAL DEMAND CURVE**

## Measuring the Slope of a Point on a Curve

Look at the U-shaped curve of Exhibit A7.

To find the slope of any point on the curve, draw a **tangent**—a straight line just touching the curve—at the point where the slope is to be measured. The **slope of the tangent** is the same as the slope of the curve at the point of tangency. What is the slope of the tangent? Look at tangent *td* at point *a* on the curve. Its slope is *ac/cd*, or numerically,

$$-10/+15 = -2/3$$

The minus sign indicates that the point of tangency lies on the downward-sloping part of the curve.

What about the slope at point *b*? Draw the tangent, *et'*. Its slope is *bf/ef*, or numerically,

$$+10/+20 = +1/2$$

Its positive value indicates it is on the upward-sloping part of the U-shaped curve.

**Tangent**
A straight line that touches a curve at only one point.

**Slope of a tangent**
The slope of a curve at its point of tangency.

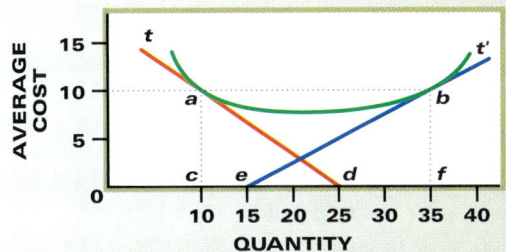

**MEASURING THE SLOPE AT A POINT ON A CURVE**

# KEY TERMS

Origin
Independent variable

Dependent variable
Slope of a curve

Tangent
Slope of a tangent

# CHAPTER 2

## PRODUCTION POSSIBILITIES AND OPPORTUNITY COSTS

Biologists talk about their field of study without worrying whether people will misunderstand the words they use. A monocotyledon is a monocotyledon—no one ever mistakes it for a screwdriver. Biologists have a language all their own.

Economists, too, have developed their own language, but the vocabulary they choose is rather commonplace. When economists talk about labor, most people feel right at home. People also know what capital, rent, profit, prices, competition, monopoly, money, income, and employment mean.

Unfortunately, what people understand these terms to mean is not always what economists understand them to mean. To understand how economists use these terms may sometimes require more effort to unlearn what we already know than to learn what the economists mean.

**THIS CHAPTER INTRODUCES YOU TO THE ECONOMIC PRINCIPLES ASSOCIATED WITH:**

- FACTORS OF PRODUCTION
- PRODUCTION POSSIBILITIES
- OPPORTUNITY COST
- THE LAW OF INCREASING COSTS
- TECHNOLOGICAL CHANGE AND ECONOMIC GROWTH
- DIVISION OF LABOR AND SPECIALIZATION
- ABSOLUTE AND COMPARATIVE ADVANTAGE

## FACTORS OF PRODUCTION

Economists refer to the resources used in the production of goods and services as **factors of production.** The four factors are labor, capital, land, entrepreneurship.

The two human factors are labor and entrepreneurship. The other two, capital and land, are nonhuman factors.

### Labor

**Labor** is the physical and mental exertion of people engaged in the production of goods and services. Labor willingly sells its skills in the resource market for agreed-upon prices. There is no coercion involved, and the agreements or contracts typically specify price per hour, per week, or per year.

The absence of coercion and the limitations specified in the contract are critical characteristics of the economists' definition of labor. No one sells his or her labor to a firm forever. To economists, slave labor is not regarded as a labor resource at all, since slaves never willingly offer their labor for a price. Bought and sold on slave markets, they are forced to work. Incredible as it may seem, slaves were regarded by slaveowners and the courts as personal property. What about prison labor today? Do inmates willingly offer their services? Who decides the price? If it's not labor, then what is it? You can see that the economists' concept of labor is narrowly defined and can be somewhat more complicated than first imagined. What about peasants who are harnessed to crude, wooden plows in Third World economies? In these economies people and animals are sometimes interchangeable, pulling plows across tough topsoils. Certainly a water buffalo isn't labor. What, then, is the peasant who substitutes for the water buffalo?

### Capital

What identifies **capital?** Capital is a manufactured good used in the production and marketing of goods and services that households consume. Because capital is not directly consumed by households, it is sometimes referred to as an intermediate good. For example, shoemakers' tools and machinery used to produce shoes are not household items. The shoes, of course, are. The stocks of shoe inventory are capital goods. The shoes in inventory become household consumption goods only when they are actually consumed by the household. Obviously, the factory that houses the machinery and inventories is a capital good.

What about robots? Robots that do what labor does are still only pieces of machinery. Store window mannequins are also capital goods because they are used to convert the finished goods inventory into household consumption. In the same way, the thousands of compact discs in record shop inventories are regarded as capital goods because the inventories are as necessary as the disc-making machinery in providing CDs for household consumption. How could you buy a particular CD if the store didn't carry it? It becomes a consumption good only when it is purchased by the consumer.

What about Michael Chang's tennis racket? It is a capital good used to produce a service. The service is our enjoyment at Wimbledon. That same racket in your hand is not capital. After all, it is used only for your own pleasure. David Letterman's stylish wardrobe is a capital good. Yours isn't.

**Factor of production**
Any resource used in a production process. Resources are grouped into labor, land, capital, and entrepreneurship.

**Labor**
The physical and intellectual effort of people engaged in producing goods and services.

**Capital**
Manufactured goods used to make and market other goods and services.

Can you think of other goods that would be capital to one person, but not to another? Go to the Interactive Study Center at http://gottheil.swcollege.com and click on the "Your Turn" button to submit your example. Student submissions will be posted to the Web site, and perhaps we will use some in future additions of the book!

**Human capital**
The knowledge and skills acquired by labor, principally through education and training.

Sometimes, capital gets mixed in with labor, so we end up with a hybrid factor. For instance, would Linda Marshall, working as a chemical engineer for Dow Chemical, be considered labor? Perhaps the most significant difference between Linda's work and the work of an unskilled laborer is her four years of college education. That education is capital. What then is the engineer, capital or labor? Economists refer to special skills, acquired through education or training, as **human capital.**

As you see, what is obvious to some people is less than obvious to economists. Is intelligence capital? If so, what's left of labor? Confusing? As you may already sense, differentiations between labor and capital as factors of production are as much philosophical issues as they are economic.

## Land

**Land**
A natural-state resource such as real estate, grasses and forests, and metals and minerals.

**Land** is a natural-state, nonhuman resource that is fixed in quantity. It includes both the real estate and the metals and minerals it contains. For example, an uncut diamond is land. A virgin forest is land. The oceans of oil underneath the North Sea are also land. To the economist, the Gobi Desert and the Pacific Ocean are land resources.

The problem with the economists' definition of land as a factor of production is that we seldom, if ever, see land in its natural state. A tree that is cut and used in production is no longer strictly a land resource. It becomes capital as well. It was cut down by labor and machines. Lumber, then, is a manufactured good. Irrigated land, too, is not strictly land. The irrigation system is capital. Any improved land is a combination of capital and land.

## Entrepreneurship

No good or service is produced by spontaneous combustion. Resources just don't come together on their own. *Somebody* has to conceive of the essential idea of production, decide what factors to use, market the goods and services produced, and accept the uncertainty of making or losing money in the venture. This somebody is the *entrepreneur,* a word that comes from the French, "to undertake." Although **entrepreneurs** who own and operate businesses typically do all these things, economists define their entrepreneurial role only in terms of the uncertainties of business they assume.

**Entrepreneur**
A person who alone assumes the risks and uncertainties of a business.

After all, entrepreneurs can delegate the buying of land, labor, and capital and the overseeing of production to a hired managerial staff. That's precisely what most modern corporations do. Managerial activity is labor. When entrepreneurs manage the production process, they function as laborers. Entrepreneurs can delegate every other function of production to labor, except the function of assuming risk and uncertainty.

We have briefly surveyed the four factors of production. Now let's put them to work.

# ROBINSON CRUSOE'S PRODUCTION POSSIBILITIES

Let's begin our analysis of production by imagining Robinson Crusoe, stranded and alone on an island. The resources at his disposal, while attractive, are limited. And being a person very much like you, he has unlimited wants. In other words, Crusoe, like all of us, faces the unshakable reality of economic scarcity. What can he do in this situation? Let's look at his options.

He can spend part of the day in leisure and part at work. He could pick mangoes right off the trees, or he can fish. He can plant and harvest crops. His principal factors of production are his own labor and the virgin land about him.

Let's suppose he decides to spend his waking hours gathering food for consumption. He climbs trees for mangoes and coconuts and spends the better part of the day trying to pick fish out of the lagoon. He ends each day with six units of consumption. It's enough to keep him going, but, of course, he wants more. How does he get it? Let's suppose he decides to make a fishing spear. That requires finding the right materials and fashioning a spear. He sets aside part of the day to find a young tree that will serve as the shank, a stone that can be sharpened to make a spearhead, and a length of vine to bind the two together.

This takes time. If he takes the time to produce the spear, he can gather only five units of consumption goods. Why then do it? Because with a fishing spear, he expects to catch more fish in the next round of production. It's a risk, of course. There's no guarantee he will catch more fish. Some expectations are never realized. But let's suppose he catches more. The spear is Robinson Crusoe's first unit of capital.

He decides to make a second spear as well to use as an extension tool so that he can reach the bigger, riper fruit at the top of the trees. He discovers that finding the right material for the second spear takes even more time than it did for the first. Why? He had already used the most available tree for the fishing spear's shank, the most available stone for the spearhead, and the most accessible length of vine to tie them together.

While he is producing both the fishing spear and the extension spear, he can manage to gather only three units of consumption goods. Why then do it? Because with both units of capital, he expects to produce considerably more consumption goods in the next round of production.

The Robinson Crusoe economy is simple, yet it contains all the elements of a modern, dynamic economy. It has capital goods production as well as consumption. Land, labor, capital, and entrepreneurship combine to create a set of goods and services.

The components of the set are variable. For example, these factors of production can be combined into any of the **production possibilities** shown in the table in Exhibit 1.

The first possibility is for Robinson Crusoe to allocate all his resources to producing consumption goods. If he does that, he ends up with six units of consumption. On the other hand, if he decides to produce a unit of capital, he ends up with only five units of consumption. As far as he's concerned, then, the unit of capital cost him one unit of consumption.

## Opportunity Cost

What economists mean by cost is **opportunity cost**—that is, the quantity of other goods that must be given up to obtain a good. That's a powerful notion of cost. It applies universally. For example, the opportunity cost of watching the L.A. Lakers play the Boston Celtics the night before an exam is the five points that could have earned an A. The opportunity cost of renovating the high school auditorium is the new biology lab that the school had been thinking about. Opportunity cost applies even where you may least suspect. For example, for a married couple, the opportunity cost of marriage to each partner is the opportunities each gives up that would have been possible had they remained single.

**CHECK YOUR UNDERSTANDING**
Why do people produce capital goods?

**Production possibilities**
The various combinations of goods that can be produced in an economy when it uses its available resources and technology efficiently.

**Opportunity cost**
The quantity of other goods that must be given up to obtain a good.

# EXHIBIT 1

### PRODUCTION POSSIBILITIES FRONTIER

Robinson Crusoe's economy can produce six consumption goods and zero capital goods, shown at point *a*. Alternatively, it can produce five consumption goods and one capital good (point *b*) three consumption goods and two capital goods (point *c*) zero consumption goods and three capital goods (point *d*) or any other combination located on this curve. The law of increasing costs accounts for the balloon-like shape of the production possibilities curve.

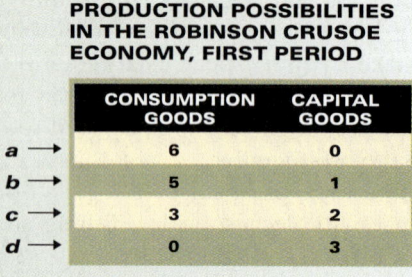

PRODUCTION POSSIBILITIES IN THE ROBINSON CRUSOE ECONOMY, FIRST PERIOD

| | CONSUMPTION GOODS | CAPITAL GOODS |
|---|---|---|
| a → | 6 | 0 |
| b → | 5 | 1 |
| c → | 3 | 2 |
| d → | 0 | 3 |

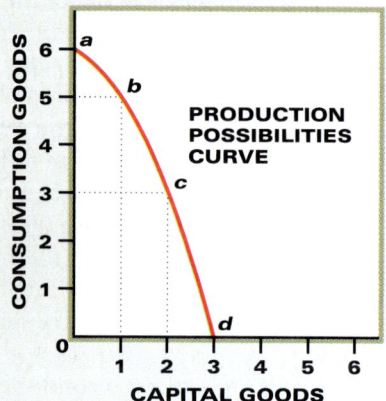

You see the connection, don't you? The thought that goes through Crusoe's mind when contemplating production is the same kind of thinking that you do before studying for an exam. You both think about the opportunities given up. But you make choices. When Crusoe gives up a unit of consumption goods to produce that first unit of capital goods, it's probably because he values that first unit of capital goods more than the consumption good given up. If you spend the evening studying for the exam, it's probably because you value the expected higher grade more than you do the Celtics game.

You may have erred. The game was the season's best and the studying didn't make a difference in your exam score. In hindsight, you find that the studying wasn't worth the cost. But what could you have done otherwise? Opportunity costs are typically subjective. How could you possibly know with certainty what opportunity costs are? Even Robinson Crusoe, making simple choices on the island, must rely on calculating *expected* gains and opportunity costs of choices made.

## The Law of Increasing Costs

If Robinson Crusoe decides to produce two units of capital, he ends up with only three units of consumption. Measured in terms of its opportunity cost, that second unit of capital costs Crusoe two units of consumption. That is more than he had to give up for the first unit of capital.

What happens if he decides to produce three units of capital? Look again at the table in Exhibit 1. Their production absorbs all the resources available. He ends up with nothing at all to consume! The opportunity cost of that third unit of capital is the remaining three units of consumption.

Do you notice what's happening? The opportunity cost of producing each additional unit of capital increases as more of the units are produced. Economists refer to this fact of economic life as the **law of increasing costs.** It applies no matter what goods are considered. For example, if Robinson Crusoe had started with three units of capital and began adding consumption, the amount of capital goods he

**Law of increasing costs**
The opportunity cost of producing a good increases as more of the good is produced. The law is based on the fact that not all resources are suited to the production of all goods and that the order of use of a resource in producing a good goes from the most productive resource unit to the least.

# APPLIED PERSPECTIVE

### DID YOU EVER FIND A PENNY ON A SIDEWALK?

How many times, strolling along a sidewalk, have you chanced upon a shiny new penny lying in your path? Picking it up is supposed to bring you good luck. But luck aside; it's fun to find it, isn't it? But what about nickels, dimes, and quarters, not to mention Susan B. Anthony dollar coins? When was the last time you saw one of those shiny silver coins lying on the sidewalk? If you're like most people, these silver coins are pretty scarce items on a sidewalk, at least compared to the copper coins we find.

Why? Is it because the supply of pennies is more plentiful than the supply of nickels, dimes, and quarters? It is more plentiful. The U.S. Mint produces about 10 billion pennies a year compared to the approximately 6 billion nickels, dimes, and quarters. But that really doesn't explain why we are more likely to see pennies on the sidewalk than silver coins.

SOME COINS YES, SOME COINS NO.

The answer has to do with opportunity cost. If you're walking home and spot a Susan B. Anthony dollar on the sidewalk, wouldn't you pick it up? You probably wouldn't turn your nose up at a quarter either. Even a dime or nickel is for many people worth the effort of bending down and picking up. A penny? Considerably less so.

The reason why you find so many pennies on the sidewalk relative to silver coins is because it takes time and energy to stop, bend down, and pick them up, and that time and energy are valued more than a penny. That's why pennies on the sidewalk are not an uncommon sight. We simply pass them up. The opportunity cost associated with picking them up is too high. The quarter? Most people place a higher value on a quarter they find than on the time and energy it takes to pick up, which explains why you find so few quarters on the street. They are quickly gobbled up. It's all a matter of opportunity cost.

would have to give up to produce each additional unit of consumption would also increase. The graph in Exhibit 1 illustrates the production possibilities of the table in graphic form.

Look at points *a, b, c,* and *d* in Exhibit 1. These are precisely the production possibilities shown in the table. Point *a,* for example, represents the choice of devoting all resources to the production of six units of consumption. The curve has a negative slope because any increase in capital goods production comes only at the cost of consumption goods production.

The bowed-out shape to the curve illustrates the law of increasing costs. When Crusoe decides to increase capital goods production from one unit to two, he is forced to use resources less suited to the production of capital goods than the

# THEORETICAL PERSPECTIVE

## GUNS AND BUTTER

**Suppose Robinson Crusoe discovers that he is not alone on the island and that his new neighbors are somewhat less than friendly. Suppose they are downright threatening.** It would be fool-hardy for Crusoe to continue producing only consumption and capital goods. After all, he may wake up one morning to find his uninvited neighbors helping themselves to his consumption and capital goods!

To protect life and property, Robinson Crusoe may have to devote some part of his working day to the production of defensive weapons. Instead of making a fishing spear, he may make several bows and arrows. Or, perhaps, remembering what the Chinese did, he might build a Great Wall to keep his neighbors out. But Robinson Crusoe knows that every bow, every arrow, and every stone in every defensive wall has an opportunity cost that reflects the quantity of nondefensive goods given up.

Crusoe's guns-versus-butter choices are the same kinds of choices every society has been forced to make from time immemorial. If an economy is operating on its production possibilities frontier, then guns can be produced only at the expense of butter. More guns means less butter.

What are choices in the Robinson Crusoe tale are also real choices for Americans. Dwight D. Eisenhower, the 34th U.S. president, was a five-star general during World War II and also the supreme commander of the Allied forces in Europe. The 1944 invasion of Nazi-occupied Europe under his command and the battles that followed led to Germany's unconditional surrender. But victory is always bittersweet. No one has expressed the costs of war better than President Eisenhower himself:

> Every gun that is made, every warship launched, every rocket fired signifies, in the final sense, a theft from those who hunger and are not fed, those who are cold and are not clothed. This world in arms is not spending money alone. It is spending the sweat of its laborers, the genius of its scientists, the hopes of its children.... This is not a way of life at all in any true sense. Under the cloud of threatening war, it is humanity hanging from a cross of iron. (Speech before the American Society of Newspaper Editors, April 16, 1953.)

### CONSIDER

Can you imagine a situation in which two people, both agreeing on the opportunity costs of war preparedness, would disagree on whether to pursue a policy of preparedness? What other issues do you think they would consider? Do you think nations go to war—or stay out of war—strictly on the basis of economic calculation?

**THAT'S AN AWFUL LOT OF STEEL AND AN AWFUL LOT OF PEOPLE THAT COULD BE PUT TO OTHER USES.**

### MORE ON THE NET

Visit a few pacifist organizations, such as the American Peace Network (http://www.apn.org/) and the Center for Economic Conversion (http://www.conversion.org/). What arguments do these organizations make for decreasing the size of the military? Do these arguments take into account the concept of opportunity cost?

resources employed in producing the first unit. After all, resources are not always of equal quality, and he obviously would use the best first. The result is a movement along the curve from point *b* to point *c* that, when plotted in Exhibit 1, traces out the bowing character of the curve. Suppose Crusoe decides on three units of consumption and two units of capital. He works busily, finishes production, eats the three consumption goods, and has available now what he had not had before—two new units of capital.

In the next period of production, he uses the two units of capital along with labor and land. The production possibilities now change. Look at the table in Exhibit 2.

Compare this table to the one in Exhibit 1. Working now with two units of capital, Robinson Crusoe can produce more. For example, ten units of consumption can now be produced when Crusoe, using the fishing spear and extension tool, devotes all his labor to consumption. Of course, he may again decide to produce more units of capital goods in order to be able to produce even more units of consumption in the following period. This can go on forever and does in most economies.

Suppose after deliberating over the production possibilities of the table in Exhibit 2, he selects seven units of consumption and two units of capital. This combination means that he not only adds two more units of capital to his resource base but also is still able to produce more consumption goods—seven—than he could have produced in the first period, even had he devoted all the resources exclusively to consumption goods production.

The graph in Exhibit 2 illustrates the change in the Crusoe economy over the two periods.

The production possibilities curve shifts outward to the right. The shift reflects the changing resource base available to Crusoe. In the second period, capital is added to the land and labor resource base of the first. The dashed curves represent later period production possibilities as long as Crusoe continues the strategy of adding units of capital to his resource base.

## SHIFTS IN THE PRODUCTION POSSIBILITIES FRONTIER

**PRODUCTION POSSIBILITIES IN THE ROBINSON CRUSOE ECONOMY, SECOND PERIOD**

| CONSUMPTION GOODS | CAPITAL GOODS |
|---|---|
| 10 | 0 |
| 9 | 1 |
| 7 | 2 |
| 4 | 3 |
| 0 | 4 |

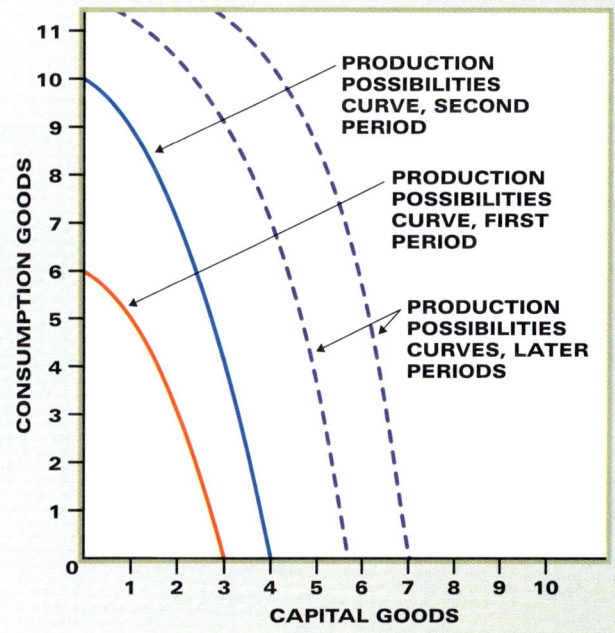

When more resources are available or when more productive technology is used, the quantity of goods and services an economy can produce increases. The increase is depicted by the outward shift to the right of the production possibilities curve.

EXHIBIT 2

## Once Rich, It's Easy to Get Richer

This rather simple way of looking at an economy's production possibilities and growth potential is instructive. Imagine two economies, shown in panels *a* and *b* of Exhibit 3, whose initial production possibilities are described by the table in Exhibit 1. The different selections of consumption and capital these economies make along their identical first-period production possibilities curve trace out their productive growth—or lack of growth—over the course of several production periods.

In the first period, panel *a* people decide to produce three units of consumption and two units of capital (point *c*), while those in panel *b* choose six units of consumption and zero capital (point *a*). Comparing themselves to the people in panel *a*, those in panel *b* may think themselves lucky to have twice the consumption goods. But they won't feel that way in the following period.

The productive powers of the two economies are no longer the same. Panel *a*'s expanded resource base, now containing the two new capital goods, allows a new and more productive set of production possibilities. Panel *a*'s production possibilities curve shifts outward. Panel *b*, on the other hand, operating on its same resource base, remains locked on its initial production possibilities curve. In fact, the people in panel *a* now actually consume more than those in panel *b*, and they can still add to their capital stock.

Time is on their side. After several periods, the outward shifts in panel *a*'s production possibilities curve generate a widening gap between this curve and that of panel *b*. In time, the outward shifts in the panel *a* economy become even easier to obtain. Why? Because a solid consumption base is already in place, the opportunity cost of shifting resources to capital goods becomes less painful. Movements along the economy's production possibilities curve further into the *cd* range—more capital, less consumption—push the curve out even further in succeeding periods.

## Once Poor, It's Easy to Stay Poor

Catching up is hard to do. If the panel *b* people decide to try, it may take some doing. Obviously, they must choose to move away from position *a* on their pro-

### EXHIBIT 3

**COMPARATIVE ECONOMIC GROWTH**

Initially, the same quantities of resources and technology are available in the economies of panel *a* and panel *b*. Panel *a* chooses to produce three consumption goods and two capital goods, while panel *b* uses all its resources to produce six consumption goods. In succeeding years, the additional capital goods created in panel *a* are added to its resource base, shifting its production possibilities curve outward, while the production possibilities curve in panel *b* remains unchanged. The production gap between the two economies widens over time.

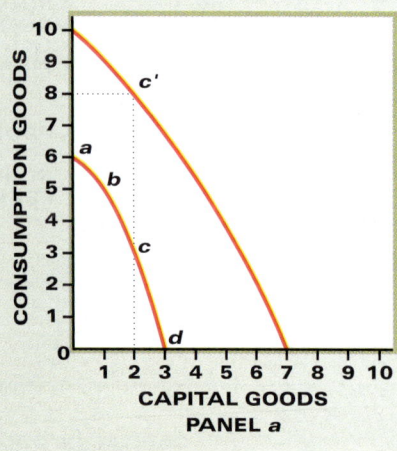
PANEL *a*

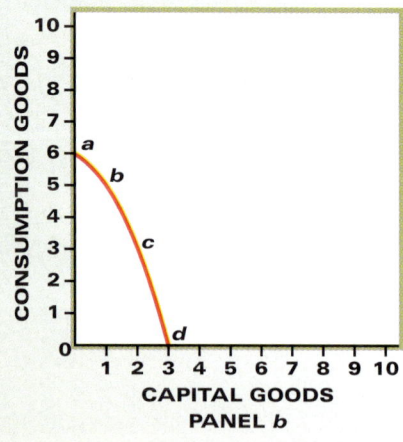
PANEL *b*

duction possibilities curve. The further away from *a*, the better. Movements along their curve into the *bc* range—much more capital, much less consumption—may force them to tighten their belts considerably. Where they position themselves along the curve depends upon how well they can tolerate low-level consumption and how quickly they want to catch up.

There are economies with resource bases so underdeveloped that they have little option but to devote all their meager resources to consumption. It is hard enough just to stay alive! Typically, these economies have high rates of population growth, so that it becomes a continuing, dispiriting struggle to feed their own people. The economies simply can't afford to produce the capital needed to shift their production possibilities curves outward. Economists refer to this condition as the vicious circle of poverty: The economies are so poor they can't produce capital; without capital, they remain poor. Poverty feeds on itself.

**CHECK YOUR UNDERSTANDING**

Why is it that focusing production on capital goods forces consumers to tighten their belts?

## THE PRODUCTIVE POWER OF ADVANCED TECHNOLOGY

Ideas, more so than any factor of production, are the most revolutionizing force able to shift the production possibilities of any economy. Ideas can shift the curve out beyond imagination. Who would have thought just a century ago that we would be walking on the moon? Who would have expected commercial space satellites to beam images from the Superdome in New Orleans to an American air base in Turkey in a matter of seconds? Economists describe ideas that eventually take the form of new applied technology as **innovations.**

Even in the simple economy of Robinson Crusoe, innovation can be shown to cause dramatic leaps forward in the production possibilities available to an economy. The fishing spear Crusoe created was an idea fashioned into a unit of capital. Two fishing spears add more to an economy's productive potential than one, shifting the production possibilities curve out to the right, but the technology is still spears.

Suppose Crusoe hits on an altogether new and creative idea: the fishing net. He sketches out this completely new technology for catching fish that requires a different combination of land and labor. Crusoe uses more vine, less wood, no stone, and more labor. The results of this new technology are dramatic. Exhibit 4 compares the production possibilities of using spear and fishing net technologies.

The net technology yields 30 units of consumption goods compared to the 10 units produced with spears when all resources are devoted to the production of consumption goods. Production possibilities based on net technology make it easier to move down along the curve—producing even more capital goods—and, therefore, shifting the curve in succeeding periods out even further to the right.

Innovations creating even more advanced technology are possible. The exciting conclusion we reach, for the simple Robinson Crusoe economy and for our own,

**Innovation**
An idea that eventually takes the form of new, applied technology.

**PRODUCTION POSSIBILITIES GENERATED BY SPEAR AND NET TECHNOLOGIES**

| CONSUMPTION | CAPITAL |
|---|---|
| 10 | 0 |
| 9 | 1 |
| 7 | 2 |
| 4 | 3 |
| 0 | 4 |

| CONSUMPTION | CAPITAL |
|---|---|
| 30 | 0 |
| 26 | 1 |
| 18 | 2 |
| 10 | 3 |
| 0 | 4 |

**CHECK YOUR UNDERSTANDING**

How are technological change and economic growth related?

is that there are no impassable limits to the growth potential of our economy. Resource limitations may impose a short-run constraint on what we are able to produce in any period of time, but given enough time and enough minds, new technology reduces the severity of scarcity. Our grandchildren will no doubt regard our technology as rather primitive, but their grandchildren will consider their technology as hardly more advanced.

## The Indestructible Nature of Ideas

Capital goods can be destroyed, but ideas are far more durable. Wars can bring havoc to any economy's resource base. People's lives are disrupted. Many do not survive the war. Whole factories, complete with machinery, and roads, bridges, railway networks, electric grids, energy facilities, and any other form of the nation's capital stock can be reduced to rubble. But capital goods can also be replaced quickly. Look at Exhibit 5.

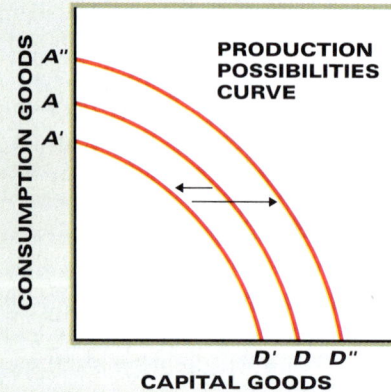

**EXHIBIT 5**

**INWARD AND OUTWARD SHIFTS OF THE PRODUCTION POSSIBILITIES CURVE**

With resources destroyed, the economy's production possibilities decrease. The decrease is depicted by the shift to the left of the production possibilities curve, from $AD$ to $A'D'$. In time, with the rebuilding of resources and the use of more advanced technology, the economy can recoup and even surpass the levels of production previously attained. This is shown in the shift to the right of the production possibilities curve, from $A'D'$ to $A''D''$.

$AD$ represents the economy's prewar production possibilities curve. The destructive effects of war, particularly on its people and capital stock, is shown as an inward shift to the left of the curve, to $A'D'$. Recovery, however, can be whole and swift because people, even with minimal capital stock, don't have to reinvent the wheel. Technological knowledge, once acquired, is virtually indestructible. In time, applying known and more advanced technology, the economy can shift its production possibilities curve back again to $AD$ and even beyond to $A''D''$.

The physical devastation of Japan and Europe caused by World War II had some rather paradoxical consequences for these war-torn economies. Because so much of their capital stock in the form of factories and machinery was destroyed, these economies were forced to start over again. But they started over with the most advanced machinery and the most up-to-date factories. The result was an incredible increase in their economies' productivity. Ironically, economies that were spared the devastation of the war had their prewar technology still intact and grew less rapidly than those whose capital stocks were destroyed and replaced with the more modern technology.

## POSSIBILITIES, IMPOSSIBILITIES, AND LESS THAN POSSIBILITIES

What an economy can produce depends upon the availability of resources and the level of technology applied. If the economy's resources are not fully employed, then obviously it cannot be producing as much as possible. For example, if the economy's labor force is not fully employed or if some of its land and capital resources remain idle, the combination of consumption goods and capital goods that it produces will be less than what is possible.

# HISTORICAL PERSPECTIVE

## THE DESTRUCTION AND RECONSTRUCTION OF ROTTERDAM

May 14, 1940, is an infamous date in the history of Holland's beautiful city of Rotterdam. It was on that day that Hitler's notorious air force (the Luftwaffe) bombed the city incessantly for 12 hours, until it lay in ashes.

Rotterdam became synonymous with disaster. German bombers, like tractors plowing a field, moved methodically back and forth until all that remained of the city was the shell of the ancient Saint Lawrence Church, the city hall, and a few buildings. Twenty-five thousand homes, 1,200 factories, 69 schools, and 13 hospitals were demolished. Overnight, 75,000 people became homeless and 900 were killed. The seaport, Rotterdam's economic lifeblood, was not spared. Thirty-five percent of the port was later gutted by the German army.

BEAUTIFUL, VIBRANT ROTTERDAM. A MARVELOUS PLACE TO VISIT AND AN IMPORTANT HISTORICAL REMINDER OF HOW CRUEL PEOPLE CAN BE AND YET HOW UNDAUNTED THE HUMAN SPIRIT IS.

But Rotterdam did not die. The city enjoys a geographical advantage by straddling the delta of the Rhine, which is the main artery of Europe's intricate network of inland waterways. Almost immediately after the war, rebuilding of the harbor began with the most up-to-date cranes, derricks, docks, and cargo-handling technology. By the end of reconstruction, ships were loading and unloading faster and at lower cost than anywhere else in the world. Rotterdam not only rebuilt but also strengthened its economic muscle, funneling a large part of the cargo trade between the prospering Common Market and the rest of the world.

### MORE ON THE NET

What does Rotterdam look like today? Visit for yourself (http://www.euronet.nl/users/frankvw/rotterdamcon.html).

---

Such a condition is described by point $u$ in the economy of Exhibit 6. At $u$, the economy is producing two consumption goods and two capital goods. Its production possibilities curve shows, however, that combination $b$ or $c$ is possible. In each case, more of one good can be produced without having to sacrifice any of the other. For example, it is possible to produce six units of consumption goods and two units of capital, or two units of consumption and six units of capital. Either combination is better than $u$.

Any point in the interior of the production possibilities curve, such as $u$, signals either the existence of unemployed or underemployed resources. What are **underemployed resources?** Some people working full time might appear to be fully employed, but in fact they still represent substantial unused resources. How come? They are producing much less than they are really capable of producing.

Imagine, for example, how much more our economy could have produced over the past 200 years if women, blacks, and other minorities had been allowed to

**Underemployed resources**
The less than full utilization of a resource's productive capabilities.

## EXHIBIT 6

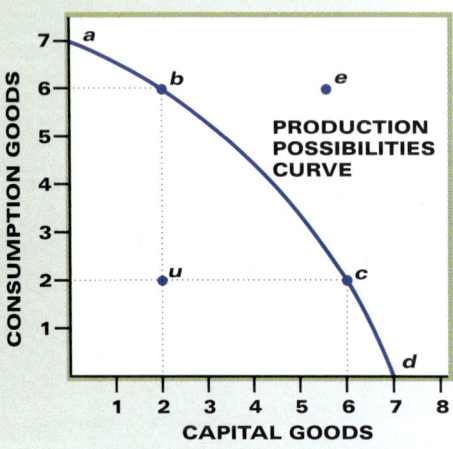

### POSSIBLE, IMPOSSIBLE, AND LESS THAN POSSIBLE

Production combinations, located outside and to the right of the production possibilities curve, such as *e*, are unattainable with the resources and technology currently available. Combinations located within the curve, such as *u*, reflect less than full use of available resources and technology. All combinations that fall on the curve, such as *b* and *c*, represent maximum use, or the full employment of the resources and technology available.

---

exercise their talents fully. How many entrepreneurs have we lost forever? How many innovations were allowed to go undiscovered? How many skilled craftspeople have wasted their talents? How much further out would our production possibilities curve be if racial, sexual, religious, and ethnic discrimination had been avoided? It staggers the imagination!

Who loses? The underemployed people and the economy. That is, the economy could be producing more, but it isn't. If these underemployed people were allowed to exercise their full productive potential, the economy's production would shift from a position inside the production possibilities curve to a position on it.

Point *u* in Exhibit 6 describes an inefficiently producing economy. **Economic efficiency** refers to the condition in which all factors of production are used in their most productive capacity. In this sense, the only points of production that represent an efficiently run economy are those *on* the production possibilities curve. No one point on the curve is more efficient than any other, since all of them reflect the full employment and maximal use of the economy's available resources.

Any point lying outside the production possibilities curve in the economy of Exhibit 6, such as *e*, is an impossible production combination. After all, points on the curve, such as *a*, *b*, *c*, or *d*, represent production combinations that fully employ the economy's usable resources. How, then, can the economy produce beyond the curve? If the economy is growing, point *e*, impossible now, need not be an impossible dream.

### CHECK YOUR UNDERSTANDING

Why does discrimination create economic inefficiency?

**Economic efficiency**
The maximum possible production of goods and services generated by the fullest employment of the economy's resources.

**Labor specialization**
The division of labor into specialized activities that allow individuals to be more productive.

## PRODUCTION POSSIBILITIES AND ECONOMIC SPECIALIZATION

The idea that labor productivity is a function of the degree of **labor specialization** goes as far back as 1776 and Adam Smith. In his *The Wealth of Nations*, Adam Smith tells about a visit to a pin factory:

> One man draws out the wire, another straightens it, a third cuts it, a fourth points it, a fifth grinds it at the top for receiving the head; to make the head requires two or three distinct operations; to put it on is a peculiar business, to whiten the pins is another; it is even a trade by itself to put them into the paper. . . .

The reason for such division of labor, he noted, is that these 10 people could make as many as 48,000 pins in a day. If they had each worked separately and independently, they could not have produced more than 200. That's an impressive point and certainly one that would not go unnoticed in the economy of Robinson Crusoe.

In Crusoe's economy, shown in the table in Exhibit 1, there is no division of labor. Alone, he is forced to produce everything—to fish, hunt, farm, and repair huts. He may be a talented carpenter, a mediocre farmer, and a terrible fisherman, but he is busy doing it all. The production possibilities shown in the table in Exhibit 1 reflect this circumstance.

## Specialization on the Island

But suppose Robinson Crusoe was one of thousands stranded on the island. He probably would not have fished a day in his life. The fishing would have been done by people who were good at it. Crusoe would have become the island's carpenter, relieving those who seem only able to hammer their thumbs. Division of labor on that island allows all the castaways to do the specific things each does best.

Labor can be divided and divided again into specialized and even more specialized activities until people are incredibly proficient at doing incredibly minute activities. The result of such specialization and cooperative production can mean enormous production. The production possibility schedule of an economy with 1,000 people, for example, may be 100,000 times more productive than a single-person economy.

Of course, with everyone working at specialized jobs, the people will need to create an exchange system that allows them to exchange the goods produced under conditions of specialization. A shirtmaker, for example, producing 1,000 shirts, may keep only 1 and trade the remaining 999 shirts for goods she needs. After all, working at making shirts all day does not allow her to fish for the evening meal. But her neighbor, fishing all day, would probably want to exchange some of his fish for her shirts. In this way, it is possible for every islander who specializes in production to end up with more of everything.

## International Specialization

If specialization among people on the island creates more goods for everyone, then imagine how much more could be produced if there were international specialization and exchange. Suppose contact was made with people on other islands, and the practice of exchanging goods with them became commonplace. Now, even more division of labor and specialization would occur. Instead of producing 1,000 shirts for the local island markets, a shirtmaker may produce 10,000 shirts for the larger islands' markets. More people would be engaged in producing shirts. But instead of every shirtworker making a complete shirt, each would specialize in a specific task in the shirt-making process, such as cutting material, sewing pieces, making buttonholes, and folding.

Perhaps four people working at specialized tasks can produce 10,000 shirts in the time it takes one shirtmaker performing all the tasks alone to produce 1,000 shirts. The more islands that are joined in international specialization and exchange, the greater are the opportunities for division of labor and specialization. Everyone produces more, exchanges more, and consumes more.

## The Principle of Comparative Advantage

Let's take this idea of international division of labor and specialization one step further to demonstrate precisely how the advantages of such specialization prevail. Imagine two island economies—Crusoe Island and Yakamaya Island—that each produce fish and shirts. Their production possibilities are shown in Exhibit 7. Crusoe Islanders can produce 2 fish per day, while Yakamayans produce 8. (The

**on the net**

*The Wealth of Nations* in its entirety is available online (http://www.bibliomania.com/NonFiction/Smith/Wealth/index.html).

## EXHIBIT 7

**PRODUCTION OF FISH AND SHIRTS PER EIGHT-HOUR DAY—ABSOLUTE ADVANTAGE**

|  | PRODUCTION OF FISH | PRODUCTION OF SHIRTS |
|---|---|---|
| CRUSOE ISLAND | 2 | 8 |
| YAKAMAYA ISLAND | 8 | 2 |

**Absolute advantage**
A country's ability to produce a good using fewer resources than the country it trades with.

**Comparative advantage**
A country's ability to produce a good at a lower opportunity cost than the country with which it trades.

## EXHIBIT 8

**PRODUCTION OF FISH AND SHIRTS PER EIGHT-HOUR DAY—COMPARATIVE ADVANTAGE**

|  | PRODUCTION OF FISH | PRODUCTION OF SHIRTS |
|---|---|---|
| CRUSOE ISLAND | 8 | 8 |
| YAKAMAYA ISLAND | 8 | 2 |

single-digit quantities are meant to keep the illustration simple.) On the other hand, Crusoe Islanders can produce 8 shirts a day, while Yakamayans struggle to produce 2.

In 2 days, then, if they each produce their own shirts and fish, total production on the 2 islands is 10 fish and 10 shirts. If, on the other hand, they agree to specialize—Crusoe Islanders producing only shirts and Yakamayans producing only fish—they can produce 16 fish and 16 shirts. As you see—and they experience—the gains from specialization are highly advantageous. Economists refer to such an advantage from specialization as **absolute advantage,** which occurs when each island can produce a good using fewer resources than the other island uses. Yakamayans have an absolute advantage in fish (1 hour of labor per fish versus 4 hours needed by Crusoe Islanders), while Crusoe Islanders have an absolute advantage in shirts (1 hour of labor per shirt versus 4 hours needed by Yakamayans).

But suppose their production possibilities look like those in Exhibit 8. Yakamaya Island now has no absolute advantage in fish. People there and on Crusoe Island produce 8 fish in an 8-hour day. On the other hand, Crusoe Islanders can still outproduce Yakamayans 4-to-1 in shirt production. Should the islands specialize? Without specialization, their total production is 16 fish and 10 shirts. With specialization, they produce 16 fish and 16 shirts. Specialization still makes them better off. But who produces what?

Look at their opportunity costs of producing fish. When Crusoe Islanders fish for a day, they catch 8 fish but give up the opportunity of producing 8 shirts. The opportunity cost, then, for each of the 8 fish they catch is 1 shirt. What about Yakamayans? When they fish for a day, catching 8 fish, they give up the opportunity of producing 2 shirts, so that the opportunity cost for each of the 8 fish they produce is ¼ of a shirt. That is, the opportunity cost associated with producing fish for Yakamayans is less than it is for Crusoe Islanders. Although Yakamayans do not have an absolute advantage in fish, they do have a **comparative advantage,** meaning that they have a lower opportunity cost producing fish than do Crusoe Islanders. The Yakamayans produce the fish.

Crusoe Islanders end up producing the shirts. Why? Look at the opportunity costs of producing shirts. When Crusoe Islanders produce 8 shirts in a day, they give up the opportunity of producing 8 fish, so that the opportunity cost associated with producing a shirt is 1 fish. What about Yakamayans? When they produce 2 shirts in a day, they give up the opportunity of producing 8 fish, so that the opportunity cost to them of producing a shirt is 4 fish. Crusoe Islanders hold a comparative advantage in shirts.

## THE UNIVERSALITY OF THE PRODUCTION POSSIBILITIES MODEL

Resource limitations confronting insatiable wants are facts of life that apply to every economic system—large or small, rich or poor, east or west, north or south, capitalist or socialist.

The universality of the production possibilities model and the law of increasing costs create the same kinds of problems and decision making for all economies. Can the economy fully employ its resources? How much of the resources should be allocated to capital goods formation? Who gets what share of the consumption goods produced?

The same questions are asked about peace and war. Just as the production possibilities curve measures out the possibilities of consumption and capital goods production, it can measure out as well the production possibilities of butter and guns. Israeli as well as Egyptian economists knew firsthand the opportunity cost of desert warfare. In no small measure, that knowledge played its part in the countries' historic 1979 peace agreement.

Imagine a couple of Martian economists landing their UFOs undetected on Earth, say, one in Beijing, China, and the other in Dayton, Ohio. If their assignments were to detail how Earthlings behave, they would be struck, upon returning to Mars and comparing notes, not by the differences they observed, but instead by the incredible similarities of our experiences and behavior. They would probably be impressed as well by how similar our economic problems and economic choices are to their own!

# CHAPTER REVIEW

1. The economy's resources—also referred to as factors of production—are labor, capital, land, and entrepreneurship. The two human resources are labor and entrepreneurship; the two nonhuman resources are capital and land. Labor is the physical and mental exertion of people willing to sell their skills for a specific period of time. Capital is a manufactured good used to produce other goods. Human capital represents the combination of labor and capital. For example, a medical education is capital, and the physician is the resulting human capital. Land, in its virgin form, is nature's gift. Entrepreneurs undertake the risks and uncertainties associated with business enterprise.

2. A production possibilities curve shows the combinations of goods that can be produced with a set of resources. The analysis of a two-goods economy in which consumption and capital goods are produced allows for fruitful discussion of issues associated with economic growth.

3. The opportunity cost of producing a unit of a good—say, a consumption good—is measured by the quantity of the other good—say, a capital good—that must be given up to produce the consumption good.

4. As more and more of a good—say, a consumption good—is produced, the quantity of the other good—say, a capital good—that must be given up to produce each additional

consumption good increases. This phenomenon is known as the law of increasing costs.

**5.** The production of capital goods in one year adds to an economy's resource base, ensuring that the quantities of goods that become possible to produce in subsequent years increase. Rich economies can more easily invest in capital goods production than can poor economies, so that, over years, greater and greater disparities among them may result.

**6.** New ideas that create innovations in the form of new technology enhance labor productivity and therefore economic growth. For example, when a few tractors replace many horse-driven plows, the production possibilities curve shifts out to the right.

**7.** An economy producing along its production possibilities curve is both at full employment and producing efficiently. If any factor is unemployed or if any factor is not being used to its fullest capacity (that is, it is underemployed), then the economy is not operating on its production possibilities curve, but somewhere inside it.

**8.** Division of labor and specialization increase labor productivity and therefore increase what an economy can produce. Absolute and comparative advantage show how nations gain when they specialize and trade among themselves.

# KEY TERMS

Factor of production
Labor
Capital
Human capital
Land

Entrepreneur
Production possibilities
Opportunity cost
Law of increasing costs
Innovation

Underemployed resources
Economic efficiency
Labor specialization
Absolute advantage
Comparative advantage

# QUESTIONS

**1.** What distinguishes entrepreneurship from the other factors of production?

**2.** Is a four-door 1998 Buick LeSabre taxi capital? Is a four-door 1998 Buick LeSabre parked in your garage capital?

**3.** Consider your economics lecture. From the point of view of your economics professor, is the lecture capital, labor, or neither? From your own point of view, is it capital, labor, or neither? What is your opportunity cost of that lecture?

**4.** Explain why the concepts of scarcity and opportunity cost are intricately related.

**5.** Explain the law of increasing (opportunity) costs. What causes costs to increase?

**6.** Everybody wants clean air. So why is the air polluted in so many of our cities? (*Hint:* Refer to the law of increasing costs in your answer.)

**7.** Why are most new technologies considered indestructible?

**8.** Suppose you were advising the government of Egypt. What policies would you recommend to achieve economic growth? Why should you expect some resistance to your policy suggestions?

**9.** Suppose government economists, on the request of the president, construct a production possibilities curve (for military and civilian goods) for the United States. Suppose also that two economics professors debate where the United States ought to be on that curve. Which set of economists is engaged in positive economics, and which in normative?

**10.** What factors or events could cause an inward shift of the production possibilities curve?

11. Why does the production possibilities curve bow out from the origin?
12. The Constitution guarantees the right to free speech. Does the *free* in *free speech* mean that there really is no opportunity cost to free speech? Explain.
13. Professor Kenneth Boulding once noted that Danish butter producers eat very little butter. They use margarine even though they produce some of the best butter in the world. Is this stupid behavior? Or is there a good reason for it?
14. What is meant by the term *vicious circle of poverty*? Draw a graph to illustrate the concept.
15. Immigration is a hot political issue these days. What arguments can an economist make to support a liberal policy of immigration? What arguments can he or she make to oppose immigration? (*Hint:* Think in terms of shifts in the production possibilities curve in the first case, and movements along the curve in the second.)

# PRACTICE PROBLEMS

1. Fill in an appropriate number (there can be more than one) for the missing number of bushels of oranges in set C and graph the following sets of production possibilities.

    | SET | BUSHELS OF GRAPEFRUIT | BUSHELS OF ORANGES |
    |---|---|---|
    | A | 200 | 0 |
    | B | 150 | 19 |
    | C | 100 |  |
    | D | 50 | 30 |
    | E | 0 | 32 |

2. Graph the following sets of production possibilities and explain why the law of increasing costs is violated.

    | SET | BUSHELS OF GRAPEFRUIT | BUSHELS OF ORANGES |
    |---|---|---|
    | A | 200 | 0 |
    | B | 150 | 19 |
    | C | 100 | 40 |
    | D | 50 | 80 |
    | E | 0 | 130 |

3. Production costs (in labor hours) of oranges and peaches in Florida and Georgia are shown in the following table.

    If the states specialize, what should each produce? Why? (*Hint:* Think in terms of absolute and comparative advantage.)

    |  | ORANGES | PEACHES |
    |---|---|---|
    | FLORIDA | 5 | 5 |
    | GEORGIA | 2 | 4 |

4. Imagine an economy with the following resource base for 2000: 100 units of labor (including entrepreneurs), 100 units of capital, and 100 acres of land. Draw a graph showing the economy's 2000 production possibilities from the following table:

    | 2000 | CONSUMPTION | CAPITAL |
    |---|---|---|
    | A | 12 | 0 |
    | B | 10 | 2 |
    | C | 6 | 4 |
    | D | 0 | 6 |

    | 2001 | CONSUMPTION | CAPITAL |
    |---|---|---|
    | A | 16 | 0 |
    | B | 14 | 2 |
    | C | 10 | 4 |
    | D | 4 | 6 |

    On the same graph, draw the economy's production possibilities curve for 2001. Which possibilities in 2000 (among A, B, C, and D) can account for the 2001 curve, and how would such a production possibilities combination affect the economy's resource base for 2001?

# WHAT'S WRONG WITH THIS GRAPH?

**THE PRODUCTION POSSIBILITIES CURVE**

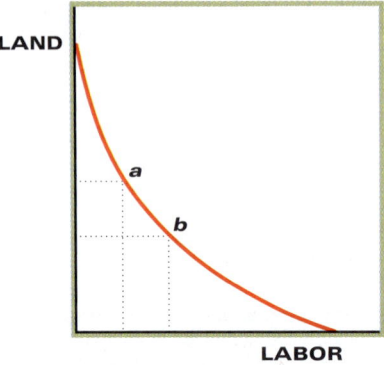

# ECONOMIC CONSULTANTS

**ECONOMIC RESEARCH AND ANALYSIS BY STUDENTS FOR PROFESSIONALS**

WaterUSA, located in Boise, Idaho, bottles and sells mineral water. This mineral water, drawn from underground springs, offers unparalleled taste and clarity. WaterUSA currently sells its water in the United States, but it is looking to expand its sales into the former Soviet Union, and into Russia in particular.

WaterUSA has approached Economic Consultants for advice on the firm's plans to expand its sales into European markets. Prepare a report for WaterUSA that addresses the following issues:

1. Are the conditions favorable in the former Soviet Union for selling mineral water? Are there businesses in Russia selling mineral water?
2. What issues does WaterUSA need to consider with regard to the principle of comparative advantage?

You may find the following resources helpful as you prepare this report for WaterUSA:

- **U.S. Department of Commerce, Business Information Service for the Newly Independent States (BISNIS)** (http://bisnis.doc.gov/bisnis/bisnis.html)—BISNIS provides economic information about Russia. In particular, BISNIS publishes market surveys and reports for common U.S. goods.
- **American Chamber of Commerce in Russia** (http://www.amcham.ru/)—The American Chamber of Commerce in Russia provides information for doing business in Russia.
- **Mineral Waters of the World** (http://www.mineralwaters.org/)—Mineral Waters of the World provides directories and ratings for various mineral waters around the globe.

# PRACTICE TEST

1. To economists, the term *capital* refers exclusively to
   a. goods used to produce other goods.
   b. money used to purchase stocks and bonds.
   c. savings accumulated by households to purchase real estate.
   d. money used by capitalists to hire workers.
   e. machinery used by workers to produce goods.

2. If an economy experiences unemployment, it would show up as a point
   a. on the production possibilities curve, but on one of the axes.
   b. outside the production possibilities curve.
   c. inside the production possibilities curve.
   d. on the production possibilities curve.
   e. on a production possibilities curve that is shifting to the right.

3. The weather in the Virgin Islands reminds us of the nursery rhyme "When she was good, she was very, very good, but when she was bad, she was horrid." A hurricane in 1996 was horrid, destroying much of the islands' infrastructure (roads, telephone systems), homes, and factories. An economist describing the effect of the hurricane on the islands' economy would show
   a. an inward shift in the islands' production possibilities curve.
   b. an outward shift in the islands' production possibilities curve.
   c. a movement along the production possibilities curve, from consumption to capital.
   d. a movement along the production possibilities curve, from capital to consumption.
   e. a movement inside the curve, the curve remaining intact.

4. Let's suppose that the day after the hurricane, the governor of the Virgin Islands addresses the population to announce the government's decision to rebuild the economy's infrastructure. Of course, it means higher taxes, which means people will have less income to spend as they please. Ceteris paribus, the tax and rebuilding will create
   a. an inward shift in the islands' production possibilities curve.
   b. an outward shift in the islands' production possibilities curve.
   c. a movement along the production possibilities curve, from consumption to capital.
   d. a movement along the production possibilities curve, from capital to consumption.
   e. a movement inside the curve, the curve remaining intact.

5. Assuming the rebuilding program is successful, in the longer run (in time) you would see
   a. an inward shift in the islands' production possibilities curve.
   b. an outward shift in the islands' production possibilities curve.
   c. a movement along the production possibilities curve, from consumption to capital.
   d. a movement along the production possibilities curve, from capital to consumption.
   e. a movement inside the curve, the curve remaining intact.

6. Which of the following is likely to cause an inward shift in Crusoe's production possibilities curve?
   a. Crusoe invents a fishnet.
   b. A typhoon destroys resources on the island.
   c. Crusoe discovers a forest of trees, perfect for use in making spears.
   d. Crusoe finds a companion, named Friday, to help him fish and make spears.

7. In Adam Smith's illustration of the pin factory, one worker draws out the wire, another straightens it, and a third cuts it. Several others serve the functions of pointing, whitening, and packaging the pins. This process is more productive than if each worker did all the tasks. This illustrates the concept of
   a. opportunity costs.
   b. labor specialization.
   c. economic efficiency.
   d. the law of increasing costs.

8. Gabe Fried is stranded on a Pacific island and realizes that, to survive, he must pick berries. He discovers that he picks more berries in the first hour than he does in the second because it becomes increasingly harder to find berries. Gabe has just discovered
   a. Engel's law.
   b. the law of opportunity cost.
   c. the law of increasing costs.
   d. the law of scarcity.
   e. the law of production possibilities.

9. Among the four factors of production is entrepreneurship. It's the only factor that
   a. does not contract to provide its services for a specific price.
   b. conceives of the essential idea of production.
   c. assumes all the risks and uncertainties involved in production.
   d. earns profit.
   e. All of the above

# CHAPTER 3

# DEMAND AND SUPPLY

One of the most exciting moments in Shakespearean drama—for economists, at any rate—has to be the final scene in *Richard III* where the king, tired and bloodied at the end of the battle, his horse slain, and standing helplessly alone upon the crest of a hill, sights the enemy about to charge at him. His sword drawn, Richard shouts in desperation: "A horse! A horse! My kingdom for a horse!"

To an economist, that's a dramatic moment, for never has so high a price been placed on a four-legged animal! Not before, and not since. Lassie and Flipper, themselves worth a small fortune, were still well within the reach of any millionaire. The legendary thoroughbred of the 1920s, Man O' War, won every race he ran but one, but even he couldn't command *that* price. Shakespeare was not an economist by profession, yet he understood the market well. In all probability, he picked the right price.

This example raises a more general question about price formation: Why are prices what they are? Why, for example, do oranges sell for 30 cents each? Why not 25 cents? Or 34 cents? Is there something magical about a 30-cent orange? And what about cucumbers? Why are they 49 cents each? Why should they be more expensive than oranges? Why is butter $1.25 per pound? Why is a fresh fish $6?

We can go on identifying thousands of goods that make up our modern economy and ask the same question about each: Why that particular price? From aircraft carriers to salted peanuts, from sweetheart roses to Buick LeSabres, why are the prices what they are?

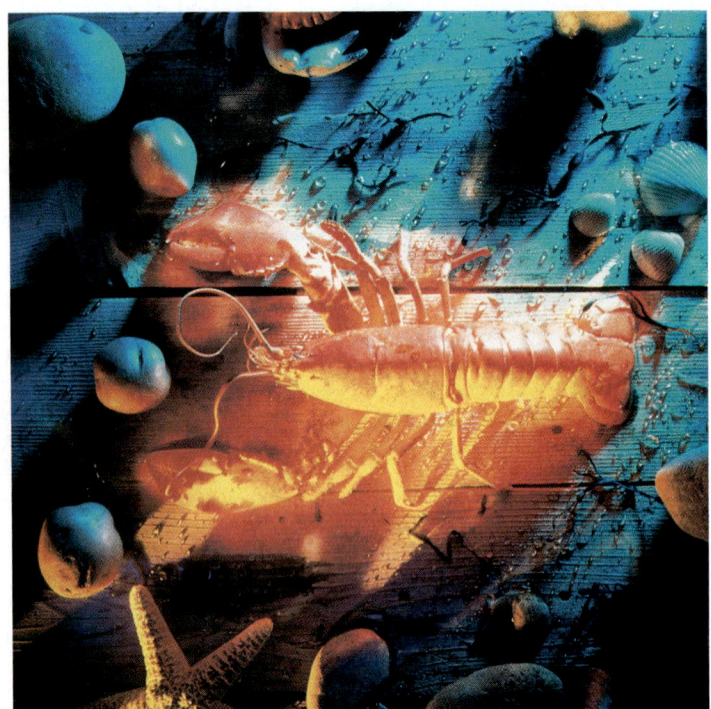

**THIS CHAPTER INTRODUCES YOU TO THE ECONOMIC PRINCIPLES ASSOCIATED WITH:**

- INDIVIDUAL AND MARKET DEMAND
- MARKET-DAY, SHORT-RUN, AND LONG-RUN SUPPLY
- THE DETERMINATION OF EQUILIBRIUM PRICE AND QUANTITY

# MEASURING CONSUMER WILLINGNESS

Price formation has to do with people's willingness to buy and sell. There is nothing mysterious about price. It has no life of its own. It has no will. Price simply reflects what people are willing to do.

Suppose that people on a small island are busily engaged each day in some productive activity that affords them a livelihood. The variety of their occupations fills up 40 Yellow Pages in their telephone directory. There are auto mechanics, dentists, farmers, plumbers, computer specialists, business consultants, and especially fishermen. After all, it's an island economy, and we should expect the community to take full advantage of its fishing grounds.

Of course, there's no sense in fishing unless some people like to eat fish. Chances are some prefer fish to filet mignon, although there must be others who wouldn't touch fish under any condition. As the Romans used to say: *De gustibus non est disputandum* (There's no disputing taste). But it would be the height of folly if fishermen went out on the water every day only to discover on returning to dock that nobody showed any interest in the fish they caught. Wouldn't you think that even the dullest of them would give up after a while? Fishermen go out every day because they know from long experience that there are always people willing to buy fish.

# MEASURING CONSUMER DEMAND

Fishermen also know that when price falls, people's willingness to buy fish increases—it's so obvious and so sensible a response to price that fishermen regard it as natural. They know, for example, that if the price of fish is outrageously high, say $25 per fish, very few people would be willing to buy. On the other hand, if the price is $10, some people unwilling to buy at $25 now would be willing to buy fish.

If the price falls to $5, more people would be willing to buy even more fish. Some who bought a few at $10 would buy more at $5, and those who had not bought before would now get into the market.

When economists refer to **change in quantity demanded** for a particular good, they always mean people's willingness to buy specific quantities at specific prices. They define the inverse relationship between price and quantity demanded as the **law of demand.** Compare the two statements "I am willing to buy four fish at a price of $6 per fish" and "I am willing to buy fish." There is considerably more information in the first statement.

## Measuring Individual Demand

Let's begin by measuring Claudia Preparata's and Chris Stefan's demand for fish. Claudia is the principal labor relations consultant on the island, and Chris is an actress. The tables in Exhibit 1 are **demand schedules** recording their willingness to buy fish at different prices.

You may not know much about these two women, but you do know that if the price of fish was $10, you wouldn't find Claudia Preparata at a fish market!

Chris Stefan, on the other hand, treats herself to a $10 poached salmon. If the price falls to $9, the quantity of fish demanded by both Claudia and Chris increases. Claudia buys one, and the quantity that Chris demands increases to three. If the price keeps falling, the quantity demanded keeps increasing.

The **demand curves** in Exhibit 1 represent Claudia's and Chris's demand for fish at different prices. They contain the same information offered in the tables. It is just a different, more visual way of looking at the information. The demand curves

**CHECK YOUR UNDERSTANDING**

How does price reflect what buyers are willing to do?

**Change in quantity demanded**
A change in the quantity demanded of a good that is caused solely by a change in the price of that good.

**Law of demand**
The inverse relationship between price and quantity demanded of a good or service, *ceteris paribus*.

**Demand schedule**
A schedule showing the specific quantity of a good or service that people are willing and able to buy at different prices.

**Demand curve**
A curve that depicts the relationship between price and quantity demanded.

# EXHIBIT 1

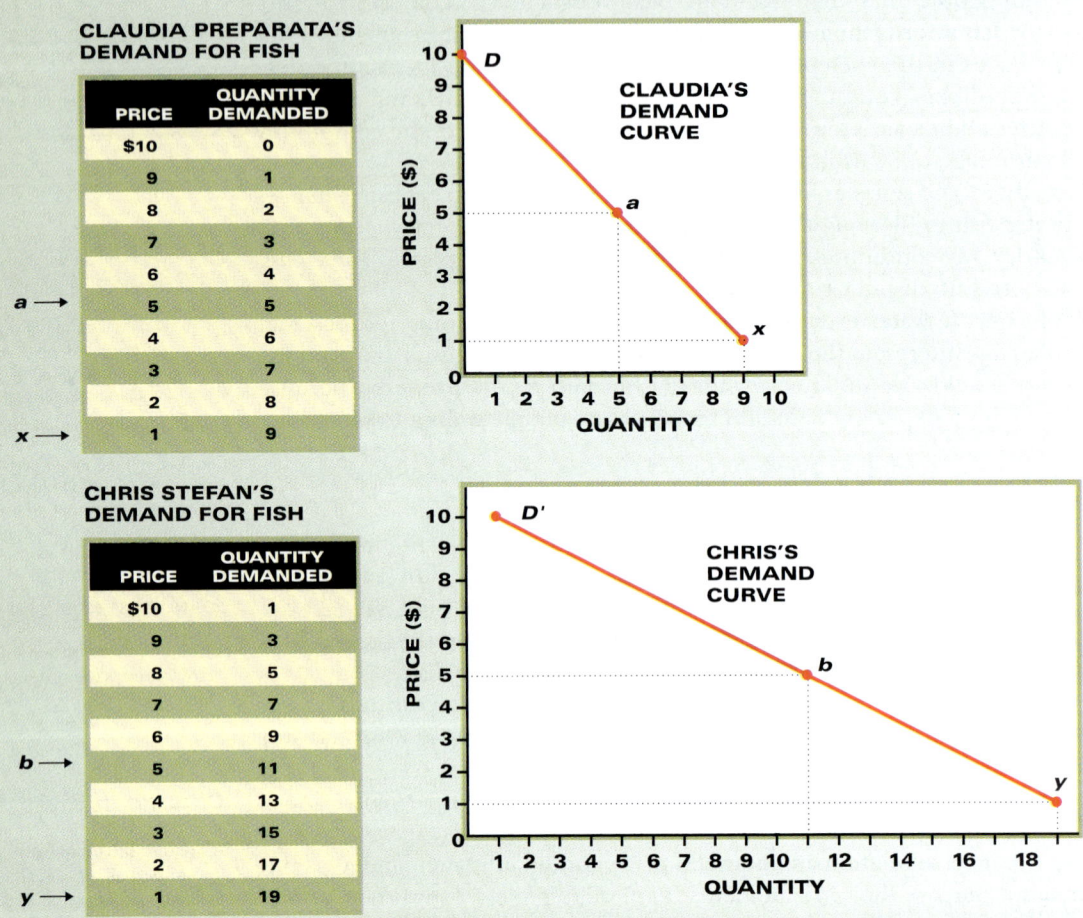

**INDIVIDUAL DEMAND CURVES FOR FISH**

Ceteris paribus, the quantity of fish demanded depends on the price of fish. At a price of $5, the quantity of fish demanded by Claudia is 5—point *a* on demand curve *D*—and the quantity demanded by Chris is 11—point *b* on demand curve *D'*. At a price of $1, the quantity demanded by Claudia increases to 9—point *x*—and the quantity demanded by Chris increases to 19—point *y*.

are downward sloping because price and quantity demanded are inversely related. When price falls, the quantity demanded increases.

## Measuring Market Demand

If we were able to record every person's willingness to buy fish at different prices, we would end up with complete information about the community's demand for fish. We can obtain such information only by observing and recording what quantities people actually buy in the market at different prices. Adding up all the individual demands for fish gives us the community demand, or **market demand**. The table and graph in Exhibit 2 represent the market demand for fish.

**Market demand**
The sum of all individual demands in a market.

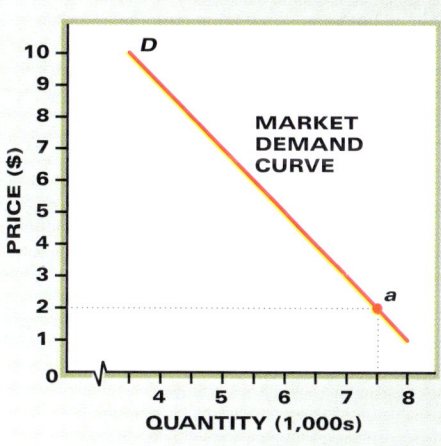

## MEASURING SUPPLY

On a beautiful April morning we see the fishermen going out in their boats. They live by the weather and by whatever daylight they can manage. At dawn, they head out to the fishing grounds while most people in the community are still asleep. Typically, they move from spot to spot, depending on the season, weather, and time of day. They search, locate, fish, and move on again.

Suppose they return home at the end of this fishing day with 6,000 fish. Imagine the scene: Fishermen unload their catch into their individual stalls, pack the fish in ice, and wash up. They sell them right on the docks. The last thing any fisherman wants to take home is a fish! They want dollars.

### Market-Day Supply

Once the fish are in, there's really no decision making concerning what quantity to supply at what price. *Whatever the price,* fishermen are willing to dispose of all 6,000 fish. What else can they do with them? Have you ever handled a day-old fish?

Even if the price was $1 per fish, $P = \$1$, fishermen would be disappointed but still willing to sell all 6,000. Some would probably start thinking about other jobs. On the other hand, if $P = \$10$, the same fishermen would still supply the same 6,000 fish, but this time would be frustrated that they hadn't caught more. But they can't change the quantity supplied once the catch is in. Regardless of price, the quantity supplied is fixed for the market day.

The table and graph in Exhibit 3 represent the **supply schedule** and corresponding supply curve for the **market-day supply.**

Just as the demand curve graphs the relationship between price and quantity demanded, the **supply curve** graphs the relationship between price and quantity supplied. The supply curve for the market day shows that whatever the price, the quantity supplied remains unchanged.

**Supply schedule**
A schedule showing the specific quantity of a good or service that suppliers are willing and able to provide at different prices.

**Market-day supply**
A market situation in which the quantity of a good supplied is fixed, regardless of price.

**Supply curve**
A curve that depicts the relationship between price and quantity supplied.

## EXHIBIT 3

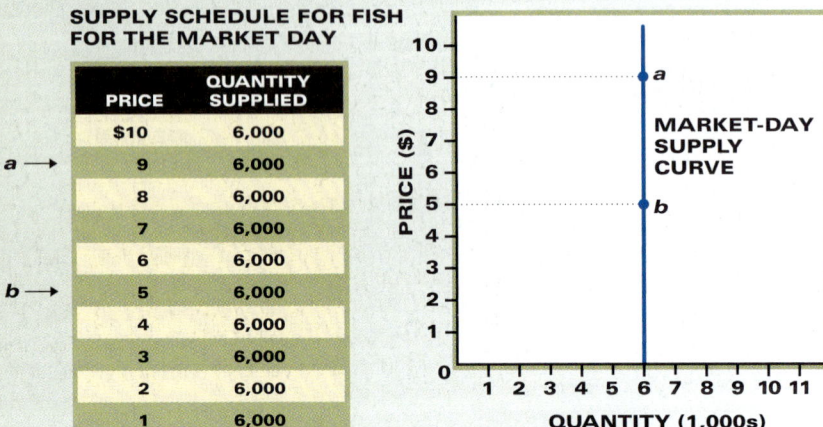

**MARKET-DAY SUPPLY CURVE**

The market-day supply curve is vertical, reflecting the fact that once the catch is in, fishermen cannot change the quantity they supply. At a price of $9, the quantity supplied is 6,000—point *a* on the supply curve. At a price of $5, the quantity supplied is still 6,000—point *b* on the supply curve.

**SUPPLY SCHEDULE FOR FISH FOR THE MARKET DAY**

| PRICE | QUANTITY SUPPLIED |
|---|---|
| $10 | 6,000 |
| 9 | 6,000 |
| 8 | 6,000 |
| 7 | 6,000 |
| 6 | 6,000 |
| 5 | 6,000 |
| 4 | 6,000 |
| 3 | 6,000 |
| 2 | 6,000 |
| 1 | 6,000 |

## DETERMINING EQUILIBRIUM PRICE

A fish market is a colorful and bustling sight. Demanders, suppliers, and flies swarm around the fish stalls, ready to strike deals. Suppliers busily encourage demanders to buy their fish, and demanders take their time looking for the best price. But fish are fish, and time is short.

Nobody knows what the other's preferences really are until they become expressed on the market through purchase and sale. But Claudia, Chris, and the many other demanders, as well as the fishermen who are the suppliers, know that 6,000 fish are on the docks for sale.

### Suppose the Price Is $8

Let's suppose that the asking price, at least at the outset of the market process, is $8 per fish. This already spells trouble. Look at Exhibit 4.

At $P = \$8$, the quantity of fish demanded is 4,500. Of this quantity, Claudia is willing to buy 2, Chris 5. But the fishermen are already nervous about the weakness they sense in the market. There is insufficient demand to absorb the entire 6,000 fish supplied. People are just not picking up fish as the fishermen had hoped. Look at the table in Exhibit 4. At $P = \$8$, there is an **excess supply** of 1,500 fish that will not be sold. Every fisherman is afraid, in the end, of being left holding the bag. Sheila Reed, one of the many fishermen on the docks, knows that the only way to protect herself from this unpleasant eventuality is to cut price. She figures that since all fish are alike, if she is willing to cut her own price to $7, chances are that she will sell out.

Of course, Sheila isn't the only fisherman who thinks this way. Fishermen Lisa Muroga and Shari Zernich had already cut their prices to $7 for the same reason. They draw a crowd. Can you imagine what happens when word spreads among the demanders and suppliers that some fishermen are willing to sell at $7? They make it virtually impossible for other suppliers to maintain the price at $8.

**Excess supply**
The difference, at a particular price, between quantity supplied and quantity demanded, quantity supplied being the greater.

# DEMAND AND SUPPLY

## EXHIBIT 4

### EXCESS DEMAND AND EXCESS SUPPLY

**PRESSURES OF EXCESS DEMAND AND EXCESS SUPPLY WHEN MARKET SUPPLY IS 6,000**

| | PRICE | QUANTITY DEMANDED | QUANTITY SUPPLIED | EXCESS DEMAND | EXCESS SUPPLY |
|---|---|---|---|---|---|
| | $10 | 3,500 | 6,000 | | 2,500 |
| | 9 | 4,000 | 6,000 | | 2,000 |
| a → | 8 | 4,500 | 6,000 | | 1,500 |
| | 7 | 5,000 | 6,000 | | 1,000 |
| | 6 | 5,500 | 6,000 | | 500 |
| b → | 5 | 6,000 | 6,000 | 0 | 0 |
| c → | 4 | 6,500 | 6,000 | 500 | |
| | 3 | 7,000 | 6,000 | 1,000 | |
| | 2 | 7,500 | 6,000 | 1,500 | |
| | 1 | 8,000 | 6,000 | 2,000 | |

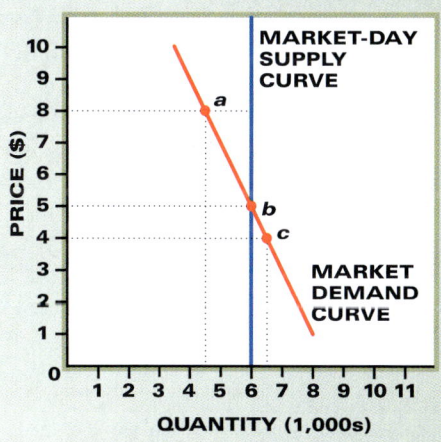

At any price other than $5, point *b* on the supply and demand curves, excess demand or excess supply will force the price to $5. At $4, point *c* on the demand curve, an excess demand of 500 fish is created, driving up price. At $8, point *a* on the demand curve, an excess supply of 1,500 fish is created, forcing price downward.

Every supplier, then, has no alternative but to reduce the price to $7. Will that do the trick? Look again at the table in Exhibit 4. At $P = \$7$, quantity demanded increases to 5,000 fish, but that still leaves an excess supply of 1,000. The pressure on suppliers persists.

As long as any excess supply exists on the market, there will always be an incentive for suppliers to cut price. The incentive is self-protection. They really don't enjoy cutting prices, but they enjoy even less the prospect of being caught at the end of the market day with unsold fish.

How much price cutting will they have to do? From the table in Exhibit 4 it's clear that suppliers will have to cut the price to $5. At $P = \$5$, quantity demanded increases to absorb the entire 6,000 fish supplied. Excess supply is zero.

## Suppose the Price Is $4

Suppose, at the beginning of the market process, price is not $8, but $4. What happens now? Market pressure is on the other side of the market. Claudia Preparata, Chris Stefan, and other demanders are the ones who become somewhat nervous.

For example, at $P = \$4$, Claudia is willing to buy 6 and Chris is willing to buy 13 fish. The quantity demanded by the community is 6,500. Both demanders and suppliers now sense that there are insufficient fish to satisfy demand at $4. Fishermen seem less worried about being caught with unsold fish. Now demanders are worried about going home fishless.

As you see in the table in Exhibit 4, **excess demand** at $P = \$4$ is 500 fish. What would you do if you were at the docks and really wanted fish? Afraid of getting caught looking at empty stalls, wouldn't you offer a little more? For example, if you announced that you were willing to pay $5, the chances are that you would draw suppliers' attention. Of course, you're not the only one with fish on your mind; many others are also willing to buy fish at $5.

**CHECK YOUR UNDERSTANDING**

What will suppliers do if there's an excess supply on the market?

**Excess demand**
The difference, at a particular price, between quantity demanded and quantity supplied, quantity demanded being the greater.

The $4 price, then, becomes untenable. Demanders, competing among themselves for the limited supply of 6,000 fish, will bid the price up. At $P = \$5$, some buyers drop out. The quantity demanded then falls to 6,000 and the excess demand disappears.

## Price Always Tends Toward Equilibrium

In the fish market on this particular day, competition among suppliers to rid themselves of their supply will always force a price greater than $5 down to $5. In the same way, competition among demanders will always force a price lower than $5 up to $5. Price is stable only at $5. Economists refer to that price where quantity demanded equals quantity supplied as the **equilibrium price.** At $P = \$5$, the market clears. There is no excess demand or excess supply.

Exhibit 4 illustrates the forces driving price to equilibrium. At any price other than $P = \$5$, excess demand or supply results, triggering bargaining activity on the part of demanders and suppliers to overcome the market's inability to clear. They force price changes. Price simply reflects their behavior. It gravitates, without exception, toward equilibrium.

**Equilibrium price**
The price that equates quantity demanded to quantity supplied. If any disturbance from that price occurs, excess demand or excess supply emerges to drive price back to equilibrium.

# MARKET-DAY, SHORT-RUN, AND LONG-RUN SUPPLY

But how realistic is this idea of a fixed supply? In Exhibit 4, the quantity supplied remains fixed at 6,000, regardless of price. Is it realistic to suppose that suppliers never think of adjusting the quantity they supply to changing prices? Do fishermen, for example, just keep fishing, day after day, bringing their catch to market without regard to the price their fish fetch on the market? Of course not. A fixed supply makes sense only for the market day. Once the catch is in, today's price cannot affect today's quantity supplied. What is done is done.

But what fishermen will do *tomorrow* depends very much on today's price. A high price today, say $10 per fish, makes fishermen happy and leaves them wishing they had more to supply. While they can't supply more today, they can prepare today to increase the quantity they supply tomorrow. A low price today, on the other hand, say $3 per fish, makes them less happy and less willing to supply fish. While they can't cut supply today—after all, the catch is in—they can prepare today to decrease the quantity they supply tomorrow. Unlike consumers, who can change their quantity demanded instantaneously when prices change, fishermen have to do something to adjust the quantity they supply to price. Doing something takes time.

Let's start with today. Suppose fishermen discover when they get to market that today's price is $10. Are they happy? They're ecstatic! The only regret they have is that their quantity supplied is only 6,000 fish. At that price they wish they had more fish to supply. But they can't undo what is done. What is done is their earlier decision to fish today with a certain amount of boats, crew, and equipment.

Well, what about tomorrow? With a $10 fish in mind, they would love to supply as many as 16,000 if they could. Look at the table in Exhibit 5, column 4.

But how can they possibly increase the quantity of fish supplied from 6,000 to 16,000 *by tomorrow*? They can't. But perhaps the first thing they can do is add more fishermen to their boats. Where would they find them? Well, suppose you are a potato farmer and not particularly happy about the money you are making in the potato business. You may be willing to try something else if that something else paid more; that is, if it met your opportunity cost. With fish now fetching $10, it may be just enough to make you switch from potato farming to fishing.

# DEMAND AND SUPPLY

## EXHIBIT 5: MARKET-DAY, SHORT-RUN, AND LONG-RUN SUPPLY

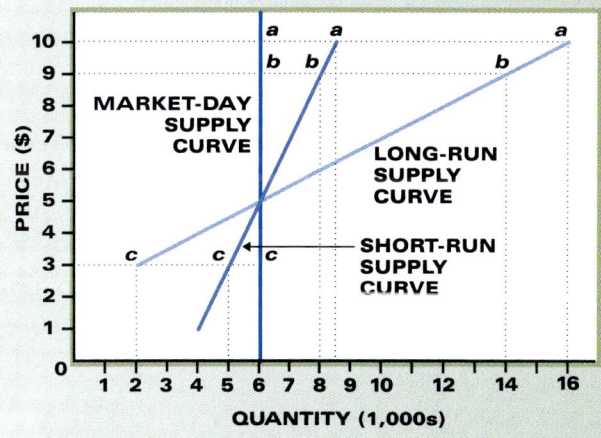

| | PRICE | MARKET DAY | SHORT RUN | LONG RUN |
|---|---|---|---|---|
| a → | $10 | 6,000 | 8,500 | 16,000 |
| b → | 9 | 6,000 | 8,000 | 14,000 |
| | 8 | 6,000 | 7,500 | 12,000 |
| | 7 | 6,000 | 7,000 | 10,000 |
| | 6 | 6,000 | 6,500 | 8,000 |
| | 5 | 6,000 | 6,000 | 6,000 |
| | 4 | 6,000 | 5,500 | 4,000 |
| c → | 3 | 6,000 | 5,000 | 2,000 |
| | 2 | 6,000 | 4,500 | 0 |
| | 1 | 6,000 | 4,000 | 0 |

All three supply curves are upward sloping. At $P = \$10$, point $a$ on the three supply curves, the quantity supplied on the market day is 6,000, the quantity supplied in the short run is 8,500, and the quantity supplied in the long run is 16,000. At $P = \$9$, point $b$ on the three curves, the quantity supplied on the market day is 6,000, the quantity supplied in the short run is 8,000, and the quantity supplied in the long run is 14,000. At $P = \$3$, point $c$ on the three curves, the quantity supplied on the market day is 6,000, the quantity supplied in the short run is 5,000, and the quantity supplied in the long run is 2,000.

But there are limits to how many people fishermen can add to their boats. If the boats are designed for crews of six, adding one or two more per boat may bring in more fish, but not the 16,000 fish that fishermen are willing to supply. Anyway, hiring more crew takes time, and the new crew may have very little experience.

What else can fishermen do to increase the quantity supplied? Another option is to stay out on the water for more hours. But staying out longer means consuming more fuel, more bait, and more ice packaging, all of which may be in short supply.

They do the best they can. Suppose their best effort, given the limitation of boat size, increases the quantity supplied from the market day's 6,000 to 8,500 fish. Look at column 3 in the table in Exhibit 5.

Now, 8,500 fish is more than 6,000 but still considerably less than the 16,000 that fishermen want to supply at $P = \$10$. But to reach 16,000 requires more boats (not just more crew or longer hours), and boat making, let's suppose, takes a full year. In other words, for tomorrow at least, they're stuck at 8,500. Until more or bigger boats are available, their only course of action is to produce as much as they can on the boats they already have. This time interval during which suppliers are able to change the quantity of some but not all the resources they use to produce goods and services is called the **short run**. The 8,500 fish, then, is the quantity supplied in the short run at $P = \$10$.

What about quantity supplied in the **long run**? What distinguishes the long from the short run? In the long run, suppliers have the time to change the quantity of *all* the resources they use to produce goods and services. In the fishing business, the long run is a year—the time it takes to acquire as many boats as fishermen wish. As we see in the table in Exhibit 5, fishermen end up in the long run acquiring enough boats to produce 16,000 fish.

**Short run**
The time interval during which suppliers are able to change the quantity of some but not all the resources they use to produce goods and services.

**Long run**
The time interval during which suppliers are able to change the quantity of all the resources they use to produce goods and services.

# THEORETICAL PERSPECTIVE

## HOW LONG DOES IT TAKE TO GET TO THE LONG RUN?

**How long does it take to reach the long run? Well, it depends.**

Focus on the time that elapses between the quantity supplied on a market day and the quantity the suppliers would have been willing to offer at that market-day price.

Consider the babysitting market of panel *a*. If the market-day price was $3 per hour on January 1, 2001, and on that day 100 hours had been supplied, babysitters would be less than ecstatic because $3 is a very unattractive price. How long will it take babysitters to find alternative employment? Not long, don't you think? Within a month or so, the quantity supplied of babysitters at $3 would fall from 100 to 30 hours, from point *a* to point *b* on the graph. On the other hand, if the market-day price was $20 per hour, then babysitters supplying those 100 hours would be delighted and it wouldn't take long—a month perhaps—for other people to switch from whatever else they were doing to babysitting. The quantity supplied would jump to 400 hours, from point *c* to point *d*.

Now think about Illinois farmers in the corn market of panel *b*. Suppose the price of corn was $20 per bushel and the market-day supply was 100 bushels. Farmers would be ecstatic, not having seen such a high price before! They would love to produce 400 bushels—but how do you supply more corn when the planting season was last spring? In order to increase the quantity supplied, they must wait for the next planting season to adjust their supply to the $20 price. That is, it takes them a full year to move from point *x* to point *y* on the graph.

How long do you suppose it takes California wine producers to increase their quantity supplied of 20-year wine from the market-day 100 bottles to the long-run 400 bottles—from point *r* to point *s* on the graph in panel *c*—when the market-day price is an attractive $20 per bottle? Think about it. How can you produce 20-year wine in less than 20 years? You see the picture, don't you? The length of time it takes to get from market-day supply to long-run supply depends on the character of the good. It takes little time for babysitting, and a much, much longer time for aged wine.

**YOU'RE A GRAPE NOW, BUT YOU'LL BE A DELICIOUS WINE IN 20 YEARS!**

Why don't suppliers shift instantaneously to the long run when p[...]

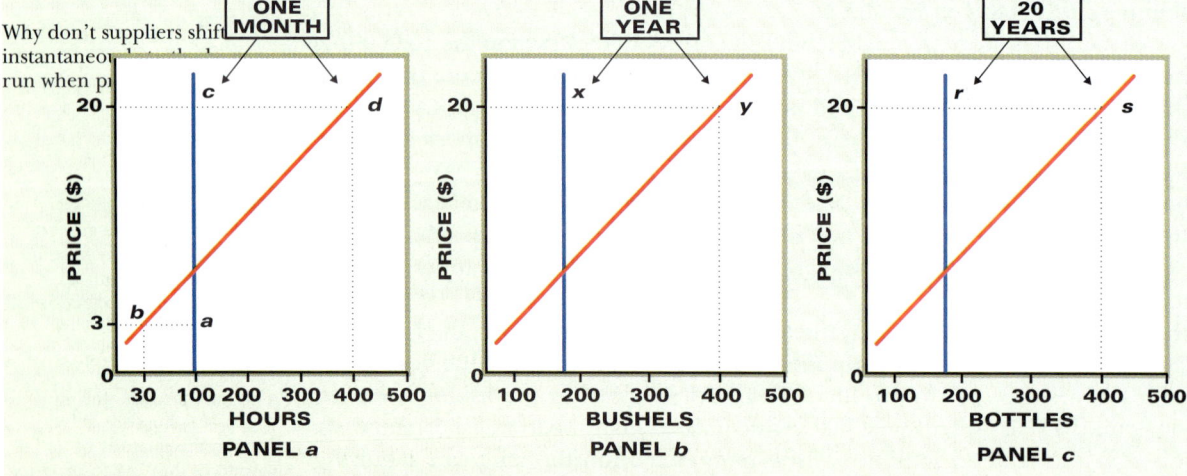

PANEL *a* — ONE MONTH

PANEL *b* — ONE YEAR

PANEL *c* — 20 YEARS

The graph in Exhibit 5 translates the table into graphic form.

The higher the price of fish, the greater the incentive to produce more. As you see for the long run in the table, when the price is $9, fishermen are willing and able to supply 14,000, slightly less than the 16,000 they are willing and able to supply at a price of $10. Why do they supply less? Fishermen will tell you that a $9 fish is not as profitable as a $10 fish. As a result, they hire a smaller crew. As well, fewer potato farmers would be sufficiently motivated to leave potato farming for a $9 fish. Fewer boats are ordered. Still, $9 is a relatively good price for fish. Compare the 8,000 quantity they are willing to supply in the short run to the 14,000 they are willing to and do supply in the long run.

But look what happens at the relatively low $3 price. The market-day supply is fixed at 6,000. If fishermen have time to adjust supply, they will adjust downward. Some who have good options may quit fishing outright. (Some may end up on a potato farm!) Others may continue to fish but produce less with smaller crews.

It isn't easy to quit outright even if there are job opportunities for fishermen elsewhere. After all, many fishermen have an emotional investment in their business and little experience at other jobs. (Ask anybody going through job retraining today.) Moreover, they have boats and equipment that represent a substantial financial investment. It may pay them to continue fishing even if the prospects are not very attractive, at least until their boats need substantial overhauling. Then the decision to shut down or stay afloat is forced.

As you see in the table in Exhibit 5, at $P = \$3$, fishermen cut back the quantity they supply in the short run to 5,000 and, given time, in the long run will trim back further to 2,000. At the much lower price of $1, very few fishermen go out on the water, cutting back further in the short run and supplying no fish at all in the long run.

All three supply curves are upward sloping, but the slope varies with the suppliers' ability to adjust to the different prices. The market-day supply curve is perfectly vertical, with no adjustment to price variations. The short-run supply curve shows moderate flexibility in adjusting quantity supplied to price, while the long-run supply curve has the most gradual slope, reflecting the fishermen's ability to adjust *fully* to price.

**CHECK YOUR UNDERSTANDING**

Why don't suppliers shift instantaneously to the long run when prices change?

## CHANGES IN DEMAND

Let's now look at the fish market of the table in Exhibit 6, whose short-run supply (column 2) is drawn from the table in Exhibit 5 and whose initial demand schedule (column 3) is drawn from the table in Exhibit 4. Now suppose that the demand for fish changes from the schedule shown in column 3 to the one shown in column 4.

Note what happens. At each price, 1,000 more fish are demanded. Prior to the **change in demand,** the quantity demanded at $P = \$10$ was 3,500 fish. It increases now to 4,500. It increases at $P = \$9$ from 4,000 to 5,000, and so on.

The graph in Exhibit 6 depicts the change in demand shown in the table. Demand curve D, graphing the initial demand schedule (column 3), shifts outward to the right to D', graphing the new demand schedule (column 4). Look at the impact on the equilibrium price of fish of the change in demand from D to D'. The old equilibrium price, $P = \$5$, is no longer tenable. Now, at that price, an excess demand of 1,000 fish emerges. The pressure of this excess demand forces the equilibrium price up to $P = \$6$, where the 6,500 quantity of fish demanded equals the 6,500 quantity supplied.

What could cause such a change in demand? There are a number of reasons why people change the quantity they demand at the same price. The principal reasons are changes in income, changes in taste, changes in other prices, changes in expectations about future prices, and changes in population size. Let's consider each.

**Change in demand**
A change in quantity demanded of a good that is caused by factors other than a change in the price of that good.

## EXHIBIT 6

### CHANGE IN DEMAND

**FISH MARKET WITH CHANGE IN DEMAND**

| PRICE | QUANTITY SUPPLIED | INITIAL QUANTITY DEMANDED | INCREASE IN QUANTITY DEMANDED | DECREASE IN QUANTITY DEMANDED |
|---|---|---|---|---|
| $10 | 8,500 | 3,500 | 4,500 | 2,500 |
| 9 | 8,000 | 4,000 | 5,000 | 3,000 |
| 8 | 7,500 | 4,500 | 5,500 | 3,500 |
| 7 | 7,000 | 5,000 | 6,000 | 4,000 |
| 6 | 6,500 | 5,500 | 6,500 | 4,500 |
| 5 | 6,000 | 6,000 | 7,000 | 5,000 |
| 4 | 5,500 | 6,500 | 7,500 | 5,500 |
| 3 | 5,000 | 7,000 | 8,000 | 6,000 |
| 2 | 4,500 | 7,500 | 8,500 | 6,500 |
| 1 | 4,000 | 8,000 | 9,000 | 7,000 |

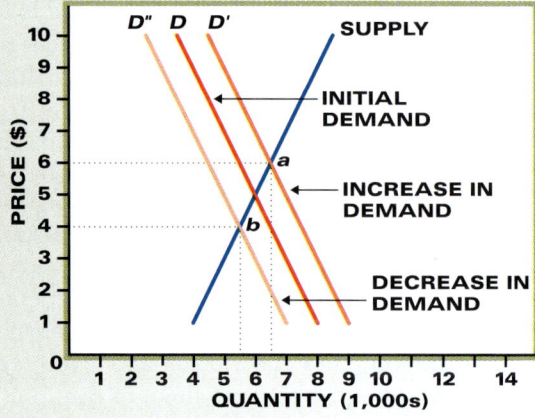

Ceteris paribus, an increase in demand from $D$ to $D'$ raises the equilibrium price from $5 to $6, point $a$ on the graph. The quantity bought and sold increases from 6,000 to 6,500. A decrease in demand from $D$ to $D''$ lowers the equilibrium price from $5 to $4, point $b$ on the graph, and reduces the quantity bought and sold from 6,000 to 5,500.

## Changes in Income

You don't suppose, do you, that when Madonna dines out in one of New York's finest restaurants, she checks the price of poached salmon to see whether she's willing to make the purchase? Wouldn't you be surprised if she orders the salmon at $P = \$5$ but passes at $P = \$10$?

The more income people have, the more they can afford to buy more of everything. If Claudia Preparata's income were to increase by 25 percent, she might be more willing to buy that first fish at $10. Before, she passed it up. It isn't surprising, then, that when people's incomes increase, the quantity demanded of fish at $P = \$10$ increases from 3,500 to 4,500. It increases as well at every other price level.

On the other hand, what do you suppose happens to the demand for fish when incomes fall? You would expect that the quantity demanded at $P = \$10$ would fall from 3,500 fish to something less and that the quantity demanded at $P = \$9$ would fall from 4,000 to something less, and so on. To economists, fish is a **normal good**—that is, a good whose demand increases (or decreases) when people's incomes increase (or decrease).

**Normal good**
A good whose demand increases or decreases when people's incomes increase or decrease.

## Changes in Taste

Tastes seldom change overnight, but they do change. Suppose that the surgeon general reports that the consumption of red meat is detrimental to health. If enough people worry about the quantity of meat they consume and make a conscious effort to cut down, the demand for fish would increase.

Sometimes, tastes are learned or cultivated. Advertising has much to do with it. Suppose McDonald's came to the island and introduced its filet of fish. Wouldn't *some* people, tasting McDonald's fish for the first time, switch from meat to fish? Can you picture the McDonald's fish commercials? If a McDonald's

# INTERDISCIPLINARY PERSPECTIVE

## WHETHER IT'S LOVE OR WISDOM, THE ANSWER IS FISH

In the Broadway musical *Carousel*, Carrie Pipperidge confides to her good friend Julie Jourdan early in the first act that she's in love with Mr. Snow, a New England fisherman. She sings:

> The first time I saw him
> A whiff of his clothes
> Knocked me flat on the floor
> Of the room
> But now that I love him
> My heart's in my nose
> And fish is my favorite perfume

That's one reason to be keen on fish, but certainly not the only one. You don't have to be lovestruck to think of fish as a favorite.

JULIE, HOW ABOUT A FISH SANDWICH AFTER THE RIDE?

Just compare a swordfish dinner to any of the fast foods listed in the following table in terms of fat content—particularly saturated fat—and you will quickly understand that although we may enjoy those foods while we're busy eating, we eventually pay the "price." You don't have to be a rocket scientist to see why people's tastes are changing from beef and even chicken to fish. The result: The demand curve for fish keeps shifting to the right. Visualize the changing equilibrium price. Fish that used to be relatively inexpensive isn't any longer.

| | WEIGHT (oz) | TOTAL FAT (g) | SATURATED FAT (g) | SODIUM (mg) | CALORIES |
|---|---|---|---|---|---|
| SWORDFISH | 8 | 11 | 02.7 | 297 | 130 |
| BIG MAC | 8 | 31 | 10.0 | 880 | 560 |
| WHOPPER | 8 | 43 | 18.0 | 920 | 660 |
| ARBY'S SANDWICH | 8 | 28 | 11.0 | 1561 | 555 |
| KFC CHICKEN PIECES | 8 | 34 | 08.5 | 1530 | 540 |
| HARDEE'S HAMBURGER | 8 | 30 | 12.0 | 1030 | 530 |
| WENDY'S HAMBURGER | 8 | 20 | 07.0 | 920 | 420 |

commercial pushed fish, people on the island would probably end up buying more fish at each price. At $P = \$10$, for example, quantity demanded might increase from 3,500 to 4,500 fish.

*Can you think of any other circumstances that could cause a change in taste? Go to the Interactive Study Center at http://gottheil.swcollege.com and click on the "Your Turn" button to submit your example. Student submissions will be posted to the Web site, and perhaps we will use some in future additions of the book!*

## Changes in the Prices of Other Goods

You don't have to be frightened by the surgeon general's report to substitute fish for beef. Prices alone can do it. For example, if the price of hamburger jumped suddenly from $1.89 to $2.45 per pound, that might be incentive enough for many people to switch from hamburger to fish. After all, fish and hamburger are **substitute goods.** When the price of one increases, the demand for the other increases.

**Substitute goods**
Goods that can replace each other. When the price of one increases, the demand for the other increases.

**Complementary goods**
Goods that are generally used together. When the price of one increases, the demand for the other decreases.

Suppose people on the island typically eat fish with fries. And suppose, as well, that the price of potatoes increases from $0.75 to $2.75 a pound. What happens to the demand for fish? It falls. People demand less fish at each price because the "fish 'n' fries" combo is more expensive. Fish and fries are **complementary goods.** When the price of one increases, the demand for the other decreases.

Can you think of other complementary goods? How about coffee and milk, milk and cookies, peanut butter and jelly, bagels and cream cheese? Coca-Cola once advertised that "Things go better with Coke." What happens to the demand for Coke when the prices of those "things" increase? It falls.

## Changes in Expectations About Future Prices

The demand for fish may change just because people change their expectations about tomorrow's fish price. If you thought that the price of fish would increase tomorrow, you might be willing to buy more fish today; that alone could explain why, at $P = \$10$, the quantity demanded increases from 3,500 to 4,500 (and increases at every price level) in the table in Exhibit 6. Of course, if you had a notion that tomorrow's price would be lower, you might delay consumption by reducing the quantity demanded today. In such a case, the demand for fish decreases.

## Changes in Population Size

Suppose an immigration wave increases the island's population by 10 percent. How does such an increase affect the demand for fish? With more mouths to feed, the quantity of fish demanded at each price increases. A baby boom on the island would have the same effect.

## A Change in Demand or a Change in Quantity Demanded?

Changes in quantity demanded and changes in demand may seem to be two ways of expressing the same idea, but they are not. What's the difference?

Economists define *change in quantity demanded* to mean only the change in quantity demanded of a good that is brought about by a change in the price of that good. They define *change in demand* to mean a shift in the entire demand curve.

Look at demand curve $D$ in Exhibit 7. When price falls from $P = \$10$ to $P = \$7$, the quantity demanded increases from 4,500 to 5,000. Economists describe this increase as "a change in quantity demanded." It traces out a movement *along the demand curve* from point $a$ to point $b$.

When demand increases for other reasons, such as population growth, the entire demand curve shifts from $D$ to $D'$. Economists call this shift "a

### EXHIBIT 7

**DISTINGUISHING CHANGES IN DEMAND FROM CHANGES IN QUANTITY DEMANDED**

Movement along the demand curve $D$ from a price of $10, at point $a$, to a price of $7, at point $b$, illustrates a *change in quantity demanded* from 4,500 to 5,000. A shift in the demand curve from $D$ to $D'$ illustrates a *change in demand*. At a price of $10, the quantity increases from 4,500 on demand curve $D$ to 6,000 on demand curve $D'$.

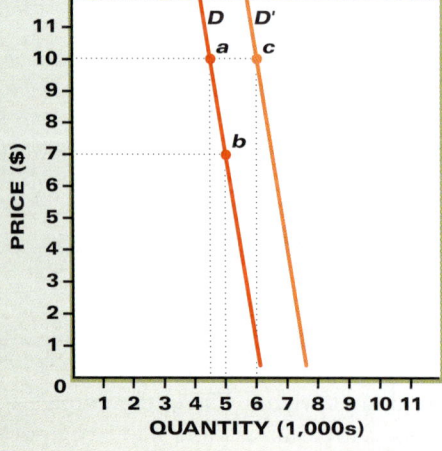

change in demand." At the same price, $P = \$10$, the quantity demanded increases from 4,500 on $D$ to 6,000 on $D'$. The shift in the demand curve from $D$ to $D'$—point $a$ to point $c$ at $P = \$10$—occurs because of a determining factor such as a change in people's tastes or income. It is not a result of a change in the price of the good.

## CHANGES IN SUPPLY

Let us now consider what happens to price when changes in short-run supply occur. Let's suppose that the demand schedule is the same as the one in column 4 of the table in Exhibit 6. The change in short-run supply is 1,000 more fish added (at every price) to the supply schedule of Exhibit 6. The table in Exhibit 8 records this market condition.

The graph in Exhibit 8 depicts the **change in supply** shown in the table.

Supply curve $S$, graphing the initial supply schedule (column 3), shifts outward to the right to $S'$, graphing the new supply schedule (column 4). Look at its impact on the equilibrium price of fish. The initial equilibrium, $P = \$6$, is no longer tenable. Now, at that price an excess supply of 1,000 fish emerges. The pressure of this excess supply drives the equilibrium price down from $P = \$6$ to $P = \$5$, and the quantities bought and sold up from 6,500 to 7,000 fish.

What could cause such a change in supply? There are a number of reasons why fishermen change the quantity they are willing to supply at every price. The principal reasons are changes in technology, changes in resource prices, changes in the prices of other goods, and changes in the number of suppliers. Let's consider each.

### Changes in Technology

Suppose Steve Scariano, an electronics tinkerer on the island, invents a sonar device that allows fishermen to detect the presence of fish at considerable depths. What a bonanza! Imagine JoAnn Weber, one of the island's fishermen, using the same boat and crew but installing Steve's sonar device on her boat. What do you

**CHECK YOUR UNDERSTANDING**
What's the difference between a change in demand and a change in quantity demanded?

**Change in supply**
A change in quantity supplied of a good that is caused by factors other than a change in the price of that good.

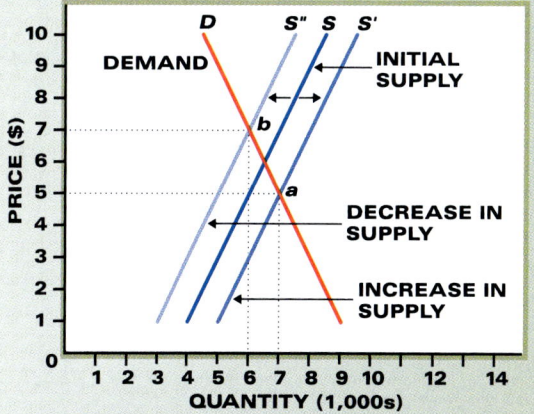

**CHANGE IN SUPPLY**

**FISH MARKET WITH CHANGE IN SUPPLY**

| PRICE | QUANTITY DEMANDED | INITIAL QUANTITY SUPPLIED | INCREASE IN QUANTITY SUPPLIED | DECREASE IN QUANTITY SUPPLIED |
|---|---|---|---|---|
| $10 | 4,500 | 8,500 | 9,500 | 7,500 |
| 9 | 5,000 | 8,000 | 9,000 | 7,000 |
| 8 | 5,500 | 7,500 | 8,500 | 6,500 |
| 7 | 6,000 | 7,000 | 8,000 | 6,000 |
| 6 | 6,500 | 6,500 | 7,500 | 5,500 |
| 5 | 7,000 | 6,000 | 7,000 | 5,000 |
| 4 | 7,500 | 5,500 | 6,500 | 4,500 |
| 3 | 8,000 | 5,000 | 6,000 | 4,000 |
| 2 | 8,500 | 4,500 | 5,500 | 3,500 |
| 1 | 9,000 | 4,000 | 5,000 | 3,000 |

Ceteris paribus, an increase in supply from $S$ to $S'$, lowers the equilibrium price from $6 to $5, point $a$ on the graph. The quantity bought and sold increases from 6,500 to 7,000. A decrease in supply from $S$ to $S''$ raises the equilibrium price from $6 to $7, point $b$ on the graph, and reduces the quantity bought and sold from 6,500 to 6,000.

suppose happens to the quantity of fish she is now capable of bringing home? At every price the quantity supplied increases.

Why? New technology, such as Steve's sonar device, typically lowers the cost of producing a good. Each fish is now cheaper to produce. That means higher profit for fishermen. That higher profit makes fishing even more attractive and becomes an incentive for fishermen to supply more at every price.

## Changes in Resource Prices

If lower costs raise profit and create incentive to supply more at every price, then any factor that contributes to lowering costs will increase supply. Consider what happens to the supply curve when resource prices associated with fishing fall. For example, suppose the price (wages) of hiring fishing crews falls. Instead of paying a boat pilot $300 a day, fishermen find that pilots are readily available at $200. Or suppose the prices of bait, fishing gear, fuel, and ice fall. These lower resource prices increase the spread between the market price a fisherman gets for a fish and the costs involved in producing it. That increased spread is greater profit per fish. In other words, lower resource prices increase the quantities of fish supplied at every price in the fish market.

Imagine what happens to the supply curve if resources associated with fish production become more expensive. The reverse occurs. More expensive resources decrease the quantities supplied at every price in the fish market. We see this in $S''$, a new supply curve to the left of $S$ in Exhibit 8.

## Changes in the Prices of Other Goods

Many boats, with minor alterations, can serve multiple purposes. For example, a sightseeing boat that transports tourists from island to island can be rigged to fish the same waters. Cargo boats can be scrubbed down and fitted for passengers. Fishing boats can haul cargo.

Suppose faltering island tourism causes the price of sightseeing boat tickets to fall. How long will it take before some of the sightseeing boat operators switch to fishing? And how will that switch affect the supply curve of fish? This change in price of other goods (sightseeing boat tickets) shifts the supply curve of fish out to the right.

Let's digress for a moment. Consider potato farmers. Their fields, too, can serve multiple purposes. If the price of corn skyrockets, many potato farmers may switch from potato to corn farming. How would the switch affect the supply schedule of potatoes? At every price in the potato market, the quantity of potatoes supplied falls. Graphed, it would show the supply curve of potatoes shifting to the left.

## Changes in the Number of Suppliers

Perhaps the first thing that comes to mind when trying to explain what could cause the shift from $S$ to $S'$ is simply more suppliers. Somewhat akin to a change in demand occasioned by a change in taste, a change in supply caused by greater numbers of suppliers might reflect changes in people's occupational "taste." More people choosing to fish means more fish at every price.

# WHY THE PRICE OF AN ORANGE IS 30 CENTS AT THE SUPERMARKET

The same factors governing the $6 equilibrium price of fish govern as well the 30-cent equilibrium price of oranges. The price of oranges depends upon the supply and demand conditions in the fruit and vegetable market.

If orange imports from Spain, Morocco, and Israel are added to our California and Florida orange supply, the supply curve in the orange market shifts out to the right, forcing the equilibrium price to fall.

Grapefruit and oranges are substitute goods. If the grapefruit harvest in both California and Florida is exceptionally large, resulting in a substantial fall in the price of grapefruit, the demand curve for oranges shifts to the left. The result? The price of oranges falls.

Suppose, on the other hand, that TV commercials sponsored by the orange-growers industry persuade people that orange juice is not only a breakfast drink but an excellent substitute for soft drinks, tea, coffee, or milk at any time of the day. What should the orange growers expect? The demand curve for their oranges shifts to the right, raising both price and quantity.

Exhibit 9 illustrates precisely how changes in demand and supply can generate changes in the equilibrium price and quantity of oranges.

Suppose both the demand for and the supply of oranges increase simultaneously. For example, health-conscious people switch from consuming soft drinks to consuming orange juice at the same time as orange growers switch to a new harvesting technology that lowers the cost of producing oranges. We see this in panels *a* and *b*, where demand shifts from D to D' and supply shifts from S to S'. But note the differences in the size of the shifts. In panel *a*, the demand shift is the more pronounced. In panel *b*, the supply shift dominates. How do these differences affect changes in the price and quantity of oranges?

Let's start with panel *a*. When either demand or supply increases, quantity increases. So when both demand and supply increase at the same time (more orange juice drinkers and newer technology), the combined result increases quantity from 100 to 200 oranges. What about price? Here, the outcome is less clear. An increase in demand, by itself, raises price. But an increase in supply, by itself, decreases price. The combined effect, then, depends on the relative size of the demand and supply increases. In panel *a*, the sizable increase in demand raises price from $0.30 to $0.50, or by $0.20. The less-than-sizable increase in supply lowers price from $0.30 to $0.20, or by $0.10. As you can see, the net effect is an

### INCREASES IN DEMAND AND SUPPLY

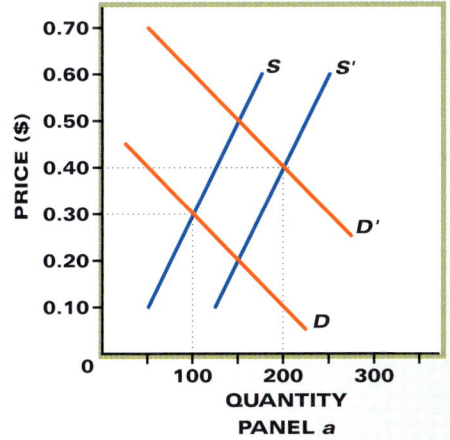

PANEL *a*

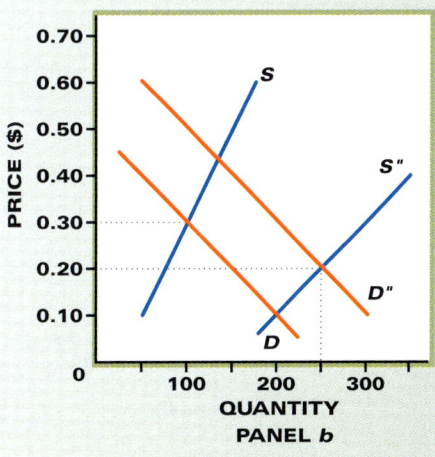

PANEL *b*

Increases in demand and supply increase the quantities demanded and supplied on the market. In panel *a*, quantity increases to 200 oranges; in panel *b*, to 250 oranges. But the effect of these increases on price depends on the relative size increases in demand and supply. When the demand increase is more sizable than the increase in supply, price rises, as we see in panel *a*, from $0.30 to $0.40. When the supply increase is more sizable than the increase in demand, price falls, as we see in panel *b*, from $0.30 to $0.20.

Why does Sunkist (http://www.sunkist.com/), a major producer of oranges, provide free orange recipes? To increase the demand for oranges, of course.

increase in equilibrium price to $0.40. This is because the effect of the change in demand dominates price.

Now look at panel *b*. Here the sizable increase occurs in supply. The increase in orange juice drinkers and new technology shifts the demand and supply curves to $D''$ and $S''$, so that the combined effect raises quantity from 100 to 250 oranges. What about price? It falls to $0.20. This is because the effect of the change in supply dominates price.

Exhibit 10 depicts another version of supply and demand changes in the market for oranges. Now the changes move in opposite directions. More orange juice drinkers (increase in demand) combine with a late spring frost that destroys orange groves (decrease in supply). What happens to price under these circumstances? Since both an increase in demand and a decrease in supply raise price, their combined effect unequivocally increases price. This we see in panel *a*, where price increases from $0.30 to $0.50. What about quantity? Here, the combined effect is less clear. The increase in demand increases quantity, while the decrease in supply decreases quantity. Because the decrease in supply is more sizable in panel *a*, the combined effect is a decrease in quantity, from 100 to 75 oranges.

Finally, look at the panel *b* variation, where the increase in demand is more sizable than the decrease in supply. Now price ends up at $0.45 and quantity increases to 200 oranges.

## POSTSCRIPT: PRICE AS A RATIONING MECHANISM

Consider again the fish market. The demand curve for fish, *D*, depicted in Exhibit 11, panel *a*, is not simply a line drawn on a graph. Each point on that curve represents somebody's willingness to buy fish at some price and, as well, that same person's unwillingness to buy at a higher one. For example, point *a* tells us that Faye Russo will pay $8 for a fish, but will not pay $9. Whether she eats fish or not depends strictly on its price. Point *b* tells us that Jackie Mathews is willing to buy a fish as long as price is no higher than $7. Kim Deal will go as high as $6, Wayne Coyne stops at $3, and Ian Rodier, who likes fish but can't put two pennies

### EXHIBIT 10

### INCREASES IN DEMAND, DECREASES IN SUPPLY

Increases in demand and decreases in supply increase price, in panel *a* from $0.30 to $0.50, and in panel *b* from $0.30 to $0.45. But the effect of the changes in supply and demand on the quantities demanded and supplied depends on the relative size of the increases and decreases in demand and supply. When the demand increase is more sizable than the decrease in supply, quantity decreases from 100 oranges to 75, as we see in panel *a*. When the supply decrease is more sizable than the increase in demand, quantity increases from 100 to 200 oranges, as we see in panel *b*.

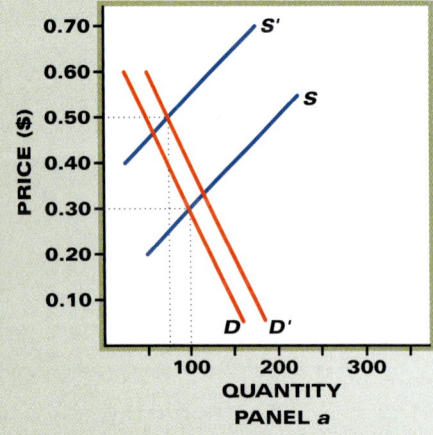
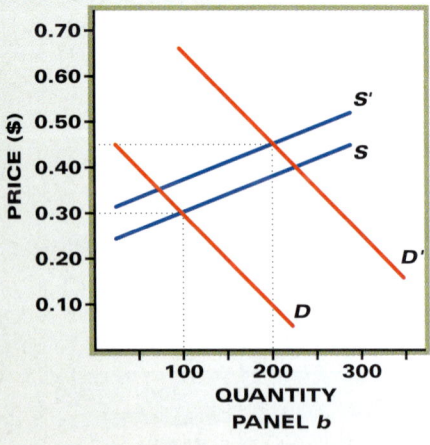

## RATIONING FUNCTION OF PRICE

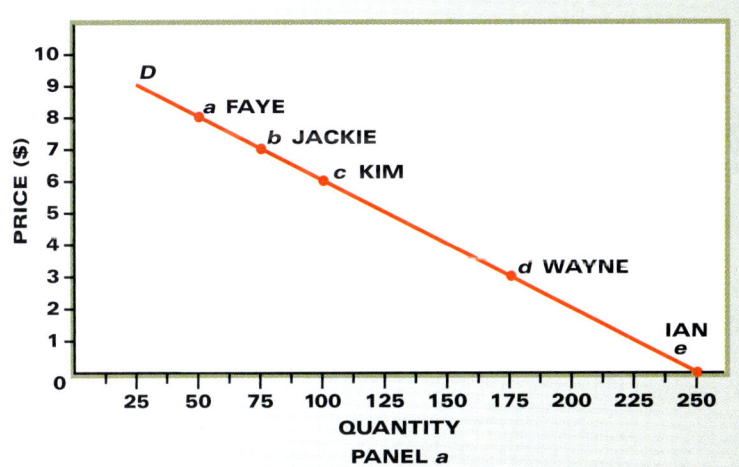

Panel *a* identifies specific people's willingness to buy fish at various prices. Altogether, 250 people express a willingness to buy fish. But who gets them? Panel *b* shows the market for fish and its equilibrium price. Only those willing to pay the market price get the fish. All others don't. The demand curve, *D*, and the supply curve, *S*, generate a market price of $6 and a quantity demanded and supplied of 100. It means 100 of the 250 end up with fish, among them Kim Deal. When the supply curve decreases to S', price rises to $7 and quantity falls to 75 fish. It means 75 people end up with fish, and 175 who want fish don't, among them Kim Deal. In this way, price services as a rationing mechanism.

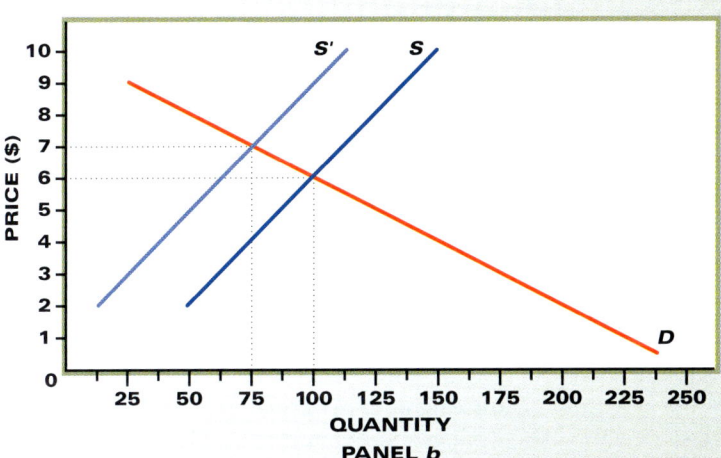

together, eats fish only when price is zero. Adding their demand for fish to everyone else's on demand curve *D* generates a total quantity demanded, albeit at different prices, of 250 fish.

Let's now introduce a supply curve, *S*, to the market. As we see in panel *b*, supply and demand create an equilibrium price of $6 and an equilibrium quantity of 100 fish bought and sold on the market.

Consider those 100 fish. How are they rationed among the 250 people who want fish? You already know the answer, don't you? Everybody positioned on the segment of the demand curve above $6 gets a fish; everyone positioned on the demand curve below $6 doesn't. *The $6 equilibrium price becomes the market's rationing mechanism.* Who are those 100 people? We know they include Faye, Jackie, and Kim. Who are the 150 people who end up without fish? We know they include Wayne and Ian.

If the supply curve shifts to the left to S′, the equilibrium price rises to $7 and the equilibrium quantity falls to 75. There are now fewer fish bought and sold. Faye and Jackie still get fish, but Kim, who would buy fish if price were $6, is shut out of the market at $7. She's disappointed. Her income hasn't changed, her taste for fish hasn't changed, but the price she confronts has. She knows, as you do, that price dictates who gets and who doesn't.

# CHAPTER REVIEW

1. Consumer demand reflects people's willingness to buy a good. People supply goods on the presumption that there will be a demand for them.

2. The demand for a good represents people's willingness to purchase specific quantities at specific prices. The law of demand is the inverse relationship between price and the quantity demanded. As the price of a good decreases, the quantity demanded increases and vice versa.

3. Graphs translate tabular data for quantities demanded at different prices into individual demand curves. Demand curves have negative slopes because price and quantity demanded are inversely related.

4. Market demand curves represent the sum of individual quantities demanded at different prices.

5. Supply involves production activity over a period of time. The market day is a time period so short that the quantity supplied cannot be changed no matter what price is paid to the supplier. Therefore, quantity supplied is constant during the market day, regardless of price.

6. Market price is determined by the intersection of demand and supply. Because quantity demanded and quantity supplied are equal at the market price, it is also called equilibrium price. If price is above its equilibrium level, an excess supply results and creates competition among suppliers, which drives price down to equilibrium. If price is below its equilibrium level, an excess demand results and creates competition among demanders, which drives price up to equilibrium. There is no excess demand or excess supply in equilibrium. The market clears.

7. In a time period longer than the market day, suppliers can respond to changes in price. The short run is a time period long enough to allow suppliers to make partial adjustments in production in response to price changes. The long run is a time period long enough to allow suppliers to completely adjust their production to changes in price. The longer the time period, the more flexible the response by suppliers to price changes. Thus, as time passes, the supply curve shifts from a vertical line to a flatter, positively sloped line.

8. Changes in demand cause changes in the equilibrium price. When demand increases (shifting the demand curve to the right), excess demand emerges at the original equilibrium, causing price to rise to a new and higher equilibrium where quantity supplied once again equals quantity demanded. When demand decreases (shifting the demand curve to the left), the excess supply at the original equilibrium causes price to fall to a new and lower equilibrium where quantity supplied once again equals quantity demanded.

9. Changes in demand are induced by changes in income, changes in taste, changes in the prices of other goods, changes in expectations about future prices, and changes in population size.

10. Complementary goods have inverse relationships such that an increase in the price of one results in a decrease in the demand for the others (for example, bread and butter). Substitute goods, on the other hand, have direct relationships among themselves such that an increase in the price of one results in an increase in the demand for the others (for example, bread and bagels).

11. Changes in supply cause changes in the equilibrium price. When supply increases (shifting the supply curve to the right), excess supply

emerges at the original equilibrium, causing price to fall to a new and lower equilibrium where quantity supplied once again equals quantity demanded. When supply increases (shifting the supply curve to the left), the excess demand at the original equilibrium causes price to rise to a new and higher equilibrium where quantity supplied once again equals quantity demanded.

12. Changes in supply are induced by changes in technology, changes in resource prices, changes in the prices of other goods, and changes in the number of suppliers.

13. Simultaneous shifts in demand and supply lead to changes in equilibrium price and quantity. Whether price increases or decreases, or whether quantity increases or decreases, depends on the direction and strength of these shifts.

14. Price serves as a rationing mechanism in our economy. As price increases, the available supply of a good is rationed to those who can still afford to buy it. A decrease in price makes a good available to a wider segment of the market because more people are able to buy it.

# KEY TERMS

Change in quantity demanded
Law of demand
Demand schedule
Demand curve
Market demand
Supply schedule

Market-day supply
Supply curve
Excess supply
Excess demand
Equilibrium price
Short run

Long run
Change in demand
Normal good
Substitute goods
Complementary goods
Change in supply

# QUESTIONS

1. Draw a demand curve representing King Richard's plea "A horse, a horse, my kingdom for a horse!"
2. Explain why the market-day supply curve for fish described in the chapter is drawn vertically.
3. Why are the slopes of the short-run supply curve and the long-run supply curve different?
4. "Prices always tend toward equilibrium." Discuss this statement by demonstrating why every other price is unsustainable.
5. Suppose NAFTA (the U.S. free trade agreement with Canada and Mexico) allows the neighboring economies to enter our slipper market. Draw a graph showing the probable effects of their entry on price and quantity of slippers demanded and supplied in the United States.
6. When the price of hamburger rises, the demand for fish rises. When the price of hamburger rises, the demand for hamburger buns falls. Why?
7. Hans Gienepp is frustrated every year. In March, the price of tomatoes is $1.75 per pound. That is sufficient incentive for him to plant tomatoes in his yard. But in August, when the crop is ready for picking, prices at the grocer have fallen to 25 cents per pound. "I always run into this bad luck," he laments. Why is his problem not a matter of luck?
8. Because there was a rumor in May that the price of compact disc players was going to increase in August, the demand for compact disc players went up in May. Explain.
9. How would each of the following events affect the international price of oil (in each case ceteris paribus): (a) the United States gives economic assistance to oil-rich Ukraine in the form of oil-drilling technology; (b) Iraq, in a war against Saudi Arabia, destroys 50 percent of Saudi oil wells; (c) a U.S. invention uses sea-water to fuel automobiles; (d) Western

European homes are heated solely by solar power; and (e) the world's population doubles.

10. How do you explain the fact that a single rose at the supermarket florist is $1.49 every day of the year except the week before and during Valentine's Day, when it increases to $3.50?

11. How do you explain the fact that years ago, cheese was considered the poor person's food, selling for less than a quarter of the price of beef? Today, beef and cheese are priced approximately the same.

12. Jeff Foxworthy is a very funny comedian. He always sells out. So how do you explain the fact that when ticket prices are $10, there are lines around the block a mile long for those tickets, and when the price is $40, he sells out, but there are no lines to be seen? Use a graph to aid your discussion.

13. Orange juice producers are dismayed and puzzled. An economist told them that the reason the demand for orange juice fell is that a new technology allows tomato producers to pick ripe tomatoes more quickly, with less damage and at lower cost. Can you make the connection?

14. Professor Carrie Meyer of George Mason University presents her students with the following scenario: "Suppose a frost destroys much of the coffee harvest in Colombia. Show why equilibrium price and quantity change. Suppose, during this period, many coffee drinkers learn to kick the coffee habit. What happens to price and quantity when coffee production returns to normal in the following year?" How would you answer her question?

# PRACTICE PROBLEMS

1. Suppose the communities of Urbana, Champaign, Rantoul, and Danville make up the east-central Illinois market for eggplant. And suppose, at a price of $2, the quantity demanded in Champaign is 2,000, in Urbana 1,000, in Rantoul 400, and in Danville 600. When price falls to $1, the quantity demanded in Champaign becomes 3,000, in Urbana 1,500, in Rantoul 500, and in Danville 700. With these data, graph the east-central Illinois market for eggplant, connecting the points to form a demand curve.

2. Suppose people leave neighboring Indiana and Iowa to settle in east-central Illinois. Show on the graph of practice problem 1 what happens to the demand curve for eggplant in the east-central Illinois market.

3. Would such an influx of people to east-central Illinois change the demand curve for eggplant or the quantity demanded of eggplant?

4. Suppose the market for holiday candles was described by the following schedule:

| PRICE | QUANTITY DEMANDED | QUANTITY SUPPLIED |
|---|---|---|
| $6 | 1,000 | 6,000 |
| 5 | 2,000 | 5,000 |
| 4 | 3,000 | 4,000 |
| 3 | 4,000 | 3,000 |
| 2 | 5,000 | 2,000 |
| 1 | 6,000 | 1,000 |

Draw the demand and supply curves and identify the equilibrium price. What effect would a 1,000-unit decrease in demand at every price level have on the demand curve, supply curve, and equilibrium price?

5. The following are the various demand and supply schedules for pizza. Let's start by assuming that the demand and supply on the pizza market are $D_2$ and $S_2$. (a) What is the equilibrium price and quantity of pizza? (b) Now suppose people's tastes switch to pizza. What happens to equilibrium price and quantity? (c) Let's add another change to the market. This time let's assume that, although with that change in taste, the price of pizza ingredients (cheese, onions, and so on) falls. What happens to equilibrium price and quan-

tity? (d) Finally, let's suppose that a new health report reveals that pizza is bad for your health and people's demand for pizza falls dramatically, even below the original $D_2$ schedule. What happens to equilibrium price and quantity?

| PRICE | $D_1$ | $D_2$ | $D_3$ | $S_1$ | $S_2$ | $S_3$ |
|-------|-------|-------|-------|-------|-------|-------|
| $5    | 6     | 10    | 14    | 12    | 14    | 18    |
| 4     | 8     | 12    | 16    | 10    | 12    | 16    |
| 3     | 10    | 14    | 18    | 8     | 10    | 14    |
| 2     | 12    | 16    | 20    | 6     | 8     | 12    |
| 1     | 14    | 18    | 22    | 4     | 6     | 10    |

# WHAT'S WRONG WITH THIS GRAPH?

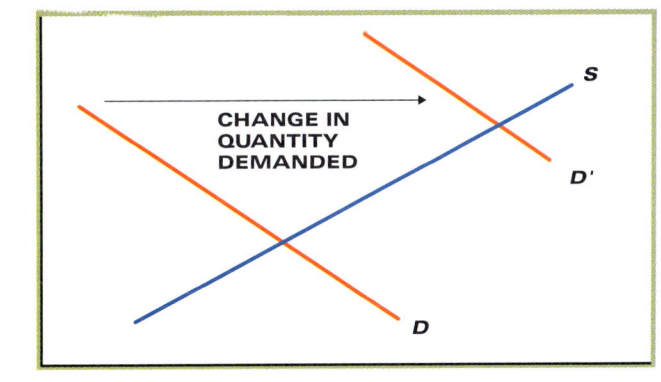

# ECONOMIC CONSULTANTS

### ECONOMIC RESEARCH AND ANALYSIS BY STUDENTS FOR PROFESSIONALS

Mort's Ostrich Farm produces high-protein, low-fat ostrich meat for restaurants and consumers. Mort's currently supplies a small number of customers, but the firm believes it can increase the quantity it produces and the price it charges with strategies to increase the demand for ostrich meat.

Mort's has approached Economic Consultants for advice on how to increase the demand. Prepare a report for Mort's that addresses the following issues:

1. What strategies can Mort's implement to increase the demand for ostrich meat?
2. Explain to Mort's the difference between changing the demand for ostrich meat versus changing the quantity demanded. Explain what strategies will cause a change in demand versus a change in the quantity demanded.

You may find the following resources helpful as you prepare this report for Mort's:

- **Ostrich Central** (http://www.connect.net/ratites/), **Ostrich Growers Meat Company** (http://www.ostrichgrowers.com), and **Warren Ostrich Foods** (http://www.warrenfoods.com/)—These suppliers of ostrich meat offer distribution across the United States.
- **The Clio Awards** (http://www.clioawards.com)—The Clio Awards highlight the best advertising campaigns in print, radio, and television.

# PRACTICE TEST

1. Dog food companies have developed a new technology that makes nutritious dog food out of garbage. We would expect, ceteris paribus, that the
   a. supply curve of dog food would shift to the left.
   b. supply curve of dog food would shift to the right.
   c. demand curve for dog food would shift to the left.
   d. demand curve for dog food would shift to the right.
   e. demand and supply curves would shift to the right.

2. We would also find that the price of dog food would
   a. fall because the supply curve shifted to the right.
   b. fall because the supply curve shifted to the left.
   c. fall because the demand curve shifted to the right.
   d. rise because the demand curve shifted to the right.
   e. rise because the demand curve shifted to the left.

3. When the demand curve for bicycles increases while the supply curve remains unchanged,
   a. the quantity demanded decreases.
   b. the equilibrium price increases and the equilibrium quantity decreases.
   c. the equilibrium price decreases and the equilibrium quantity increases.
   d. quantity supplied increases.
   e. quantity supplied decreases.

4. Which of the following will not shift the market short-run supply of corn?
   a. A change in the price of corn
   b. A change in the price of soybeans
   c. A change in the price of herbicides and pesticides
   d. A change in the storage of technology
   e. A change in the number of acres planted of corn

5. As long as an excess demand for fish exists on the market, there will always be an incentive
   a. for demanders to bid the price up.
   b. for demanders to buy fewer fish.
   c. for fishermen to produce and supply fish.
   d. for fishermen to lower the price of fish.
   e. for demanders and suppliers to seek the equilibrium price.

6. In March, if consumers expect the price of in-line skates to increase as the summer approaches,
   a. the market-day supply of in-line skates in March will shift to the right.
   b. the demand for in-line skates in March will shift to the right.
   c. the demand for in-line skates in March will shift to the left.
   d. the current price of in-line skates will fall.
   e. there will be a movement along the demand curve for in-line skates.

7. Ty manufactures Beanie Baby dolls. The market-day supply curve for Beanie Baby dolls is vertical because
   a. Ty is very responsive to price changes.
   b. the consumer demand curves are very responsive to even small price changes.
   c. the price will not change as the quantity supplied changes in the market.
   d. the equilibrium price dictates how many Beanie Babies will be sold each day.
   e. Ty cannot increase its supply during a given day in response to price changes.

**SUPPLY AND DEMAND FOR BRIEFCASES**

| PRICE | QUANTITY SUPPLIED | QUANTITY DEMANDED |
|---|---|---|
| $50 | 100 | 600 |
| 60 | 200 | 500 |
| 70 | 300 | 400 |
| 80 | 350 | 350 |
| 90 | 400 | 300 |

8. The preceding table illustrates the supply and demand schedules for briefcases. The equilibrium price for briefcases in this market
   a. is $50.
   b. is $60.
   c. is $70.
   d. is $80.
   e. cannot be determined without more information.

9. The preceding table illustrates the supply and demand schedule for briefcases. If there is a reduction in the price of leather used to make briefcases, enabling manufacturers to supply 100 additional briefcases at each price, the new equilibrium price
   a. will be the same as the old equilibrium price.
   b. will cause a rightward shift in the market demand curve for briefcases.
   c. will cause a leftward shift in the market demand curve for briefcases.
   d. will be $90.
   e. will be $70.

10. If both the demand and supply curves in the market for oranges shift to the right,
    a. price falls and quantity increases.
    b. price rises and quantity decreases.
    c. price and quantity both decrease.
    d. price increases and it is unclear what happens to quantity.
    e. quantity increases and it is unclear what happens to price.

# APPENDIX
## ON READING GRAPHS

## HOW MUCH IS THAT DOGGIE IN THE WINDOW?

The image of a young child's face pushed flush up against the window of a pet shop, watching puppies at play, is a sight that would warm the cockles of anyone's heart. Is it too great a leap from fish markets to the puppy market? Not really. After all, both fish and puppies are produced for and sold on markets. Supply and demand determine the price of puppies just as supply and demand determine the price of fish.

Look at Exhibit A1. In 1993, the supply, S, and demand, D, for Jack Russell terrier pups generated an equilibrium price of $600 and an equilibrium quantity of 1,000 pups. That was then. This is now. When the sitcom *Frasier* became a sensation on prime-time TV, the market for Jack Russell terriers changed dramatically. Why? Because the sitcom included a Jack Russell terrier named Eddie who was the darling pet of Frasier's dad. The popularity of the TV sitcom increased the popularity of the Jack Russell terrier as a pet dog. As we see in Exhibit A1, the demand curve for Jack Russell terrier pups shifted from D to D', which caused the equilibrium price of the puppies to rise from $600 to $900 and quantity to increase from 1,000 to 1,400.

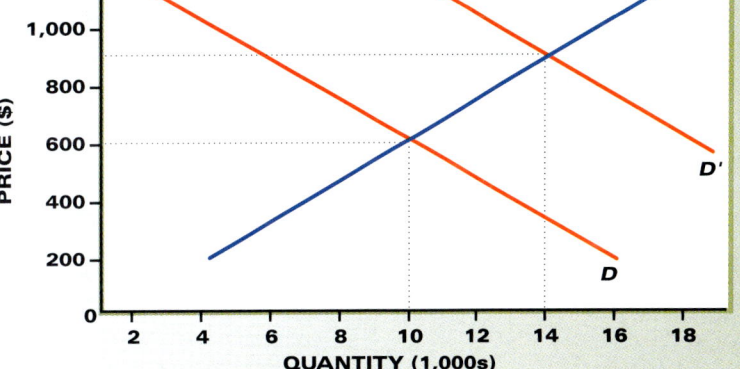

What about the child at the pet shop window? Try as he might—clutching 25 cents in his tiny fist—the Jack Russell terrier pup is far beyond his financial means. He may want that pup as badly as any child wants a puppy, but he confronts the rationing function of price and is just out of luck. The pup goes to someone who is willing and able to pay $900. It's as simple as that. It has nothing to do with love of animals, or love of children, or concern for the pup. It has all to do with willingness and ability to pay the price.

**CHECK YOUR UNDERSTANDING**
Why can't the child get the puppy?

## THE CASE OF THE GUIDE DOG

Let's look at a different dog market, this time for guide dogs, which as you know are indispensable to many blind people. Look at Exhibit A2. The supply curve, S, reflects the relatively high cost of training these animals; the demand curve, D,

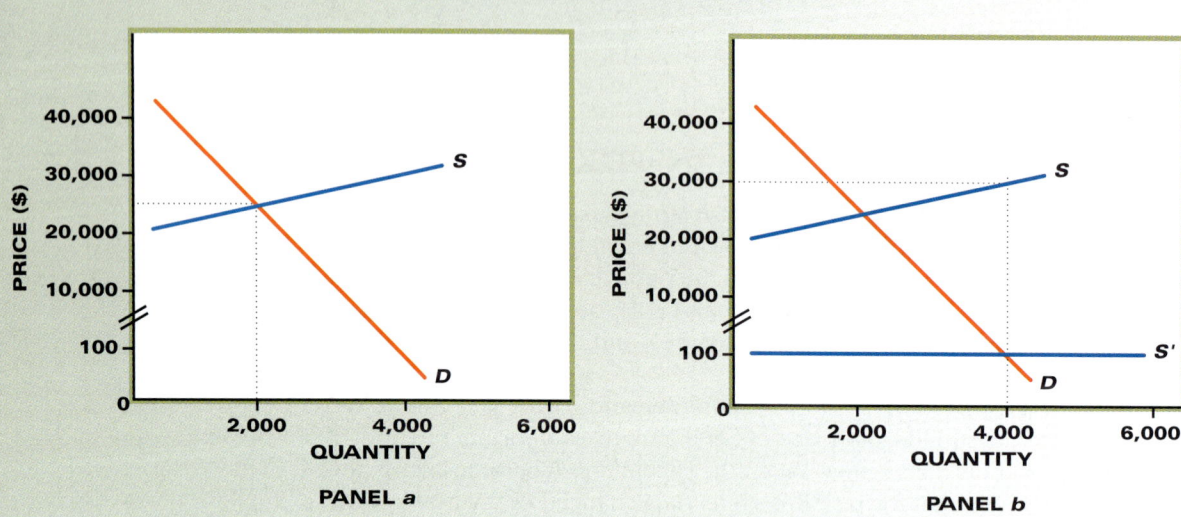

**EXHIBIT A2**

**MARKET FOR GUIDE DOGS**

**PANEL a**

**PANEL b**

reflects the relatively high value sightless people place on having such a dog. Market equilibrium occurs at a price of $25,000 and a quantity of 2,000 dogs. It is pointless to dispute the market's $25,000 equilibrium price. Reasonable or not, it simply records the interaction of supply and demand on the market. Who gets these dogs depends solely on who can afford to pay $25,000.

But is that *really* the way we want to ration those dogs among demanders? Perhaps we can tolerate a child's longing for but not having a Jack Russell terrier puppy, but can we tolerate a sightless person longing for but not having a guide dog? If that's unacceptable, then how do we go about providing these people with guide dogs at affordable prices?

After all, the willingness and ability of suppliers to supply a good depends, as you know, on the opportunity cost of producing the good. Look at the supply curve in the guide dog market of Exhibit A2, panel *a*. What does it tell us? The willingness and ability of suppliers to supply those dogs depends on the opportunity cost of producing them. For example, suppliers' willingness and ability—measured by opportunity cost—to supply 100 dogs is $20,000. It takes $30,000 to create a quantity supplied of 4,000 dogs. How then can suppliers supply *any* quantity of guide dogs at affordable prices?

Look at Exhibit A2, panel *b*. The actual supply curve that functions in the market is the horizontal supply curve, S′, which shows that suppliers are willing and able to supply as many as 5,000 guide dogs at $100 each. But how can suppliers supply those dogs at $100 when the opportunity cost of producing them—reflected in supply curve S—is considerably higher than $100? The answer is that the suppliers are supported financially by people like yourself. These suppliers solicit donations—by direct mail, collection cans, and boxes at cashier counters—whose sums are sufficient to make up the $30,000 opportunity cost shown on supply curve S at the quantity of 4,000. (Have you ever slotted a quarter in their donation card?)

Why do these suppliers set their supply curve, $S'$, at $100? It is an arbitrarily picked, very affordable price to indicate to their eventual owners that the dogs are not free goods. Can we create a similar donation-supported market for Jack Russell terriers? Of course. But why?

## FROM DOGS TO HUMAN BEINGS

If it isn't a great analytical leap from the fish market to the dog market, is it any greater a leap from the pet puppy and guide dog markets to markets for human body parts? Not really. The powerful tools of supply and demand allow us to analyze the highly emotional and ethical issues associated with the buying and selling of human organs. How do we deal with these demands and supplies? Do we put these human body parts on the market as we do fish and puppies? Are their prices market-derived?

### The Market for Organ Transplants

Perhaps the most emotionally charged and ethically engaged market we will ever encounter is the market for human organ transplants. At one time—not too many years ago—transplanting a human organ, such as a kidney or lung, from one person to another was strictly science fiction. Today it's a reality. Organ transplantation technology along with genetic engineering has allowed us to defy Mother Nature. How long will it be before we can order through the Internet an upgraded IQ, or a set of lungs, heart, and legs that would allow each of us to break the four-minute mile? Ludicrous? Don't bet on it.

**THE MARKET FOR HUMAN KIDNEYS** That's the good news. The bad news is depicted in Exhibit A3, panel $a$, the market for human kidneys. As you see, demand and supply generate an equilibrium price of $120,000, which is far beyond the financial reach of most who need a kidney. The demand curve, $D_a$, reflects the urgency and intensity of that demand; the supply curve, $S_a$, reflects the difficulty people have parting with a nonreplenishable organ of their own—a kidney, in this case—or even parting with one after death, or with that of a deceased relative.

Is there a problem with that $120,000 price? Theoretically, not any more so than the $900 price tag on a puppy. Price serves as the rationing function in both markets. People willing and able to pay the price get the kidneys and puppies. Others don't. The question is, Should price serve as the rationing function?

**THE NATIONAL TRANSPLANT ORGAN ACT OF 1984** While people may hold strong opinions on this subject, this normative economic issue was resolved, at least legally, with the passage in Congress of the National Transplant Organ Act of 1984. This act disallowed the private sale of organs, making the only legal market for kidneys—and other human organs—the not-for-profit market of Exhibit A3, panel $b$.

Note the difference. Volunteer donors alone provide the entire supply of 25,000 kidneys, *and that supply has nothing to do with price*. The horizontal supply curve, $S_b$, reflects the willingness of suppliers—in this case, hospitals—to supply any quantity up to 25,000 kidneys at a price of $20,000, a price that simply covers the cost of harvesting the kidney procured from an unpaid donor.

What about demand? Before the advent of organ transplantation technology, people who suffered an organ failure simply didn't survive. Now, with transplant technology accessible, there is reason to hope—and this hope translates into the Exhibit A3, panel $b$, demand for kidneys, $D_b$.

**CHECK YOUR UNDERSTANDING**

Why is the supply curve horizontal at $20,000?

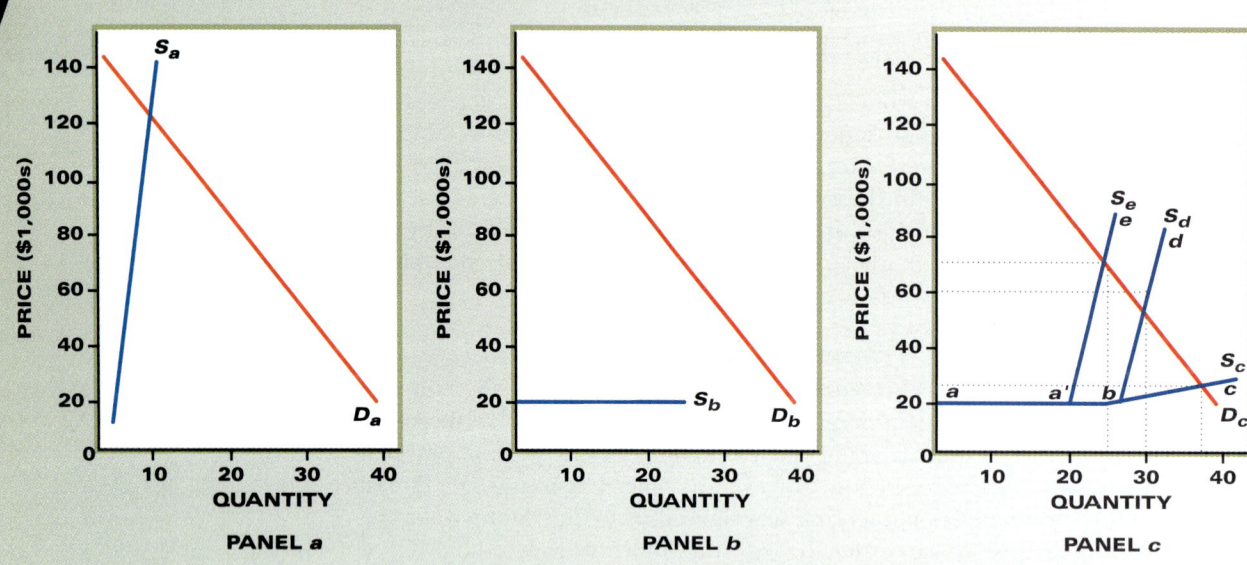

Suppliers (hospitals) supply the 25,000 kidneys at $20,000, but at that price, the quantity supplied falls considerably short of the 40,000 quantity demanded, creating a *chronic* excess demand of 15,000 kidneys.

How, then, are the kidneys allocated among demanders? The rationing function of price is not permitted to clear the market. Some other rationing function—such as age, urgency, or geography—must take its place. However reasonable and fair these rationing systems may appear to be, many who need a kidney transplant still end up without one. To these people, and to many others, the outcome generated by the strictly donor-supplied market is simply intolerable. Is there some way to improve the outcome?

**WOULD ORGAN-FOR-A-PRICE SUPPLIERS HELP?** Look at the horizontal supply curve, $S_b$, in Exhibit A3, panel *b*. It shows the willingness of hospitals to supply 25,000 unpaid-donor kidneys at a price of $20,000. This reliance on unpaid-donor kidneys acts as a formidable barrier to any increase in quantity supplied.

What incentive scheme motivated these unpaid donors to volunteer one of their two kidneys, or both upon death? For most donors, it is strictly a matter of altruism, touched perhaps by a history of some personal loss or otherwise moved by compassion and social responsibility.

It would be lovely (certainly for those needing kidney transplants) if more people volunteered an organ, extending the supply curve, $S_b$, to the right. But if that prospect were not immediately forthcoming, then perhaps another way of increasing supply would be to simply pay people for organs supplied.

Organ-for-a-price supply curves are depicted in Exhibit A3, panel *c*. If it takes just a modest payment to induce many people to supply one or more of their kidneys before or after death, then the supply curve of kidneys may very well look like $S_c$ (line *abc*).

At $20,000, quantity supplied is 25,000 kidneys (line *ab*), reflecting the unpaid organ donors' supply. But thereafter, quantity supplied increases as payments kick in (line *bc*). For example, at a payment of $8,000, the equilibrium price for a kidney increases slightly—from $20,000 to $28,000, but the equilibrium quantity increases more than slightly, from 25,000 to 38,000. An attractive option, don't you think?

On the other hand, if the organ-for-a-price supply curve were $S_d$ (line *abd*), it would take a significant payment to induce just a slight increase in quantity supplied. For example, a $40,000 payment to paid donors increases price from $20,000 to $60,000 and quantity supplied by only 3,000—from 25,000 to 28,000.

Consider yet a third organ-for-a-price supply curve possibility, $S_e$, (line *aa'e*). Here we see a rather perverse outcome. Suppose some unpaid donors are offended by what they consider to be a callous and coldhearted move toward the organ-for-a-price market and respond by reducing their unpaid organ supply by 5,000 so that quantity supplied at a $20,000 price falls from 25,000 to 20,000 kidneys (line *aa'*). If the organ-for-a-price supply curve is $S_d$-shaped, then $S_e$ becomes the operative supply curve. Now a $50,000 payment for a kidney drives price to $70,000 and quantity supplied to 24,000. That's 1,000 short of the 25,000 kidneys that would have been supplied by unpaid donors in the absence of an organ-for-a-price market.

Which of these organ-for-a-price supply curves reflects the real world we live in? There is no strong consensus among economists on this vital question.

## SCALPING TICKETS AT A YANKEE GAME

Let's end the discussion of supply and demand applications on a less somber note. Suppose you were thinking of going to a Yankee baseball game. Here's the picture. The stadium's capacity is 70,000 seats and when the Yankees are hot, many of their games are sold out. But a sellout doesn't mean you can't buy a ticket! It just means that you will probably have to buy your ticket from a scalper in a **scalper's market.** What does this market look like?

Let's first look at the scalpers' supply curve. People with season tickets or who have bought tickets in advance may be willing to sell their tickets to a scalper instead of attending the game "if the price is right." If the Yankees are playing well, Yankee fans holding tickets may be reluctant to part with them unless they're paid handsomely for them. For example, a scalper could probably buy a few $35 tickets for $50 each. To get more tickets to resell, the scalper would probably have to pay even more than $50 because it would take a higher price to induce the more devoted fans to give them up. As a result, the supply curve for scalpers' tickets is upward sloping.

If the Yankees are having a rough season, losing many of their games, scores of fair-weather fans may be more than willing to sell their tickets for less than the original $35 price. A scalper may get a few $35 tickets for $20 each and more than a few if the supply price is raised to $30.

What about demand? As there are fair-weather suppliers, there are also fair-weather demanders. If the Yankees are doing well, people without tickets would be willing to pay more than $50 for a $35 ticket at a sold-out game. If the scalper lowers price, the quantity demanded increases. You see the outcome, don't you?

The equilibrium price on the scalper's market for a Yankee ticket depends upon supply and demand, as depicted in Exhibit A4; these supply and demand curves reflect the willingness of ticket holders to sell their tickets and the willingness of

**Scalper's market**
A market in which a good is resold at a price higher than the original or officially published price.

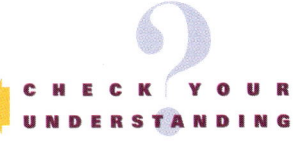

**CHECK YOUR UNDERSTANDING**

What determines the scalper's price?

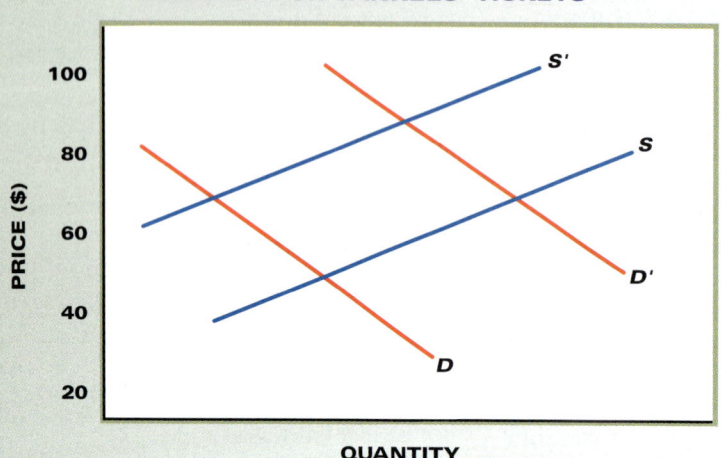

**MARKET FOR YANKEES' TICKETS**

ticket buyers to pay for those tickets. The scalper is the agent that makes these demands and supplies come to life. If the Yankees are pennant-bound, the demand curve may shift to the right, from $D$ to $D'$, while the supply curve shifts to the left, from $S$ to $S'$, driving the equilibrium price upward from $50 to $90. Is there anything wrong or unethical about a scalper's market? Not really. It actually represents an honest-to-goodness free market for baseball tickets.

# QUESTIONS

1. Think about the market for drug-detecting police dogs and the market for pet dogs. Why would their equilibrium prices differ?
2. Make a case for allowing the market to determine the price and quantity of human body parts. Make the countercase that opposes such a pure market determination.
3. Why is the supply curve in the market for kidneys drawn horizontally when the kidneys obtained by the suppliers (hospitals, in this case) are provided by unpaid donors?

# PRACTICE PROBLEMS

1. Let's get ready for the Super Bowl! Suppose the game is played in Chicago at Soldier Field, which has a capacity of 105,000 seats. Ticket prices are $75. The game is sold out, which brings the scalper's market to life. The willingness of ticket holders to sell their $75 tickets is shown in the Quantity Supplied column in the following table. The willingness of people to buy those tickets is shown in the Quantity Demanded column. If you were one of those suppliers, how much would you get for your $75 ticket?

| PRICE | QUANTITY SUPPLIED | QUANTITY DEMANDED |
|---|---|---|
| $1,000 | 7,000 | 500 |
| 800 | 6,000 | 1,000 |
| 600 | 5,000 | 2,000 |
| 400 | 4,000 | 4,000 |
| 200 | 3,000 | 6,000 |

2. Now suppose the hype before the game was extraordinary and ticket holders were more reluctant to part with their $75 tickets. At each price level, 1,000 fewer tickets are offered. Fill in this quantity supplied in the following table. At the same time, more people were willing to pay a higher scalper's price. At each price level, 4,000 more tickets are demanded. Fill in this quantity demanded in the table. If you were still one of those suppliers, how much would you get for your $75 ticket?

| PRICE | QUANTITY SUPPLIED | QUANTITY DEMANDED |
|---|---|---|
| $1,000 | | |
| 800 | | |
| 600 | | |
| 400 | | |
| 200 | | |

# PART 2

# EMPLOYMENT, INFLATION, AND FISCAL POLICY

## CHAT ECONOMICS

**T**une into the conversation. It's about *your* course. Just change the names, and it's *your* campus, *your* classroom, *your* professor, *your* classmates, and *you.*

Professor Gottheil walks into his 9 A.M. Monday class. Everyone is in his or her usual place except Wayne Coyne. He normally sits in the back of the room, but this morning he is seated up front, sporting a rather perplexed look on his face.

**WAYNE:** (*Waving his hand to draw Professor Gottheil's attention.*) Professor Gottheil, before you start today's lecture, could you explain something that has been puzzling me all weekend?

**GOTTHEIL:** Fire away!

**WAYNE:** Well, I was home this weekend and my father asked me what courses I was taking this semester, and I told him about this macroeconomics course. He asked me if I was learning anything.

**GOTTHEIL:** And what did you say? (*The class laughs.*)

**WAYNE:** I said I think I was.

**GOTTHEIL:** Well, I know you are! Your work has been good.

**WAYNE:** Thank you! My dad quizzed me about something I think I should have known, but I couldn't answer him. I felt pretty dumb. I think he was tricking me.

**GOTTHEIL:** What did he ask you?

**WAYNE:** It was sort of a riddle. He said: Suppose someone, let's say Nick Rudd, goes to Bob Diener's Good Vibes shop and buys a $100 CD player, paying for it by check. And Bob later, using the check—he endorses it by signing his name on the back of the check—buys a $100 pair of boots at Lisa Burnett's Leather Shop. And then Lisa, using the same check, endorses it as well—buying $100 groceries at Geoff Merritt's Foods. Geoff also endorses the check, and this goes on through 10 such endorsements. The last person, Louise Gerber, takes the $100 check to her bank, and the bank discovers that Rudd's check is worthless. Louise notes the 10 names signed on the back of the check and invites them to her shop. She tells them that the check they were all passing is worthless and that she is out $100. However, if each gave her $10, half of the $20 profit they made on their sales, she would recoup the $100. Considering the proposal quite fair, they each contribute $10. Now here's the weird moral to my dad's story: Nick Rudd, the bad-check passer, gets his CD player, and the 10 who endorsed his worthless check come out ahead as well, each making a profit.

**GOTTHEIL:** So what's the problem?

**WAYNE:** How can everyone come out a winner when the check was worthless in the first place?

**GOTTHEIL:** (*Turning to the class, and noticing Jennifer Busey looking away.*) Anyone want to explain it? Jennifer?

**JENNIFER:** I think Wayne is right. There's a flaw somewhere in the story. It's a trick. It can't really happen.

**GOTTHEIL:** No flaw, no trick. Wayne's dad tells a good story that makes a very good point. Look at all the $100 sales that the worthless $100 check created. Those sales represent a lot of goods produced and a lot of people employed. If Bob, the first one to get the check, had called the bank to verify it at the very beginning, all those sales the check generated would never have taken place, and all that employment would never have occurred. In a way, you can thank the bad-check writer, Nick Rudd, for stimulating the economy!

**WAYNE:** But that's cheating. It's like getting something for nothing.

**GOTTHEIL:** But the nothing actually created something. Wayne, your dad's story is very useful. Remember it when you read the next few chapters. Whether he knew it or not, your dad was describing the mechanics of the income multiplier, something we will study in the next few chapters.

**WAYNE:** Frankly, I don't think he knew!

# CHAT ECONOMICS

Over the next 6 chapters, you will encounter a number of new economic concepts, such as the income multiplier, the business cycle, the consumption function, aggregate demand, and aggregate supply. These, and others, are concepts we use in economics to describe how our economy works. Read carefully and keep track of each of these new key concepts, and, like Wayne, ask questions when you don't understand. You will be surprised at what you discover.

# CHAPTER 4

# AGGREGATE DEMAND AND AGGREGATE SUPPLY

Suppose you've been out of work for four months and spent the first month trying unsuccessfully to find a job like the one you had. Then, in the second month, you lowered your sights and were willing to take a job that at least had some potential. Finally, in the last two months of being out of work, you were willing to take anything at all. The last thing you want to hear is somebody telling you that if you *really* wanted a job, you would hustle and find one.

Most likely, you didn't lose your job through any fault of your own. It wasn't because your wages were too high or because you didn't give the job 100 percent of your talents and energies. It was simply because people cut back on buying the goods you and your co-workers were making. After all, if people buy fewer automobiles, Ford needs fewer MBAs and engineers.

The trouble with finding another job is not that you aren't hustling. It may be that people are not only buying fewer automobiles, but also buying fewer of everything. It isn't just Ford that has cut back on its workforce. Cutting back employment may be a nationwide phenomenon. With firms everywhere in the economy downsizing production, who is hiring?

That's why the job placement agencies you have tried are crowded with people like you. The economy could be producing more, but isn't. People could be consuming more, but aren't. More workers than those employed could be working, but aren't. Economists identify this economic malaise as a **recession** if the decline in GDP persists for six consecutive months.

A relatively long and deep recession is sometimes described as a **depression.** The distinction is meant to convey a difference like that between first- and second-degree burns: How intense is the inflicted pain?

### THIS CHAPTER INTRODUCES YOU TO THE ECONOMIC PRINCIPLES ASSOCIATED WITH:

- THE PHASES OF THE BUSINESS CYCLE
- GROSS DOMESTIC PRODUCT (GDP)
- THE CPI AND GDP DEFLATOR
- NOMINAL AND REAL GDP
- AGGREGATE DEMAND AND AGGREGATE SUPPLY
- MACROECONOMIC EQUILIBRIUM
- DEMAND-PULL AND SUPPLY-PUSH INFLATION

**Recession**
A phase in the business cycle in which the decline in the economy's real GDP persists for at least a half-year. A recession is marked by relatively high unemployment.

**Depression**
Severe recession.

**Prosperity**
A phase in the business cycle marked by a relatively high level of real GDP, full employment, and inflation.

**Inflation**
An increase in the price level.

**Business cycle**
Alternating periods of growth and decline in an economy's GDP.

**Trough**
The bottom of a business cycle.

**Recovery**
A phase in the business cycle, following a recession, in which real GDP increases and unemployment declines.

**Peak**
The top of a business cycle.

**Downturn**
A phase in the business cycle in which real GDP declines, inflation moderates, and unemployment emerges.

## WHY RECESSION? WHY PROSPERITY?

But why recession? Why do so many people who are willing and able to work lose their jobs? Why do people cut back their consumption? What triggers recession, and how does an economy climb out of the economic doldrums?

Depressed enough? Well, picture a different and much more pleasant scenario. Suppose you are working your regular shift at Ford and the plant manager asks you, almost begs you, to work overtime. Apparently, people are buying more automobiles than Ford and the other automakers had anticipated. You also learn that General Motors needs more workers and is offering wages that are higher than you are earning at Ford. You point this out to your plant manager, who immediately matches the General Motors offer. Under these circumstances, morale among management and labor at Ford is understandably high.

But suppose that people are not only buying more automobiles, but also trying to buy more of everything. They are demanding more residential housing than is available on the market, so more electricians and carpenters are put to work. More people are flying, so more flight crews are operating. More people are crowding into department stores, as if every day were the day before Christmas. Everywhere in the economy, excess demand for goods and services drives prices up. Trying to take advantage of this robust nationwide consumer demand, producers look for more workers, even hiring workers away from each other. They don't mind paying higher wages under these circumstances. Producing more is paramount. And suppose more goods and services are produced until all available resources—land, labor, and capital—are fully employed. What happens if the unrelenting demand for goods and services in the now fully employed economy continues? Prices would rise like a hot-air balloon!

Economists define such a period of economic activity as **prosperity**—an economic boom. And an overall increase in prices is called **inflation.**

But why prosperity and inflation? Why do people try to consume more goods and services than producers have planned to produce? Why can people, without much hustle at all, find almost any kind of job at good wages? Sound attractive? Alas, prosperity, like recession, never lasts.

## The Business Cycle

Historical experience shows that our economy roller-coasters from periods of prosperity and inflation to periods of recession, then, recovering from recession, it heads back again to prosperity and inflation. Economists describe this roller-coaster pattern of economic activity as the **business cycle.** Exhibit 1 depicts the course an economy takes through such a cycle.

The vertical axis records the economy's production of goods and services, that is, the economy's output. The horizontal axis records time, measured in years.

The first phase of the cycle depicted in Exhibit 1 is recession, that time period when the economy's unemployment rate is greatest and output declines to the cycle's minimum level (or **trough**). The **recovery** phase follows recession. During a recovery, output increases, unemployment decreases, and pressure on the economy's price level begins to build. In time, recovery evolves into the prosperity phase, where output reaches its maximum level (or **peak**), the labor force is fully employed, and increasing pressure on prices is likely to generate inflation. Unable to sustain prosperity, the economy enters its **downturn** phase. Output falls, unemployment once again reappears, and inflation tends to moderate as the downturn becomes recession. The business cycle has run its course and the cyclical process

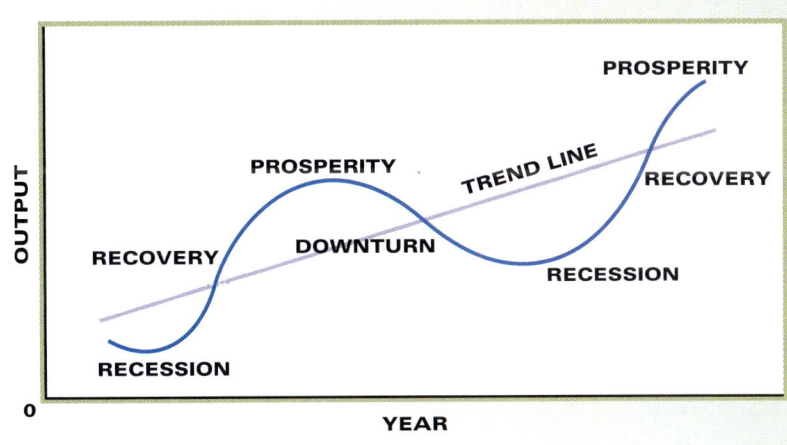

**THE BUSINESS CYCLE**

The national economy moves through four phases of the business cycle: recession, recovery, prosperity, and downturn. The cycles repeat. The trend line depicts long-run economic growth.

repeats, although no two business cycles are identical. The number of months in any given phase of the cycle, as well as the output levels of peaks and troughs, varies from cycle to cycle.

## Economic Growth

Note the upward-sloping trend line cutting through the cycle. It traces the economy's output performance over the course of a business cycle, measured either from recession to recession or from prosperity to prosperity. The upward-sloping character of the trend line signifies economic growth. It shows that the economy's output—production of goods and services—increases, cycle after cycle. The steeper the trend line, the higher the economy's rate of growth. When no growth occurs, the trend line is horizontal.

What causes economic growth? What factors contribute to the increase in the production of goods and services cycle after cycle? Addressing this question (along with questions concerning the economy's cyclical behavior) is what the study of macroeconomics is about.

Understanding why cycles and growth occur is important not just to macroeconomists who study them, but to you and everyone like you who hopes to work for and achieve a growing and reasonable standard of living. Can we harness the disturbing swings in our business cycles? That is to say, can we moderate the inflationary pressures on the economy when it is on the upswing of the business cycle, pressing upon full employment? Can we moderate the inevitable unemployment that occurs when the economy, after reaching its peak, begins its slide into recession? Can we also learn how to engineer an attractive rate of economic growth?

**CHECK YOUR UNDERSTANDING**

What does macroeconomics attempt to explain?

## MEASURING THE NATIONAL ECONOMY

Let's look into these questions. Where do we begin? Perhaps the first thing we ought to do is define precisely what we mean by the economy's output and compare the different ways we go about measuring it.

# INTERDISCIPLINARY PERSPECTIVE

## THE PHENOMENON OF CYCLICAL ACTIVITY

Cyclical activity—the occurrence of recurring events—is an integral part of our world. Things happen, happen again, and happen once again, sometimes with uncanny regularity. At the heart of this cyclical experience are the earth's precise and rhythmic movements. These create our alternating days and nights, our seasons, and the multiplicity of natural occasions, such as ocean tides and spectacular geysers with their mighty rhythmic upheavals—the kind we delight in visiting at our national parks.*

Meteorologists describe the phenomenon of climatic cycles—the skyward rise of earth-warmed air to form rain clouds that subsequently burst upon earth as rain and rise again to re-create the clouds. These climatic cycles nourish and replenish life.

Our biological world is rhythmic and cyclical as well. The seasonal migrations of large animals, birds, and butterflies are never-ending. Observable recurring patterns of activity (and inactivity) are commonplace in the animal kingdom. In winter, bears retreat into a state of hibernation, then reemerge to activity in early spring, year in and year out. Salmon, born in spawning pools, make their way downstream to the ocean where they live their adult life in the open water and return to complete their life cycle in the very pools in which they were spawned. Even human physiology is replete with rhythms and cycles, and psychologists report the cyclical nature of our moods and behavior.

This phenomenon of cyclical activity is found in the world of economics as well. Economists identify four sequential and recurring phases of economic activity: prosperity, downturn, recession, and recovery. These repeating phases describe the business cycle.

AGAIN, AND AGAIN, AND AGAIN, AND . . .

### MORE ON THE NET

Find out more about Yellowstone's many geysers by visiting http://www.geyserstudy.org/geyser_main.htm.

*The water at the geyser Old Faithful in Yellowstone National Park is 350 degrees Fahrenheit and is thrust approximately 60 feet into the air for about three or four minutes. It repeats every 35 to 120 minutes, day and night, year after year. Barometric pressure, the moon, the tides, and the earth's tectonic stresses determine the height of the geyser and the time between eruptions.

---

**Gross domestic product (GDP)**
Total value of all final goods and services, measured in current market prices, produced in the economy during a year.

The definition is simple enough: The economy's output, or **gross domestic product (GDP)**, is the *total value, measured in current market prices, of all final goods and services produced in the economy during a given year.*

Let's analyze this definition phrase by phrase. Consider first "final goods and services." This refers to everything produced—from acorn squash to Ziploc bags—that is not itself used to produce other goods. For example, if we produce and eat an acorn squash, it's a final good and counted in GDP. But if we use the acorn squash to make an acorn squash pie, then it's the pie that's counted in GDP, not the acorn squash. After all, we don't want to count the acorn squash twice! The pie is the *final* good, not the acorn squash.

What about "during a given year"? This phrase refers to a specific calendar year. An acorn squash pie baked on December 31, 2000, is counted as part of 2000 GDP.

An acorn squash pie produced the next day is counted as part of 2001 GDP. If more pies, along with other goods and services, are produced in 2001 than were produced in 2000, the rate of GDP growth in 2001 is greater than zero.

What about "measured in current market prices"? This phrase refers to the pie's price in the year it was made. If your grandmother tells you that when she was a young lass, acorn squash pies sold for $0.25, it doesn't mean that an acorn squash pie baked in 2000 and priced at $7 adds only $0.25 to 2000 GDP! It's the $7—the current market price—that counts.

What about "produced in the economy"? That's the *domestic* part of gross domestic product. It makes no difference who produces the pie—a U.S.-owned company in Philadelphia or a Canadian-owned company in Davenport, Iowa—it's counted as part of the GDP as long as it is produced domestically, that is, in the United States. On the other hand, a pie made by a U.S.-owned company in Halifax, Nova Scotia, is not counted as part of U.S. gross domestic product. It's counted in Canada's gross domestic product.

Suppose the 2000 GDP in the United States adds up to $8 trillion, twice the $4 trillion GDP that was produced in 1990. Does this doubling of GDP over a decade indicate that we really doubled our production of goods and services?

Not necessarily. Over time, prices may have drifted upward. That is, it may have been the *prices* of pies and other goods and services, not necessarily the *number* of pies and other goods and services produced, that have increased. Since GDP for any year measures the value—in *current* market prices—of that year's production of final goods and services, price changes alone might have changed the size of GDP over time.

Consider this simple example. Imagine an economy where the only good produced is corn. If total production in 1990 was 100 bushels, and if the 1990 price of corn was $2 per bushel, then GDP in 1990 would be $200.

Now suppose, for some reason, the price of corn a decade later doubled to $4 per bushel, while production remained at 100 bushels. The 2000 GDP, measuring all final goods and services at 2000 market prices, would increase to $400. Even though *real* production in the economy remained unchanged—100 bushels is still 100 bushels—the economy's GDP doubled. Under these conditions, would it make any sense to describe the 2000 economy as being twice as large as the 1990 economy? Not really. After all, eating $4 corn is no more satisfying than eating $2 corn. And even though a $400 GDP is twice the $200 GDP, people are still eating only 100 bushels of corn.

## Adjusting for Prices

If we want to use GDP as a reliable measure of how well an economy performs—in producing goods and services over time—we must devise some way of eliminating the effect of price changes. To compare GDP in different years, we want to remove the effect of inflation. Economists have created a number of price indexes to do just that. The indexes transform **nominal GDP**—GDP unadjusted for price changes—into **real GDP**—GDP adjusted for price changes. The consumer price index and the GDP deflator are the two indexes most used. How do they work?

**THE CONSUMER PRICE INDEX (CPI)** Let's start with the **consumer price index (CPI)**. Pick a year—any year will do—as a point of reference, or **base year**. Let's pick 1996. Suppose in 1996 we shopped for a basket of goods and services that represented what a typical consumer in an urban household buys. The items we put in the basket probably wouldn't include caviar or yachts but would include

For the latest measure of GDP, visit the Economic Statistics Briefing Room (http://www.whitehouse.gov/fsbr/esbr.html) and the Bureau of Economic Analysis (http://www.bea.doc.gov/).

**CHECK YOUR UNDERSTANDING**

Does a $100 increase in GDP indicate a $100 increase in goods and services?

**Nominal GDP**
GDP measured in terms of current market prices—that is, the price level at the time of measurement. (It is not adjusted for inflation.)

**Real GDP**
GDP adjusted for changes in the price level.

**Consumer price index (CPI)**
A measure comparing the prices of consumer goods and services that a household typically purchases to the prices of those goods and services purchased in a base year.

**Base year**
The reference year with which prices in other years are compared in a price index.

clothing, food, fuel, and a variety of household goods and services, such as kitchen appliances, transportation, and health care. Suppose that when we took that basket to the cash register, it cost $350. Using 1996 as our base year, the $350 converts to a price level index of 100, $P = 100$.

Now suppose in the following year, 1997, we purchase the same basket of consumer items, and their cost again sums to $350. Some prices may have risen, but just enough to offset those that declined. The 1997 consumer price index, then, is $P = 100$.

**Price level**
A measure of prices in one year expressed in relation to prices in a base year.

An unchanging **price level** is a rarity. Let's suppose, instead, that the basket purchased in 1997 adds up to $385. That is, the items in the basket remain unchanged, but the total cost of the items increased by $35. The 1997 CPI, measured against the 1996 base year of 100, is now 110 ($P = \$385/\$350 \times 100$). What does a 1997 $P = 110$ indicate? It shows that from 1996 to 1997, the cost of the goods and services that consumers typically buy increased by 10 percent.

The CPI for any year is constructed by calculating the ratio between the cost of the basket for that year and its cost in the base year. We can shop for the same basket in 2000, calculate its cost, and draw the comparison to the 1996 cost to derive the 2000 CPI. Or we can go back to 1952, calculate the basket's cost in 1952 prices, then compare it to the 1996 cost to derive the 1952 CPI.

The usefulness of such comparisons, however, diminishes the more distant a year is from the base year. Why? First, new goods and services appear on the market every year. Over time, the consumer basket of a base year becomes increasingly less representative of the things consumers buy. For example, if we used a 1952 base year, we could not have included personal computers, CDs, or VCRs, which are typical consumer purchases today. Second, the quality of the items in the basket changes as well. The automobile in a 1952 basket is not the same as the automobile we drive today. Power steering, power brakes, seat belts, radial tires, and air bags make price comparisons between the two less meaningful. Third, the importance of specific items in the basket changes over time. Food purchases may have accounted for 40 percent of the consumer basket in 1952 but only 25 percent in 1996. If food prices increase more rapidly than other prices in 1996 and if we still count their importance at 40 percent of the basket, then the influence of food prices in 1996 is exaggerated.

The Bureau of Labor Statistics publishes the latest consumer price index measurements (http://stats.bls.gov/cpihome.htm). The Federal Reserve Bank of Minneapolis publishes historical CPI measurements, with corresponding inflation rates (http://woodrow.mpls.frb.fed.us/economy/calc/hist1913.html).

That is why the Bureau of Labor Statistics (BLS) of the U.S. Department of Labor, which is charged with the task of composing the CPI, periodically updates the base year. When it does so, it also revises the specific items and their importance in the consumer basket.

**THE GDP DEFLATOR** The CPI measures the prices of consumer items only. There are other price indexes that include different sets of items. For example, price indexes are constructed for farm goods, producer goods, crude materials, services, capital equipment, and export goods.

The most inclusive of all price indexes is the **GDP deflator.** It contains not only the prices of consumer goods and services, but also the prices of producer goods, investment goods, and exports and imports, as well as goods and services purchased by government. It is the price index generally used to differentiate nominal GDP and real GDP.

**GDP deflator**
A measure comparing the prices of all goods and services produced in the economy during a given year to the prices of those goods and services purchased in a base year.

## From Nominal to Real GDP

The GDP deflator converts nominal GDP, measured in current prices for any year, to real GDP, which is adjusted for price changes. Economists sometimes refer to real GDP as GDP expressed in constant dollars.

# APPLIED PERSPECTIVE

## WHAT'S IN THE CPI BASKET?

As you know, the consumer price index (CPI) is a measure of the average change over time in the prices paid by urban consumers for a fixed market basket of consumer goods and services. Sounds simple enough, but how do we know what to put in that basket and what prices to use?

Here's how it's done. The basket is derived from detailed information provided by about 7,000 families who are interviewed quarterly by the BLS (Bureau of Labor Statistics). A second source of information is drawn from another 5,000 families who keep diaries listing everything bought during a two-week period. Altogether, about 36,000 individuals and families contribute information to determine what items are bought and the relative importance of each to the basket.

The result is that the thousands of goods and services purchased are classified into 200 categories and these are put into eight major groups, with percentage weights—derived from the data—attached to each. For example, in 1997 the groups were as follows: (1) housing (such as rent of primary residence, owners' equivalent rent, fuel oil, bedroom furniture), weighted at 39.6 percent of the basket; (2) transportation (such as new vehicles, airline fares, gasoline, motor vehicle insurance), weighted at 17.6 percent; (3) food and beverages (such as breakfast cereal, milk, coffee, chicken, wine, full-service meals, snacks), weighted at 16.3 percent; (4) recreation (such as televisions, cable television, pets and pet products, sports equipment, admissions), weighted at 6.1 percent; (5) medical care (such as prescription drugs and medical supplies, physicians' services, eyeglasses and eye care, hospital services), weighted at 5.6 percent; (6) education and communication (such as college tuition, postage, telephone services, computer software and accessories), weighted at 5.5 percent; (7) apparel (such as men's shirts and sweaters, women's dresses, jewelry), weighted at 4.9 percent; and (8) other goods and services (such as tobacco and smoking products, haircuts and other personal services, funeral expenses), weighted at 4.3 percent.

How do economists determine the "right" price? Each month, BLS data collectors visit or call thousands of retail stores, service establishments, rental units, and doctors' offices to obtain price information on the 80,000 items used to track and measure price changes. If the item is no longer in use—for example, quart-size glass milk bottles—or there's been a quality change in any usable item, adjustment is made to prevent the change from distorting the CPI measure.

IT'S EVERYBODY'S BASKET.

Picking the "right" item is no easy task either. Consider milk. If the BLS selects the specific kind of fresh whole milk that will be priced over time, each kind of whole milk is assigned a probability of selection based on the quantity sold. If vitamin D, homogenized milk in half-gallon containers makes up 70 percent of the sales of whole milk, and the same milk in quart containers accounts for 10 percent of all whole milk sales, then the half-gallon container will be seven times as likely to be chosen as the quart container.

This painstaking way of selection of item and price is absolutely essential if the CPI is to be regarded as a reliable measure. Want a job?

### MORE ON THE NET

To look up details on the most recent Consumer Price Indexes, visit the government's CPI site at http://stats.bls.gov/cpihome.htm.

The conversion formula is

$$\text{real GDP} = \frac{\text{nominal GDP} \times 100}{\text{GDP deflator}}$$

Let's see how it works. Exhibit 2 traces the conversion of nominal GDP into real GDP for the period 1995–2000.

Using 1996 as the base year, 1996 nominal and real GDP are identical. But look at 1997. Nominal GDP increased from $7,813.2 billion in 1996 to $8,318.4 billion in 1997, or by $505.2 billion. Not all of that $505.2 billion represented an increase in real production of goods and services. Part of it simply reflected the higher prices in 1997. But how much of it?

In 1997, the GDP deflator was 101.95. The formula to convert 1997 nominal GDP to real GDP—measuring 1997 GDP in 1996 prices—is

$$\frac{\$8,318.4 \times 100}{101.95} = \$8,159.5$$

We can now calculate how much of that $505.2 billion increase in 1997 GDP represented more real goods and services, and how much really reflected an increase in prices. The increase attributed to prices alone was $8,318.4 − $8,159.2, or $158.9 billion. The remaining $346.3 billion represented more real goods and services.

If you were describing the 1996–97 change in GDP to a friend, which number would you use? Would you say that GDP increased from $7,813.2 billion to $8,318.4 billion, or would you choose to compare the $7,813.2 billion to the $8,159.2 billion? Both are honest-to-goodness changes in GDP. They just represent different evaluations. One set includes changes in both production and prices, the other includes just changes in production. If what you mean to convey to your friend is how much better off people were in 1997 than in 1996, wouldn't changes in real GDP be the appropriate one to use?

Look at Exhibit 2. Again, differences between nominal and real GDP growth rates are rather striking. If we calculate the economy's 1995–2000 performance in nominal GDP, the economy's annual growth rate was 6.2 percent. But if the calculation is made for real GDP, the growth rate was 4.4 percent. Which GDP we choose to express, then, makes a difference.

## EXHIBIT 2

**CONVERTING NOMINAL GDP TO REAL GDP: 1995–2000 ($ BILLIONS, 1996 = 100)**

|      | NOMINAL GDP | GDP DEFLATOR | REAL GDP |
|------|-------------|--------------|----------|
| 1995 | $7,400.5    | 098.10       | $7,543.8 |
| 1996 | 7,813.2     | 100.00       | 7,813.2  |
| 1997 | 8,318.4     | 101.95       | 8,159.5  |
| 1998 | 8,790.2     | 103.22       | 8,515.7  |
| 1999 | 9,299.2     | 104.77       | 8,875.8  |
| 2000 | 10,063.3    | 107.26       | 9,382.2  |

Source: U.S. Department of Commerce, Bureau of Economic Analysis.

## DERIVING EQUILIBRIUM GDP IN THE AGGREGATE DEMAND AND SUPPLY MODEL

Understanding the difference between nominal and real GDP for 1997 still doesn't tell us why 1997 GDP ended up being what it was. Why was 1997 nominal GDP $8,159.5 billion? Why not $10,000 billion or $7,000 billion? What determines its size?

Several competing theories explain how the equilibrium levels of GDP are derived. We will examine some in detail in later chapters. For now, we focus on one—the aggregate demand and aggregate supply model—to explain how GDP is determined.

The aggregate demand and aggregate supply model is a good place to start. It bears some similarity to the demand and supply model we used to explain equilibrium price and quantity of goods and services. In the case of fish, we saw how the downward-sloping demand curve for fish intersected the upward-sloping supply curve of fish to determine its price and quantity. In what appears to be an analogy, the downward-sloping aggregate demand curve intersects the upward-sloping aggregate supply curve to determine the economy's price level and GDP.

But there the similarity ends. The factors that cause the demand curves in both models to slope downward are quite different. The factors explaining why the supply curves in both models are upward-sloping are different as well.

The demand curve for fish slopes downward because a decrease in the price of fish occurs while all other prices remain unchanged. Fish, then, becomes *relatively* cheaper. As a result, people increase the quantity demanded of fish.

This cause-and-effect analysis cannot explain why the aggregate demand curve slopes downward. After all, the price level reflects all prices, so when it falls, *all* prices are assumed to fall. As a result, the relative prices of fish and everything else remain unchanged. If people demand more of everything, it cannot be because everything becomes relatively cheaper.

What are the forces governing the aggregate demand and supply model? **Aggregate supply** is the total supply of goods and services that all firms in the national economy are willing to offer at varying price levels. **Aggregate demand** is the total quantity demanded of these goods and services by households, firms, foreigners, and government at those varying price levels.

Panel *a* in Exhibit 3 shows the relationship between aggregate supply and the price level. Panel *b* in Exhibit 3 shows the relationship between aggregate demand and the price level.

## Explaining Aggregate Supply

Look at the economy's aggregate supply curve in panel *a*. Three distinct segments are apparent. The horizontal segment shows that real GDP can increase up to point *a* without affecting the economy's price level. The upward-sloping segment of the supply curve depicts, from point *a* to point *b*, a positive relationship between real GDP and the price level. The vertical segment marks the full-employment level of real GDP. All resources are fully employed, so that real GDP cannot increase.

**THE HORIZONTAL SEGMENT** Why the horizontal segment? For any level of GDP in this range—that is, far below full employment—there are ready supplies of unused resources. All these idle resources can be put to work before there is any upward pressure on prices. For example, the economy can increase aggregate supply—the production of goods and services—say, from $5 trillion to $6 trillion GDP, without prices going up. Producers can hire more workers without having to raise the wage rate. They can use more capital without having to pay higher interest rates because unused capital in the form of unused plants and machinery is already available. As you see in panel *a*, any increase in real GDP within the range $0 to $8 trillion can occur with the price level remaining unchanged at $P = 100$.

**THE UPWARD-SLOPING SEGMENT** What about aggregate supply beyond $8 trillion? It becomes upward sloping. Increases in output are linked to increases in the price level. Why? Because unused resources become less available at higher levels of real GDP. Faced with the difficulty of finding ready resources,

**Aggregate supply**
The total quantity of goods and services that firms in the economy are willing to supply at varying price levels.

**Aggregate demand**
The total quantity of goods and services demanded by households, firms, foreigners, and government at varying price levels.

**CHECK YOUR UNDERSTANDING**

Why would an increase in real GDP, within some output range, cause the price level to increase?

## EXHIBIT 3

### AGGREGATE SUPPLY AND AGGREGATE DEMAND

The aggregate supply curve in panel *a* shows the aggregate quantity of goods and services that firms are willing to supply at varying price levels. For levels of real GDP within the range $0 to $8 trillion, the price level remains unchanged at 100. Beyond $8 trillion, increases in real GDP are accompanied by rising price levels. At real GDP = $9 trillion, $P = 110$. Full-employment real GDP is $9.5 trillion. The aggregate supply curve becomes vertical at that point. An increase in the price level beyond $P = 115$ is not accompanied by increases in real GDP.

The downward-sloping aggregate demand curve in panel *b* shows the aggregate quantity demanded at varying price levels. For example, an increase in the price level from $P = 100$ to $P = 110$ is accompanied by a decrease in the aggregate quantity demanded, from $10 trillion to $8.5 trillion.

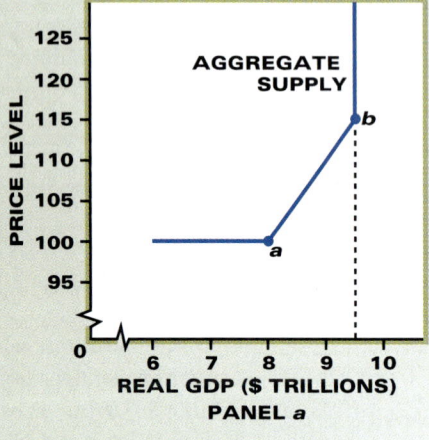
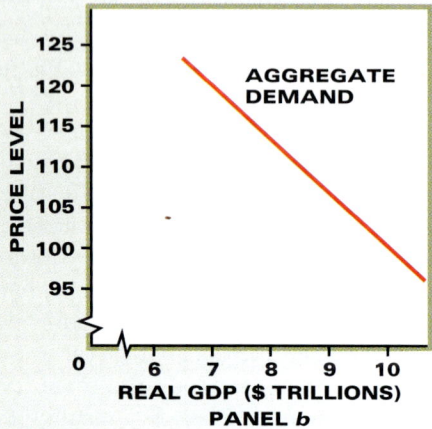

### CHECK YOUR UNDERSTANDING

Why would an increase in the price level, in some instances, lead to an increase in real GDP?

firms resort to offering higher prices for them. For example, to get more labor, firms are willing to pay higher wages. These higher wages increase the cost of production, which in turn raises the prices of goods produced. Beyond $8 trillion GDP, the price level begins to rise above $P = 100$. The higher the level of GDP—say, $8.5 trillion—the greater is the economy's absorption of the dwindling unused resources, and the more intense the upward pressure on the price level. At GDP = $9 trillion, $P = 110$.

The upward-sloping relationship between aggregate supply and the price level can be explained in another way. Instead of dwindling unused resources pushing up prices, increasing prices can pull up resource costs. Suppose the price level increases from $P = 110$ to $P = 115$. As the spread between prices and costs widens, producers earn higher profits. Higher profits attract new firms into production and stimulate existing firms to produce more. The higher production levels tap into unused resource availability, driving resource costs upward.

**THE VERTICAL SEGMENT** When resources are fully employed, aggregate supply reaches an impassable limit. Full employment is shown in panel *a* of Exhibit 3 at $9.5 trillion GDP. At that level of real GDP, producers may try to hire more workers, but how can they? They can bid away *already* employed workers from each other by offering higher wage rates. But what one producer gains in output by hiring a worker away from another, the other loses. In the end, competition among producers for already employed resources can succeed only in raising the economy's price level. Its aggregate supply remains unchanged. In our example, real GDP stays constant at $9.5 trillion.

## Explaining Aggregate Demand

The aggregate demand curve shown in panel *b* is downward sloping. For example, as the price level increases from $P = 100$ to $P = 110$, aggregate demand of households, firms, foreigners, and government falls from $10 trillion to $8.5 trillion. Why? Because increases in the price level affect people's real wealth, their lending and borrowing activity, and the nation's trade with other nations in such a way that the demand for goods and services produced in the economy declines.

For current wealth and income data, visit the Economic Statistic Briefing Room (http://www.whitehouse.gov/fsbr/income.html) and the Bureau of Economic Analysis (http://www.bea.doc.gov/).

**THE REAL WEALTH EFFECT** Consider the effect of a price level increase on the value of people's wealth, and the effect of changes in the value of wealth on aggregate demand. Suppose your own wealth consisted of $100,000 held in the form of cash, bank deposits, and government bonds. You know that, if needed, these holdings can be cashed in, allowing you to buy $100,000 of real goods and services. In fact, that is how you view your wealth: as things it can buy for you.

But suppose while you are holding these financial assets, the economy's price level increases. Videotape recorders that formerly cost $400 now cost $480. Automobiles that formerly cost $16,000 now cost $18,500. With prices rising everywhere, what happens to the real worth of your $100,000? It can no longer buy the same quantity of goods and services, can it?

That is, the *real* value of your $100,000 wealth decreases. You feel yourself becoming less wealthy. And you're not mistaken! To replenish the value of your real wealth, you would save more and consume less. In other words, when the price level increases, the quantity demanded by most people for goods and services in the economy falls.

What happens to the value of your wealth when the price level increases?

**THE INTEREST RATE EFFECT** Consider the effect of a higher interest rate on aggregate demand. Few people buy homes with cash. Typically, high-priced items such as homes and automobiles are purchased with borrowed money.

Suppose mortgage rates increase from 10 percent to 15 percent per year. Monthly payments on a home with a $100,000 mortgage, carrying a 20-year loan at 10 percent, are $965.03. At 15 percent, these monthly payments jump to $1,316.79. Wouldn't that difference cut many prospective home buyers out of the market?

Students, too, feel the pinch of higher interest rates. Wouldn't the number of students attending college be affected by higher interest rates on student loans? Even the quantities demanded of restaurant lunches, concert tickets, and designer jeans are linked to the interest rate. Many pay for these items with Visa, MasterCard, or Discover cards. These plastic cards allow people to build up interest-carrying debt. If interest rates on these cards rise, people tend to cut back on these purchases, depressing the aggregate quantity of goods and services demanded.

The Federal Reserve Board publishes current and historical data on interest rates (http://www.federalreserve.gov/releases/).

Firms' demands for investment goods are sensitive to the interest rate as well. A firm contemplating an investment in new machinery may calculate making 15 percent profit on the investment. If the interest rate is 10 percent, the 5 percent spread between profit and the interest rate may be sufficient inducement to buy the new machinery. If the interest rate rises to 15 percent, the firm's demand for the new machinery disappears along with the spread, contributing to the decrease in quantity demanded.

# GLOBAL PERSPECTIVE

## ECONOMIC SUCCESS? DEPENDS ON WHAT YOU MEASURE

**If you want to make the case that** Mexico's economic performance in the first half of the 1990s was impressive, just point to the graph depicting the 16.2-percent-per-year rate of growth of its nominal GDP. But be careful. Why? Because if it's really economic performance you want to measure, the 16.2 percent rate may be illusory. If you distill out price increases, the rate of Mexico's real GDP growth falls to zero! That's the striking difference between nominal and real GDP.

For the six economies depicted in the accompanying graphs, nominal GDP growth over the period 1991–95 is considerably higher than real GDP growth, indicating—as we always knew—that there's some price bloating embedded in the nominal data. How far nominal GDP diverges from real GDP in each case depends not only on relative price increases, but also on the time lapse between the current and base years. Look, for example, at France. In 1991, nominal GDP was approximately twice the value of real GDP largely because the base year used was 1980. That is to say, there is a decade of price increases separating the two measures of French GDP. Compare Canada's 1991 nominal and real GDP to the Netherlands'. The four years separating their base years—1986 and 1990—create the very visible difference between their nominal and real GDPs.

**MEXICO CITY: SYMBOL OF MEXICO'S BRIGHT FUTURE AND PRODUCT OF DECADES OF PHENOMENAL ECONOMIC GROWTH. BUT THE PAST FEW YEARS HAVE BEEN TROUBLESOME.**

### MORE ON THE NET

Visit the Organisation for Economic Co-operation and Development (OECD) (http://www.oecd.org/std/mei.htm) and the *World Factbook* (http://www.odci.gov/cia/publications/factbook/), which both publish macroeconomic data on nations around the world.

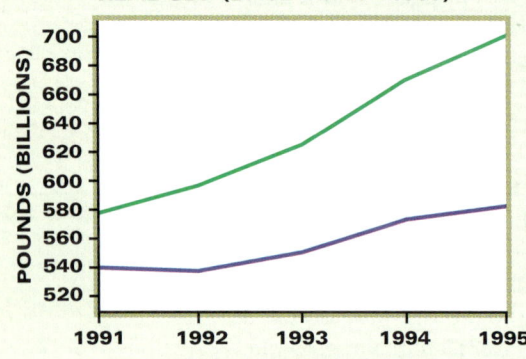

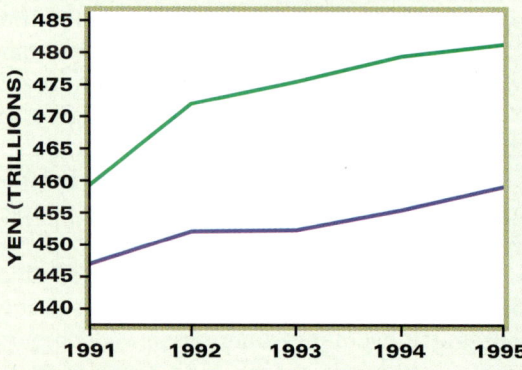

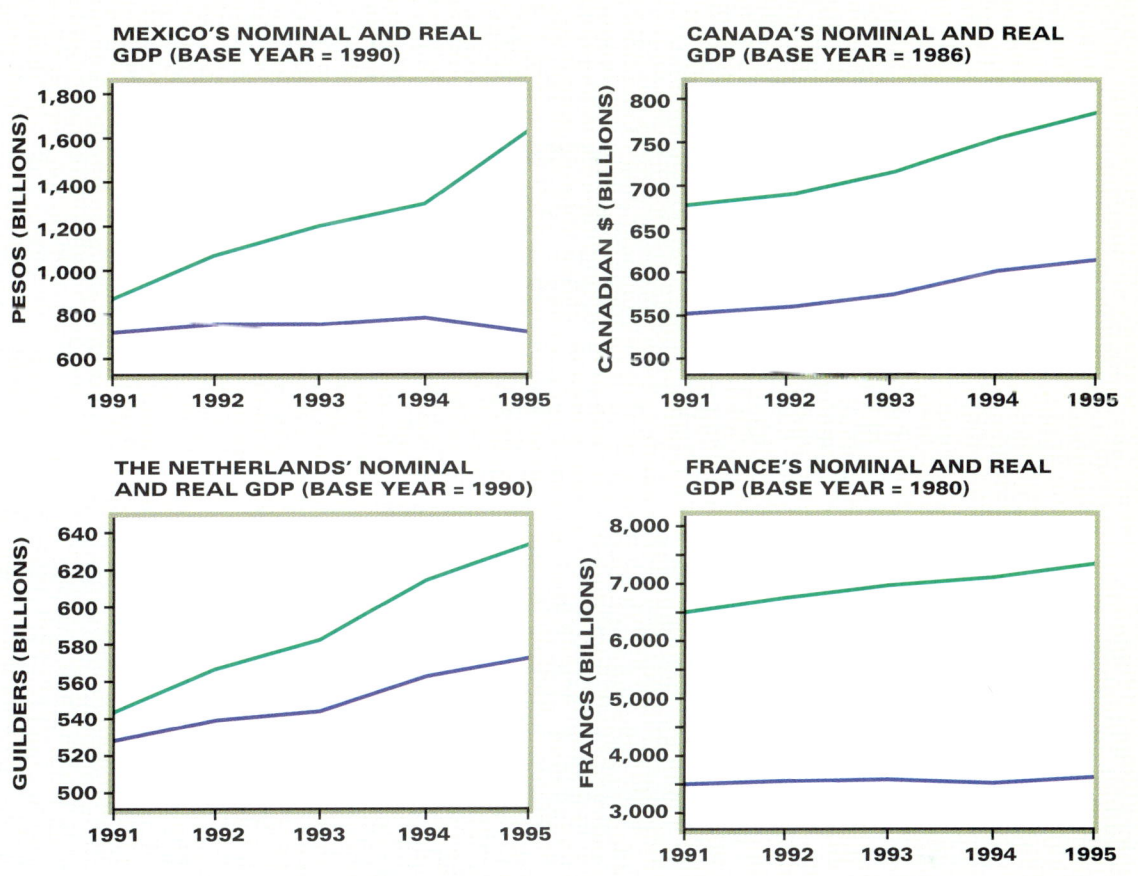

**THE INTERNATIONAL TRADE EFFECT** Suppose the price level in the United States rises while price levels elsewhere in the world remain unchanged. Wouldn't we tend to buy more foreign goods and reduce the demands for our own goods? After all, when prices for domestically produced goods such as wines, lumber, and automobiles increase while other nations' prices remain unchanged, wouldn't French wines, Canadian lumber, and Japanese automobiles become more attractive? Our demand for imports would rise, and our demand for domestic goods would fall.

At the same time, the French, Canadians, and Japanese would find our now higher-priced exports less attractive. Many wouldn't buy them. The quantity demanded of our goods and services, then, would fall.

For current international trade data, visit the Economic Statistics Briefing Room (http://www.whitehouse.gov/fsbr/international.html) and the Census Bureau (http://www.census.gov/ftp/pub/indicator/www/ustrade.html).

## Shifts in the Aggregate Demand and Aggregate Supply Curves

Let's again consider the analogy between the demand and supply model used to explain equilibrium price and quantity of fish that we developed in Chapter 3 and the model of aggregate demand and aggregate supply that we are using to explain equilibrium GDP and price level. In Chapter 3, we distinguished between *changes in quantity demanded* (or *quantity supplied*) of fish—that is, changes along the demand (or supply) curve—and *changes in demand* (or *supply*) of fish—that is, shifts in the demand (or supply) curve.

Let's now draw that same distinction for changes in the aggregate quantity demanded (or supplied) and shifts in the aggregate demand (or aggregate supply) curve.

**SHIFTS IN THE AGGREGATE DEMAND CURVE** The aggregate demand curve relates the quantity of goods and services demanded in the economy to varying price levels. A change in the quantity of goods and services demanded at a particular price level, however, is represented by a shift in the curve itself. Exhibit 4, panel *a*, maps two shifts in aggregate demand. What could cause such shifts to occur?

Suppose the government decides to overhaul our economy's infrastructure. It programs major construction on highways, bridges, railroad lines, airports, research hospitals, public housing, and other facilities that are in the public domain. These programs represent new investment demands that shift the aggregate demand curve to the right, from *AD* to *AD'*.

Or consider what would happen to aggregate demand when incomes abroad increase. Canadians, with higher incomes, buy more U.S. imports, shifting our *AD* curve to the right. If we decide to consume more goods and services ourselves—even when prices remain unchanged—aggregate demand increases.

What would cause a change in our consumption behavior? A tax cut could do it, or perhaps changes in our expectations of future income. After all, if we expect to have more money in the future, we may feel more comfortable about buying more today by borrowing or saving less.

Just reverse the direction of change in these factors, and the aggregate demand curve shifts to the left, from *AD* to *AD"*. For example, a cut in government spending, a decrease in income abroad, an increase in taxes, or an expectation that future income will fall would all tend to lower aggregate quantity demanded at every price level.

## EXHIBIT 4

### SHIFTS IN AGGREGATE DEMAND AND AGGREGATE SUPPLY

The aggregate demand curve in panel *a* shifts with changes in government spending, foreign incomes, and consumer or firms' expectations about the future. The aggregate demand curve increases—shifts to the right—when government spending, incomes, and expectations rise. It decreases—shifts to the left—when they fall.

The aggregate supply curve in panel *b* shifts with changes in the availability of resources. More resources shift the aggregate supply curve to the right.

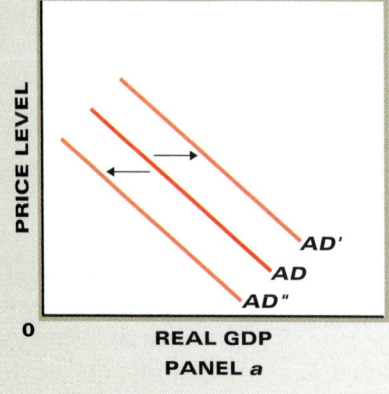

PANEL *a*

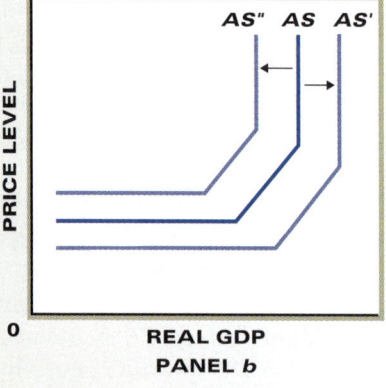

PANEL *b*

**SHIFTS IN THE AGGREGATE SUPPLY CURVE** One of the principal factors accounting for a shift in the aggregate supply curve from AS to AS′ in panel b is an increase in resource availability. Simply put: More workers, more land, more capital, and more entrepreneurial energies—no matter what the price level—result in greater aggregate supply. The prices of these resources affect aggregate supply as well. If wage rates or interest rates or rents decrease while the economy's price level remains unchanged, profit margins will expand, making producers more willing to supply greater quantities of goods and services.

Anything that reduces resource availability or increases the prices of resources would, of course, have the opposite effect; that is, it would shift the aggregate supply curve from AS to AS″.

> **CHECK YOUR UNDERSTANDING**
> What would shift the aggregate supply curve to the right?

## MACROECONOMIC EQUILIBRIUM

Let's bring both aggregate demand and aggregate supply together in a national market for goods and services. This is done in Exhibit 5.

Does it look familiar? As with all markets, Exhibit 5 expresses a relationship between price and quantity. The vertical axis measures the economy's price level. The horizontal axis measures real GDP.

We can now explain—at least according to the aggregate demand and aggregate supply model—why 1997 real GDP was $8,159.5 billion. The quantity of aggregate demand equaled the quantity of aggregate supply at $8,159.5 billion real GDP. The equilibrium price level was $P = 101.95$. This **macroequilibrium** position for 1997 persisted only as long as the aggregate demand and aggregate supply curves remained unchanged.

To illustrate why the economy gravitates toward an equilibrium of $8,159.5 billion real GDP and $P = 101.95$, let's suppose the economy was not in equilibrium. Instead, suppose the price level was $P = 110$. What happens? With that price level, consumers, firms, government, and foreigners demand fewer goods and services. We see in Exhibit 5 that at $P = 110$, the aggregate quantity demanded falls to $5,000 billion.

What about aggregate supply? How would firms react to the higher price level? At $P = 110$, they are willing to produce more GDP. The aggregate quantity of GDP that firms are willing to supply increases to $9,000 billion.

A problem now emerges. At $P = 110$, the aggregate quantity demanded is insufficient to absorb the aggregate quantity supplied, generating an excess aggregate supply of $9,000 − $5,000 = $4,000 billion GDP. Competition among suppliers will force overall prices downward. That is, given the aggregate demand and aggregate supply curves in Exhibit 5, the economy is unable to sustain a price level of 110.

Now suppose the price level is 90. What happens?

**Macroequilibrium**
The level of real GDP and the price level that equate the aggregate quantity demanded and the aggregate quantity supplied.

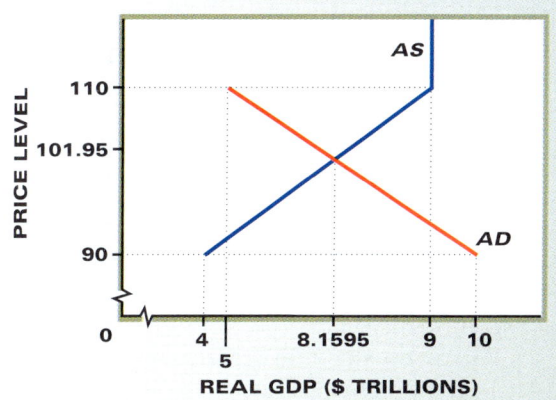

**ACHIEVING MACROECONOMIC EQUILIBRIUM**

Macroequilibrium is achieved when aggregate supply, AS, and aggregate demand AD, intersect at real GDP = $8,159.5 billion and $P =$ 101.95. At higher price levels, such as $P = 110$, excess aggregate quantity supplied would emerge, depressing the price level. At lower price levels, excess aggregate quantity demanded would emerge, forcing the price level to increase.

EXHIBIT 5

# APPLIED PERSPECTIVE

## "IF WINTER COMES, CAN SPRING BE FAR BEHIND?"

The 18th-century English poet Percy Bysshe Shelley, finding beauty in the harsh realities of cold and stormy autumns and winters, ends his poem *Ode to the West Wind* with expectation and perhaps even promise: "Oh wind, if Winter comes, Can Spring be far behind?"

How harsh must our economic autumns and winters be? Do economists find anything beautiful about a harsh economic winter? And how far behind is the promising spring?

Recent swings in the business cycle are shown in the accompanying table. Since the Great Depression of the 1930s, the U.S. economy experienced ten recessions, some steeper than others, but all marked by hard times, with high rates of unemployment and declining real GDP.

Those are a lot of months of hard times. In more than 20 percent of our economic life, we find ourselves struggling through the downturns and recession phases of a business cycle. The brighter side of the picture is that for almost 80 percent of our economic life, we bask in the economic springs and summers of recovery and prosperity. If we can't change the flow of these economic seasons, can we at least change their length? Or perhaps, modify the harshness of economic autumns and winters?

### MORE ON THE NET

The National Bureau of Economic Research (NBER) (http://www.nber.org/) measures U.S. business cycle expansions and contractions (http://www.nber.org/cycles.html). The Bureau of Economic Analysis provides current and historical data for real GDP (http://www.bea.doc.gov/bea/sumnip-d.html), and the Bureau of Labor Statistics provides current and historical unemployment data (http://stats.bls.gov/cpshome.htm).

**Source:** NBER and the Federal Reserve Bank of Boston.

**RECESSIONS SINCE 1945**

| RECESSION OF | DURATION (MONTHS) | DEPTH DECLINE IN REAL GDP (PERCENTAGE) | PEAK RATE OF UNEMPLOYMENT |
|---|---|---|---|
| 1945 | 8 | | 4.3 |
| 1948–49 | 11 | | 7.9 |
| 1953–54 | 10 | –3.0 | 6.1 |
| 1957–58 | 8 | –3.5 | 7.5 |
| 1960–61 | 10 | –1.0 | 7.1 |
| 1969–70 | 11 | –1.1 | 6.1 |
| 1973–75 | 16 | –4.3 | 9.0 |
| 1980 | 6 | –3.4 | 7.6 |
| 1981–82 | 16 | –2.6 | 10.8 |
| 1990–92 | 30 | | 7.3 |

The aggregate quantity demanded is $9,000 billion and the aggregate quantity of GDP that firms are willing to supply is $4,000 billion. Competition among the demanders—consumers, firms, government, and foreigners—now forces the price level upward.

Where do the price level and GDP come to rest? The aggregate quantity demanded and aggregate quantity supplied equate at $8,159.5 billion GDP and $P = 101.95$. Macroequilibrium is achieved.

# EQUILIBRIUM, INFLATION, AND UNEMPLOYMENT

Macroeconomists use this simple aggregate demand and supply model of GDP and price level to show how an economy can move from stable to rising price levels, and from unemployment to full employment. For example, it gives us some understanding of the economic forces that were at work during the depression of the 1930s, during the war-related recovery of the 1940s, during the Vietnam-induced inflation of the 1960s, during the OPEC-induced inflation of the 1970s and early 1980s, and during the recession and economic stagnation of the early 1990s.

## The Depression of the 1930s

The 1930s produced one of the poorest GDP performance records in our economic history. For most of the decade, real GDP was either falling or recovering slightly, only to fall once again. It fell by 30 percent in the first four years of the decade, recovered to its 1929 level by 1937, but fell again in 1939. Nobody had any reason to feel optimistic about the future. Unemployment was massive. It rose from 3.2 percent in 1929 to a peak of 25.2 percent in 1933. It fell to 14.3 percent by 1937, only to climb back to 19.1 percent in 1938. How would you have felt about our economic future on New Year's Day 1939?

By December 1939, however, the fate of the world had changed. Germany invaded Poland in September, bringing Europe to war. Moving swiftly westward, German forces took Holland and Belgium, then overtook an ill-prepared France. Paris fell without a single shot fired.

The German war against England, however, was another matter. German warplanes, in unending waves, crossed the English channel during the cold winter of 1940 to strike at England's aircraft factories on its eastern coast. English cities, including London, absorbed almost daily bombings. England's prime minister, Winston Churchill, appealed to the United States for material support. We obliged with what he was later to describe as the most generous response any nation afforded another in recorded history. These events of 1939 and 1940 changed the pace and direction of our national economy significantly.

Exhibit 6, panel *a*, illustrates the impact on GDP of the 1930s depression and of our later wartime commitment.

Consider, first, the effects of a shift in aggregate demand on the economy's prewar position. The prewar depression GDP equilibrium is shown where the aggregate demand curve, *AD*, cuts the aggregate supply curve, *AS*, at point *a* along its horizontal range. With double-digit unemployment and substantial plant capacity remaining idle, real GDP could increase considerably without putting any pressure on the price level.

But the war in Europe changed all that. Our idle factories were put to work producing tanks, fighter planes, cannons, armored cars, aircraft carriers, battleships, munitions, and millions of uniforms. Army bases were built overnight, and entirely new military-related factories mushroomed to meet the demands of war. Government's war-related spending shifted the aggregate demand curve outward to the right, to *AD'*, creating a new GDP equilibrium at point *b* and a higher price level.

The Japanese attack on Pearl Harbor in December 1941 and the subsequent war in the Pacific added even more to the demand for war materials, shifting the aggregate demand curve once again. With the aggregate demand curve at *AD"*, the economy moved to full-employment GDP and exerted substantial upward pressure on the price level (point *c*).

**CHECK YOUR UNDERSTANDING**

How does a war affect aggregate demand?

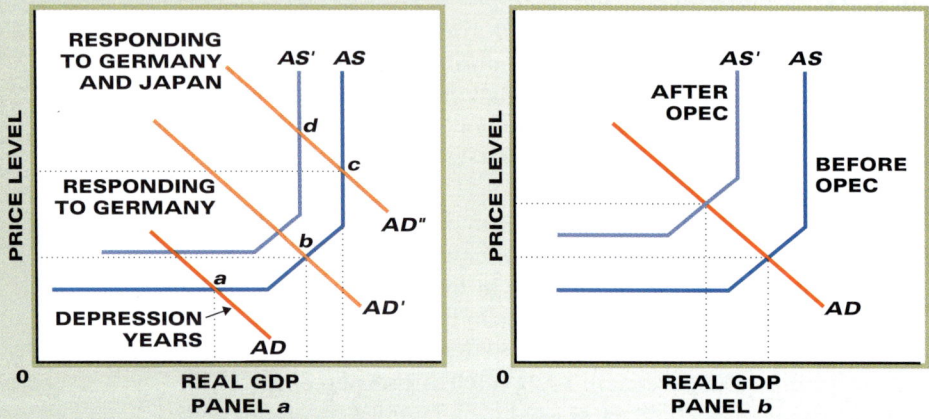

**AGGREGATE DEMAND AND AGGREGATE SUPPLY DURING THE DEPRESSION AND WAR PERIOD AND THE OIL PRICE INCREASES**

The 1930s depression GDP equilibrium occurred at the intersection of the aggregate demand curve, AD, and the aggregate supply curve, AS, in panel a. The demand created by the war in Europe shifted the aggregate demand curve from AD to AD', creating a new macroequilibrium at a higher level of GDP. The extension of the war to the Pacific shifted the aggregate demand curve even further to the right, to AD", creating a new macroequilibrium at a much higher price level.

The transfer of men and women out of civilian employment into the armed forces shifted the aggregate supply curve to the left, from AS to AS', increasing further the pressure on the price level.

The dramatic increase in the price of crude oil during the 1970s and early 1980s pushed overall costs of production upward, which shifted the aggregate supply curve of panel b to the left. A new equilibrium was obtained at a lower level of real GDP and at a higher price level.

What about aggregate supply? Millions of men and women volunteered or were drafted into the armed forces, reducing the size of the civilian labor force. With fewer resources available, the aggregate supply curve shifted from AS to AS', increasing further the upward pressure on the price level (point d).

## Demand-Pull Inflation: The Vietnam War

That same simple model can be used to describe the effect of the Vietnam war on GDP from 1964 to 1975. Before the war, the economy was relatively vigorous. Aggregate demand intersected aggregate supply on the upward-sloping segment of the aggregate supply curve. In fact, GDP was approaching the impassable limits imposed by full employment, but only moderate pressure was being exerted on the price level.

But in just three years, 1965 to 1968, government spending on defense increased more than 40 percent. The aggregate demand curve shifted to the right, pressing GDP to its limit and forcing the price level upward. In fact, the price level during the 1965–75 decade rose from 72.8 to 125.8 (1972 = 100). Economists refer to such price inflation as **demand-pull inflation** because the factor contributing most to the rising price level was the increased demand for military goods and the subsequent rightward shift of the aggregate demand curve. This shift *pulled*

**Demand-pull inflation**
Inflation caused primarily by an increase in aggregate demand.

GDP to full employment and *pulled* the price level up along the vertical segment of the aggregate supply curve.

## Cost-Push Inflation: The OPEC Legacy

The aggregate demand and aggregate supply model of Exhibit 6, panel *b*, may help explain the puzzling phenomenon of concurrent inflation and unemployment—economists call it **stagflation**—during the 1970s and 1980s. The model illustrates the inflation and unemployment effects generated by the oil-producing countries, particularly those associated with the Organization of Petroleum Exporting Countries (OPEC).

In October 1973, the price of Arabian light crude oil was $2.10 per barrel. By November 1974, OPEC had cut oil production substantially and raised the price to $10.46. By January 1979, the price had drifted upward to $13.34. While our economy was still trying to adjust to this greater-than-fivefold price increase, a second major oil price shock hit us broadside. By April 1980, OPEC had raised the price to $28, and by January 1982 to $34.

The impact of these OPEC-designed oil price increases on the costs of producing almost everything in our economy—and in the rest of the world—shifted the aggregate supply curve from *AS* to *AS'*. As the model illustrates, GDP declined while the price level increased. The OPEC-induced inflation is described as **cost-push inflation** because the factor contributing most to the rising price level was the increase in cost of a basic good and the subsequent shift to the left of the aggregate supply curve.

**Stagflation**
A period of stagnating real GDP, inflation, and relatively high levels of unemployment.

**Cost-push inflation**
Inflation caused primarily by a decrease in aggregate supply.

## The Recession and Economic Stagnation of the Early 1990s

For the half-decade preceding the 1990–91 recession, the economy was performing about as well as it ever had in the past quarter century. A number of factors contributed to the relatively high rates of economic growth and low rates of inflation and unemployment. First, the 1986 tax reform fueled consumers' demands for goods and services. In addition, banks and other financial institutions accommodated consumers' tastes for more goods and services by providing ready credit. The financial system also provided the credit for large **leveraged buyouts** and extensive office building. The commercial real estate boom created many construction jobs. Expectations that the good times would continue added even more strength to an already strong aggregate demand.

**Leveraged buyout**
A primarily debt-financed purchase of all the stock or assets of a company.

But the economic storm clouds were gathering. After all, the tax reform that created tax breaks for many also created the largest government deficits in history. By the end of the 1980s, these deficits became a primary political issue. The government simply couldn't continue with business as usual. In an attempt to harness the deficits, the federal government reduced its revenue sharing with state and local governments, who in turn were unwilling or unable to raise their own taxes to compensate for the lost revenues. Instead, they downsized their budgets by cutting their demands for goods and services. The end of the Soviet Union and the cold war triggered a cut in our demands for military goods and services. Many defense workers became unemployed in the early 1990s.

Consumers, too, felt the pressures to curb spending. The easy credit that banks made available to them led to exceptionally high levels of consumer debt, so that by the end of the 1980s these consumers had little choice but to change their consumption behavior. And just as expectations can reinforce the good times when times are good, so they can reinforce caution when the economy appears less buoyant.

But consumers weren't the only ones assuming debt in the 1980s. Many firms went into considerable debt by buying new assets and acquiring others through leveraged buyouts. If the economic growth of the 1980s had continued into the 1990s, the revenues these firms needed to service their debts would have been available. But the recession of 1990–91 and the economic sluggishness that followed cut sharply into their revenue flows, making it difficult—and in some cases impossible—for them to pay their debts. Many responded by trimming their workforce.

How do these events play out in the aggregate demand and aggregate supply model of Exhibit 6? The recession and economic stagnation of the early 1990s can be explained by focusing on aggregate demand. Assuming a given aggregate supply curve, the recession could be viewed as the consequence of an inward shift of aggregate demand—that is, from a period of full employment with moderate inflation to one with lower levels of real GDP, higher levels of unemployment, and even more moderate inflation.

## CAN WE AVOID UNEMPLOYMENT AND INFLATION?

If government had a wish list, it would certainly include an economy in equilibrium at full employment with no inflation. In fact, that GDP condition would appear on almost everyone's wish list, wouldn't it? But how realistic are wish lists? Is there anything government can do to make wishes come true? Look at Exhibit 7.

The aggregate supply curve, AS, creates three different GDP levels of equilibrium with the three different aggregate demand curves, AD, AD', and AD".

If aggregate demand in the economy was described by AD, then real GDP would come to rest at $10 trillion, $5 trillion below the economy's full-employment real GDP. The price level would be 100. If, on the other hand, aggregate demand was AD', the level of equilibrium GDP would be at full employment at $15 trillion. The price level would be 103. If aggregate demand was AD", the level of equilibrium GDP, already at full employment, would stay at $15 trillion, but the price level would rise to 115.

EXHIBIT 7

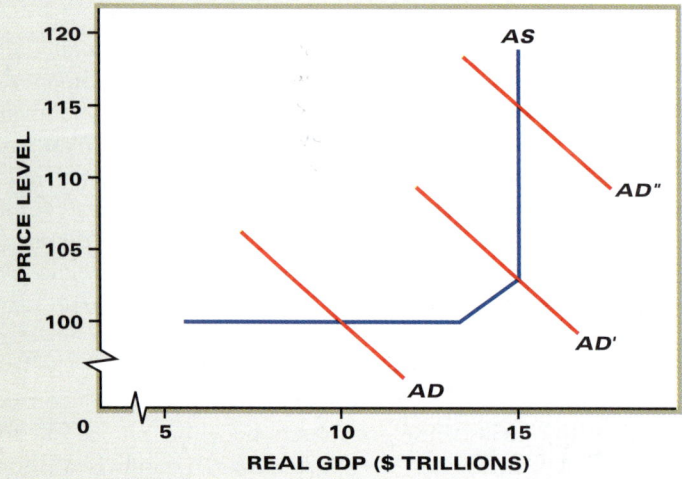

**OBTAINING FULL-EMPLOYMENT GDP WITHOUT INFLATION**

There is no reason to suppose that the aggregate demand curve will necessarily intersect the aggregate supply curve at a level of real GDP consistent with full employment and no inflation. If the aggregate demand curve is AD, unemployment results. On the other hand, if the aggregate demand curve is AD", inflation results. The government can intervene—adding to or cutting its spending and taxes—to shift the aggregate demand to AD', where full employment occurs with moderate inflation—that is, at P = 103.

Now if government had a choice in the matter, it would no doubt wish for the aggregate demand curve AD'. But wishing, as you know, doesn't always make a wish come true! Why suppose that because the *desired* aggregate demand curve is AD', the independently derived demands for goods and services by households, firms, foreigners, and government will actually generate an aggregate demand of AD'? The unsettling fact is that there is no more reason to expect aggregate demand to be AD' than AD, AD'', or any other aggregate demand curve that can be mapped in Exhibit 7.

Suppose, for example, that aggregate demand is AD. Must the economy, saddled with that level of aggregate demand, accept the consequences? Is there any way to move aggregate demand to AD'? That's where some economists believe the government should come into the picture. One way the government can shift aggregate demand to AD' is by increasing its own spending. And it isn't necessary to start a war to do this! *Any* increase in government spending will do the job. How about increased spending on the economy's infrastructure? Or on health care? Or on education? You can surely think of a few other ways, too. The options are almost unlimited.

What kinds of spending would you introduce to raise aggregate demand from AD to AD'? Go to the Interactive Study Center at http://gottheil.swcollege.com and click on the "Your Turn" button to submit your example. Student submissions will be posted to the Web site, and perhaps we will use some in future editions of the book!

Other government policies can influence aggregate demand as well. Reducing income taxes, for example, puts more money in the hands of people who will then spend part of it on more goods and services. That spending shifts the aggregate demand curve to the right. If government cuts the corporate income tax, it leaves corporations with higher after-tax income, which may increase demands for investment goods. That, too, shifts the aggregate demand curve.

Can there be *too much* aggregate demand in the economy? If the aggregate demand curve generated by households, firms, foreigners, and government was AD'' instead of AD', it would push real GDP to full employment at $15 trillion, but not without pushing the price level up to $P = 115$. In other words, the aggregate demand curve AD'' creates inflation.

What could the government do under these conditions? The appropriate policy would be to reverse gears—to reduce government spending and increase taxes. Either strategy could shift the aggregate demand curve to the left, from AD'' to AD'.

To many, these government actions seem very simple, almost mechanical. Add spending or reduce taxes to increase aggregate demand. Reduce government spending or increase taxes to cut aggregate demand. But the truth is that our real economy isn't nearly as manageable as the aggregate demand and aggregate supply model suggests. Exhibit 7 is about as simple an abstraction of the world we live in as economists can design. In the real world it is difficult enough just to identify full-employment real GDP, let alone create a government policy that puts aggregate demand right on the mark.

Why then bother with the model? Because it is still a useful first approximation of the world we live in. Understanding aggregate demand and aggregate supply gives us a useful handle in understanding the basic movements of the primary factors in our national economy. It allows us to see how problems of unemployment and inflation can emerge, and how the government might intervene to orchestrate change. At least it's a start!

# CHAPTER REVIEW

1. The business cycle consists of GDP roller-coasting from periods of prosperity, marked by inflation, to periods of recessions, marked by relatively high rates of unemployment. Two intermediate periods, downturn and recovery, describe the cycle's transition from prosperity to recession and from recession to prosperity.
2. Macroeconomics focuses on how the national economy works.
3. The CPI and GDP deflator are the most commonly used indices for converting nominal GDP, measured in current prices, to real GDP, measured in prices associated with a base year.
4. The aggregate demand and aggregate supply model is used to explain how an economy arrives at an equilibrium level of real GDP.
5. The aggregate supply curve—relating the price level to real GDP—has three distinguishing segments. The horizontal segment reflects the availability of unused resources. The upward-sloping segment reflects increasing pressure on the price level as firms bid for resources. The vertical segment reflects the full employment of all resources.
6. The aggregate demand curve relates the price level to aggregate quantity demanded. Its downward-sloping character reflects three principal influences: People's desire to maintain real wealth holdings, the interest rate, and international trade. For example, an increase in the price level decreases people's real wealth. To restore real wealth levels, people increase savings and reduce consumption.
7. Macroeconomic equilibrium occurs at the level of real GDP and at the level of price where aggregate demand intersects aggregate supply. That equilibrium may be associated with either inflation or unemployment and, on occasion, with both simultaneously.
8. Demand-pull inflation occurs when the aggregate demand curve shifts to the right, intersecting the aggregate supply curve on its upward-sloping or vertical segment.
9. Cost-push inflation occurs when the aggregate supply curve shifts to the left while the aggregate demand curve remains unchanged.
10. By manipulating aggregate demand, the government can reduce unemployment and/or inflation.

# KEY TERMS

- Recession
- Depression
- Prosperity
- Inflation
- Business cycle
- Trough
- Recovery
- Peak
- Downturn
- Gross domestic product (GDP)
- Nominal GDP
- Real GDP
- Consumer price index (CPI)
- Base year
- Price level
- GDP deflator
- Aggregate supply
- Aggregate demand
- Macroequilibrium
- Demand-pull inflation
- Stagflation
- Cost-push inflation
- Leveraged buyout

# QUESTIONS

1. What is macroeconomics?
2. Describe the phases of the business cycle. In what ways is the business cycle illustrated in Exhibit 1 like a roller-coaster ride? In what ways is it different? (*Hint:* What does the trend line look like on a roller-coaster ride?)
3. How do economists measure an economy's performance?
4. What is the difference between nominal and real GDP?

**AGGREGATE DEMAND AND AGGREGATE SUPPLY**

5. What is a consumer price index? How is it constructed? Why does the index become increasingly unreliable over time?
6. What is the difference between a consumer price index and a GDP deflator?
7. Which price index is generally used to transform nominal GDP into real GDP? Write the conversion formula.
8. What is aggregate demand? Draw an aggregate demand curve and explain its shape. What factors influence aggregate demand?
9. What is aggregate supply? Draw an aggregate supply curve and explain its shape. What factors influence aggregate supply?
10. What does *macroequilibrium* mean?
11. Draw a diagram illustrating macroequilibrium at less than full employment.
12. What is demand-pull inflation? Draw a diagram illustrating such an inflation. Give an example.
13. What is cost-push inflation? What might cause it?
14. What can the government do to change macroeconomic equilibrium?
15. If you were teaching economics, how would you explain the Great Depression? Assume your students know the *AD/AS* model.
16. Graph the economy's macroequilibrium position, using the following data.

| PRICE LEVEL | AGGREGATE DEMAND | AGGREGATE SUPPLY |
|---|---|---|
| 160 | $1,000 | $7,000 |
| 150 | 2,000 | 7,000 |
| 140 | 3,000 | 7,000 |
| 130 | 4,000 | 6,000 |
| 120 | 5,000 | 5,000 |
| 110 | 6,000 | 4,000 |
| 100 | 7,000 | 3,000 |

17. Suppose aggregate supply shifts to the left by $2,000 at each price level. What happens to the economy's macroequilibrium position?
18. Suppose aggregate demand shifts to the right by $4,000 at each price level. What happens to the economy's macroequilibrium position?

# PRACTICE PROBLEMS

1. Calculate the GDP deflator for the following years for the U.S. economy, using 1982 as the base year.

| | NOMINAL GDP ($ BILLIONS) | REAL GDP ($ BILLIONS) | GDP DEFLATOR |
|---|---|---|---|
| 1981 | $3,052.6 | $3,248.8 | |
| 1982 | 3,166.0 | 3,166.0 | |
| 1983 | 3,405.7 | 3,279.1 | |
| 1984 | 3,772.2 | 3,501.4 | |

2. Calculate the real GDP for the following years for the U.S. economy, given data for nominal GDP and the GDP deflator (1987 is the base year).

| | NOMINAL GDP ($ BILLIONS) | REAL GDP ($ BILLIONS) | GDP DEFLATOR |
|---|---|---|---|
| 1986 | $4,268.6 | 4405.2 | 96.9 |
| 1987 | 4,539.9 | | 100.0 |
| 1988 | 4,900.4 | | 103.9 |
| 1989 | 5,250.8 | 4839.4 | 108.5 |

3. Compute the percentage change in nominal GDP shown in practice problem 2 over the period 1986–89, and compare that figure to the percentage change in real GDP over the same period.

# WHAT'S WRONG WITH THIS GRAPH?

**AGGREGATE SUPPLY AND AGGREGATE DEMAND MODEL**

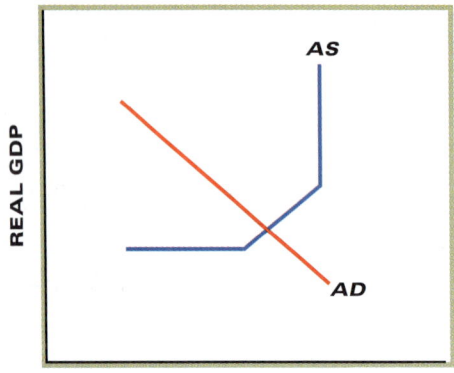

# ECONOMIC CONSULTANTS

**ECONOMIC RESEARCH AND ANALYSIS BY STUDENTS FOR PROFESSIONALS**

Charles Edwards, a young businessman in Minneapolis, Minnesota, is considering whether to run against the incumbent U.S. senator in his district, who is up for reelection in the next year. Charles hasn't had formal training in economics, but, based on his observations, he thinks that incumbents fare better when the economy is strong and worse when the economy is weak.

Charles wants to know if this is an accurate assessment. He also wants to know how to track the state of Minnesota's economy. For help with these questions, Charles has hired Economic Consultants. Prepare a report for Charles that addresses the following issues:

**1.** Review real GDP, unemployment, inflation, and business cycle data. Using presidential elections as a point of comparison, have incumbent presidents tended to win reelection if the economy is strong and lose if the economy is weak?

**2.** What conclusions, if any, can you draw from this analysis? What assumptions are being made in this analysis?

**3.** What is the current state of the economy in Minnesota? What resources are available for tracking the Minnesota economy?

You may find the following resources helpful as you prepare this report for Charles:

- **Bureau of Economic Analysis (BEA)** (http://www.bea.doc.gov/)—The BEA publishes data on the GDP.
- **Bureau of Labor Statistics (BLS)** (http://stats.bls.gov/)—The BLS publishes data on consumer prices and unemployment.
- **The National Bureau of Economic Research (NBER)** (http://www.nber.org/)— The NBER measures U.S. business cycle expansions and contractions.
- **MultiEducator History of Presidential Elections Site** (http://www.multied.com/elections/)—The MultiEducator History of Presidential Elections Site provides presidential election statistics.
- **Federal Reserve Bank of Minneapolis** (http://woodrow.mpls.frb.fed.us/)—The Federal Reserve Bank of Minneapolis publishes regional economic data (http://woodrow.mpls.frb.fed.us/economy/9index.html) and forecasts (http://woodrow.mpls.frb.fed.us/economy/analysis.html).

# PRACTICE TEST

1. A recession can be defined as a period in which
   a. there is an increase in the price level.
   b. the business cycle is at its peak.
   c. inflation and unemployment occur simultaneously.
   d. there is high unemployment.
   e. the business cycle is at its trend line.

2. The phases of the business cycle include all of the following except one. Which one?
   a. Peak
   b. Equilibrium
   c. Recovery
   d. Prosperity
   e. Trough

3. Which of the following would not be counted as part of the gross domestic product for the United States?
   a. The value of Japanese automobiles sold in the United States and produced in Akron, Ohio
   b. The value of Ford automobiles sold in the United States and produced in Detroit, Michigan
   c. The value of Japanese automobiles sold in foreign markets and produced in Akron, Ohio
   d. The value of Ford automobiles sold in foreign markets and produced in Detroit, Michigan
   e. The value of Ford automobiles sold in the United States and produced in Canada

4. If real GDP in the economy is $8 billion in the current year and nominal GDP is $6 billion in the same year, then
   a. the GDP deflator equals 0.75.
   b. the GDP deflator equals 1.33.
   c. the current year is the base year.
   d. the price level is higher in the current year than in the base year.
   e. the price level in the economy is rising at an increasing rate.

5. One similarity between the aggregate supply and aggregate demand curves is that they both
   a. have positive slopes.
   b. have negative slopes.
   c. shift to the right when prices rise.
   d. are assumed to be linear (straight lines).
   e. relate the price level to real GDP.

6. The price level does not rise along the horizontal section of the aggregate supply curve because
   a. firms do not have to increase wages to hire more workers.
   b. real GDP rises as the aggregate demand curve shifts to the right.
   c. higher wages will not entice any additional individuals to enter the labor force.
   d. the economy is already at full employment along this segment of the aggregate supply curve.
   e. wages and the price level move in opposite directions.

7. Suppose that the economy is producing output at a point along the horizontal segment of its aggregate supply curve. Which of the following strategies would be effective in increasing real GDP?
   a. Decreasing wages paid to workers in the economy
   b. Reducing income taxes
   c. Decreasing government spending
   d. Reducing incomes for foreigners
   e. Increasing the price level in the economy

8. If the aggregate demand and aggregate supply curves intersect at a point along the vertical portion of the aggregate supply curve, then spending increases in the economy will
   a. lead to increases in real GDP.
   b. lead to decreases in real GDP.
   c. shift the aggregate supply curve to the right.
   d. lead to no change in real GDP.
   e. lead to higher levels of employment.

9. If the economy is in macroequilibrium at a point along the positively sloped section of the aggregate supply curve, then an increase in the quantity of resources in the economy will lead to
   a. higher prices and higher real GDP.
   b. lower prices and higher real GDP.
   c. lower prices and lower real GDP.
   d. no change in prices and higher real GDP.
   e. no change in output and lower prices.

10. Inflation created by rightward shifts in the aggregate demand curve is referred to as
    a. cost-push inflation.
    b. hyperinflation.
    c. demand-push inflation.
    d. demand-pull inflation.
    e. cost-pull inflation.

# CHAPTER 5

# GROSS DOMESTIC PRODUCT ACCOUNTING

Imagine yourself in Vegas, playing the 25-cent slot machines. Suppose that every time you put in a quarter and pull down on the lever, you win a quarter. After a while, it may get to be monotonous and perhaps no fun at all, but the quarter-in-quarter-out machine, if nothing else, exemplifies a perfect circular flow of money. The quarter flows from you, through the machine, back to you, time and again.

Economists see money, resources, goods, and services moving through the national economy in much the same way. Substitute households and firms for the slot machine. Resources (in the form of land, labor, capital, and entrepreneurship) flow into firms, which crank out goods and services. (See Exhibit 1.) And just as the slot machine took in quarters only to spit out quarters, the value of the resources flowing into the firms is precisely the value of the goods and services flowing out of the firms.

But here the analogy ends. The **circular flow of goods, services, and resources** through the national economy is not a game of chance. Households don't bet their resources in the hope of winning goods and services. They supply the flow of resources to firms because firms pay for them. Firms pay wages, interest, and rent, and they give profit. These payments make up household incomes. Exhibit 2 shows these payments as part of the **circular flow of money.**

What's the other part? The money firms pay out to households comes right back to them. How? Households use the money they receive from the firms to buy the goods and services that the firms produce. After all, firms don't give those goods and services away. They sell them. So the money ends up, once again, in their hands. Money makes a circuit, from firms to households and back to firms again. It's a money merry-go-round.

**THIS CHAPTER INTRODUCES YOU TO THE ECONOMIC PRINCIPLES ASSOCIATED WITH:**

- THE CIRCULAR FLOW OF RESOURCES, GOODS, AND SERVICES
- THE CIRCULAR FLOW OF MONEY
- THE EXPENDITURE APPROACH TO MEASURING GDP
- THE INCOME APPROACH TO MEASURING GDP
- THE RELATIONSHIP BETWEEN GDP, NDP, AND NATIONAL INCOME
- THE LIMITATIONS OF GDP AS A MEASURE OF ECONOMIC WELL-BEING

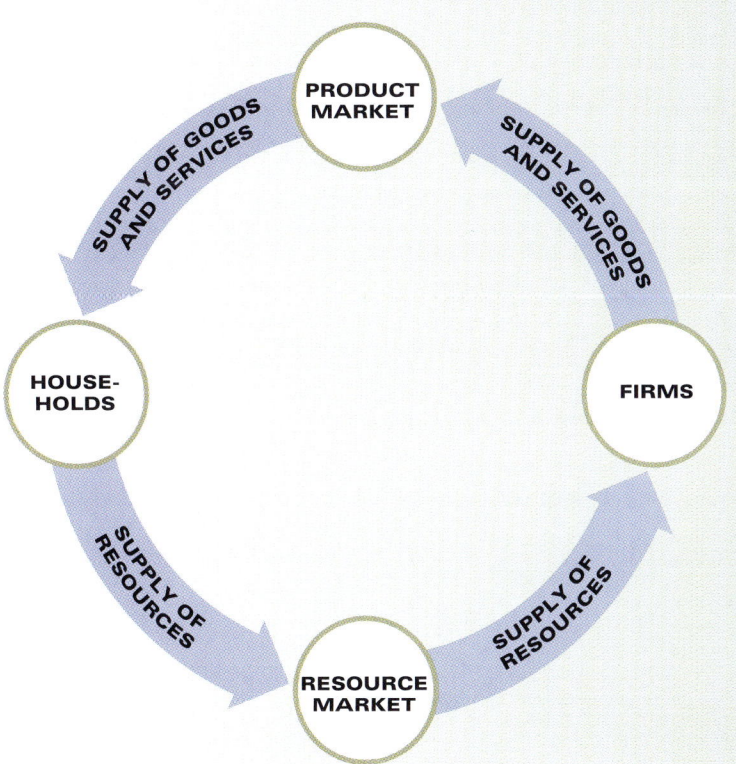

**THE CIRCULAR FLOW OF GOODS, SERVICES, AND RESOURCES**

The circular flow of goods, services, and resources shows the interdependence of households and firms. Households supply their resources—labor, capital, land, entrepreneurship—to the firms in the resource market and, in turn, demand in the product market the goods and services produced by the firms. The firms go to the resource market to demand resources that households supply and, in turn, provide households with the goods and services produced for the product market.

## TWO APPROACHES TO CALCULATING GDP

As you already know, gross domestic product (GDP) is a measure of the total value of all final goods and services produced in the economy in a given year. One way of calculating GDP for, say, 2000 is to add up the market value of all final goods and services produced in 2000. Another way is to add up the total value of the resources used in producing the 2000 final goods and services. The values should be equivalent. After all, goods and services reflect the value of the resources used to make them.

Economists calculate GDP both ways. They add up the total value of all final goods and services produced in the economy in a given year and add up the total value of the resources used in making these goods and services. The former calculation is called the *expenditure approach* to GDP; the latter is called the *income approach* to GDP.

## THE EXPENDITURE APPROACH

### Counting Final Goods and Services

Let's start with the **expenditure approach.** One of the first concerns you have when adding up the market prices of all final goods and services is to make certain the

**Circular flow of goods, services, and resources**
The movement of goods and services from firms to households, and of resources from households to firms.

**Circular flow of money**
The movement of income in the form of resource payments from firms to households, and of income in the form of revenue from households to firms.

**Expenditure approach**
A method of calculating GDP that adds all expenditures made for final goods and services by households, firms, and government.

## EXHIBIT 2

### THE CIRCULAR FLOW OF MONEY

Start with the flow of money—in the form of wages, interest, rent, and profit—that firms in the resource market pay to households for resources supplied. These resource payments are the incomes that enable households to purchase goods and services from firms. The money circuit is completed when the payments flow from households, through the product market, to the firms for the goods and services they supply.

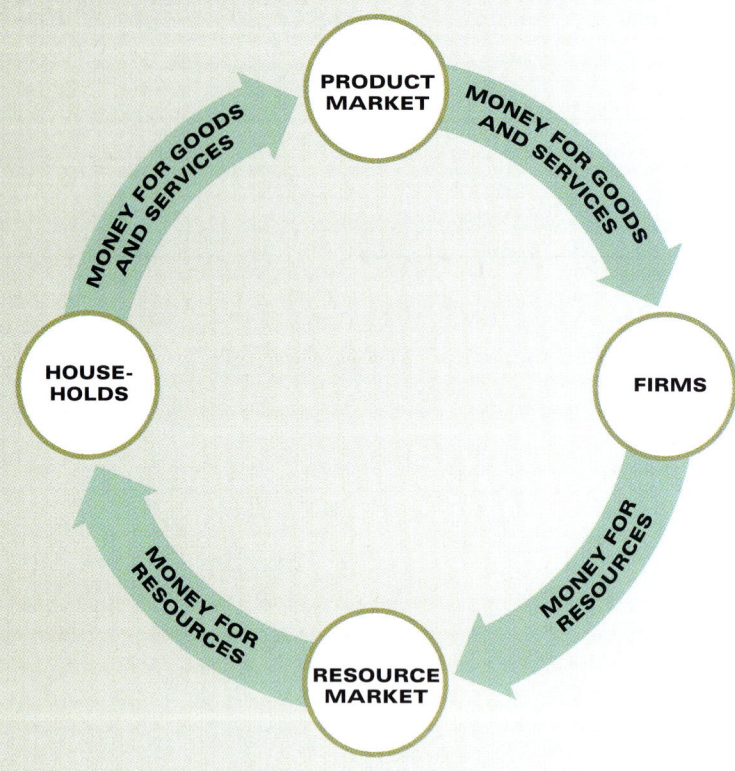

**on the net**

The Bureau of Economic Analysis (BEA) (http://www.bea.doc.gov/), an agency of the Department of Commerce, is the nation's economic accountant, preparing data on all components of GDP (http://www.bea.doc.gov/bea/glance.htm). The BEA also maintains international data (http://www.bea.doc.gov/bea/di1.htm) and regional data (http://www.bea.doc.gov/bea/regional/data.htm).

goods and services whose prices you add are, in fact, *final* goods and services. If you simply add the prices of all goods and services produced in the year, you end up double counting—counting some goods and services more than once. How so? Exhibit 3 illustrates the point.

How much market value is contributed to GDP in Exhibit 3? As you see, five different firms are involved in producing woolen sweaters. In the first, wool is actually being produced on the sheep. Let's suppose the value of the wool, determined by the market price of wool still on the hoof, is $4. A second firm, producing bulk wool, pays the sheep owner $4—its market price—for the sheep's wool. After shearing, washing, drying, and sizing the wool, the second firm sells it at the $7 bulk wool price.

A knitting mill buys the wool and knits it into a fine wool fabric. At the end of this third stage of economic activity, the market price of the fabric is $13. It is sold to a sweater-making firm that fashions it into a wool sweater, priced at $20.

The firm-to-firm process is finally completed with the sale of the sweater by a clothing store. Here, the sweater is put on display, and a salesperson finally sells it, gift wrapped, for $50.

How do we transfer the information of Exhibit 3 into GDP? We don't simply add up the total values of the goods and services produced by the five firms to get $94.

## EXHIBIT 3

**MARKET VALUE AND VALUE ADDED OF GOODS PRODUCED**

| FIRM | GOOD | MARKET VALUE | VALUE ADDED BY FIRM |
|---|---|---|---|
| 1. SHEEP RANCH | WOOL ON SHEEP | $4 | $4 |
| 2. SHEARING SHEEP | BULK WOOL | 7 | 3 |
| 3. KNITTING MILL | WOOL FABRIC | 13 | 6 |
| 4. MANUFACTURING | SWEATER | 20 | 7 |
| 5. STORE | SWEATER | 50 | 30 |
| TOTAL | | $94 | $50 |

That $94 counts the $4 raw wool five times over. The $4 makes up part of the value of the $7 price of bulk wool and is counted again as part of the value of the $13 price of the fabric, counted once more as part of the $20 price of the manufactured sweater, and counted again as part of the sweater's $50 retail price at the store.

How do we overcome overcounting? By counting only values of **final goods** produced, that is, *goods that are not resold.* The only good not resold in Exhibit 3 is the $50 sweater. What about the raw wool, the bulk wool, the fabric, and the sweater in the sweater factory? These are **intermediate goods,** goods sold by firms to other firms. They are goods used to produce other goods. Their values are accounted for in the value of the final good.

Another way of arriving at the $50 value that is counted as part of GDP is by considering only the **value added** by each of the five firms of Exhibit 3. Look at column 4.

The sheep ranch, where the wool is actually grown, adds $4 to value. The firm producing bulk wool buys the wool for $4 and adds $3 to its value. The knitting mill buys the bulk wool for $7 and adds $6 to its value. The sweater firm buys the $13 fabric and adds $7 to its value. Finally, the store buys the sweater for $20 and adds $30 to its value. The firms' value added sums to $50. That is precisely the market value of the *final* good.

### The Four Expenditure Categories of GDP

What kinds of final goods and services are produced in our economy, and who buys them? Economists classify final goods and services according to whether they are produced to satisfy (1) consumption demands by households, (2) investment demands by firms, (3) demands by government, or (4) exports minus imports (net exports)—that is, the demands by foreigners for our goods and services minus our demands for foreign goods and services.

All final goods and services that make up GDP, then, can be expressed in the form

$$GDP = C + I + G + (X - M),$$

where $C$ is **personal consumption expenditures,** $I$ is **gross private domestic investment,** $G$ is **government purchases,** and $(X - M)$ is **net exports,** or exports minus imports.

What did 2000 GDP add up to? Look at Exhibit 4.

**Final goods**
Goods purchased for final use, not for resale.

**Intermediate goods**
Goods used to produce other goods.

**Value added**
The difference between the value of a good that a firm produces and the value of the goods the firm uses to produce it.

**Personal consumption expenditures**
All goods and services bought by households.

**Gross private domestic investment**
The purchase by firms of plant, equipment, and inventory goods.

**Government purchases**
All goods and services bought by government.

**Net exports**
An economy's exports to other economies, minus its imports from other economies.

## EXHIBIT 4

### EXPENDITURE APPROACH TO 2000 GDP ($ BILLIONS)

| | | | |
|---|---|---|---:|
| C | = | PERSONAL CONSUMPTION EXPENDITURES | $6,816.7 |
| | | DURABLE GOODS | 825.5 |
| | | NONDURABLE GOODS | 2,032.0 |
| | | SERVICES | 3,959.0 |
| I | = | GROSS PRIVATE DOMESTIC INVESTMENT | 1,872.4 |
| | | NONRESIDENTIAL | 1,392.5 |
| | | RESIDENTIAL | 412.5 |
| | | CHANGE IN BUSINESS INVENTORY | 67.4 |
| G | = | GOVERNMENT PURCHASES | 1,749.2 |
| | | FEDERAL | 594.4 |
| | | DEFENSE | 375.1 |
| | | NONDEFENSE | 219.3 |
| | | STATE AND LOCAL | 1,154.9 |
| X – M | = | NET EXPORTS OF GOODS AND SERVICES | –386.1 |
| | | EXPORTS | 1,135.1 |
| | | IMPORTS | (1,521.2) |
| GDP | = | GROSS DOMESTIC PRODUCT | 10,052.2 |

**Source:** Bureau of Economic Analysis, U.S. Department of Commerce, November 29, 2000.

**Durable goods**
Goods expected to last at least a year.

**CHECK YOUR UNDERSTANDING**

Why is a car considered a durble good?

GDP equals $10,052.2 billion. Look at the sums and specific character of the goods and services in each of the expenditure categories.

**PERSONAL CONSUMPTION EXPENDITURES** The $6,816.7 billion personal consumption expenditures make up 67.8 percent of the $10,052.2 billion 2000 GDP. These are the goods and services consumed directly by households. They are grouped into categories of durable goods, nondurable goods, and services.

**Durable goods** account for $825.5 billion. These include familiar household items such as kitchen appliances, television sets, carpeting, personal computers, washing machines, and lawn mowers. Durables include, as well, automobiles, electric saws, and hearing aids.

What sets durables apart from other consumption goods and services? Essentially, their durability. Unlike tuna salad sandwiches, they're not consumed soon after being produced. A refrigerator, for example, once produced, outlasts years of tuna salad sandwiches. Of course, all refrigerators eventually wear out. But it takes time. Economists describe a durable good as one that is expected to last at least a year. For example, a new Ford is *expected* to last more than a year. Even if Alice Gorman buys it today and totals it this afternoon on the way home from the dealership, it is still classified as a durable good.

Purchases of durable goods help economists identify the phases of the business cycle. During recessions, consumers tend to hang on to their durables (say, by getting them repaired), so that sales of new durables are relatively weak. As prosperity returns, consumers are more inclined to discard old durables than to repair them. As a result, sales of new durables are relatively strong.

# HISTORICAL PERSPECTIVE

## THE WEALTH OF NATIONS

**G**ross domestic product (GDP) is defined as the total value of all final goods and services, measured in current market prices, produced during a year. The only exceptions are illegal goods and services, such as the production of cocaine or the services offered in prostitution. Everything else counts.

The rationale behind such a measure of GDP is consumer sovereignty. If people value a good or service, then regardless of what the good or service is, that value should be considered as contributing to the wealth or well-being of the nation. For example, if people value cotton candy, then despite the fact that it contains no nutritional value and probably rots your teeth, the production of that cotton candy contributes to the wealth of the nation and should be counted as part of its GDP. So too a questionable performance of an off-Broadway production of *Hamlet*.

Classical economists of the 18th and 19th centuries had a very different take on what should be counted in GDP. Adam Smith in his *Wealth of Nations* (1776) argued that only the production of goods that promote economic growth should be regarded as contributing to the wealth of nations. For example, the production of a potato is part of GDP because the potato promotes economic growth. Once planted, it reproduces itself and more. To Smith, all goods that sustain the physical well-being of people are both productive and contributing to the wealth of nations because having and using the goods allow people to reproduce those goods and more.

TAKING A BITE OUT OF GDP.

What kind of production, then, doesn't serve to promote the wealth of nations? Adam Smith is explicit here: All services, *however useful*, fail the economic-growth test. Using his own criterion, Smith would regard himself as unproductive and his services as a professor not contributing to GDP! It's not that Smith underappreciated his place in society. It's simply that he believed his services did not add materially to society. And that's what the wealth of nations was about. He elaborates:

> The sovereign with all the officers of both justice and war who serve under him, the whole army and navy are unproductive laborers. Their service, however honorable, produces nothing for which an equal quantity of services can afterwards be procured. In the same class must be ranked some of the most gravest and most important, and some of the most frivolous professions: churchmen, lawyers, physicians, men of letters of all kinds; players, buffoons, musicians, opera-singers, opera dancers, etc. Like the declamation of the actor or the tune of the musician, the work of all of them perishes in the very instant of its production.

It's an interesting way of looking at GDP and perhaps not too surprising for the 18th and 19th centuries. After all, what the "wealth of nations" (or GDP) is, is in truth highly subjective. It depends ultimately on one's conception of value. Does two dollars' worth of cotton candy contribute twice as much to society as a dollar's worth of nursing care? Yes, say 21st-century economists. What say you?

---

What about **nondurable goods?** These include goods consumed within a relatively short period of time, usually less than a year, such as food, clothing, gasoline, drugs, tobacco, and toiletries. Some things are easy to classify as nondurables—such as bananas—whereas it may take years to consume some spices. Also, many of us wear clothes and shoes for more than a year, yet the U.S. Department of Commerce

**Nondurable goods**
Goods expected to last less than a year.

# THEORETICAL PERSPECTIVE

## AN EXPANDED CIRCULAR FLOW

The exhibit on the following page, illustrating the income and expenditure approaches to GDP, is an expanded version of the circular flow models shown in Exhibits 1 and 2. A government sector and international trade have been added.

Let's begin by looking at the resources (labor, capital, land, and entrepreneurship) that flow through the purple artery from households to the resource market, and then from the resource market to firms that use the resources to produce goods and services. Now follow the flow of these goods and services from firms through the three purple arteries on the right side of the figure. The first leads from firms to households through the product market. These represent the households' private consumption. The second artery carries the flow to government. Note that the goods-and-services flow that government buys from firms is passed on to households (as public goods). The third artery carries the flow of goods and services in the form of exports from firms to foreign economies. The foreign economies' contribution is depicted in the flow through the purple artery from the foreign economies to households. The difference between the import and export flows represents net exports. Finally, some of the firms' output flow is absorbed by the firms themselves in the form of investment. Combined, these flows of goods and services, all channeled through purple arteries, make up the expenditures approach in the circular flow model:

$$C + I + G + (X - M)$$

The circular flow model also depicts a counterbalancing money flow carried through green arteries that represent payments made by households, government, firms, and foreign economies for goods and services received. Note the green and yellow arteries that carry money flows from households to firms for the goods and services purchased on the product market, from households to government in the form of taxes, and from households to foreign economies for imports. Households receive money from firms in the form of payments flows for resources provided and from government in the form of transfer payments. Firms pay taxes to government and receive a payments flow from government for goods and services provided. Firms also receive money from foreign economies in the form of a payments flow for exports.

What about saving and investment? The money that households set aside as saving is equal to the value of the goods and services firms set aside for investment.

**Services**
Productive activities that are instantaneously consumed.

*Can you think of other firms that sell both durable goods and services? Go to the Interactive Study Center at http://gottheil.swcollege.com and click on the "Your Turn" button to submit your example. Student submissions will be posted to the Web site, and perhaps we will use some in future editions of the book!*

classifies them as nondurables. Households spend more on nondurables than on durables. In fact, the value of nondurables consumed in 2000 was more than twice the value of durable items.

**Services** are intangible (nonphysical) consumption items consumed as they are being produced. Think about health care. You consume your doctor's service precisely when it is being given. An Economics 101 lecture is consumed as your professor lectures. The Chicago Symphony is consumed as Daniel Barenboim conducts.

Some industries (often those that produce durable goods) produce services as well. AT&T, for example, sells telephones (durable goods) and telephone calls (ser-

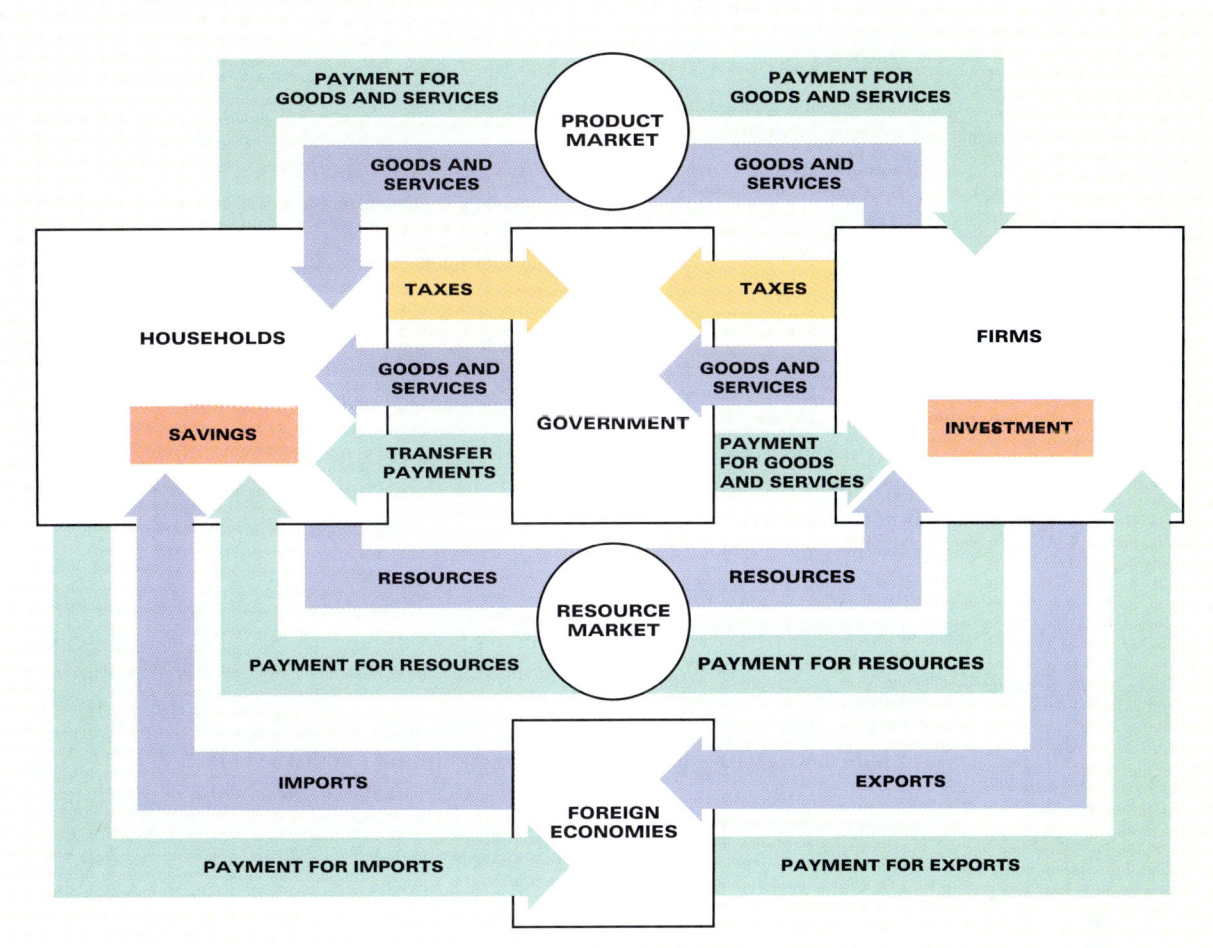

vices). Sears sells washing machines (durable goods) and washing machine repair (service). As you see in Exhibit 4, we spend more on services than we do on durable and nondurable goods combined.

**GROSS PRIVATE DOMESTIC INVESTMENT** Not all production of final goods and services in 2000 was consumed by households. Some goods and services—$1,872.4 billion of the $10,052.2 billion—were actually purchased by firms themselves in the form of gross private domestic investment. What kinds of goods? The oil rigs produced in 2000 by firms that make oil-drilling equipment were bought by Exxon and Texaco, not by you. The rigs are used by the oil companies to produce energy for households. Construction companies built automobile plants for General Motors and Ford, not for households. These plants turn out the automobiles demanded by households.

The goods that firms buy from each other are classified as new structures (or plants) and equipment. Some plant and equipment purchases merely replace plants and equipment that have worn out producing consumption goods. But some purchases are made to increase the quantity of plants and equipment in use. For example, United Airlines bought aircraft to replace those no longer usable. But it also bought aircraft to expand its fleet.

**Inventory investment**
Stocks of finished goods and raw materials that firms keep in reserve to facilitate production and sales.

What about residential investment? Houses and apartment buildings produced in 2000 and used as residences are classified as investment goods, even though a case can be made to classify a homeowner's house—as we do a homeowner's automobile—as a durable consumption good.

Changes in business inventories are counted as **inventory investment.** Why? Inventories are unsold output. Firms keep stocks of finished final goods, as well as stocks of resources used to produce those goods, in reserve in order to promote efficiency in production and sales. How can a clothing store expect to sell sweaters if it doesn't stock a variety of styles, sizes, and colors? How can Goodyear expect to run a smooth production line if it doesn't stock the raw materials used in manufacturing tires?

What does the $67.4 billion business inventory change in 2000 signify? That some goods produced in 2000 were *added* to 2000 inventory—that is, they were produced in 2000 but not sold in that year.

Business inventory changes, positive or negative, are not always intended. Suppose that Rockport Shoes planned to produce and sell $200 million of shoes in 2000, but by year's end was able to sell only $180 million. The remaining unsold $20 million would be recorded as an addition to business inventory, even though Rockport intended the shoes for sale, not inventory. Rockport would end up with more shoes in inventory than it wanted.

**CHECK YOUR UNDERSTANDING**
Why do some goods produced for consumption end up being investment?

**GOVERNMENT PURCHASES** Government, too, is a buyer of goods and services. In 2000 federal, state, and local government purchases amounted to $1,749.2 billion, or 17.4 percent of the economy's $10,052.2 billion production of goods and services. The largest slice of federal government purchases—$375.1 billion—went to national defense. It bought food and clothing for the armed forces, F-15 fighter planes, Bradley tanks, Navy uniforms, and countless other military hardware and software items that make up our military preparedness.

Defense goods were not the federal government's only purchases. It also bought interstate highways, dry docks, post offices, and services such as justice, transportation, and education. It spent money on Amtrak service, for example, and airport construction. Without federal spending on these items, many people could not afford to travel.

Yet, in spite of all the media attention focused on the appetite of the federal government, the biggest government spender doesn't live in Washington, D.C. State and local government expenditures account for approximately 66 percent of all government spending. These expenditures and the means used by governments to finance them are described in later chapters.

**NET EXPORTS OF GOODS AND SERVICES** The final item in the expenditure approach to GDP is net exports. We produced for export $1,135.1 billion of goods and services. How does this item affect our GDP account?

We include exports in calculating GDP because they represent goods and services we produced, even though they do not appear as part of our own expenditures. On the other hand, the imported goods and services we buy from other economies are part of our expenditures even though we didn't produce them. In calculating GDP by the expenditure approach, we include exports and subtract imports. In 2000, net exports—the difference between exports and imports—was negative, a minus $386.1 billion.

# THE INCOME APPROACH

**Income approach**
A method of calculating GDP that adds all the incomes earned in the production of final goods and services.

An alternative approach to calculating GDP is the **income approach.** How does this differ from the expenditure approach? Instead of determining GDP by computing the total value of all final goods and services produced in the economy, the income approach computes the total payments made to households that provide the resources used in producing the final goods and services.

The resources used in production—labor, capital, land, and entrepreneurship—receive income payments in the form of wages and salaries, interest, rent, and profit. These income payments are rearranged in GDP accounting into five categories: (1) the compensation of employees, (2) interest, (3) corporate profit, (4) rental income, and (5) proprietors' income. The sum of these income payments is **national income.**

National income for 2000 is shown in Exhibit 5.

National income equaled $8,091.9 billion. Look at the sums and specific character of each of the income categories shown in Exhibit 5.

**National income**
The sum of all payments made to resource owners for the use of their resources.

## Compensation of Employees

In every morning rush hour, an incredible crush of people head to work. They spend their working life producing the economy's goods and services. Some people work production lines as hourly workers earning wages; others sit behind desks as salaried workers pushing the paper flow that modern production requires. Still others are journalists, teachers, or firefighters.

In 2000 firms, organizations, and government entities paid out to their employees $4,803.8 billion in wages and salaries, and another $874.6 billion in fringe benefits, such as bonuses, paid vacations, and contributions to employees' Social Security. All that compensation of employees was money paid for labor supplied.

No surprise, then, that our national economy appears to be labor generated. After all, the $5,678.4 billion income payment to workers accounts for 70.2 percent of our national income. That percentage hasn't changed much over the years.

## Interest

How is capital incorporated into the income approach to GDP? People who provide firms with capital—for example, by buying interest-bearing bonds issued by the firms—receive interest, just as people who provide labor services receive wages and salaries. Firms also borrow capital from banks, which in turn borrow from individual savers. In each case, interest is earned. In 2000, $578.7 billion was received by people in the form of interest.

## Corporate Profit

Corporate profit represents the return to owners of incorporated firms. Part of corporate profit is distributed to stockholders as *dividends,* part is retained by the corporation as investment, and a third part ends up with government as corporate taxes. The income approach to GDP includes all of corporate profit, which in 2000 amounted to $972.2 billion.

What about the income of corporate managers? These are the people making key corporate decisions. Are their

**EXHIBIT 5**

**2000 NATIONAL INCOME ($ BILLIONS)**

| | |
|---|---|
| COMPENSATION OF EMPLOYEES | $5,678.4 |
| WAGES AND SALARIES | 4,803.8 |
| SUPPLEMENTS | 874.6 |
| RENTAL INCOME | 138.6 |
| CORPORATE PROFIT | 972.2 |
| NET INTEREST | 578.7 |
| PROPRIETORS' INCOME | 725.0 |
| FARM | 31.7 |
| NONFARM | 693.3 |
| NATIONAL INCOME | 8,091.9 |

**Source:** Bureau of Economic Analysis, U.S. Department of Commerce, November 29, 2000.

incomes included as part of corporate profit? No. Their incomes, typically salaries, are counted as employee compensation.

## Rent

Rent is payment for use of property. The most common property forms are land, housing, and office space. People using their own property typically don't pay themselves rent, but the rent is nonetheless estimated in GDP accounting and counted along with contractual rental leases. Imputed rents associated with owner-occupied dwellings are also counted. In 2000 these rental forms amounted to $138.6 billion.

## Proprietors' Income

Although our economy is dominated by large corporations, the largest number of businesses are unincorporated firms. Many people own their own businesses, earning income for the goods and services they produce. How are these incomes classified? They don't fall into the category of corporate profit, because the firms are not corporations. They aren't wages or salaries, because owners don't hire themselves as employees. They obviously aren't rent or interest. They are regarded as proprietors' income.

Imagine an ethnic restaurant in Brooklyn owned and operated by a husband and wife. They work hard, save their pennies, rent the premises, and set up a 12-table restaurant. They prepare the meals, serve, and clean up after a 14-hour workday. They gross $172,000 in 2000. But they must also pay rent and utilities, buy ingredients for meals, and repair wear and tear on their plant and equipment. After paying out all 2000 expenses, they end up with a net income of $44,000. Economists define that net income as proprietors' income. In 2000, unincorporated firms generated $725.0 billion for their owners.

# BRINGING GDP AND NATIONAL INCOME INTO ACCORD

How do economists reconcile differences between the $10,052.2 billion 2000 GDP and the $8,091.9 billion 2000 national income? First they derive gross domestic product (GDP), then subtract two items from it—depreciation of capital and indirect business taxes.

## From GDP to GNP

**Gross national product (GNP)**
The market value of all final goods and services in an economy produced by resources owned by people of that economy, regardless of where the resources are located.

The difference between GDP and **gross national product (GNP)** is ownership and location. Gross domestic product measures location, that is, what is produced and earned *in the domestic economy*. In 2000 GDP equaled $10,052.2 billion. Gross national product, on the other hand, measures ownership, that is, what the *nation's people and their property* produce and earn. In 2000 GNP was $10,040.0 billion. If the nation's entire resources were employed wholly within the economy, then GDP would be exactly the same as GNP.

The reality, however, is that some U.S. workers and other resources are employed outside the country. And some of the resources employed in this country are not owned by U.S. citizens. The value of the automobiles produced by a General Motors plant in Spain is not included in our GDP (it is counted in Spain's GDP). On the other hand, it is included in our GNP. Conversely, a Nissan plant's output in Tennessee is part of our GDP, but not our GNP. In 2000 foreign workers and the property owned by foreigners in the United States created $387.7 billion

# GLOBAL PERSPECTIVE

## IS THE 2000 COMPOSITION OF GDP FOR THE UNITED STATES UNIQUE?

Suppose we hadn't seen the composition of 2000 GDP shown in Table A. Could we have guessed it? Probably, if we had access to GDP data for any other year. The consumption expenditures by households, the investment expenditures by firms, the government purchases, and the net exports shares of GDP vary little from year to year, as Table A indicates. In the 40-year period 1960–2000, the consumption share each year varied only slightly from 65 percent of GDP. Investment clustered around 15 percent and government's share was approximately 20 percent.

These shares not only remain reasonably stable over time, but also are not too dissimilar from the composition shares of GDP for most other market economies. Look at Table B.

The variations, although greater, are still remarkably narrow. For most of the European economies in 1999, consumption shares vary only slightly around the 60 percent mark. Denmark's 51.2 percent, while relatively low, is counterbalanced by its higher 25.5 percent government share, reflecting Denmark's history of Social Democrat policies.

FAMILIAR SCENE? IT COULD BE IN MOST ANY TOWN, ANY COUNTRY. CONSUMER SPENDING HABITS ARE PRETTY MUCH THE SAME EVERYWHERE.

### MORE ON THE NET

Review the *World Factbook* (http://www.odci.gov/cia/publications/factbook/) for GDP measurements and descriptions for nations around the world.

**TABLE A: COMPOSITION OF U.S. GDP: 1960–2000**

|  | 1960 | 1970 | 1980 | 2000 |
|---|---|---|---|---|
| CONSUMPTION | 64.7 | 64.0 | 64.6 | 67.8 |
| INVESTMENT | 15.3 | 14.9 | 17.3 | 18.6 |
| GOVERNMENT | 19.4 | 21.0 | 18.7 | 17.4 |
| NET EXPORTS | 0.5 | 0.1 | −0.5 | −3.8 |
|  | 100.0 | 100.0 | 100.0 | 100.0 |

Source: *Economic Report of the President, 1997* (Washington D.C., February 1997).

**TABLE B: COMPOSITION OF GDP FOR SELECTED ECONOMIES: 1999**

|  | CONSUMPTION | INVESTMENT | GOVERNMENT | NET EXPORTS |
|---|---|---|---|---|
| ITALY | 59.1 | 18.9 | 18.6 | 2.0 |
| FRANCE | 54.2 | 19.7 | 23.8 | 0.0 |
| UNITED KINGDOM | 66.4 | 19.4 | 18.8 | −4.7 |
| GERMANY | 57.8 | 20.9 | 19.0 | 1.0 |
| CANADA | 57.8 | 20.9 | 19.0 | 2.0 |
| JAPAN | 59.3 | 20.3 | 18.2 | 2.3 |
| DENMARK | 51.2 | 20.9 | 25.5 | 1.7 |
| THE NETHERLANDS | 59.5 | 20.0 | 13.6 | 6.4 |

Source: *Economist Intelligence Unit,* London, England.

**CHECK YOUR UNDERSTANDING**

If you worked in Japan for an American-owned company, would what you produce be part of American GDP or GNP?

of income that was included in our GDP but excluded from our GNP. On the other hand, the $375.5 billion of 2000 U.S. assets abroad and income earned by U.S. citizens working in foreign economies was excluded from our GDP but included in our GNP.

## From GDP to NDP

To create the 2000 GDP of $10,052.2 billion, people were busy turning out, day after day, automobiles and computers, corn and health care. They worked in factories and hospitals and on farms. They welded frames, operated tractors, and took X rays. These factories, hospitals, welding machines, tractors, and X-ray machines—along with other factories and machinery—make up the capital stock in our economy. Wouldn't you think that during 2000 part of this capital stock would be used up producing the economy's 2000 GDP? After all, nothing is forever. Machines in use wear out, as do hospitals and factories.

Shouldn't they be replaced? Typically, they are. During 2000 *new* factories and machinery were produced. New hospitals were built, new tractors manufactured, and new automobile assembly lines constructed.

But if the value of all investment goods produced in 2000 only replaces the value of the capital stock used up in 2000, then 2000 GDP may be giving us an inflated view of our economy's 2000 performance.

For example, suppose each of two fishermen caught 1,000 pounds of fish, but one used 100 pounds of fish bait to do the catching, the other 500 pounds of fish bait. Wouldn't the difference in their *used-up capital* influence your evaluation of their performance? Or suppose we discover that firms in 2000 used up $2,000 billion, not $1,272.3 billion, of plants and equipment to produce the $10,052.2 billion GDP. Wouldn't that give us a very different reading of the economy's 2000 performance?

By deducting used-up capital, or **capital depreciation,** *d*, from GDP, we derive **net domestic product (NDP):**

$$NDP = GDP - d$$

By way of illustration, let's compare the 2000–2001 growth rates of NDP, assuming different hypothetical values for capital depreciation and rates of GDP growth.

As you see in Exhibit 6, the 5 percent rate of GDP growth could be coupled with a 10.0 percent, an 8.8 percent, and a 7.7 percent growth rate of NDP, depending on how much plant and equipment is used up in the process of producing the $10,052.2 billion GDP. Which of the two rates of growth, GDP or NDP, would you consider the more informative measure of the economy's performance?

**Capital depreciation**
The value of existing capital stock used up in the process of producing goods and services.

**Net domestic product (NDP)**
GDP minus capital depreciation.

**EXHIBIT 6**

**INFLUENCE OF CAPITAL DEPRECIATION ON THE GROWTH RATE OF NDP ($ BILLIONS)**

|  | GDP | RATE OF GDP GROWTH | CAPITAL DEPRECIATION | NDP | RATE OF NDP GROWTH |
|---|---|---|---|---|---|
| 2000 | $10,052.2 |  | $1,272.3 | $8,779.9 |  |
| 2001 | 10,554.8 | 5.0% | 900.0 | 9,654.8 | 10.0 |
| 2001 | 10,554.8 | 5.0% | 1,000.0 | 9,554.8 | 8.8 |
| 2001 | 10,554.8 | 5.0% | 1,100.0 | 9,454.8 | 7.7 |

## From NDP to National Income

The reduction of NDP to national income involves removing indirect business taxes—that is, general sales taxes, excise taxes, customs duties, business property taxes, and license fees—from the NDP accounts. They are called indirect taxes because they are not levied on the firm directly, but on the good or service. Why must we remove them from NDP to get national income? Because they are embodied in the price of the good or service. And because government is not viewed as a resource, or factor of production, these tax revenues to government are not viewed as compensation for production. That is, the taxes are not paid to any factor of production.

As we saw in Exhibit 5, payments to households for resources provided defines national income. It is the sum of wages and salaries, corporate profit, rent, interest, and proprietors' income. The exclusion of indirect taxes from the NDP accounts, then, generates national income.

Why bother measuring national income? Isn't NDP a good enough measure? National income provides us with more specific information. It offers, in some instances, a much sharper picture of the population's economic well-being. After all, national income is what eventually ends up in people's hands.

## GDP, GNP, NNP, and National Income for 2000

Exhibit 7 summarizes the relationships between GDP, GNP, NNP, and national income for 2000.

# PERSONAL INCOME AND PERSONAL DISPOSABLE INCOME

National income is what people earn. **Personal income,** on the other hand, is what they receive. What people receive in any year is not always equal to what they earn. Consider, for example, the income earned and received by corporate shareholders in 2000.

Since shareholders own the corporation, what they earn as shareholders is the profit the corporation makes. But shareholders don't end up with that profit. First, the corporation is obliged to pay corporate income tax. What it pays out in taxes, its shareholders don't receive. Second, the corporation typically retains some of its

**Personal income**
National income, plus income received but not earned, minus income earned but not received.

**THE RELATIONSHIP BETWEEN GROSS DOMESTIC PRODUCT, GROSS NATIONAL PRODUCT, NET NATIONAL PRODUCT, AND NATIONAL INCOME: 2000 ($ BILLIONS)**

|        | GROSS DOMESTIC PRODUCT | $10,052.2 |
|--------|------------------------|-----------|
| MINUS  | FACTOR PAYMENTS TO THE REST OF THE WORLD | -387.7 |
| PLUS   | FACTOR PAYMENTS FROM THE REST OF THE WORLD | 375.5 |
| EQUALS | GROSS NATIONAL PRODUCT | 10,040.0 |
| MINUS  | CAPITAL DEPRECIATION   | -1,272.3 |
| EQUALS | NET NATIONAL PRODUCT   | 8,767.7 |
| MINUS  | INDIRECT BUSINESS TAXES | -675.8 |
| EQUALS | NATIONAL INCOME        | 8,091.9 |

Note: Net domestic product = $8,767.7 billion. The use of NNP instead of NDP to derive national income conforms to the derivation of national income used by government sources. Note also that because GDP and GNP are almost identical, NDP and NNP are almost identical.
**Source:** Bureau of Economic Analysis, U.S. Department of Commerce, November 29, 2000.

EXHIBIT 7

after-tax profit for its own internal investment. What it retains for investment, its shareholders don't receive. And third, the corporation is obliged to contribute to Social Security. That represents yet another deduction from corporate earnings that its shareholders don't receive.

What about employees? They don't bring home total employee compensation, either. Employees are obliged to pay Social Security taxes as well. They end up, then, with less than the full measure of their earnings.

On the other hand, some people in 2000 received more income than they earned. How is that possible? People received income from government in the form of retirement benefits, veteran benefits, unemployment insurance benefits, disability payments, Aid to Families with Dependent Children, and subsidies to farmers. Economists refer to this form of income as **transfer payments** because the government—acting as receiver and dispenser of income—transfers income from taxpayers (who earned the income in the first place by providing resources) to those receiving benefits. These income transfers, prior to the actual transfers, are counted as part of national income because they represent income earned. They are not counted as national income again when they end up in the hands of the benefit recipients.

**Transfer payments**
Income received but not earned.

**CHECK YOUR UNDERSTANDING**

Why is a $20 lottery win considered part of your personal income, but not part of national income?

Another form of income is the interest people receive on the government savings bonds, notes, and bills they own. This interest is part of their personal income but is not included in national income. Why not? Because the bonds, notes, and bills that government sold to them were primarily incurred to finance *past* recessions and defense, which—however essential they *were*—were not income yielding in 2000. That is, the interest paid out by government in 2000 had no equivalent 2000 income source.

In 2000 the economy's $8,351.0 billion of personal income exceeded the $8,091.9 billion of national income.

Households, however, were not free to dispose of the entire $8,351.0 billion personal income as they wished. Why not? Because they were still obligated to pay direct taxes to federal, state, and local governments. What remains after subtracting these taxes out of personal income is **disposable personal income.** In 2000, this disposable personal income was $7,042.9 billion. It is what households have at their disposal to spend on final goods and services or to save.

**Disposable personal income**
Personal income minus direct taxes.

## HOW COMPREHENSIVE IS GDP?

Does GDP really measure everything produced in the national economy? Is what we produce an adequate measure of our economic well-being? GDP tries to measure everything that *appears on the market*. But not everything produced in the economy gets onto the market. And there are things that contribute to our economic well-being that aren't even produced.

### Value of Housework

One of the most glaring exclusions from GDP accounts is the value of housework done by householders. Nobody with any sense at all would argue that housework is any less a productive activity contributing to our economic well-being than, say, manufacturing automobiles. In fact, housework is included in GDP accounts as long as it isn't done by a member of the household. Hired housekeepers, nannies, and cooks working in households are either employees or self-employed persons earning incomes for productive services that are counted in GDP. In most cases, however, the housekeepers, nannies, and cooks are the householders themselves, and because their productive labor is not supplied through a market—they are neither employees nor self-employed—their contributions are not recorded in GDP accounts.

One explanation for the omission is that GDP was never meant to measure all productive activity in the economy, and, anyway, housework is extremely difficult if not impossible to evaluate. On the other hand, economists have found ways to include other forms of nonmarket productive activity in GDP. Is it really more difficult to impute value to housework than to impute value to goods produced and consumed by farm families on family farms? Yet, GDP includes farmers' self-consumed food, but not the value of housework.

## The Underground Economy

Some economic activities other than housework also do not get reported—and for good reason. Drug trafficking, money laundering, bribery, prostitution, fraud, illegal gambling, and burglary are activities that aren't negotiated openly in the marketplace. Yet they represent sets of demanders and suppliers, and they generate unreported incomes that can be sizable.

Other activities, legal and mainstream, go unreported by people trying to evade taxes. There is ample opportunity for people who receive payments for service, such as lawyers, physicians, consultants, domestics, tailors, car mechanics, babysitters, and taxi drivers, to understate income earned.

A driving force of the **underground economy** is tax avoidance. If you and a friend swap services ("I'll fix your car if you paint my house"), you both avoid paying taxes. But the car repair and painting are not counted in GDP. Your 9-to-5 economic activity may be counted, but your moonlighting activities are not.

A growing population of legal and illegal immigrants has swelled the not-so-mainstream workforce. Many earn less than minimum wages working in off-the-books entry-level jobs such as sidewalk vendors of electronics, jewelry, and flowers; serving as casual labor in sweatshops and construction; doing illegal piecework at home; and toiling as domestics. Many immigrants apply their entrepreneurial talents in flea markets, greengrocers, and the garment trade. These activities go unreported. Illegal immigrants are sought-after workers by some employers because, typically, they work for lower-than-prevailing-rate market wages, and because the employer makes no contribution to Social Security or unemployment insurance.

How sizable is this unreported underground economy? Some economists estimate it at 10 percent of GDP. Professor Peter Gutmann of Baruch College estimated that $902 billion—$261 billion illegal, $641 billion legal—of U.S. economic activity was underground in 1993, representing 13 percent of GDP. Other economists believe that underground activity in the United States is closer to 25 percent. In some European economies, the underground economy is estimated to be as high as 40 percent.

## Leisure

What about the economic value of leisure? What about reading a book, or taking a walk, or playing baseball, or visiting friends? The fact that people choose to spend time consuming some quantity of leisure over producing and consuming more final goods and services indicates that adding up the market value of goods and services may not give us the whole picture of a person's or a society's economic well-being. Going to a Dodgers-Expos game on Sunday afternoon is purchased entertainment and included in GDP, but playing tennis with friends on that same afternoon is not.

**Underground economy**
The unreported or illegal production of goods and services in the economy that is not counted in GDP.

# APPLIED PERSPECTIVE

## UNDERGROUND ECONOMY DOING THRIVING BUSINESS

What does skid row in Nashville tell us about the American economy? Or drug smuggling in Belize, the black market in Cuba, or one of those sleazy traveling carnival games?

A lot, says Bruce Wiegand, a sociologist at the University of Wisconsin at Whitewater, who has made his career the study of what is diplomatically called the underground economy. It is also known as the black market.

According to Wiegand, that shady, off-the-books economy may be one of America's largest and fastest-growing industries.

It includes drug dealers, teenage baby-sitters, physicians who ask patients to pay in cash, flea market operators, moonlighting carpenters, small businesspeople who inflate their deductions, and multinational corporations that fudge on the value of goods transferred between their far-flung subsidiaries.

"My guess," says Wiegand, "is that the underground economy is about 25 percent the size of the national economy, and that does not include the illegal sector, like drugs and prostitution."

The illicit underground economy—activities such as drugs and loan-sharking that are by their nature illegal—is probably only about a third the size of the legal underground economy, which comprises otherwise legal enterprises that simply cheat on taxes.

The black market really began with Prohibition in 1920, after the 18th Amendment banned booze, and entrepreneurs such as Al Capone began smuggling it to a thirsty public. Prohibition was repealed in 1933, but depression-era shortages of goods and money and then World War II restrictions resulted in a thriving underground economy.

After the war, the big-city ghettos became the reservoir of the underground economy, because for many entrepreneurial blacks, that was the only way to survive, scholars say.

Middle-class whites began to rediscover the black market in the 1970s, and according to Wiegand, it was finally noticed by economists late in that decade.

IRS estimates on tax avoidance give some clues to the nature of the underground economy. Individuals account for an estimated 75 percent of tax cheating and corporations 25 percent, according to the most recent IRS research reports.

RECEIPT? I'M SORRY, LADY, WE DON'T GIVE RECEIPTS. IT'S $5, NO RECEIPTS, NO TAXES.

Among individuals who file federal tax returns, almost 57 percent underreport income. The biggest offenders are sole proprietorships (including doctors, lawyers, accountants, sweatshops, and operators of cottage industries), at almost 20 percent of the national total.

Informal suppliers, such as flea market merchants, account for 9 percent, and the underreporting of capital gains by people wealthy enough to claim them accounts for almost 8 percent.

The best compliance, as might be suspected, is by employees who have their income reported to the IRS on their annual W-2 forms. They account for only 1.7 percent of the cheating.

### MORE ON THE NET

The Internal Revenue Service (http://www.irs.gov/) maintains extensive tax statistics (http://www.irs.ustreas.gov/prod/tax_stats/).

**Source:** David Young, "Underground Economy Doing Thriving Business," *Chicago Tribune*, July 10, 1992. © Copyrighted Chicago Tribune Company. All rights reserved. Used with permission.

## Quality of Goods and Services

People chronically complain about how our goods and services don't live up to their advertised claims. What's the real value of a new automobile, advertised as high quality, when its transmission fails four days after the warranty runs out? How commonplace is that experience? What value should we place on a toaster that cannot be repaired because there are no shops to service the toaster?

Notwithstanding these and tens of thousands more complaints, quality has nevertheless improved dramatically over time. While transmissions do sometimes go out and toasters become instant junk when one part malfunctions, most of the goods and services we consume have increased in quality and serviceability. Radial tires are considerably more durable than the tires available 25 years ago. Automobiles are more reliable, microwave ovens more convenient, and home furnaces more efficient than they ever were. New technologies make health care more accessible and more successful. Higher-quality goods are continually replacing inferior ones even though they do not always meet our more demanding expectations. These quality improvements may not register in our GDP accounts because the prices of the higher-quality goods may actually be less than the prices of the inferior goods they replace.

## Costs of Environmental Damage

While firms keep churning out the goods and services that make up our GDP, they churn out pollution that fouls our environment as well. No-deposit bottles and aluminum cans are convenient but litter our physical space. Automobiles provide us with valued mobility but also with rush-hour traffic, noise, and carbon monoxide. We have polluted air, land, and water, and our poor record in cleaning up our atmosphere threatens to damage the ozone layer that protects us from excessive radiation. We have allowed soil erosion to replace forests in parts of our deforested landscape. Destruction of habitat and species follow. How do these negative attributes of our quest for more goods and services fit into our system of GDP accounts? The cleaning-up expenses associated with the pollution we create contribute to GDP, but the actual pollution created is not subtracted.

Although that's precisely how our GDP accounting works, there's something inherently wrong with this system of accounting. After all, if we were to allocate all our resources to producing and cleaning up garbage, we would end up with a GDP and no goods or services!

In the past 25 years, the government has legislated environmental codes and standards that firms are required to observe. Pollution control has been costly. Billions of dollars that could have been invested in new plants and machinery has been spent instead on pollution control devices. On the other hand, ignoring the effects of economic activity on the environment merely postpones payment and increases the damage.

The polluting activities of the recently defunct communist states were nothing short of horrendous. They simply ignored the environmental effects of their polluting factories. After investing almost nothing in pollution control for decades, it is no longer possible for them to postpone the difficult task of cleaning up a costly environmental mess. Perhaps the communist economists should have seen the U.S. television commercial advertising automobile air filters. It showed a mechanic in the foreground holding an air filter to the screen, while in the background we saw an automobile with its hood raised and engine smoking. The mechanic looked straight at the viewer and said: "You can pay me now [the air filter], or pay me later [the engine]."

Do exclusions from GDP measurement of such items as the value of housework, leisure, and the underground economy seriously undermine the usefulness economists ascribe to GDP accounting? Not really. Having a measure of real GDP that can accurately depict recessions and recoveries is worth the exclusion of some economic activities incapable of being accurately measured on a consistent basis. Simply put: The few items excluded involve too much guesswork. What we end up with is a measure of GDP sufficiently comprehensive to be a highly reliable indicator of the changes in the overall performance of the economy.

# CHAPTER REVIEW

1. The circular flow model illustrates the resource flow from households to firms and the goods and services flow from firms to households. Money flows through the economy in the opposite direction, as resource payments from firms to households and as goods and services purchases from households to firms. The dollar value of the resource flow equals the dollar value of the goods and services flow.

2. The expenditure approach to measuring GDP adds consumption expenditures by households, investment expenditures by firms, government expenditures, and net exports. In 2000, GDP was $10,052.2 billion.

3. The income approach to measuring GDP adds compensation of employees, interest, rent, corporate profit, and proprietors' income.

4. Gross national product, GNP, is GDP plus receipts of factor income from the rest of the world, minus payments to factor income to the rest of the world. Net domestic product, NDP, is GDP minus capital depreciation. Net national product, NNP, is GNP minus capital depreciation. National income is derived by deducting indirect taxes from NNP. National income in 2000 was 8,091.9 billion.

5. Derivative measures calculated from national income include personal income and personal disposable income.

6. GDP fails to include economic activity such as the value of housework performed by householders and the value of production in the underground economy. GDP also fails to account for improvements in the quality of goods and for environmental costs.

# KEY TERMS

Circular flow of goods, services, and resources
Circular flow of money
Expenditure approach
Final goods
Intermediate goods
Value added
Personal consumption expenditures
Gross private domestic investment
Government purchases
Net exports
Durable goods
Nondurable goods
Services
Inventory investment
Income approach
National income
Gross national product (GNP)
Capital depreciation
Net domestic product (NDP)
Personal income
Transfer payments
Disposable personal income
Underground economy

# QUESTIONS

1. Sketch a circular flow of goods, services, and resources through households and firms. Draw a similar one for money flows. Indicate the direction of each of the flows.
2. What categories of expenditures are included in the expenditure approach to calculating GDP?
3. What categories of income are included in the income approach to calculating GDP?
4. Distinguish between GDP and GNP.
5. How does the problem of double counting arise in calculating GDP, and how is it corrected?
6. Distinguish between intermediate and final goods.
7. Distinguish between durable goods, non-durable goods, and services.
8. What is an investment good? Why are some investment goods unintended?
9. How do economists bring GDP and national income into accord?
10. How does GDP differ from NDP? From national income?
11. In what ways do NDP and national income provide more specific information about an economy's performance than does GDP?
12. What are some of the limitations in using GDP as a measuring rod of our economic well-being?
13. If Madonna married her personal bodyguard, what effect might it have on national income?
14. Professor Kangoh Lee asks his students at Towson State University, "Suppose that in an economy, real consumption, real investment, and real government purchases remain the same from one year to another, while the real trade deficit increases. Can we conclude that real GDP must fall during the same period?" Explain.

# PRACTICE PROBLEMS

1. Use the following data to calculate GDP, GNP, NNP, national income, personal income, and personal disposable income.

   | | |
   |---|---|
   | PERSONAL CONSUMPTION EXPENDITURES | $800 |
   | INTEREST | 80 |
   | CORPORATE PROFIT | 120 |
   | GOVERNMENT PURCHASES | 300 |
   | DEPRECIATION | 80 |
   | RENT | 40 |
   | GROSS PRIVATE DOMESTIC INVESTMENT | 100 |
   | COMPENSATION OF EMPLOYEES | 750 |
   | EXPORTS | 100 |
   | IMPORTS | 60 |
   | INDIRECT BUSINESS TAXES | 70 |
   | PROPRIETORS' INCOME | 110 |
   | INCOME TAX | 100 |
   | INCOME EARNED BUT NOT RECEIVED | 120 |
   | INCOME RECEIVED BUT NOT EARNED | 140 |
   | RECEIPT OF FACTOR INCOMES FROM THE REST OF THE WORLD | 60 |
   | PAYMENT OF FACTOR INCOMES TO THE REST OF THE WORLD | 50 |

2. Suppose, in the following year, the changes in economic activity that occur in practice problem 1 are as follows.

   | | |
   |---|---|
   | DURABLE GOODS | +30 |
   | BUSINESS INVENTORY | +10 |
   | IMPORTS | +20 |
   | INCOME TAX | +10 |

   What effect would these changes have on GDP?

3. Imagine a three-firm, three-stages-of-production economy that produces one final good: a desk. Calculate the value added at each stage of production.

   | FIRM | GOOD | TOTAL VALUE OF GOOD PRODUCED | VALUE ADDED |
   |---|---|---|---|
   | LOGGING FIRM | LOG | $40 | |
   | LUMBER FIRM | LUMBER | 65 | |
   | DESK-MAKING FIRM | DESK | 150 | |

# ECONOMIC CONSULTANTS

## ECONOMIC RESEARCH AND ANALYSIS BY STUDENTS FOR PROFESSIONALS

Diane Pecknold owns an independent grocery store that has been in operation for 25 years. Over time Diane has enjoyed good and weathered bad economic times, and she has hired and, unfortunately, had to fire dozens of employees. Diane pays taxes and has a savings account. She pays wages to her employees from the money her grocery store brings in, and she buys goods and services for herself and her family from the profits her store makes. Like most people, Diane is worried that the government spends too much money on frivolous programs and not enough on those that matter.

Diane read in the paper about the latest measurement for the GDP. While she recognizes that this is an important economic measure, Diane doesn't understand how the GDP relates to her life and her business. Moreover, she knows a number of businesspeople like her who are similarly confused. One of her employees, who works part time while attending college, suggested that she speak with Economic Consultants about conducting a community workshop to explain what the GDP is and what it measures. Diane contacted Economic Consultants, and the firm agreed to conduct this workshop as a service to the community. Prepare a presentation for this community workshop that addresses the following issues:

**1.** What is the gross domestic product and what does it measure? What components of the economy are included? What components of the economy aren't reflected in the GDP?

**2.** How does the government measure GDP? How do the actions of someone like Diane affect the GDP?

**3.** What is the current measure of GDP, and generally, what does it say about the health of the U.S. economy? What resources are available for learning more about the GDP?

You may find the following resources helpful as you prepare this presentation for the community workshop:

- **Bureau of Economic Analysis** (http://www.bea.doc.gov/)—The Bureau of Economic Analysis publishes current GDP measurements along with analysis and commentary.
- **The Dismal Scientist** (http://www.dismal.com/)—The Dismal Scientist is an economic news and analysis service, part of which is devoted to the GDP (http://www.dismal.com/economy/gdp.stm).

# PRACTICE TEST

1. In the circular flow of money,
   a. households supply resources to the product market.
   b. households supply money for goods and services to the product market.
   c. firms supply goods and services to the product market.
   d. households are not viewed as suppliers.
   e. the resource market supplies resources to firms for production.

2. The circular flow of GDP shows the movement of _____ from firms to households.
   a. income
   b. revenue
   c. resources
   d. goods and services
   e. wealth

3. Under the expenditure approach to calculating GDP,
   a. personal consumption expenditures are excluded from the calculation to avoid double counting.
   b. expenditures for all goods and services (intermediate and final) are added together.
   c. exports are not included in the final total.
   d. only intermediate goods are included in the final total.
   e. expenditures on all final goods and services are added together.

4. All of the following are included in the calculation of GDP under the expenditure approach, except one. Which one?
   a. Gross private domestic investment
   b. Net exports
   c. Services
   d. Net interest
   e. Government purchases

5. Changes in inventories would be included in which of the following expenditure categories?
   a. Gross private domestic investment
   b. Net exports
   c. Government purchases
   d. Personal consumption on durable goods
   e. Personal consumption on nondurable goods

6. National income includes all but which of the following components?
   a. Employee compensation
   b. Corporate profits
   c. Gross private domestic investment
   d. Rental income
   e. Net interest

7. Which of the following income payments for the United States represents the smallest proportion of national income?
   a. Net interest
   b. Employee compensation
   c. Proprietors' income
   d. Corporate profit
   e. Rental income

8. The gross national product for Armenia will exceed the gross domestic product for Armenia when
   a. payments to Armenians in other countries exceed payments to foreigners residing in Armenia.
   b. payments to foreigners residing in Armenia exceed payments to Armenians in other countries.
   c. capital depreciation is positive.
   d. capital depreciation is less than indirect business taxes.
   e. capital depreciation exceeds indirect business taxes.

9. National income can be calculated in which of the following ways?
   a. GDP minus indirect business taxes
   b. GNP plus capital depreciation
   c. GNP minus capital depreciation minus indirect business taxes
   d. Personal consumption expenditures plus gross private domestic investment, government purchases, and net exports
   e. Personal income minus taxes and transfers

10. GDP calculations have been criticized for omitting all of the following except one. Which one?
    a. The value of housework
    b. The value of leisure
    c. The level of corporate profits
    d. The level of activity in the underground economy
    e. The costs of damage to the environment

# CHAPTER 6
## CONSUMPTION AND INVESTMENT

If we could put a satellite in space to observe every person's activity in the marketplace, we would be watching millions of people deciding what kinds of goods to consume. At the same time, we would be watching millions of other people deciding what consumption goods to produce. We would also see that these people make these consumption-spending and consumption-production decisions *simultaneously and independently of each other.*

The fact that producers and consumers make their production and consumption decisions simultaneously and independently of each other may explain why an economy slides into recession or rockets to prosperity. Think about it. How can producers know that what they produce for consumption is what consumers want to consume? And if they're off the mark, what happens? For example, suppose Beth Dollins, Dollins's CEO, decides to produce 1 million pairs of cross-training shoes, but when these shoes reach the market, consumers decide to buy only 600,000 pairs. Suppose, at the same time, that Paola Flygare, producer of the Flygare fiberglass bass boat, produces 8,000 boats only to discover later that consumers take fewer than 3,000 off the market. And suppose that their experiences are common among producers. That is, *consumers just aren't buying enough of everything produced.* The most plausible consequence in this scenario is a cutback in overall production (a decrease in real GDP) and an increase in the economy's unemployment.

Let's now change the scenario. Suppose that Beth Dollins's decision to produce 1 million pairs of cross-training shoes is still off base, but this time it's because consumers want to buy more pairs of shoes than Dollins produced. Suppose also that Paola Flygare's 8,000 bass boats are substantially fewer than the number of boats consumers want. And to complete the picture, let's suppose other producers discover that they, too, underproduced for the market.

**THIS CHAPTER INTRODUCES YOU TO THE ECONOMIC PRINCIPLES ASSOCIATED WITH:**

- KEYNES'S ABSOLUTE INCOME HYPOTHESIS
- DUESENBERRY'S RELATIVE INCOME HYPOTHESIS
- FRIEDMAN'S PERMANENT INCOME HYPOTHESIS
- MODIGLIANI'S LIFE-CYCLE HYPOTHESIS
- THE MARGINAL PROPENSITY TO CONSUME
- THE MARGINAL PROPENSITY TO SAVE
- AUTONOMOUS INVESTMENT

Now the problem is reversed: *Producers are not producing as much as people want to consume.* The most plausible consequence of this scenario is greater overall production (an increase in real GDP) and a decrease in the economy's unemployment.

The uncomplicated fact that production and consumption decisions are made simultaneously and independently of each other is critically important in understanding the forces that determine the level of real GDP.

## WHAT DETERMINES CONSUMPTION SPENDING?

How do people choose their level of consumption spending? What factors are involved in their decisions to increase or decrease the amount of goods and services they consume? Are we just creatures of habit? Or impulse?

If you had to guess the single most important factor influencing a person's consumption spending, you would probably be right on the first try. It's the level of a person's disposable income. (For now, let's assume no government spending or taxes, so that a person's income is the same as his or her disposable income.) You would also be right to suppose that rich people consume more than poor people because rich people have more income. You don't have to be a Nobel laureate in economics to figure that out! Economists refer to this simple, but powerful, relationship between consumption and income as the **consumption function.** It is written as

$$C = f(Y),$$

where $C$ represents consumption and $Y$ represents income. It means that consumption is a function of income, or in other words, that the amount of consumption depends on the amount of income.

Let's use real numbers to illustrate this relationship. Suppose Brenda Nielsen, a manager at Record Swap, enjoys a $1,000 raise in salary. What would happen to her consumption? Does it increase by the $1,000? Or by less? And if by less, by how much less? A number of hypotheses have been offered to explain how changes in an individual's income and, taken collectively, changes in national income affect individual and national consumption.

### Keynes's Absolute Income Hypothesis

John Maynard Keynes, whose 1936 book *The General Theory of Employment, Interest and Money* became the bedrock upon which Keynesian economics was built, advanced the hypothesis that although people who earn high incomes spend more on consumption than people who earn less, they are less inclined to spend as much *out of a given increase in income* than are those earning less. For example, Madonna's consumption spending is greater than Brenda's. Yet, if both were given $1,000, Madonna would likely spend less of the $1,000 on consumption than Brenda.

Why? Keynes believed that consumption behavior reflects a psychological law that links changes in our consumption spending to the absolute levels of our income. He explains:

> The fundamental psychological law, upon which we are entitled to depend with great confidence both *a priori* from our knowledge of human nature and from the detailed facts of experience, is that men are disposed, as a rule and on the average, to increase their consumption as their income increases, but not by as much as their increase in their income. . . . [A] higher absolute level of income will tend, as a rule, to widen the gap between income and consumption. For the satisfaction of the immediate primary needs of a man and his family is usually a

**CHECK YOUR UNDERSTANDING**

What is the principal factor determining the level of a person's consumption spending?

**Consumption function**
The relationship between consumption and income.

The Census Bureau (http://www.census.gov/hhes/www/income.html), the Bureau of Economic Analysis (http://www.bea.doc.gov/bea/dn/pitbl.htm), and the Bureau of Labor Statistics (http://stats.bls.gov/eag/eag.map.htm) publish income data for the United States.

stronger motive than the motives towards accumulation, which only acquire effective sway when the margin of comfort has been attained.

**Absolute income hypothesis**
As national income increases, consumption spending increases, but by diminishing amounts. That is, as national income increases, the MPC decreases.

Does this **absolute income hypothesis** seem reasonable to you? Imagine a millionaire receiving a gift of $500. It's unlikely that you would find him running off to buy more food, clothing, or shelter. He would probably just add the $500 to his savings. Why? In Keynes's view, the millionaire's "margin of comfort" is already provided, and the "stronger motive" guiding his behavior, then, becomes "accumulation."

But suppose the $500 were given to an inner-city welfare recipient. What do you suppose he would do? Consult his broker? Do you think he would save a penny? Wouldn't the "immediate primary needs of [him] and his family"—as Keynes aptly put it—lead straight to consumption?

**AN INDIVIDUAL'S MARGINAL PROPENSITY TO CONSUME** Let's pursue Keynes's idea further. Keynes believed that if Brenda's income were increased by increments, say, of $1,000—getting richer with every $1,000 added—the amount she would spend on consumption *out of each additional $1,000* would decrease.

Exhibit 1 illustrates this point.

Look what happens to Brenda's level of consumption as her income increases in increments of $1,000 from $0 to $5,000. Her consumption increases as well, but

## EXHIBIT 1

### THE INDIVIDUAL'S MARGINAL PROPENSITY TO CONSUME

The marginal propensity to consume measures the slope of the consumption function. It is the ratio of the change in consumption to the change in income. When income increases by $1,000—from $1,000 to $2,000—the change in consumption is $2,200 − $1,400 = $800. MPC is ($2,200 − $1,400)/($2,000 − $1,000) = 0.80. Note how consumption spending increases by diminishing amounts as the income level increases, tracing out the curvature of the consumption curve, C.

#### THE MARGINAL PROPENSITY TO CONSUME

| TOTAL INCOME (Y) | CHANGE IN INCOME | CONSUMPTION (C) | CHANGE IN CONSUMPTION | MARGINAL PROPENSITY TO CONSUME (MPC) |
|---|---|---|---|---|
| 0 | | $ 500 | | |
| $1,000 | $1,000 | 1,400 | $900 | 0.90 |
| 2,000 | 1,000 | 2,200 | 800 | 0.80 |
| 3,000 | 1,000 | 2,900 | 700 | 0.70 |
| 4,000 | 1,000 | 3,500 | 600 | 0.60 |
| 5,000 | 1,000 | 4,000 | 500 | 0.50 |

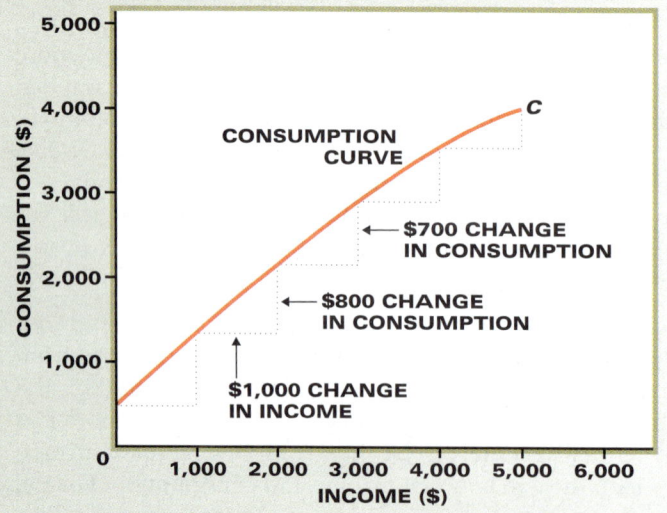

note the incremental changes. The first $1,000 addition to income—raising income from $0 to $1,000—induces a change in consumption from $500 to $1,400, or by $900. Keynes defines the change in consumption induced by a change in income as the **marginal propensity to consume (MPC).**

$$MPC = \frac{\text{change in } C}{\text{change in } Y}$$

**Marginal propensity to consume (MPC)**
The ratio of the change in consumption spending to a given change in income.

The marginal propensity to consume, *MPC*, is a quantifiable and behavioral relationship. It measures our inclination, Keynes calls it our propensity, to consume *specific* amounts out of *specific* income changes.

At the income level of $1,000, the marginal propensity to consume is ($1,400 − $500)/($1,000 − $0) = 0.90.

What happens to consumption when the second $1,000 of income is added? Consumption increases from $1,400 to $2,200, or $800. Therefore, at $Y = $2,000, Brenda's *MPC* is ($2,200 − $1,400)/($2,000 − $1,000) = 0.80. Brenda increases consumption, but by less than she did before. Her *MPC* falls from 0.90 to 0.80.

Note what's going on. As more units of $1,000 are added to Brenda's income, her total consumption continues to increase, but each time by lesser amounts. At $Y = $3,000, $C = $2,900 and the corresponding *MPC* = 0.70. At $Y = $4,000, $C = $3,500 and *MPC* = 0.60, and so on. MPC *falls as the absolute level of income increases.*

**THE NATION'S MARGINAL PROPENSITY TO CONSUME** To Keynes, national economies behave like individuals. Just as Brenda's *MPC* depends upon the level of her income, so does a nation's *MPC* depend upon its level of national income. Exhibit 2 describes Keynes's view of the nation's consumption behavior.

The nation has its own *MPC*. When national income increases from $300 billion to $400 billion, national consumption increases by $360 − $300 = $60 billion. At $Y = $400 billion, *MPC* = 0.60. Look at the *MPC* column. As the absolute level of national income increases, the nation's *MPC* decreases.

Look at the graph. Note the step increases along the consumption curve, *C*. They become increasingly smaller as national income increases; the curve flattens out to almost no increase at all at high levels of national income.

The nation's consumption curve reflects Keynes's *absolute* income hypothesis. It shows that the nation's *MPC* depends upon the *absolute* level of national income. Does this make sense? Do you find Keynes's view of consumption spending behavior convincing?

If your intuition tells you Keynes was right, you would be dead wrong! Five years after Keynes's *The General Theory of Employment, Interest and Money* appeared, Simon Kuznets published his *National Income and Its Composition*, which pioneered analysis of national income data. (He won the Nobel Prize in economics in 1971 for his work.) Kuznets's findings—as well as the mountains of empirical research that followed— showed that, in spite of intuition, *a nation's* MPC *tends to remain fairly constant regardless of the absolute level of national income.* Where did Keynes go wrong?

Review an autobiography of Simon Kuznets (http://www.nobel.se/economics/laureates/1971/index.html).

## Duesenberry's Relative Income Hypothesis

James Duesenberry offered an alternative income hypothesis. Every economy, whatever its level of national income, includes people earning different incomes. Knowing someone's absolute income tells us little about that person's income status. For example, Brenda earning $20,000 a year would be considered a low-income person if others in the economy earned more, say $40,000 and $80,000. On the other hand,

## EXHIBIT 2

### THE NATION'S MARGINAL PROPENSITY TO CONSUME

Note the similarity between the individual's marginal propensity to consume of Exhibit 1 and the nation's. When the national income increases, national consumption increases as well, but by diminishing amounts. *MPC* decreases from 0.90 to 0.50 as national income increases from $0 to $500 billion, tracing out the upward-sloping consumption curve, *C*.

**THE NATION'S MARGINAL PROPENSITY TO CONSUME ($ BILLIONS)**

| NATIONAL INCOME (Y) | CHANGE IN NATIONAL INCOME | CONSUMPTION (C) | CHANGE IN CONSUMPTION | MARGINAL PROPENSITY TO CONSUME (MPC) |
|---|---|---|---|---|
| $ 0 |  | $ 60 |  |  |
| 100 | $100 | 150 | $90 | 0.90 |
| 200 | 100 | 230 | 80 | 0.80 |
| 300 | 100 | 300 | 70 | 0.70 |
| 400 | 100 | 360 | 60 | 0.60 |
| 500 | 100 | 410 | 50 | 0.50 |

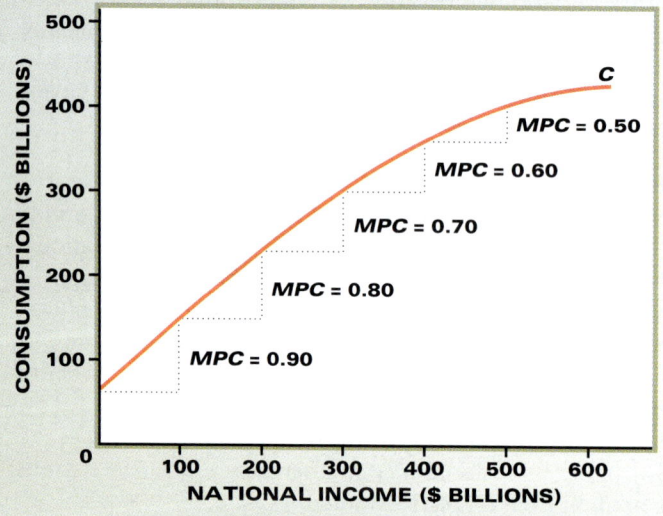

that same $20,000 makes her a high-income person if others in the economy earn less, say, $5,000 and $10,000.

If Brenda's income doubled to $40,000, but at the same time everybody else's income also doubled—say, from $40,000 to $80,000 and from $80,000 to $160,000—then Brenda, at $40,000 income, would still be regarded as low income.

The distinction between Brenda's relative income (that is, income relative to other incomes) and her absolute income level provided Duesenberry with an alternative view of the consumption function. It explains why the marginal propensity to consume in the economy does not decline as national income increases—as Keynes believed it does—but instead remains constant.

According to Duesenberry, *consumption spending is rooted in status*. High-income people not only consume more goods and services than others, but also set consumption standards for everybody else. They own the most comfortable homes, drive the most expensive cars, enjoy the newest consumer technologies, and read *Architectural Digest* without feeling deprived.

Everybody else takes their cues from the rich. The middle-income people try to stay within reach. Low-income people struggle to keep their consumption within

# HISTORICAL PERSPECTIVE

## JOHN MAYNARD KEYNES: A NEW MACROECONOMICS

Although he was celebrated for his contributions to economic theory, John Maynard Keynes's creative energies were focused primarily on solving real-world issues. He was interested in changing the world, not simply in understanding it.

In the 1930s the economic world Keynes observed was in turmoil. The reality of a persisting and deepening economic depression seemed to contradict everything economists knew about how an economy works. The conventional wisdom of classical economics argued that depression was only a short-run, temporary departure from full-employment equilibrium and that in the long run the economy would return to it. Keynes's response to this conventional wisdom was that "in the long run, we're all dead."

But Keynes really didn't see the issue—what to do about the depression—as a matter of patience. He was convinced that the economy could not correct itself even in the very long run and explained his reasoning in *The General Theory of Employment, Interest and Money* (1936). *The General Theory* offered an entirely new set of ideas about macroeconomics that, almost instantaneously, became a new school of economic thought. There was ready acceptance of his ideas among the bright young economists in Britain and in the United States, in part because of the collapse of confidence in classical economics during the depression but also because Keynes was already Britain's preeminent economist. Had he proposed that the world was flat, many of his fellow economists would probably have given him the benefit of the doubt and flattened their globes.

From the very beginning, Keynes was an intellectual phenomenon. Born and raised in Cambridge (his father, Neville, was an economics pro-

JOHN MAYNARD KEYNES CHANGED THE WAY WE THINK ABOUT THE WORLD OF ECONOMICS.

fessor) and schooled at Eton, he returned to Cambridge to do his undergraduate studies at King's College in mathematics and philosophy (which resulted in a highly esteemed book on the theory of probability). His mentor, Alfred Marshall, persuaded him to switch to economics.

Although a rising star at Cambridge, Keynes did not limit himself to academic research. The real world was his natural venue. He divided his time between London and Cambridge, working in London at the Treasury during the week and lecturing at Cambridge on weekends. Quickly establishing a formidable reputation at the Treasury, he became a major participant in international diplomacy, a task he initially relished but later came to dislike. He was the chief economic counsel to the British delegation at Versailles after World War I and there warned against a peace treaty that would impose harsh retribution on defeated Germany, believing that such a policy would ensure the collapse of the European economy. His two-volume work *A Treatise on Money* (1930) established him as the heir apparent to Marshall. During all this time, Keynes was editor of *The Economic Journal*, the premier scholarly research journal in Britain (and, arguably, the world). In 1944, as the principal architect of the Bretton Woods agreement, he once again tried to prepare Europe and the United States for the difficult task of reconstructing a stable world economy in the aftermath of war.

Keynes also put his financial wizardry to work in stock speculations, which he made in the early morning by phone while still in bed, and which made him a millionaire. While bursar of King's College, he speculated on the college's behalf, increasing its endowment tenfold.

Although new ideas have come to challenge Keynesian economics, many Keynesians still revere him

*continued on next page*

as Shakespeare's Anthony did Caesar: "Here was a Caesar! When comes such another?"

**MORE ON THE NET**

For a sample of Keynes's writing, review his May 1932 *Atlantic Monthly* article, "The World's Economic Outlook" (http://www.theatlantic.com/unbound/flashbks/budget/keynesf.htm), and his text *The Economic Consequences of Peace* (http://socserv2.mcmaster.ca/~econ/ugcm/3ll3/keynes/peace.htm).

**CHECK YOUR UNDERSTANDING**

What explains the constant *MPC*?

**Relative income hypothesis**
As national income increases, consumption spending increases as well, always by the same amount. That is, as national income increases, *MPC* remains constant.

**Permanent income hypothesis**
A person's consumption spending is related to his or her permanent income.

**Life-cycle hypothesis**
Typically, a person's *MPC* is relatively high during young adulthood, decreases during the middle-age years, and increases when the person is near or in retirement.

**Permanent income**
Permanent income is the regular income a person expects to earn annually. It may differ by some unexpected gain or loss from the actual income earned.

**Transitory income**
The unexpected gain or loss of income that a person experiences. It is the difference between a person's regular and actual income in any year.

sight of middle-income consumption. For example, if Brenda's *MPC* is 0.80 at an income of $20,000, it remains 0.80 even if her income doubles to $40,000 *as long as her relative income position remains unchanged*. If everybody's income doubles so that their relative income positions remain unchanged, then everybody's *MPC* remains unchanged. That's how Duesenberry explains why, contrary to what Keynes thought, the nation's *MPC* is constant while national income increases.

The logic is compelling and is supported by historical data as well. Keynes's consumption function of Exhibit 2 is modified in Exhibit 3 to reflect Duesenberry's **relative income hypothesis.**

As national income increases by increments of $100 billion, the economy's consumption spending increases by increments of $80 billion. That is, the marginal propensity to consume, *MPC*, is constant at 0.80.

Of course, low-income people have higher incomes when national income is $500 billion than when it is $200 billion. And because they have higher incomes, they spend more on consumption. But because their relative income has not changed—everyone, rich and poor, is richer—their *MPC*, and the economy's, remain unchanged.

Notice the steplike increases in consumption in Exhibit 3. Because *MPC* = 0.80, every dollar increase in income generates an $0.80 increase in consumption—the steps are the same height—so that the consumption curve, *C*, is a straight line.

Economists have continued to study the consumption function, providing additional insights into our consumption behavior. The two most influential are Milton Friedman's **permanent income hypothesis** and Franco Modigliani's **life-cycle hypothesis.**

## Friedman's Permanent Income Hypothesis

Milton Friedman, who won the Nobel Prize in economics in 1976, believes that people distinguish between their regular income and the income they may happen to make (or lose) in any one year. He refers to regular income as **permanent income,** and to the unanticipated income that adds to (or subtracts from) the permanent income as **transitory income.**

Why make these distinctions? Because, according to Friedman, how much we spend on consumption depends strictly on our permanent income.

Why? Why doesn't transitory income contribute to our consumption spending? Because people don't usually go about changing lifestyles when they suffer a temporary loss of income or even when they enjoy a temporary gain. Consumption spending is generally tied to long-run earning capacity.

Imagine two people, Natasha Rubel and Peter Holsapple, each earning $50,000 in 1998. But suppose Natasha, a self-employed artist who conducts art-therapy classes for teachers and counselors, had a bad year. A broken leg put her out of work for three months, so that her 1998 income was $15,000 less than the $65,000 she typically earns.

## THE MARGINAL PROPENSITY TO CONSUME REMAINS CONSTANT

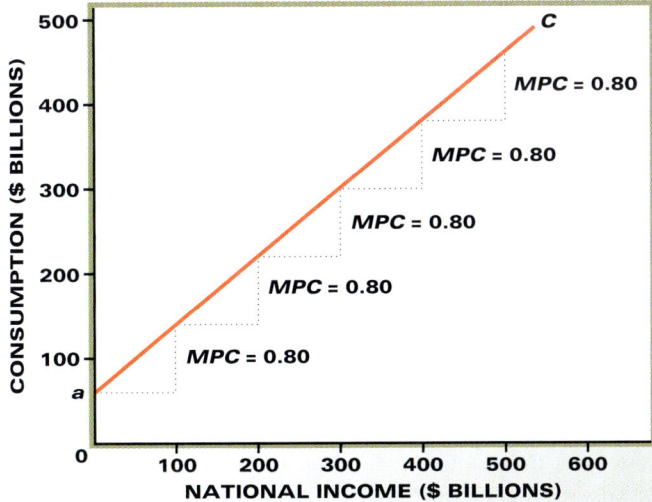

With every $100 billion increase in national income, the nation's consumption spending increases by $80 billion, tracing out a straight-line consumption curve, $C$. The $MPC = 0.80$ at every level of national income.

What would Natasha's 1998 consumption look like? The permanent income hypothesis suggests that, assuming $MPC = 0.80$, Natasha's consumption would be $0.80 \times \$65,000 = \$52,000$. The effect of her negative $15,000 transitory income shows up as reduced saving. Her saving in 1998 becomes $50,000 - \$52,000 = -\$2,000$. Her negative transitory income creates, then, negative saving, or dissaving. The important point is that she still thinks of herself as a $65,000 person and consumes like one.

What about Peter Holsapple? He's a high school teacher who typically earns $35,000. But in 1998 he received a $15,000 teaching award. Would this $15,000 transitory income affect his $35,000 lifestyle? Not likely. Assuming his $MPC = 0.80$, his 1998 consumption, fixed by his permanent income, is $0.80 \times \$35,000 = \$28,000$. The effect of the $15,000 positive transitory income shows up as saving, which in 1998 becomes $50,000 - \$28,000 = \$22,000$.

Friedman's point is simple. To appreciate what influences consumption spending, we must distinguish between transitory and permanent income.

Review an autobiography of Milton Friedman (http://www.nobel.se/economics/laureates/1976/index.html).

Review an autobiography of Franco Modigliani (http://www.nobel.se/economics/laureates/1985/index.html).

## Modigliani's Life-Cycle Hypothesis

Franco Modigliani of MIT, who won the Nobel Prize in economics in 1985, makes his own observation about our consumption behavior. He identifies three consumption phases—young adult, middle age, and near or in retirement—in a person's life cycle. Each specific phase has its specific *MPC*.

The *MPC* for young adults is relatively high. They are busy building families and careers. They buy first homes, first new automobiles, stocks of household durables, sets of clothing for growing children, and streams of services. These items tend to eat quickly into their modest incomes.

When they become middle-aged, enjoying their highest and most rapidly growing incomes, their consumption spending also increases, but modestly, at least compared to earlier years. After all, their homes are virtually mortgage-free, their car payments not nearly so demanding, their children finally graduating from college, and the basics of life already taken care of. They tend to consume more because they earn more, but the ratio of changes in consumption to changes in income tends to fall. That is, their *MPC* falls.

In the third phase, nearing or in retirement, their *MPC* tends to rise. Why? Their incomes don't grow very much, and in many cases, actually decline. But what about their consumption? They become more careful about their spending, but habits are hard to break. People don't change their lifestyles that much.

Modigliani explains why differing *MPCs* over a person's life cycle are still consistent with the observed stability in our national *MPC*. As long as birth and death rates are relatively stable, the percentage of population passing through these three consumption phases at any time remains stable as well.

## Autonomous Consumption Spending

The idea that consumption depends primarily on the level of income is so consistent with our experience that very few people have trouble making the connection. But consumption based on income is not the whole story. Look again at Exhibit 3.

When $Y = 0$, $C = \$60$ billion. Some consumption is autonomous, that is, independent of the level of income. Economists call it **autonomous consumption.**

**Autonomous consumption** Consumption spending that is independent of the level of income.

Why autonomous? Because some consumption spending is simply unavoidable. The spending takes place regardless of the level of income. For example, we might spend less on food, clothing, and shelter when our incomes fall, but there are limits to how deeply we can cut into our consumption of these basics. At some point, we simply cannot consume less and still survive. We make some minimum consumption spending even if we have to borrow, use our savings, or sell off part of our assets. Put simply: If we have no other means of putting food on the table, we may sometimes be forced to sell the table! That explains why in the economy of Exhibit 3, when income is 0, autonomous consumption is positive. The consumption curve, *C*, in Exhibit 3 begins at *a*, above the origin on the vertical axis, at $60 billion.

## Shifts in the Consumption Curve

Look at the consumption curve, *C*, in Exhibit 4. A change in national income from, say, $200 billion to $300 billion induces a change of $80 billion in consumption—from $220 billion to $300 billion. We see this change in consumption as a movement *along* the consumption curve *C*.

But consumption spending can change even when the level of national income remains unchanged. These changes in consumption are caused by shifts in the consumption curve itself. What factors shift the consumption curve in Exhibit 4 upward from *C* to *C'*?

**REAL ASSET AND MONEY HOLDINGS** Suppose Sara Cook wins the $12 million Florida state lottery. That's everyone's fantasy! And suppose she decides to keep her $50,000 job at Disney World. It's hard to believe that her lottery winnings would not *eventually* affect her consumption spending. The probability is high that even though she continued to work at her $50,000 job, she would end up consuming more goods and services than before.

Or suppose George Paaswell, who rents a studio apartment in midtown Manhattan, inherits a mortgage-free house on Park Avenue. That's not exactly $12 million, but to George, it's a real asset of considerable value. Wouldn't you think an inheritance like that would affect his consumption spending?

Suppose people's real assets and money holdings in the economy increase. National consumption spending should increase as well. These increases are shown in Exhibit 4 as an upward shift in the consumption curve from $C$ to $C'$. A decrease in the nation's real assets or money holdings would have the opposite effect, shifting the curve from $C$ to $C''$.

**CHECK YOUR UNDERSTANDING**
What happens to the consumption curve when people's real asset holdings increase?

**EXPECTATIONS OF PRICE CHANGES** People are always anticipating the future. Suppose, for some reason, they expect inflation to increase from 3 to 12 percent in one year and to continue in double digits for the following six years. Wouldn't it be smart for people, *even though they don't expect their income to change*, to increase the level of their consumption spending now, before the expected inflation hits? Such an increase shifts the consumption curve from $C$ to $C'$.

**CREDIT AND INTEREST RATES** People's consumption of relatively costly durables, such as automobiles, personal computers, and major kitchen appliances, is typically financed by interest-carrying credit. For many, interest payments on these items make up a significant part of their monthly expenditures. If, then, credit is made more available or if the credit terms are made more attractive, say, by a cut in the interest rate, won't people increase their consumption spending even if their incomes haven't changed? The consumption curve would shift upward from $C$ to $C'$.

**TAXATION** We are all obligated to pay taxes. But how much? Suppose the government decides to cut the income tax. Then imagine Meg Weinbaum's delight when she discovers more dollars in her pay envelope at the end of the week, even though her salary remains unchanged. What do you suppose she would do with the extra money? Spend some of it, wouldn't she? She and many millions more would shift the consumption curve from $C$ to $C'$. If their pay envelopes were lighter because of increased taxes, the consumption curve would shift from $C$ to $C''$.

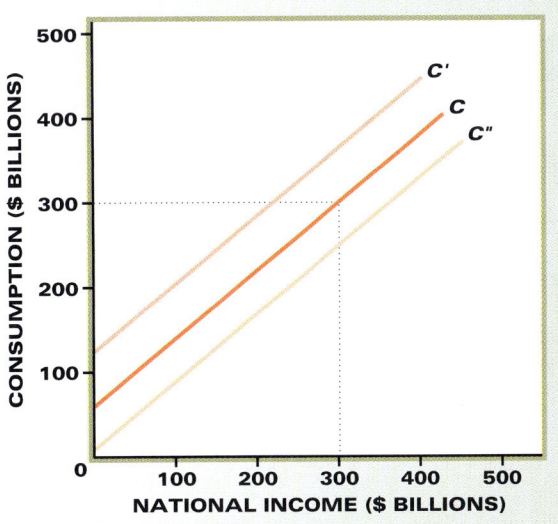

**SHIFTS IN THE CONSUMPTION CURVE**

Shifts in the consumption curve are distinguished from movements along the curve. The shifts are unrelated to changes in national income. Among the principal factors causing the shifts in the consumption curve are changes in the economy's asset and money holdings, in people's expectations of price changes, in interest rates, and in taxation. Anything that causes autonomous consumption to change will shift the consumption curve.

**EXHIBIT 4**

# THEORETICAL PERSPECTIVE

## THE LONG AND SHORT OF IT: THE CONSUMPTION FUNCTION IN THE UNITED STATES

Panel *a* of the figure on the next page plots national income and consumption data for the United States for selected years during the period 1970–91. The data trace out a straight-line consumption curve, *which appears to run through the origin.* The curve shows average propensities to consume—that is, $C/Y$, falling within the range 0.697 and 0.768.

This data-constructed consumption function (see table) seems to contradict the consumption function depicted in the text—such as Exhibit 3—which shows the consumption curve intercepting the vertical axis above the origin.

Which function is correct? The answer is both! The seeming contradiction between the two is resolved by noting that the straight-line-through-the-origin consumption function is a long-run function, while the intercept-above-the-origin function represents a short-run consumption function.

Panel *b* shows how the two functions relate. Look at the short-run consumption curve, $C$. It depicts the relationship between national income and consumption *for the short-run period of 1970.* For example, the actual levels of national income and consumption for 1970, as shown in the accompanying table, are $928 billion and $646.5 billion. Now suppose that in 1970 national income was not $928 billion but, say, $1,439.2 billion. At that level of national income, the short-run consumption function for 1970 shows that consumption would have been at point *b*—$825 billion. One more example: If national income in 1970 had been $2,000 billion, consumption in 1970 would have been $980 billion, point *a*.

But suppose that after five years of continuing economic growth, people's holdings of wealth and their permanent income increase, shifting the short-run consumption function from $C$ to $C'$. In 1975, then, actual levels of national income and consumption are $1,439.2 billion and $1,024.9 billion, respectively. Compare this actual $1,024.9 billion to the $825 billion plotted in the short-run consumption curve, $C$, for 1970. *The difference is explained in the shifts in short-run consumption curves that take place over the long run,* in this case, the five years from 1970 to 1975. In 1975, people consume $1,024.9 billion, not $825 billion, because they are wealthier than they were in 1970.

Panel *b* shows a series of short-run consumption curves—one for each year of actual data shown in the accompanying table—that identify actual points on the short-run curves. The long-run consumption function of panel *a*, then, connects the points of the series of short-run consumption functions.

|  | NATIONAL INCOME ($ BILLIONS) | PRIVATE CONSUMPTION ($ BILLIONS) | C/Y |
|---|---|---|---|
| 1991 | $5,062.8 | $3,889.1 | 76.8% |
| 1990 | 4,929.8 | 3,742.6 | 75.9 |
| 1989 | 4,673.7 | 3,517.9 | 75.3 |
| 1988 | 4,374.3 | 3,296.1 | 75.4 |
| 1985 | 3,599.1 | 2,667.4 | 74.1 |
| 1980 | 2,430.2 | 1,748.1 | 71.9 |
| 1975 | 1,439.2 | 1,024.9 | 71.5 |
| 1970 | 928.0 | 646.5 | 69.7 |

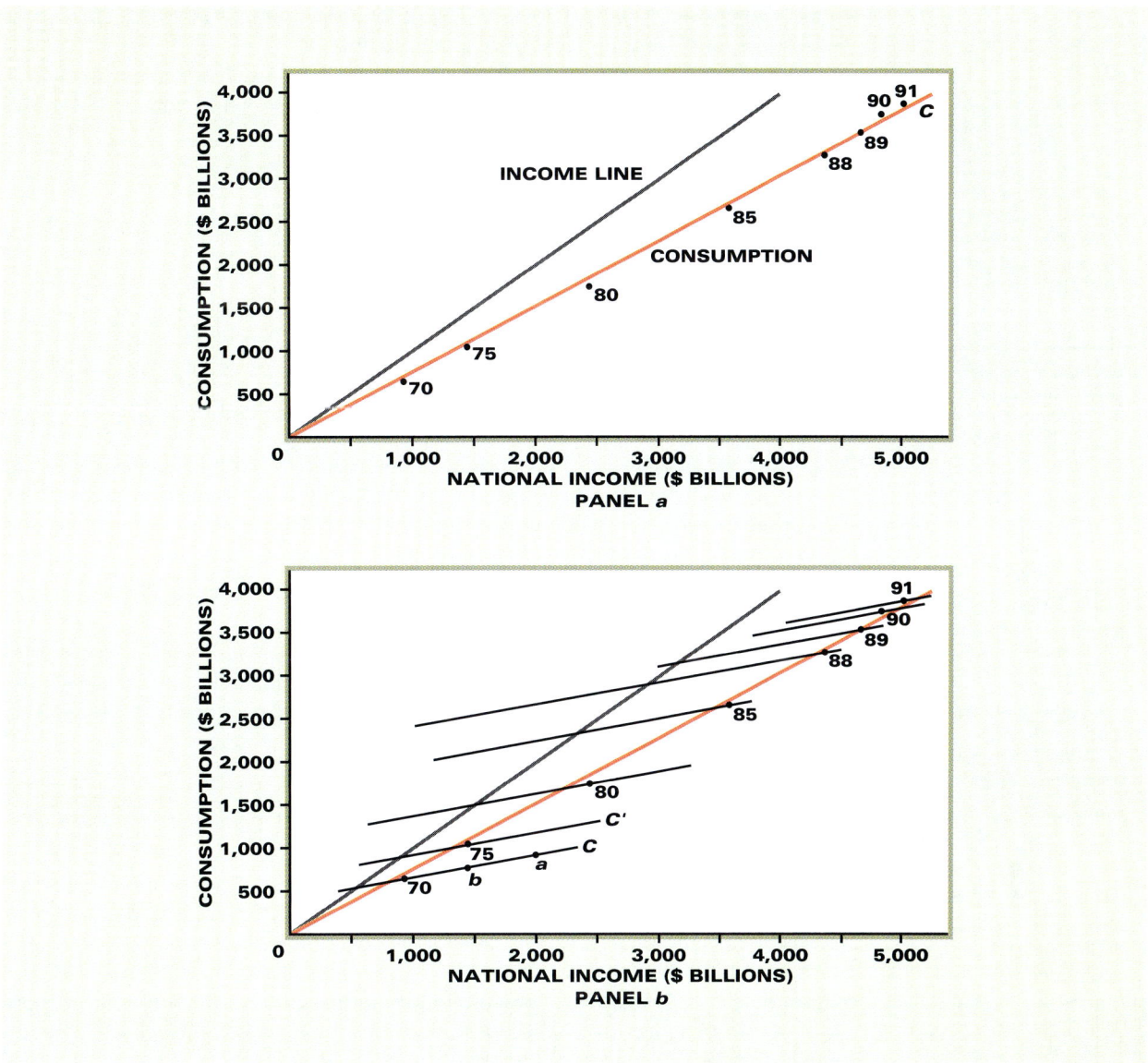

## THE CONSUMPTION EQUATION

As you see, there are two key factors influencing the character of our consumption spending. Keynes's conception of the marginal propensity to consume, and the insightful modifications to the consumption function that followed—by Duesenberry, Friedman, and Modigliani—show that our level of consumption spending is primarily determined by our level of income. Economists refer to this consumption as *induced* consumption, meaning induced by the level of income. A second factor contributing to consumption spending is autonomous consumption.

Adding autonomous consumption to consumption spending induced by income generates a specific form of the consumption function:

$$C = a + bY,$$

One estimate of future consumption is the consumer confidence index (http://www.conference-board.org/products/frames.cfm?main=c-consumer.cfm). Each month, about 5,000 households respond to questions about expectations for their jobs, their incomes, their careers, and their spending plans. From these responses, economists can gauge whether consumption will likely increase or decrease over the next month.

**Saving**
That part of national income not spent on consumption.

**Marginal propensity to save (MPS)**
The change in saving induced by a change in income.

How are *MPC* and *MPS* related?

where *a* equals autonomous consumption spending, *b* equals marginal propensity to consume, and *Y* equals level of national income.

Let's see how the equation is used to determine how much consumption spending occurs when $Y = \$800$ billion, $MPC = 0.80$, and $a = \$60$ billion. We simply plug the appropriate values into the equation:

$$\begin{aligned} C &= a + bY \\ &= \$60 \text{ billion} + 0.8(\$800 \text{ billion}) \\ &= \$60 \text{ billion} + \$640 \text{ billion} \\ &= \$700 \text{ billion} \end{aligned}$$

When national income is $900 billion—assuming *MPC* and autonomous consumption remain unchanged—consumption spending is $780 billion.

## WHAT DETERMINES THE LEVEL OF SAVING?

People do two things with their income. They either spend it on consumption or they do *not* spend it on consumption. When people make a decision about one, they automatically make a decision about the other. After all, if you decide to spend 80 percent of your income, you have also made a decision *not* to spend 20 percent, haven't you? The income not spent on consumption is defined as **saving**:

$$S = Y - C$$

That's the economy's saving equation. Moreover, in the same way we derive the marginal propensity to consume, we derive the **marginal propensity to save (MPS)**. The *MPS* measures the change in saving generated by a change in income:

$$MPS = \frac{\text{change in } S}{\text{change in } Y}$$

If $MPC = 0.80$, then $MPS = 0.20$. Why? Because if our marginal propensity to consume is 80 percent of any additional income, then it stands to reason that our marginal propensity to save is the rest. That's the remaining 20 percent.

We could just as well have stated the relationship between *MPC* and *MPS* the other way. That is, if we save 20 percent of any additional income, then our propensity to consume the rest is 80 percent. Either way, the marginal propensities to consume and to save add up to 100 percent:

$$MPC + MPS = 1$$

The equation can be rewritten to focus on the derivation of *MPS*.

$$MPS = 1 - MPC$$

The table in Exhibit 5 shows the relationship between national saving, national consumption, *MPC*, and *MPS*.

As you see, in the unlikely income range of $Y = \$0$ to $Y = \$200$ billion, saving is actually negative. How can people consume more than their income allows? By running down their savings or other forms of accumulated wealth. In this same way, nations can end up with negative saving. As we already noted, economists refer to negative saving as dissaving.

Let's see how the equation is used to determine how much saving occurs when $Y = \$400$ billion and $C = \$380$ billion.

The Bureau of Economic Analysis publishes data on savings and investment (http://www.bea.doc.gov/bea/dn/nipatbls/nip5-1.htm).

## THE SAVING CURVE

**MARGINAL PROPENSITY TO SAVE ($ BILLIONS)**

| Y | CHANGE IN Y | C | S | MPC | MPS |
|---|---|---|---|---|---|
| $ 0 | | $ 60 | $-60 | | |
| 100 | $100 | 140 | -40 | 0.80 | 0.20 |
| 200 | 100 | 220 | -20 | 0.80 | 0.20 |
| 300 | 100 | 300 | 0 | 0.80 | 0.20 |
| 400 | 100 | 380 | 20 | 0.80 | 0.20 |
| 500 | 100 | 460 | 40 | 0.80 | 0.20 |

Saving is defined as income not spent on consumption. When $Y$ is less than $300 billion, $C$ is greater than $Y$, so that saving is negative, that is, the nation is dissaving. Saving is $0 at $300 billion, and then positive and increasing as national income increases beyond $300 billion. Panel *a* shows saving as the difference between the income and consumption curves. Panel *b* depicts the saving curve.

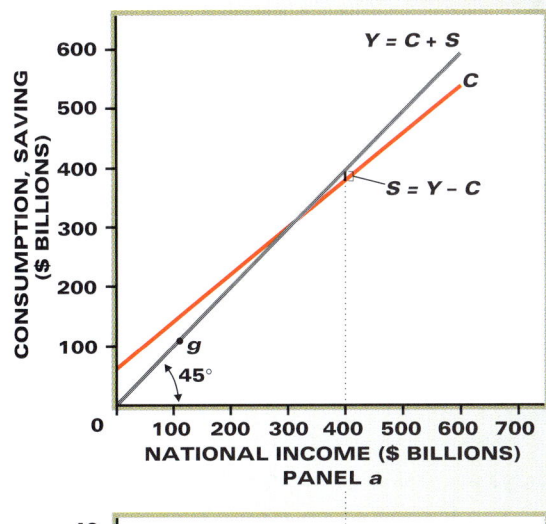

PANEL *a*

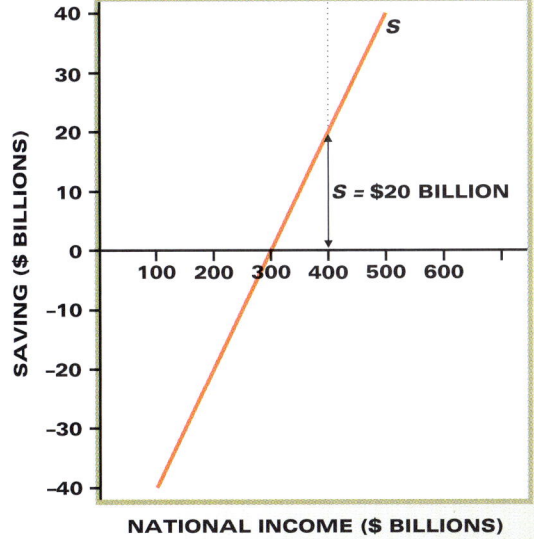

NATIONAL INCOME ($ BILLIONS)
PANEL *b*

# HISTORICAL PERSPECTIVE

## PROPENSITY TO SAVE

**Why do people save? Seems obvious, doesn't it? Or does it?** If you were living in late 19th-century England and attended Cambridge University, you would no doubt have heard Professor Alfred Marshall lecture on the subject. He eventually put his ideas on savings into his celebrated *Principles of Economics* (1891). To Marshall, ". . . family affection is the main motive for saving." He elaborates:

> That men labor chiefly for the sake of their families and not for themselves, is shown by the fact that they seldom spend, after they have retired from work, more than the income that comes in from their savings, preferring to leave their stored-up wealth intact for their families. . . ."

A man can have no stronger stimulus to energy and enterprise than the hope of rising in life, and leaving his family to start from a higher rung of the social ladder than that on which he began.

A lot of economic and social change has occurred since Marshall wrote these lines. Do we still think about family in the same way? Do Marshall's views on our propensity to save make sense in the 21st century?

Professor Christopher Carroll at The Johns Hopkins University has a different take on why we save. It is not to finance our future consumption or that of our heirs, he says, in his paper "Why Do The Rich Save So Much?"* Instead, the reason we save is to create a "flow of services (such as power or social status)." That is, Carroll believes we derive a value from saving as we would from buying any good. In this case, the goods we buy *having savings* are power and social status. It's an interesting and very un-Marshallian idea.

If you haven't thought about it, you will! In the near future, you will become an income earner and a saver and will have to make up your mind about how much of your income you will spend and save. You will eventually have an answer to the question: Why save?

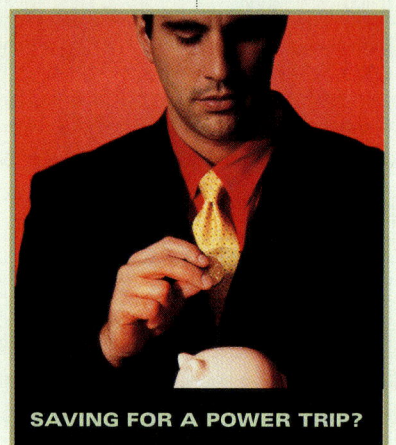

SAVING FOR A POWER TRIP?

*Carroll's article appears in *Does Atlas Shrug? The Economic Consequences of Taxing the Rich,* ed. Joel Shimrod (Cambridge, Mass.: Harvard University Press, 2000).

$$S = Y - C$$
$$= \$400 \text{ billion} - \$380 \text{ billion}$$
$$= \$ 20 \text{ billion}$$

When $Y = \$500$ billion and $C = \$460$ billion, then $S = \$40$ billion. Throughout the income range $Y = \$0$ to $Y = \$500$ billion in the table, saving increases by \$20 billion for every \$100 billion increase in national income. *MPS* is constant at 0.20.

In panel *a* of Exhibit 5, the 45° diagonal line serves as a point of reference. Since $Y = C + S$, every point on the 45° line equates the level of *Y* measured on the horizontal axis to the level of $C + S$ measured on the vertical axis. For example, *g* on the diagonal measures \$100 on both axes. The **45° line** measuring $Y = C + S$ is also called the *income curve*.

How do we derive the level of saving in panel *a*? Look, for example, at $Y = \$400$ billion. By using the equation $S = Y - C$, and substituting $(a + bY)$ for *C*, we derive

**45° line**
A line, drawn at a 45° angle, showing all points at which the distance to the horizontal axis equals the distance to the vertical axis.

$$S = Y - (a + bY)$$
$$= \$400 \text{ billion} - [\$60 \text{ billion} + (0.8 \times \$400 \text{ billion})]$$
$$= \$20 \text{ billion}.$$

Now look at $Y = \$400$ billion in panel $b$ of Exhibit 5. Panel $b$ is another way of looking at panel $a$, showing only the saving curve, which, as we have seen in panel $a$, is derived from subtracting consumption from national income. At $Y = \$400$ billion, the $20 billion difference between $Y$ and $C$, shown in panel $a$, shows up as $20 billion in the saving curve of panel $b$.

Because the absolute $(Y - C)$ gap in panel $a$ increases as the level of $Y$ increases, the saving curve in panel $b$ is upward sloping.

## THE INVESTMENT FUNCTION

At the same time that people are deciding how much of their income to spend on consumption and how much to save, producers in the economy are deciding how much to spend on new investment.

What determines how much they invest? Producers have to decide whether to replace used up or obsolete machinery, whether to expand production, whether to increase raw material or finished goods inventories, and even whether to build completely new facilities for entirely new products.

Each producer makes these investment decisions independently of others. For example, the giant Caterpillar, in Peoria, Illinois, may decide to expand its forklift production line at the same time that a small retail bookstore in Phoenix, Arizona, decides to move into larger space.

Sears may decide to open an outlet in Raleigh, North Carolina. The Artistic Headwear Company in Bangor, Maine, protecting itself from inadequate supplies, may decide to increase its raw material inventories.

These and thousands of other investment decisions made by producers make up the **intended investment** for the national economy. As we shall see, intended investment doesn't always end up realized.

**Intended investment**
Investment spending that producers intend to undertake.

## WHAT DETERMINES INVESTMENT?

Consider two different levels of national income: Does your intuition tell you that intended investment should be greater when national income is higher? That at $Y = \$800$ billion, producers would tend to invest more than at $Y = \$500$ billion?

Then think again. What if the economy at $Y = \$800$ billion is in a downturn phase of a business cycle; the year before, $Y$ was $900 billion. Why, then, in a year of declining national income, should producers consider buying more machinery or expanding production lines or building new factories? Why gear up for more production when consumers are not gearing up for more consumption? Shouldn't we expect intended investment, even at the higher level of national income, to be relatively weak under these bleak conditions?

**CHECK YOUR UNDERSTANDING**

Why isn't the level of income important in determining investment?

What about intended investment at $Y = \$500$ billion? Suppose the economy now is in the recovery phase of a business cycle. Wouldn't you expect to find producers busy purchasing new machinery, adding more production lines, and stocking up on inventories if the $500 billion is $100 billion more than the national income of the year before? After all, people with growing incomes are also people whose consumption spending is growing. Intended investment under these spirited conditions would tend to be relatively high.

## EXHIBIT 6

### THE INVESTMENT CURVE

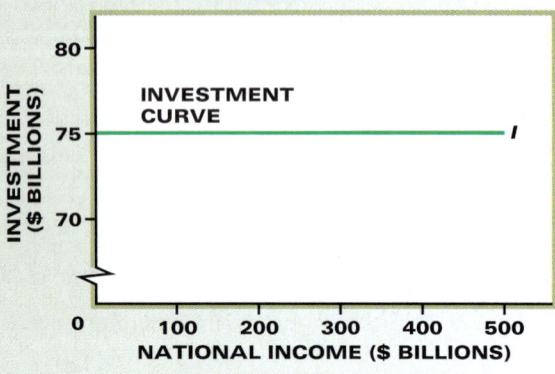

The investment curve is horizontal, independent of the level of national income. Intended investment is $75 billion at every level of national income.

It would seem then that the level of national income doesn't play the decisive role in determining investment that it plays in determining consumption spending. Exhibit 6 illustrates this point, showing investment as autonomous, that is, independent of the level of national income.

The investment curve, $I$, is a horizontal straight line. If $I = \$75$ billion, it is $75 billion regardless of the level of national income. For example, when $Y = \$100$, $I = \$75$ billion. When $Y = \$200$ billion, $I = \$75$ billion. And so on.

## Determinants of Investment

But why $75 billion? What factors determine the size of the economy's **autonomous investment**? There are four principal determinants of autonomous investment: the level of technology, the rate of interest, expectations of future economic growth, and the rate of capacity utilization.

**TECHNOLOGY LEVEL** The introduction of new technologies is one of the mainsprings of investment. For example, when the railroad displaced water transport as the principal means of long-distance transportation, it sparked massive investment spending not only in the railroad industry, but in the secondary industries that grew up alongside it. Investments in mining, steel, lumber, and construction were needed to feed the expanding railroads. But that was only the surface of railroad-led investment. The railroads opened up the West, generating decades of spectacular investment spending in roads and commercial and residential building, as well as in goods that filled these new structures.

Similar technological leaps, such as the automobile, steam power, electricity, the telephone, petrochemicals, television, nuclear energy, drugs, computers, and genetic engineering have produced, in their own times, extensive networks of investment spending.

**Autonomous investment**
Investment that is independent of the level of income.

While we cannot predict technological breakthroughs, we can measure the amount of technological research and development happening in the economy. The National Science Foundation, Division of Science Resources Studies (http://www.nsf.gov/sbe/srs/), does just that.

*Can you think of other technological leaps that can or have produced extensive networks of investment spending? Go to the Interactive Study Center at http://gottheil.swcollege.com and click on the "Your Turn" button to submit your example. Student submissions will be posted to the Web site, and perhaps we will use some in future editions of the book!*

There is no connection between these technological breakthroughs and the levels of national income they feed, and it is also impossible to fit them into any defined timetable. Like volcanoes, they seem to erupt in their own time and place.

**INTEREST RATE** Producers undertake investment when they believe that the rate of return generated by the investment will exceed the interest rate, that is, the cost of borrowing investment funds. For some types of investment, the difference between the expected rate of return and the interest rate is so wide that even a 4 or 5 percent change in the interest rate has no influence on the investment decisions.

There are other investment projects, however, typically large scale and long term, such as housing construction or expansion of automobile assembly lines, for which interest charges are an important cost factor. Slight changes in the rate of interest—even fractions of a point—may be a sufficient incentive or deterrent to such investment spending.

Picture the scene. Michelle Vlasminski, CEO of Michelle Enterprises, asks five of her executives to present investment projects that would cost roughly $1 million each and to estimate their expected rate of return. The following week, Michelle, with the five projects in hand, considers which, if any, to undertake. Their expected rates of return are as follows: project $A$ = 12 percent, project $B$ = 7 percent, project $C$ = 10 percent, project $D$ = 9 percent, and project $E$ = 8 percent. If the interest rate (what Michelle pays to borrow investment funds) is 15 percent, which, if any, investment project will she accept? None, of course. She would not borrow at a 15 percent interest rate if she can get, at best, only a 12 percent rate of return.

What if the interest rate is 11 percent? Then, project A is feasible. If the interest rate is 9.5 percent, then both projects A and C are advantageous. At 8.5 percent interest, projects A, C, and D increase the profitability of her firm. As you can see, a lower interest rate makes more investment projects feasible. In other words, there is an inverse relationship between the rate of interest and the quantity of investment spending.

That's what panel $a$ of Exhibit 7 depicts.

The demand curve for investment in the economy as a whole is downward sloping. That is, as the interest rate falls, the quantity demanded of investment increases. For example, when the rate falls from 8 to 6 percent, investment increases from $75 billion to $80 billion. *Note that this increase in investment has nothing to do with changes in national income.* This new level of investment is represented, in panel $b$, by the upward shift of the investment curve from $I$ to $I'$, from $75 billion to $80 billion.

**CHECK YOUR UNDERSTANDING**

How is the interest rate related to the level of intended investment?

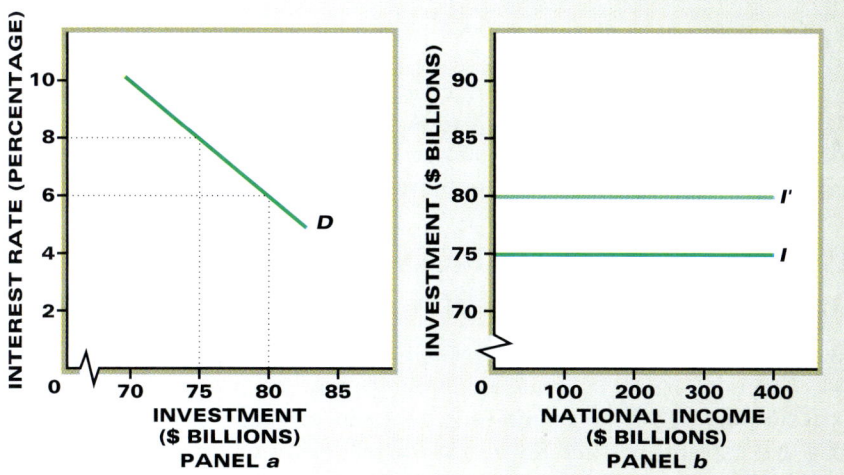

**THE EFFECT OF CHANGES IN THE RATE OF INTEREST ON THE LEVEL OF INVESTMENT**

In panel $a$, the level of investment is determined by the interest rate. The demand curve for investment, $D$, is downward sloping. As the rate of interest decreases from 8 to 6 percent, the level of investment in the economy increases from $75 billion to $80 billion. This increase in investment is depicted in panel $b$ as an upward shift in the investment curve, from $75 billion to $80 billion.

EXHIBIT 7

One estimate of how producers view the economic future is the Measure of Business Confidence (http://www.conference-board.org/products/frames.cfm?main=c-consumer.cfm). Every quarter, about 150 business leaders from various industries respond to questions about their businesses.

**EXPECTATIONS OF FUTURE ECONOMIC GROWTH** Investment spending reflects how producers view the future. They expand production lines or build entirely new factories if they expect sales to grow. What influences expectations?

Many producers base their expectations of the future on past experience. If the economy grew rapidly in the past, many producers—lacking any contrary information—expect it to continue to grow rapidly in the future. If they expect it to grow, they prepare for the growth by increasing investment spending. On the other hand, if the economy was sluggish in the past, these same producers would expect it to continue being sluggish. Investment spending may be the furthest thing from their minds. That is to say, investment spending takes its cue from past performance. It's the changes in national income and the projections of those changes into the future, not the absolute level of national income, that influence producers.

**RATE OF CAPACITY UTILIZATION** Producers seldom choose to operate at 100 percent capacity. Why not? Because to produce at capacity reduces their ability to expand production on demand. They typically choose a capacity utilization rate that gives them some short-run flexibility. For example, by operating at 85 percent capacity, they can increase production by as much as 15 percent without having to wait for new machinery or raw material inventories. In the highly competitive business world, differences of months, weeks, or even days can make the difference between success and failure.

There is, however, a cost to flexibility. Carrying excess productive capacity can be an expensive way of overcoming short-run production bottlenecks. How much flexibility producers end up choosing, then, influences the economy's level of investment. For producers who choose to operate close to full capacity, a moderate increase in sales may shift them quickly into strong investment spending.

The Federal Reserve Board publishes monthly data on capacity utilization and industrial production (http://www.federalreserve.gov/releases/g17/default.htm).

## The Volatile Nature of Investment

Any one of the factors just discussed can excite or depress the level of investment. In some years, these factors pull in opposite directions. For example, the interest rate may increase at the same time a new round of technologically induced investments are introduced. One stimulates, the other dampens investment spending.

On the other hand, there are times when, *by chance,* these factors work in unison. A fall in the interest rate combines with an increase in the rate of technological change, with a shift to greater capacity utilization and with impressive economic growth. In such a situation, dramatic upward shifts in the investment curve occur.

The investment curve in Exhibit 8 shows the possible volatility of investment spending in the U.S. economy.

In some years, a specific combination of factors influencing investment drives the level of investment to new heights, only to be followed by a sharp plunge in investment driven by a reversal in those same factors. Most of the time, the direction—let alone the levels—investment will take is, for everyone, a big unknown.

## COMBINING CONSUMPTION SPENDING AND INVESTMENT SPENDING

Let's pause for a moment. The two principal building blocks in the Keynesian model—consumption and investment spending—have been put in position. What follows is an analysis of the relationship between consumption and investment spending that explains how the Keynesian model derives national income.

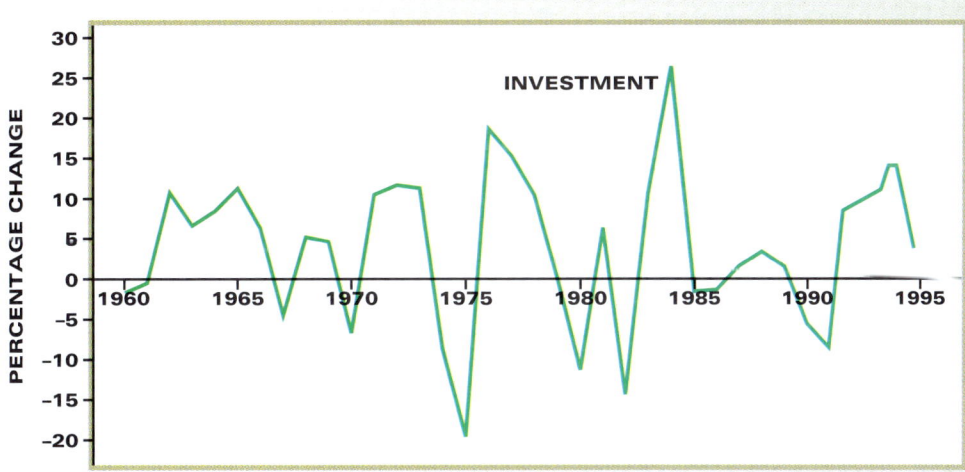

**THE VOLATILITY OF INVESTMENT**

Unlike consumption, which is fairly stable over time, investment is subject to erratic fluctuations even through very short periods of time. The economic and technological factors that influence investment can sometimes create the conditions for rapid expansion of investment and, just as quickly, reverse to cause investment to fall just as rapidly, as we see in the annual rate of change in real investment spending over the years 1960 to 1995.

**Source:** *Economic Report of the President 1994* (Washington, D.C.: United States Government Printing Office, 1994), p. 270; and U.S. Department of Commerce, *Survey of Current Business* 76 (January/February 1996), Table 2.

That's the task we assign to the following chapter. It should be viewed as a continuation or second half of this chapter, since both chapters develop the Keynesian model of national income determination.

# CHAPTER REVIEW

1. The consumption function relates the level of consumption to the level of income. The relationship is causal: An increase in income increases consumption.
2. Keynes's absolute income hypothesis suggests that as income increases, consumption increases, but at a decreasing rate. Keynes believed that the rich have a lower marginal propensity to consume than do the poor. Extending his theory from individuals to the national economy, Keynes argued that a nation's marginal propensity to consume depends on the absolute level of national income.
3. Empirical work on the national marginal propensity to consume by Simon Kuznets found that contrary to Keynes's hypothesis, the nation's marginal propensity to consume is constant. Duesenberry's relative income hypothesis helps to explain Kuznets's empirical finding. When national income increases and relative incomes remain unchanged, the marginal propensity to consume for the nation is unchanged. Duesenberry's hypothesis suggests a straight-line consumption function.
4. Friedman's permanent income hypothesis distinguishes between permanent income and transitory income. Friedman argues that consumption is dependent on permanent income.
5. Modigliani's life-cycle hypothesis of consumption behavior suggests that a person's marginal propensity to consume changes during one's lifetime. Young people tend to have high marginal propensities to consume. People in

middle age have lower marginal propensities to consume. When people are in retirement, the *MPC* increases again.

6. Autonomous consumption is independent of income. Shifts in the consumption function involve changes in autonomous consumption. The consumption function shifts due to changes in real asset and money holdings, expectations of changes in the price level, changes in interest rates, and changes in taxes.

7. The consumption equation expresses consumption as a function of national income. Consumption is equal to autonomous consumption ($a$) plus national income ($Y$) multiplied by the marginal propensity to consume ($b$): $C = a + bY$.

8. The saving equation is $S = Y - C$. The marginal propensity to save is $1 - MPC$.

9. Changes in investment tend to be unrelated to the level of national income. Investment is regarded as autonomous. Variables that influence investment include technological change, interest rate changes, changes in the rate of growth of national income, and the rate of capacity utilization. Autonomous investment can be quite volatile.

## KEY TERMS

Consumption function
Absolute income hypothesis
Marginal propensity to consume (MPC)
Relative income hypothesis
Permanent income hypothesis
Life-cycle hypothesis
Permanent income
Transitory income
Autonomous consumption
Saving
Marginal propensity to save (MPS)
45° line
Intended investment
Autonomous investment

## QUESTIONS

1. What is the consumption function?
2. How does Keynes's comment: "The satisfaction of the immediate primary needs of a man and his family is usually a stronger motive than the motives toward accumulation" relate to his absolute income hypothesis?
3. Accepting the absolute income hypothesis, would you expect the *MPC* in the U.S. economy in 1995 to be higher, lower, or about the same as the *MPC* in the Haitian 1995 economy? Why? How would it compare to the *MPC* in the U.S. economy in 1925?
4. Accepting the relative income hypothesis, would you expect the *MPC* in the U.S. economy in 1995 to be higher, lower, or the same as the *MPC* in the U.S. economy in 1925? Why?
5. Give an example of transitory income. What effect does this income have on the marginal propensity to consume?
6. What is autonomous consumption?
7. Why would a change in asset or money holdings shift the consumption curve?
8. What factor explains movements along the consumption curve?
9. Why is *MPC* + *MPS* always equal to 1?
10. What is dissaving? Describe a situation that would create dissaving in an economy.
11. What factors determine autonomous investment?
12. Draw a graph depicting consumption for an economy through the range $Y = \$100$ billion to $Y = \$500$ when autonomous consumption is $100 billion and $MPC = 0.6$.

# PRACTICE PROBLEMS

**1.** Calculate the marginal propensity to consume, the marginal propensity to save, and the level of saving for each income level in the accompanying table.

| Y | C | MPC | MPS | SAVING |
|---|---|---|---|---|
| $ 0 | $ 50 | | | |
| 100 | 100 | | | |
| 200 | 150 | | | |
| 300 | 200 | | | |
| 400 | 250 | | | |
| 500 | 300 | | | |

**2.** Calculate consumption for each level of national income, given the accompanying levels of autonomous consumption, $C_a$, and marginal propensities to consume.

| Y | $C_a$ | MPC | C |
|---|---|---|---|
| $100 | $50 | 0.50 | |
| 200 | 60 | 0.60 | |
| 300 | 70 | 0.70 | |
| 400 | 80 | 0.80 | |
| 500 | 90 | 0.90 | |

**3.** Calculate the level of autonomous investment, I, for each level of national income.

| Y | C | I |
|---|---|---|
| $100 | $ 50 | 60 |
| 200 | 100 | |
| 300 | 150 | |
| 400 | 200 | |
| 500 | 250 | |

**4.** Accepting Milton Friedman's permanent income hypothesis, calculate the marginal propensities to consume (MPCs) for each of the four scenarios.

| PERMANENT INCOME | TRANSITORY INCOME | TOTAL INCOME | CONSUMPTION | MPC |
|---|---|---|---|---|
| $ 8,000 | $ 2,000 | $10,000 | $ 6,400 | |
| 14,000 | 6,000 | 20,000 | 7,000 | |
| 25,000 | 5,000 | 30,000 | 19,500 | |
| 30,000 | 10,000 | 40,000 | 21,000 | |

**5.** For each of the three income levels shown, provide appropriate data to satisfy or be consistent with the absolute and relative income hypotheses.

| | COMPSUMPTION | | MPC | |
|---|---|---|---|---|
| INCOME | ABSOLUTE INCOME HYPOTHESIS | RELATIVE INCOME HYPOTHESIS | ABSOLUTE INCOME HYPOTHESIS | RELATIVE INCOME HYPOTHESIS |
| $1,000 | | | | |
| 2,000 | | | | |
| 3,000 | | | | |

**6.** For each of the three income levels shown, provide appropriate data to satisfy or be consistent with the absolute and relative income hypotheses.

| | SAVING | | MPS | |
|---|---|---|---|---|
| INCOME | ABSOLUTE INCOME HYPOTHESIS | RELATIVE INCOME HYPOTHESIS | ABSOLUTE INCOME HYPOTHESIS | RELATIVE INCOME HYPOTHESIS |
| $4,000 | | | | |
| 5,000 | | | | |
| 6,000 | | | | |

**7.** Calculate the 2000 and 2001 *MPC*s for each of the countries.

|  | 2000 | | | 2001 | |
|---|---|---|---|---|---|
|  | ΔY | ΔC | MPC | ΔY | MPC |
| FRANCE | 1,000 FRANCS | 6,000 FRANCS |  | 1,000 FRANCS |  |
| ITALY | 1,000 LIRE | 7,000 LIRE |  | 1,000 LIRE |  |
| BRITAIN | 1,000 POUNDS | 7,500 POUNDS |  | 1,000 POUNDS |  |
| IRELAND | 1,000 PUNTS | 8,000 PUNTS |  | 1,000 PUNTS |  |

**8.** Calculate the 2000 and 2001 *MPC*s for each of the countries *when national income falls* by 1,000.

|  | 2000 | | | 2001 | |
|---|---|---|---|---|---|
|  | ΔY | ΔC | MPC | ΔY | MPC |
| FRANCE | −1,000 FRANCS | −6,000 FRANCS |  | −1,000 FRANCS |  |
| ITALY | −1,000 LIRE | −7,000 LIRE |  | −1,000 LIRE |  |
| BRITAIN | −1,000 POUNDS | −7,500 POUNDS |  | −1,000 POUNDS |  |
| IRELAND | −1,000 PUNTS | −8,000 PUNTS |  | −1,000 PUNTS |  |

# WHAT'S WRONG WITH THIS GRAPH?

### THE CONSUMPTION CURVE (SHORT-RUN)

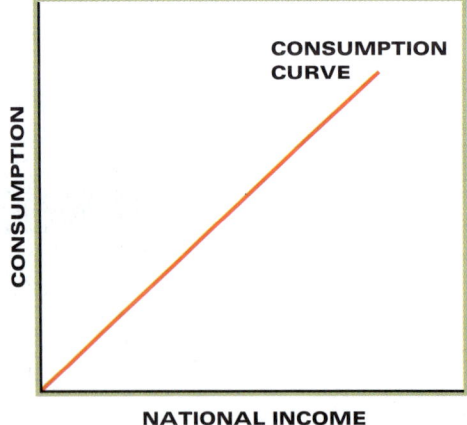

# ECONOMIC CONSULTANTS

### ECONOMIC RESEARCH AND ANALYSIS BY STUDENTS FOR PROFESSIONALS

Gary Behrman is regional manager of the Wal-Mart stores in Dallas, Texas. As manager, Gary must decide every month how much inventory to stock and how many people to hire (or fire). He has a layman's understanding that these decisions depend on the state of the national economy and, more specifically, on the economic climate in the Dallas region, but he would like to be better informed about the connection.

One of his part-time employees, a student at Dallas Community College, suggests that he might get the information he seeks by hiring Economic Consultants to show him what specific factors influence people's consumption and how these influences affect the decisions he must make at Wal-Mart concerning its inventory and hiring. Prepare a presentation for Gary that addresses the following issues:

**1.** What factors (or variables) influence how much consumers spend on consumption goods? What factors influence the amount of consumption goods produced?

**2.** What resources are available to make short-run forecasts concerning expected consumer sales, wage rates, and production for retail in Texas and in Dallas?

You may find the following resources helpful as you prepare this presentation for Gary:

- **Consumer Confidence Index** and the **Measure of Business Confidence** (http://www.conference-board.org/products/frames.cfm?main=c-consumer.cfm)—The Consumer Confidence Index and the Measure of Business Confidence, released monthly, provide a short-term forecast of consumption and production.
- **Summary of Commentary on Current Economic Conditions by Federal Reserve District (The Beige Book)** (http://www.federalreserve.gov/FOMC/BB/current/)—The Beige Book—so named because the report has a beige cover—is published eight times a year. Each Federal Reserve bank gathers anecdotal information on current economic conditions in its district through reports from bank and branch directors and interviews with key businesspeople, economists, market experts, and other sources. The Beige Book summarizes this information by district and sector (including Dallas, Texas).
- **Federal Reserve Bank of Dallas** (http://www.dallasfed.org/)—The Dallas Fed publishes annual reports (http://www.dallasfed.org/htm/pubs/annual.html) and publications (http://www.dallasfed.org/htm/pubs/pubindex.html).
- **The *Dallas Morning News*** (http://www.dallasnews.com/)—The *Dallas Morning News* provides business news (http://www.dallasnews.com/business/) for the Dallas area.

# PRACTICE TEST

1. According to Keynes's absolute income hypothesis,
   a. individuals have relatively fixed income levels in real (inflation-adjusted) terms over their lifetimes.
   b. wealthy people consume a larger proportion of their wealth then do poor people.
   c. an individual's marginal propensity to consume is constant.
   d. consumption rises as income rises, but at a decreasing rate.
   e. consumption rises proportionately with changes in income.

2. George earns $50,000 per year and spends $40,000 consuming goods and services such as housing and food. Suppose that George receives a lottery prize of $10,000, and he spends $8,000 on a new car and saves the remaining $2,000. Which of the following is true?
   a. George's behavior is consistent with Duesenberry's income hypothesis.
   b. George's marginal propensity to consume is falling.
   c. George reacts differently to marginal changes in income than he does to permanent changes in income.
   d. George's behavior is consistent with Modigliani's income hypothesis.
   e. George's behavior is consistent with Friedman's income hypothesis.

3. The life-cycle hypothesis asserts that
   a. the *MPC* is constant over a person's lifetime.
   b. young and old people typically have higher *MPC*s than middle-aged people.
   c. people base consumption decisions on their nontransitory income.
   d. the *MPC* rises as income rises.
   e. transitory income changes are treated differently by individuals than are permanent income changes occurring during their life cycle.

4. The notion that people do not radically alter their consumption patterns due to transitory changes in income is referred to as the
   a. life-cycle hypothesis.
   b. absolute income hypothesis.
   c. transitory income hypothesis.
   d. relative income hypothesis.
   e. permanent income hypothesis.

5. If an individual's income is $0, the consumption level for the individual
   a. must equal 0.
   b. is referred to as transitory consumption.
   c. is referred to as permanent consumption.
   d. is referred to as autonomous consumption.
   e. is negative if the individual has to borrow money to pay for necessities.

6. If there is a fall in interest rates from 8 percent to 7 percent, then
   a. the consumption function will shift downward.
   b. permanent income will rise by 1 percent.
   c. there will be an upward movement along the consumption function.
   d. there will be a downward movement along the consumption function.
   e. the consumption function will shift upward.

7. Suppose that a $6,000 increase in income is accompanied by a $4,500 increase in consumption. The marginal propensity to save
   a. is 0.75.
   b. is 0.25.
   c. is 1.33.
   d. is 0.20.
   e. cannot be determined without knowing the initial levels of income and consumption.

8. If the consumption equation is given to be $C = \$80 + 0.7Y$ and $Y = \$1,000$, then the level of saving in a two-sector economy (saving and consumption)
   a. equals $220.
   b. equals $700.
   c. equals $300.
   d. equals $780.
   e. cannot be determined without information about the savings function.

9. Along the 45° line,
   a. income always equals consumption.
   b. the economy has a declining *MPS*.
   c. the level of saving falls as income rises.
   d. income always equals consumption plus saving.
   e. the consumption function is equal to one.

10. The autonomous investment curve will shift upward when which of the following occurs?
    a. There is a fall in the level of technology.
    b. Interest rates rise.
    c. The level of income rises.
    d. The level of income falls.
    e. There is a rise in capacity utilization in firms.

# CHAPTER 7

# EQUILIBRIUM NATIONAL INCOME

Which blade in a pair of scissors cuts the cloth? Silly question? The answer is apparent, isn't it? Both blades do the cutting. It is almost inconceivable to suppose that one blade alone can do the cutting. That's what Alfred Marshall, the celebrated 19th-century economist, said when asked whether demand or costs of production determine equilibrium price. His reply (*Principles of Economics,* 1891)—using the scissors metaphor—was that both, equally, and in particular, *the interaction of both,* determine equilibrium price.

About a half-century later, a similar question was asked about the determination of the equilibrium level of national income. Which blade does the cutting? Is it aggregate expenditure—that is, spending by consumers on consumption goods, spending by businesses on investment goods, spending by government, and spending by foreigners on net exports—or aggregate supply? You might think that by this time the answer was obvious. But Marshall's most renowned student, J. M. Keynes, while acknowledging that the

**THIS CHAPTER INTRODUCES YOU TO THE ECONOMIC PRINCIPLES ASSOCIATED WITH:**

- AGGREGATE EXPENDITURE
- THE EQUILIBRIUM LEVEL OF NATIONAL INCOME
- THE RELATIONSHIP BETWEEN SAVING AND INVESTMENT
- THE INCOME MULTIPLIER
- THE RELATIONSHIP BETWEEN AGGREGATE EXPENDITURE AND AGGREGATE DEMAND
- THE PARADOX OF THRIFT

interaction of aggregate expenditures and aggregate supply determines the equilibrium level of national income, still felt that—using Marshall's scissors metaphor again—one blade in particular is responsible for most of the cutting. That blade, he was convinced, is aggregate expenditures.

Why he was so convinced is the subject of this chapter. What determines the equilibrium level of national income was an important issue for Keynes then—and is perhaps for us today—because he believed that the economy is always heading toward equilibrium (even if it might never get there) and that its equilibrium level might be a rather troublesome one. Keynes was trying to explain why the 1930s economy was mired in depression and massive unemployment. If he could figure out how an economy's equilibrium level ends up being a depression, he thought, then maybe he could figure out how an economy can be extricated from that situation. That is, is it possible to change an equilibrium level?

Let's build an economic model to represent an economy heading toward or being in equilibrium. Let's first make some simplifying assumptions about the economy in this model so that we can focus on the primary forces that determine the economy's level of national income. Although aggregate expenditures include consumption, investment, government spending, and net exports, let's assume no government spending or foreign trade. Aggregate expenditures then become consumption spending and investment spending alone. Our assumption—excluding government, and therefore taxes—also means that disposable income is the same as total income, since people pay no taxes.

## INTERACTION BETWEEN CONSUMERS AND PRODUCERS

Two very different kinds of people are always at work making decisions concerning consumption spending, saving, and investment that affect each other. As we saw in the previous chapter, people, acting as consumers, spend part of their income on consumption and save the rest. This is represented in

$$Y = C + S.$$

At the same time, other people, acting as producers, produce both consumption goods and investment goods, partly in response to and partly in anticipation of the demands that consumers make for consumption goods and producers make for investment goods. This is represented in

$$Y = C + I_i.$$

Now suppose, *by chance*, that the investment producers intend to make equals the same billions of dollars that consumers actually save out of their income. It follows, then, that what producers intend to produce for consumption ($C_i = Y - I_i$) turns out to be precisely what consumers intend to consume ($C_i = Y - S$). (The subscript *i* indicates *intended* as distinct from *actual*.) This perfect match between intended investment and savings is written as

$$I_i = S.$$

Perhaps it is worthwhile to note again that the $I_i = S$ equation is a chance event arrived at, in this illustration, by decision making on the part of producers and consumers that, unbeknownst to both, created the perfect fit. After all, the producers of investment goods do not know *with certainty* what people who do the saving are intending to save. Nor can the people making saving decisions take into consideration what the producers of investment goods, responding to or anticipating investment demand, are intending to produce.

How fortunate, then, if this chance event generates for both producers and consumers the condition in which all consumption, investment, and saving intentions in the economy are realized!

*The $I_i = S$ equation describes the economy in macroequilibrium.* After all, no excess demand or supply exists. All the consumption goods supplied by producers are taken off the market by consumers; **aggregate expenditure** equals aggregate supply.

But what if the intended investment of producers is not equal to the saving people choose to make?

**Aggregate expenditure**
Spending by consumers on consumption goods, spending by businesses on investment goods, spending by government, and spending by foreigners on net exports.

# THE ECONOMY MOVES TOWARD EQUILIBRIUM

The national economy, if not already in equilibrium, is always moving toward it. *But not by chance.* Let's suppose the economy is at $Y = \$900$ billion, which is *not* the **equilibrium level of national income.** Suppose as well that autonomous consumption is $60 billion and $MPC = 0.80$. Consumption spending, then, is

$$C = \$60 + (0.80 \times \$900) = \$780.$$

**Equilibrium level of national income**
$C + I_i = C + S$, where saving equals intended investment.

Suppose also that the producers in the economy have decided that of the $900 billion of goods they produced, $100 billion is intended for investment. That's their intended investment demand:

$$I_i = \$100$$

## How Consumers and Producers Behave When $Y = \$900$ Billion

Let's focus on how consumers and producers behave under these circumstances. What do consumers do at $Y = \$900$ billion? What do the producers do at $Y = \$900$ billion? These two sets of people make their consumption and investment decisions simultaneously and independently of each other. We can imagine them thinking through their choices and reacting to realized and unrealized outcomes.

Exhibit 1 summarizes their behavior.

Look at the top rows of Exhibit 1. The left-hand side, describing consumers' behavior, simply spells out the fact that consumers divide their income $Y = \$900$ billion into $C + S$. The right-hand side, describing producers' behavior, shows that producers, responding to and anticipating demands for consumption and investment goods, divide their production of $Y = \$900$ billion into $C + I_i$.

But how much of the $Y = C + S$ is in the form of $C$, and how much of the $Y = C + I_i$ is in the form of $C$? The consumption equation, $C = a + bY$, provides part of the answer. At $Y = \$900$ billion, consumers spend $[\$60 + (0.8 \times \$900)] = \$780$ billion on consumption. They save, then, $120 billion.

But producers have other ideas. At $Y = \$900$ billion, they intend to invest $100 billion. That means they intend to produce for consumption $800 billion. They immediately run into a vexing problem. How can they sell $800 billion, when consumers are prepared to buy up only $780 billion? They can't.

Just what happens to the $800 − \$780 = \$20$ billion of consumption goods that are produced but remain unsold? Retail stores, unable to move the $20 billion across the counter as final goods, discover they have more inventory than they want. Their shelves are crammed with these unsold goods, many boxed in stockrooms and

**CONSUMERS' AND PRODUCERS' INTENTIONS AND ACTIVITIES, BY STAGES, WHEN $Y = \$900$ BILLION**

| CONSUMERS | PRODUCERS |
|---|---|
| $Y = \$900$ | $Y = \$900$ |
| $Y = C + S$ | $Y = C + I_i$ |
| $C = a + bY$ | $I_i = \$100$ |
| $C = \$60 + 0.8\,(Y)$ | $C = Y - I_i$ |
| $= \$60 + 0.8\,(\$900)$ | $= \$900 - \$100$ |
| $= \$780$ | $= \$800$ |
| $S = Y - C$ | $I_a = \$120$ |
| $= \$900 - \$780$ | |
| $= \$120$ | |

# APPLIED PERSPECTIVE

## INTERVIEW WITH THE AUTHOR'S BROTHER, IRVING GOTTHEIL, CEO OF THE ARTISTIC HAT COMPANY, MONTREAL, CANADA

**FRED:** Let's talk about business. What's going on this year? Are you doing anything different?

IRVING: We're coming out with new colors and new styles. And producing a lot more hats.

FRED: Who decides how many hats to produce?

IRVING: I do! Come to think about it, it's also the firms I sell to. After all, they retail the hats. You know, the big ones like the Hudson Bay Company, the T. Eaton Company, Zeller's Incorporated, Sears, and Kmart. Then there are the hundreds of boutique shops across Canada.

FRED: How do these firms know how many hats to order?

IRVING: Well, when you get right down to it, it's a guessing game. They have to anticipate what consumers want. It's hard. We really can't get into consumers' heads. Of course, we hope to get on their heads.

FRED: Be more specific.

IRVING: Well . . . we make decisions on the basis of what we think people will demand. And what they demand depends upon a lot of things. For example, if it's a cold winter (like last year), they buy. Remember three years ago? It hardly snowed. People didn't need hats. Only Santa Claus wore a hat! We ended up with an overload of unsold inventory. You saw the problem when you were in Montreal that February. Who wore hats? We couldn't give them away. It was a bad year. Some years are really bad for other reasons. Remember when I moved the factory from 124 McGill Street to 5445 de Gaspe Street? I doubled my space expecting a great season. It was a heck of a decision. I was wrong! How did I know the economy was going into a recession. What a recession! I took an awful beating.

FRED: What about Sears and Hudson Bay?

IRVING: They took a beating too! Listen, they're no *mavens* [a maven is a sage]. They were left holding half the hats they ordered. By the way, this is a good year despite the warm weather. It goes to show you. You think you know, and you don't.

FRED: What's in store for next year?

IRVING: I'm optimistic. Not crazy optimistic, but optimistic. The factory is running now at full capacity. I'm even replacing the stamping presses I bought in Milan, Italy, just two years ago. Technology changes so quickly in this business. There's a new press out of Sweden that is top of the line. I figure it will cut my stamping press labor costs by 25 percent. Oh yes, those handmade aluminum molds that come from England . . . a company in Toronto does the same quality work and is much less expensive. I'm going to give them a try.

**EVERY SNOWFLAKE COUNTS. LET IT SNOW! LET IT SNOW! LET IT SNOW!**

FRED: Looks like you're banking on a lot of people buying hats.

IRVING: That's right! But you know, Freddie, it's always risky. Someone has to make the decision on how much to produce. And that someone is me. Next year? I need cold weather. I can use an ice age. By the way, why these questions?

FRED: I will use them in the book as an example of firms making decisions concerning production of consumption and investment goods. You're my consumption goods decision-maker.

IRVING: Spell my name right!

FRED: Any message for my students?

IRVING: Yeah. Stay out of the hat business!

FRED: How about giving the student who scores the highest grade in my economics class a hat as a prize?

IRVING: Let's wait until the end of the season, OK? If the season's bad, I could give your entire class hats!

warehouses. That is to say, *although produced as consumption goods, the $20 billion—by default—becomes investment goods* in the form of **unwanted inventories.**

In other words, producers intended to invest $100 billion, but their **actual investment,** $I_a$, turns out to be $120 billion, that is, $20 billion more than the intended investment, $I_i$:

$$I_a > I_i$$

As you can see, whether producers' investment intentions are realized or not depends on what consumers do. After all, how much people choose to consume out of their income dictates how much of what producers produce for consumption gets sold.

You can imagine what happens next. Retail stores, saddled with unwanted inventories, scale down their orders for resupply. After all, why reorder when they can't sell what they already have? Producers, in turn, feeling the pinch of fewer reorders, will be unable to maintain production levels.

What follows next? Both retailers and producers lay off workers. And there's nothing employers or workers can do about it. What room is there for compromise? With consumption and investment functions being what they are, the $900 billion level of national income simply cannot support employment for all the workers. Unemployment results. With fewer people working, production and income fall.

## How Consumers and Producers Behave When $Y = \$700$ Billion

Now let's suppose national income is not at $Y = \$900$ billion but at $Y = \$700$ billion. What happens to consumer and producer intentions at $Y = \$700$ billion? Look at Exhibit 2.

As you see, the basic consumption and investment functions, $C = \$60 + 0.8Y$ and $I_i = \$100$, remain unchanged. Consumers still spend $60 billion on autonomous consumption and 0.80 of national income. Producers still intend to invest $100 billion.

But note what has changed. The level of national income is $700 billion, and a very different set of circumstances emerges. Consumers now spend [$60 + (0.8 × $700)] = $620 billion on consumption goods. Producers, on the other hand, intending to invest $100 billion in new factories, new equipment, new vehicles, and so on, produce only $700 − $100 = $600 billion of consumption goods.

What happens now? With consumers spending $620 billion on consumption but finding only $600 billion of consumption goods available, producers and retail stores find that inventories they had wanted to hold as investment end up sold as consumption goods.

Picture, for example, David Tietlebaum's Poster and Frame store. Its wall and freestanding

**CHECK YOUR UNDERSTANDING**

Why are some inventories unwanted?

**Unwanted inventories**
Goods produced for consumption that remain unsold.

**Actual investment**
Investment spending that producers actually make—that is, intended investment (investment spending that producers intend to undertake), plus or minus unintended changes in inventories.

**CONSUMERS' AND PRODUCERS' INTENTIONS AND ACTIVITIES, BY STAGES, WHEN Y = $700 BILLION**

| CONSUMERS | PRODUCERS |
|---|---|
| Y = $700 | Y = $700 |
| Y = C + S | Y = C + $I_i$ |
| C = a + bY | $I_i$ = $100 |
| C = $60 + 0.8 (Y) | C = Y − $I_i$ |
| = $60 + 0.8 ($700) | = $700 − $100 |
| = $620 | = $600 |
| S = Y − C | $I_a$ = $80 |
| = $700 − $620 | |
| = $80 | |

EXHIBIT 2

shelves are filled with stocks of posters. People can walk into the store and choose from among precut Lucite, steel, and wood frames. As you can well imagine, it would be very difficult for David to sell framed posters if he didn't have a ready supply on hand—that is, an inventory—of posters and frames. (Recall, inventories are part of investment.)

How does David fit into the $Y = \$700$ billion scenario? Because consumers spend \$620 billion on consumption goods while producers only produce \$600 billion of consumption goods, David discovers, along with many other producers and retailers, that the inventories they want *and need* will be reduced. In response, David will reorder greater quantities of posters and frames from the producers of posters and frames, not only to meet consumption needs but also to restock depleted inventories.

Once again, intended investment will be unrealized. But this time, actual investment will be less than intended:

$$I_a < I_i$$

You can bet producers will be more than delighted! Retail stores will be on the phones pleading with them for more goods. Producers, in response, will hire more workers. With more workers producing goods and earning incomes, national income rises above \$700 billion.

## How Consumers and Producers Behave When $Y = \$800$ Billion

Let's now suppose national income is at $Y = \$800$ billion. How would consumers and producers behave? Look at Exhibit 3.

The consumption and investment functions remain unchanged. Look what consumers do now. Consumption spending is [\$60 + (0.8 − \$800)] = \$700 billion. Producers, still intending to invest \$100 billion, produce \$700 billion of consumption goods.

Although producers really didn't know with certainty what consumers intended to do with their incomes, and consumers really didn't know what producers intended to produce, the match is perfect. People's consumption spending turns out to be exactly what producers have produced for consumption. At $Y = \$800$ billion, producers, responding to or anticipating investment demand, intend to invest \$100 billion and end up actually investing \$100 billion:

$$I_i = I_a$$

Retail stores sell the consumption goods that they had hoped to sell and have left as inventory precisely what they want. What will they do? They will reorder from producers exactly what they had ordered before—no more, no less. Why order more? The market

**EXHIBIT 3**

**CONSUMERS' AND PRODUCERS' INTENTIONS AND ACTIVITIES, BY STAGES, WHEN $Y = \$800$ BILLION**

| CONSUMERS | PRODUCERS |
|---|---|
| $Y = \$800$ | $Y = \$800$ |
| $Y = C + S$ | $Y = C + I_i$ |
| $C = a + bY$ | $I_i = \$100$ |
| $C = \$60 + 0.8\ (Y)$ | $C = Y - I_i$ |
| $= \$60 + 0.8\ (\$800)$ | $= \$800 - \$100$ |
| $= \$700$ | $= \$700$ |
| $S = Y - C$ | $I_a = \$100$ |
| $= \$800 - \$700$ | |
| $= \$100$ | |

gives no indication that they could sell more than $700 billion. But why order less when experience tells them the market will absorb $700 billion?

Producers, then, will maintain their production level at $800 billion. They will keep in employment precisely that number of workers who produce the $800 billion. At $Y = \$800$ billion, there is no incentive for producers or consumers to change what they do. *The economy is in equilibrium.*

## EQUILIBRIUM NATIONAL INCOME

Panels *a* and *b* of Exhibit 4 illustrate what Exhibits 1, 2, and 3 describe. They depict the economy moving to national income equilibrium.

Look at panel *a*. The upward-sloping, straight-line consumption curve, *C*, is a straight line because the marginal propensity to consume is constant—it intersects

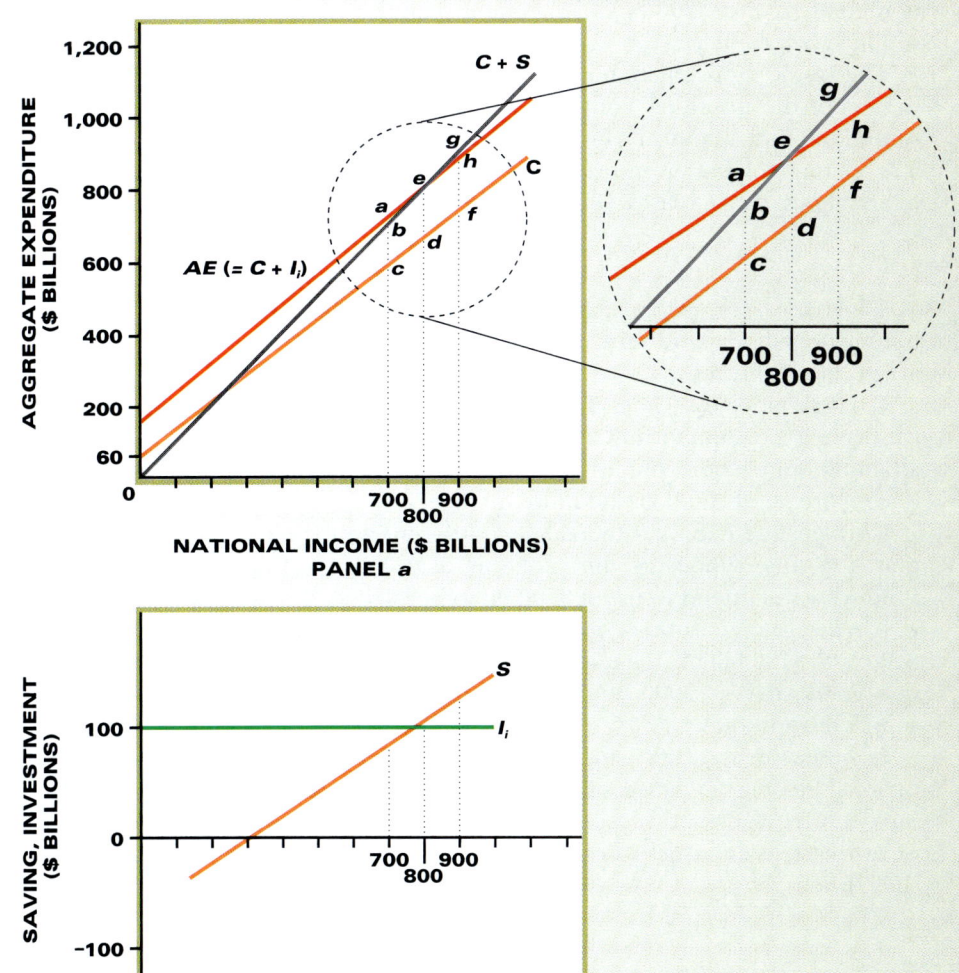

**THE EQUILIBRIUM LEVEL OF NATIONAL INCOME**

In panel *a*, the economy is in equilibrium at *e*, where $Y = \$800$ billion. When national income is below equilibrium, say at $Y = \$700$, aggregate expenditure, that is, people's consumption spending plus producers' intended investment spending, $AE = C + I_i$, is greater than the $700 billion national income, $C + S$. As a result, part of the producers' intended investment, *ab*, is not realized, driving national income up to $800 billion. When national income is above equilibrium, say at *g*, where $Y = \$900$, aggregate expenditure, $AE = C + I_i$, at *h*, is less than the $900 billion national income. The difference, *gh*, drives national income down to $800 billion.

Panel *b* focuses on the relationship between saving and intended investment. The inequalities, $S > I_i$ and $I_i > S$, drive national income to its $800 billion equilibrium level.

**Aggregate expenditure curve (AE)**
A curve that shows the quantity of aggregate expenditures at different levels of national income or GDP.

The Bureau of Economic Analysis maintains current data on the national income (http://www.bea.doc.gov/bea/dn1.htm).

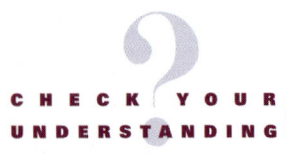

**CHECK YOUR UNDERSTANDING**

What happens to the economy when the actual level of national income is greater than the equilibrium level?

the vertical axis at $60 billion. The intended investment curve, $I_i = \$100$ billion, which is independent of the level of national income, is added to the consumption curve to generate the $C + I_i$ curve, which is the **aggregate expenditure curve (AE).** (At every level of $Y$, $AE$ differs from $C$ by $100 billion of investment demand.)

The 45° income line (the $C + S$ curve) in panel $a$ represents the economy's total production, or aggregate supply. Recall from the GDP accounting chapter our analysis of the income and expenditure approaches to national income accounting. There we saw that national income can be derived either by adding up income ($C + S$) or by adding up expenditures, that is, consumers' and producers' spending on consumption and investment goods ($AE = C + I_i$). Note that the 45° income (or $C + S$) line intersects the $AE$ (or $C + I_i$) curve at $e$, where $Y = \$800$ billion. *The intersection identifies the economy's equilibrium position.*

Suppose the economy is operating at a lower-than-equilibrium income and production level, say, at $Y = \$700$ billion. What happens? At $Y = \$700$ billion, producers still intend to invest $100 billion, which is the distance marked off by $ac$ in panel $a$, while consumers save ($Y - C$), or $cb$, which is $700 - [\$60 + (0.80 \times \$700)] = \$80$ billion. That is, the quantity demanded by consumers of consumption goods at $Y = \$700$ billion is greater than the quantity of consumption goods supplied by producers.

The result? Consumers buy up $20 billion of inventory (the purchase by consumers of the inventory converts that inventory from investment goods to consumption goods), and producers respond by hiring more workers to replace the $20 billion depleted inventories. More workers means more income. That is to say, national income increases. In a nutshell, when

$$I_i > S,$$

$Y$ increases *and continues to increase until* $I_i = S$. Note where $I_i = S$. At $800 billion, aggregate expenditure, $AE$, equals aggregate output, $C + S$. The economy arrives at equilibrium.

What about prices? Does the strain of excess aggregate expenditure that drives the economy to equilibrium also force up prices? Not if at equilibrium there is still an ample supply of resources available, at existing prices, that can be used to produce more goods (and create more income).

Now let's use Exhibit 4 to analyze a different nonequilibrium state of the economy, this time supposing the economy is at $Y = \$900$ billion. What happens? Producers still intend to invest $100 billion, which is the distance marked off by $hf$ in panel $a$, and consumers save ($Y - C$), or $gf$, which is $900 - [\$60 + (0.80 \times \$900)] = \$120$ billion. That is, the quantity demanded by consumers of consumption goods at $Y = \$900$ billion is less than the quantity of consumption goods supplied by producers.

In other words, when national income is greater than the equilibrium level of national income, an excess supply of consumption goods emerges and inventories build up. How does the economy respond to this excess supply? Producers lay off workers in an effort to reduce unwanted inventories. Incomes fall. In a nutshell, when

$$S > I_i,$$

national income falls and continues to fall until it reaches equilibrium, where $I_i = S$.

An alternative illustration of the panel $a$ approach to national income equilibrium is shown in panel $b$. The upward-sloping saving curve, $S$, of panel $b$ depicts the vertical distance between panel *a*'s income curve, $C + S$, and consumption curve, $C$. It is upward sloping because the distances between $C + S$ and $C$ in panel *a* become larger as national income increases.

The planned investment curve in panel *b* is a horizontal curve at $100 billion. It intersects the saving curve at $800 billion, the equilibrium level of national income. As panel *b* shows, when national income is below equilibrium, say at $700 billion, $S < I_i$, creating an excess demand for consumption goods that drives national income up to equilibrium. When national income is above equilibrium, say at $900 billion, $S > I_i$, creating an excess supply of consumption goods that drives national income down to equilibrium.

## CHANGES IN INVESTMENT CHANGE NATIONAL INCOME EQUILIBRIUM

There is no reason to suppose, *as long as the consumption function and the investment demand function remain unchanged,* that the level of national income would move away from equilibrium at $800 billion. As long as aggregate expenditure—that is, consumers' spending on consumption goods and producers' spending on investment goods—exactly matches consumption goods and investment goods production, there is no incentive for producers to increase or decrease their production. Inventories would not be too large or too small. That's what an equilibrium position implies.

But functions do, in fact, change. We noted in the prior chapter how volatile investment can be, and it is not unreasonable to expect that the investment demand function will shift up or down, perhaps even before the economy reaches an equilibrium position.

Suppose producers decide to take advantage of new technologies and add an additional $30 billion to planned investment spending. Intended investment increases, then, from $100 billion to $130 billion.

As we see in Exhibit 5, the $800 billion equilibrium level of national income is no longer tenable.

Intended investment is now $130 billion. How does that affect the equilibrium level of national income? At $Y = \$800$ billion, consumers will still want to spend $700 billion on consumption. But since producers now intend to invest $130 billion of the $800 billion they produce, they supply only $670 billion of consumption goods. That simply isn't enough for consumers.

What will consumers do? What can they do? They will, of course, consume the $670 billion in consumption goods that producers supplied. In addition, they will buy up $30 billion of the inventories that producers had intended to hold as investment. That is to say, consumers convert

**EXHIBIT 5**

**CONSUMERS' AND PRODUCERS' INTENTIONS AND ACTIVITIES, BY STAGES, WHEN INVESTMENT INCREASES TO $130 BILLION AND $Y = \$800$ BILLION**

| CONSUMERS | PRODUCERS |
|---|---|
| $Y = \$800$ | $Y = \$800$ |
| $Y = C + S$ | $Y = C + I_i$ |
| $C = a + bY$ | $I_i = \$130$ |
| $C = \$60 + 0.8\,(Y)$ | $C = Y - I_i$ |
| $= \$60 + 0.8\,(\$800)$ | $= \$800 - \$130$ |
| $= \$700$ | $= \$670$ |
| $S = Y - C$ | $I_a = \$100$ |
| $= \$800 - \$700$ | |
| $= \$100$ | |

intended investment into consumption goods. (Imagine the stripped window displays in retail stores after consumers buy up $30 billion of inventories.) The result is that actual investment ends up being $30 billion less than intended investment.

How will the retailers respond? By faxing producers to replenish their depleted inventories. The producers, excited by this surge in orders, hire more workers. National income increases beyond $800 billion.

### $Y = \$950$ Billion: The New Equilibrium

We trace the economy's path to a higher equilibrium level in Exhibit 6.

The consumption and investment spending curve, which is really the aggregate expenditure curve, $AE$, shifts from $C + I_i$ (with $I_i = \$100$ billion) to $C + I_i'$ (with $I_i' = \$130$ billion). How does the shift affect the equilibrium level of national income?

## EXHIBIT 6

If producers' intended investment spending is $100 billion, then $S = I_i (= ed)$ at $e$, where equilibrium $Y = \$800$ billion. If producers' intended investment spending increases to $130 billion, then at $Y = \$800$ billion, $I_i > S$ ($jd - ed = je$). National income would increase to $e'$, the new equilibrium level of $950 billion, where $I_i = S = \$130$ billion ($e'd'$).

**DERIVING EQUILIBRIUM AT $Y = \$950$ BILLION**

**CONSUMERS' AND PRODUCERS' INTENTIONS AND ACTIVITIES BY STAGES**

| CONSUMERS | PRODUCERS |
|---|---|
| $Y = \$950$ | $Y = \$950$ |
| $Y = C + S$ | $Y = C + I_i$ |
| $C = a + bY$ | $I_i = \$130$ |
| $C = \$60 + 0.8\,(Y)$ | $C = Y - I_i$ |
| $= \$60 + 0.8\,(\$950)$ | $= \$950 - \$130$ |
| $= \$820$ | $= \$820$ |
| $S = Y - C$ | $I_a = \$130$ |
| $= \$950 - \$820$ | |
| $= \$130$ | |

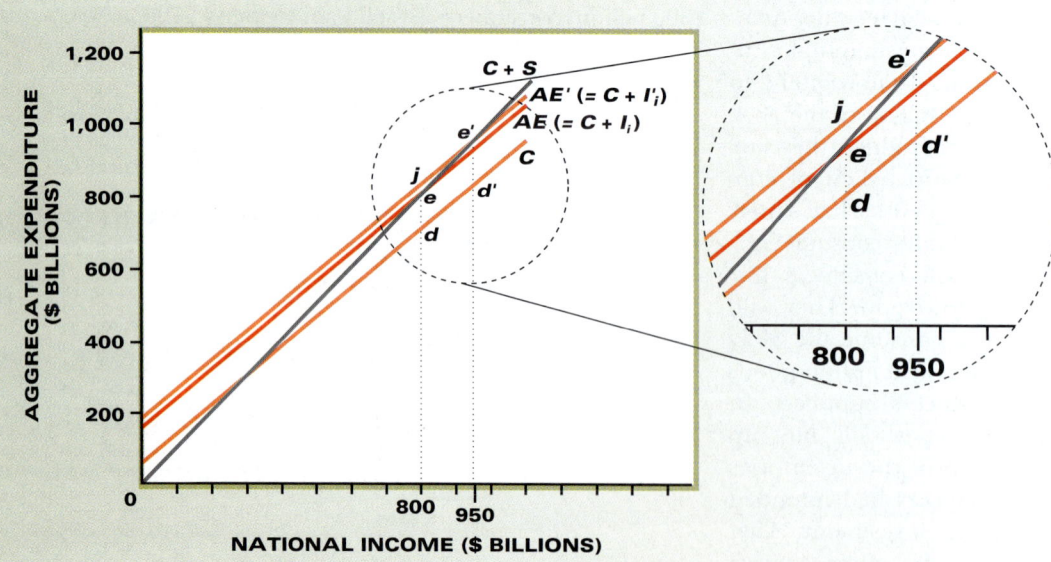

## INTERDISCIPLINARY PERSPECTIVE

### A FRACTURED VERSION OF THE EXODUS STORY

"Pyramid-building, earthquakes, and even wars may serve to increase wealth. . . ."*

In the days of the old Pharaoh, many loyal Egyptians were lacking work and those with jobs were earning far less than a livable wage. There was much grumbling among the people. Sensing the possibility of an uprising, Pharaoh's chief economist advised him to open the royal purse to the poor and unemployed.

"Nonsense," said the Pharaoh. "I'm the Pharaoh. They serve me. I don't serve them. I prefer pyramid building. The royal purse will be used to honor me!"

"Where will we find cheap labor?" asked the economist.

"We'll use the cheapest. I have tens of thousands of foreign slaves. Put them to the task."

The Pharaoh's wishes were obeyed. Giant stones were cut from the quarries at Aswan, pulled and rolled to the banks of the Nile and floated down the river to the delta. Slaves were cutting stone, hauling stone, lifting stone, and setting stone upon stone, every day of every week of every month of every year. But they had to be fed. Pharaoh used his royal purse to buy the food. Now Egyptian farmers had to increase their planting and harvesting. As well, toolmakers, rope makers, shipbuilders and road and ramp builders were busier than ever before. Slowly, the pyramid began to take form. And the farmers, toolmakers, rope makers, shipbuilders, and road and ramp builders had more employment and income than they thought possible. They used their newly acquired money to buy more goods for themselves and their families, creating even more income and employment in Egypt.

During a royal house meeting several years later, the economic adviser confessed to Pharaoh. "You know," he said, "Your idea of a pyramid wasn't such a bad idea after all. No need now to subsidize anybody. Your people have ample jobs and income."

"Good!" said the Pharaoh. "You see, by satisfying me, everybody's satisfied."

"Well, not exactly. There's still the slaves," said the economist.

"I don't think we have to worry about them," replied the Pharaoh.

"Well, maybe not. But there's this fellow Moses . . ."

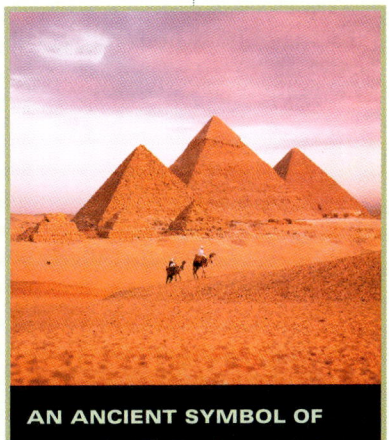

AN ANCIENT SYMBOL OF ECONOMIC PROSPERITY?

#### CONSIDER

How was Egypt's aggregate expenditure increased? What did this increase mean for the national income? How does this story relate to the income multiplier?

*Keynes, J. M., *The General Theory of Employment, Interest, and Money* (London: Macmillan and Co., 1954), p. 129.

---

Look at $Y = \$800$ billion. Before the shift, $I_i = S$ (the distance $ed$). The economy is in equilibrium. After the shift, saving is still $ed$, but intended investment is $jd$. In other words, $I_i > S$. The result: Excess demand for consumption goods at $Y = \$800$ billion propels national income upward.

But to where? The new equilibrium level of national income is at $950 billion. Here, both saving and intended investment are $130 billion (this is the distance $e'd'$, which is the same distance as $jd$). The table in Exhibit 6 lays out the particulars of this new equilibrium position.

Look at the left column. At $Y = \$950$ billion, consumers intend to spend $820 billion on consumption goods and save the remaining $130 billion. The right column shows that producers, responding to and anticipating the demand for investment goods, intend to invest $130 billion and produce $820 billion of consumption. The $I_i = S$ equilibrium condition is met:

$$I_i = S = \$130$$

## An Alternative Method of Calculating Equilibrium

A quick way of calculating the equilibrium level of national income, given specific values for (1) autonomous consumption, (2) *MPC*, and (3) intended investment, is to substitute $(a + bY)$ for $C$ into the aggregate expenditure equation $Y = C + I_i$. For example, since

$$\begin{aligned} \text{in equilibrium} \quad & Y = C + I_i \\ \text{and} \quad & C = \$60 + 0.8Y \\ \text{and} \quad & I_i = \$130, \\ \text{then} \quad & Y = (\$60 + 0.8Y) + \$130. \end{aligned}$$

Subtracting $0.8Y$ from both sides reduces the equation to

$$0.2Y = \$60 + \$130 = \$190.$$

Finally, dividing both sides by 0.2 reduces the equation to

$$Y = \$950.$$

Change any of the values for autonomous consumption, *MPC*, or intended investment, and a new equilibrium level of national income results.

# THE INCOME MULTIPLIER

What's likely to change? Consumption spending has tended to be more stable than investment spending in the past. The *MPC* can be counted on to remain pretty much unchanged. Autonomous consumption, a creature of habit, is hardly likely to change either. Investment spending, on the other hand, is considered rather volatile.

Economists identify changes in aggregate expenditure, in particular investment spending, as the key to our understanding of why national income changes. Changes in investment have highly magnified effects on national income.

For example, we saw in the table in Exhibit 6 that a $30 billion increase in investment spending generated an increase in national income five times that size, from $800 billion to $950 billion, or by $150 billion.

Economists define the change in national income that is generated by a change in aggregate expenditure as the **income multiplier**. It is written

$$\text{multiplier} = \frac{\text{change in } Y}{\text{change in } AE}.$$

**Income multiplier**
The multiple by which income changes as a result of a change in aggregate expenditure.

## Deriving the Multiplier

But why precisely fivefold, as in the case of Exhibit 6? *The degree of multiplication depends on the marginal propensity to consume.*

Let's consider once more the $30 billion increase in investment spending. It reflects, we supposed, a series of new technologies that were introduced at one time into the economy. Let's follow through the impact on the level of national income of one such technological change, say, a $1,000 investment.

Suppose John Flygare, the owner of a tennis shop in Evanston, Illinois, reads an article in *Sports Illustrated* describing a new machine that restrings tennis rackets in half the time it formerly took. The new technology costs $1,000. Suppose John decides to make the investment.

*Can you think of other examples to illustrate the beginning of an income multiplier process? Go to the Interactive Study Center at http://gottheil.swcollege.com and click on the "Your Turn" button to submit your example. Student submissions will be posted to the Web site, and perhaps we will use some in future editions of the book!*

Let's trace the sequence of events that follow that $1,000 increase in investment. First, a *new* order is placed for the machine. John's decision to invest represents a *new* order for Bradley Hastings, the machinist and inventor of the restringing equipment. He produces the machine, sells it to John, and ends up with a $1,000 increase in income. Of course, John ends up with a new machine.

What do you suppose Bradley does with the additional $1,000 income earned? Since we suppose $MPC = 0.80$, we know, then, that he increases his consumption spending by $800. Let's suppose he spends $800 on a custom-made water bed.

Think about what follows. The carpenter, Jay Malin, makes the bed and earns $800, which represents for him an addition to income. Once again, real output and real income are created simultaneously. And, of course, Jay will do with his new income what Bradley did with his—spend part, and save the rest. With $MPC = 0.80$, $640 of the $800 is put to consumption spending.

The sequence of additions to real output, additions to income, and additions to consumption spending and saving is shown in Exhibit 7.

The initial $1,000 change in investment spending sets in motion a chain of events that creates—in successive rounds of income earning, consumption spending, and saving—a $5,000 change in national income. And, as you see, it creates also water beds, violins, computers, health care, auto repair, space heaters, and a host of other real outputs whose total value is $5,000.

**CHECK YOUR UNDERSTANDING**

How does a change in investment create a larger change in income?

### THE MAKING OF THE INCOME MULTIPLIER

| ROUND | CHANGE IN $I_i$ | OUTPUT | Y | C | S |
|---|---|---|---|---|---|
| 1 | $1,000 | RESTRINGER | $1,000.00 | $ 800.00 | $ 200.00 |
| 2 | | WATER BED | 800.00 | 640.00 | 160.00 |
| 3 | | VIOLIN | 640.00 | 512.00 | 128.00 |
| 4 | | COMPUTER | 512.00 | 409.60 | 102.40 |
| 5 | | HEALTH CARE | 409.60 | 327.68 | 81.92 |
| 6 | | AUTO REPAIR | 327.68 | 262.14 | 65.54 |
| 7 | | SPACE HEATER | 262.14 | 209.71 | 52.43 |
| . | | | . | . | . |
| . | | | . | . | . |
| . | | | . | . | . |
| n | | | . | . | . |
| TOTAL | $1,000 | $5,000.00 | $5,000.00 | $4,000.00 | $1,000.00 |

EXHIBIT 7

Note that as economic activity progresses through the successive rounds, the additions to national income become smaller and smaller. For at each round, some of the income is set aside as saving. The lower the *MPC* (or the higher the *MPS*), the greater is the sum set aside.

**THE ALGEBRA OF THE INCOME MULTIPLIER** As we see in Exhibit 7, the total income created is the sum of a series of incomes, each one reduced in the succeeding round by the *MPS*, that is, by 0.20. The series for the $1,000 change in aggregate expenditure, then, is written as

$$\$1,000 + (0.8 \times \$1,000) + [0.8(0.8 \times \$1,000)] + \ldots$$

More generally, this is written

$$\$1,000 + \$1,000 \, (MPC) + \$1,000 \, (MPC^2).$$

The initial $1,000 change in spending is multiplied by

$$1 + MPC + MPC^2 + MPC^3 + \ldots + MPC^n,$$

where $n$ represents the $n$th round of spending. (The next round of spending, the $n$th + 1, is so close to 0 that it becomes totally unimportant.)

Finally, the generalized sum reduces to

$$\frac{1}{1 - MPC}.$$

Since $(1 - MPC) = MPS$,

$$\frac{1}{1 - MPC} = \frac{1}{MPS}.$$

Why does national income increase five times as much as the increase in aggregate expenditure? If *MPC* = 0.80, then

$$\frac{1}{1 + 0.80} = \frac{1}{0.20} = \frac{1}{2/10} = 5$$

You can see, then, what happens to national income when $30 billion is added to aggregate expenditure. With *MPC* = 0.80, the economy generates a $30 billion × 5 = $150 billion increase in national income. Were aggregate expenditure to increase by $100 billion, national income would increase by $500 billion.

## What If $MPC = 0.90$?

Suppose *MPC* = 0.90. What would happen to the level of national income if the same $30 billion of aggregate expenditure were added to the economy? The income multiplier now becomes

$$\frac{1}{1 - 0.90} = 10.$$

With $30 billion of aggregate expenditure added, national income increases by $300 billion. In a nutshell, any change in *MPC* changes the income multiplier and consequently the level of national income that the aggregate expenditure would generate.

# GLOBAL PERSPECTIVE

## HOW THE INCOME MULTIPLIER INTENSIFIES THE IMPACT OF AGGREGATE EXPENDITURE SHIFTS WITHIN DIFFERENT ECONOMIES

Stanford economist Hollis Chenery once observed that the huge increases in aggregate expenditure in northern Italy during the 1950s triggered not only huge increases in northern Italy's income—the income multiplier at work—but contributed as well to southern Italy's economic stagnation.

Why would one region's economic gain come at another region's expense? Think of it this way: The robust economic activity in northern Italy drew the "best and brightest" out of the less robust south and sapped as well southern investment expenditure that would otherwise have been infused into southern Italy's economy. That loss—magnified by the income multiplier effect—dampened southern Italy's growth potential. For example, a 100-million-lire drain on the south's aggregate expenditure—magnified, say, by an income multiplier of five—creates a *negative* 500-million-lire impact on the south's regional income.

Many Canadian economists today see a similar regional disparity problem working against them. They have long viewed living just north of the United States as a mixed blessing. Although the American "economic giant" casts both shadows and light on its northern neighbor, Canadians seem habitually to depreciate the importance of American investment in Canada—which, magnified by the income multiplier, contributes significantly to Canadian economic growth—and instead focus on a Chenery-like idea that the presence of such a powerful and vibrant southern neighbor serves as a magnet for the unending outflow of Canada's "best and brightest" as well as its investment capital. This is seen as robbing Canada of its productive potential.

Many of the newly developing countries of Asia, Africa, and Latin America share this concern about the impact of a reverse multiplier on their national incomes. They see not only their meager supplies of investment capital leave for the greener and more lucrative pastures in the developed economies of the world, but see as well their "best and brightest" make the same trek. Their concern parallels the Chenery observation of 1950s Italy: Different levels of economic activity among nations or regions within nations, through the operations of the income multiplier, exacerbate the economic successes and problems within and among them.

SMILE? HOW CAN I WHEN I'M ABOUT TO LEAVE MY FRIENDS AND FAMILY?

Even European economists were not immune to this line of thinking. During the oil crisis of the 1980s, they argued that the oil-producing cartel OPEC—and notably Saudi Arabia—bled potential investment capital out of the European economies that were later invested by OPEC in the United States. Some called it an American conspiracy! The migration of European capital to the United States via the OPEC cartel—magnified by the reverse income multiplier in Europe—was seen as intensifying the recession in Europe.

In this way, the income multiplier raises the ante of regional resource shifts. It is, to some economists, an economics application of the old adage "One man's meat is another man's poison."

## The Income Multiplier Works in Either Direction

Just as increases in aggregate expenditure stimulate the economy, cuts in aggregate expenditure drag it down. Suppose an increase in the rate of interest shifts the demand curve for investment from $100 billion to $75 billion.

The White House's Economic Statistics Briefing Room has current data on prices (http://www.whitehouse.gov/fsbr/prices.html).

The income multiplier now works in reverse. In the first round of the cutback, national income falls by $25 billion. People whose employment had been supported by the $25 billion investment find themselves with $25 billion less income. But that $25 billion had financed $25 \times 0.80 = \$20$ billion of consumption spending, which was the source of second-round income. That, too, now disappears, creating in turn successive cuts in income and consumption through to the $n$th round. What is the total loss of national income? With a multiplier of 5 ($MPC = 0.80$), the $25 billion investment cutback decreases national income by $25 billion $\times$ 5 = $125 billion. National income falls from $800 billion to a new equilibrium level of $675 billion.

## Aggregate Expenditure and Aggregate Demand

Up to this point in our analysis, we ignored changes in prices. Movements in the economy toward equilibrium occurred without any change in the price level. We assumed an ample supply of resources available, so that any increase in aggregate expenditure, say, an increase in investment demand, would set off a chain reaction of mutually reinforcing increases in income, production, and consumption, without creating any pressure on the price level.

Let's change that now by relaxing the assumption of fixed prices and considering what happens to aggregate expenditure when prices do change. Let's start by supposing that the economy of Exhibit 8, panel a, is in equilibrium at $800 billion and at a price level of 100.

Suppose a general fall in prices occurs, cutting the price level from 100 to 75. Consumer and investment goods are now cheaper. If you lived in that economy, how would you respond to these lower prices? As a consumer, you would probably buy more consumer goods. As a producer facing lower investment goods prices, you would probably invest more. And wouldn't you expect other consumers and producers in the economy to respond the same way?

### EXHIBIT 8

### CONVERTING AGGREGATE EXPENDITURE TO AGGREGATE DEMAND

Increases in the price level shift the $AE$ curve in panel a downward, creating lower equilibrium levels of national income. Decreases in the price level shift the $AE$ curve upward, creating higher equilibrium levels of national income. This relationship between price levels and aggregate expenditure shifts is depicted in panel b by the downward-sloping $AD$ curve.

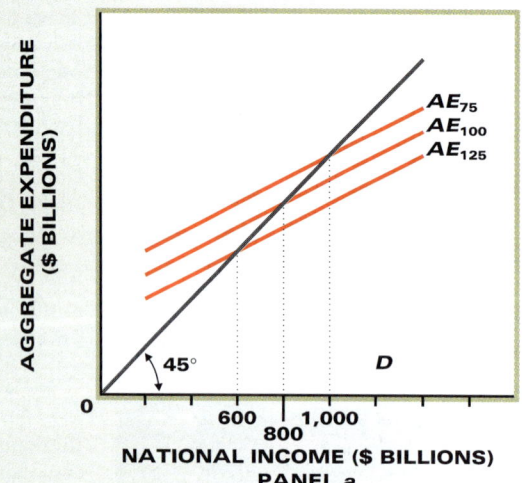

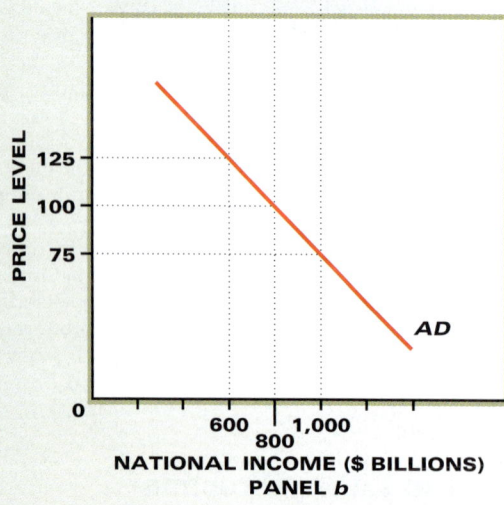

# EQUILIBRIUM NATIONAL INCOME

In other words, when the price level falls, aggregate expenditure increases. This response is shown in panel *a* as an upward shift in the aggregate expenditure curve, from $AE_{100}$ to $AE_{75}$, moving the equilibrium level from $800 billion to $1,000 billion.

If the price level increases, say, from 100 to 125, the opposite responses take place. Now facing higher consumer goods prices, you would probably buy less, and producers, facing higher investment goods prices, would probably invest less. The result: a downward shift in the aggregate expenditure curve, from $AE_{100}$ to $AE_{125}$, moving the equilibrium level from $800 billion to $600 billion.

Positioning panels *a* and *b* as we do allows us to see the relationship between the price-induced shifts in the aggregate expenditure curve in panel *a* and the formation of the downward-sloping aggregate demand curve in panel *b*. At a price level of 125, aggregate demand is $600 billion. When the price level falls to 100, aggregate demand increases to $800 billion. At a price level of 75, aggregate demand is $1,000 billion.

What about the income multiplier? How can we show it in an economy of changing prices? We saw that in the fixed-price model, a change in aggregate expenditure changes the equilibrium level of national income. Look at Exhibit 9, panel *a*. Assuming the economy is in equilibrium at $800 billion and at a price level of 100, a $40 billion increase in aggregate expenditure creates—if $MPC = 0.80$—a $200 billion increase in the equilibrium level of national income *without changing the price level*. How can we show this multiplier effect in the nonfixed-price model of aggregate demand? By a $200 billion outward shift in the aggregate demand curve in panel *b*, from $AD$ to $AD_{+40}$ *at the same price level of 100*, the +40 signaling the $40 billion increase in investment demand.

## EXHIBIT 9

### THE MULTIPLIER EFFECT IN THE *AE* AND *AD* MODELS OF INCOME DETERMINATION

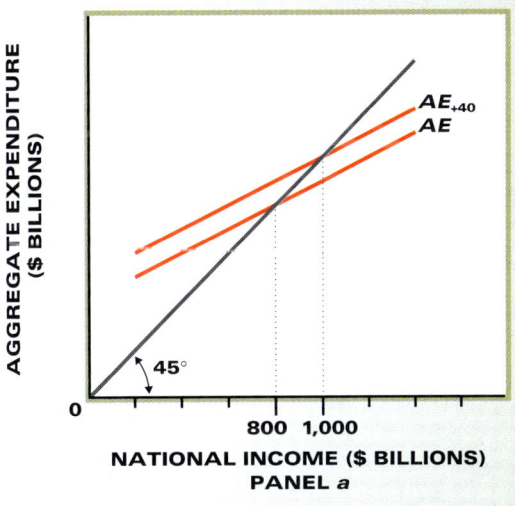

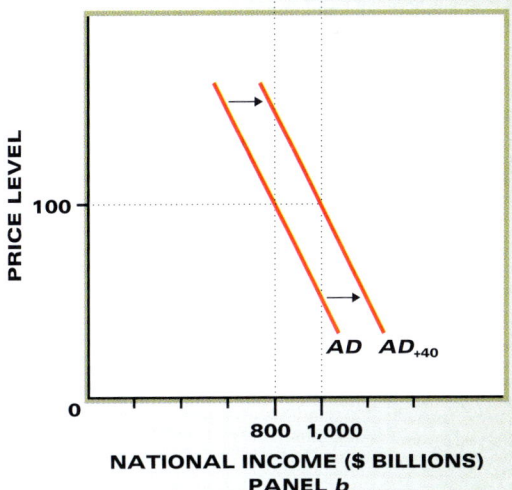

In panel *a*, the multiplier effect of a $40 billion increase in aggregate expenditure increases national income by $200 billion. Prices are assumed not to have changed. In panel *b*, this multiplier effect is shown as an outward shift in the *AD*, so that aggregate demand is $200 billion more, without the price level changing.

**The paradox of thrift**
The more people try to save, the more income falls, leaving them with no more and perhaps with even less saving.

## THE PARADOX OF THRIFT

Suppose people, afraid that their economic future is not nearly as promising as they once thought, decide to put a higher percentage of their income into saving. Increased saving, they feel, will provide greater economic security. But does their shift out of consumption spending to higher saving really provide them with greater economic security? Do they *really* end up saving more? Not necessarily. In fact, by *trying* to save more, they may actually end up saving less, or at least saving no more. That's what economists call the **paradox of thrift.** But why should trying to save more lead to no greater saving and perhaps even less? The answer depends on how income (and production) responds to a change in saving.

Suppose people decide to increase their saving by $30 billion whatever the level of national income. And suppose the economy is in equilibrium at $800 billion. What happens?

Exhibit 10, panel *a*, illustrates the effect of that intention to save on the equilibrium level of national income. The saving curve shifts upward, from $S$ to $S'$, causing the equilibrium level of national income to fall from $800 billion to $650 billion. Follow the logic. Before the saving-curve shift, people intended to save $100 billion, and producers intended to invest $100 billion.

$$S = I_i = \$100$$

With the shift to $S'$, people *intend* to save $130 billion at $Y = \$800$ billion. But can they? If producers still intend to invest only $100 billion, then

$$S > I_i$$

The economy slips into reverse gear. National income falls. The multiplier, when applied to the $30 billion increase in saving ($30 billion cut in consumption),

## EXHIBIT 10

The intentions of people in panel *a* to save more out of their income shifts the saving curve to the left, from $S$ to $S'$. But their intentions will not be realized because the shift will cause the equilibrium level of national income to fall from $800 billion to $650 billion, leaving saving unchanged and equal to investment spending at $100 billion.

In panel *b*, the investment curve is upward sloping, so that the shift in the saving curve from $S$ to $S'$ not only causes the equilibrium level of national income to fall from $800 billion to $550 billion but saving to fall from $100 billion to $75 billion.

### THE PARADOX OF THRIFT

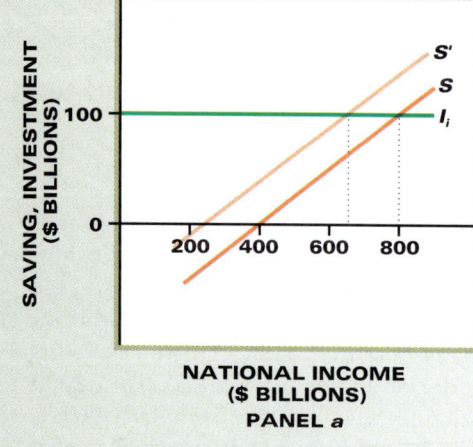
**PANEL a**

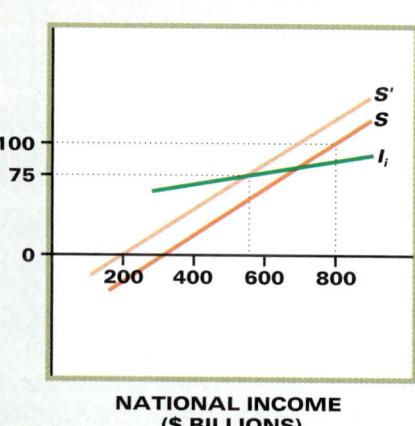
**PANEL b**

# APPLIED PERSPECTIVE

## GM'S MONEY MACHINE

As General Motors' decision to sell its Powertrain foundry in Tilton, Illinois, begins to sink in, the question arises, Just how important is GM to the area?

"Let's not try to wrap what could happen in a pretty package with pretty ribbon," said state representative Bill Black, R-Danville. "If that foundry closes and we can't find a buyer, devastating is not, perhaps, a strong enough word as to what it would do to the area's economy."

Though no economic impact study has been done on the importance of the foundry, most officials agree with Black that a closing would devastate Danville and much of Vermilion County. And economists have studied similar situations enough to offer a thumbnail sketch of the foundry's local influence.

GM's annual payroll for its more than 1,300 employees—about $60 million, according to the United Auto Workers union—probably has the most dramatic and direct impact in the area, said Steve Downing, an economics instructor at Danville Area Community College.

Those dollars, in turn, multiply out into the economy, say Downing and other economists, supporting more dollars and more jobs.

For every payroll dollar at the foundry, Downing guesses that about four more are generated throughout the area.

According to federal statistics, the foundry's $60 million payroll would make up roughly 5 percent of Vermilion County's entire personal income in 1990, which was $1.29 billion.

And the state has estimated that those dollars, on top of production costs paid by GM, have helped create three spinoff jobs in the community tied to every foundry job.

So the foundry's 1,300 employees help support the jobs of roughly 3,900 other workers in the area, from the dozens of local industries and businesses that service the foundry to the waitresses and cooks at area restaurants.

"The foundry is integrally linked to the community from its payroll point of view as well as the subcontractors that provide services to it," said Thomas Byrket, president of the Danville Area Chamber of Commerce.

"It is also linked to the entire corridor along Interstate 74, east and west, Champaign and Indianapolis," Byrket said. "There is no question that it is a major player in east central Illinois, central Illinois and western and central Indiana."

Whether the foundry closes or finds a buyer, the change does not bode well for local governments, most of which rely heavily on local property taxes.

According to the Vermilion County treasurer's office, the Danville school district, in dire budget straits of its own, is the biggest direct recipient of property tax revenues.

"This ripples out into our economy in more ways than are imaginable," Downing said.

THIS SILENCE IS AS DEAFENING AS A RAMPAGING FLOOD—AND OFTEN JUST AS DEVASTATING TO A COMMUNITY.

### CONSIDER

Steve Downing, an economics instructor at Danville Area Community College, estimates that every foundry dollar supports four more dollars in the community. If his estimate is accurate, what is the marginal propensity to consume in Danville?

### MORE ON THE NET

Take a virtual visit to Danville (http://www.danville.net/~danville/homes.html) and visit the Danville Area Economic Development Corporation (http://www.daedc-il.com/). What is the state of Danville's economy today? What incentives for economic development initiatives does the city offer?

**Source:** *Champaign-Urbana News-Gazette,* March 1, 1992.

generates a 5 × $30 billion fall in national income. The new equilibrium level of national income is $650 billion. At $650 billion,

$$S = I_i = \$100.$$

Do you see what has happened? Since people's decision to increase saving to $130 billion caused a fall in national income, they cannot save $130 billion! There's the paradox. *The more people try to save, the more they force a fall in national income, which, in spite of their intentions, results in the level of saving remaining unchanged.*

If we relax the assumption that the investment curve is horizontal and instead assume that it is upward sloping, then the consequences of attempting to increase saving are even more severe. Look at panel *b*. Because the investment curve is upward sloping, the shift in the saving curve from *S* to *S'* results not only in a lower equilibrium level of national income but in a fall in the level of investment. And since $S = I_i$ in equilibrium, the paradox now reads: *The more people try to save, the less they end up saving.*

The discovery of this thrift paradox was nothing short of revolutionary, for the paradox of Exhibit 10 challenges the folk wisdom that many of us believe. Benjamin Franklin taught us that a penny saved is a penny earned. We now see how a penny saved can cause national income to fall! Thrift is no longer an unqualified virtue.

Is increased saving *always* detrimental to our economic health? Not by a long shot. If accompanied by increased investment, increased saving is both inevitable and desirable. After all, if intended investment increases to $130 billion along with intended saving, national income increases to $950 billion. The increased saving that people intended to make is actually made. And we're all the better for it. But if saving increases unattended by a complementary increase in intended investment, some economists—notably Keynesians—see economic trouble.

# CHAPTER REVIEW

**1.** Because consumers and producers make their consumption and production decisions independently and simultaneously, it is only by chance that what consumers purchase for consumption is equal to what producers produce for consumption. If consumers purchase just as much as producers produce for consumption, then the investment that producers intend to make will equal the saving consumers make. The economy is in equilibrium when producers' intended investment equals consumers' saving.

**2.** When producers intend to invest more than consumers save, there are more consumption goods demanded by consumers than producers have produced. Wanted inventories (investment goods) are converted into consumption goods, so that actual investment ends up being less than intended. Producers hire more workers to replenish their inventory stock. National income and employment increase.

**3.** When producers intend to invest less than consumers save, there are fewer consumption goods demanded by consumers than producers have produced. Unwanted inventories (investment goods) accumulate, so that actual investment ends up being more than intended. Producers lay off workers to decrease actual investment to intended levels. National income and employment decrease.

**4.** The size of the income multiplier depends on the size of the marginal propensity to consume. The higher the *MPC*, the larger the income multiplier. The income multiplier is the result of an initial change in aggregate expenditure that creates income for some people who spend part of it on consumption, which then becomes income for other people. These people, too, spend part of their income on consumption, which generates income for still other people. This income/consumption-generating process continues, each round of income created being less than that of the previous round. (The shrinkage is accounted for by the marginal propensity to save.)

5. A fall in the price level creates an upward shift in aggregate expenditure, which results in an increase in the equilibrium level of national income. The aggregate demand curve traces the relationship between changes in aggregate expenditure (corresponding to changing equilibrium levels of national income) brought about by changes in the price level.

6. The paradox of thrift contends that the more people try to save, the more income falls, leaving them with no more, and perhaps with even less, saving.

# KEY TERMS

Aggregate expenditure
Equilibrium level of national income
Unwanted inventories

Actual investment
Aggregate expenditure curve *(AE)*

Income multiplier
The paradox of thrift

# QUESTIONS

1. Why is the Keynesian model of national income determination considered to be a demand-side model as opposed to a supply-side model? (*Hint:* Recall the analogy of the two cutting blades of a pair of scissors, made at the beginning of the chapter.)
2. The chapter emphasizes that two different groups of people in the economy operate simultaneously and independently of each other. Who are these groups, and why is it important to emphasize that they operate in this way?
3. What happens to the level of national income when intended investment is greater than actual investment?
4. What happens to the level of national income when intended investment is greater than saving?
5. The creation of unwanted inventories or the depletion of wanted inventories signals coming changes in the level of national income. Explain.
6. What effect would an upward shift in the investment curve have on the equilibrium level of national income?
7. Describe how the income multiplier works.
8. What is the numerical value of the income multiplier when $MPC = 0$? When $MPC = 1$? Describe what happens to national income in each case.
9. What is paradoxical about the paradox of thrift?
10. Professor Arvind Jaggi asks his students at Franklin and Marshall College the following question: Upon hearing that the Boeing Corporation received a massive order for commercial aircraft from the Saudi Arabian government, the governor of Washington optimistically proclaimed the order to be a massive boon not only for Boeing but for the entire state. Using insights from the income multiplier phenomenon, explain the reasons for the governor's enthusiasm.
11. Explain the relationship between aggregate expenditure and aggregate demand.

# PRACTICE PROBLEMS

1. Fill in the missing cells for $C$, $S$, and $I_a$ in the following table, given that autonomous consumption = $100, MPC = 0.50, and intended investment = $200. Indicate whether the economy is in equilibrium.

   | CONSUMERS | PRODUCERS |
   |---|---|
   | Y = $600 | Y = $600 |
   | C = | C = |
   | S = | $I_a$ = |

2. Fill in the missing cells for $C$, $S$, and $I$ in the following table, given that autonomous consumption = $100, MPC = 0.50, and intended investment = $150. Indicate whether the economy is in equilibrium.

   | CONSUMERS | PRODUCERS |
   |---|---|
   | Y = $600 | Y = $600 |
   | C = | C = |
   | S = | $I_a$ = |

3. Fill in the missing cells in the following table.

   | MPC | MPS | INCOME MULTIPLIER |
   |---|---|---|
   | 0.40 | | |
   | 0.60 | 0.25 | |
   | | | 0.10 |

4. Suppose investment spending increases by $200 and $MPC = 0.90$. Calculate the effect of that increase on the first five rounds of changes in income, changes in consumption, and changes in saving. Illustrate these changes by describing the changes in real output (use your imagination).

   | ROUND | Y | C | S | OUTPUT |
   |---|---|---|---|---|
   | 1 | | | | |
   | 2 | | | | |
   | 3 | | | | |
   | 4 | | | | |
   | 5 | | | | |

5. Imagine an economy with the consumption function $C = \$100 + 0.90Y$. Now consider four scenarios of intended investment: (1) $I_i = \$100$, (2) $I_i = \$150$, (3) $I_i = 250$, and (4) $I_i = 350$. Calculate the equilibrium levels of national income under these four scenarios.

   | INTENDED INVESTMENT | NATIONAL INCOME |
   |---|---|
   | $100 | |
   | $150 | |
   | $250 | |
   | $350 | |

6. Use your imagination to create the first five rounds of a $1,000 change in aggregate expenditure. Show the final effect on national income when $MPS = 0.10$.

   | ROUND | GOOD | $\Delta Y(\$)$ | $\Delta C(\$)$ |
   |---|---|---|---|
   | 1 | | | |
   | 2 | | | |
   | 3 | | | |
   | 4 | | | |
   | 5 | | | |
   | | | TOTAL = | |

# WHAT'S WRONG WITH THIS GRAPH?

**DERIVING EQUILIBRIUM NATIONAL INCOME (EQ Y)**

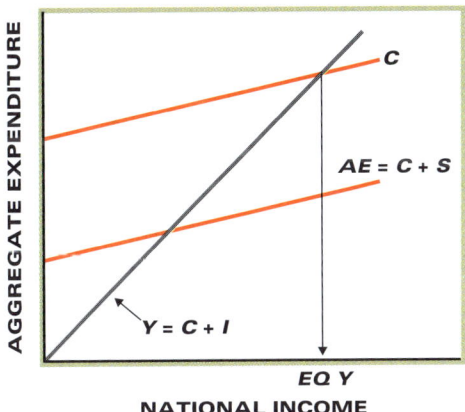

# ECONOMIC CONSULTANTS

**ECONOMIC RESEARCH AND ANALYSIS BY STUDENTS FOR PROFESSIONALS**

Beth Dollins, mayor of New Orleans, LA, is trying to secure a new NHL franchise that will involve both private and city financing. Beth knows that although the franchise has many supporters, there are still many people who oppose the idea principally because they anticipate increases in their city taxes. There has been much discussion in the media about the projected costs, job and income creation, and the taxes associated with the creation of the franchise, but no reliable data have been presented. Beth is convinced that if accurate estimates of costs and benefits were given, the proposed franchise would win overwhelming support in New Orleans.

To make her case, Beth has hired Economic Consultants to prepare a report for Beth that addresses the following issues:

1. How much annual income would the hockey franchise create in the New Orleans downtown region—increased revenues for restaurants, retail stores, hotels, and the like—and what impact would this new income have on the surrounding areas?

2. How would the proposed franchise contribute to job creation in the New Orleans region?
3. What kinds of arguments have been made by other cities that have used public funding to help finance new professional sport franchises?
4. What strategies should Beth pursue to convince the citizens of New Orleans that a professional hockey team in the city is in each citizen's own self-interest?

You may find the following resources helpful as you prepare this presentation for Beth:

- **NHL.COM** (http://www.nhl.com/)—NHL.com is the official site of the National Hockey League.
- **Progessive Minnesota** (http://www.progressivemn.org/)—This site gives the background on one group that opposes public financing for stadiums.
- **The Unofficial reject Bob Bedinghaus Web Site** (http://www.bedinghaus.org)—This site demonstrates the reaction of some voters when they feel they've been taken advantage of for the sake of a new stadium.

# PRACTICE TEST

1. John Maynard Keynes believed that
   a. aggregate supply was most responsible for determining national income.
   b. both aggregate expenditure and supply contribute equally to determining the rate of inflation.
   c. aggregate expenditure is most responsible for determining national income.
   d. both aggregate expenditure and supply contribute equally to determining national income.
   e. aggregate expenditure has no effect on national income.

2. Macroequilibrium occurs when
   a. consumption plus saving equals national income.
   b. planned investment equals actual investment.
   c. saving equals consumption.
   d. aggregate expenditure equals planned investment.
   e. actual investment equals saving.

3. Suppose that the consumption function is $C = 110 + 0.7Y$, and national income is $800 billion. If producers intend to invest $100 billion, then
   a. the economy will be in macroequilibrium.
   b. savings will equal $100 billion.
   c. national income will fall because actual investment exceeds intended investment.
   d. national income will rise because actual investment is less than intended investment.
   e. savings exceeds actual investment in equilibrium.

4. Unwanted inventories arise when
   a. intended investment is less than savings.
   b. intended investment exceeds savings.
   c. the economy is in macroequilibrium.
   d. actual investment is $0.
   e. the aggregate expenditure curve lies below the consumption curve.

5. National income rises when intended investment exceeds actual investment because
   a. interest rates rise so that additional income can be generated.
   b. additional workers are hired to produce more output.
   c. workers are laid off in response to lower demand for goods and services.
   d. planned consumption is less than planned savings.
   e. the economy is moving upward along its aggregate demand curve.

6. The Keynesian $C + I = C + S$ model assumes that prices
   a. rise when the aggregate expenditure curve shifts upward.
   b. rise when the aggregate supply curve shifts upward.
   c. are determined by aggregate demand and aggregate supply.
   d. are constant because the economy always tends toward equilibrium.
   e. are constant because there is an excess supply of resources that can be drawn upon to increase real GDP.

7. Consider the relationship between aggregate demand and aggregate expenditure. A fall in the price level in the $AD$ model will, in the $AE$ model,
   a. shift the $AE$ curve upward.
   b. shift the $AE$ curve downward.
   c. leave the $AE$ curve unchanged, but increase the level of $AE$.
   d. leave the $AE$ curve unchanged, but decrease the level of $AE$.
   e. leave the $AE$ curve and the level of $AE$ unchanged.

8. If the consumption function for an economy is $C = 180 + 0.75Y$, and intended investment rises by $800, then the resulting change in national income is
   a. +$2,400.
   b. −$3,200.
   c. +$3,200.
   d. −$800.
   e. +$1,133.

9. If the marginal propensity to save decreases, then
   a. changes in intended investment would have larger effects on national income.
   b. the marginal propensity to consume would fall by the same amount.
   c. changes in intended investment would have smaller effects on national income.
   d. the economy cannot attain macroequilibrium.
   e. the income multiplier will fall.

10. According to the paradox of thrift,
    a. as national income falls, consumption rises, thereby offsetting any change in planned saving.
    b. if individuals try to save more, they may actually save less, because national income will increase.
    c. when the aggregate expenditure curve shifts upward, it is exactly offset by the change in saving in the economy.
    d. if individuals try to save more, they end up saving no more and may actually save less, because national income will decrease.
    e. the multiplier effect makes it impossible for the level of saving in the economy to exceed national income in equilibrium.

# FISCAL POLICY: COPING WITH INFLATION AND UNEMPLOYMENT

## CHAPTER 8

As we discussed in the previous chapter, only three factors—autonomous consumption, intended investment, and the marginal propensity to consume—dictate precisely where the level of national income will come to rest. That understanding is a good foundation upon which to build added dimensions. As we saw, tens of millions of consumers and producers, each acting independently, make consumption and investment decisions that drive the economy toward equilibrium.

But what's so great about being in equilibrium? What's really so great about people consuming and investing what they intended to consume and invest? Perhaps their intentions weren't very good in the first place! After all, poor people intend to consume very little and, because they are poor, actually do consume very little. Do you suppose

**THIS CHAPTER INTRODUCES YOU TO THE ECONOMIC PRINCIPLES ASSOCIATED WITH:**

- FRICTIONAL, STRUCTURAL, AND CYCLICAL UNEMPLOYMENT
- DISCOURAGED AND UNDEREMPLOYED WORKERS
- THE NATURAL RATE OF UNEMPLOYMENT
- WINNERS AND LOSERS FROM INFLATION
- RECESSIONARY AND INFLATIONARY GAPS
- THE TAX MULTIPLIER
- THE BALANCED BUDGET MULTIPLIER
- FISCAL POLICY OPTIONS

they're happy about the fact that their intentions were realized? When the economy is in equilibrium, it can sometimes be distressful.

In the economy described in the preceding chapter, we first assumed that at equilibrium $Y = \$800$ billion. Consumers chose to spend $700 billion on consumption, precisely the amount that producers, acting independently, chose to produce for consumption. As a result, the actual investment producers made was exactly what they intended to make.

But is $Y = \$800$ billion, itself, particularly attractive? Were people, in fact, satisfied with their lot? *Equilibrium tells us nothing about satisfaction* or the general state of the economy.

171

# EQUILIBRIUM AND FULL EMPLOYMENT

Let's consider the relationship between the economy's equilibrium position and the level of national income that would support full employment. After all, the equilibrium position is determined by the consumers' and producers' specific consumption and investment decisions, and these have little to do with how large the labor force is or how many of those in the labor force are actually working.

The economy can be in equilibrium and at the same time still be unable to provide employment to those wanting jobs. In fact, that's precisely what Keynes saw in the 1930s. He and millions of other people who experienced unemployment or who had to live under its threat didn't think that kind of national income equilibrium was anything to celebrate.

## Identifying Unemployment

When is an economy at full employment? When everybody is working? Although this sounds like a reasonable enough criterion, it's far from useful. Why? Because there are always some people who, at prevailing wage rates, *choose* not to work. Suppose, for example, that Brian Vargo, an auto repair mechanic, refuses to work unless he is paid $1,000 per hour. Who would hire him at that wage? It would be silly, then, to count him among the unemployed. In defining full employment, therefore, we need to look at the reasons why people may not have jobs.

The Bureau of Labor Statistics provides current data (http://stats.bls.gov/) on unemployment.

**THE FRICTIONALLY UNEMPLOYED** What about people who voluntarily quit a job to spend time looking for a better one? Most people, particularly in the early years of their working life, are relatively mobile. They are always thinking about the possibilities of an upward move. They may have read about the prospects in Alaska, or heard about the new Japanese auto plant being built in Tennessee. Their antennas are always up, searching for new and better employment.

Many times, they do more than think about changing jobs. They actually do it. A real lead or a passed-over promotion could trigger their decision to quit. They gamble on improvement. For a short period—days, weeks, or perhaps even months—they explore their opportunities. It takes energy and patience. Some may decide to return to school to complete a degree or develop new technical skills.

How would you classify these between-jobs people or people entering the labor force for the first time and looking for their first job? Economists use the term **frictional unemployment** to convey the idea that initial job hunting or job switching for improvement is seldom smooth or instantaneous, but quite natural in a dynamic economy.

**Frictional unemployment**
Relatively brief periods of unemployment caused by people deciding to voluntarily quit work in order to seek more attractive employment.

**THE STRUCTURALLY UNEMPLOYED** It is quite another matter when workers wake up one morning to find their jobs gone because of a technological change in the production process or because of a change in demand for the goods they were producing. And it is hardly a comfort to them to know that both technological change and changes in demand are quite natural phenomena in a dynamic economy. Economists describe such a loss of jobs as **structural unemployment**.

When a new technology displaces an old one, it typically displaces the old technology's operators as well. For example, when the steam-driven locomotive was the principal mode of moving passengers and freight across the country, railroad firemen were needed to fuel the engines. But when the railroads switched from steam to diesel, these formerly indispensable firemen became technologically obsolete.

**Structural unemployment**
Unemployment that results from fundamental technological changes in production, or from the substitution of new goods for customary ones.

The firemen soon discovered they weren't alone. As rail transportation gave way to trucks and airplanes, many locomotive engineers, porters, stationmasters, switch operators, rail repairmen, and others employed in the manufacture of rails, locomotives, boxcars, refrigerator cars, and railway stations found themselves out of work. What could they do? Not every ex–railway worker can pilot a Boeing 747.

Changes in consumer tastes, too, destroy jobs. Wisconsin dairy farmers lost their farms and employment when consumer preferences shifted from butter to margarine. When people switched from reading newspapers to watching television, a stream of editors, columnists, reporters, printing press workers, and newspaper vendors found themselves out of work. Should we not watch television because editors need jobs?

What do you suppose will happen to fur trappers, traders, tanners, and fur-coat makers if activists struggling for animal rights succeed in convincing millions of consumers? What happens to tobacco workers when people stop smoking? When people in France switch from wine to Coke—and they seem to be doing so in increasing numbers—vineyard workers in southern France join the ranks of the structurally unemployed.

Unemployment-creating changes in technology and consumer taste strike workers indiscriminately—no industry or worker is immune—but the impact of such change falls particularly hard on older workers. After all, they acquired years of on-the-job experience to match a specific technology. When the technology changes, their work experience and skills often count for zero. What can they do? It is difficult for them to start over again. They find themselves competing for lower-paying jobs against the preferred younger workers.

Can we avoid structural unemployment? Only by avoiding the modern conveniences of life such as central heating, paved streets, electric lights, personal computers, and vacuum cleaners. That is to say, if people are to enjoy the benefits that advanced technology affords, then the pain of structural unemployment has to be paid. But for those who pay it, the question always is: Why me?

**THE CYCLICALLY UNEMPLOYED** Why me? is the same question asked by people who lose their jobs not to technological change but because the economy happens to be languishing in a downturn or recession phase of a business cycle. In these economically depressed phases, many businesses are forced to cut back on production and consequently cut back as well on the number of workers they are able to employ.

Economists define this kind of joblessness as **cyclical unemployment** because it is governed by the rhythms of the business cycle—increasing as the cycle moves into its recession phase and decreasing as it moves out.

If you're among the unfortunate workers who are cyclically unemployed during some part of the recession, you would probably find it difficult to get a new job. After all, who is hiring during a recession? You may be eager to work, but eagerness is not the issue.

**THE DISCOURAGED WORKER** How long can you search for a job without becoming totally discouraged and give up? Many of the unemployed do just that. Perhaps you would too if, day after day, week after week, you confront only rejection. After a while you may no longer even think of yourself as a worker or as part of the labor force. Many **discouraged workers** end up in a nonwork culture and remain permanently separated from the productive society. And once in that culture, it may take more than the availability of jobs to get them back into productive life.

**THE UNDEREMPLOYED WORKER** Take the case of Nancy Krasnow, an aeronautical engineer who once earned $60,000 working for Lockheed in Los Angeles. In the midst of a recession, Lockheed laid her off, along with 2,000 of her coworkers. After months of fruitless job searching, and with savings close to zero,

**Cyclical unemployment**
Unemployment associated with the downturn and recession phases of the business cycle.

**Discouraged workers**
Unemployed people who give up looking for work after experiencing persistent rejection in their attempts to find work.

# INTERDISCIPLINARY PERSPECTIVE

## FROM JOHN STEINBECK'S *CANNERY ROW*

It was a lazy day. Willard was going to have to work hard to get up any excitement. "I think you're a coward, too. You want to make something of that?" Joey didn't answer. Willard changed his tactics. "Where's your old man now?" he asked in a conversational tone.

"He's dead," said Joey.

"Oh yeah? I didn't hear. What'd he die of?"

For a moment Joey was silent. He knew Willard knew but he couldn't let on he knew, not without fighting Willard, and Joey was afraid of Willard.

"He committed—he killed himself."

"Yeah?" Willard put on a long face. "How'd he do it?"

"He took rat poison."

Willard's voice shrieked with laughter. "What'd he think—he was a rat?"

Joey chuckled a little at the joke, just enough, that is.

"He must of thought he was a rat," Willard cried. "Did he go crawling around like this—look, Joey—like this? Did he wrinkle up his nose like this? Did he have a big old long tail?" Willard was helpless with laughter. "Why'n't he just get a rat trap and put his head in it?" They laughed themselves out on that one, Willard really wore it out. Then he probed for another joke. "What'd he look like when he took it—like this?" He crossed his eyes and opened his mouth and stuck out his tongue.

"He was sick all day," said Joey. "He didn't die 'til the middle of the night. It hurt him."

Willard said, "What'd he do it for?"

"He couldn't get a job," said Joey. "Nearly a year he couldn't get a job. And you know a funny thing? The next morning a guy come around to give him a job."

### CONSIDER

Judging from that snippet of conversation, would you describe Joey's father as having been a discouraged worker? Why or why not?

*Source:* From CANNERY ROW by John Steinbeck. Copyright 1945 by John Steinbeck. Renewed © 1973 by Elaine Steinbeck, John Steinbeck IV, and Thom Steinbeck. Used by permission of Viking Penguin, a division of Penguin Putnam Inc.

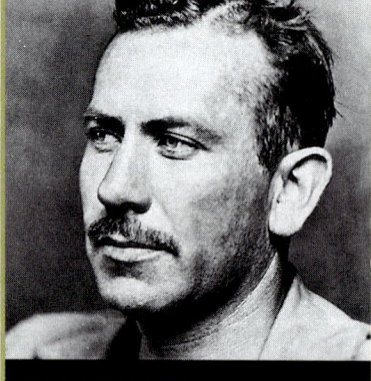

JOHN STEINBECK: HIS MUSE WAS THE SUFFERING POOR; HIS GENIUS WAS CONVEYING THEIR PATHOS.

---

Nancy's only viable prospect (other than slipping into the world of the discouraged worker) was flipping hamburgers at McDonald's, which earns her slightly more than minimum wage. Reluctantly, she sets aside her talents and experience and takes the job. But what is she now, an aeronautical engineer or a hamburger flipper?

If she were asked whether she was unemployed and looking for a job, how would she answer? The fact is that she *is* employed. But how would *you* define her status? In periods of recession, the number of people who end up as discouraged workers or among the **underemployed workers** can be rather significant.

**Underemployed workers**
Workers employed in jobs that do not utilize their productive talents or experience.

## Calculating an Economy's Rate of Unemployment

Imagine an economy with the employment/unemployment characteristics shown in Exhibit 1.

How would you go about determining the economy's rate of unemployment? Do you simply sum up the unemployed—that is, the 150 + 200 + 500 = 850 and divide by the total number of workers? That reckoning would generate an unemployment rate of 850/10,250 = 8.3 percent.

But what about the 300 underemployed workers? A tough call, isn't it? After all, is an aeronautical engineer flipping hamburgers at McDonald's really employed? If you're inclined to answer no and count such workers among the unemployed, the economy's unemployment rate increases to 1,150/10,250 = 11.2 percent.

But look again at Exhibit 1. There are 250 discouraged workers who have no jobs. Are you prepared to write them off the list of unemployed because they have given up looking? If you include them, the rate of unemployment increases to 1,400/10,250 = 13.7 percent. As you see, the unemployment rate for the Exhibit 1 economy depends on your decision about who belongs in the unemployment pool.

### EXHIBIT 1

**NUMBER OF WORKERS AND TYPES OF UNEMPLOYMENT**

| | |
|---|---|
| NUMBER OF WORKERS | 10,250 |
| FRICTIONAL UNEMPLOYMENT | 150 |
| STRUCTURAL UNEMPLOYMENT | 200 |
| CYCLICAL UNEMPLOYMENT | 500 |
| DISCOURAGED WORKERS | 250 |
| UNDEREMPLOYED WORKERS | 300 |

## The Bureau of Labor Statistics Definition of Unemployment

How does the rate of unemployment you choose as being appropriate compare to the rate chosen by the Bureau of Labor Statistics (BLS) of the U.S. Department of Labor? Each month, the bureau conducts a nationwide employment survey of 60,000 households. The critical question asked is: *Are you presently gainfully employed or actively seeking employment?* Only those answering yes are counted in the labor force. That is, according to the BLS, the **labor force** consists of working people plus the unemployed who are looking for work.

Suppose, for example, that Elisa Kilhafer, a homemaker in St. Louis, Missouri, is surveyed by the BLS and reports that she is neither gainfully employed nor looking for work. According to the BLS, Elisa is neither unemployed nor a part of the labor force. On the other hand, if she had said that she was looking for work but couldn't find any, she would be counted not only among the unemployed but also as a member of the labor force.

How does the BLS treat the underemployed? As long as the underemployed are working somewhere at some job, they are counted as employed and in the labor force. Discouraged workers, on the other hand, are viewed differently. Why? Because it makes no difference to the BLS *why* discouraged workers have no jobs. The fact that they are not actively looking is reason enough to exclude them from the labor force and from the lists of the unemployed.

According to the BLS, then, the labor force in Exhibit 1 is 10,250 − 250 discouraged workers = 10,000. The number of workers unemployed—now excluding discouraged and underemployed workers—is 150 + 200 + 500 = 850. The BLS-derived rate of unemployment is 8.5 percent.

## The Natural Rate of Unemployment

Does an 8.5 percent unemployment rate signal that the economy is 850 jobs short of full employment? Not exactly. Economists recognize that some of that unemployment is natural, that is, it does not necessarily reflect an economy unable to

**Labor force**
People who are gainfully employed or actively seeking employment.

The Bureau of Labor Statistics maintains statistics and information from its monthly report of households, called the Current Population Survey (http://stats.bls.gov/cpshome.htm). Included is a Labor Department report on how the government measures unemployment (http://stats.bls.gov/cps_htgm.htm).

absorb its unemployment. After all, they argue, even if the economy of Exhibit 1 were bursting with energy and the demand for workers outstripped the supply, there would still be workers looking for better positions, and others displaced from their jobs because of technological improvements. If we accept the fact that these forms of unemployment are both natural and inevitable, then—setting that unemployment aside—if all other workers are employed, the economy is at full employment.

The 350 frictionally and structurally unemployed of Exhibit 1 make up what economists describe as the economy's 3.5 percent **natural rate of unemployment**. What remains are the 500 cyclically unemployed, accounting for 5.0 percent of the labor force.

Economists distinguish between the 8.5 percent actual rate of unemployment, the 3.5 percent natural rate, and the 5.0 percent rate of cyclical unemployment. *To economists, the economy is at full employment when the actual rate of unemployment equals the natural rate.* Put differently, the economy is considered to be at **full employment** when the rate of cyclical unemployment is zero.

## Full-Employment Level

Let's apply the concept of full employment to the aggregate supply curve developed in the aggregate demand and aggregate supply chapter and redrawn here in panel *a* of Exhibit 2.

**Natural rate of unemployment**
The rate of unemployment caused by frictional plus structural unemployment in the economy.

**Full employment**
An employment level at which the actual rate of employment in the economy is equal to the economy's natural rate of unemployment.

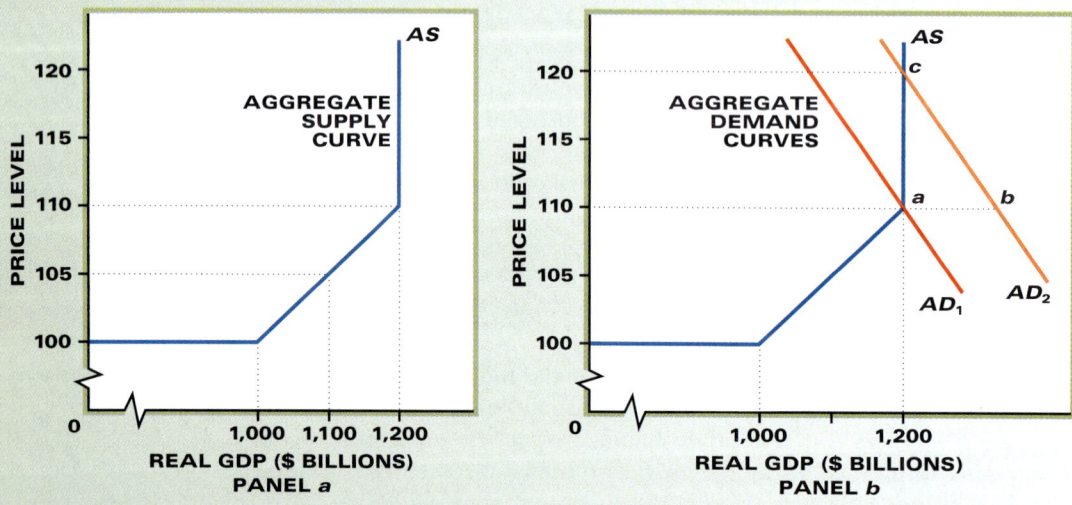

**THE FULL-EMPLOYMENT LEVEL OF THE AGGREGATE SUPPLY CURVE AND THE EFFECTS OF AN INCREASE IN AGGREGATE DEMAND**

Within the real GDP range of $0 to $1,000 billion, GDP can increase without triggering an increase in the economy's price level. This is depicted in panel *a* by the horizontal segment of the aggregate supply curve at $P = 100$.

Beyond that point, producers must offer higher wage rates to induce more people into the labor force. Higher wages cause higher price levels, shown in the upward-sloping segment of the aggregate supply curve. At GDP = $1,200 billion, everyone who is capable of working at *any* wage rate is working. No further increase in the price level can generate more real GDP. That is why the aggregate supply curve becomes perfectly vertical at $1,200 billion.

The shift in aggregate demand from $AD_1$ (point *a*) to $AD_2$ creates excess aggregate demand—aggregate quantity demanded minus aggregate quantity supplied—at $P = 110$ (point *b*). Since output and income at $Y = \$1,200$ billion are already at full-employment level, the pressures of excess aggregate demand force prices upward to $P = 120$ (point *c*).

The shape of the aggregate supply curve reflects the view (expressed in the preceding chapter) that the price level is constant at low levels of employment. Output and income can increase anywhere along the horizontal segment without any upward pressure on the price level because there is a ready pool of unemployed workers to draw upon at current wage rates.

The price level is constant only up to a level of $1,000 billion. From $1,000 billion to $1,200 billion, the price level rises from $P = 100$ to $P = 110$. At $GDP = \$1,000$ billion, everyone willing to work at the current wage rate is employed. There are others in the economy who are not working but would be willing to work—but only at wage rates higher than the current rate. If they can't get the higher rates, they prefer not to be members of the labor force.

How, then, can the economy get beyond $1,000 billion to, say, $1,100 billion? By inducing more people into employment with higher wage rates. But higher wage rates raise the cost of producing goods, and producers pass these higher costs on to consumers, with varying degrees of success, by raising prices. In the end, higher wage rates are accompanied by higher prices. Note that at $1,100 billion, $P = 105$. In other words, real GDP and employment both increase, *but only under conditions of price level increases.*

That's why the aggregate supply curve slopes upward within the range $Y = \$1,000$ billion to $Y = \$1,200$ billion. Increases in both GDP and employment occur, but only with increasing doses of inflation.

What happens beyond $1,200 billion? *There is no beyond $1,200 billion.* At $1,200 billion, the aggregate supply curve becomes vertical. The economy's employment potential is *fully* exhausted. There are no more workers available at any wage rate to increase national income. The only increase that occurs at $1,200 billion is in prices. This is illustrated in panel *b* of Exhibit 2. The combination of the aggregate demand curve, $AD_1$, and the aggregate supply curve, $AS$, creates an equilibrium of real GDP of $1,200 billion at a price level of 110, point *a*. But look what happens to real GDP and the price level when the aggregate demand curve shifts upward to $AD_2$. At the price level of 110, the quantity of output demanded—point *b* on $AD_2$—is now greater than the quantity supplied.

Although production of goods and services cannot increase beyond $1,200 (the economy's maximum output is depicted by the vertical segment of the aggregate supply curve), the prices of the goods and services can. Excess aggregate demand at the price level $P = 110$ drives the price level up along the $AD_2$ curve from point *b* to point *c*, where a new equilibrium occurs at $1,200 billion and $P = 120$.

# UNDERSTANDING INFLATION

Suppose you were living in the economy of Exhibit 2, panel *b*, and could choose between $GDP = \$900$ billion and $P = 100$ (moderate unemployment with no inflation) and $GDP = \$1,200$ billion and $P = 110$ (full employment with inflation). Which would you choose? If you are like most people, you would probably choose the second option because you can more easily identify with the pain associated with being out of a job than you can with the pain associated with inflation. Unlike unemployment, whose victims are personal and recognizable, inflation covers the economy like a fog, affecting everything and everybody, making it sometimes difficult to distinguish inflation's victims from its nonvictims. In fact, there are many in the economy who actually benefit from inflation.

## Winners and Losers from Inflation

Inflation redistributes people's incomes. Who wins in this redistribution? Who loses?

**WHO LOSES FROM INFLATION?** Perhaps more than any other single group, people living on fixed incomes, such as retirees, have reason to worry about inflation. Why? Listen to Tina Eckstrom's sad story. Back in 1960, she and her husband bought a deferred annuity that cost them $100 monthly. In 2001, it started to pay them $700 a month in retirement benefits. They were excited about the prospect of living comfortably in retirement on the $700 monthly check, along with the savings they had accumulated. After all, back in 1960 when they put their retirement plans together, their rent was $125 per month, a new automobile was $1,500, milk was $0.25 a quart, and a first-run movie was $0.35. What they didn't factor into their plans was inflation.

When they retired in 2001, they began to receive their $700 each month. But their retirement dreams were shattered. Why? The $700 doesn't come close to covering their condominium rent, and a new car—now at $20,000—is simply out of the question. They, along with millions of other people who live on fixed incomes, are big losers from inflation.

For the same reason, landlords worry about inflation, especially those whose incomes are tied to long-term rental leases. So too do workers who accepted union-negotiated, multiyear, fixed-wage contracts. Imagine how you would feel if you were working for minimum wage during the 1990s. The annual inflation rate was 2.2 percent, and the minimum wage was fixed at $5.15. If you bought $100 worth of groceries in 1990, by 2000 you could buy only $75.07 worth of groceries (assuming the price of groceries went up at the same rate as the price level).

**CHECK YOUR UNDERSTANDING**

Why are savers sometimes losers from inflation?

Savers can lose as well. How? Suppose you saved $100 last year, giving up the option of buying a $100 pair of Nike cross-training shoes. This year, you decide to use the savings to buy the shoes. You withdraw $105 from the bank—your savings earned 5 percent interest—only to discover that the shoes now cost $110. While your money was in the bank, inflation was 10 percent. You're in a relatively worse position. Imagine if you had saved $10,000, not $100.

Remember Benjamin Franklin's comment: A penny saved is a penny earned. Think about it. In inflationary times, it simply isn't true.

**WHO GAINS FROM INFLATION?** Not everyone loses from inflation. Borrowers, for example, are among those who benefit. Let's consider those shoes again. Suppose that last year you borrowed $100 at 5 percent interest to buy the shoes. This year, you repay the bank with interest, $105, and come away a winner. Why? *Inflation!* Had you waited until this year to buy the shoes, with inflation at 10 percent, it would have cost you $110. Of course, if inflation works in favor of borrowers, it works against lenders. What you won through inflation, the bank lost. The $105 that the bank now holds buys less goods and services for the bank than the $100 it held (and loaned you) last year.

Let's paint another scenario. Suppose you considered buying a beautiful brick ranch house sitting on a ¼-acre lot. It had three bedrooms, two baths, a sunken living room with fireplace, a large study, wood-floored dining room, and a two-car garage. The owner, eager to sell, will accept $140,000. The bank offers you a 30-year fixed-rate mortgage at 6½ percent. Your monthly payments amount to $850. That's $300 more than the two-bedroom apartment you now rent, but the difference in comfort is so striking that you decide to buy the house. Six years later you

# HISTORICAL PERSPECTIVE

## INFLATION AND HYPERINFLATION

Suppose you earned $70,000 a year as a garage mechanic, specializing in foreign sports cars. You planned to save 20 percent or $14,000 and spend the remaining $56,000 on a shopping list of marvelous things. Good idea? Sounds great.

But then it happens. A 10 percent inflation descends on the economy. What had cost $20 before, say a toaster oven, now costs $22. The new fully equipped Saturn was once $17,000; it's now $18,700. The rent on your apartment jumps from $700 per month to $770. Everything goes up except wages and salaries. Your $70,000 annual income is still $70,000. The $56,000 you commit to consumption still buys $56,000 of consumption goods. But because prices rose, it buys fewer goods. The $20,000 is still in the bank but it too has lost purchasing power.

Let's now suppose that the inflation rate is 50 percent and not 10 percent. You get the picture, don't you? That Saturn now costs $25,500! The toaster oven is $30. The $56,000 looks less and less powerful, doesn't it?

Let's bump that inflation rate up to 100 percent. Wow! That $34,000 Saturn alone eats away most of your $56,000 consumption. You're hardly able to toast your bread!

Rates of inflation are measured in percentages, which may seem somewhat esoteric until you consider the things inflation prevents you from buying. That's why inflation is considered a real cost. How high the cost you pay is depends on the rate of inflation.

While there is no specific percentage that economists use to differentiate inflation from very high inflation, economists will grant that any rate in the 50 percent to 100 percent range is mighty high inflation! Out of the ordinary. Extremely troublesome.

Yet as disturbing and costly as very high inflation may be to people, it is still qualitatively different from the sociopathological rate that economists identify as hyperinflation. The difference? When economists think of hyperinflation, they think 50 percent or higher *per month*. Imagine: A toaster in January costs $20; in February, $30; in March, $45, in April, $67.50, and if you're thinking about a Christmas gift, think $1,730. Crazy, isn't it? People have actually lived through months and years of hyperinflation. Look at the accompanying table of hyperinflations.

| GERMANY | 1922 | 5,000% |
| HUNGARY | 1946 | 20,000% |
| BOLIVIA | 1985 | 10,000% |
| ARGENTINA | 1989 | 3,100% |
| PERU | 1990 | 7,500% |
| BRAZIL | 1993 | 2,100% |
| UKRAINE | 1993 | 5,000% |
| YUGOSLAVIA | 1993–95 | 5,000,000,000,000,000% |

**I JUST STARTED SHOPPING AND I ALREADY RAN OUT OF MONEY.**

German workers, during Germany's hyperinflation, insisted on being paid twice a day so they could buy their groceries during lunch break. If they waited until the end of the workday, they could not have afforded the food! It was ridiculous to save because their savings would lose its value overnight.

Yugoslav's 5 quadrillion percent inflation—from October 1993 to January 24, 1995—represents the worst episode of hyperinflation in recorded history. The average daily rate was nearly 100 percent. Money became virtually useless. One story suffices to illustrate the irrationality of its money economy. Postmen collected telephone bills. One postman found that by the time he collected the 780 bills on his route, their value was virtually zero. So he decided to stay home and pay the bills himself, which cost him the equivalent of a few U.S. pennies!

*continued on next page*

His time was worth more than the few pennies he would spend on the bills. If someone told yo to go downtown and pick up a free stick of gum, you would stay home, too.

How safe would you feel if you had to cope with such price increases? Even if wages soared as well, there would be no anchor to your economic life. How would you know what tomorrow would look like? How could you plan for your family's future? Could you feel any sense of security?

It's no surprise, then, that economists view any kind of inflation as problematic. Moderate inflation can escalate into high inflation and high inflation may end up being a ticking time bomb that explodes into that dreaded twilight zone of hyperinflation. Like a bogeyman in a closet, hyperinflation is very, very scary. And unlike a bogeyman, it's sometimes very real. It can happen!

drive by your old apartment building and notice a For Rent sign sitting on the front lawn. What shocks you is the advertised rent: $885 per month! More than your present monthly mortgage payments. You may have made silly purchases in your lifetime, but the house, thanks to 10-percent-per-year-inflation, was not one of them. You come away a winner.

What ends up as gains from inflation to borrowers like you also works for government. After all, government is the largest single borrower. Interest payments every year on its more than $4 trillion national debt exceed $200 billion. And just as your $850 mortgage payments every month became less and less burdensome through inflation, so too does inflation, with time, reduce the *real* cost to government of carrying the national debt.

Inflation could help the government in yet another way. If prices of goods and services increase at about the same rate as wage rates and other sources of income, you end up paying more income tax. Why? Because a higher money income may put you in a higher tax bracket. Suppose, for example, that 10 years ago, your income was $40,000 and the last $1,000 of it was taxed at 20 percent; you paid $200 tax on it. Now, after 10 years of inflation, you earn $75,000, and the last $1,000 of it is taxed at 31 percent. You now pay $310 tax on that $1,000. You have been bumped into a higher tax bracket, even though the $75,000 buys the same groceries now as the $40,000 did 10 years ago. In other words, even though your real income remains the same, your disposable income decreases because government collects more.

Changes in the consumer price index (CPI)—a measure of the average change in prices paid by urban consumers for a fixed market basket of goods and services—is a standard measure of inflation. The Bureau of Labor Statistics provides current and historical data on the CPI (http://stats.bls.gov/cpihome.htm).

**MODERATING THE WINS AND LOSSES** Wouldn't you think that habitual losers of inflation would get tired of losing and try to do something about it? Many do, and succeed. For example, many banks offer home mortgages whose rates vary directly with the rate of inflation. Instead of charging 6½ percent on a 30-year mortgage, they may charge 5 percent *plus the inflation rate.* In this way, they check the loss of future income through inflation. Unions understand as well that they could end up being big losers if they sign multiyear fixed-wage contracts. Most union contracts now include a built-in cost-of-living adjustment (COLA) that covers the rate of inflation. Even taxpayers now can get some relief from "bracket creep" because the federal government recently adjusted the income levels associated with tax brackets to the rate of inflation.

# LIVING IN A WORLD OF INFLATION AND UNEMPLOYMENT

Look at the economy of Exhibit 3. It's in equilibrium at $Y = \$800$ billion, where aggregate expenditure, $AE_2$, intersects the 45-degree line. But note: that's $400 billion below the economy's $1,200 billion full-employment level.

At $Y = \$800$ billion, firms responding to or anticipating demands for consumption and investment goods continue to produce $700 billion of consumption goods and $100 billion of investment goods, and if at the same time consumers continue to spend $700 billion on consumption and save $100 billion, then the number of people employed in the economy remains stuck at less than full employment. Moreover, there is no reason for those unemployed to expect to find employment, no matter how hard they may try.

Wouldn't it be cruel, under these circumstances, to accuse people willing to work but unable to find a job of being lazy or listless? If they can persuade an employer to hire them, it likely means that they have displaced other workers in a game of employment musical chairs. After all, at $Y = \$800$ billion, only so many workers will be employed.

**Recessionary gap**
The amount by which aggregate expenditure falls short of the level needed to generate equilibrium national income at full employment without inflation.

## Identifying the Recessionary Gap

A $400 billion national income deficiency separates the $Y = \$800$ billion equilibrium level from the $Y = \$1,200$ billion full-employment level. What it takes to drive the equilibrium level of national income up to full employment is more aggregate expenditure; how much more depends principally on the marginal propensity to consume. For example, if $MPC = 0.80$ and generates an income multiplier of 5, then it would take an additional spending of $80 billion—which is the amount represented by the distance $hg$—to shift the equilibrium level of national income up from $Y = \$800$ billion to $Y = \$1,200$ billion. This $80 billion deficiency in aggregate expenditure is called the **recessionary gap**.

### RECESSIONARY AND INFLATIONARY GAPS

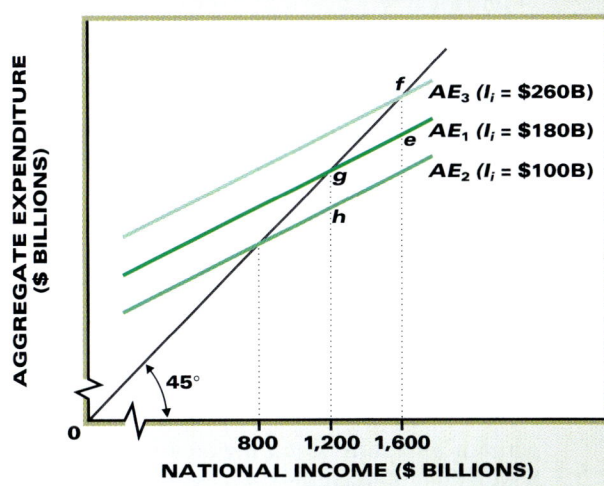

PANEL a

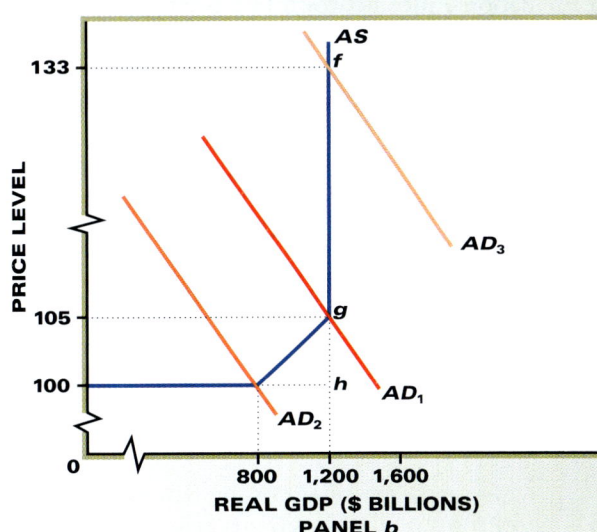

PANEL b

EXHIBIT 3

The $800 billion equilibrium level of national income in panel a is $400 billion short of the economy's $1,200 billion full-employment national income level. To achieve full-employment equilibrium, aggregate expenditures must increase by $80 billion (the income multiplier is 5), from $AE_2$ to $AE_1$, which defines the recessionary gap $hg$. The $1,600 billion equilibrium level of national income is $400 billion above the zero-inflation full-employment level. To eliminate the inflationary gap, $ef$, aggregate expenditures must be cut $80 billion, from $AE_3$ to $AE_1$. In the real GDP version of the economy, panel b, $gh$ defines the $80 billion recessionary gap and $fg$ defines the $80 billion inflationary gap.

**CHECK YOUR UNDERSTANDING**

Why don't producers simply increase their investment to close a recessionary gap?

In Exhibit 3, the recessionary gap reflects the difference between the $100 billion that producers invest (investment being part of aggregate expenditures) and the $180 billion total investment demand required to bring equilibrium to full employment.

The fact that many people are jobless when producers invest only $100 billion is unfortunate, not only for the unemployed but for producers as well. After all, they would love to produce more. But they confront the economy's consumption and investment spending, which tells them that producing more would be foolhardy. They can't be expected to increase investment when there's no evidence that demand exists for the investment goods. That is to say, neither the unemployed nor the producers can be faulted for the economy's recessionary gap.

This recessionary gap can also be illustrated in the aggregate demand and aggregate supply model of real GDP shown in Exhibit 3, panel $b$. If aggregate demand is $AD_2$, then the economy comes to equilibrium at $800 billion real GDP, when $AD_2 = AS$. What would it take to bring panel $b$'s economy to its $1,200 billion full-employment equilibrium? An increase in investment demand from $100 billion to $180 billion, which would shift the aggregate demand curve from $AD_2$ to $AD_1$. This distance $hg$ marks the recessionary gap. But note: The move to full employment creates in this version of the economy a moderate inflation, shown in panel $b$ as a price level increase from 100 to 105.

### Identifying the Inflationary Gap

Let's go back to panel $a$ in Exhibit 3 for a moment. Let's now suppose that the aggregate expenditures curve is $AE_3$. The economy is then propelled to an equilibrium level of $Y = \$1,600$ billion. But is that possible?

Think about it. How can an economy be in equilibrium at $Y = \$1,600$ billion when the full-employment level is $1,200 billion? That is to say, how can the economy create more goods and services when all its resources are fully engaged producing $1,200 billion? The answer: It can't. What then explains the difference between the $1,200 billion full-employment level and the $1,600 billion equilibrium level? Inflation. National income above the $1,200 billion level reflects only price increases.

What would it take to bring the economy to equilibrium at full employment without inflation? Assuming again that $MPC = 0.80$ and the income multiplier is 5, an $80 billion cut in aggregate expenditure would draw the equilibrium level of national income down by $400 billion to the $Y = \$1,200$ billion full-employment level. This need for an $80 billion aggregate expenditure cutback defines the economy's **inflationary gap**.

**Inflationary gap**
The amount by which aggregate expenditure exceeds the aggregate expenditure level needed to generate equilibrium national income at full employment without inflation.

The inflationary gap can be illustrated as well in the aggregate demand and aggregate supply model of panel $b$. If investment demand increases from $180 billion to $260 billion, shifting the aggregate demand curve upward to $AE_3$, the economy achieves equilibrium at full employment, at $1,200 real GDP, but with a matching price level of 133. (The $1,200 billion real GDP multiplied by the 133 price level creates a nominal GDP of $1,600 billion, corresponding to the inflationary $1,600 billion national income equilibrium of panel $a$.) The distance $fg$ in panel $b$ identifies the inflationary gap.

## CLOSING RECESSIONARY AND INFLATIONARY GAPS

Suppose the president of the United States asks for your advice. The economy he confronts is the recessionary one of Exhibit 3, and his goal is to bring the economy to equilibrium at full employment. What do you tell him?

# HISTORICAL PERSPECTIVE

## J. M. KEYNES AND SAY'S LAW

**For the economy as a whole, the total quantity of goods and services supplied equals the total quantity of goods and services demanded, because the very act of producing goods and services for supply necessitates the purchase and use of resources to produce them.** The incomes that the resource owners earn producing the goods and services are used by the resource owners to purchase them. In other words, supply always creates its own demand.

This statement of the classical argument—*supply creates its own demand*—is known as Say's law, named after the 19th-century French economist Jean Baptiste Say, who was among the first to maintain that *general* overproduction or underconsumption in the economy was impossible. It is possible that the quantity supplied can exceed the quantity demanded in specific markets. But since the total value of all goods supplied creates an equivalent total value of all goods demanded, if an excess supply exists in some markets, an excess demand equivalent in value to the excess supply must exist in other markets. Eventually, competitive forces and flexible prices establish equilibrium in all markets.

Say's law applied to the capital market means that, in the long run, the quantity of capital supplied equals the quantity of capital demanded. In other words, saving equals investment. If saving is greater than investment in the short run, the interest rate will fall to equate saving and investment. If investment is greater than saving in the short run, the interest rate will increase to equate saving and investment.

Applied to the labor market, it means that unemployment may exist, but only in the short run. Given enough time, demand and supply forces in the labor market will adjust to bring about full employment.

During the Great Depression of the 1930s, the persistence of extraordinarily high unemployment and chronic deficiency in investment demand seemed to undermine the validity of Say's law. The idea that supply creates its own demand didn't seem to reflect the depressing conditions of oversupply of both goods and resources. Investment demand, it seemed, was insufficient to absorb the availability of saving. What went wrong with Say's law? Why didn't it work?

According to J. M. Keynes, Say's law didn't work because the assumptions underlying Say's law are fallacious. With few exceptions, markets are not competitive, nor are prices flexible.

In the labor market, for example, Keynes believed that unions dominate supply—little if any competition exists among workers supplying labor—while large corporate firms dominate demand, providing little competition among themselves for labor. Moreover, the wages that the noncompetitive labor market generate are anything but flexible. Unions and workers typically reject wage cuts even if it means accepting unemployment. And Keynes argued that even if the unions and workers accept wage cuts, unemployment still persists. Why? Because wage cuts decrease workers' incomes and consequently decrease their demand for consumer goods. Firms react to the decrease in consumer demand by cutting employment.

**IF SUPPLY CREATES ITS OWN DEMAND, WHAT AM I DOING HERE SELLING APPLES?**

In the capital market the rate of interest is not effective in equating the quantity of capital supplied to the quantity of capital demanded—that is, saving to equal investment. To Keynes, investment demand depends less on low interest rates or the availability of saving, than on the expectation of a continuing robust economy.

If Keynes's view of labor and capital markets, interest rates, wages, and employment is right, what's left of Say's law? According to Keynesians, not very much!

### MORE ON THE NET

Review a biography of Jean Baptiste Say (http://www.cpm.ll.ehime-u.ac.jp/AkamacHomePage/Akamac_E-text_Links/Say.html).

How about presidential persuasion? You could advise the president to invite the economy's most influential producers to a White House breakfast and there explain the importance of increasing aggregate expenditure.

It would be marvelous if all it took was a little presidential sweet talk to get producers to add another $80 billion to investment. But even producers who voted twice for the president couldn't justify a penny more investment when the economy is already in equilibrium at $Y = \$800$ billion. Where, then, do you find the $80 billion?

## Enter Government

If nobody else will do it, government can. How does government get into an $80 billion investment business? It designs a public investment package that totals $80 billion. In ten minutes the president can probably come up with projects that would completely close the recessionary gap.

For a detailed account of how much the federal government spends on what, review the federal budget of the United States (http://www.gpo.gov/usbudget/index.html).

There are always more superhighways to build, more public housing to construct, more pollution control facilities to finance, more space shots to make, more health care schemes to fund, and more defense to procure. In fact, the least of his problems would seem to be finding suitable projects to absorb the $80 billion.

What about Congress? Would it go along? Members of Congress have to be sensitive to voters' concerns back home, and among their concerns in times of recession are jobs.

The government now becomes an integral part of the economy's aggregate expenditures. What was once $AE_2$ is now $AE_1 =$ the $80 billion increase representing government purchases of goods and services.

*What would you like to see government do? List one or more things that add up to $80 billion. Go to the Interactive Study Center at http://gottheil.swcollege.com and click on the "Your Turn" button to submit your example. Student submissions will be posted to the Web site, and perhaps we will use some in future editions of the book!*

Suppose the president asks you to brief the White House staff on your $80 billion recommendation. You prepare Exhibit 3, panels *a* and *b*, which shows the economy struggling along without the $80 billion of government spending on goods and services, and how the economy fares with the government spending.

They would see the difference immediately.

## Government Spending Is Not Problem-Free

Simple? Perhaps too simple. Critics of the Keynesian view of closing a recessionary gap offer a series of objections. First, they warn that once the $80 billion of government spending is introduced into the economy, it takes on a life force of its own. *Once in, always in.* Whether or not it is needed to close recessionary gaps in subsequent years, the politics of the spending—such as defense and road building—guarantees its continuity. In addition, *once in, always grows.* That is, $80 billion of government spending today, because of the vested political interests it creates, might push to $500 billion in a decade.

One critic of government spending is the Cato Institute (http://www.cato.org/), a nonpartisan public policy research foundation.

Second, they insist that advocates of government intervention fail to appreciate the self-correcting nature of the economy. Given sufficient time, market forces will shift private-sector investment upward to the right, narrowing the recessionary gap. For example, changes in prices and wage rates may make investment more attractive to producers. Time also takes its toll on the economy's machinery and physical plants. Eventually, they must be replaced, and thus they contribute also to the upsurge in demand for investment.

## APPLIED PERSPECTIVE

### THE RECORD ON DEFICIT BUDGETS UNDERMINES THE IDEA THAT THEY ARE STRICTLY TOOLS OF COUNTERCYCLICAL FISCAL POLICY

Back in 1980, economist Irwin Kellner, writing about Keynes and deficits, said: "Those who have written about Keynes in an effort to interpret his writings have drawn the conclusion that budget deficits are quite acceptable during periods of economic slack. I would agree. Some authors believe that Keynes had a cavalier attitude toward budget deficits, pointing to the views of many of his disciples who assert that deficits do not matter. With this I would disagree. If Keynes did not place great emphasis on the implications of a budget deficit beyond that of stimulating the economy, it is simply because he believed that deficits should not be used as a main tool of economic policy, and when they were, they were to be used during periods of slack. It is Keynes's followers and the politicians whom they educated that are to blame for the 'cavalier' attitude toward budget deficits that subsequently developed in the 1950s and 1960s."

EVER COMING DOWN? NOT WITH DEFICITS AT THE OTHER END!

Whether Kellner is right or wrong about Keynes, the record on deficits and surpluses tells the story.

During the 1940s, 1950s, and 1960s, 22 of the 30 years had deficit budgets. Since then, from 1970 through 1997, *every year* was a deficit year. In other words, only 8 of the 57 years since 1940 had surplus budgets. Obviously, in the many years of robust economic growth during that period, the budget was still generating deficits. Even though the 1998–2000 period generated surpluses, as Kellner noted, the data do not support the idea that deficits necessarily reflect countercyclical fiscal policy.

#### MORE ON THE NET

The Bureau of the Public Debt (http://www.publicdebt.treas.gov/) and the Concord Coalition (http://www.concordcoalition.org/) publish data and information about federal budget deficits and the public debt.

**Source:** Adapted from Irwin L. Kellner, *Economic Report* (New York: Manufactures Hanover Trust Company, November 1980); and *Statistical Abstract of the United States, 1994* (Washington, D.C.: U.S. Department of Commerce, 1994).

---

Third, the critics note the obvious: Government spending is not cost-free. The funding for $80 billion in government spending must come from somewhere, and, too often, it is debt financed. Apart from the other objections to spending, this debt financing—the national debt—places a new burden on the economy that can sap the vitality of the economy's future.

### Closing the Inflationary Gap

What about closing the inflationary gap? Do you simply reverse the process that closes the recessionary gap? That's just about it. The idea is to bring $AE_3$ down to $AE_1$ in panel *a* of Exhibit 3 (or $AD_3$ down to $AD_1$ in panel *b*). How do you do that? By cutting $80 billion out of investment demand. Either government spending gets chopped or private-sector investment shrinks, or both. If consumers won't cut their spending on consumption and producers won't cut their demand for investment goods, then the president must cut government spending. It means, of course, less highway construction, less public housing, and less defense spending. You can imagine, can't you, some strong resistance back home! If it's your highway, your public housing, or your defense factory that gets cut, then your voice will get heard in Congress. For this reason, Congress may be less willing to go along with curbing inflation than promoting full employment.

How much cutting is necessary? The $80 billion cut multiplied by 5 (the income multiplier) creates the $400 billion cut needed to bring the economy down from $1,600 billion to $1,200 billion.

## MAKING FISCAL POLICY

Let's again consider the recessionary gap of Exhibit 3. Knowing that government spending of $80 billion will drive national income from $800 billion to the desired $1,200 billion is an important initial step in the formation of fiscal policy. But that information doesn't tell us where the government *gets* the $80 billion. It doesn't materialize out of nowhere.

Perhaps the first thing the president considers is taxation. If the government needs $1, it can raise taxes by $1. If it needs $80 billion, then it simply taxes the people $80 billion. Of course, the people always have the final say. If taxes become too burdensome, it may be the last time the president sees the inside of the White House.

Suppose the president shows a strong reluctance to tax. Is it hopeless? Not yet. The government can borrow the $80 billion. From whom? From people like you who are willing to lend the government money in exchange for its interest-bearing IOUs. These IOUs take the form of government securities, such as Treasury bills, notes, and bonds. As long as the interest rate the government offers on these securities is competitive with the rate in the private market, the government should be able to finance the $80 billion of government spending.

The use of government spending and taxation to make changes in the level of national income is what economists call **fiscal policy.**

**Fiscal policy**
Government spending and taxation policy to achieve macroeconomic goals of full employment without inflation.

**Balanced budget**
Government spending equals tax revenues.

### Choosing the Tax Option

Let's suppose the government decides against borrowing and instead chooses the tax option. For every dollar the government decides to spend, it gets that dollar by taxing the people one dollar. This one-to-one correspondence between government spending, $G$, and tax revenue, $T$, results in a **balanced budget:**

$$G = T$$

Of course, balanced budgets come in all sizes. The government can program a $100 billion, or even a $500 billion, recession-fighting balanced budget. As long as it collects in taxes what it spends on programs, that is, if $G = T$, the budget is balanced.

### Full Employment, Zero Inflation, and a Balanced Budget

If the president insists on a balanced budget, he cannot simply inject $80 billion of government spending into the economy and allow the income multiplier to shift the equilibrium level of national income from $Y = \$800$ billion to $Y = \$1,200$ billion. He now has to worry about the effects of financing the $80 billion spending with taxes.

If government imposes a tax, most people would be scrambling about trying to come up with the money to pay it. Where would they find it? Obviously, right at home. To pay the tax, people will have to consume less and save less. But consuming less during recession adversely affects the level of national income. And that's a new problem.

Does the negative impact of higher taxes on national income simply cancel out the positive impact of government spending? Not at all. Any increase in the government's balanced budget—that is, government spending and taxes increase by the same amount—actually adds to the level of national income. Why is this so?

**DERIVING THE TAX MULTIPLIER** The answer is linked to the relationship between the income multiplier and the tax multiplier. Like the income multiplier, which magnifies the effect of government spending on the level of national income, the **tax multiplier** magnifies the effect of taxes on the level of national income. *But income magnification from taxes is the weaker of the two.* Why?

**Tax multiplier**
The multiple by which the equilibrium level of national income changes when a dollar change in taxes occurs. The multiple depends upon the marginal propensity to consume. The equation for the tax multiplier is $-MPC/(1 - MPC)$.

Suppose Bob Diener, an attorney working for the FBI in Santa Fe, earns $50,000 annually. And suppose that he spent $40,500 of that income on consumption and put the remaining $9,500 into savings.

Now suppose Congress agrees with the president and imposes a 20 percent income tax. Come April 15, Bob is obligated to transfer $50,000 × 0.20 = $10,000 of his income to the government. Where would he get it? Would he take it all from savings? Or all from consumption? Neither is likely.

In fact, we know precisely how much he will draw from each source. Since his $MPC = 0.80$ and $MPS = 0.20$, he will give up $8,000 of what would have been consumption spending and $2,000 of what would have been saved.

That $8,000 cutback in consumption sends shock waves through the economy. After all, what Bob no longer spends on consumption, others no longer earn as income.

Picture the scene. Unaccustomed to being frugal, Bob must nonetheless cut back. But where? Suppose that among the consumption items he picks to trim are his catered parties. Prior to the tax, he had spent $1,000 annually on catering. He now cuts that out completely.

The first to feel the effect of his consumption cut is, of course, his caterer, Ayala Donchin. Ayala now discovers she has $1,000 less income, and with less income she consumes less herself. How much less? With $MPC = 0.80$, she cuts her consumption by $0.80 × \$1,000 = \$800$. That, in turn, means $800 less income for some other person. And so this shock wave, initiated by a $1,000 cut in catering, continues.

**CHECK YOUR UNDERSTANDING**

Why isn't the tax multiplier equal to the income multiplier?

You should see a *tax-induced multiplier* at work. But note what triggers the rollback in income. It is Bob's $8,000 cutback in consumption, not the entire $10,000 tax. After all, $2,000 of the $10,000 tax came from his would-be savings. Only $8,000 would have gone through the income stream. The multiplying factor associated with such a tax multiplier when $MPC = 0.80$ is

$$\frac{-MPC}{1 - MPC} = \frac{-0.80}{1 - 0.80} = \frac{\text{change in } Y}{\text{change in } T} = -4.$$

The $10,000 tax, then, generates a $10,000 × -4 = \$40,000$ decline in national income.

**GOVERNMENT USES THE $10,000 TAX FOR $10,000 OF SPENDING** The government now has Bob's $10,000 in tax revenue. What does it do with the tax? If it were to save $2,000 and spend the remaining $8,000 on, say, sewage repair, then the income multiplier effect of that spending would exactly offset the $40,000 cut in national income induced by the tax. That is, if the government saved

$2,000, the net effect on national income of a $10,000 increase in taxes and spending, $G = T$, would be $0.

*But the government doesn't save.* It spends the entire $10,000 of Bob's taxes. The income multiplier effect is not on $8,000, but on the entire $10,000. The income multiplier on that $10,000, with $MPC = 0.80$, is 5:

$$\frac{1}{1 - MPC} = \frac{1}{1 - 0.80} = \frac{\text{change in } Y}{\text{change in } G} = 5$$

The increase in national income that government creates by spending the $10,000 is $10,000 \times 5 = $50,000$.

## The Balanced Budget Multiplier

In brief, things aren't always what they seem. When the government levies a $10,000 tax on people's income and puts the $10,000 back into the economy, national income does not remain the same. It expands. For example, a $10,000 increase in both $G$ and $T$ generates a $50,000 - $40,000 = $10,000 expansion of national income. We get this result from

$$\frac{1}{1 - MPC} + \frac{-MPC}{1 - MPC} = \frac{1}{0.2} + \frac{-0.8}{0.2} = 5 - 4 = 1,$$

subtracting the government's tax multiplier of 4, operating on $T$, from the income multiplier of 5, operating on $G$. This gives us a **balanced budget multiplier** of $5 - 4 = 1$. *No matter what the specific income multiplier and tax multiplier may be, the balanced budget multiplier always equals 1.*

> **Balanced budget multiplier**
> The effect on the equilibrium level of national income of an equal change in government spending and taxes. The balanced budget multiplier is 1.

## Balancing the Budget at $80 Billion

Suppose the president recommends an $80 billion balanced budget. Its effect on national income, then, is a matter of simple arithmetic. With a balanced budget multiplier equal to 1, national income increases by $80 billion.

The tax multiplier applied to an $80 billion $G = T$ budget reduces national income by $80 \times 4 = $320 billion. But at the same time the government gets the $80 billion tax revenue and converts it into $80 billion of government spending. The effect of that spending on the economy adds $80 \times 5 = $400 billion to national income.

What do we end up with? The net effect on the economy of the $80 billion $G = T$ is a $400 - $320 = $80 billion increase in national income. As we already know, it is precisely the size of the balanced budget. But is it enough to pull the economy out of recession?

## How to Get to Full-Employment National Income and Balance the Budget

The only way to drive the recessionary economy of Exhibit 3 out of its equilibrium position at $Y = $800 billion to a $Y = $1,200 billion equilibrium at full employment, *and balance the budget at the same time,* is to generate a government budget of $400 billion—that is, $400 billion of taxes and $400 billion of government spending. This budget produces the desired $400 billion increase in national income.

But that's strong fiscal policy! You can see why the president, bent on full employment, might think twice about balancing the budget. What would you advise?

## Just a Spoonful of Deficit Makes the Medicine Go Down

It's worth exploring other ways to bring the economy out of recession. Why not modify the balanced budget slightly? Or perhaps even more than slightly. The government has several fiscal policy options. Look at Exhibit 4.

Every fiscal policy budget option in Exhibit 4 produces the same results. In each, national income increases by the targeted $400 billion. That is, each budget option completely closes the $400 billion recessionary gap.

The first option, $G = T$ at $400 billion, does the job. Moreover, it creates no budget deficit. But a $400 billion tax may be more than Congress is willing to impose.

The president can choose the second fiscal policy option, that is, couple a $100 billion tax revenue with $160 billion of government spending. That budget combination creates the targeted $400 billion increase in national income, but it also creates a $60 billion **budget deficit**, $G > T$.

The third option couples a $50 billion tax revenue with $120 billion of government spending. This lower tax budget (compared to the first and second options) may look attractive, but the drawback is that it creates a larger budget deficit, $70 billion. The fourth fiscal policy option is tax-free! The income multiplier (of 5) applied to $80 billion of government spending creates the targeted $400 billion increase in national income. But the economy is saddled with an $80 billion budget deficit as well.

Why even think of such complex combinations of government spending and taxes when the simple balanced budget at $400 billion would do? Because the president and Congress may find it more acceptable politically to have deficit budgets than a balanced budget that depends on $400 billion in taxes. On the other hand, the fourth option would work, but it might be more deficit than the president is willing to tolerate politically.

Is the only issue in choosing a fiscal policy option, then, the political future of Congress and the president? Are their chances for getting reelected and their personal tolerance for taxing and borrowing all that matter? Not really. Another consideration is at issue.

**Budget deficit**
Government spending exceeds tax revenues.

## How Mixed Is the Mixed Economy?

Although all the fiscal policy budget options of Exhibit 4 lead to $Y = \$1,200$ billion at full employment, they don't all produce the same mix of government and private sector economic activity.

For example, if the president chooses the first option from Exhibit 4—the balanced budget option at $G = T = \$400$ billion—government becomes a major participant in the national economy. This is an important consideration that the president and Congress must address. As you know, much of the political debate in the United States and other countries focuses on this one issue: How much government is the right amount of government?

**CHECK YOUR UNDERSTANDING**

Why is it sometimes inappropriate to rely on the balanced budget multiplier to close a recessionary gap?

**SAMPLE BUDGET OPTIONS TO CLOSE A RECESSIONARY GAP ($ BILLIONS)**

| OPTION | GOVERNMENT SPENDING | TAX REVENUE | BUDGET DEFICIT | TARGET CHANGE IN INCOME |
|---|---|---|---|---|
| 1 | $400 | $400 | $ 0 | $400 |
| 2 | 160 | 100 | 60 | 400 |
| 3 | 120 | 50 | 70 | 400 |
| 4 | 80 | 0 | 80 | 400 |

EXHIBIT 4

## Creating Surplus Budgets

Let's look again at the economy of Exhibit 3. An inflationary gap of $80 billion creates an equilibrium level of national income that is $400 billion *higher* than the full-employment equilibrium level of $1,500 billion. What fiscal policy measures should the president pursue now? The government has several options. Look at Exhibit 5.

The first option reduces both taxes and government spending by $400 billion. Note the negative signs. They indicate cuts. The balanced budget multiplier, with both taxes and government spending cut by $400 billion, reduces national income by the targeted (negative) $400 billion. But that's about as drastic a fiscal policy as the government could possibly design. People would love to see their taxes cut substantially, but cutting $400 billion out of government spending would probably mean drastic cuts in interstate repairs, Medicare, funding of higher education, job-retraining programs, and almost everything else that government does. It would probably be politically unworkable.

**Budget surplus**
Tax revenues exceed government spending.

Other fiscal policy options are shown in Exhibit 5. For example, in the second option, the government reduces spending by $160 billion and taxes by $100 billion—creating a **budget surplus**, $T > G$, of $60 billion. That reduces national income by the targeted $400 billion.

If the government chooses, it can cut government spending and at the same time raise taxes. Each reduces national income. For example, in the third option, applying the tax multiplier of $-4$ to a $50 billion increase in taxes reduces national income by $200 billion. Applying the income multiplier of 5 to a $40 billion cut in government spending reduces national income by an additional $200 billion. The combined effect of the government spending cut and tax increase reduces national income by the targeted $400 billion. Or the government can choose the fourth option, that is, not to increase taxes at all but rely exclusively on decreasing government spending by $80 billion to reduce national income by the targeted $400 billion.

## Are Fiscal Policy Options Really That Straightforward?

Are our fiscal policy options really that simple? Does the president really face recessionary gaps and inflationary gaps that emerge when equilibrium levels of national income deviate from no-inflation full-employment levels? Can the president and Congress play with taxes and spending to close those gaps with balanced budgets, deficit budgets, and surplus budgets such as those shown in Exhibits 4 and 5?

Many economists believe that the Keynesian model of national income determination and the fiscal policy prescriptions (to close recessionary and inflationary gaps) that follow from it are accurate enough reflections of our economic reality to make them useful. As a policy adviser, you may find that the president not only is a good listener and a quick learner, but also is interested to know what *other* economic models are available.

It will not take the president long to discover that there are many competing approaches to national income determina-

**EXHIBIT 5**

### SAMPLE BUDGET OPTIONS TO CLOSE AN INFLATIONARY GAP ($ BILLIONS)

| OPTION | GOVERNMENT SPENDING | TAX REVENUE | SURPLUS BUDGET | TARGET ΔY |
|---|---|---|---|---|
| 1 | -$400 | -$400 | $ 0 | -$400 |
| 2 | -160 | -100 | 60 | -400 |
| 3 | -40 | 50 | 10 | -400 |
| 4 | -80 | 0 | 80 | -400 |

tion, that there really is no consensus among economists concerning the "correct" income determination model or the "correct" fiscal policy.

The president has a dilemma, doesn't he? What advice should he accept? We will return to this obviously important question in later chapters when we consider alternative views on economic stabilization policy. For now, it is important to understand how the Exhibit 3 model works. After all, it has dominated economic thinking on issues of inflation and unemployment ever since the 1930s and still influences a great deal of economic thinking today.

# CHAPTER REVIEW

1. An economy in equilibrium tells us very little about the general state of the economy. After all, it could be in equilibrium with high levels of unemployment.

2. The types of unemployment that can exist include frictional unemployment, structural unemployment, cyclical unemployment, discouraged workers, and the underemployed. The Bureau of Labor Statistics calculates the rate of unemployment by conducting a survey in which it asks people whether they are working or seeking employment. People who answer yes to this question are part of the labor force. The number of people who are seeking work, divided by the labor force, is the unemployment rate.

3. The natural rate of unemployment consists of workers who are frictionally and structurally unemployed. Full employment exists when the unemployment rate is equal to the natural rate. Full employment is represented by the vertical portion of the aggregate supply curve. As wage rates increase, more workers can be attracted to the labor force, up to a point where the aggregate supply curve becomes vertical.

4. Some groups of people hurt by inflation include people living on fixed incomes, landlords, and savers. Those who gain from inflation include borrowers and the government, which is a major borrower. Bankers have developed ways to moderate their losses from inflation. Unions bargain for cost-of-living allowances in their wage contracts to protect themselves from the erosion of real wages.

5. A recessionary gap exists when the equilibrium level of national income is below the full-employment level. The amount by which spending must increase to achieve full employment is the recessionary gap. An inflationary gap exists when the equilibrium level of national income is above the full-employment level. The inflationary gap is the amount by which spending must decrease to achieve full employment.

6. A recessionary gap can be closed by government spending. When the government spends, a multiple expansion in national income arises. Government spending is not without its problems. For one, it may raise the deficit. Also, it is possible that the economy will adjust back to full employment automatically, without any government spending.

7. Cuts in government spending are the means by which inflationary gaps can be closed. The problem with cuts in government spending is that those who are hurt by the cuts will oppose them, so that Congress and the president are less likely to follow through.

8. Fiscal policy involves choosing both the level of government spending and the level of taxation. A recessionary gap can be eliminated by a simultaneous increase in government spending and taxes to match the size of the recessionary gap. This result derives from the balanced budget multiplier, which equals 1. A variety of fiscal policy options to close recessionary gaps exists. Gaps can be closed in such a way as to leave the deficit unchanged, or they can be closed with various-sized budget deficits. Closing an inflationary gap involves the creation of a surplus budget where tax revenues exceed government spending.

9. Not all economists accept the idea that fiscal policy can be an effective tool for stabilizing the economy at a full-employment level of national income.

# KEY TERMS

Frictional unemployment
Structural unemployment
Cyclical unemployment
Discouraged workers
Underemployed workers
Labor force

Natural rate of unemployment
Full employment
Recessionary gap
Inflationary gap
Fiscal policy

Balanced budget
Tax multiplier
Balanced budget multiplier
Budget deficit
Budget surplus

# QUESTIONS

1. Why are people not always delighted when national income finally reaches its equilibrium level?
2. What is frictional unemployment? Why is it not regarded as a serious economic problem?
3. What is structural unemployment? Why is such unemployment particularly hard on older workers? Cite examples.
4. What is cyclical unemployment? Why is it difficult for people who are cyclically unemployed to find jobs?
5. Who are discouraged workers? Underemployed workers? Are they counted as part of the labor force? As part of the unemployed?
6. What is the relationship between the full-employment level in an economy and the economy's natural rate of unemployment?
7. Who are the winners and losers from inflation?
8. Professor Scott Fausti asks his students at South Dakota State University to answer the following question: Assume Harry receives a $10,000 bank loan. The loan is due at the end of one year. The interest charge is 10 percent and the inflation rate is 4 percent per year. Who benefits from the inflation, Harry or the bank? Explain.
9. Draw graphs showing recessionary and inflationary gaps and explain how these gaps emerge.
10. What fiscal policy measures can the government employ to close a recessionary gap? An inflationary gap?
11. What is a tax multiplier? How does it differ from the income multiplier?
12. What effect would a $100 billion tax cut have on the level of national income, assuming $MPC = 0.50$?
13. Why is the balanced budget multiplier always equal to 1?
14. Why shouldn't the government *always* program a balanced budget?

# PRACTICE PROBLEMS

1. Calculate the following rates of unemployment and size of the labor force from the following data: frictional unemployment = 20; structural = 30; cyclical = 40; discouraged workers = 10; underemployed = 25; employed workers = 375.

   | SIZE OF LABOR FORCE | |
   |---|---|
   | NATURAL RATE OF UNEMPLOYMENT | |
   | ACTUAL RATE OF UNEMPLOYMENT | |
   | BLS'S RATE OF UNEMPLOYMENT | |

2. Fill in the missing cells in the following table.

   | MPC | MPS | TAX MULTIPLIER |
   |---|---|---|
   | 0.50 | | |
   | | 0.50 | |
   | 0.75 | | |
   | | | 0.40 |

3. Fill in the missing cells to raise national income by $100, assuming $MPC = 0.80$.

| TAX | GOVERNMENT SPENDING | CHANGE IN NATIONAL INCOME |
|---|---|---|
| $25 | | $100 |
| | $60 | $100 |
| $30 | | $100 |
| | $50 | $100 |

4. Calculate the values for the recessionary or inflationary gaps for each of the four cases in the following tables.

| MPC | EQUILIBRIUM Y | FULL EMPLOYMENT Y | RECESSIONARY GAP | INFLATIONARY GAP |
|---|---|---|---|---|
| 0.60 | $400 | $300 | | |
| 0.70 | 400 | 900 | | |
| 0.80 | 500 | 900 | | |
| 0.90 | 500 | 200 | | |

5. Calculate both the tax revenue required to generate the surplus budget shown and the change in national income that will result in each of the three cases in the following table.

| MPC | SURPLUS BUDGET | GOVERNMENT SPENDING | TAX REVENUE | CHANGE IN NATIONAL INCOME |
|---|---|---|---|---|
| 0.70 | $100 | $50 | | |
| 0.80 | 200 | 60 | | |
| 0.90 | 300 | 70 | | |

# WHAT'S WRONG WITH THIS GRAPH?

**THE RECESSIONARY GAP**

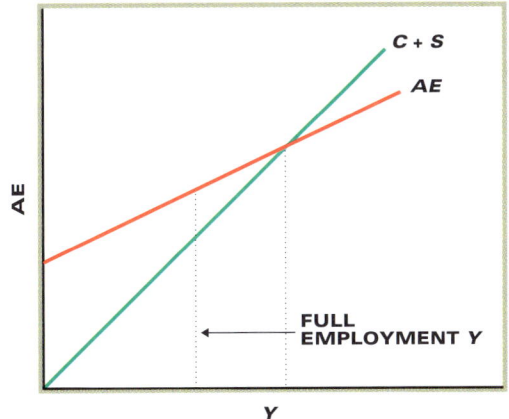

# ECONOMIC CONSULTANTS

## ECONOMIC RESEARCH AND ANALYSIS BY STUDENTS FOR PROFESSIONALS

Jobs for Everyone (JFE) is a private, not-for-profit corporation in Chicago, Illinois, that helps people find new or better jobs. For several years, JFE has been assisting people in the Chicago area, but Gordon Kay, its director, now finds that the number of people seeking JFE's assistance far exceeds JFE's ability to accommodate them. Strapped by its limited resources, Gordon is convinced that the only way to provide adequate assistance is to encourage government to become more actively involved in job creation. He believes government has the potential to help thousands of job-needing people in Chicago and, given a broader focus, can even address the job-related concerns of millions of Americans nationwide. Thus, Gordon has decided to use some of JFE's time and energy to lobby government agencies to do more to create jobs. Before JFE can do this, it needs to get a better understanding of the issues associated with unemployment in Chicago and nationwide, and what the government is currently doing about the problem.

Economic Consultants, aware of JFE's good work and success, has offered its services to the organization, and Gordon has accepted. Prepare a report for JFE that addresses the following issues:

1. What is the current rate of unemployment in the United States, as defined by the Bureau of Labor Statistics? What is that rate for Chicago? What other kinds of information concerning unemployment would you want to consider?
2. What does government currently do to provide jobs for people or to help people find jobs?
3. JFE believes everyone should have a job. What are the possible costs and benefits of full employment?

You may find the following resources helpful as you prepare this report for JFE:

- **Department of Labor** (http://www.dol.gov/)—The Department of Labor provides a number of employment-related programs, such as America's Job Bank (http://www.ajb.dni.us/) and Welfare to Work (http://wtw.doleta.gov/).
- **Bureau of Labor Statistics (BLS)** (http://stats.bls.gov/)—The BLS is the primary source for labor data for the federal government. The BLS also publishes the *Occupational Outlook Handbook* (http://stats.bls.gov/ocohome.htm), which provides job descriptions, working conditions, training and educational requirements, and similar information on various jobs.
- **Bureau of the Census** (http://www.census.gov/)—The Census Bureau maintains labor data (http://www.census.gov/hhes/www/laborfor.html).
- **Chicago Fact Book** (http://www.cityofchicago.org/Planning/ChgoFacts/)—The Chicago Fact Book, maintained by the city of Chicago, provides extensive labor and demographic information.

# PRACTICE TEST

1. Technological change has the largest impact on which form of unemployment?
   a. Frictional
   b. Structural
   c. Cyclical
   d. Discouraged workers
   e. Underemployed workers

2. Suppose there are 1,100 people in the economy. Of these, 700 are employed, 100 are underemployed, 200 are looking for work, and the remaining 100 are either retired or in school. According to the BLS, the unemployment rate is
   a. 20 percent.
   b. 18 percent.
   c. 29 percent.
   d. 27 percent.
   e. 36 percent.

3. The natural rate of unemployment refers to the rate(s) of
   a. cyclical unemployment.
   b. frictional and structural unemployment.
   c. underemployed and discouraged workers.
   d. actual unemployment.
   e. cyclical, frictional, and structural unemployment.

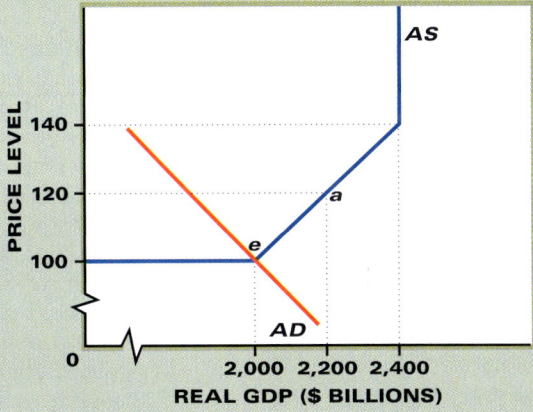

4. The graph shows the economy in equilibrium at $2,000 billion real GDP. Which of the following explains how the equilibrium-level real GDP increases to $2,200 billion?
   a. A shift in the aggregate demand curve to the left
   b. A shift in the aggregate demand curve to the right
   c. A shift in the aggregate supply curve to the left
   d. Movement along the supply curve from point $e$ to point $a$
   e. A fall in price level

5. If an increase in aggregate demand does not lead to inflation, we can assume that
   a. there are sufficient resources available at prevailing prices.
   b. the full-employment level of real GDP has been reached.
   c. the economy's equilibrium level of real GDP is positioned along the vertical segment of the aggregate supply curve.
   d. the aggregate supply curve must have decreased, offsetting the increase in aggregate demand.
   e. wages fell as real GDP increased.

6. During periods of high inflation,
   a. people on fixed incomes, such as retirees, benefit.
   b. money lenders who earn fixed rates of interest on their loans benefit.
   c. landlords who negotiated long-term rental leases benefit.
   d. people who borrowed money at fixed rates of interest benefit.
   e. people who pay fixed mortgage rates on their purchased homes lose.

7. Suppose the full-employment level of national income is $2 billion and the equilibrium level of national income is $1.4 billion. If $MPS = 0.25$, then there is a(n) _____ gap that can be closed by
   a. recessionary/increasing aggregate expenditure by $600 million.
   b. inflationary/increasing aggregate expenditure by $600 million.
   c. recessionary/decreasing aggregate expenditure by $600 million.
   d. inflationary/decreasing aggregate expenditure by $150 million.
   e. recessionary/increasing aggregate expenditure by $150 million.

8. A deficit budget occurs when
   a. the inflationary gap is larger than the recessionary gap.
   b. the inflationary gap is smaller than the recessionary gap.
   c. tax revenues are greater than government spending.
   d. tax revenues are less than government spending.
   e. $MPC$ is greater than $MPS$.

9. The tax multiplier is
   a. positive and smaller than the income multiplier.
   b. negative and smaller than the income multiplier.
   c. positive and larger than the income multiplier.
   d. negative and smaller than the income multiplier.
   e. positive and equal to the income multiplier.

# CHAPTER 9

# LONG-RUN ECONOMIC GROWTH AND BUSINESS CYCLES

Have you heard about the fellow who, enjoying the effects of his seventh martini, accidentally slipped off a 35-story penthouse sundeck? While falling to earth, he passed an open window. A college student looking out the window asked the unfortunate fellow in flight, "How's life treating you?" Summing up quickly, the falling man replied, "So far, so good!"

Is there a moral to this story? If so, it may be that it is sometimes difficult to tell just where we are and where we're going.

Or think about a time when you were driving to visit a friend. Despite your friend's assurances about accurate directions, you still manage to get lost.

The good news is that, more often than not, you eventually get to where you are going. Our economy also occasionally gets lost, slows down, or heads in the wrong direction despite our best directions, but then eventually it gets back on track. Economists study these movements.

**THIS CHAPTER INTRODUCES YOU TO THE ECONOMIC PRINCIPLES ASSOCIATED WITH:**

- CAPITAL-LABOR AND CAPITAL-OUTPUT RATIOS
- TECHNOLOGY AND LABOR PRODUCTIVITY
- LABOR PRODUCTIVITY AND ECONOMIC GROWTH
- SAVING, INVESTMENT, AND ECONOMIC GROWTH
- EXTERNAL AND INTERNAL THEORIES OF THE BUSINESS CYCLE
- THE INTERACTION OF THE MULTIPLIER AND ACCELERATOR
- COUNTERCYCLICAL FISCAL POLICY

How do we really know whether an economy in motion is moving toward equilibrium? All we actually observe is its motion.

If national income equilibrium is more a theoretical construct than an observed reality, why do economists spend so much time analyzing it? Isn't that what we did in the previous two chapters? Because understanding a simplified economy, which is assumed to approach equilibrium, can tell us a great deal about how a real economy—even one that never approaches equilibrium—works.

Analysis of national income equilibrium allows us to see how changes in aggregate expenditure can generate changes in national income and employment. When government is brought into the analysis, we can measure its impact on national income and employment as well. These cause-and-effect relationships are significant findings that apply to any economy, whether it is in equilibrium or not.

If an economy is not in or moving toward equilibrium, what, then, is it doing? Perhaps the only thing we can say with some degree of confidence is that it is never at rest; it is in a continuous state of motion.

# LONG-RUN ECONOMIC GROWTH

Let's look at the continuous motion path of the U.S. economy through the years 1900–2000. What do you see?

What must strike you about Exhibit 1 is the coupling of year-to-year fluctuations in GDP with a pronounced long-run upward thrust. The long-term average annual growth rate of real GDP is 3.5 percent (a doubling of GDP every generation).

The economic policy considerations associated with the year-to-year fluctuations in real GDP typically focus on solving the short-run unemployment problem depicted in panel *a* of Exhibit 2. How do we get from point *a* to point *b* on the aggregate supply curve, $AS_1$?

A very different set of policy considerations is associated with long-run growth of real GDP depicted in panel *b* of Exhibit 2. The question here is: How do we get from point *b* on $AS_1$ to point *c* on $AS_2$, to point *d* on $AS_3$, and so on? That is, what factors contribute to the outward shifts in aggregate supply?

## Creating the Environment for Long-Run Growth

Understanding why some nations grow—by experiencing outward shifts in aggregate supply—and others don't, or why some grow quite robustly and others less so, has as much to do with an appreciation for the sociopolitical environment that nurtures economic growth as with the economic factors governing the growth process itself.

"In the state of nature," says philosopher Thomas Hobbes, "life is nasty, brutish, and short." If you've seen any television program about animals in their natural habitat, you get the picture. It's not fun being a yearling with a pride of lions hanging around.

Imagine living in a world where no laws prevail and where protection and respect for personal property are entirely absent. Not much sense planting an apple tree, is there? After all, as soon as apples appear, you can bet they will disappear! And if, by chance, you catch the culprit in the act of "acquiring" the fruit of your labor, who ends up with the fruit becomes strictly a matter of who's the lion and who's the yearling. Then why bother planting? Why bother investing in any productive enterprise when the fruits of enterprise are so insecure?

### on the net

The Federal Reserve Bank of St. Louis's FRED (Federal Reserve Economic Data) database (http://www.stls.frb.org/fred/) provides historical U.S. economic and financial data, including quarterly GDP data since 1959 (http://www.stls.frb.org/fred/data/gdp/gdp).

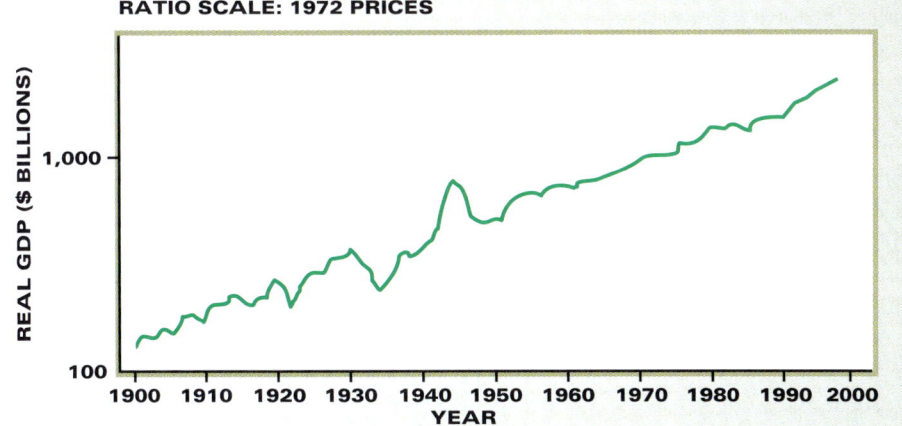

**U.S. ECONOMIC PERFORMANCE: 1900–2000**

From 1900 to 2000, U.S. real GDP, measured in 1972 dollars, increased approximately 15-fold. But year-to-year changes over the period deviated from the approximate 3.5 percent average rate of growth, and in some years the deviations were considerable. What stands out sharply is the real GDP decline during the 1930s—the years of the Great Depression.

EXHIBIT 1

## EXHIBIT 2

### LONG-RUN ECONOMIC GROWTH

Points *a* and *b* on the aggregate supply curve, $AS_1$, in panel *a* show the possibilities of real GDP positioning, given a fixed set or resources. Point *b*, *c*, *d*, and *e* on aggregate supply curves $AS_1$, $AS_2$, $AS_3$, and $AS_4$ in panel *b* show the possibilities of attaining higher levels of real GDP with changing levels of the economy's resources. Panel *a* reflects policy consideration for the short run; panel *b* reflects policy considerations affecting the long run.

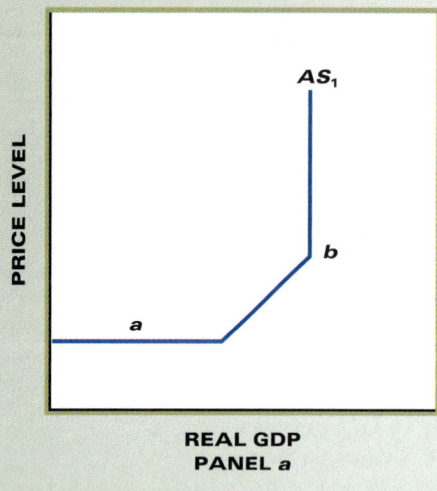
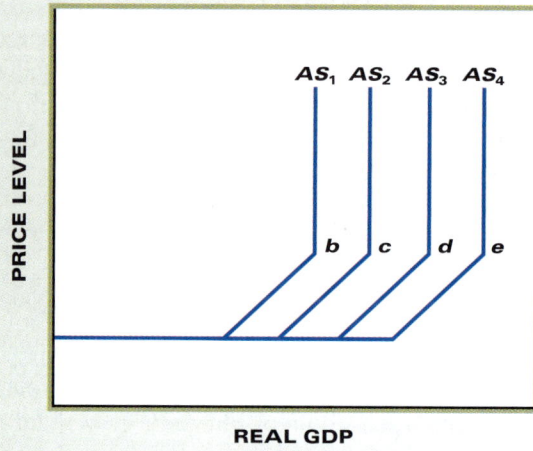

That's the question Thomas Malthus addressed in his *Principles of Political Economy* (1820). In the first page of Chapter One, Book II, titled *On the Progress of Wealth*, he writes: "Among the primary and most important causes which influence the wealth of nations, must unquestionably be placed, those which come under the head of politics and morals. Security of property, without a certain degree of which, there can be no encouragement to individual industry, depends mainly upon the political constitution of a country, the excellence of its laws and the manner in which they are administered."

How comfortable would you be living in a society where the laws governing property and rights to property change at the whim of those holding political power? What expectations about the future can you make when laws and constitution become means to political ends? The absence of confidence in the dependability of laws must dull the creative edge.

It's a matter of linking effort and reward. Legitimate rights to personal property and having a sense of security concerning those rights create the incentive for personal effort and expected reward. It is inconceivable to think of economic progress without such a linkage.

Most economists would also insist that the market system—the freedom and ability to exchange goods, resources, and money for each other—is an indispensable agent of economic growth. It allows individuals to engage with each other as producer and consumer, to specialize and trade, and to save and invest. The productiveness of these activities is limited only by the size of the market. In the long run, market size is virtually boundless because people's imaginations are boundless,

## INTERDISCIPLINARY PERSPECTIVE

### POLITICAL UNCERTAINTY HAMPERS QUEBEC'S LONG-RUN ECONOMIC GROWTH

**If** you visit Quebec, the predominantly French-speaking province of Canada, you couldn't help but notice if you're backed up in traffic—as you will be—the motto on Quebec license plates: *Je Me Souviens*. It means "I remember." But remember what?

What French Canadians in Quebec remember is the 1756–63 war between England and France in which France ceded Quebec to the English crown. That may have been a long time ago, but memories and passions live on undiminished.

These memories and passions have taken on a political life that thrives in the 21st century. Many French Canadians, exasperated by what they see as English domination of their culture and commerce, want to create an independent Quebec state, separate from Canada. Turn the clock back 250 years? Is it possible? Is it probable?

What about the English-speaking minority in Quebec? It opposes the separatist movement in Quebec, fearing French Canadian malevolence once Canadian constitutional rights are discarded. These polar positions concerning Quebec's sovereignty make for an unhealthy political climate in the province, which becomes increasingly unhealthy each time the separatist issue is put to a provincial referendum. This has happened several times during the past two decades, each time unsuccessful, but the closeness of the votes keeps the issue alive and heightens the fear among the English-speaking minority that the separatists in Quebec may yet prevail.

Are the English-speaking minority fears of a non-Canadian Quebec justified? There is, some think, enough evidence to support this apprehension. To some extent, the separatists have already created a *de facto* French state in Quebec in the absence of *de jure* sovereignty. The French-dominated provincial government has enacted provincial laws that the English-speaking minority consider unconstitutional and downright prejudicial—chief among them laws restricting the use of English in commerce, education, and public service.

The implementation of these anti–English language laws and the uncertainty concerning what may follow with Quebec independence has had a significant impact on Quebec's long-run economic growth. The initial shock of the language laws sparked a mass migration in the late 1970s and early 1980s of the English-speaking minority out of Quebec to the neighboring province of Ontario and, to a lesser extent, to other western provinces and the United States. As well, many business executives left along with the head offices of many major Canadian corporations. These migrations created a leftward pressure on Quebec's aggregate supply curve.

What continues to hamper Quebec's long-run economic growth is the continuing uncertainty surrounding Quebec's political future and the rather capricious way it tends to violate Canada's constitution. Until the uncertainty of Quebec's political future is laid to rest, Quebec will face an uncertain economic future.

#### MORE ON THE NET
To learn more about busines activities in Quebec, visit http://www.quebecweb.com.

---

creating always newer and more productive technologies that generate even greater specialization, more trade, and increased market size. The process is interactive: Expanding markets excite the creative nerve and whet the appetite for newer technologies. In this way, long-run economic growth and markets are inexorably connected.

**Economic growth**
An increase in real GDP, typically expressed as an annual rate of real GDP growth.

This connection is dramatically illustrated in Adam Smith's *Wealth of Nations*. You can almost feel his excitement: "The discovery of America, and that of a passage to the East Indies by the Cape of Good Hope, are the two greatest and most important events recorded in the history of mankind." That's as bold and assertive a statement as any you will ever read. And also incredibly perceptive! Smith saw these two events as creating the global market, and with it, the limitless potential for economic growth.

## What Causes Economic Growth?

What causes long-run **economic growth**? If you look at the title page of *The Wealth of Nations*—published in 1776 and still very readable—you will discover that its complete title is *An Enquiry into the Nature and Causes of the Wealth of Nations*. Smith struggled with the same question we ask about our economy today, and, interestingly, what economists today know about the causes of long-run economic growth is not terribly dissimilar from the insightful observations Smith made more than 200 years ago.

Adam Smith identified four principal factors that contribute to a nation's economic growth: (1) the size of its labor force, (2) the degree of labor specialization (or the division of labor), (3) the size of its capital stock, and (4) the level of its technology.

That is to say, if more people are employed, more goods and services are produced. If people are better educated, they can produce more goods and services. If they use more capital, the goods and services they produce increase even more. And the more advanced the level of technology, the higher their productivity.

## A Simple Model of Economic Growth

Let's look more closely at some of the factors Smith identified as contributing to economic growth and see how they work. To illustrate, let's look at a lumber-producing economy with a labor supply, $L$, of 100 laborers and a capital stock, $K$, of \$20,000. The relationship between capital and labor—how much capital each laborer uses—is referred to as the **capital-labor ratio** and is shown as

$$K/L = \$20{,}000/100 = \$200.$$

**Capital-labor ratio**
The ratio of capital to labor, reflecting the quantity of capital used by each laborer in production.

Smith argued that the more capital a laborer works with, the more output the laborer is able to produce. Imagine the 100 laborers using only \$10,000 of capital in the form of 50 double-bladed axes. Suppose they are able to fell 400 trees a day, or 4 trees per laborer. Now imagine what would happen to the number of trees felled if the capital stock they worked with doubled to \$20,000, or 100 axes. Wouldn't you expect each to be more productive, that is, to cut down more than 4 trees a day?

That's what we suppose in the economic growth model of Exhibit 3. We link the capital-labor ratio to **labor productivity** by supposing that each laborer, working with \$200 of capital, contributes \$50 of cut trees to GDP.

$$GDP/L = \text{output per laborer} = \$50$$

**Labor productivity**
The quantity of GDP produced per worker, typically measured in quantity of GDP per hour of labor.

Point *a* in Exhibit 3 shows the cause-and-effect relationship between $K/L$ of \$200 and the resulting $GDP/L$, or output per laborer, of \$50.

How do increases in capital stock contribute to economic growth? Imagine a \$2,000 investment that raises the economy's capital stock from \$20,000 to \$22,000. It raises the capital-labor ratio from \$200 to \$220. Economists refer to such an increase in the capital-labor ratio as **capital deepening**.

**Capital deepening**
A rise in the ratio of capital to labor.

What's the connection between capital deepening and labor productivity? Look at point *b*. When the capital-labor ratio increases to $220, output per laborer increases to $55 of cut trees. This cause-and-effect relationship between capital deepening and labor productivity traces out the output-per-laborer curve, *Q*, whose arching reflects the law of diminishing returns.

What do points *a* and *b* on the *Q* curve have to do with economic growth? At point *a*, prior to the $2,000 investment, GDP was $5,000 (output per laborer × 100 laborers, or $50 × 100). At point *b*, after the investment is added to capital stock, GDP is $5,500 (output per laborer × 100 laborers, or $55 × 100), creating an investment-induced economic growth of 10 percent ($5,500/$5,000 − 100).

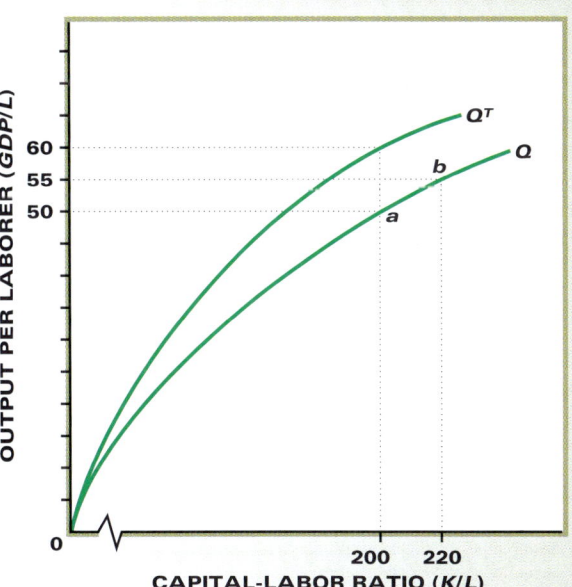

**THE LABOR PRODUCTIVITY CURVE**

The curve *Q* shows the relationship between labor productivity and capital deepening. The more capital per laborer, the greater the laborer's productivity. For example, at point *a*, a laborer working with $200 of capital produces an output of $50. Raising the capital-labor ratio to $220 raises the laborer's output to $55, point *b*. New technology can increase the laborer's productivity. This is shown as an upward shift in the labor productivity curve, from *Q* to $Q^T$. At $K/L = \$200$, the new technology raises output per laborer from $50 to $60.

**THE ROLE OF SAVING** How does saving fit into this economic growth scenario? According to Adam Smith and many economists today, saving automatically converts to investment, so that investment-induced growth is dependent on saving.

Exhibit 4 illustrates the saving-investment link to economic growth. Look at the left-hand side of the exhibit. In year 1, capital stock = $20,000, *L* = 100, *K/L* = $200, and *GDP* = $5,000. Economists define the relationship between capital stock and GDP as the **capital-output ratio,** in this case, $20,000/$5,000 = 4.

What do people do with the $5,000 income earned producing the $5,000 GDP? They spend some and save the rest. Look at the *C* + *S* rectangle. Of the $5,000 income, $3,000 is consumed and $2,000 is saved. Look at the saving conversion to investment in the *C* + *I* rectangle. The $2,000 saving becomes a $2,000 investment.

Follow the red arrow from year 1 to year 2, shown on the right-hand side of Exhibit 4. The $2,000 of year 1 investment adds to capital stock in year 2, which grows to $22,000. Because capital deepens to $220 per laborer, labor productivity increases to $55, so that GDP in year 2 is $5,500. The growth rate over the period year 1 to year 2, then, is 10 percent.

Applying the saving-rectangle analysis of economic growth to the U.S. economy, Exhibit 5 traces the ratios of saving to GDP for the United States over the years 1960 to 1999.

Slightly above 20 percent for the early 1960s, the national (or gross) ratio took an erratic but plodding slide to approximately 16 percent for 1993, and recovered partially during the last six years to the 18 percent ratio for 1999.

**Capital-output ratio**
The ratio of capital stock to GDP.

## EXHIBIT 4

### THE GROWTH PROCESS

In year 1, a $20,000 capital stock generates a $5,000 GDP. Two-fifths, or $2,000 of the $5,000 GDP, is put into investment, which appears as an addition to capital stock in year 2. The $2,200 capital stock in year 2 generates $5,500 GDP, creating a rate of economic growth of 10 percent.

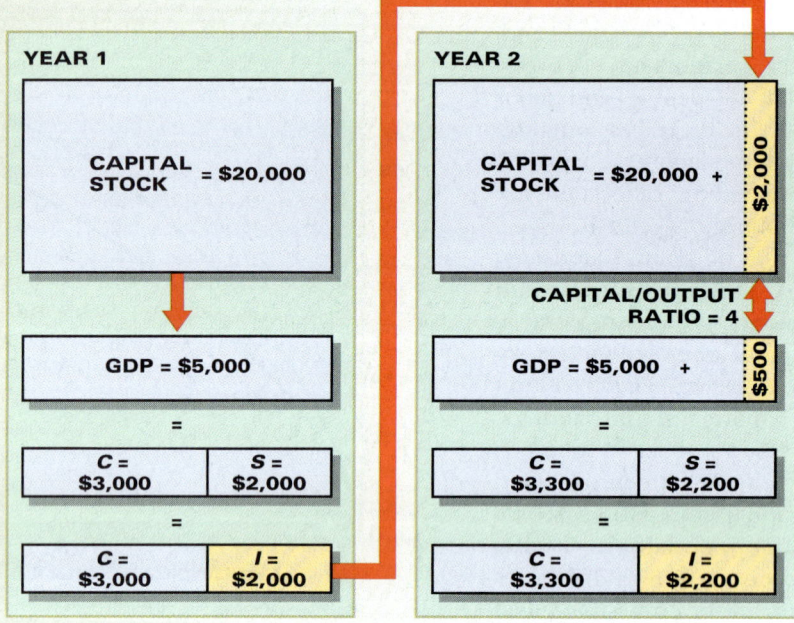

## EXHIBIT 5

### GROSS NATIONAL SAVING IN THE UNITED STATES: 1960–99

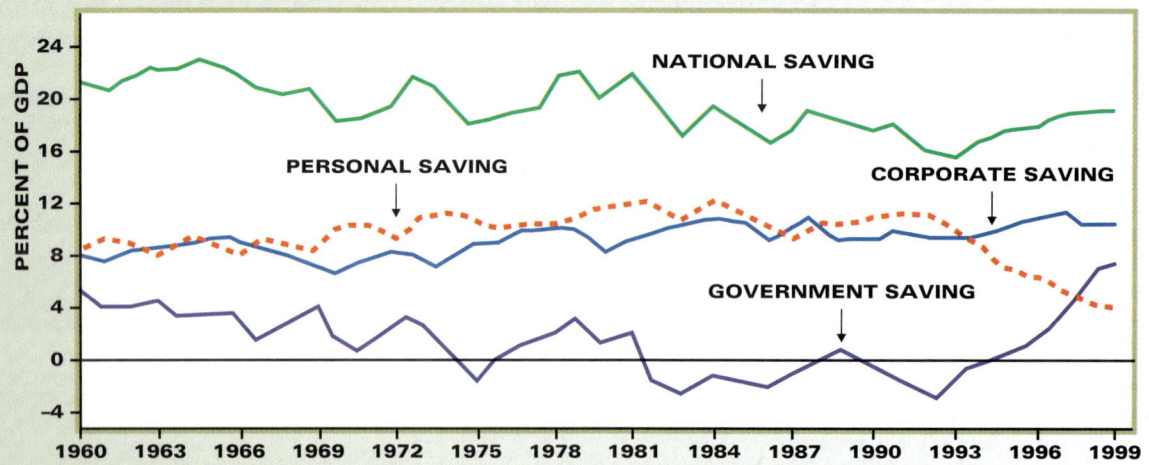

**Source:** Council of Economic Advisers, *Economic Report of the President* (Washington, D.C.: U.S. Government Printing Office, 2000), p. 73.

Relative to GDP, gross national saving held steady in 1999 as an increase in government saving offset a decline in personal saving, which fell to its lowest level in at least 40 years.

# THEORETICAL PERSPECTIVE

## A VIEW FROM THE PAST: ZERO LONG-RUN ECONOMIC GROWTH

The classical economists of the 19th century had a pretty grim vision of where the economy was heading. In their view, the economy's growth rate will steadily drop to zero and remain at zero thereafter. No ifs and no buts. Zero. As if that weren't enough to wipe the smile off anyone's face, it gets worse! Not only will the economy cease to grow, but its performance level will sustain only minimal subsistence for the majority of its population. Grim may be too sanguine a description of what 19th-century economists saw as our economic future.

Of course they were wrong. In hindsight, we may be puzzled at how mind-bogglingly mistaken these brilliant minds were. What they never fully appreciated was the impact that technology and capital deepening could have on labor productivity. The idea of a computerized world was as alien to their thinking as UFOs are to ours. They would likely have dismissed Exhibit 3 as highly improbable.

What they saw instead is the world depicted in the accompanying graph. The production function, $Q$, represents the quantity of GDP generated by a specific population size. Its curvature reflects the law of diminishing returns: As population grows, GDP grows but by smaller and smaller additions.

Line $M$ represents the GDP per person needed for minimal subsistence. If minimal subsistence is $50 and population is 500, then $25,000 GDP is needed just to keep the population alive.

How do we get to zero long-run economic growth? Start with a population of 1,000 that generates $100,000, or $50,000 GDP greater than needed for subsistence. This over-subsistence GDP is put into investment. The economy grows, the demand for labor grows, wages are ($100,000/1,000) = $100 or $50 above subsistence, and with the higher than subsistence wages, *people have more children.* Suppose population grows to 1,500. The GDP generated is $110,000. The over-subsistence GDP falls to $35,000, slowing the economy's rate of growth. GDP per person falls to ($110,000/1,500) = $73.34. Because it's still above $50 minimal subsistence, population continues to grow.

This process continues until population reaches 2,400, generating a GDP of $120,000. Wages equal the $50 minimal subsistence. There is now no above-subsistence GDP, no investment, and no economic growth.

The difference between their rather dismal forecast of our future and the one we have come to experience and enjoy is the incredible impact on productivity of capital deepening and technology. Amen to them both!

### CONSIDER

What are some recent technologies besides the computer that have increased economic growth? Are there any that you think will come along in the future?

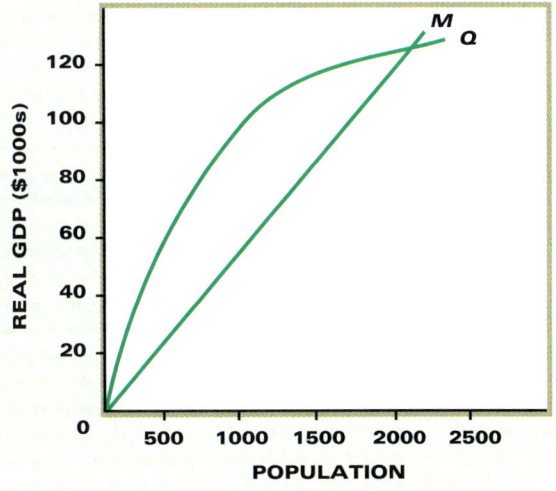

This recent upward trend in the national saving ratio is explained by changes in household, business, and government saving. Notably, the federal government transformed itself from a major borrower to a major saver. Saving ratios for state and local governments increased as well. Corporate saving also contributed to the upward trend. Together, these increases more than compensated for the near 5-point decline in personal saving.

The 2000 *Economic Report of the President* makes note of this upward shift in the national saving ratio and its relationship to economic growth. It sees it as "an encouraging sign regarding the Nation's preparations for the future." In the context of the growth model depicted in Exhibit 4, it is clear why President Clinton's Council of Economic Advisers, who authored the *Report,* believes, as most economists do, that saving matters.

**THE ROLE OF TECHNOLOGY** Changes in technology can increase labor productivity and GDP *without any change in the value of capital stock.* Imagine the laborers in Exhibit 3 trading in their capital stock of 100 axes for an equivalent value of capital stock in the form of 20 high-powered, gas-driven circular saws. As you would suspect, the same $20,000 of capital stock now cuts considerably more trees. This is shown in Exhibit 3 as an upward shift from $Q$ to $Q^T$. Even though $K/L$ remains at $200, GDP increases to $6,000 ($60 \times 100$).

## U.S. Economic Growth: 1947–2000

The Council of Economic Advisers and the Department of Labor estimate the factors contributing to the 1947–92 U.S. GDP growth. The author's own estimates extend the data to 2000. The Council's findings are shown in Exhibit 6.

The factors identified by the Council of Economic Advisers and the Department of Labor and the estimates they offer are clearly more explanatory than the analysis offered by the simple investment model of GDP growth. Exhibit 6 estimates a 3.94 percent average annual rate of GDP growth for the 1947–73 period, a more moderate 2.3 percent rate for the 1973–92 period, and a robust 4.0 percent annual rate for 1992–2000.

What explains these rates? The most significant factor in 2 of the 3 periods appears to be capital inputs. In explains 36.8 percent of the annual growth rate in

**EXHIBIT 6**

### SOURCES OF U.S. GROWTH: 1947–2000

| SOURCE | 1947 TO 1973 | 1973 TO 1992 | 1992 TO 2000 |
|---|---|---|---|
| LABOR INPUTS | 1.01 | 0.88 | 1.50 |
| CAPITAL INPUTS | 1.45 | 1.07 | 2.10 |
| TECHNOLOGICAL CHANGE | 1.63 | 0.40 | 0.40 |
| ADJUSTMENTS | −0.14 | −0.40 | — |
| TOTAL (GDP GROWTH) | 3.94 | 2.30 | 4.00 |

**Source:** Council of Economic Advisers, *Economic Report of the President* (Washington, D.C.: U.S. Government Printing Office, 1994), p. 44, and author's estimates.

# GLOBAL PERSPECTIVE

## I'VE GOT TO ADMIT IT'S GETTING BETTER, A LITTLE BETTER ALL THE TIME

The incredible Beatles album *Sgt. Pepper's Lonely Hearts Club Band* has, among its list of enduring hits, the optimistic song *Getting Better*. The lyric "I've got to admit it's getting better, a little better all the time" came to Beatle Paul McCartney during a walk on Primrose Hill in London, on the first sunny day of spring in 1967. Remarking on the weather, Paul commented offhand to journalist Hunter Davies that it was "getting better." It struck him then as a good idea to work on. It also reflected the cheerfulness he felt then because the weight of a stressful tour had been lifted.

Economists, too, could tell the same story, although perhaps not with the poetry of a Paul McCartney lyric or the loveliness of a John Lennon musical composition.

TANGERINE TREES AND MARMALADE SKIES.

Still, economists know that there is good reason to feel optimistic about our economic future if you look back at data on long-run growth of real GDP from, say, 1967—the year of the Beatles song—to 1998, as shown in the accompanying table.

There are no negatives in any of the 14 economies in the table. All experienced some degree of economic growth, although it was more than "a little better" for some. Eleven of the 14, including the United States, achieved average annual rates of growth of 2.5 percent or more. Small economies such as Ireland, as well as major leaguers such as Japan, France, and the United States, enjoyed that "little better all the time" year after year and, along with most economies of the world, have reason to expect that the 21st century will be even a little better.

### LONG-RUN GROWTH OF REAL GDP FOR 14 SELECTED ECONOMIES: 1967–98 (BILLION $US, 1995)

|  | 1967 GDP | 1998 GDP | AVERAGE ANNUAL GROWTH RATE, 1967–98 |
|---|---|---|---|
| AUSTRALIA | $139 | $410 | 3.5% |
| BELGIUM | 130 | 294 | 2.7 |
| CANADA | 234 | 620 | 3.2 |
| DENMARK | 94 | 199 | 2.5 |
| FRANCE | 705 | 1,646 | 2.8 |
| GREECE | 46 | 127 | 3.3 |
| IRELAND | 18 | 87 | 5.2 |
| ITALY | 487 | 1,127 | 2.8 |
| JAPAN | 1,487 | 5,319 | 4.2 |
| NETHERLANDS | 181 | 442 | 2.9 |
| SPAIN | 227 | 616 | 3.3 |
| SWEDEN | 132 | 245 | 2.0 |
| UNITED KINGDOM | 606 | 1,195 | 1.9 |
| UNITED STATES | 3,458 | 8,023 | 2.8 |

**CHECK YOUR UNDERSTANDING**

What factor is the most significant contributor to economic growth?

1947–1973; 46.5 percent for 1973–92; and 52.8 for 1992–2000. Additions to the labor force and technological change were important as well. Loot at the 1992–2000 period. Additions to the labor force account for 1.5 of the 4.0 percent growth rate, while technological change explains the remaining 0.40 percent. Working smarter seems to be more effective than working harder.

## THE BUSINESS CYCLE

Look again at Exhibit 1, this time focusing not on the dominant, long-run, upward thrust of the GDP growth path, but instead on the path's twists and turns. As you see, in some years the path rose steeply, while in others the incline was more moderate. There were also years in which the path dipped, that is, in which real GDP was actually declining.

Exhibit 7 tells the same story but shows the twists and turns as year-to-year deviations from a horizontal trend line that depicts the economy's long-run average annual growth rate (1860–1990).

These deviations *seem* to map out a picture of recurring cycles, that is, periods of rapid GDP growth followed by periods of less rapid GDP growth, or even decline. Some of the cycles appear to be mild, while others seem particularly severe. It isn't hard to pick out the depression of the 1930s and the sharp recovery after World War II, is it?

Although economists have no trouble identifying the major business cycles during the 1860–1990 period, they are hard-pressed to agree on *why* the cycles occur.

**EXHIBIT 7**

The year-to-year change in GDP is depicted as percentage deviations from the long-term trend growth rate. Sharp upturns are clearly marked by the Civil War, World War II, the Korean War, and the Vietnam War. The Great Depression of the 1930s and the sharp economic recovery following World War II dominate the picture.

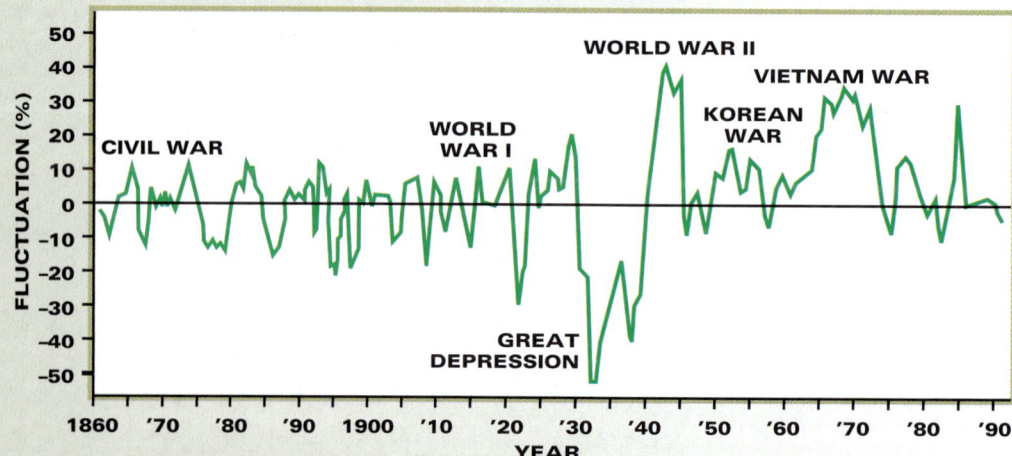

Source: Ameritrust Company, Cleveland, Ohio.

# TRADITIONAL THEORIES OF THE BUSINESS CYCLE

What economists do agree on is that there is no one cycle or one explanation for cycles (some economists are even reluctant to acknowledge the existence of cycles, contending that just because the economy has its twists and turns does not mean it cycles through them).

Some cycles are thought to be triggered by *external*, random events, such as wars, changes in climate, population booms, clustering of innovations, changes in consumer confidence, changes in government spending, or changes in international exchange rates. Other cycles are thought to be *internal* to the economy—like seasons of the year—and natural consequences of essentially normal economic activity.

Identifying cycles and their causes is tricky business. For example, a cycle whose upward and downward swings appear to be moderate may in fact be a composite of a set of not-so-moderate cycles whose phases—recession, recovery, prosperity, downturn—by chance counteract each other. One cycle's recession phase may overlap another's prosperity phase; thus, the appearance of a moderate cycle. On the other hand, a cycle that leads to economic depression, such as the Great Depression of the 1930s, may in fact be a composite of moderate cycles whose phases, by chance, are synchronized. One cycle's recession phase overlaps another's recession phase, producing exaggerated twists and turns in the economy's growth path.

Let's examine some of these internal and external cycle theories to see if any fit into the historical record mapped out in Exhibit 7.

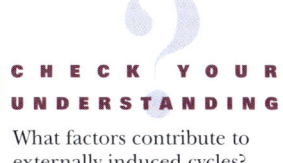

**CHECK YOUR UNDERSTANDING**

What factors contribute to externally induced cycles?

The Conference Board (http://www.tcb-indicators.org/) and the National Bureau of Economic Research (http://www.nber.org/) publish and maintain data on business cycle indicators.

## External Theories of Cycles

Some theories linking cycles to random events seem plausible. Others appear far less plausible, and still others seem downright silly. Yet even the silly ones can sometimes make sense. Consider, for example, William Stanley Jevons's sunspot theory of cycles, developed in the early part of the 19th century.

**THE SUNSPOT THEORY** To explain the English economy's erratic growth path, Jevons linked the economy's movements to the earth's path through the solar system. The causation he found ran from cosmic influences on weather, to weather influences on agricultural yields, and finally to the influences of these yields on the nation's economic performance.

Jevons noted that good harvests occur when the number of sunspots—nuclear storms on the sun—are at a minimum. The resulting abundant food supply lowers food prices and raises real incomes and employment. The national economy prospers.

But when the number of sunspots reaches a maximum, the economic consequences are reversed. Poor climate produces poor crops, higher food prices, lower real incomes, and greater unemployment. Jevons observed:

Learn more about William Stanley Jevons (http://home.tvd.be/cr27486/Jevons.html).

> If, then, the English money market is naturally fitted to swing or roll in periods of ten or eleven years, comparatively slight variations in the goodness of harvest repeated at like intervals would suffice to produce these alternations of depression, activity, excitement, and collapse *which undoubtedly occur in marked succession.*

Ingenious, wasn't he? But the explanatory value of Jevons's business cycles theory seems pretty much confined to agricultural economies. What relevance could it have to our economy today? After all, the "harvests" of automobiles, VCRs, dishwashers, and financial services seem to have little to do with nuclear explosions on the sun.

# APPLIED PERSPECTIVE

## YOU GOT THE DATES? WE GOT THE GROWTH RATES

Want to know what the average annual rate of growth in the U.S. economy's real GDP was for any two years between 1970 and 1996? Just consult the table on the following page. It shows the average annual percentage change in real GDP for any set of years between 1970 and 1996.

For example, suppose you wanted to know how the economy fared between the year you were born and the year you got your first bike. Let's suppose you were born in 1981 and your first bike was a birthday gift 10 years later. Read down the 1981 column and across on the 1991 row. Result: 2.6 percent per year.

In fact, just a cursory glance at the table reveals that a 2.6 percent per year rate of GDP growth is not uncommon. It seems to pop up everywhere, between any two initial and terminal years of the table.

Consider the exceptions to the rule. The 7.0 percent growth rate for 1983–84, for example, is impressive, but it represents only a one-year growth rate. If we stretch it into the decade of 1983–93, we're at 2.9 percent.

Look at your 1981 birth year again. Your first year may have been tough for your parents. The 1981–82 rate of GDP growth was $-2.1$ percent. Although you were a godsend, they may have thought the timing was not the greatest. Unemployment may have accompanied your arrival! But by the time you were five years old, the average annual rate of GDP growth—since your birth—evened out to a cool 3.1 percent. Not bad at all.

The 1981 birth year was just illustrative, of course. Look for your birth year in the table and any year of significance in your youth. How was the economy then?

I'M PROUD TO SAY WE'VE BROUGHT THE CRIME RATE DOWN. HOW? BY KEEPING THE ECONOMY'S GROWTH RATE UP.

### MORE ON THE NET

The *Survey of Current Business* (http://www.bea.doc.gov/bea/pubs.htm), a monthly publication of the Bureau of Economic Analysis, provides the latest data and commentary about the GDP. In fact, the table included on the next page came from this publication.

---

**WAR-INDUCED CYCLES** Are we destined always to go to war? From time immemorial, wars have been viewed as innate to the human experience. Admittedly, the evidence is frightfully confirming. Whether or not wars can be avoided, economists have long observed a link between wars and business cycles.

Does such a link make sense? Think about it. Wars create instantaneous demands for all kinds of goods and services. Once the decision is made to go to war, supporting the war effort becomes high priority. Armies need to be staffed, fed, clothed, housed, transported, equipped, and mended.

That requires considerable spending. You can see the income multiplier working overtime. In each of our major wars—the 1861–65 Civil War, the 1914–18 World War I, the 1939–45 World War II, the 1950–53 Korean War, the 1964–74 Vietnam War—military production spurred the economy into rapid expansion. And in at least some, if not all, of them, the end of war brought an end to the economy's war-induced prosperity.

**REAL GROSS DOMESTIC PRODUCT AVERAGE ANNUAL PERCENTAGE CHANGE, BASED ON CHAINED (1992) DOLLAR ESTIMATES**

| TERMINAL YEAR | INITIAL YEAR | | | | | | | | | | | | | | | | | | | | | | | | | |
|---|---|---|---|---|---|---|---|---|---|---|---|---|---|---|---|---|---|---|---|---|---|---|---|---|---|---|
| | '70 | '71 | '72 | '73 | '74 | '75 | '76 | '77 | '78 | '79 | '80 | '81 | '82 | '83 | '84 | '85 | '86 | '87 | '88 | '89 | '90 | '91 | '92 | '93 | '94 | '95 |
| 1996 | 2.8 | 2.7 | 2.6 | 2.5 | 2.6 | 2.8 | 2.7 | 2.6 | 2.4 | 2.4 | 2.6 | 2.6 | 2.9 | 2.8 | 2.5 | 2.4 | 2.3 | 2.3 | 2.1 | 1.9 | 2.0 | 2.6 | 2.6 | 2.6 | 2.2 | 2.4 |
| 1995 | 2.8 | 2.8 | 2.6 | 2.5 | 2.7 | 2.8 | 2.7 | 2.6 | 2.4 | 2.4 | 2.6 | 2.6 | 2.9 | 2.9 | 2.5 | 2.4 | 2.3 | 2.2 | 2.0 | 1.8 | 1.9 | 2.6 | 2.6 | 2.7 | 2.0 | |
| 1994 | 2.8 | 2.8 | 2.7 | 2.5 | 2.7 | 2.9 | 2.7 | 2.6 | 2.4 | 2.4 | 2.6 | 2.6 | 3.0 | 2.9 | 2.5 | 2.4 | 2.4 | 2.3 | 2.0 | 1.7 | 1.9 | 2.8 | 2.9 | 3.5 | | |
| 1993 | 2.8 | 2.8 | 2.6 | 2.5 | 2.6 | 2.8 | 2.7 | 2.5 | 2.4 | 2.3 | 2.5 | 2.6 | 3.0 | 2.9 | 2.4 | 2.3 | 2.2 | 2.1 | 1.7 | 1.3 | 1.3 | 2.5 | 2.3 | | | |
| 1992 | 2.8 | 2.8 | 2.6 | 2.5 | 2.7 | 2.8 | 2.7 | 2.6 | 2.4 | 2.3 | 2.6 | 2.6 | 3.1 | 3.0 | 2.5 | 2.3 | 2.2 | 2.0 | 1.6 | 1.0 | .9 | 2.7 | | | | |
| 1991 | 2.8 | 2.8 | 2.6 | 2.5 | 2.7 | 2.9 | 2.7 | 2.5 | 2.3 | 2.3 | 2.5 | 2.6 | 3.1 | 3.0 | 2.4 | 2.2 | 2.1 | 1.9 | 1.2 | .1 | -.9 | | | | | |
| 1990 | 3.0 | 3.0 | 2.8 | 2.7 | 2.9 | 3.1 | 3.0 | 2.8 | 2.6 | 2.6 | 2.9 | 3.0 | 3.6 | 3.6 | 3.0 | 2.9 | 2.8 | 2.8 | 2.3 | 1.2 | | | | | | |
| 1989 | 3.1 | 3.1 | 2.9 | 2.8 | 3.0 | 3.3 | 3.1 | 3.0 | 2.7 | 2.7 | 3.1 | 3.2 | 4.0 | 4.0 | 3.4 | 3.3 | 3.4 | 3.6 | 3.4 | | | | | | | |
| 1988 | 3.1 | 3.1 | 2.9 | 2.7 | 3.0 | 3.2 | 3.1 | 2.9 | 2.7 | 2.7 | 3.0 | 3.1 | 4.1 | 4.1 | 3.4 | 3.3 | 3.4 | 3.8 | | | | | | | | |
| 1987 | 3.0 | 3.0 | 2.9 | 2.7 | 2.9 | 3.2 | 3.0 | 2.8 | 2.6 | 2.5 | 2.9 | 3.0 | 4.1 | 4.1 | 3.2 | 3.0 | 2.9 | | | | | | | | | |
| 1986 | 3.0 | 3.0 | 2.9 | 2.6 | 2.9 | 3.2 | 3.0 | 2.8 | 2.5 | 2.5 | 2.9 | 3.1 | 4.4 | 4.5 | 3.3 | 3.1 | | | | | | | | | | |
| 1985 | 3.0 | 3.0 | 2.8 | 2.6 | 2.9 | 3.2 | 3.0 | 2.8 | 2.4 | 2.4 | 2.9 | 3.1 | 4.8 | 5.3 | 3.6 | | | | | | | | | | | |
| 1984 | 3.0 | 3.0 | 2.8 | 2.5 | 2.8 | 3.2 | 2.9 | 2.7 | 2.2 | 2.1 | 2.7 | 2.9 | 5.5 | 7.0 | | | | | | | | | | | | |
| 1983 | 2.7 | 2.6 | 2.4 | 2.1 | 2.4 | 2.7 | 2.3 | 2.0 | 1.3 | .9 | 1.3 | .9 | 4.0 | | | | | | | | | | | | | |
| 1982 | 2.6 | 2.5 | 2.2 | 1.9 | 2.2 | 2.5 | 2.1 | 1.6 | .6 | -.1 | .1 | -2.1 | | | | | | | | | | | | | | |
| 1981 | 3.0 | 3.0 | 2.7 | 2.4 | 2.8 | 3.3 | 2.9 | 2.5 | 1.6 | 1.0 | 2.3 | | | | | | | | | | | | | | | |
| 1980 | 3.1 | 3.1 | 2.8 | 2.4 | 2.9 | 3.6 | 3.1 | 2.6 | 1.2 | -.3 | | | | | | | | | | | | | | | | |
| 1979 | 3.5 | 3.5 | 3.2 | 2.8 | 3.5 | 4.6 | 4.3 | 4.1 | 2.8 | | | | | | | | | | | | | | | | | |
| 1978 | 3.6 | 3.6 | 3.3 | 2.8 | 3.7 | 5.1 | 5.0 | 5.4 | | | | | | | | | | | | | | | | | | |
| 1977 | 3.3 | 3.3 | 2.9 | 2.2 | 3.2 | 5.0 | 4.7 | | | | | | | | | | | | | | | | | | | |
| 1976 | 3.1 | 3.1 | 2.5 | 1.4 | 2.4 | 5.4 | | | | | | | | | | | | | | | | | | | | |
| 1975 | 2.7 | 2.5 | 1.5 | -.5 | -.4 | | | | | | | | | | | | | | | | | | | | | |
| 1974 | 3.4 | 3.5 | 2.5 | -.6 | | | | | | | | | | | | | | | | | | | | | | |
| 1973 | 4.9 | 5.6 | 5.8 | | | | | | | | | | | | | | | | | | | | | | | |
| 1972 | 4.4 | 5.5 | | | | | | | | | | | | | | | | | | | | | | | | |
| 1971 | 3.3 | | | | | | | | | | | | | | | | | | | | | | | | | |

Look again at Exhibit 7. Note the link between wars and economic upturns. For World War I, World War II, and the Korean War, the war-induced expansion came *when the economy was in the downswing or trough phase of an already existing cycle.* We were still in the throes of the Great Depression when Japan attacked Pearl Harbor in 1941.

In fact, the link between war and economic prosperity is so suggestive that some economists—Marxists, in particular—are inclined to believe that some wars were engineered principally to get us out of economic crises!

But most economists are unwilling to suppose that war conspiracies account for the economy's recovery from a cycle's trough. More likely, these war-induced cycles are random shocks to an economy already in continuous cyclical motion.

**THE HOUSING CYCLE** Another externally induced cycle is the 15- to 20-year housing cycle, also known as the Kuznets cycle, named for Nobel Laureate Simon Kuznets, who pioneered research on the relationship between cycles and housing construction.

Review an autobiography of Simon Kuznets (http://www.nobel.se/economics/laureates/1971/kuznets-autobio.html).

How do housing cycles originate? What could touch off an extraordinarily large investment in housing within a relatively short period of time? Imagine what happened to the demand for housing in 1992 after Hurricane Andrew hit south Florida. The calamities of nature, Midwest floods and California earthquakes, may be the most obvious, but certainly they are not the only causes of housing cycles.

For example, if interest rates are unusually high for an unusually long period of time, housing construction suffers. If people don't buy houses, they tend also not to buy house furnishings. Picture the income multiplier at work. When interest rates finally fall, mortgage payments once again become affordable. Housing investment booms to satisfy the backlog of housing and housing-related demands.

But at some point the investment slows down and the cycle's downturn phase begins. The housing cycle reappears with far less intensity. After all, not all housing depreciates at once. Some houses seem to last forever; others, poorly built or maintained, are torn down much sooner. Typically, a first-wave housing cycle lasts 15 to 20 years.

**THE INNOVATION CYCLE** Like housing investments, innovations are sometimes introduced into an economy in clusters and thus produce their own variety of cycle. What accounts for a clustering of innovations?

Joseph Schumpeter explained innovation clustering by identifying specific innovations that create major breakthroughs in technology. These pioneering innovations not only require massive investment themselves but promote a host of supporting innovations that together create an economic upswing that could last as long as 30 years.

What do these innovations look like? We live in their shadow. The railroad, the automobile, petrochemicals, television, nuclear energy, computers, genetic engineering, and space technologies are innovations that changed the character of our economy. Each, in its time, stimulated the development of entirely new industries that dictated for generations the specific pace and direction of our economic life.

Consider, for example, the railroad. It revolutionized the size of our markets and, therefore, almost everything marketable. It created industries where none could have existed before, bringing millions of previously remote idle acres into the productive economy.

Yet even the mighty railroad ultimately exhausted its potential. What happens to the economy when the initial investment momentum subsides? The income multiplier effect of reduced demand and employment triggers the downturn phase of this long-wave innovation cycle.

The automobile and the myriad industries it fostered created its own long-wave cycle. Petrochemicals and television followed, creating superstructures of investments that revolutionized the way we live. Are space and genetic engineering innovations now about to revolutionize our economic life? What kinds of earthbound investments will outer space inspire?

## Internal Cycles

Many economists believe that cycles need not wait upon wars or population explosions for momentum. The economy's continuous motion is *inherently* cyclical. But why should this be so?

We know something about the income multiplier. It tells us that any change in the level of investment triggers a series of changes in people's incomes. It explains how we move from one specific equilibrium level of national income to another.

That makes sense as far as it goes, *but it doesn't go far enough*. The very change in national income that the original change in investment generated *now feeds back to generate changes in investment*.

Why should a change in national income feed back to induce a new change in investment? Think about it. When national income increases, businesspeople see investment opportunities. Expecting sales to increase, they add to their inventories, buy new machinery, or expand their physical plant.

In other words, changes in investment and changes in national income are mutually reinforcing, and it is the mutual reinforcement that gives the economy its cyclical character. Just how does this mutual reinforcement work?

## THE INTERACTION OF THE MULTIPLIER AND ACCELERATOR

Let's start with the idea of the **accelerator**. It relates the level of investment to the change in the level of national income. To explain how the accelerator works, we suppose that there is a fixed relationship between the stock of capital in the economy—plants and machinery—and expected sales. That is to say, if you plan to produce goods for sale, you need the appropriate quantity of capital to produce them.

Suppose, then, that an initial injection of new investment into the economy triggers the income multiplier into action. As a result, people's income and consumption spending grow. Buoyed by this growth in sales, firms *expect the growth to continue*. They react accordingly. To gear up for the expected increase in sales, firms purchase more investment goods—more plants and machinery—to maintain the appropriate relationship between their stock of capital and their *expected* sales. The coupling of the effects of the accelerator and the effects of the income multiplier creates the upward phases of the business cycle.

But having acquired the capital stock needed to meet their expected sales, firms producing consumer goods must experience even higher sales just to keep the investment industries busy producing the same level of investment goods. After all, once the capital stock is built, it lasts for some time. To justify more capital stock, *you must keep growing!*

And there's the problem. If consumers simply maintain their already high levels of consumption, it's not good enough. The demand for new investment goods weakens, along with the level of economic activity it generates. This weakening forces firms to revise downward their expectations of future sales, leading to cuts in investment. The multiplier and accelerator now work in reverse. Since less capital stock is needed to maintain declining sales, the downward phase of the business cycle kicks in and feeds upon itself.

Where does it stop? Capital stock eventually wears out. Plants and machinery depreciate, become out-of-date, or both. The investment needed to replace worn-out capital stock in due time becomes larger than the fall in investment caused by declining sales. As a result, the economy's net investment becomes positive again, and the income multiplier once again works to generate higher levels of national income. These higher levels stimulate higher levels of expected sales and, through the accelerator, higher levels of investment. The economy once again swings into the upward phase of the business cycle. And the cycle repeats.

The idea that this interaction of the multiplier and accelerator, *by itself*, generates repeating business cycles supports the view that the economy is inherently unstable. That is to say, we suffer the business cycle not because the cycle is dependent on outside or external shocks to get it going, but because it is in the nature of the way the economy works.

**CHECK YOUR UNDERSTANDING**

What factors contribute to internally induced cycles?

**Accelerator**
The relationship between the level of investment and the change in the level of national income.

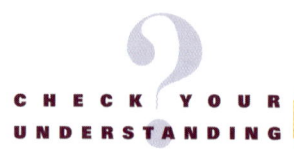

**CHECK YOUR UNDERSTANDING**

Why is the real business cycle theory not a cycle theory?

For more about real business cycle theory, visit the Quantitative Macroeconomics and Real Business Cycle Home Page (http://ideas.uqam.ca/qmrbc/index.html).

# REAL BUSINESS CYCLE THEORY

Some economists challenge the idea that internal or external cycles exist (even though their own theory is called the real business cycle). They believe that the idea of an economy actually moving through regular and distinct phases of a business cycle is a misreading of our economic reality. They argue that the economy is highly dynamic and competitive, operating close to if not at full employment, and that what other economists diagnose as cycles are in fact variations in the rate of growth of a full-employment economy. (Imagine a production possibilities curve shifting outward year after year but with a different-sized shift each year.) These variations—tracing out an uneven growth path of twists and turns or, more appropriately, robust spurts, not-so-robust spurts, and, very occasionally, short, moderate dips in real GDP—are misconceived of as the business cycle.

The principal factor shaping the unevenness (not cycles) in the economy's growth path, they argue, is the random injection by firms of individually minor but still large numbers of unconnected technological changes that cumulatively raise the level of productivity in the economy. They emphasize both the *large numbers of minor, unconnected technological changes* and their *randomness*.

Consider first their idea that technological change in the economy is the result of numerous minor innovations that occur regularly in all industries. This characterization of technological change is consistent with their view that the economy is both dynamic and competitive. The key to success and to ultimate survival for the great numbers of firms that compete is to develop or at least adopt new technology. *New technology raises real productivity,* which allows for lower costs and prices. Firms that don't adopt new technology cannot be price competitive with those that do. In the end, they drop out of the market. The real productivity increases that occur in this competitive environment make up the increase in the economy's real GDP.

Second, the randomness of these technological changes accounts for the variations in year-to-year increases in real productivity. For example, one year may bring in a host of technological changes, followed by a year with relatively few changes. These changes are independent of one another. Their frequency and numbers are randomly distributed over time and space.

Compare this characterization of technological change to the one described in Joseph Schumpeter's innovation business cycle theory. Schumpeter assumes that technological change typically is clustered and connected, triggered by a few very major innovative investments that represent breakthroughs in technology. These clustered innovation investments create the economic activity that causes the dramatic upswing phase in the innovation cycle theory. In time and sequence, the economic impact of these clustered investments peaks then weakens, bringing the cycle into its downturn phase.

In other words, while both views—the Schumpeterian innovation cycle and the real business cycle—focus on technological change, the former projects clear and discernable business cycles while the latter sees no such cyclical pattern, only unevenness in the economy's growth path.

The difference between traditional theories of the business cycle—from the external cycles, such as the housing or war-induced cycles, to the internal cycles, such as the interaction between the multiplier and accelerator—and the real business cycle theory is the role assigned to government. While economists associated with traditional business cycle theories, in particular with the internally generated ones, see cycles as a problem and government as an instrument to correct the problem, real business cycle theorists see the unevenness in the economy's growth path not as a problem but as a natural, anticipated, and positive outcome of technological change and increased productivity. That is, in the one case government is viewed as a contributor to the economy's long-run growth and stability, while in the other it is viewed as a long-run economic growth obstructionist. (A more complete analysis of the competing theories and ideas concerning the proper role of government awaits us in the chapter "Can Government Really Stabilize the Economy?")

## COUNTERCYCLICAL FISCAL POLICY

The real business cycle theory notwithstanding, let us recall from the previous chapter how fiscal policy was used to close inflationary and recessionary gaps and now put that policy to work on business cycles, whatever their origin. The idea is the same, but the problems of fiscal policy management become a little more complicated.

For example, picture a White House cabinet meeting in January 2001. President Bush is concerned about the state of the economy. He came into office following 8 Clinton years of high rates of economic growth. But even before President Bush was able to occupy the Oval Office, there were strong indications that the economy was beginning to cool off and perhaps heading into the first recession phase of the 21st century. Is it time to think about recession-prevention economic policy? What about defense spending? What about the tax cut he had proposed during the election campaign?

Robert Hubbard, chair of the president's Council of Economic Advisers, seems more cautious than the president about going ahead with increased spending or the tax cut. His concern is the deficit it may create in the president's first budget year. As well, it isn't entirely clear to him just where the economy is really heading. **Countercyclical fiscal policy** makes sense only if you know what it is you want to counter! He is uncertain whether the intensity of the presumed recessionary pressures deserve the kind of budgetary response the president has in mind.

Suppose that, to make his point, he goes to the chalkboard in the cabinet room and draws Exhibit 8.

"The economy this morning," he says, "is positioned at *a*. It *seems* to be heading into a downturn phase of a business cycle. What is less clear is whether the downturn will be troubling. If the cyclical path that the economy will take is along the dotted line *ab*, then perhaps some anti-recessionary countercyclical fiscal policy is appropriate. But if the actual cyclical path is along dotted line *ac*, then that policy may end up being an overreaction and counterproductive.

"If it is *ac*," he continues, "it is not a serious fiscal concern now. At some point in the cycle, the economy will turn around on its own. *The problem is knowing just where the turning point is.* If we opt now for strong anti-recessionary countercyclical policy—which the president's tax cut and defense spending appear to be—it may in

**Countercyclical fiscal policy**
Fiscal policy designed to moderate the severity of the business cycle.

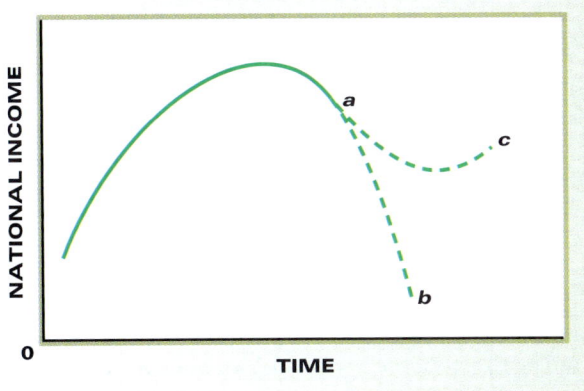

**DESIGNING COUNTERCYCLICAL POLICY**

At the time when policy is being discussed, the economy at *a* is thought to be entering the recession phase. Whether the economy will follow the *ab* or *ac* path through the cycle is unknown to policy makers. Each path has its own (and different) appropriate policy.

EXHIBIT 8

# INTERDISCIPLINARY PERSPECTIVE

## CONGRESSIONAL PHASE OF AN ADMINISTRATIVE LAG

The accompanying graphic shows the most typical way in which legislation is enacted into law. The hypothetical bill in this illustration refers to a $4.3 billion proposal for a CVN-76 aircraft carrier. It is introduced into the House of Representatives on January 3, 1999, as House Bill No. 203 (HR 203) and into the Senate the following day as Senate bill No. 70 (S 70).

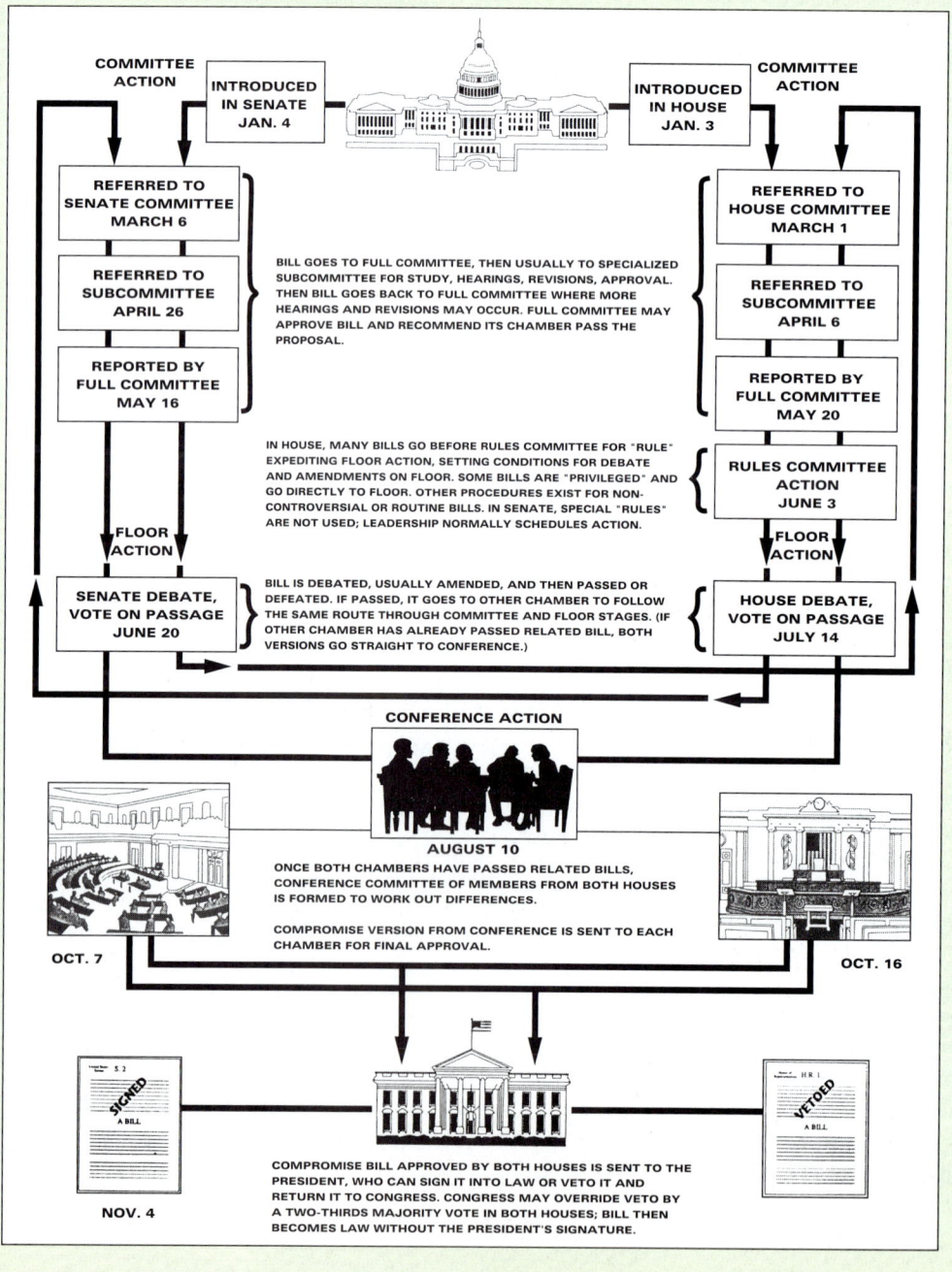

fact contribute to inflationary problems we want to avoid." In other words, Hubbard warns that an anti-recessionary policy at *a* in an *ac* cycle may be overkill.

"But what if the economy's on the *ab* path?" asks the president, looking intensely at Exhibit 8. "Then," replies Hubbard, "the anti-recessionary countercyclical measures are appropriate. Although how much budgetary deficit is needed," he adds, "is another question."

Everyone stares at Exhibit 8. Don Evans, the secretary of commerce, thinks aloud: "Exhibit 8 explains a lot, yet not enough." Everyone agrees. "It isn't enough to know where the economy is on the cycle—although that alone is difficult to gauge—but we have to be fairly confident as well that we know the path the economy is taking into the future. Deciding *when* to use *how much* fiscal policy is crucial in avoiding fiscal overkill or underkill."

"It seems to me," says President Bush, attempting to lift the cabinet's deflating spirits, "that practicing good fiscal policy is much loke doing good comedy: *it's all in the timing*."

"There's still another problem," Hubbard warns. "There is an **administrative lag** to think about. After all, if we decide this morning to decrease taxes and increase defense spending by, say, $200 billion, we couldn't simply implement that policy tomorrow. To be responsible, we would have to carefully weigh the competing projects already in place or on the drawing boards. I know that Secretary of State Colin Powell, Secretary of Defense Donald Rumsfeld, and Vice President Dick Cheney have their own ideas about what is needed. There are political as well as economic issues. Whatever we propose has to be reviewed by Congress, and that takes time. In fact, knowing Congress, it may take a great deal of time. And by the time we actually end up with an agreed upon $200 billion increase in defense—not to mention the other increases that are pressing the Oval Office—the economy may be in a very different phase of this cycle. In other words, administrative lag time, however unavoidable, may itself undermine the effectiveness of countercyclical fiscal policy."

"But I've heard there's no such thing as a business cycle!" adds the secretary of agriculture, Ann Veneman. "So why the excitement? I'm told the economy's growth path is naturally uneven, reflecting the increase in real productivity that is associated with current levels of technological change. In all probability, those levels will change tomorrow. Is there any truth to this argument?" The president's chief economic adviser nods his head and replies, "Ann, the truth is that there is a lot of theorizing going on out there about cycles and long-run economic growth, some making good sense, some less so, but all of them struggling to understand the real world. Whether it's a honest-to-goodness cycle phase or merely a slowdown in an uneven growth path we're in, I think we're involved in a lot of guesswork. I wish we knew more about this than we do, but we simply don't."

"And the buck stops here," the president mutters to himself. He knows that the countercyclical problems of administrative lag—identifying where on the cycle's phase the economy is, and what path it will follow—are critical to intelligent policy making. He also knows that however helpful a team of economists may be, they are no substitutes for a crystal ball!

**Administrative lag**
The time interval between deciding on an appropriate policy and the execution of that policy.

# CHAPTER REVIEW

1. Although an economy at any time may be viewed as tending toward GDP equilibrium, there is no reason to believe it actually gets there. During its progress toward that equilibrium, new economic circumstances may arise to change its equilibrium level, making the economy's equilibrium more a moving target than a specifically fixed GDP.

2. An economy's GDP performance record, such as the one describing the United States over the years 1860–1990, traces out a long-run economic growth path marked by cyclical fluctuations.

3. The four factors identified in Adam Smith's *The Wealth of Nations* (1776) as principal contributors to economic growth—and that are still relevant today—are the size of the economy's labor force, the degree of its labor specialization, the size of its capital stock, and the level of its technology.

4. Increases in the economy's capital-labor ratio, described as capital deepening, and changes in technology raise labor productivity and real GDP. As well, increasing rates of saving and investment, raising the economy's capital-output ratio, generate higher rates of economic growth.

5. Traditional theories explaining the causes of business cycles can be viewed as belonging to one of two sets: (1) external theories, such as the sunspot cycle theory, the war-induced cycle theory, the housing cycle theory, and the innovation cycle theory; and (2) the internal cycle theory, triggered by the interaction of the multiplier and accelerator.

6. Real business cycle theorists reject the idea of the business cycle, believing instead that the economy is highly dynamic, operating close to, if not at, full employment. What explains variability in the economy's year-to-year real GDP is the variability and highly random nature of the year-to-year changes in new technology.

7. Countercyclical fiscal policy, as its name implies, is fiscal policy (such as changing taxes, government spending, or both) used to counter or moderate the inflationary or recessionary phases of the business cycle. Its effectiveness depends on its proper use at the appropriate time. Adding to the difficulty of knowing how much to use when is the administrative lag that marks the time lapse between a government's decision to use a specific fiscal policy and its actual implementation.

# KEY TERMS

Economic growth
Capital-labor ratio
Labor productivity
Capital deepening
Capital-output ratio
Accelerator
Countercyclical fiscal policy
Administrative lag

# QUESTIONS

1. What are the principal factors contributing to U.S. economic growth in the latter half of the 20th century?
2. What is a trend growth rate?
3. What is an externally induced cycle? Give some examples.
4. Suppose the government prepares for war during the prosperity phase of a cycle. What effect would the war preparation activity most likely have on real GDP, employment, and inflation?
5. Suppose war preparation occurred during the trough phase of a cycle. What effect would it

most likely have on real GDP, employment, and inflation?
6. Explain why a housing cycle tends to dampen out over time.
7. What causes an innovation cycle?
8. What is an internally generated cycle?
9. What is the acceleration principle? How does it differ from the income multiplier?
10. Explain how interactions of the multiplier and accelerator generate cycles of national income.
11. Real business cycle theory is not a theory about cycles. Explain.
12. In the end, effective countercyclical fiscal policy relies on guesswork. Explain.
13. How does administrative lag undermine the effectiveness of countercyclical fiscal policy?
14. The long-term trend growth rate for the following set of GDPs is 2.7 percent:

| YEAR | GDP |
|---|---|
| 0 | 100.0 |
| 1 | 102.5 |
| 2 | 105.6 |
| 3 | 106.6 |
| 4 | 110.9 |
| 5 | 114.2 |

Graph the deviation of the economic growth rate from the trend line for each year.

15. In trying to explain economic growth, what kind of evidence can economists offer to demonstrate that saving matters?

# PRACTICE PROBLEMS

1. In 1990, the economy's resource base consists of 10 laborers and a capital stock of $50. Its capital-output ratio is 2. In 1991, its capital stock increases to $75, while the number of laborers and capital-output ratio remain unchanged. Calculate (1) the 1990–91 rate of economic growth, (2) the capital-labor ratio in 1991, (3) the GDP in 1991, and (4) the 1990–91 capital deepening.

2. Consult the Added Perspective box "You Got the Dates? We Got the Growth Rates" to complete the following table.

| TIME PERIOD | AVERAGE ANNUAL RATE OF GROWTH |
|---|---|
| 1970–95 | |
| 1985–95 | |
| 1990–95 | |
| 1994–95 | |
| 1981–82 | |

# WHAT'S WRONG WITH THIS GRAPH?

**THE LABOR PRODUCTIVITY CURVE**

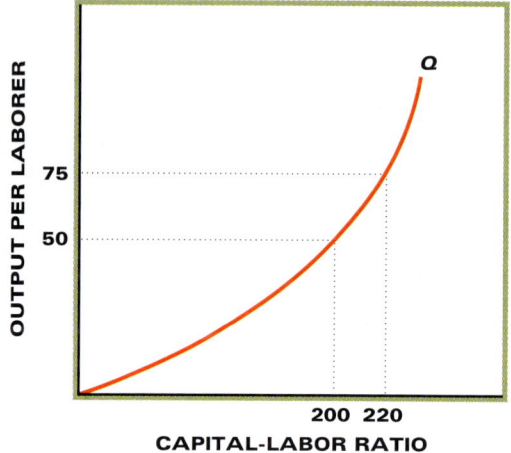

# ECONOMIC CONSULTANTS

## ECONOMIC RESEARCH AND ANALYSIS BY STUDENTS FOR PROFESSIONALS

Future Now! is an organization of business leaders in both the biotechnology industry and the computer industry. It is actively involved in educating the public—business and government people, in particular—about the economic benefits to society of having a cutting-edge biotechnology industry. In this way, it hopes to create an economic environment favorable to its business interests. Future Now! has been invited to testify before the Senate Subcommittee on Science, Technology, and Space about a congressional proposal to downsize government spending on technology research and development.

Alice Gorman is the public relations director of Future Now! Having interned with Economic Consultants while at college, she is familiar with its expertise and has hired the firm to help her prepare her statement before the Senate subcommittee. You are assigned the project and asked to work with her on the following issues:

1. What has government done in the past to promote technological development in the economy and in the biotechnology industry in particular?
2. What effects might new advancements in biotechnology have on the economic growth of the industry and the economy in general?
3. What effects would a cut in government spending on biotechnology research have on the industry and the economy in general?
4. What existing government programs fund biotechnology research?

You may find the following resources useful as you prepare your report for Future Now!:

- **Senate Subcommittee on Science, Technology, and Space** (http://www.senate.gov/~commerce/subcmte.htm#STS)—This Senate subcommittee has jurisdiction over federal research and development funding, among other areas.
- **National Science Foundation (NSF)** (http://www.nsf.gov/)—The NSF is an independent U.S. government agency responsible for promoting science and engineering through programs that invest over $3.3 billion per year in almost 20,000 research and education projects in science and engineering. Biotechnology research is handled through the Directorate for Biological Sciences (http://www.nsf.gov/bio/start.htm).
- **Biotechnology Information Resource** (http://www.nal.usda.gov/bic/)—The Department of Agriculture sponsors the Biotechnology Information Resource, a library of resources for biotechnology.
- **National Institute of Standards and Technology** (http://www.nist.gov/public_affairs/nandyou.htm)—This is an agency of the U.S. Department of Commerce (http://www.doc.gov/) that works with industry to develop and apply technology.
- **BioChemLinks: Biotechnology** (http://biochemlinks.com/bclinks/bclinks.cfm)—BioChemLinks provides links to biotechnology resources.

# PRACTICE TEST

1. All of the following can lead to economic growth except one. Which one?
   a. Increases in the capital stock
   b. Increased specialization of labor
   c. Improvements in the level of technology in the economy
   d. Increases in the capital-output ratio
   e. Increases in the size of the labor force

2. Suppose that the capital-output ratio in the economy is equal to 5. If GDP is equal to $200 billion, then the capital stock
   a. must equal $1 trillion.
   b. must equal $40 billion.
   c. is also equal to $200 billion.
   d. must be falling.
   e. cannot be determined without more information.

3. Which of the following statements best describes economic growth in the U.S. economy between 1947 and 1973?
   a. Overall, the economy experienced negative growth for the period.
   b. The rate of growth was lower than that for the period 1974–92.
   c. The primary cause of growth was technological change.
   d. The primary cause of growth was capital accumulation.
   e. The primary cause of growth was increases in the size of the labor force.

4. Suppose that an economy consists of 200 workers (L) and a capital stock of $50,000 (K). Assume that each worker can contribute $100 to GDP. Given this information,
   a. labor productivity is $2,500.
   b. the capital-output ratio is 2.5.
   c. the capital-labor ratio is 4.
   d. the capital-output ratio is 4.
   e. the capital-labor ratio is $2,500.

5. Capital deepening is said to occur when
   a. the capital-labor ratio increases.
   b. decreases in the capital stock increase the quantity of labor in the economy.
   c. labor productivity decreases.
   d. workers can produce more output per unit of labor than before.
   e. the capital-output ratio moves in the same direction as the capital-labor ratio.

6. The business cycle focuses attention on
   a. shifts in the long-run economic growth for the economy.
   b. deviations in GDP growth from its long-run path.
   c. how changes in the capital-labor ratio affect the capital-output ratio.
   d. whether the capital stock is rising or falling.
   e. comparisons across nations in the long-run level of economic growth.

7. Which business cycle theory suggests that spurts of technological innovations are a major cause of business cycle fluctuations?
   a. The innovation cycle
   b. The sunspot theory
   c. The housing cycle
   d. The high-technology cycle
   e. The accelerator principle

8. The accelerator is used to show that
   a. wars increase the speed at which national income changes over time.
   b. there is no such thing as a regular business cycle.
   c. business cycles are created by the multiplier effect relating induced investment to changes in national income.
   d. countercyclical fiscal policy can be an effective tool in reducing the magnitude of the business cycle in the economy.
   e. administrative lags reduce the effectiveness of countercyclical fiscal policy.

9. Real business cycle theorists
   a. argue that business cycles are actually variations in the growth rate of the economy.
   b. believe that natural phenomena such as sunspots can create business cycles.
   c. advocate strong countercyclical policy to reduce the effects of the business cycle on the economy.
   d. believe that clusters of innovations in the economy lead to the appearance of business cycles.
   e. argue that the accelerator is the primary cause of the business cycle.

10. The time interval between choosing a fiscal policy and having the policy executed is known as
    a. fiscal lag.
    b. administrative lag.
    c. countercyclical lag.
    d. the long run.
    e. the short run.

# PART 3

## MONEY, BANKING, AND MONETARY POLICY

**Tune into the conversation.** It's about *your* course. Just change the names, and it's *your* campus, *your* classroom, *your* professor, *your* classmates, and *you*.

Before beginning the morning lecture, Professor Gottheil asks for questions. Two hands shoot up. The first belongs to Gen Clark, a freshman who hopes to major in fine arts. The second belongs to Chris Stefan, also a freshman, who has philosophy in mind.

**GOTTHEIL:** Gen, you have your hand up. What's the problem?
**GEN:** Well, I think I have an intuitive feeling about real GDP. I mean, I can understand the idea that people produce things—and that's real GDP, right?—and they consume things and save. I can see them actually doing these things. But I'm having trouble visualizing how money—you know, dollar bills—fits into the picture. After all, it's just paper.
**GOTTHEIL:** OK. Let's talk about it. In fact, that's what our next few lectures are about, anyway. Let's see if we can grasp the vital connection between the real world of GDP and the world of money, even before we sink our teeth into the money chapters. We'll get to your question next, Chris.
**CHRIS:** It's really the same question! I was thinking about banks and money. They don't seem to have much to do with the real things that make up our GDP, like the food we eat or the house we live in.
**GOTTHEIL:** OK. Let's pick up on the idea of the house we live in. Chris, do you know what scaffolding is?
**CHRIS:** You mean the scaffolding used in construction?
**GOTTHEIL:** That's right. Describe to the class what scaffolding is.
**CHRIS:** Well, it's everywhere you see buildings going up. It's a wood-and-piping, skeleton-like structure that frames the outside of the building site. It's actually a series of temporary platforms used to support construction workers who are building a building. Is that what you mean?
**GOTTHEIL:** That's a fairly accurate description. It is not actually part of the building, is it, but it is what the building must have if it's going to be built at all. OK, now, what happens when the building is completed?
**CHRIS:** They remove the scaffolding.
**GOTTHEIL:** Right. And what do they do with it?
**CHRIS:** I guess they can use it again to construct another building.
**GOTTHEIL:** But suppose only 80 percent of the scaffolding is usable. Some of it can get pretty well banged up in construction. So if they had put up a five-story building before, what remains of the scaffolding limits them to a four-story second building. Right? And when that's done, the scaffolding is disassembled and removed to a third site, where there would be only enough scaffolding to support a three-story building. Got the idea?
**CHRIS:** Makes sense. I guess if you told me what the initial scaffolding was and its rate of wear and tear, I could figure out the total number of stories that could be built.
**GOTTHEIL:** I'm glad you said *could* be built, not *would* be built. Because suppose after the five-story building is up, nobody wants another building. You disassemble the scaffolding and it just lies there. All you have, then, is a total of five stories.
**CHRIS:** That's right. I got a strong feeling that you're about to make a connection between the use of scaffolding in building a house and the use of money in making real things.
**GEN:** Chris, I think I know where Professor Gottheil's going with this. Suppose you want to build a $100,000 house. You go to the bank to get a $100,000 loan—that's the scaffolding—and use the money to buy the materials

*continued on next page*

# CHAT ECONOMICS

and labor. In other words, the money supports the building of the house, although it's not part of the actual house. When you sell the house, the money is returned to the bank, just as scaffolding is disassembled to be used again.

**CHRIS:** OK. Loans are equivalent to scaffolding. But where's the wear and tear on money?

**GOTTHEIL:** Good question. There's no wear and tear on money, but suppose we insist that banks must retire a certain percentage of the money, say, 20 percent, from active duty after each loan is completed. That is, every time the bank receives $100 in money, it can loan out only $80. When the $80 is repaid, it can lend out $64, and so on.

**GEN:** Got it! Money isn't the real things built, but to get the real things built, you need the support system of money. The scaffolding analogy makes sense.

Keep this scaffolding analogy in mind when you review the chapters on banks and money creation. And always remember, it's producing real things, like houses, that matters. Money is only the scaffolding to get there.

# CHAPTER 10

# MONEY

Indulge yourself! Imagine that you are on an island loaded with fruits, berries, rabbits, and exotic fowl, and teeming with a wide variety of fish always accessible in the shallows of the island's crystal-clear lagoons. All at your disposal.

Sounds marvelous, doesn't it? Now suppose, during the late hours of a summer afternoon, while leisurely digging for truffles with your pet pig, you chance upon a treasure chest filled with 1,000 gold coins. Each bears the imprint of an ancient Spanish realm.

An exciting find? Well, perhaps. What would you do with the coins? You couldn't eat them, wear them, or sleep on or under them, could you? They may be beautiful to look at, but so too are clouds! You may end up deciding that a sensible thing to do with the find is to bury it again.

Suppose, months later, another person arrives on the island. Nature's abundance is now shared. You both agree to divide the daily chores: You pick berries, he does the hunting and fishing. At the end of each day, you exchange the rewards of your specialized labor. For example, one bowl of berries for one fish. Or one egg for two pieces of fruit, depending, say, on the time required to produce these goods.

If one of you were an economist, you would know straight away that this kind of direct goods-for-goods exchange is defined as **barter**.

Now suppose a third person appears. This situation creates even more possibilities for specialization, doesn't it? The chores are now divided among three. One specializes in fishing, another in berry and fruit picking, while the third hunts. You set up a flourishing three-way barter exchange.

Let's add a fourth person. And a fifth. Berry and fruit picking are divided, and egg gathering, once handled by the person raising fowls, becomes a specialized activity. Barter

**THIS CHAPTER INTRODUCES YOU TO THE ECONOMIC PRINCIPLES ASSOCIATED WITH:**

- BARTER EXCHANGE
- THE CHARACTERISTICS OF MONEY
- GOLD-BACKED AND FIAT MONEY
- LIQUIDITY
- THE EQUATION OF EXCHANGE
- THE QUANTITY THEORY OF MONEY
- THE CLASSICAL VIEW OF MONEY
- THE KEYNESIAN VIEW OF MONEY
- MONETARISM

**Barter**
The exchange of one good for another, without the use of money.

exchange now becomes a little more complex, and exchange-matching problems are bound to occur.

For example, suppose the egg gatherer wants to exchange eggs for berries, but the berry picker, worried about cholesterol, is not an egg eater. Or suppose the berry picker wants rabbit for dinner, but the hunter has no taste for berries, preferring eggs instead. You can see the problems.

If they all got together in one place at one time they could probably straighten out this no-match exchange mess. But it would still involve some degree of risk taking. After all, the hunter would have to accept unwanted eggs in exchange for rabbit in the hope of later exchanging those eggs for berries. He would like to have prior knowledge, however, that the berry picker will really want eggs. That's a lot of indirect arranging to do.

As you see, barter can be an excellent means of exchanging goods as long as the people and goods involved are few and simple. But it breaks down quickly when the numbers increase. To function effectively, barter requires *the double coincidence* of each party to the exchange wanting precisely what the other has to offer. That's difficult to achieve among five people, impossible among five thousand.

## THE INVENTION OF MONEY

If you find yourself stuck in a barter situation, what can you do? One solution—common to all societies—is to pick one of the available goods as a medium of exchange, that is, as **money.** All other goods are measured in units of the one selected. Suppose the choice is eggs. By common consent, eggs are the accepted currency. A rabbit exchanges for 14 eggs, a peahen exchanges for 10, a basket of berries for 2, and a banana for 1.

**Money**
Any commonly accepted good that acts as a medium of exchange, a measure of value, and a store of value.

This wouldn't last very long. People will quickly discover that eggs are a poor money form. They are too fragile. If the hunter sells 3 rabbits and receives in exchange 42 eggs, most likely many would break before the day is out. There goes the money! How would you feel walking about with 42 eggs in your pocket?

Money must be *durable* and *portable*. Eggs are out on both counts. What about fish? They are too perishable. You wouldn't want to keep that money form in your pocket for very long, would you?

Rabbits? They are more durable than eggs or fish, but how would you buy an egg with a unit of rabbit? How could you measure out one-fourteenth of a rabbit? And what would you do with the remaining thirteen-fourteenths? You see the problem: money must be *divisible* as well.

Another problem with rabbits as a money form is that some rabbits are big and fluffy, others are not. Some are cute, others less so. As long as some are preferred to others, people will tend to hoard preferred rabbits and use only the less preferred ones as money. In such cases, then, not all of the money form actually serves as money. To overcome this problem, the units of any money form selected must be *identical*, or homogeneous.

There's still another problem with rabbits. They breed like rabbits! If rabbits are money, it becomes impossible to control the money supply. The supply of fish and eggs, too, can be expanded without much effort. If money is to serve as a reliable store of value, its supply, at least in the short run, must be fairly *stable*.

As you can see, almost any choice on the island creates a problem. But we all do the best we can. Some Native Americans, before Europeans arrived, used wampum, strings of beads made of shells, as money. During the colonial period, fish, furs, corn, cattle, whiskey, and, at various times, even gunpowder was used as money.

Elsewhere, other goods served as the medium of exchange. In the South Pacific, the tiny island of Yap came to use large stone wheels, one of them 12 feet in diameter, as its money form. In Homer's day, cattle were used as money. The ancient Egyptians used necklaces, hatchets, and daggers. U.S. prisoners of war during World War II used cigarettes. In fact, most common goods, including beans, fishhooks, pearls, cocoa seeds, nails, rum, tea, pepper, sheep, pigs, dates, salt, rice, sugar, skins, silk, reindeer, and whale teeth have served somewhere at some time as money.

## Gold as Money

Economies tend to select whatever goods they have that come closest to satisfying the prerequisites for perfect money. What money form would *you* choose if you were on the island? Think about it. If homogeneity, divisibility, portability, durability, and unchanging supply count, what about that gold buried among the truffles? Before exchange, it was useless. Now it appears to satisfy all five prerequisites:

- Its supply—the 1,000 coins—is fixed. In the real world, supplies of gold are hard to come by. People have searched the globe for gold, but whatever the discovery, even the San Francisco Gold Rush of 1849, year-to-year additions to total stock have been less than dramatic. Gold is just hard to find.
- It's perfectly homogeneous. Gold is gold. One ounce is identical to any other. No ounce is preferred to another.
- It's incredibly durable. Just try destroying a nugget of gold. It doesn't rot, rust, fade, overripen, or dry up. Its luster withstands the elements of time.
- It's perfectly divisible. Gold can be melted down and remolded into any shape or size. Think of gold jewelry. Gold nuggets can be reduced to standard-sized ounces, and ounces cut to minute fractions. Gold dust is still gold.
- It's portable. It can be held, pocketed, or carried about. There's a limit, of course, to the quantity a person could carry, but for most people, the quantities required are quite manageable.

Because gold has these marvelous physical properties, it satisfies the primary functions of money. That is, it serves as (1) a *medium of exchange* (a payment for any purchase), (2) a *measure of value* (a yardstick for measuring the value of other goods), and (3) a *store of value* (a means of holding wealth from one time period to another).

Its divisibility, portability, and homogeneity make gold a perfect medium of exchange and measure of value. Its durability and relative scarcity make it an excellent store of value. People feel confident that they can store it away knowing that when they choose to spend it, it will buy as much as it would today. In this sense, money transfers goods from our past to the present and from our present into the future.

## Gold-Backed Paper as Money

If the island switched its money form to gold, it would not be the first economy to do so. In fact, gold coinage dates back to the eighth century B.C., when coins were issued by the Kingdom of Lydia, by the Greek coastal cities, and by the Persian Empire.

Exchanging rabbits for gold, eggs for gold, and fish for gold works very well. In time, gold becomes the most recognizable good in the economy. Even children know how it works. It is carried about, stored away, traded for real goods, borrowed, and loaned. It represents the power to purchase any good at any time.

But somebody comes up with a new idea. Why not print paper money to represent the gold? It's more convenient than carrying the physical gold around. It can be easily tucked away in a pocket or purse, and simply by printing higher numbers

# HISTORICAL PERSPECTIVE

## FLUFFY RABBITS AND GRESHAM'S LAW

**I**t seems reasonable, doesn't it, that if rabbits were money and the price of a video rental were two rabbits, you would use the two least attractive rabbits from your rabbit stock to rent the video? Or imagine if you were a lawyer and charged three rabbits per hour; the three you receive from your client would probably be scrawny looking. After all, why would anyone give up the more attractive rabbits from their money supply? In other words, if the economy's money supply consisted of 1,000 rabbits, half adorable and fluffy, the other half cross-eyed and scruffy, only the 500 cross-eyed, scruffy ones would actually circulate as money.

Or suppose the economy's money form was gold, but unscrupulous people minted coins of fool's gold as well as coins of pure gold. Wouldn't you very quickly become expert in detecting which of the coins in your supply were pure and which were debased? And if there were 1,000 coins—500 pure and 500 debased—wouldn't everybody use only the debased coins as money, hoarding the pure coins? That is, the money supply used in everyday transactions would end up being only the 500 debased coins.

Debasing coins is a practice almost as old as coinage itself. Sir Thomas Gresham, a 16th-century merchant and advisor to the English crown, observed that *bad money drives out good*. He observed that debased coinage drove the good coins not only out of circulation, but out of Britain. He wrote to Queen Elizabeth:

THE TWO MOST BEAUTIFUL WORDS TO A BANKER'S EAR: SOLID GOLD!

> Ytt may please your majesty to understande, thatt the first occasion of the fall of exchange did growe by the Kinges majesty, your latte ffather, in abasinge the quoyne ffrome vi ounces fine too iii ounces fine . . . which was the occasion that all your fine gold was convayed ought of this your realme.

This passage explains why gold was conveyed out of Britain. Elizabeth's father, Henry VIII, had debased the coinage. Gresham's observation prompted the 19th-century economist H. D. MacLeod to write, "As he was the first to perceive that a bad and debased currency is the cause of the disappearance of good money, we are only doing what is just in claiming this great fundamental law of the currency by his name."

### CONSIDER

What happens to the price level when bad money drives out good money?

### MORE ON THE NET

For more on the history of money, visit History of Money from Ancient Times to the Present Day (http://www.ex.ac.uk/~RDavies/arian/llyfr.html).

on the paper, it can be made to represent great quantities of gold. Of course, a unit of paper money would be backed by a specific quantity of gold, so that paper money could always be cashed—converted back—for gold.

It's a revolutionary idea, almost as revolutionary as gold money itself. If it works, why not? What, then, should we do with the physical gold? Bury it once more! As long as people have confidence that paper money will serve the functions of money, then it's as good as gold.

## Fiat, or Paper, Money

One good idea leads to another. Suppose a violent storm washes away the entire supply of gold. Does the island lose its money? Not at all. Why couldn't the paper money, or **fiat money**, still continue to serve as the medium of exchange? Is the gold backing really necessary? As long as everyone continues, as before, to accept the paper as money—why worry?

Still, there is reason for concern. If we no longer link the quantity of paper money to a specific quantity of gold, then what's to limit the supply of paper money? Nothing. It seems reasonable to suppose that people, knowing that money serves as a store of value only if its supply is relatively stable, would be careful about overprinting paper money. But sometimes reason is of no avail. There is a temptation for economies to print more money. If a society chooses fiat money as its money form, then it must be particularly vigilant about controlling the quantity of money.

**Fiat money**
Paper money that is not backed by or convertible into any good.

## MONEY IN A MODERN ECONOMY

When was the last time you saw a gold coin, let alone bought anything with it? What, then, do we use as our money form? For a start, look in your pocket.

Coins and dollar bills are money in the form of **currency**. Look closely at the dollar bill. Although it says in bold and large print: "The United States of America," it is not government-issued currency. It is, instead, issued by our central bank, the Federal Reserve System (commonly referred to as the Fed). The dollar bill is a Federal Reserve Note. In your pocket, it represents the Fed's IOU. Why do we hold it? Read the fine print. It says: "This note is legal tender for all debts, public and private." That is to say, the Fed assures you that the dollar (its note) can be used by you or by anyone else as a medium of exchange and as payment for debts. Nowhere on the bill does it say anything about gold, because there is no gold backing it. The dollar bill is fiat money.

It works. No one hesitates to accept the dollar bill as payment for pizza, popcorn, or photographic equipment. We can even buy other nations' currencies with it. Canadians gladly accept our dollars in exchange for theirs. Japanese accept our dollar for their yen. Russians would be thrilled to exchange rubles for dollar bills.

**Currency**
Coins and paper money.

The Federal Reserve (http://www.federalreserve.gov/) issues the money we use to buy our favorite goods and services.

## Money and Liquidity

If you were to play a word-association game with economists and say "money," chances are they would all respond with "liquidity." **Liquidity** is what distinguishes money from any other asset form. Liquidity is the ease with which an asset can be converted into a medium of exchange. Look around your room. What assets do you have that can be readily converted into a medium of exchange? How about that dollar bill on your desk? That's instant. The dollar is a perfectly liquid form of asset. That is to say, the dollar, *in its present form,* can be used as a medium of exchange. A pizza maker, for example, will accept your dollar *as is* in exchange for pizza. A physician will accept it as payment for services.

**Liquidity**
The degree to which an asset can easily be exchanged for money.

*Try the word game with friends. What do they come up with? Go to the Interactive Study Center at http://gottheil.swcollege.com and click on the "Your Turn" button to submit your example. Student submissions will be posted to the Web site, and perhaps we will use some in future editions of the book!*

What about your other assets? Consider, for example, your ticket to next week's basketball game. Can you use it now, *in its present form,* to buy a pizza? Not likely.

**Money supply**
Typically, M1 money. The supply of currency, demand deposits, and traveler's checks used in transactions.

The Federal Reserve (http://www.federalreserve.gov/) maintains current and historical data on M1, M2, and M3 money.

**M1 money**
The most immediate form of money. It includes currency, demand deposits, and traveler's checks.

**M2 money**
M1 money plus less-immediate forms of money, such as savings accounts, money market mutual fund accounts, money market deposit accounts, repurchase agreements, and small-denomination time deposits.

Even if the ticket is refundable, you still must go to the refund office to convert it back into dollars. The ticket, *in its present form,* is not a perfectly liquid form of money. What about your stereo? It's worth something, isn't it? But *in its present form,* it is highly illiquid. What about the U.S. savings bond in your top drawer? It's more liquid than your stereo, but not nearly as liquid as your dollar bill.

As you see, each one of those assets in your room—the financial as well as the real goods—can be ordered according to liquidity. Some assets are perfectly liquid, that is, can serve immediately as money. Others are less liquid, representing a less-than-perfect money form. Most are highly illiquid, that is, far removed from a money form.

How much money we have, then, depends on how much (or how little) liquidity we accept for a money form. Let's consider the various qualities of money that make up our **money supply.**

## The Liquidity Character of Our Money Supply

Do we just add up the dollar bills and coins issued by the Fed to compute our money supply? That is to say, is our money supply simply all currency?

Not quite, although currency is part of our money supply. Consider the other money forms we use as a medium of exchange. If you saw a T-shirt you liked, what kind of money would you use to make the purchase? Most likely, currency. But how do you pay your rent? If you're like most people, you write a check on your checking account. The landlord accepts it as payment. As far as the landlord is concerned, your check is money.

**THE M1 MONEY SUPPLY** In fact, the check is the most commonly used money form. Most working people receive their wages and salaries in the form of checks. Corporations pay out dividends by check. Most large-ticket items are bought by check. How do you pay your telephone bill? How did you pay your college tuition? Next time you're in line at the supermarket, watch the cashier. Three-bag purchases are often paid for by check.

How many checks you can write depends, of course, on the size of your checking account. That is, your checking account balance represents your money supply.

After all, if you were asked to add up your own money supply, wouldn't you count the dollars and cents you have in your pocket, and then add the money you have on deposit in your checking account?

Economists describe these money forms as **M1 money.** M1 money is highly liquid (immediately available) money. Currency is about as liquid as money could be. Checking accounts? Banks are legally obligated to give you any fraction or all of your deposit immediately *upon demand.* That's pretty liquid, and that is why economists describe checking account balances as demand deposits.

Traveler's checks, too, are M1 money. Think about it. There are times when traveler's checks are more convenient and even more liquid than checks drawn on local banks. They are particularly useful when we're away from home. If you were in Italy, for example, you would probably find it easier to buy a leather jacket with a traveler's check than with a check drawn on your local bank. The Italian merchant may not know much about your bank balance at home but has confidence that the traveler's check you offer can be readily converted into Italian lire.

**THE M2 MONEY SUPPLY** A broader definition of money is **M2 money.** M2 money includes M1 money and more. How much more? What about your savings deposits? What about your time deposits (or certificates of deposit, commonly

# APPLIED PERSPECTIVE

## HAVE YOU WRITTEN A CHECK LATELY?

**M**oney in your wallet? When was the last time you used cash—dollar bills and coins—to make a purchase?

If you're like most consumers, the average value of your cash transaction is $5. But it adds up. Cash transactions account for as much as 36 percent of the total value of all family expenditures. In terms of volume (numbers) of transactions, cash was used to pay for 73 percent of all transactions; checks account for another 17 percent; and credit and debit cards, along with electronic devices, make up the remaining 10 percent.

What about those checks? They add up to mountains of paper. Approximately 65 to 70 billion of them are written every year. Who writes them? Who receives them?

Individuals writing checks to businesses account for 50 percent of all checks written. Another 25 percent are written by businesses to businesses, 15 percent more are written by businesses to individuals, and the remainder involve payments among individuals or payments to or by federal, state, and local governments.

When consumers take out their checkbooks, 85 percent of their checks are made out to businesses, 35 percent of these at point of sale and 50 percent from home for recurring bills.

Are all these percentages making you dizzy? Here's one more: Ninety percent of Americans have checking accounts and use them extensively. Enough, the point is made. The check, like cash, is a marvelous invention! It's as highly liquid as any M1 money and reliable. Only slightly more than 1 percent of all checks written bounce, most of them representing sloppy record keeping, not fraud.

THE FIRST STEP TO MONEY LIQUIDITY.

### CONSIDER

How might debit cards affect the use of checking accounts? Do debit cards affect the money supply?

---

referred to as CDs)? Are they money? Yes, indeed. But they are not nearly as liquid a form of money as M1. Why not?

Consider your savings deposit. It may come as a surprise to you, but banks are not obligated to release all or any part of that deposit to you without you first giving them 30 days' notice. That's pretty illiquid, isn't it? Still, as you have probably experienced, banks seldom exercise that 30-day notice privilege. A savings deposit is a less perfect form of money than M1 for yet another reason: It isn't a medium of exchange. For example, you can't pay your rent with a check drawn on your savings account.

What about your time deposit? As its name implies, you are committed to leave your money with the bank for a specified period of time. If you want to convert the time deposit into M1 money—think of cashing in a CD prior to its maturity date—you pay a penalty. The CD's not quite as handy as your checking account, is it? But you think of it as money, don't you?

Why, then, bother with savings and time deposits? Because they typically yield higher rates of interest to depositors than do checking accounts.

**M3 money**
M2 money plus large-denomination time deposits and large-denomination repurchase agreements.

**THE M3 MONEY SUPPLY** An even broader concept of money is M3. **M3 money** includes M2 money as well as a set of other money forms that have less liquidity than M2. For example, M3 includes large-denomination ($100,000 or more) time deposits, typically in the form of certificates of deposit held in banks and other financial institutions.

Eurodollars are M3 money as well. They are U.S. dollar deposits held in foreign banks. For example, you can set up a dollar account at the Midland Bank in London, England, and use those dollars instead of having to transfer U.S. dollars to England every time you want to negotiate a transaction in U.S. dollars there.

## Money and "Near" Money

If you received a $100 U.S. savings bond as a birthday gift, would you regard it as a money gift? Would you treat it the same way you would a gift of $100? Have you ever sold a U.S. savings bond before its maturity date? If you have, you know why it isn't a perfectly reliable money form or store of value. Although you can sell the bond anytime at *some* price, the price it will fetch on the bond market will be less than the stated maturity value.

What about corporate bonds? Is an AT&T bond any more reliable a money form than a U.S. savings bond? It too is marketable (and therefore convertible into cash), but at what price? There is even greater risk attached to the corporate bond. Economists refer to these financial assets as near money.

## What Isn't Money?

When you think about it, what isn't money? After all, can't you really convert any asset you own into money? Couldn't you sell your wristwatch at *some* price? That's why pawnshops are in business. They allow you to convert your belongings (or someone else's!) into money by purchasing them from you. But do you really think of your watch as a form of money?

Think about the credit card applications you receive in the mail, or visit Visa (http://www.visa.com/) and MasterCard (http://www.mastercard.com/). Is it clear from these advertisements that credit cards aren't money?

Unquestionably, people regard their checking accounts as money. That's what they look at when they worry about making it through the month. They know they can always dip into savings, but savings is something they prefer to protect. It was never really intended as a medium of exchange. Few people think of their homes as money, even though second mortgages are a common way of financing expenditures.

Nevertheless, every asset we own is potential money. At some price, it can be converted into money. Still, we make distinctions between our money, near money, and nonmoney assets, don't we? These distinctions, however problematical, depend not only upon how liquid these assets are, but also upon the intended purpose we ascribe to them.

**CHECK YOUR UNDERSTANDING**

Are your credit cards a form of money?

What about your Visa and MasterCard? Are they money? Not at all. They may be accepted as readily as money, but the reason these cards are honored at shops, restaurants, and hotels is because merchants expect to be paid by the financial institution that issued the card. Eventually, you pay off your bill by writing a check to the financial institution or bank that issued the card. But without an adequate checking account, Visa would soon discover that the credit receipt it received with your signature on it was virtually worthless.

Using credit cards is often more convenient than writing checks. Because we travel farther and more frequently than we ever did, these plastic cards have become indispensable. They are readily accepted in other cities and even in other countries by people who would otherwise refuse a check on an unknown bank. And

## HISTORICAL PERSPECTIVE

### EXPLAINING THE IMPRESSIVE GROWTH OF M2 MONEY

Bank robber Willie Sutton was once asked why he robbed banks. He replied, "Because that's where the money is." And, indeed, that's where it was. But since the late 1970s, and particularly since the deregulation of the banking industry in the early 1980s, money deposits in the form of M2 money found a haven in financial institutions such as credit unions, savings and loan associations, and investment companies that competed directly with banks. How did the competition come about?

Let's start with investment companies. They got into the banking business in the late 1970s by creating money market mutual funds (or MMMFs). These funds were preferred by many depositors over the traditional savings accounts or time deposits of banks because they paid higher rates of interest. (Using the deposits, the investment companies bought government securities and business debt, which yielded even higher rates of return.)

But the MMMFs had a downside. They were a much less convenient form of M2 money for depositors. Originally, the investment companies placed severe restrictions on the number of withdrawals allowed each month on an MMMF and on the minimum size—$500 to $1,000—allowable for each withdrawal. Although many of these restrictions have since been relaxed, restrictions are still imposed.

How did the banks react? In the 1970s, they couldn't. Banks were unable to compete with the MMMFs because they were prohibited by state law from paying comparable interest rates on savings deposits. As a result, money market mutual funds became a preferred M2 money form. But in 1980, when the state-imposed interest rate ceilings were lifted, banks created their own version of the MMMF called the money market deposit account, MMDA.

The competition between the MMMFs and the MMDAs made these money forms more and more accessible—providing depositors greater and greater liquidity—so that the old distinctions between M1 and M2 forms of money became increasingly blurred.

Adding to this blurring process was an innovation of the savings and loan associations (S&Ls)—the NOW account, or negotiable order of withdrawal. This allowed depositors to use S&L savings accounts as honest-to-goodness checking accounts. Not to be left behind, credit unions created the share-draft account, their own version of NOW.

Banks didn't sit idly by. They met the NOW competition by creating the ATS account, or automatic transfer of savings, which allowed depositors to automatically transfer funds from savings to checking when their checking accounts were depleted.

This intense competition for depositors between banks and other financial intermediaries since the 1970s resulted in depositors moving energetically into these many forms of M2 money deposits, creating an impressive rate of M2 growth.

the best part of all is that every time you use a credit card, you receive an interest-free loan for a month or two. You don't need to have money in hand (or in your checking account) until the time comes to pay the bill.

## Adding Up Our Money Supply

Exhibit 1 totals the M1, M2, and M3 money supply for the 2000 U.S. economy.

Look at currency, the money form most people would describe as money. It amounts to less than 8 percent of the M3 money supply.

Much of the M2 money supply growth since the 1960s, and particularly through the 1970s, can be explained by the introduction of money market mutual funds and deposit accounts into the banking system. They were the right money form at the right time. People favored an asset that could perform both as investment

## EXHIBIT 1

### U.S. MONEY SUPPLY: 2000 ($ BILLIONS)

| M1 | | $1,094.9 |
|---|---|---|
| | CURRENCY | $523.9 |
| | TRAVELER'S CHECKS | 8.8 |
| | DEMAND DEPOSITS | 323.8 |
| | OTHER CHECKABLE DEPOSITS | 238.3 |
| M2 | | $4,860.9 |
| | M1 | $1,094.9 |
| | SAVINGS DEPOSITS, MMDAs | 1,839.4 |
| | SMALL TIME DEPOSITS | 1,027.5 |
| | MMMFs | 899.0 |
| M3 | | $6,899.1 |
| | M2 | $4,860.9 |
| | LARGE TIME DEPOSITS | 760.8 |
| | INSTITUTIONAL MMMFs | 724.1 |
| | EURODOLLARS | 190.3 |
| | OTHER | 362.9 |

**Source:** *Federal Reserve Bulletin* (Washington, D.C.: Federal Reserve, December 2000), p. A13, table 1.21.

and as reasonably accessible money. As you can see in Exhibit 2, M2 has grown considerably faster since 1960 than any other money form.

Another factor that contributed to the rapid growth of M2 during the 1970s was the sluggish stock market. High-interest-yielding accounts looked good compared to the stock market performance. People shifted out of the stock market into these M2 money forms.

Although the broadest notion of money supply—M3—amounts to $6,899.1 billion, unless otherwise specified, *economists mean M1 when they refer to money.* It is what people and businesses use in their day-to-day market transactions.

**CHECK YOUR UNDERSTANDING**

What specific money form do economists have in mind when they refer to *money*?

## THE QUANTITY THEORY OF MONEY

How does the money supply affect prices? To show the money-price connection, imagine an economy consisting exclusively of 100 apple trees producing a real GDP of 5,000 apples. Suppose also that the economy's money supply is $10,000. Under these conditions, the price of apples is $2. The total value of the apples (or nominal GDP) is 5,000 × $2 = $10,000.

The equation of exchange relating the economy's price level, *P*, the quantity of goods, *Q*, and the money supply, *M*, is written as

$$P = \frac{M}{Q}.$$

If the money supply doubles to $20,000 and *Q* doesn't change, the price level doubles to $20,000/5,000 = $4. If the money supply falls to $5,000 and *Q* is still unchanged, the price level falls to $5,000/5,000 = $1.

Look at the other correspondences in the equation of exchange. If *Q* (real GDP) doubles from 5,000 to 10,000 apples and *M* doesn't change, the price level falls to $10,000/10,000 = $1. Simple enough?

### The Velocity of Money

Actually, it's too simple. The equation of exchange shown in our apple illustration does not take into account the **velocity of money.** The price level depends not only on *Q* (real GDP) and *M* (the quantity of money), but also on velocity—that is, on the number of times a dollar is used during a year transacting *Q*.

**Velocity of money**
The average number of times per year each dollar is used to transact an exchange.

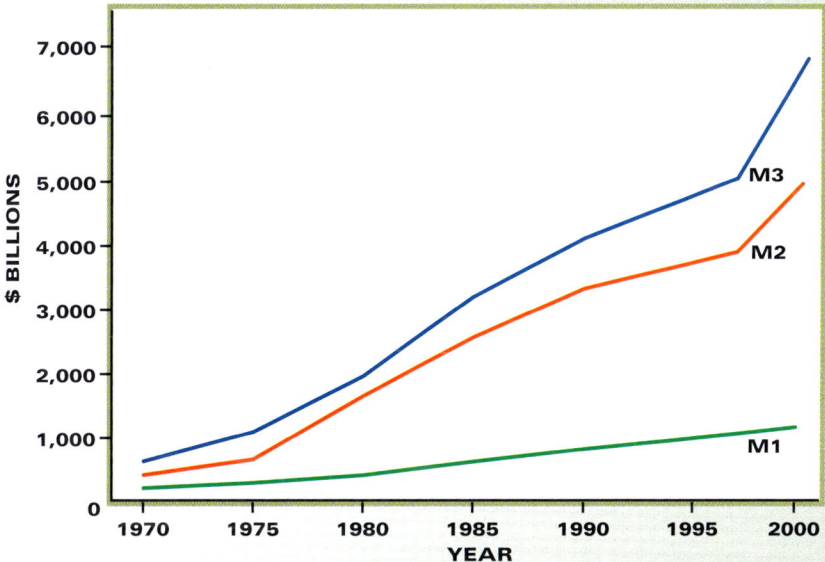

**EXHIBIT 2**

**GROWTH OF THE MONEY SUPPLY: 1970–2000**

**MONEY SUPPLY ($ BILLIONS)**

| DATE | M1 | M2 | M3 |
|------|-----|-------|-------|
| 1970 | 214 | 419 | 634 |
| 1975 | 295 | 663 | 1,092 |
| 1980 | 415 | 1,651 | 1,963 |
| 1985 | 627 | 2,566 | 3,200 |
| 1990 | 825 | 3,328 | 4,112 |
| 1997 | 1,065 | 3,904 | 5,053 |
| 2000 | 1,095 | 4,861 | 6,899 |

M1 money increased from $214 billion in 1970 to $1,095 billion in 2000, or by an annual rate of 5.1 percent. The M2 money components (M1 − M2) increased by 10.2 percent, and the M3 components (M3 − M2) increased by 7.8 percent.

D. H. Robertson illustrates the importance of money velocity in a rather amusing story:

> On Kentucky Derby day, Bob and Joe invested in a barrel of beer and set off to Louisville with the intention of selling at the racetrack at a dollar a pint. On the way, Bob, who had one dollar left in the world, began to feel a great thirst, and drank a pint of beer, paying Joe the dollar. A little later, Joe yielded to the same desire, and drank a pint of beer, returning the dollar to Bob. The day was hot, and before long Bob was thirsty again, and so, a little later, was Joe. When they arrived at the track, the dollar was back in Bob's pocket, but the beer was all gone. One single dollar had performed a volume of transactions which would have required many dollars if the beer had been sold to the public in accordance with the original intention.[1]

---

[1] D. H. Robertson, *Money* (New York: Harcourt, 1922), p. 35. The original text referred to the famous Derby at Epsom, in England, not the Kentucky Derby, and to shillings, not dollars. The derby and currency were changed here to make the illustration more familiar to the reader.

# APPLIED PERSPECTIVE

## MONEY CHALLENGE QUIZ

**When it comes to money, you probably think you know a lot, don't you? Let's find out just how much you really know about the money in your pocket.** See how many of these facts you know. (The answers are below, but no peeking!)

1. The U.S. Department of Treasury first issued paper currency for the Unitd States during which war?
   a. Revolutionary War
   b. War of 1812
   c. Civil War
   d. World War I
2. What has been the largest denomination of currency printed since 1946?
   a. $500
   b. $100
   c. $1000
   d. $5000
3. Which is the only coin that has the portrait facing to the right?
   a. penny
   b. nickel
   c. dime
   d. quarter
4. What is the most widely used denomination of coin currently in circulation?
   a. penny
   b. nickel
   c. dime
   d. quarter
5. Which U.S. president's portrait is featured on the fifty-dollar bill?
   a. McKinley
   b. Grant
   c. Jackson
   d. Cleveland
6. The first design of the 50 state quarters series commemorates the first colony and the first state to sign the consitution. It was
   a. Georgia.
   b. Pennsylvania.
   c. New Jersey.
   d. Delaware.
7. How many state commemorative quarters will be issued every year in the 50 state quarters program?
   a. one
   b. three
   c. five
   d. ten
8. What symbol on the back of the one-dollar bill symbolizes durability, endurance, permanence, and strength?
   a. pyramid
   b. eye
   c. flag
   d. eagle
9. Whose portrait is featured on the new dollar coin?
   a. Susan B. Anthony
   b. John F. Kennedy
   c. Abraham Lincoln
   d. Sacajawea
10. Th approximate life span of a United States coin is
    a. 15 years.
    b. 25 years.
    c. 35 years.
    d. 45 years.

Answers: 1. c; 2. b; 3. a; 4. a; 5. b; 6. d; 7. c; 8. a; 9. d; 10. b.

**Source:** Federal Reserve Bank of St. Louis (http://www.stls.frb.org/pubinfo/econed/quiz.html).

---

**Equation of exchange**
$MV = PQ$. The quantity of money times its velocity equals the quantity of goods and services produced times their prices.

A busy dollar working 50 times a year can do the same money-work as 50 one-dollar bills that work only once a year. In one case, the velocity of money, $V$, is 50; in the other, it is 1.

Adding the velocity of money completes the **equation of exchange:**

$$MV = PQ$$

Consider once more the apple economy. If $Q = 5{,}000$ apples, $M = \$10{,}000$, and $V = 8$, the price level $P$ skyrockets to $\$16$. The velocity of money, as you see, can be important.

Although the equation of exchange seems to be a matter of simple arithmetic, economists are nowhere near agreeing on how changes in $M$, for example, *really* affect $P$. Some economists, notably Keynesians, believe that if a change in $M$ occurs, it may not affect only $P$, as we see in the equation of exchange, but also and at the same time $Q$. If that happens, then the one-to-one correspondence between $M$ and $P$ in the equation of exchange is lost. They also see an interdependence between changes in $M$ and changes in $V$; that is, changes in $M$ cause changes in $V$. On the other hand, classical economists disagree, arguing that the velocity of money is unchanging, regardless of changes in $M$, $P$, or $Q$.

Classical and Keynesian economists offer two opposing views on the characteristics of $V$ and on the interdependence of the variables in the equation of exchange. Their differing views lead to differing theories concerning the relationship between money and prices.

## The Classical View

The classical view of the relationships among money, real GDP, money velocity, and prices fits into the broader picture that classical economists present of an economy in equilibrium at full-employment GDP. Real GDP—$Q$ in the equation of exchange—depends upon the amount of resources available in the economy. If the amount of resources does not change—a condition supposed by classical economists for short-run equilibrium—$Q$ does not change. Prices, on the other hand, are flexible in the classical world, adjusting the value of the goods produced, $Q$, to the money supply.

What about the velocity of money? According to classical economists, the velocity of money is constant. After all, they argue, people tend not to change the way they use money.

Think about it. How much money we need to purchase the goods and services we buy in a year depends, in part, on how often we get paid during the year. Suppose Kirsten Gentry earns $\$52{,}000$ annually and is paid that $\$52{,}000$ in one lump sum, say, on December 31. That is, there is only one payday per year. She would use that $\$52{,}000$ a dollar at a time throughout the year to buy goods and services. On the other hand, suppose there were 52 paydays per year so that she received $\$1{,}000$ weekly. In that case, the same $\$1{,}000$, used over and over in each of the 52 weeks, could buy the same $\$52{,}000$ worth of goods and services. That is to say, $\$1{,}000$ $M$, with $V = 52$, can transact for as many goods and services as $\$52{,}000$ $M$ with $V = 1$. As long as the number of paydays is an established practice in the economy, velocity remains fairly stable.

Our spending and saving behavior is habitual as well. As impulsive as we think we are, the truth of the matter is that we use approximately the same quantity of money week after week to buy our goods and services, and even on exceptional occasions such as vacations and holidays, our spending is fairly conventional.

Classical economists convert the equation of exchange into a **quantity theory of money.** Since they believe that both $V$ and $Q$ are constants for an economy in short-run equilibrium, the equation of exchange becomes a theory in which the *quantity of money explains prices*:

$$P = \frac{MV}{Q}$$

**CHECK YOUR UNDERSTANDING**

Why do classical economists believe velocity is constant?

**Quantity theory of money**
$P = MV/Q$. The equation specifying the direct relationship between the money supply and prices.

# INTERDISCIPLINARY PERSPECTIVE

## VELOCITY OF ANOTHER KIND

**Suppose you're one of 100 students taking Economics 101 and every student, including yourself, is fully aware that having *and reading* the assigned economics textbook is essential to a good grade.** The 100 students, then, would buy 100 books. Make sense?

But suppose these students didn't take the class in the same semester. Suppose, instead, class size was limited to 20 students so that the 100 students were forced to take the course over 5 semesters. The first semester's class of 20 students would need only 20 textbooks.

And suppose, after finals, these first 20 students sold their 20 textbooks back to the campus bookstore, who resold them as used books to the second set of 20 students enrolled in next semester's class. At the end of the second semester, those students resold their texts to the same bookstore, who resold them again as used books to the third-semester class, and so on.

Sound familiar? It should on two counts. First, that's probably what you will end up doing with your textbook. Second, the *idea* of velocity of textbooks is identical to the *idea* of velocity of money in a money economy. Each of the 20 textbooks over the course of 5 semesters "worked" 5 times as hard—or 5 times as much—as 100 textbooks used in the class of 100 students taking the course in one semester. The equivalence? Twenty texts working 5 times equals 100 texts working once.

**LOOK! THIS IS LISA'S OLD BOOK.**

Causality is clear and mechanical. If *M* increases, then because *V* and *Q* are constants, the price level, *P,* increases.

For the sake of argument, even if the economy tends to be at full employment, there is nothing that compels us to believe that *Q* must remain constant *in the long run*. In fact, there's good reason to suppose it doesn't. Why not? Because in the long run, the supply of resources available, such as labor and capital, increases. And since classical economists believe that the economy operates at full employment (always using its available resources and the most advanced technology), then with more resources used, more *Q* is produced.

To illustrate the classical view of the relationship between money and prices in the long run, let's suppose that the economy's resource supply increases by 5 percent every year.

The simple proportionality between money and prices supposed in short-run equilibrium breaks down. With more resources available every year, full-employment *Q* increases every year by 5 percent. How does that full-employment *Q* growth affect prices? If the money supply *M* grows by 5 percent every year as well, then with velocity constant, the price level remains unchanged year after year. If, on the other hand, *M* grows at 7 percent while *Q* grows at 5 percent, then the price level, *P,* increases by 2 percent (inflation) every year. And if *M*'s growth is lower than *Q*'s— say, 3 percent compared to *Q*'s 5 percent—then *P* falls (deflation) by 2 percent.

Classical economists saw the quantity theory of money as proof that money cannot influence how much we produce but that it does influence the prices of the goods we produce.

## Monetarism: A Modification of the Classical View

The idea that money velocity is constant was challenged in the 1970s by economists *within the classical tradition*. Their reformulation of the classical view on money became known as monetarism.

In a sense, the monetarist view of money was an attempt to rescue the classical view from the onslaught of empirical evidence that showed that M1 money velocity was anything but constant. Look at Exhibit 3.

As you see, M1 money velocity is quite erratic. Its long-run trend was downward until the 1950s, when it reversed and rose steadily until the mid-1980s. Since then, it has been even more erratic.

Monetarists accept the idea that velocity is not constant; nonetheless, they believe that it is still highly predictable, well behaved, and independent of money supply.

They explain the steady increase in money velocity since the 1950s by pointing to the technological changes associated with the transactions demand for money. For example, the use of computers speeds up the banking process. Also, the widespread use of credit cards allows people to buy and sell goods and services with less cash and lower bank balances relative to nominal GDP. The result: higher money velocity. Since technologies in money and banking are still developing and pay periods are becoming more frequent, monetarists believe it is reasonable to predict increases in velocity over time, and for the short run at least, they believe the increases will be well behaved.

If money velocity is known—that is, relatively stable and highly predictable—and if $Q$ is at full-employment real GDP, then the quantity theory of money—expressing the relationship between money and prices—remains intact. In the end the monetarist version of the quantity theory of money still leads to the same classical conclusion: Although money cannot influence how much we produce, it does influence the prices of the goods and services we produce.

**CHECK YOUR UNDERSTANDING**

According to classical economists and monetarists, what does a change in the money supply affect? What can it not affect?

## The Keynesian View

Keynesians offer a different view of the quantity theory of money. They reject the idea that $V$ is either stable or predictable and that $Q$ always reflects full-employment GDP. If they're right—that is, if $V$ is neither stable nor predictable and if $Q$ is not necessarily at full employment—then changes in the supply of money may end up affecting more than prices. They may affect $Q$ as well.

Consider how Keynesians view the velocity of money. They do not challenge the classical or monetarist view that

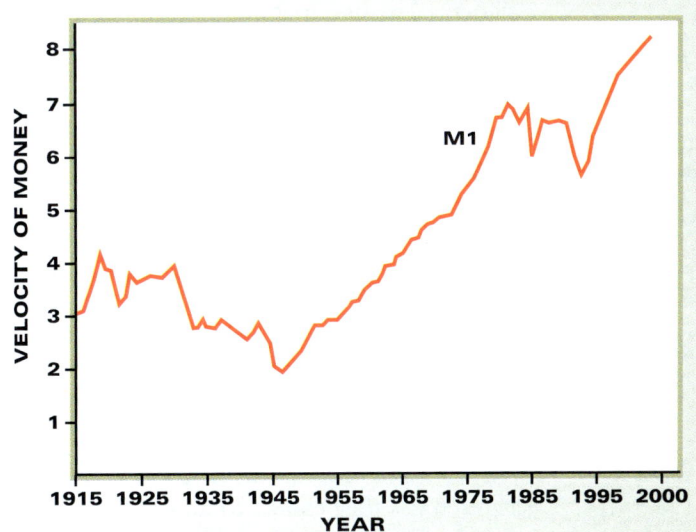

**HISTORICAL RECORD OF MONEY VELOCITY**

Until World War II, the velocity of money drifted downward, with some short-run upward swings, from approximately 4.0 in the 1920s to 2.0 in 1945. The trend reverses dramatically thereafter, increasing, with some short-run downturns, from 2.0 in 1945 to more than 8 in 2000.

EXHIBIT 3

payment schedules and patterns of spending and saving are basically stable. What they do challenge, however, is that these are the principal determinants of money velocity.

What is missing? To Keynesians, velocity is also affected by changes in people's *expectations*. A price increase, for example, may lead to an increase in money velocity. Why? Because people typically expect past performance to continue into the future. If prices increase, people will expect them to increase again; that is, they expect future prices will be higher. In that case, people will buy more now to avoid the higher future prices. In other words, price increases today can change spending habits today. To accommodate the increase in spending, the velocity of money increases.

What reduces velocity? The same logic is applied. This time, if prices decrease, people expect lower future prices, so they decrease present consumption in order to buy cheaper later. The decrease in spending today decreases the velocity of money.

Setting aside the issue of whether money velocity is stable or predictable or unpredictably variable, the idea that $Q$ always reflects full-employment real GDP is totally unacceptable to the Keynesians because it contradicts their central argument that an economy can be in equilibrium at less than full employment. If we really don't live in a world characterized by full-employment real GDP, then the tight relationship between money and prices that classical economists supposed existed comes completely unglued. (The Keynesian idea that changes in the money supply can affect real GDP is developed in the next section.)

## THE DEMAND FOR MONEY

### The Classical View

Classical economists regard the quantity theory of money as the key to our understanding of the economy's demand for liquidity, that is, money. The quantity theory of money equation is transposed to

$$M = \frac{PQ}{V}.$$

Since $PQ$ is nominal GDP (the quantity of goods produced multiplied by the price level) and since classical economists assume $V$ is constant, the quantity of money demanded by households and businesses to transact the buying and selling of the goods produced is derived by dividing nominal GDP by the velocity of money. That's it!

This **transactions demand for money** is the only motive classical economists see for anyone demanding money. If either the price level or real GDP increases, more money would be demanded to meet the needs of increasing nominal GDP.

**Transactions demand for money**
The quantity of money demanded by households and businesses to transact their buying and selling of goods and services.

### The Keynesian View

Keynesian economists see a more complex set of motives influencing the demand for money. They identify three principal motives for demanding money. These are the transactions motive (which classical and monetarist economists accept as the only motive), the precautionary motive, and the speculative motive.

**THE TRANSACTIONS MOTIVE** People hold money (liquid assets) to transact purchases they expect to make. This notion is fairly classical. People prefer to avoid the inconvenience of having to convert their nonmoney assets into money every time they decide to buy something. Can you imagine the headache converting nonmoney assets into money every time you buy a tuna sandwich? People learn, then, to hold a specific quantity of money for the groceries, theater tickets, gasoline, clothes, film, and other items they habitually purchase. The quantity of money demanded to satisfy transactions needs increases with the level of nominal GDP. The more people buy, the more money they need to make the purchases.

**THE PRECAUTIONARY MOTIVE** People also hold money as insurance against *unexpected* needs. Let's suppose Joel Spencer plans a trip that he estimates will cost $1,000. Is that the quantity of money he will take along? Most unlikely. Joel will probably add another $100 *just in case*. More-cautious people may add more. The motive? Precautionary.

And what about unexpected problems? A smashed fender. A broken furnace. A slipped disc that keeps you out of work for three weeks. A pink slip in your pay envelope. All is possible and, at *some* time, most probable. People hold money, giving up interest-bearing accounts, just to cover these eventualities.

**THE SPECULATIVE MOTIVE** Another major consideration for demanding money is the speculative motive. People have the choice of holding their assets in the form of either money or other financial assets, such as interest-bearing notes, bills, and CDs. How much they choose to hold of each depends on the interest rate. Look at Exhibit 4.

Why is the speculative demand curve for money downward sloping? If the rate of interest is high, say, $i_1$, people will choose to hold only $M_1$ and use the rest of their money to buy interest-bearing assets. After all, the opportunity cost of holding more than $M_1$ is the relatively high $i_1$ interest rate.

But if the interest rate falls to $i_2$, people will most likely shift out of holding interest-bearing assets into holding money. In Exhibit 4, the quantity of money demanded increases to $M_2$. Why? Because the opportunity costs associated with holding money and holding interest-paying assets have changed. Holding money now costs less because the interest to be earned is less. Holding the now lower-interest-yielding assets increases the cost of not having the money immediately available to take advantage of any unforeseen good prospect that may arise suddenly. That is to say, when interest rates fall, people feel more inclined to *speculate*. According to Keynesians, then, the demand for money is not just to satisfy people's transactions and precautionary needs, but to satisfy their speculative proclivities as well.

**MONEY AFFECTS REAL GDP** We are now prepared to explain why Keynesians believe money affects real GDP. Look at Exhibit 5.

Suppose the money supply increases from $S_1$ to $S_2$. (The demand curve is assumed to be $D_1$.) The effect of that increase lowers the equilibrium interest rate from $i_1$ to $i_2$, as shown in panel *a*. The fall in the interest rate increases the investment spending from $I_1$ to $I_2$, which is shown in panel *b*. (Note the steepness of the investment curve. It

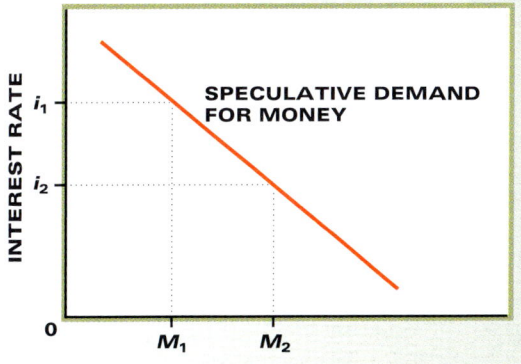

**THE SPECULATIVE DEMAND FOR MONEY**

When the interest rate falls, people shift out of interest-yielding asset holdings into holding money. And because the interest rate falls, the opportunity cost of holding money also falls. Why favor money? The primary reason is speculation. The interest rate could continue to fall, remain unchanged, or rise. In the expectation that it may rise, holding money (instead of nonmoney assets) puts money holders in a better position to take advantage of any future rise in the interest rate.

EXHIBIT 4

## EXHIBIT 5

### MONEY AFFECTS REAL GDP

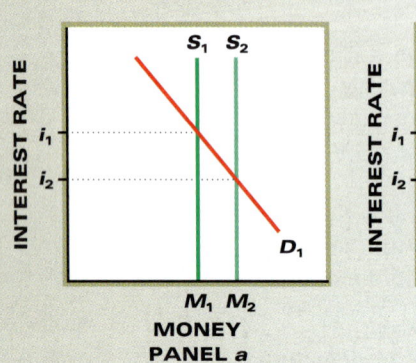
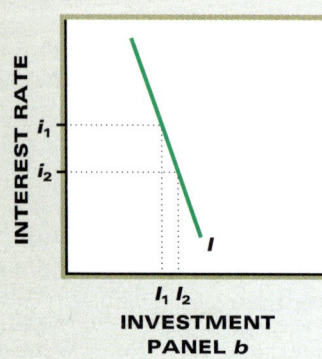
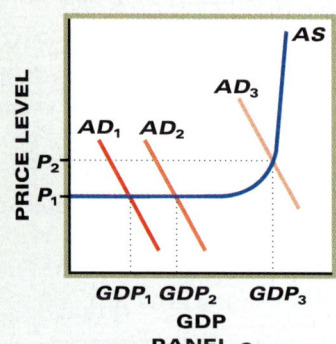

Follow the sequence of events through panels a, b, and c. When the money supply increases from $S_1$ to $S_2$, the interest rate falls from $i_1$ to $i_2$, which increases the quantity demanded of investment goods from $I_1$ to $I_2$. This increase in investment shifts aggregate demand from $AD_1$ to $AD_2$. The result is an increase in real GDP from $GDP_1$ to $GDP_2$.

**CHECK YOUR UNDERSTANDING**

Why do Keynesians believe that an increase in the money supply raises GDP and not price?

reflects the Keynesian view that changes in investment are relatively insensitive to changes in the interest rate.) Since investment is an integral part of aggregate demand, the increase in investment shifts the aggregate demand curve to the right, from $AD_1$ to $AD_2$, shown in panel c. And because Keynesians believe that the economy typically operates below the full employment level, the shift in aggregate demand raises real GDP from $GDP_1$ to $GDP_2$.

What about the price level? If the shift in aggregate demand and the consequent change in real GDP occur along the horizontal segment of the aggregate supply curve—and that's how Keynesians view the world—then the price level remains unaffected by changes in money supply. A different outcome would occur, however, if the economy were operating along the upward-sloping segment of the aggregate supply curve. In this situation, an increase in the money supply that raises aggregate demand to $AD_3$ raises both real GDP and prices.

The cause-and-effect sequence depicted in panels a, b, and c can be made to show what happens when the money supply falls. Interest rates (in panel b) increase, which reduces the quantity of investment undertaken in the economy. The fall in investment, in turn, shifts the aggregate demand curve to the left, thus decreasing real GDP.

How do classical economists and monetarists view the linkages shown in Exhibit 5? They believe that the investment curve (in panel b) is much more sensitive to changes in the interest rate than Keynesians suppose. Since they also believe that the economy operates at full-employment real GDP—that is, along the vertical segment of AS—any increase in the money supply (which lowers the interest rate and raises the quantity of investment and consequently aggregate demand) can only end up raising the price level. Nominal GDP increases, but real GDP does not.

# CHAPTER REVIEW

1. Barter exchange requires a double coincidence of wants. As the number of people and the number of goods increase, barter becomes increasingly more difficult. One good then becomes chosen as the money form. The characteristics of a good money form are durability, portability, divisibility, homogeneity, and stability. Gold is an exemplary money form.
2. Money serves three functions: It is a medium of exchange, a measure of value, and a store of value. Paper (or fiat) money can substitute for gold as long as it is universally accepted as the medium of exchange.
3. The different measures of our money supply depend upon the degree of liquidity we use. M1, the most liquid form of money, is essentially currency and checkable deposits, such as NOW and ATS accounts. M2 includes M1 plus small-denomination time deposits, such as MMDAs, and savings accounts. M3 includes M2 plus large-denomination time deposits and overnight repurchase agreements.
4. The equation of exchange is written as $MV = PQ$. Classical economists believe that because output, $Q$, is constant at full-employment equilibrium, and because the velocity of money, $V$, is constant, then the price level in the economy, $P$, varies directly with the money supply, $M$.
5. Monetarists accept the classical idea that the economy operates at full-employment equilibrium, but unlike the classicists, they believe that the velocity of money is not constant but nonetheless stable and predictable enough to ensure the usefulness of the equation of exchange linking prices to the money supply.
6. Keynesians believe that because output and velocity are neither constant nor stable and predictable, changes in the money supply can affect real GDP as well as prices.
7. According to classical economists, the demand for money is strictly a transactions demand. Keynesians, on the other hand, use the transactions, precautionary, and speculative motives as determinants of money demand.

# KEY TERMS

Barter
Money
Fiat money
Currency
Liquidity

Money supply
M1 money
M2 money
M3 money

Velocity of money
Equation of exchange
Quantity theory of money
Transactions demand for money

# QUESTIONS

1. Why does barter exchange become increasingly less useful as the number of people engaged in exchange increases?
2. What are the essential properties of money?
3. What are the three principal functions of money?
4. What are the principal components of M1, M2, and M3 money?
5. What is the relationship between money and liquidity?
6. What is "near" money?
7. Are Visa and MasterCard balances part of M1? Why or why not?
8. What is money velocity?
9. How do the classical and Keynesian views of money velocity differ?
10. In the classical view, what is the principal reason for people demanding money?
11. In the Keynesian view, what are the principal reasons for people demanding money?

**12.** Why does the quantity demanded of interest-yielding assets fall and the quantity demanded of money increase when the interest rate falls?

**13.** Explain graphically how the interest rate affects the Keynesian demand for money.

# WHAT'S WRONG WITH THIS GRAPH?

**THE SPECULATIVE DEMAND FOR MONEY**

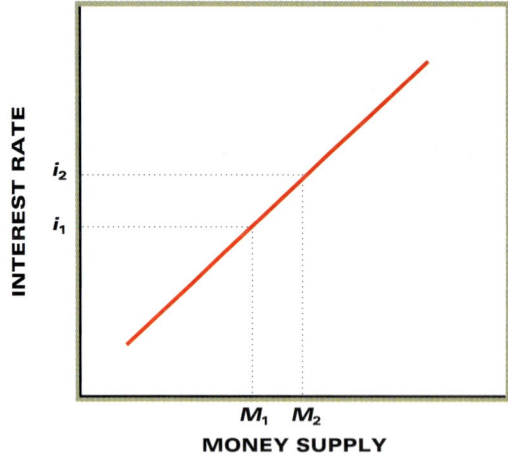

# ECONOMIC CONSULTANTS

## ECONOMIC RESEARCH AND ANALYSIS BY STUDENTS FOR PROFESSIONALS

JoAnn Weber is an economics teacher at Washington High School in Miami, Florida. For her honors economics class, JoAnn has decided to include a section on the history, uses, and quantity of money in the United States.

As part of an arrangement with school districts in the Miami area, Economic Consultants helps economics teachers create their curricula. JoAnn has contacted Economic Consultants to prepare background materials on money. You are assigned to the project and asked to prepare a report for JoAnn that addresses the following issues:

1. Why and in what ways do we use money?
2. What economic institutions have been instrumental in the historical development of money in the United States?
3. What is meant by liquidity and how is it used to distinguish different money forms? Who actually produces the money we commonly use?
4. What resources are available for students interested in learning more about money?

You may find the following resources helpful as you prepare this report for JoAnn:

- **Fundamental Facts about U.S. Money** (http://www.frbatlanta.org/publica/brochure/fundfac/money.htm)—The Atlanta Federal Reserve publishes an online brochure about U.S. money.
- **Monetary Museum** (http://www.frbatlanta.org/atlantafed/tours_museum/monet/index.html)—The Atlanta Federal Reserve maintains a physical and virtual museum devoted to money.
- **Our Money** (http://minneapolisfed.org/econed/curric/money.html)—The Minneapolis Federal Reserve provides information on U.S. currency and new designs, counterfeit protections, and the history of money.
- **Your Money Matters** (http://www.treas.gov/currency/)—The U.S. Treasury Department publishes information on every denomination of U.S. paper money.
- **The U.S. Mint** (http://www.usmint.gov/)—The U.S. Mint provides extensive information about the composition, production, and history of coins.
- **Bureau of Engraving and Printing (BEP)** (http://www.bep.treas.gov/)—The BEP designs and manufactures paper money, among other securities. The BEP has extensive information about paper money, including videos that show how currency is printed and information on what happens to mutilated money.
- **Currency Facts** (http://www.bep.treas.gov/currencyfacts.htm)—The Bureau of Printing and Engraving has dozens of facts and trivia about currency.
- **Know Your Money** (http://www.treas.gov/usss/index.htm?know_your_money.htm&1)—The U.S. Secret Service, which, in addition to protecting the president, protects against counterfeiting, provides information for spotting fake money.

# PRACTICE TEST

1. Barter becomes difficult to implement in a large economy because
   a. individuals are less willing to trade in large economies.
   b. individuals have fewer wants in large economies.
   c. it becomes more difficult to find a double coincidence of wants in large economies.
   d. fiat is usually not available in large economies.
   e. there are many places that individuals in large economies can gather to find double coincidences of wants.

2. Suppose that a professional racquetball player suggests using racquetballs as the standard for money in the economy. Racquetballs would be a _____ choice for money because
   a. poor/they are not portable.
   b. good/they have low durability.
   c. poor/they are not very homogeneous.
   d. good/they are all the same color.
   e. poor/they are not easily divisible.

3. Which of the following assets is the most liquid form of money?
   a. Currency
   b. U.S. savings bonds
   c. Commercial water
   d. An automobile
   e. Gold

4. All of the following are components of the M1 money supply except one. Which one?
   a. Coins
   b. Savings accounts
   c. Checking accounts
   d. Dollar bills
   e. Traveler's checks

5. Large-denomination time deposits are included in which the following definitions of the money supply?
   a. M1 only
   b. M2 only
   c. M3 only
   d. Both M1 and M3
   e. Both M1 and M2

6. The velocity of money represents
   a. whether individuals are increasing or decreasing the quantity of money spent in the economy.
   b. the quantity of money available in the economy.
   c. the level of prices determined by the equation of exchange.
   d. how often money is used in a specific period of time.
   e. whether currency is accepted as a medium of exchange in the economy.

7. According to the quantity theory of money,
   a. increases in the money supply, ceteris paribus, will lead to inflation.
   b. the level of inflation is independent of the money supply.
   c. the money supply times velocity is equal to real GDP.
   d. when real GDP rises, the money supply must fall by the same proportion.
   e. the velocity of money is assumed to fluctuate wildly over time.

8. Monetarists differ from classical economists in their view of money in that monetarists believe that
   a. the velocity of money is relatively constant over time.
   b. prices are not influenced by real GDP.
   c. prices are not influenced by the money supply.
   d. the level of unemployment is directly related to the money supply.
   e. the velocity of money varies over time.

9. According to classical economists,
   a. individuals desire to hold money only because of the precautionary demand for money.
   b. individuals do not hold money for either precautionary or speculative reasons.
   c. the velocity of money is not constant but is predictable.
   d. the velocity of money is not constant and cannot be predicted with any degree of certainty.
   e. individuals have no reason for wanting to hold onto money.

10. The speculative demand for money suggests that
    a. individuals hold onto money for the purpose of engaging in transactions.
    b. as the rate of interest rises, the demand for money will rise.
    c. when the economy becomes more uncertain, people are more likely to hold onto money.
    d. the velocity of money is constant.
    e. as the rate of interest falls, the demand for money will rise.

# MONEY CREATION AND THE BANKING SYSTEM

## 11

If you don't believe in magic, this chapter may make you change your mind. The magic performed is the creation of money. Like pulling a rabbit out of a hat, money seemingly appears from nowhere. Not only does the magician make money appear, but the money created ends up in the hands of those who have reason to use it.

Let's start our analysis of money creation with a simple tale. Imagine a premodern economy where gold is used to satisfy the people's transactions and precautionary money needs. But here, life can be quite nasty, brutish, and short, particularly for those holding large quantities of gold. People in this economy without banks have a problem. Where do they put their gold for safekeeping?

Amar Bazazz is the answer. Why him? He owns a deep cave and an enormous, unfriendly dog. He uses the cave as a depository where people can keep their gold. With the dog pacing the cave's entrance, nobody would dare try their luck.

Amar charges depositors 10 percent per year for guarding the gold they deposit in his cave. They regard that percentage as an insurance premium.

Sounds uneventful so far, but the plot thickens. What people don't know is that Amar is addicted to gambling. Every night, he takes some of the deposited gold to the casino in the next town and loses it all in a matter of hours. In fact, he gambles away fully 80 percent of the deposits in the cave.

*But what he discovers, to his shock, is that it doesn't really matter.* Nobody is the wiser! Everybody thinks their gold is in the cave, and when they come to withdraw some of it—few withdraw all, and certainly not everyone at once—*enough* is always there. Gold is

**THIS CHAPTER INTRODUCES YOU TO THE ECONOMIC PRINCIPLES ASSOCIATED WITH:**
- THE FRACTIONAL RESERVE SYSTEM
- THE LEGAL RESERVE REQUIREMENT
- A BANK'S BALANCE SHEET, ITS ASSETS AND LIABILITIES
- DEMAND DEPOSITS AND BANK LOANS
- THE POTENTIAL MONEY MULTIPLIER
- BANK FAILURE
- THE FEDERAL DEPOSIT INSURANCE CORPORATION (FDIC)

245

gold. Perfectly homogeneous. That's the way Amar Bazazz makes his living, earning 10 percent per year on gold that isn't there.

Let's now suppose that in the twilight of his life, Amar confesses his gambling to his only son who, although shocked at the disclosure, is quick enough to see the possibilities. Inheriting the cave and the dog's ferocious pups, he goes into his father's gold-keeping business.

Amar's son doesn't gamble in casinos. Instead, he takes the deposited gold to other towns and gambles there on what he thinks are sound investments. In this way he earns money both by safekeeping the gold *and* on the investments. To get his hands on more gold, he lowers the security rate he charges to 5 percent. People are so moved by his generosity, they elect him mayor.

He is a smart businessman. He holds to a sound fractional reserve rule. He always keeps 20 percent of the deposited gold in reserve to handle the transactions demands of the depositors. That, of course, still leaves 80 percent free for investments. He even hires people to locate good investment projects for him.

To encourage growth in his investment business, he not only cuts the security rate to 0 percent but offers to pay his depositors a small percentage to deposit their gold in his cave. For fear they would think him insane, he comes clean. He tells them about his father's gambling, his own investments, and explains how the security of their deposits is guaranteed in a **fractional reserve system.**

**Fractional reserve system**
A banking system that provides people immediate access to their deposits but allows banks to hold only a fraction of those deposits in reserve.

Should the depositors panic? Should they be concerned that only 20 percent of their gold deposits are in reserve? Not at all. They accept his assurance that they can get their entire deposit returned upon demand. Some even refer to their deposits as *demand deposits.* It works. Now they actually draw interest on their entire deposit although only a fraction of their gold is being safely kept in the cave.

Who said life can't be wonderful? The tale may be simple, *but this is essentially the basis of all modern banking.*

## HOW BANKS CREATE MONEY

Let's update the story to a modern economy. Suppose we want to go into the banking business. What would it take? What would we do? Why do it?

The last question is easy. The reason people go into banking is to earn profit. Bankers are like barbers, automobile makers, and coal mining entrepreneurs. These others cut hair, make automobiles, and dig coal because that's how they make a profit. Bankers hope to make a profit by borrowing your money at low prices and lending it to others at higher prices. That's all there is to it. Nothing really complicated.

Well, let's do it! Let's set up the Paris First National Bank (PFN) in downtown Paris, Texas. We pick out an imposing, gray stone building. We hire cashiers, loan officers, and other personnel. We're ready.

### Attracting Depositors

We run a series of radio and television commercials inviting depositors to bank at PFN. The commercials also invite people looking for bank loans to come by.

Let's suppose Jeff Kaufman decides to bank with PFN. He opens a checking account by depositing $1,000. He knows, of course, that he can withdraw that sum of M1 money any time he pleases. It is, after all, a demand deposit.

PFN's **balance sheet**—a summary of the bank's assets (what it has) and liabilities (what it owes)—after this initial $1,000 demand deposit is

**Balance sheet**
The bank's statement of liabilities (what it owes) and assets (what it owns).

**Paris First National Bank**

| Assets | Liabilities |
|---|---|
| Reserves $1,000 | Demand Deposits $1,000 |

Look at PFN's assets and liabilities. Its assets, held by the bank as reserves in its vaults, are $1,000. What does that mean? Simply that it has Jeff Kaufman's $1,000 in cash. Is the bank, then, $1,000 richer than it was before Kaufman came in? No. Although it has the $1,000, it also has a $1,000 obligation to give the money back to Kaufman. In fact, Kaufman can demand the money back any time he pleases. The bank may *use* the money, but it's not the bank's. It's Jeff Kaufman's. In fact, if you ask Kaufman how much money he has, he would tell you. It's $1,000.

## Making Loans

Demand deposits are only half of PFN's business. Loans are the other. PFN makes a profit only on the loans it provides, not on its deposits. So PFN is now willing and able to lend money, but it can do so only if borrowers show up. And they do. Some borrow to finance consumption purchases, such as automobiles and houses; others borrow to finance business investments.

*Can you think of any other reasons people borrow from banks other than consumption purchases or business investments? Go to the Interactive Study Center at http://gottheil.swcollege.com and click on the "Your Turn" button to submit your example. Student submissions will be posted to the Web site, and perhaps we will use some in future editions of the book!*

Let's suppose Matt Taylor approaches the bank with an idea of setting up a Japanese food carry-out. His presentation to the bank is impressive. He explains that there are many pizza, taco, hot dog, and hamburger places in town, as well as Chinese restaurants. But no one offers Japanese food. He has also done his homework. He shows that he could renovate a vacated Pizza Hut for $800 and make a 25 percent profit in the first year. What he needs is an $800 loan.

PFN likes the idea and loans Matt $800 at an interest rate of 10 percent. In fact, $800 is the maximum it can loan because, by law, banks are required to keep 20 percent of their demand deposits on reserve, either in their own vaults or at the Federal Reserve Bank. The Federal Reserve decides what the **legal reserve requirement** will be. The 20 percent legal reserve requirement in this story is only hypothetical. In fact, the legal reserve requirement that the Fed actually picks for our economy is typically less than 10 percent. (We'll say more about the Federal Reserve later.)

**Legal reserve requirement**
The percentage of demand deposits banks and other financial intermediaries are required to keep in cash reserves.

Let's look at PFN's balance sheet after the loan is made:

**Paris First National Bank**

| Assets | Liabilities |
|---|---|
| Reserves $1,000<br>Loans 800 | Demand Deposits $1,800 |

Note what happens to the bank's assets. They change from $1,000 in reserves to $1,800 in reserves and loans. By agreeing to loan Matt $800, PFN has a new asset in the form of Matt's signed $800 IOU to the bank (shown as the $800 loan in the asset column of the balance sheet). What does PFN give Matt Taylor in return? The bank

# THEORETICAL PERSPECTIVE

## VIRTUAL BANKS RAISE REGULATORY CHALLENGES

As more and more of the people surfing the Net seem willing to bring their checkbooks with them, banking industry officials are wondering how to get them to hang ten at their banks. And government regulators are wondering how to ensure that the surfing is safe and fair.

Electronic banking in the form of automatic teller machines and telephone services has been around for more than a decade, but these services have offered mostly traditional transactions through traditional banks. Since 1995, however, several cyberspace banks have been online, offering the electronic transfer of funds and bill-paying services over the Internet. To combat this threat, traditional banks have begun to offer similar services.

All this activity has banking industry regulators watching with interest. Most such regulators want to encourage cyberbanking as a way to help the banking industry—an electronic transfer of funds, after all, costs a bank far less than the same transaction processed by a human teller. But cyberbanking raises a number of issues that worry regulators.

The first is determining exactly what a cyberspace bank is. A myriad of federal laws mandates that banks serve their local community by lending a certain percentage locally and to certain minority groups. Cyberspace banks, however, exist only electronically. How can regulators ensure that they compete fairly with other banks that must follow current regulations?

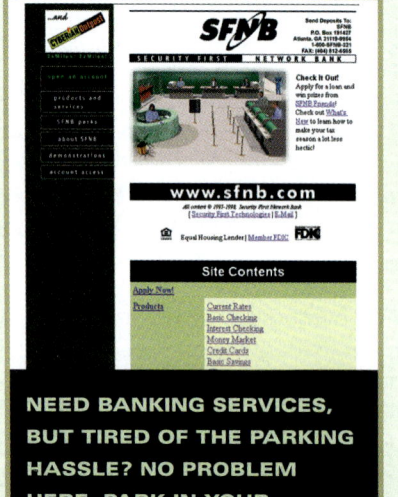

NEED BANKING SERVICES, BUT TIRED OF THE PARKING HASSLE? NO PROBLEM HERE. PARK IN YOUR OWN GARAGE!

The second issue is security. Although more and more people seem comfortable making transactions online, regulators wonder if a certain amount of enforced encryption is necessary to encourage more online banking activity and help prevent fraud. And they wonder if the different forms of electronic banking—via phone, personal computer software, and the Internet—require different forms of regulation.

Because technology and banking habits are changing so rapidly, many regulators and industry officials have taken a wait-and-see attitude toward further regulation. In general, however, most industry officials would like to see some changes to current regulations to encourage, they hope, a variety of cyberbanking services, and they would like to see better coordination between government agencies that regulate banking.

In the meantime, regulators and banking officials hope more Americans will be surfing—and banking—with their computers.

### MORE ON THE NET

Visit a few cyberspace banks, such as U.S. Bank Online (http://www.usbank.com/online/) and Security First Network Bank (http://www.sfnb.com/). How are their services different from those of your local bank? Also review Office of Thrift Supervision materials on electronic banking (http://www.ots.treas.gov/ebanking.html). The OTS regulates federally chartered savings and loans.

**Source:** Cindy Skrzycki, "OTS Eyes Challenges of Rule-Making for 'Virtual Banks,'" *Washington Post,* September 5, 1997, p. G1.

---

opens an $800 demand deposit for him. Note what's happened. *The loan creates the demand deposit.* There is now $1,800 in demand deposits, up from $1,000 before the loan. That is, loans create money.

Does the bank give Matt the $800 in currency? Not likely. Instead, it gives Matt a checkbook—like yours—and the right to write checks up to the amount of the $800 demand deposit. It really makes no difference to Matt whether he has checking privileges or currency. It's still M1 money. He can just as easily write checks as use currency to buy labor and materials needed for the carryout.

## The Interaction of Deposits and Loans

Suppose Matt Taylor hires Charlie Dold, a skilled carpenter, who can do the work for $800. Dold completes the project in a week. Taylor, satisfied with the job, writes out a check to Dold for $800. Dold accepts the check as his week's income and deposits it in *his* bank, Paris Second National (PSN).

Let's see what happens to the balance sheet at the Paris First National Bank after the check clears:

**Paris First National Bank**

| Assets | | Liabilities | |
|---|---|---|---|
| Reserves | $200 | Demand Deposits | $1,000 |
| Loans | 800 | | |

The $800 check to Charlie Dold wipes out Matt's $800 demand deposit at PFN. The bank's total demand deposits fall from $1,800 to $1,000. At the same time, PFN's reserves fall from $1,000 to $200. After all, PFN paid out $800 to the Paris Second National Bank.

Let's now look at PSN's balance sheet:

**Paris Second National Bank**

| Assets | | Liabilities | |
|---|---|---|---|
| Reserves | $800 | Demand Deposits | $800 |

Dold's $800 demand deposit creates an $800 asset and an $800 liability for PSN. Imagine a conversation between Jeff Kaufman and Charlie Dold. Dold could ask, "How much money do you have?" Jeff would respond, "$1,000 in Paris First National. What about you?" Charlie would reply, "$800, in Paris Second National." They are both right. *What was once $1,000 in Kaufman's pocket now becomes, through the banking process, $1,800 of money in the form of demand deposits.*

Of course, PSN doesn't sit on Dold's $800 demand deposit. It is eager to loan. Let's now suppose Laura Spears, a city park district director, wants to refinish her old 1936 Packard. She plans to sell it on the antique car market and needs a loan of $640 to rebuild the engine and transmission. She's sure she can make a 50 percent profit on the car, and after checking out her car and the market, PSN agrees. Laura Spears gets the loan. Let's look at PSN's revised balance sheet, right after the loan has been credited to Laura's checking account:

**Paris Second National Bank**

| Assets | | Liabilities | |
|---|---|---|---|
| Reserves | $800 | Demand Deposits | $1,440 |
| Loans | 640 | | |

The two depositors in PSN are Charlie Dold (with $800) and now Laura Spears (with a new account set up in her name for $640, which is the amount of her loan). *Remember, the loan creates the new demand deposit.* Let's suppose Spears hires Balty Deley, a mechanic with a passion for classic automobiles, to rebuild the engine and transmission for the agreed $640. He is paid with a PSN check, which he promptly deposits in his bank, the Paris Third National (PTN).

Once Laura writes a check to Balty for $640 and the check clears PSN, her demand deposit at PSN is wiped out. The bank's new balance sheet looks like this:

**Paris Second National Bank**

| Assets | | Liabilities | |
|---|---|---|---|
| Reserves | $160 | Demand Deposits | $800 |
| Loans | 640 | | |

Look at its assets. Reserves are reduced from $800 to $160 (it paid out $640, the amount of Laura's check) and it has $640 in loans. Its $160 in reserves is 20 percent of its $800 demand deposit. In other words, PSN is also completely loaned out. That's precisely what PSN had hoped for. It makes profit on the $640 loan.

What about PTN after Balty deposited Laura's $640 check? Look at its balance sheet:

**Paris Third National Bank**

| Assets | | Liabilities | |
|---|---|---|---|
| Reserves | $640 | Demand Deposits | $640 |

PTN, too, is now ready and able to loan money. Like other banks, it is obligated to keep at least 20 percent of its demand deposits in reserve, which entitles it to loan out a maximum of $512.

Do you see what's happening throughout the banking system? Kaufman's original $1,000 demand deposit in PFN set in motion a chain reaction of loans and demand deposits that created not only a series of new money but also bank loans that make the creation of real goods, such as carry-out restaurants and rebuilt cars, possible.

What does it take to create money? There are three prerequisites.

First, there must be a fractional reserve system operating within **financial intermediaries**, such as banks, savings and loan associations, or credit unions, that are able to loan out some fraction of their deposits.

Second, there must be people willing to make demand deposits.

Third, there must be borrowers prepared to take out consumption loans or loans to finance investment projects.

Without borrowers like Matt Taylor, Jeff Kaufman's original $1,000 demand deposit in the PFN would remain completely sterile.

**HOW MUCH MONEY CAN THE BANKING SYSTEM ULTIMATELY CREATE?** Let's add up the creation of money that takes place in the first 10 rounds of our example, from the initial deposit made in the Paris First National Bank through to one placed in the Paris Tenth National Bank:

**Total Demand Deposits in the Banking System after 10 Rounds of Deposits and Loans**

| Bank | Demand Deposits |
|---|---|
| Paris First National | $1,000.00 |
| Paris Second National | 800.00 |
| Paris Third National | 640.00 |
| Paris Fourth National | 512.00 |
| Paris Fifth National | 409.60 |

**Financial intermediaries**
Firms that accept deposits from savers and use those deposits to make loans to borrowers.

**CHECK YOUR UNDERSTANDING**

What three factors are needed for a banking system to create money?

| | |
|---|---|
| Paris Sixth National | 327.68 |
| Paris Seventh National | 262.14 |
| Paris Eighth National | 209.72 |
| Paris Ninth National | 167.77 |
| Paris Tenth National | 134.22 |
| Total M1 | $4,463.13 |

After 10 rounds, the initial $1,000 deposited by Jeff Kaufman has triggered a series of financial transactions that creates an additional $3,463.13 of M1 money. But the process continues. With a new demand deposit of $134.22, the Paris Tenth National can loan out $107.38. As long as there is a sufficient number of people willing to borrow, each demand deposit created by a preceding loan creates the reserves for the succeeding one. With the legal reserve requirement, LRR, set at 20 percent, the *total* amount of money—the initial $1,000 plus all the money potentially created by the banking system—is

$$M = \frac{ID}{LRR},$$

where $M$ is the total demand deposits in the banking system, $ID$ is the initial deposit, and $LRR$ is the legal reserve requirement. When $ID = \$1,000$ and $LRR = 20$ percent, $M$ is $5,000.

$$M = \frac{ID}{LRR} = \frac{\$1,000}{.20} = \$5,000$$

It's a pretty neat system, isn't it? That's why economists marvel at its performance. When you think about it, it's almost magical.

Let's sum up. How is money created? Borrowing creates it, automatically, when the borrower's checking account at a bank is credited as a result of a loan. Why do borrowers demand money? To produce goods and services. So there we have it. The banking system is perfectly synchronized with real-world production. As more goods and services are produced, the banking system automatically creates the equivalent money.

**THE POTENTIAL MONEY MULTIPLIER** Of course, the amount of money created depends on the legal reserve requirement and on borrowers *actually* utilizing the maximum permissible loans. If $LRR = 10$ percent, a demand deposit of $1,000 will generate—assuming willing borrowers—an increase in the money supply of $10,000. If $LRR$ increases to 50 percent, the money supply grows by only $2,000.

Another way of describing this process of money creation is by developing the concept of the banking system's **potential money multiplier,** $m$. It is simply

$$m = \frac{1}{LRR}.$$

When $LRR = 20$ percent, the potential money multiplier is $1/0.2 = 5$. That is, a new demand deposit of $1,000 placed in any bank can potentially support $5,000 of demand deposits.

**LIVING WITH EXCESS RESERVES** Why do we call it a *potential* money multiplier? Because we can't assume that there will always be sufficient borrowers to take advantage of the available loanable reserves. Suppose Jeff Kaufman deposits

**Potential money multiplier**
The increase in the money supply that is potentially generated by a change in demand deposits.

**CHECK YOUR UNDERSTANDING**

Why are there excess reserves?

$1,000 in PFN, but only $400 is demanded by Matt Taylor. Although PFN is willing and able to loan twice that sum, the potential simply isn't realized. What happens?

Look at PFN's revised balance sheet:

**Paris First National Bank**

| Assets | | Liabilities | |
|---|---|---|---|
| Required Reserves | $200 | Demand Deposits | $1,000 |
| Excess Reserves | 400 | | |
| Loans | 400 | | |

Kaufman's $1,000 shows up, as before, as the PFN bank's liability. But look at its assets' composition. Although the legally required reserve remains $200, PFN's *actual* reserves are $600. It holds, then, **excess reserves,** reserves in excess of those legally required, of $400.

**Excess reserves**
The quantity of reserves held by a bank in excess of the legally required amount.

The presence of excess reserves changes how much money the banking system *actually* creates. With PFN now loaning out only $400, the second-round demand deposits in PSN fall to $400. Even if every other bank in the series loans out the maximum permissible, the money created by Kaufman's initial $1,000 deposit shrinks from $4,000 to 400/0.20 = $2,000. Adding Kaufman's own $1,000, the total demand deposits in the banking system are $3,000 instead of $5,000.

But this $3,000 assumes that no other bank aside from PFN holds excess reserves. That's a strong assumption. If other banks, too, do not loan out the maximum permissible, then the actual demand deposits created in the economy by Kaufman's original $1,000 deposit could be most any sum less than $5,000.

The role played by the borrower in money creation cannot be overstated. Without someone actually coming into the bank to demand a loan, there is no process of money creation.

## REVERSING THE MONEY CREATION PROCESS

In our example, we have focused on Kaufman's initial $1,000 demand deposit, and for good reason. We were interested in understanding the mechanics of creation, and the simplicity of the example was useful.

Obviously, Jeff Kaufman cannot be PFN's only depositor. Let's add 2,000 more depositors. Now look at PFN's new, fully expanded balance sheet:

**Paris First National Bank**

| Assets | | Liabilities | |
|---|---|---|---|
| Required Reserves | $ 4,000,000 | Demand Deposits | $20,000,000 |
| Loans | 16,000,000 | | |

PFN is a thriving bank. Deposits are $20 million. Look at its asset position. With the legal reserve requirement at 20 percent, PFN is fully loaned out. The bank has $4 million in required reserves and the remaining $16 million of its assets in outstanding loans.

Why 20 percent? Because, in our illustrative scenario, that's what the Federal Reserve instructs. Let's change the instruction. Let's now suppose that the Federal Reserve increases the legal reserve requirement from 20 to 40 percent. All financial intermediaries—commercial banks, savings and loan associations, and credit unions—are obliged to comply. How would PFN react?

It knows what it has to do. It must raise its reserves from $4 million to $8 million. But how? By converting loans back into reserves. Perhaps the least painful way

# INTERDISCIPLINARY PERSPECTIVE

## IF WILLIAM SHAKESPEARE RAN THE FED

Suppose William Shakespeare gave up his job as playwright to become the chair of the Federal Reserve System. In all likelihood, both the principles and practices of the Fed and of the banking system would be dramatically different.

Imagine Shakespeare writing his first position paper. His instruction to all banks would probably begin with: "Neither a borrower nor a lender be, for loan oft loses both itself and friend and borrowing dulleth the edge of husbandry."[1] Doesn't leave banks much room for creating loans, does it?

The reserve requirement consistent with such an instruction is 100 percent. If you deposited $1,000 in the Stratford-upon-Avon Bank, the bank would have $1,000 in the form of liabilities and $1,000 in the form of assets. Its balance sheet would be as follows:

### Stratford-upon-Avon Bank

| Assets | Liabilities |
| --- | --- |
| $1,000 cash reserve | $1,000 |

With a reserve requirement of 100 percent, the bank has no excess reserves. It can make no loans. Without the ability to make loans on the strength of its deposits, the banking system's money creation process grinds to a halt. And that's precisely what Shakespeare intended.

Shakespeare's 100 percent reserve requirement idea would probably not be the most popular idea to hit the banking community. After all, banks would lose their most profitable activity. Would-be borrowers would not be entirely happy either. Without access to bank loans, they would have to find an alternative source of financing.

What would a Shakespeare-run Fed advise? Probably that would-be-borrowers should rely on their *own* savings, because using other people's money—borrowing from banks—to finance enterprise "dulleth the edge of husbandry." Does such a Fed opinion sound reasonable to you? Are people more inclined to take risks if the money involved is not theirs?

And even if most business people are prudent, regardless of whose money is involved, borrowing can end up being riskier than imagined. Shakespeare tells the story[2] about Antonio, a Venetian merchant, who borrowed 3,000 ducats for three months from the moneylender Shylock. Unable to repay the loan because his own business ventures went awry—four laden ships were lost at sea—Antonio would have forfeited his life were it not for a prejudicial court that, violating the spirit of the loan contract, ruled in his favor against Shylock.

While no financial institution, including the Fed, can protect either borrower or lender *completely* against the uncertainties associated with enterprise, a 100 percent reserve requirement minimizes the possibility of any set of failed investments triggering a negative, spiral reaction throughout the money economy. Shakespeare's Fed presented the trade-off: Monetary stability versus money creation—or in real terms, less GDP but less fluctuation in GDP as well.

---

[1] *Hamlet*, Act I, Scene 3.
[2] *The Merchant of Venice*, Act I, Scene 3.

---

of converting loans into reserves is to wait until some of them are paid off—every day some of them are being paid off—and instead of loaning them out again, keep them in reserves.

Imagine the bank's loan department at work loaning money and then recovering loans that come due. By redirecting some of this flow, the bank can pull in the reins. In the end, its balance sheet is revised:

### Paris First National Bank

| Assets | | Liabilities | |
| --- | --- | --- | --- |
| Required Reserves | $ 8,000,000 | Demand Deposits | $20,000,000 |
| Loans | 12,000,000 | | |

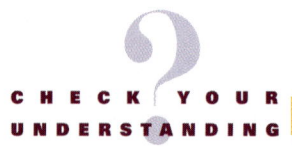

**CHECK YOUR UNDERSTANDING**

What happens to bank loans when the Fed raises the reserve requirement?

Nothing, of course, changes in the PFN bank's liabilities. Demand deposits remain at $20 million. But look at its asset position. The bank shifted $4 million out of loans into reserves to comply with Federal Reserve instructions. Its loan position contracted from $16 million to $12 million.

With a potential money multiplier of 5, that's an awful lot of money shrinkage. That is, the Fed's effect on PFN alone reduced the economy's money by $4 million × 5 = $20 million. With 15,000 banks operating in the United States, that's an awful lot of play in the money supply. It makes you appreciate the Fed's awesome power.

## WHY BANKS SOMETIMES FAIL

Suppose Matt Taylor's Japanese carryout restaurant is less than a great success. Because people still prefer hamburgers to Matt's sushi, he is in a mess of trouble. But so, too, is the PFN bank. What seemed at first like a great idea to both Taylor and PFN just didn't work out.

What, then, happens to PFN's $800 loan to Taylor? As much as Taylor would like to, he simply can't repay it. He used the bank's money in an honest effort but ended up with a lot of unsold sushi and little money. When the carryout finally closes, the bank can claim its used equipment. And that's about it.

Most likely, the bank survives the Taylor folly. After all, PFN has a diversified loan portfolio and can absorb a loss here and there. In fact, it probably expected something, somewhere, to go afoul. If you were the bank, wouldn't you? Not *everything* works out as planned. That's life.

But what if Taylor's failure was the bank's usual experience—the rule, not the exception? What if too many of PFN's loans to promising business ventures turn out to be not so promising? How many loan defaults can PFN absorb without running into problems of survival itself? On occasion, banks do fail.

Any business failure is an unhappy event. Everyone associated with the enterprise suffers. Some never recover. But when a bank fails, not only do bank owners and bank staff lose the money they invested in the bank and their jobs, but the people who deposited money in the bank discover they no longer have deposits.

Unfair, isn't it? People who deposit money in banks don't regard themselves as being in the banking business. That was not the intent of their deposit. Yet, *unless they are protected in some way,* they become unsuspecting partners in the bank's financial losses.

**CHECK YOUR UNDERSTANDING**

Why does bank failure represent a potentially destabilizing threat to the economy?

Moreover, any bank failure can undermine an entire banking system. Imagine a rumor spreading that a bank just failed completely, wiping out its depositors' money. How secure would you feel about your own bank deposit? After all, what happens to one bank could happen to any other. Could yours be next? How could you protect yourself? You would probably do what everyone else was doing. Run quickly to withdraw your money.

Such a run on the bank creates the very problem it tries to avoid. Obviously, no bank, including your own, can expect to satisfy all deposit withdrawal requests at once, even though it is legally obligated to do so. It keeps less than 100 percent in reserve. The entire banking system could collapse if people lose confidence in its ability to function.

The United States has had bank runs brought about by numerous bank failures. It happened in 1907 and triggered an economic downturn. Then, in March 1933, people panicked and set off a run on the banks that forced President Roosevelt to declare an unprecedented week-long "bank holiday." The bank shutdown was

## THEORETICAL PERSPECTIVE

### FEDERAL DEPOSIT INSURANCE AND MORAL HAZARD

**W**hy do banks fail? One reason, ironically enough, has to do with the very mechanism that protects depositors in case a bank should fail: deposit insurance. The Federal Deposit Insurance Corporation (FDIC), created by Congress in 1933, protects depositors from incurring losses in the event of a bank failure. Prior to the creation of the FDIC, banks had been plagued by capricious, rumor-fed, panicked runs on deposits. Congress believed that federal deposit insurance would prevent this from happening. Once people understood that their deposits were safe even if the bank failed, fear of bank failure would no longer lead inexorably to panicked withdrawals and bank runs.

There is a problem, however, with the FDIC. Fully insuring deposits leads to a costly side effect known as moral hazard. Once a person is insured, the insured has an incentive to take on more risk than he or she otherwise would. This is why, for example, fire and auto insurance policies have deductibles. With deductibles, the insured has more incentive to pick up old paint cans and drive cars more carefully. Deposit insurance in most cases doesn't require a "deductible" of banks and depositors, thereby providing incentive to profit-maximizing banks and depositors to assume an immoderate amount of risk. And, as the numerous bank failures in the 1980s and early 1990s demonstrated, the taxpayers are left to pay the hefty bill for bailing out the failed banks.

What can be done to counteract the effects of moral hazard? Two primary alternatives to the current system have been offered. The first is to privatize the deposit insurance system. The second is to reduce the scope of the current system and thus rely more on the markets to discipline the banking system. But Ricki Helfer, chairman of the FDIC, argues that any change in the current deposit insurance system is itself risky: "We know federal deposit insurance works to stabilize the banking system in times of great stress. Can we be sure that another approach will work as well?"

HEY, THAT'S MY MONEY IN THERE. IS IT SAFE?

#### CONSIDER

Why is it that deposit insurance, created to reduce the risks of banking, actually may increase that risk? In your opinion, is it the role of government, the free market, or both to regulate how banks operate?

#### MORE ON THE NET

Visit the FDIC (http://www.fdic.gov/). What is the latest information on moral hazard?

**Source:** *The Margin,* September/October 1989; Ricki Helfer, FDIC Symposium, 1997 (http://www.fdic.gov/publish/speeches/97spchs/sp23jan.html); and Gary H. Stern, "The Too Big to Fail Problem," *The Region,* 1997 (http://woodrow.mpls.frb.fed.us/pubs/region/97-09/gs-fixFDICIA.html).

meant to calm the troubled financial waters and to signal that government would come to the people's rescue.

## SAFEGUARDING THE SYSTEM

When banks fail and people panic, how can the banking system protect itself from its inherently explosive vulnerability? Is there no way to protect depositors from the frightening consequences of bank failure?

**Federal Deposit Insurance Corporation (FDIC)**
A government insurance agency that provides depositors in FDIC-participating banks 100 percent coverage on their first $100,000 of deposits.

The Federal Deposit Insurance Corporation (FDIC) (http://www.fdic.gov/) insures demand deposit accounts in participating banks.

## The Federal Deposit Insurance Corporation

Why not an insurance policy? Why can't banks insure demand deposits just as you insure your automobile? If your automobile disappears, you're covered. Well, if a bank fails and your demand deposits disappear, you're covered as well.

That's precisely what the **FDIC—Federal Deposit Insurance Corporation**—does. It insures all demand deposit accounts up to $100,000 in banks choosing FDIC protection. The protection costs the participating bank an insurance premium that represents only a small percentage of its deposits. It makes sense for depositors and banks. Most everyone, including Jeff Kaufman, can now relax. If PFN goes under, no small depositor is hurt.

The FDIC, which is a government-owned corporation, was created in 1933, too late for the tens of thousands of people who had been financially wiped out by bank failures in the Great Depression. Today, bank failures still occur, but their sting has been localized and most of the depositors are compensated.

## Bank Audits and Examinations

But why close the barn door *after* the horse escapes? While the FDIC is the insuring institution that protects depositors against bank failure, why allow a financially unsound bank to get into trouble in the first place?

Bank audits and examinations are designed to prevent bank failure. The task of auditing and examining falls upon the FDIC, which regularly evaluates bank performance to detect weaknesses in operations. Recognized early enough, serious damage can be avoided.

## Still, Banks Do Go Under

Bank failures used to be rare events, as we see in Exhibit 1. Only 43 of approximately 14,000 banks failed in the 1950s. That is less than 5 failures per year. The number per decade increased during the 1960s to 63, and to 83 during the 1970s. Still, there were less than 10 failures per year.

In the early 1980s, however, bank failures became somewhat more visible. In 1981 alone, 48 banks went under. Many were small, located in rural communities, but a few were large banks involving substantial sums of money and numbers of people. Why the increase?

**THE BANK DEBACLE OF THE 1980s AND 1990s** These bank failures reflected the severe shocks that troubled specific sectors of our real economy, such as agriculture. High farm prices in the 1970s misled many farmers. As land values rose to reflect these higher prices, farmers brought more land under cultivation, bought more machinery, and expanded production. They financed these activities with loans extended to them by accommodating banks that accepted the price-inflated land as collateral for the loans.

The honeymoon ended abruptly when farm prices and land values collapsed in the early 1980s. Many farmers, caught between falling farm prices and rising costs, went bankrupt and defaulted on their bank loans. Some unfortunate banks, whose loan portfolios were heavily involved in these farm ventures, could not survive.

What about the large urban banks? A few, with heavy international loan commitments, were hit as well. The circumstance that led to their problems was the unexpected slide in oil prices. Anticipating that oil prices in the 1980s would remain as high as or even higher than they were in the 1970s, major U.S. banks loaned billions to oil export economies such as Mexico and Venezuela. The banks anticipated that the oil economies would have no problems meeting their interest and loan obligations.

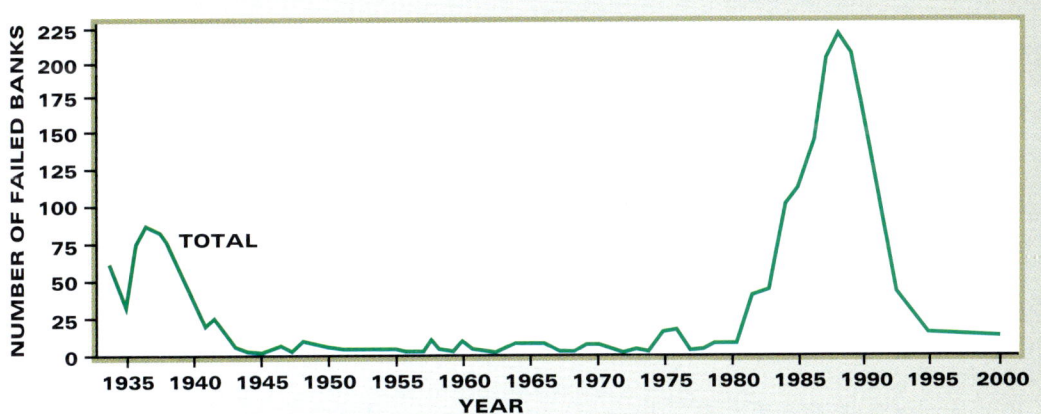

**BANK FAILURES: 1930–2000**

For years after the Great Depression the number of bank failures was insignificant. All that changed in the 1980s. With the recession of 1982, bank failures increased dramatically. In 1988 alone there were more bank failures than the combined total for the previous 25 years.

But they guessed wrong. The dramatic fall in oil prices during the 1980s sent many of the oil exporters, even Saudi Arabia, into deficit. Mexico alone incurred a $100 billion bank debt, and after the first shock of falling oil prices, it was forced to seek new terms on its loan repayments. To press its need for loan restructuring, Mexico even threatened default.

Mexico was not alone among the less-developed economies seeking relief from excessive loan obligations. Brazil, for example, had to borrow extensively during the 1970s to finance its trade deficit—the difference between its imports and exports. Here, too, oil was at the heart of the problem. OPEC's ability to increase the price of oil tenfold during the 1970s accounted for the dramatic rise in Brazil's oil import bill and, consequently, in its trade deficit.

The connection between the plight of agriculture and the oil industry and bank failures shows up clearly in the numbers of bank failures by state for the latter part of the 1980s. Look at Exhibit 2.

Note the large number of failures in the oil-based economies of Texas, Oklahoma, and Louisiana. Look also at bank failures in the farm states of Iowa, Kansas, Florida, California, and Minnesota. The disproportionality is striking, isn't it?

**EVEN THE MIGHTY FALL** Perhaps the most dramatic bank failure of the 1980s was the demise of Chicago's Continental Illinois Bank. The cause of its death: overdosing on high-risk loans. In one dramatic but fatal move, Continental enhanced its loan portfolio by buying up

**BANK FAILURES, SELECTED STATES: 1987–89**

| TEXAS | 296 | NEBRASKA | 8 | OHIO | 2 |
|---|---|---|---|---|---|
| OKLAHOMA | 66 | ARIZONA | 7 | ALABAMA | 2 |
| LOUISIANA | 46 | MISSOURI | 7 | IDAHO | 1 |
| COLORADO | 30 | ILLINOIS | 6 | KENTUCKY | 1 |
| KANSAS | 19 | MONTANA | 6 | MICHIGAN | 1 |
| MINNESOTA | 19 | ALASKA | 5 | MISSISSIPPI | 1 |
| CALIFORNIA | 12 | ARKANSAS | 5 | PENNSYLVANIA | 1 |
| IOWA | 12 | NEW YORK | 5 | OREGON | 1 |
| FLORIDA | 11 | UTAH | 5 | WYOMING | 1 |

**Source:** Federal Deposit Insurance Corporation, Annual Report, 1989 (Washington, D.C., 1989), p. 11.

# GLOBAL PERSPECTIVE

## DEPOSIT INSURANCE, ASSURANCE-DÉPÔTS, TUTELA DEI DEPOSITI, PROTECCIÓN AL AHORRO BANCARIO, ETC., ETC.

**It is no great surprise that the first deposit insurance scheme was born in the United States during the Great Depression of the 1930s. Necessity, an old adage goes, is the mother of invention.** What *is* perhaps surprising is that for the following two decades, the United States remained the only country with such deposit protection. But the idea finally spread. Germany, Finland, and Canada introduced their own systems in 1966–67. Japan followed in 1971, followed by Belgium and Sweden in 1974. France and the Netherlands created their deposit insurance schemes in 1979–80 and Italy, a latecomer, followed in 1987. By 1995, all countries within the European Union were expected to have deposit guarantee schemes that met the minimum conditions with respect to types of coverage and eligible deposits. And more recently, many European countries that aspire to join the European Union—among them Hungary, Poland, Slovenia, and the Czech Republic—have adopted deposit insurance schemes of their own.

Many countries in Asia, Africa, and Latin America provide deposit guarantees. India adopted its system as early as 1962, long before most European countries. In the mid-1980s, countries such as Mexico, Chile, Venezuela, and Kenya introduced theirs.

The accompanying table compares the coverage provided to depositors in a randomly selected set of developed and developing countries.

### COMPARISON OF SELECTED DEPOSIT INSURANCE SCHEMES

| COUNTRY | TYPE OF DEPOSITS COVERED | COVERAGE (MEASURED IN $US) |
|---|---|---|
| BELGIUM | ALL DEPOSITS EXCEPT FOREIGN AND INTERBANK | $11,750 |
| CANADA | DEMAND AND TIME DEPOSITS, PENSIONS | $40,000 |
| FINLAND | ALL DEPOSITS | 100% |
| FRANCE | DOMESTIC CURRENCY, INCLUDING INTERBANK | $57,840 |
| GERMANY | MOST DEPOSITS EXCEPT INTERBANK | 90% |
| HUNGARY | ALL DEPOSITS EXCEPT INTERBANK | $3,580 |
| INDIA | ALL DEPOSITS EXCEPT INTERBANK | $640 |
| IRELAND | DOMESTIC CURRENCY | 80% OF 1ST $6,000 |
|  |  | 70% OF 2ND $6,000 |
|  |  | 50% OF 3RD $6,000 |
| ITALY | ALL DEPOSITS EXCEPT INTERBANK | 100% OF 1ST $100,000 |
|  |  | 80% OF NEXT $400,000 |
| JAPAN | DEMAND AND TIME DEPOSITS | $86,000 |
| MEXICO | MOST DEPOSITS, INCLUDING FOREIGN CURRENCY | 100% |
| NETHERLANDS | ALL DEPOSITS | $17,200 |
| NORWAY | ALL DEPOSITS | NO LIMIT |
| PHILIPPINES | ALL DEPOSITS EXCEPT INTERBANK | $1,960 |
| UNITED STATES | ALL DEPOSITS | $100,000 |

more than $1 billion in loans from the Penn Square Bank of Oklahoma City. Continental believed it was acquiring high-performing assets. In fact, the Penn Square loans were basically unsound. The loss was more than Continental could digest.

The FDIC took Continental over and, to everyone's surprise and the depositors' delight, announced it would cover *every* deposit, not just accounts under $100,000. It then tried to sell Continental to another bank. But even at bargain prices, no bank showed any interest. In the end, the FDIC invested billions of its own money to make the bank solvent once again.

Why didn't the FDIC just allow Continental to fold, as it did the smaller rural banks? Size was the difference. The FDIC's decision to keep Continental alive was taken to protect the confidence people place in our banking system. In the view of the FDIC, Continental was simply too important a bank to be allowed to go under.

## THE SAVINGS AND LOAN DEBACLE OF THE 1980s AND 1990s

What about savings and loan associations (S&Ls)? They, too, felt the sting of financial bankruptcy. Look at Exhibit 3.

Why the dramatic growth in S&L failures in the 1980s? Prior to the 1980s, S&Ls were busy providing long-term (20- to 30-year) mortgages to private homeowners. They had a virtual monopoly in the home mortgage market because government regulations prohibited banks from competing in that market and prohibited S&Ls from competing in any other. And because government also set ceilings on the interest rates that banks and S&Ls were allowed to pay depositors (Regulation Q), S&Ls enjoyed the spin-off effect of competing with banks for depositors at relatively low rates of interest, while making loans to homeowners at much higher mortgage rates. In other words, long-term private residential mortgage loans not only were fairly safe investments for the S&Ls, but were quite lucrative as well.

But deregulation of economic activity became the new focus of government policy during the 1980s and the undoing of the S&Ls. Among the industries affected by deregulation was banking. The deregulation created an open-season banking environment. Investment houses, such as Merrill Lynch, were allowed to compete with banks and S&Ls for depositors. They offered money market mutual funds at rates higher than those offered by banks and S&Ls. These funds gave depositors the best of two worlds: sound investments at attractive interest rates and the privilege of using these funds as checking accounts. To create a level playing field for

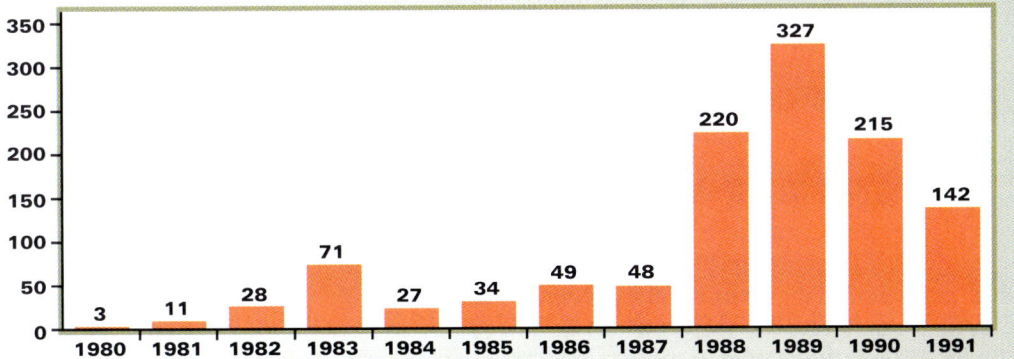

**EXHIBIT 3**

**THRIFT FAILURES: 1980–91**

| Year | Failures |
|------|----------|
| 1980 | 3 |
| 1981 | 11 |
| 1982 | 28 |
| 1983 | 71 |
| 1984 | 27 |
| 1985 | 34 |
| 1986 | 49 |
| 1987 | 48 |
| 1988 | 220 |
| 1989 | 327 |
| 1990 | 215 |
| 1991 | 142 |

The combination in the late 1980s of banking deregulation, higher-risk loans made by the S&Ls, and outright S&L banking fraud led to the collapse of the S&L industry and the extraordinary number of S&L failures in the 1988–91 years.

banks and S&Ls, the government discarded Regulation Q so that banks and S&Ls now had the opportunity to raise interest rates to keep their depositors from switching to the competing investment houses. These events sealed the fate of many S&Ls.

Why? Because the S&Ls were locked into fixed long-term mortgage loans at rates that were often lower than the rates they now had to pay depositors. To recoup losses, they moved into new loan markets, such as speculative land development, that earned more, *but were much riskier* than the private residential home mortgage market they had once dominated.

Another factor contributing to the S&Ls' demise was the substantial fraud that crept into their deregulated banking environment. "Loans" were made to S&L management friends and families that, upon later investigation, amounted to outright theft. In the end, as Exhibit 3 shows, disaster struck. By 1987 a third of S&Ls had gone bankrupt.

What about their depositors? They were protected by the government-created FSLIC—Federal Savings and Loan Insurance Corporation—the S&L counterpart to the FDIC. But the extraordinary number of S&L failures during the 1980s and 1990s was too much for the FSLIC to absorb. The FSLIC itself was driven into financial crisis, forcing the government to enact the Financial Institutions Reform, Recovery and Enforcement Act in 1989. The act established the Resolution Trust Corporation, which handles the disposal of all failed S&Ls. The act also transferred the defunct FSLIC's insuring functions to the FDIC.

Although the FSLIC (like the FDIC) was set up to provide depositors with some measure of security against S&L (or bank) failure, it is somewhat paradoxical that the FSLIC may have actually contributed to the S&L demise. Why? Because the S&Ls, having that FSLIC-backed security, had less incentive to prevent failure from occurring. That is, having the FSLIC insurance as a guaranteed safety net, they were more inclined to venture into high-risk loans that would not have been considered loanworthy otherwise.

## CONTROLLING THE FINANCIAL INSTITUTIONS THAT CONTROL THE MONEY SUPPLY

Georges Clemenceau, the French statesman who served as war minister during the First World War, once remarked: "War is too important to be left to the generals." Had he looked at the banking system, he might well have added: "And the money supply is too important to be left to the banks."

Few economists would disagree. We have seen how the banking system, almost by magic, creates money.

But the relationship between the money that financial institutions are willing and able to create and the economy's need for the money is *not always* one-to-one.

Paradoxical as it may seem, it is when the economy most needs injections of money that the financial institutions are most reluctant to supply it. And only when the economy least needs it do they show a willingness—sometimes an eagerness—to offer money.

And that's a problem. In periods of prosperity—when prices, wage rates, interest rates, employment, and consumer spending are relatively high—banks, S&Ls, and credit unions feel confident in the economy's future and, therefore, in borrowers' ability to repay loans. Under these conditions, most bankers are eager to lend the maximum permissible. Such loan behavior, coupled to the money multiplier, creates maximum permissible supplies of money. But it is precisely in the heady times of prosperity, with the economy already at full employment, that maximum permissible money can push the economy into unintended inflation.

On the other hand, in periods of recession—when prices, wage rates, interest rates, employment, and consumer spending are relatively low—the financial institutions' expectations of the economy's future change from confidence to caution. Their loan policies, reflecting this change, become increasingly hesitant. Their concern now is to minimize loan defaults. They are more willing, then, to hold greater excess reserves. In other words, precisely when the economy could use more investment money, banks and other financial institutions are more inclined to forego the opportunities of creating money.

Frustrating, isn't it? The marvelous invention of modern banking allows us to create the money supply to promote maximum real goods production. Sometimes, however, it overindulges, and at other times it denies that supply and exacerbates the economy's bouts with inflation and unemployment.

If the financial institutions cannot be counted upon to create the proper money flows to foster economic activity with minimal inflation and unemployment, then perhaps *some* control over their control of the money supply is needed. That's where the Federal Reserve System comes in.

# CHAPTER REVIEW

1. Fractional reserve banking is based on the idea that a bank need not keep all of its deposits on hand as reserves. Loans can be made based on deposits, with only a fraction of the deposits held as reserves. In this way, a bank can earn interest on loans while paying depositors interest for their deposits.

2. A fractional reserve banking system is able to create money. When a bank receives a new deposit, it can loan a portion of this deposit, leaving enough of the deposit on hand to satisfy the reserve requirement. The borrower spends the proceeds from the loan. These expenditures end up as a new deposit in a second bank. The second bank is able to loan a fraction of its new deposit. And in this way, a sequence of events occurs that causes the money supply to expand by a multiple of the original deposit.

3. The banking system can create new deposits equal to the initial demand deposit divided by the legal reserve requirement. The potential money multiplier is calculated by dividing 1 by the legal reserve requirement. The money supply may not expand to the extent determined by the potential money multiplier, because banks may elect to hold some of their excess reserves, people may not want to borrow, and not all the loans made find their way back into bank deposits.

4. The money creation process can run in reverse. When loans are paid back, checks are written on bank accounts, which decreases deposits and forces banks holding loans up to their legal reserve requirements to reduce their loans. The potential money multiplier can be used to calculate the extent to which the money supply will shrink as deposits decrease.

5. Banks sometimes fail when a large portion of the loans they have made are not repaid. When people learn of bank failures, they tend to become nervous about their own deposits and withdraw them. As deposits are withdrawn, loans must be called in, and the money supply shrinks. Serious bank failures can trigger waves of failures and drastic reductions in the money supply.

6. Federal deposit insurance is intended to assure depositors of the safety of their deposits, so they won't be easily inclined to withdraw their funds. Bank audits and examinations help improve faith in the banking system by making

certain that banks operate according to sound principles and legislated regulations.

7. In spite of the FDIC and bank auditing on a regular basis, banks do fail sometimes. During the 1980s and the first years of the 1990s, bank failure rates rose significantly. Savings and loan associations also went through a difficult period during the 1980s as banks began to compete with them for customers in the home mortgage market. S&L failures were so extensive in the 1980s that a special government-sponsored corporation, the Resolution Trust Corporation, had to be established to dispose of the failed S&Ls.

8. If left to their own devices, financial intermediaries would tend to make downturns in the business cycle more pronounced and upturns more extreme. During a downturn, a bank or other intermediary is less likely to lend, for fear of not being repaid. The money supply shrinks as outstanding loans are repaid, causing the interest rate to rise and investment to fall. Thus, the downturn is made more severe. During an economic expansion, banks are more inclined to lend, which causes the money supply to grow more rapidly than it would otherwise, resulting in lower interest rates and more borrowing. As the economy approaches full employment, there is upward pressure on the price level.

# KEY TERMS

Fractional reserve system
Balance sheet
Legal reserve requirement
Financial intermediaries
Potential money multiplier
Excess reserves
Federal Deposit Insurance Corporation (FDIC)

# QUESTIONS

1. Why was Amar Bazazz able to convince people who deposited gold in his cave for safekeeping that it was all there when, in fact, he had gambled most of it away?
2. What relationship is there between the Amar Bazazz story and the fundamentals of modern banking?
3. Why is it important to have a legal reserve requirement imposed on banks? What could happen to the banking system if there were no such requirement?
4. What is the potential money multiplier? Why is it called *potential*?
5. What are the three principal requirements for the banking system to create money?
6. What is the significance of calling the deposits you make in your checking account *demand deposits*?
7. Explain how a new demand deposit of $100 can potentially create $500 of new money if the legal reserve requirement is 20 percent.
8. If the legal reserve requirement is 50 percent, how much new money could the $100 deposit create?
9. How does a bank end up with excess reserves?
10. Suppose your neighborhood bank has no excess reserves and the legal reserve requirement is raised from 20 percent to 50 percent. What must it do to conform to the new requirement?
11. What can cause a bank to fail?
12. What has been the record of bank failures in the United States over the past 4 decades?
13. Which states have been hardest hit by bank failures? Why?
14. What safeguards have we created to protect ourselves against the fallout of bank failure?

# PRACTICE PROBLEMS

1. Suppose you land your first job with Columbia Records in New York City and, after your first week at work, you deposit $100 in your checking account at Chase Manhattan Bank. If the reserve requirement is 10 percent, show how your $100 deposit can create money. Illustrate the process by filling in the missing data for the cells through 5 stages in the following table.

| BANK | DEMAND DEPOSIT | LOANS |
|---|---|---|
| CHASE MANHATTAN | $100 | |
| CHEMICAL BANK | | |
| HANOVER TRUST | | |
| CITIBANK | | |
| 1ST NATIONAL BANK OF NY | | |

2. Suppose the Federal Reserve raised the reserve requirement to 50 percent. Show how that would affect the value of money creation through the first 5 stages of deposit and loan in practice problem 1.

| BANK | DEMAND DEPOSIT | LOANS |
|---|---|---|
| CHASE MANHATTAN | $100 | |
| CHEMICAL BANK | | |
| HANOVER TRUST | | |
| CITIBANK | | |
| 1ST NATIONAL BANK OF NY | | |

3. Using the potential money multiplier equation and the values in the following table, show what the initial deposit, the total money supply created (that is, initial deposit plus subsequent deposits), and the reserve requirement must be in each of 5 situations.

| INITIAL DEPOSIT | RESERVE REQUIREMENT | TOTAL MONEY CREATED |
|---|---|---|
| $100 | 40 percent | |
| | 10 percent | $1,000 |
| $200 | | $1,000 |
| $1,000 | | $1,000 |
| $0 | 50 percent | |

# ECONOMIC CONSULTANTS

## ECONOMIC RESEARCH AND ANALYSIS BY STUDENTS FOR PROFESSIONALS

Steve Scariano graduated from the University of Toronto with a degree in journalism. After a brief stint with CJAD radio in Montreal, Steve was hired by CNN as a researcher in its news department. His first project is to write a primer for the network's business correspondents on banks and the banking system in the United States.

While Steve, a native Canadian, studied economics in college, he is unfamiliar with the intricacies of the U.S. banking system. He can write succinctly, but he desperately needs a refresher course on money and banking if he is to do the job well. He has heard great things about Economic Consultants, and he asked CNN to hire the firm to assist him. CNN has agreed. You are assigned the task of preparing a report for Steve that addresses the following issues:

1. What do banks do with the money deposited in their accounts, and how are banks interrelated?
2. Why are banks sometimes in financial trouble? Are such troubles inherent in the banking system? What safeguards can prevent banks from getting into trouble?
3. What role does government play in the banking system?
4. What sources are available to provide readers with up-to-date information on banking news?

You may find the following resources helpful as you prepare this report for Steve:

- **FDIC's Learning Bank** (http://www.fdic.gov/about/learn/learning/index.html)—The Federal Deposit Insurance Corporation (FDIC) educates the public about banks, banking, and the FDIC.
- **The Federal Reserve** (http://www.federalreserve.gov/)—The Federal Reserve provides a detailed description of its operations (http://www.federalreserve.gov/general.htm).
- **The Federal Reserve System's National Information Center (NIC)** (http://www.ffiec.gov/nic/)—The NIC has news, data, and information about banks.
- **The Fed: Our Central Bank** (http://www.chicagofed.org/publications/index.cfm)—The Chicago Federal Reserve bank publishes this pamphlet on the workings of the Federal Reserve.
- *MyBank* (http://www.mybank.com/)—This comprehensive directory will help you locate banks in the United States and abroad.
- *American Banker* (http://www.americanbanker.com/)—*American Banker* is a journal providing banking and financial services information.
- **Fitch** (http://www.bankwatch.com/)—Fitch provides research and analysis on over 1,000 financial institutions in more than 85 countries.
- *bankinfo.com* (http://www.bankinfo.com/)—*bankinfo.com* is a daily online magazine for the banking and financial services industry.
- *ABA Banking Journal* (http://www.banking.com/aba/)—*ABA Banking Journal* is an online magazine devoted to the banking industry.
- **Faulkner & Gray** (http://www.faulknergray.com/)—Faulkner & Gray publishes a number of banking journals and newsletters, many of which are available online.
- **Bankrate.com** (http://www.bankrate.com/brm/default.asp)—Bankrate.com regularly surveys 4,000 institutions in 50 states to provide current interest rates.

# PRACTICE TEST

1. The various entries in the balance sheet of a bank can all be grouped into which of the following 2 categories?
   a. Assets or demand deposits
   b. Liabilities or assets
   c. Reserves or demand deposits
   d. Checking accounts or savings accounts
   e. Loans or reserves

2. Suppose that the Gamehendge First National Bank has initial reserves of $4,000. If the legal reserve requirement is 15 percent, then the initial level of liabilities that the bank must have had is equal to
   a. $4,000.
   b. $600.
   c. $4,600.
   d. $3,400.
   e. $7,400.

3. If Betty secured a $5,000 loan from the First National Bank and then deposited the money in the Second National Bank,
   a. it would be listed as an asset with only the First National Bank.
   b. it would be listed as an asset with only the Second National Bank.
   c. it would be listed as an asset with both the First and Second National Banks.
   d. it would lead to a reduction in the money supply, since the same money is held in two separate locations.
   e. she would make a profit when the Second National Bank pays interest on all deposits.

4. What is the maximum amount by which the money supply can increase due to an initial deposit of $20,000 when the legal reserve requirement equals 25 percent?
   a. $60,000
   b. $25,000
   c. $20,000
   d. $65,000
   e. $100,000

5. Banks hold excess reserves
   a. when the rate of inflation is low.
   b. when the amount they loan out is less than they are permitted to loan out.
   c. to earn more money on their loans to customers.
   d. to put pressure on the Federal Reserve to raise the legal reserve requirement.
   e. so that the potential money multiplier will rise.

6. The government agency that protects deposits up to $100,000 in member banks is known as the
   a. federal government.
   b. Federal Deposit Insurance Corporation.
   c. Federal Savings and Loan Insurance Corporation.
   d. fractional reserve system.
   e. World Bank.

7. All of the following except one contributed in part to the large number of bank failures that occurred during the 1980s. Which one?
   a. Risky investments by banks
   b. Loans to oil-exporting countries
   c. Loans to developing countries
   d. Falling farm prices
   e. High interest rates

8. When deregulation of the banking industry occurred in the 1980s, savings and loan associations
   a. became more profitable due to less competition from the banking industry.
   b. faced more competition and thus underwrote riskier investments.
   c. chose to reduce the number of loans made to customers.
   d. increased interest rates and increased their excess reserves.
   e. chose to invest their funds in banks.

9. Some have argued that the FSLIC contributed to the demise of many savings and loan associations by
   a. raising interest rates.
   b. not providing protection for depositors as the FDIC does for banks.
   c. setting the legal reserve requirement too high.
   d. lowering the risks faced by member S&Ls.
   e. reducing competition with traditional banks.

10. One of the roles of the FSLIC was to
    a. set the legal reserve requirement for banks.
    b. provide insurance for bank depositors.
    c. increase interest rates in the economy.
    d. provide insurance for depositors in savings and loan associations.
    e. ensure that there is adequate competition in the market between banks and savings and loan associations.

# CHAPTER 12

# THE FEDERAL RESERVE SYSTEM AND MONETARY POLICY

If there is anything you've learned in school, in your home, and in your daily life, it is that we are a society that jealously cherishes individual freedom. Freedom to travel around. Freedom to say what we please. Freedom to take any job we like or none at all. Only *very* reluctantly do we agree to compromise our personal freedoms.

We resisted the regulation of our money system. We allowed private banks guided by the profit motive to determine their own reserve requirements, and we allowed interest rates, which govern the quantity of money demanded and supplied in our economy, to be determined in an unregulated market by an unregulated banking system.

**THIS CHAPTER INTRODUCES YOU TO THE ECONOMIC PRINCIPLES ASSOCIATED WITH:**

- THE FEDERAL RESERVE SYSTEM AS A CENTRAL BANK
- RESERVE REQUIREMENTS AS A TOOL OF MONETARY POLICY
- THE DISCOUNT RATE AS A TOOL OF MONETARY POLICY
- OPEN MARKET OPERATIONS AS A TOOL OF MONETARY POLICY
- MONEY SUPPLY VERSUS INTEREST RATE TARGETS
- COUNTERCYCLICAL MONETARY POLICY

American resistance to control over our monetary system finally broke down in the early part of the 20th century. It had become unmistakably clear that unregulated banking had too often triggered financial panics that endangered the economic well-being of nearly everyone.

The core problem until the 20th century seemed to be the money system itself. From the very beginning of our republic through the 19th century, the overriding and chronic money problem we faced was the banks' *inclination to overissue currency*. The early and hesitant attempts by Congress to curb the banks' tendency to overissue repeatedly ended in failure and finally led to the enactment of the more assertive Federal Reserve Act of 1913. We need to consider the principal historical events that led to the creation of the Federal Reserve.

# A GLIMPSE AT HISTORY

In colonial times, before banks printed their own **bank notes,** our money was simply a collection of foreign currencies. The French guinea, the Spanish pistole, and the English crown, among many others, circulated as money on the streets of New York, Baltimore, Philadelphia, and Boston. They were exchanged readily for each other. The nation had no currency of its own. But the system worked.

**Bank note**
A promissory note, issued by a bank, pledging to redeem the note for a specific amount of gold or silver. The terms of redemption are specified on the note.

## Continental Notes

Then came the American Revolution. It transformed our money system as well as our political system. It took a great deal of money to recruit, equip, feed, and pay a growing army. The Continental Congress, pressed for funds, turned to the states. But little help was forthcoming. With no real alternative, the Continental Congress took to the printing presses.

Between 1775 and 1780, $242 million of Continental Notes, our first real money, were printed. Since Congress had no taxing authority, it turned to the printing press for money. As the quantity of Continentals multiplied, their value depreciated. In 1777 they traded 2 for 1 against silver. By 1779, as more and more of these notes came on the market, the exchange rate jumped to 20 to 1. By 1781, with printing presses still churning them out, the notes traded 1,000 to 1 against silver. Continentals were rapidly becoming worthless.

To create some semblance of monetary order, Thomas Jefferson proposed a new money, based on the Spanish dollar, metrically divisible, and *backed by gold and silver.* His recommendations were accepted by the Continental Congress, and in 1786, the government established the dollar as the country's unit of account.

## The Chartering of State Banks

But who was to supply the dollars, and how many of them? In those pre-banking years, this simple money system became increasingly incapable of providing adequate supplies to satisfy our monetary needs. Farmers pushing westward needed credit to finance their homesteads. Businesspeople back east sought credit to expand their growing manufacturing operations. Some form of banking system that could offer credit was not only desirable but imperative.

In 1781 the Bank of North America, chartered by the State of Pennsylvania, was formed. It was the first bank in the United States to accept deposits and issue bank notes. Soon, other **state-chartered banks** sprang up—the Bank of New York and the Massachusetts Bank in 1784—each printing and issuing its own bank notes. Exhibit 1 traces the growth of state-chartered banks.

With each new bank issuing its own bank notes, with no established rule on specie backing, and with little discipline on what

**State-chartered bank**
A commercial bank that receives its charter or license to function from a state government and is subject to the laws of that state.

**EXHIBIT 1**

**GROWTH OF STATE BANKS: 1784–1860 ($ MILLIONS)**

|      | NUMBER OF BANKS | CAPITAL |
|------|-----------------|---------|
| 1784 | 3               | $ 2.1   |
| 1801 | 31              | 22.4    |
| 1805 | 75              | 40.4    |
| 1811 | 88              | 42.6    |
| 1816 | 246             | 89.8    |
| 1829 | 329             | 110.1   |
| 1839 | 840             | 327.1   |
| 1859 | 1,476           | 402.9   |

**Source:** U.S. Bureau of the Census, *Historical Statistics of the United States, 1789–1945* (Washington, D.C.: U.S. Government Printing Office, 1949,) pp. 261–263.

should be acceptable collateral, was there any way the government could have controlled the banks' control of the money supply? Should it have tried?

There were opposing views on this issue. Some felt that the states had the right to charter banks and that banks should have the right to issue notes unimpeded by the federal government. They were very reluctant to interfere with a bank's freedom to give or not give credit. They did not like the idea of creating a government monitor over the money supply. But others, no less supportive of a banking system, were still worried about the unconstrained behavior of the banks. They were fearful that these profit-making, state-chartered banks would end up overissuing bank notes, which would undermine the stability of the monetary system.

## The First Bank of the United States

The worriers prevailed. In 1790, Congress proposed that the Bank of North America take on the functions of a central bank. Its primary function would be to control the economy's money supply. It would have the power to dictate what banks could and could not do. The idea of central banking was anything but novel. Central banks were already functioning in Sweden, England, and Holland.

An alternative proposal was put forward by Alexander Hamilton. Instead of the state-chartered Bank of North America acting as the country's central bank, he proposed the creation of a **nationally chartered bank** that would exercise control over the nation's money supply *and* be authorized to extend credit to the government.

Thomas Jefferson and James Madison opposed the idea of a central bank altogether because, in their view, establishing a central bank exceeded the powers of the federal government under the strict interpretation of the Constitution. Moreover, they were convinced that central bank activity would favor the already powerful northern merchant class.

Congress bought the Hamilton plan. In 1791, it set up the First Bank of the United States. The bank's charter was designed to expire after 20 years but could be renewed by Congress.

Actually, the First Bank of the United States performed reasonably well. It served as the government's fiscal agent and even succeeded in dampening the inclination of the state-chartered banks to overissue notes. How? Since many of the state bank notes found their way to the First Bank, the bank could present the notes to the state banks for payment in gold or silver. Aware of this prospect, the state banks became more careful about issuing bank notes in excess of their gold and silver.

## The Second Bank of the United States

And yet in 1811, when the time came to renew the First Bank's charter, Congress declined to do so. The advocates of states' rights won out. Over the next five years, the number of state-chartered banks almost tripled, from 88 in 1811 to 246 in 1816. Left without a central bank's restraining influence on the issuance of bank notes, bank note depreciation and fraud became commonplace. By 1814, most banks had suspended specie payment; that is, they would no longer convert paper bank notes into gold and silver. Would you put your gold into such a bank?

It didn't take Congress long to regret having disposed of the First Bank. It became painfully clear that something had to be done to stabilize the money supply. The answer, just five years after the demise of the First Bank, was to establish the Second Bank of the United States. This time, Congress gave the national bank the right to issue its own notes. These soon became the most widely accepted currency in the nation, preferred to the less-trusted notes of the state-chartered banks.

When the Second Bank took on the task of making specie payment in exchange for its notes, it confronted strong regional resistance. Many state banks in the West

> **Nationally chartered bank**
> A commercial bank that receives its charter from the comptroller of the currency and is subject to federal law as well as the laws of the state in which it operates.

and South catered to the unrestrained money demands of farmers, merchants, and land speculators. Many banks ended up holding excessive quantities of overvalued real estate collateral that they, in turn, used to fuel their bank note issues.

Recognizing the weakness of these issues, the Second Bank pressed for sounder specie backing. The southern and western banks balked, viewing this pressure as discriminatory. Animosity toward the Second Bank intensified when it instructed northern banks not to accept bank notes from the southern and western banks that could not back their currency with gold and silver.

Like the First Bank, the Second Bank had a laudable performance record. And like the First, it was abandoned. When Andrew Jackson, an opponent of central banking, was reelected to the presidency in 1832, the Second Bank's constitutionality was an election issue, and its fate was virtually sealed. Jackson shifted Treasury funds from the Second Bank back to state banks, which undermined the Second Bank's ability to control the issuance of notes by state banks. By 1836 it had become just another bank in Pennsylvania.

From the demise of the Second Bank as a central bank until Congress passed the National Banking Act in 1864, the economy's money supply was once again left in the hands of the state banks. And once again, unsound loans and overissuing of notes led to an unhealthy climate of unreliable money. The Civil War pressured Congress to rediscover central banking.

## The National Bank Act

The cost of the Civil War pushed Congress far beyond its financial capabilities. The steady outflow of specie from the Treasury made it impossible for it to continue buying back its notes. Congress reluctantly allowed the Treasury to begin to print money. The Treasury printed Greenbacks, so called because of the ink used on the back side of the notes. They became the economy's most common, but rapidly depreciating, currency.

Once again, the government faced two classic problems: how to provide itself with the financial resources it needed to carry on the affairs of government and, at the same time, stabilize the monetary system. This time, it came up with a novel idea that ultimately was legislated in 1864 as the National Bank Act.

The idea was to develop a national banking *system*. The act created a new office, comptroller of the currency, housed in the Treasury, which chartered national banks. A national bank had to buy Treasury bonds equal to one-third of its capital, and could issue notes only in proportion to its Treasury bond holdings.

Now how do you reestablish people's confidence in the banking system? Banks were no longer allowed to accept real estate as collateral for loans, nor lend more than 10 percent of the value of their capital stock to any single borrower. Also, each bank was required to provide financial reports to the comptroller of the currency and was subject to periodic bank audits.

To encourage state banks to switch over to the national system, the comptroller levied a 10 percent annual tax on state-chartered bank note issues. This was a steep tax, but there wasn't a rush to conversion. For one thing, not all state-chartered banks could afford the minimal capital required to obtain a national charter. As a result, state-chartered and nationally chartered banks coexisted within the banking industry.

The National Bank Act did tighten the money supply, but it was by no means the banking industry's panacea. It could not stem the credit expansion that banks generated by holding each other's deposits. This practice of credit expansion heightened the banking system's volatility.

For example, in winter, when farmers' demands for funds were relatively weak, country banks would deposit some of their reserves in the larger city banks to earn

Review the National Bank Act (http://www.law.cornell.edu/uscode/12/38.shtml).

interest. Counting these deposits as their own reserves, the city banks would create new loans.

Then came spring. Farmers, now ready to get back into the fields, needed money for seed and equipment. The country banks, ready to service farmers, withdrew their winter deposits from city banks, leaving them with much-depleted reserves. There was nothing city banks could do but call in outstanding loans. At times, these wholesale shifts of deposits touched off financial panics and recessions.

## The Knickerbocker Trust Disaster

The 1907 Knickerbocker disaster was the straw that broke the camel's back. Both state and national banks, along with mushrooming financial trusts, were caught up in a whirlwind of speculative loans. In October, frightened depositors looked in horror at the collapse of the Knickerbocker Trust Company, a highly reputable and seemingly sound financial institution. The thought in everyone's mind—as it would have been in yours—was, Who's next? Panic spread. People ran to their banks to withdraw their deposits, and hard-pressed banks in turn scrambled for liquidity by calling in outstanding loans. Investment projects, in various stages of incompletion, were suspended. Sound businesses, drained dry of credit, were forced into bankruptcy. The result was almost instant recession.

Once again, Congress was forced to intervene. This time, with Knickerbocker still fresh in mind, Congress broadened its concerns from simply coping with the chronic problems of overissue of bank notes and inadequate collateral to addressing a newly perceived menace, the overreach of powerful financial trusts. The response came in the form of the Federal Reserve Act of 1913.

Review the Federal Reserve Act of 1913 (http://www.law.cornell.edu/uscode/12/221.shtml).

## THE FEDERAL RESERVE SYSTEM

The Federal Reserve Act of 1913 created the **Federal Reserve System,** commonly referred to as **the Fed.** Why the Federal Reserve *System* and not the Federal Reserve *Bank*? The Fed was designed as a system because Congress wanted a decentralized central bank. The decentralization was essentially geographic, reflecting people's desire for regional monetary independence.

Why was the Fed designed as a decentralized central bank?

**Federal Reserve System (the Fed)**
The central bank of the United States.

The need for such regional autonomy has since dissipated, but the structure remains intact. The Fed's structure is simple. It consists of 12 district Federal Reserve banks, each serving a region of the country. The larger district Federal Reserve banks have smaller branches. Under this arrangement, a bank in a specific district would use its own district Federal Reserve bank as its central bank. In this way, banks in Omaha, Nebraska, or Ocala, Florida, would not have to depend upon banking decisions made in New York. Exhibit 2 maps the geographic domain of the 12 district Federal Reserve banks and their locations.

### Who Owns the Fed?

Unlike the Bank of Canada, the Bank of France, the Bank of England, and other central banks in democratic market economies, the Federal Reserve System is not owned by the government. Although created by and responsible to Congress, the Fed pursues an independent monetary policy that at times can conflict with government's economic policy. For example, the government may be pursuing a stimulative fiscal policy (lower taxes, increased government spending), while the Fed may be more interested in controlling inflation.

The Board of Governors of the Federal Reserve System (http://www.federalreserve.gov/) provides links to the 12 district Federal Reserve banks (http://federalreserve.gov/otherfrb.htm).

Who owns the Fed, then, if not the government? Each district Federal Reserve bank is owned by its member banks. Each member bank contributes 3 percent of

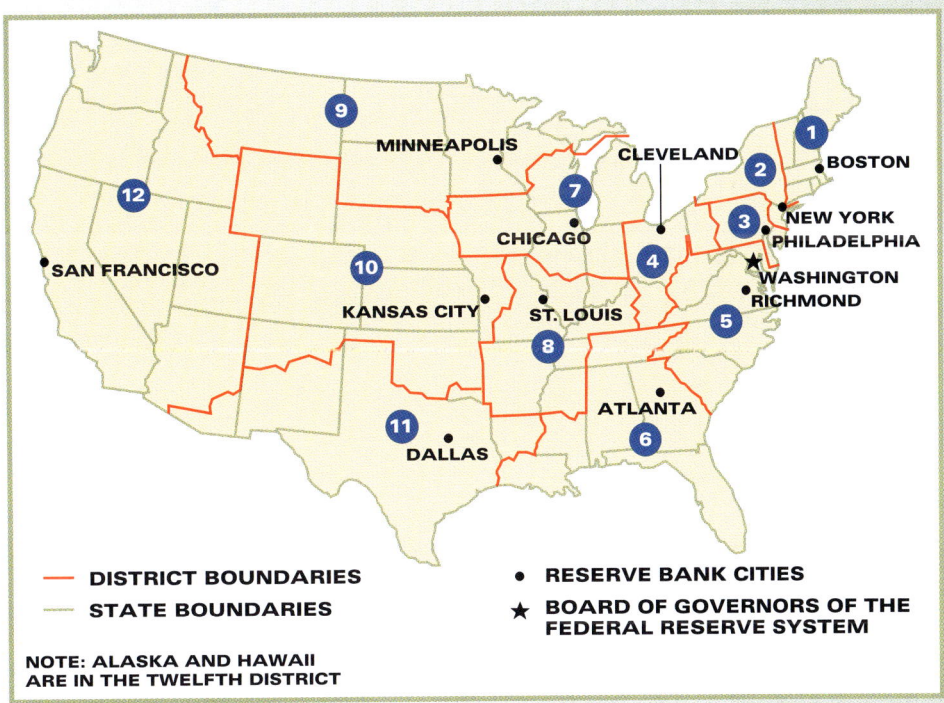

its capital stock to the Federal Reserve bank in its district, and another 3 percent is subject to call by the Fed.

Of the 9,988 banks in the country, fewer than 3,000 are chartered nationally; the rest remain state chartered. You can identify some national banks just by name. The Chicago First *National*, the First *National* of Toledo, the First *National* of Fresno, and so on. Look at Exhibit 3.

All nationally chartered banks must be members of the Fed. The state-chartered banks can choose to be members. Even though less than 17 percent of the state-chartered banks are members of the Federal Reserve System—1,003 out of 6,133 banks in 2000—they, along with nationally chartered banks, hold more than 50 percent of all deposits in our economy.

**NATIONAL BANKS, STATE BANKS, AND TOTAL DEPOSITS: 2000 ($ BILLIONS)**

|  | NUMBER OF BANKS | ASSETS |
|---|---|---|
| TOTAL | 9,988 | $7,268 |
| COMMERCIAL BANKS | 8,375 | 6,064 |
| NATIONAL | 2,242 | 3,363 |
| STATE (FED MEMBER) | 1,003 | 1,573 |
| STATE (NONFED MEMBER) | 5,130 | 1,126 |
| SAVINGS INSTITUTIONS | 1,613 | 1,204 |

**Source:** Federal Deposit Insurance Corporation, *Statistics on Banking, 2000* (Washington, D.C.: FDIC, 2000).

## The Fed's Purpose and Organization

The Federal Reserve System's main charge is to safeguard the proper functioning of our money system. It is the watchdog of our money supply, our interest rates, and the economy's price level.

Obviously, if it's going to do that job at all, it has to monitor the activities of the nation's financial institutions, anticipate what they will do, prevent them from doing some things, and encourage them to do others, and all this without interfering too much in the conduct of private business. Impossible? Some people think so. But these same people are unable to imagine a modern economy operating without a central bank.

The Fed's organizational structure is not very complicated. Look at Exhibit 4.

The nucleus of the Federal Reserve System is its Board of Governors, which meets in Washington, D.C. The board consists of seven members, appointed by the president and confirmed by the Senate. Each serves a 14-year term. Appointments are staggered, one every other year, so that no president or Senate session can manipulate the composition of the board. This also ensures continuity. The chairman is a board member appointed by the president to a 4-year term. Chairmen may be reappointed, but they cannot serve longer than their 14 years on the board.

Typically, chairmen are reappointed for lengthy periods that overlap Republican and Democratic presidents. Paul Volcker, who preceded current chairman Alan Greenspan, was appointed by Jimmy Carter and twice reappointed by Ronald Reagan. Greenspan has continued into the George W. Bush administration. Much earlier, William McChesney Martin chaired through the Eisenhower, Kennedy, and Johnson administrations and even into the early Nixon years.

**EXHIBIT 4**

### ORGANIZATIONAL STRUCTURE OF THE FEDERAL RESERVE SYSTEM

**BOARD OF GOVERNORS (7 APPOINTED MEMBERS)**
- SETS RESERVE REQUIREMENTS AND APPROVES DISCOUNT RATES AS PART OF MONETARY POLICY
- SUPERVISES AND REGULATES MEMBER BANKS AND BANK HOLDING COMPANIES
- ESTABLISHES AND ADMINISTERS PROTECTIVE REGULATIONS IN CONSUMER FINANCE
- OVERSEES FEDERAL RESERVE BANKS

*EXERCISES GENERAL SUPERVISION* →

**FEDERAL RESERVE BANKS (12 DISTRICTS)**
- PROPOSE DISCOUNT RATES
- HOLD RESERVE BALANCES FOR DEPOSITORY INSTITUTIONS AND LEND TO THEM AT THE DISCOUNT WINDOW
- FURNISH CURRENCY
- COLLECT AND CLEAR CHECKS AND TRANSFER FUNDS FOR DEPOSITORY INSTITUTIONS
- HANDLE U.S. GOVERNMENT DEBT AND CASH BALANCES

*ADVISE* ↑

**CONSUMER ADVISORY COUNCIL**

**FEDERAL ADVISORY COUNCIL**

**THRIFT INSTITUTIONS ADVISORY COUNCIL**

*COMPOSE* ↓

**FEDERAL OPEN MARKET COMMITTEE (BOARD OF GOVERNORS AND 5 RESERVE BANK PRESIDENTS)**
- DIRECTS OPEN MARKET OPERATIONS (BUYING AND SELLING OF U.S. GOVERNMENT SECURITIES), WHICH ARE THE PRIMARY INSTRUMENT OF MONETARY POLICY

**Source:** Board of Governors of the Federal Reserve System, Division of Support Services, *Purposes & Functions*, 1984.

More often than not, board members are drawn from within the banking industry, either from commercial banks or from the Fed's district banks. Volcker, for example, came from the New York Fed. Such ties to banking experience can be both helpful and problematic. While members must understand the complexities of banking, their strong connection to the industry seems to compromise, for some people, their role as guardians of the public trust. But not all come from banking. Arthur Burns, for example, left his professorship at Columbia University to serve as chairman during the late Nixon years.

**DISTRICT FEDERAL RESERVE BANKS** The 12 district banks make up the second tier of the Fed's structure. Each is managed by a board of nine directors, six chosen by the member banks of the district, the other three appointed by the Board of Governors. The president of each district bank is selected by its nine directors.

**FEDERAL OPEN MARKET COMMITTEE** The nerve center of the Fed is its **Federal Open Market Committee**. Here, the Fed exercises monetary control over the economy through its open market operations (discussed below). The 12-person committee is composed of all seven members of the Board of Governors, the president of the New York Fed, and four district presidents who rotate voting on the Committee. Each member has one vote. Its composition reflects the power of the board, the unique position held by the New York Fed, and the Fed's commitment to regional representation.

**Federal Open Market Committee**
The Fed's principal decision-making body, charged with executing the Fed's open market operations.

## The Fed as Money Printer

The Fed has a monopoly on printing our paper currency. Occasionally, others try it, but typically they end up in federal prison. The actual printing presses are located in Washington, D.C. There, the U.S. Bureau of Engraving and Printing prints up stocks of Federal Reserve bank notes in various denominations for each district bank. These are stored until the district banks call for specific quantities.

Until they are actually used by the district Federal Reserve banks, the notes are just so much printed paper (actually, cloth—75 percent cotton and 25 percent linen). They are not counted as part of the money supply. But once the district Feds put the printed paper into circulation by transferring it to their member banks, the printed paper becomes currency. How much currency we have at any one time, then, is determined by the wishes of commercial banks and especially by the public.

The Federal Open Market Committee posts minutes from its recent meetings (http://www.federalreserve.gov/fomc/minutes/).

We all know what currency looks like. All dollar bills are Federal Reserve notes, representing the Fed's liability. Each bears a seal—placed to the left of George Washington on the $1 bill—identifying the district bank that issued it. The fine print on the seal spells out the particular district bank, but a large letter makes identification easier.

Exhibit 5 matches the letter markings on the seal to specific district Federal Reserve banks.

Check the seals on your own dollar bills. How many different district Federal Reserve bank notes do you have? Chances are that out of five notes in your wallet, two or three will be different bank issues. How do you suppose the San Francisco Fed's note ends up in a Boston wallet? Or a Kansas City Fed's ends up in Dallas? We are an open, active, and wide-ranging economy. When you can fly from Los Angeles to New York in less than six hours, it doesn't take long for currency to travel across the country.

The Bureau of Engraving and Printing (http://www.bep.treas.gov/) prints Federal Reserve bank notes.

## EXHIBIT 5

### IDENTIFYING LETTERS AND DISTRICT BANKS

| LETTER | FEDERAL RESERVE BANK OF |
|---|---|
| A | BOSTON |
| B | NEW YORK |
| C | PHILADELPHIA |
| D | CLEVELAND |
| E | RICHMOND |
| F | ATLANTA |
| G | CHICAGO |
| H | ST. LOUIS |
| I | MINNEAPOLIS |
| J | KANSAS CITY |
| K | DALLAS |
| L | SAN FRANCISCO |

## The Fed as the Bankers' Bank

The Federal Reserve System is often called the bankers' bank because it provides specific services to its member banks that in some respects are like the services banks provide to us. For example, member banks can create their own accounts at the Fed, allowing them to deposit and withdraw their funds on demand. They can even borrow from the Fed, just as we borrow from banks. The Fed provides them with check-clearing services and, of course, with currency.

**HOLDING RESERVES** As you know, banks are obligated to keep some fraction of their demand deposits in reserve. But they can also hold reserves in excess of the reserve requirement set by the Fed. Suppose that the Paris First National Bank (PFN), a member of the Federal Reserve System, with $1,000,000 in demand deposits, holds $300,000 in reserve, $200,000 more than the 10 percent legal reserve requirement.

What does it do with the $300,000? Some of it, say $75,000, stays in Paris in PFN's vaults. The remaining $225,000 is sent to Dallas, where it is deposited in PFN's account at the Dallas Fed, just as you deposit money in your account at your own bank. PFN can always add to or subtract from its account at the Dallas Fed.

**PROVIDING BANKS WITH CURRENCY AND LOANS** Suppose PFN finds that its depositors are demanding much more currency than it has available in Paris. What does it do? It simply calls the district Federal Reserve bank in Dallas. The Dallas Fed ships the currency in an armored car (or mails it—insured, of course!) to PFN and deducts that amount from PFN's deposits at the Dallas Fed.

If, on the other hand, PFN discovers that the amount of currency it has on hand is abnormally large, it can transfer some of it to the Dallas Fed. The Fed then simply credits PFN's account with that amount. This is the same process you go through with your bank.

Now suppose the PFN wants to make a loan to Shara Gingold but has no excess reserves it can draw upon. It holds only the legally required reserves. Are PFN and Shara out of luck? Not necessarily. PFN can borrow from the Dallas Fed just as we can borrow from banks. If the Dallas Fed decides to make the loan to PFN, it charges PFN an interest rate on the loan—called the **discount rate**—just as we are charged an interest rate on bank loans. Obviously, the discount rate charged to PFN is lower than the rate of interest PFN charges Shara if Shara is to get the loan.

Why is the Fed so generous? These Fed loans to member banks provide the Fed not only with a means to service member banks, but also with a means to control what banks do.

**Discount rate**
The interest rate the Fed charges banks that borrow reserves from it.

**CLEARING BANKS' CHECKS** Suppose Brian Mosley, watching David Letterman on TV one night, sees a Rock Classics commercial for five Billy Bragg CDs and decides to get them. He writes a check for $49.95 on his bank, the First National of Cincinnati, FNC, and mails the check to Rock Classics in Athens, Georgia. He expects the CDs in six weeks.

Exhibit 6 traces the sequence of bank transactions that Brian triggers with his $49.95 check. Two days after it is mailed, Brian's check arrives in Athens. Rock Classics deposits the check in its account at the First National Bank of Athens, FNA. Rock Classics's account at FNA is richer by $49.95.

It never occurs to Rock Classics that FNA would refuse Brian's check. But why not? Why should an Athens bank accept a check drawn on a bank in Cincinnati? How does the Athens bank collect the $49.95 from Cincinnati?

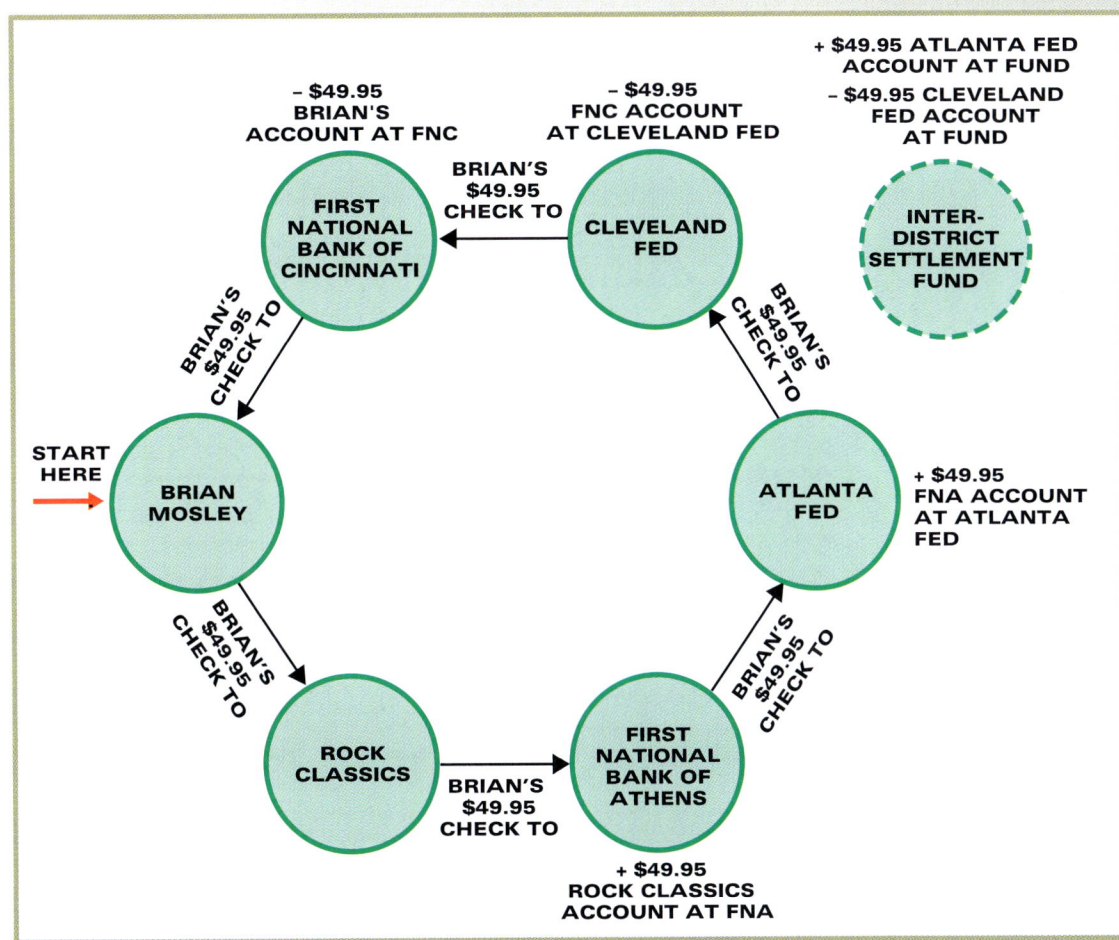

**BANK TRANSACTIONS TRIGGERED BY BRIAN'S PURCHASE**

The circular flow of Brian Mosley's $49.95 check through Rock Classics, the First National Bank of Athens, the Atlanta Fed, the Cleveland Fed, and the First National Bank of Cincinnati.

# GLOBAL PERSPECTIVE

## CHECK OUT THE CENTRAL BANKS

Are all central banks alike? Not exactly. While their principal functions are very much the same—providing and controlling the money supply, maintaining price stability, regulating and directing monetary policy, and being a bank for commercial banks—there are notable differences. Some central banks are owned and run by government; others are independent. Among those that are independent, some are more obliged to follow government directives than others. Central banks in many developing economies not only control the money supply and engage in monetary policy but also are directly involved in the financing of economic development. Sample some of the central bank Web sites listed here and note their similarities and differences.

| COUNTRY | CENTRAL BANK | http://www. |
|---|---|---|
| ALBANIA | BANK OF ALBANIA | bankofalbania.org/ |
| ARGENTINA | BANCO CENTRAL DE LA REPÚBLICA ARGENTINA | bcra.gov.ar/ |
| ARMENIA | CENTRAL BANK OF ARMENIA | cba.am/ |
| ARUBA | CENTRALE BANK VAN ARUBA | cbaruba.org/ |
| AUSTRALIA | RESERVE BANK OF AUSTRALIA | rba.gov.au/ |
| AUSTRIA | OESTERREICHISCHE NATIONALBANK | oenb.at/oenb/ |
| BELGIUM | NATIONALE BANK VAN BELGIË | bnb.be/sg/index.htm |
| BOLIVIA | BANCO CENTRAL DE BOLIVIA | bcb.gov.bo/ |
| BOSNIA | CENTRALNA BANKA BOSNE I HERCEGOVINE | cbbh.gov.ba |
| BOTSWANA | BANK OF BOTSWANA | bankofbotswana.bw/ |
| BRAZIL | BANCO CENTRAL DO BRASIL | bcb.gov.br/ |
| BULGARIA | BULGARIAN NATIONAL BANK | bnb.bg/ |
| CANADA | BANK OF CANADA | bankofcanada.ca/en/ |
| CHILE | BANCO CENTRAL DE CHILE | bcentral.cl/ |
| COLOMBIA | BANCO DE LA REPÚBLICA | banrep.gov.co/ |
| COSTA RICA | BANCO CENTRAL DE COSTA RICA | bccr.fi.cr/ |
| COTE D'IVOIRE | BANQUE CENTRALE DES ETATS DE L'AFRIQUE DE L'OUEST | bceao.int/ |
| CROATIA | HRVATSKA NARODNA BANKA | hnb.hr/ |
| CYPRUS | CENTRAL BANK OF CYPRUS | central bank.gov.cy/ |
| CZECH REPUBLIC | CESKÁ NÁRODNI BANKA | cnb.cz/ |
| DENMARK | DANMARKS NATIONALBANK | nationalbanken.dk/uk |
| EAST CARIBBEAN | EASTERN CARIBBEAN CENTRAL BANK | eccb-centralbank.org/ |
| ECUADOR | BANCO CENTRAL DEL ECUADOR | bce.fin.ec/ |
| EGYPT | CENTRAL BANK OF EGYPT | cbe.org.eg/ |
| ESTONIA | EESTI PANK | ee/epbe/ |
| EUROPEAN UNION | EUROPEAN CENTRAL BANK | ecb.int/ |
| FIJI | RESERVE BANK OF FIJI | reservebank.gov.fj/ |
| FINLAND | SUOMEN PANKKI | bof.fi/ |
| FRANCE | BANQUE DE FRANCE | banque-france.fr/ |
| GERMANY | DEUTSCHE BUNDESBANK | bundesbank.de/ |
| GREECE | BANK OF GREECE | bankofgreece.gr/ |
| GUATEMALA | BANCO DE GUATEMALA | banguat.gob.gt/ |
| HONDURAS | BANCO CENTRAL DE HONDURAS | bch.hn/ |

| COUNTRY | CENTRAL BANK | http://www. |
|---|---|---|
| HONG KONG | HONG KONG MONETARY AUTHORITY | info.gov.hk/hkma/ |
| HUNGARY | MAGYAR NEMZETI BANK | mnb.hu/ |
| ICELAND | SEDLABANKÍ ISLANDS | sedlabanki.is/ |
| INDIA | RESERVE BANK OF INDIA | rbi.org.in/ |
| INDONESIA | BANK INDONESIA | bi.go.id/ |
| IRELAND | CENTRAL BANK OF IRELAND | centralbank.ie/ |
| ISRAEL | BANK OF ISRAEL | bankisrael.gov.il/ |
| ITALY | BANCA D'ITALIA | bancaditalia.it/ |
| JAMAICA | BANK OF JAMAICA | boj.org.jm/ |
| JAPAN | BANK OF JAPAN | boj.or.jp/en/index.htm |
| JORDAN | CENTRAL BANK OF JORDAN | cbj.gov.jo/ |
| KENYA | CENTRAL BANK OF KENYA | centralbank.go.ke/ |
| KOREA | BANK OF KOREA | bok.or.kindex_e.html |
| LATVIA | LATVIJAS BANKA | bank.lv/ |
| LITHUANIA | LIETUVOS BANKAS | lbank.lt/ |
| LUXEMBOURG | BANQUE CENTRALE DU LUXEMBOURG | bcl.lu/html/en/ |
| MEXICO | BANCO DE MEXICO | banxico.org.mx/ |
| MOZAMBIQUE | BANCO DE MOÇAMBIQUE | bancomoc.mz/ |
| NETHERLANDS | DE NEDERLANDSCHE BANK | dnb.nl/ |
| NEW ZEALAND | RESERVE BANK OF NEW ZEALAND | rbnz.govt.nz/ |
| NICARAGUA | BANCO CENTRAL DE NICARAGUA | bcn.gob.ni/ |
| NORWAY | NORGES BANK | norges-bank.no/ |
| PARAGUAY | BANCO CENTAL DEL PARAGUAY | bcp.gov.py/ |
| PERU | BANCO CENTRAL DE RESERVE DEL PERU | bcrp.gob.pe/ |
| POLAND | NARODOWY BANK POLSKI | nbp.pl/ |
| PORTUGAL | BANCO DE PORTUGAL | bportgual.pt/ |
| ROMANIA | NATIONAL BANK OF ROMANIA | bnro.ro/def_en.htm |
| RUSSIA | CENTRAL BANK OF RUSSIA | cbr.ru/eng/ |
| SAUDI ARABIA | SAUDI ARABIAN MONETARY AGENCY | sama.gov.sa/ |
| SINGAPORE | MONETARY AUTHORITY OF SINGAPORE | mas.gov.sg/ |
| SLOVAKIA | NÁRODNÁ BANKA SLOVENSKA | nbs.sk/ |
| SOUTH AFRICA | THE SOUTH AFRICAN RESERVE BANK | resbank.co.za/ |
| SPAIN | BANCO DE ESPAÑA | bde.es/ |
| SRI LANKA | CENTRAL BANK OF SRI LANKA | lanka.net/centralbank/ |
| SWEDEN | SVERIGES RIKSBANK | riksbank.se/ |
| SWITZERLAND | SCHWEIZERISCHE NATIONALBANK | snb.ch/d/index3.html |
| TANZANIA | BANK OF TANZANIA | bot_tz.org/ |
| THAILAND | BANK OF THAILAND | bot.or.th/ |
| TUNISIA | BANQUE CENTRALE DE TUNISIE | bct.gov.tn/ |
| TURKEY | TÜRKIYE CUMHURIYET MERKEZ BANKASI | tcmb.gov.tr/ |
| UNITED KINGDOM | BANK OF ENGLAND | bankofengland.co.uk/ |
| UNITED STATES | FEDERAL RESERVE SYSTEM | federalreserve.gov/ |
| VENEZUELA | BANCO CENTRAL DE VENEZUELA | bcv.org.ve/ |
| ZIMBABWE | RESERVE BANK OF ZIMBABWE | rbz.co.zw/ |

Here's where the Federal Reserve System comes in. FNA transfers the check to its district Federal Reserve bank, the Atlanta Fed, for deposit. FNA now has an additional $49.95 on deposit at the Atlanta Fed, and the Atlanta Fed now has Brian's check. What does the Atlanta Fed do? It wants to be reimbursed. After all, its liabilities to FNA just increased by $49.95.

The Atlanta Fed transfers the check to the Cleveland Fed and informs the Interdistrict Settlement Fund in Washington about the transfer. The fund credits the Atlanta Fed's account at the fund by $49.95—the Atlanta Fed is now reimbursed—and debits the Cleveland Fed's account at the fund by $49.95.

What does the Cleveland Fed do? It deducts $49.95 from the First National Bank of Cincinnati's account with it. The FNC, in turn, gets reimbursed by reducing Brian Mosley's account by $49.95. The trail ends with the cancelled check sent back to Brian.

Imagine how busy the banks, the district Feds, and the fund must be on any banking day. Millions of accounts in banks, at the district Feds, and at the fund are in a state of constant change. The Fed processes over 30 billion of these migrating checks each year, serving millions of people and businesses. It is hard to imagine how our economy could survive without such an arrangement.

## CONTROLLING THE MONEY SUPPLY

As we noted earlier, a primary function of the Fed is to control the money supply. Focusing on the flow of money in the economy allows the Fed to exercise some control over the economy's price level, interest rates, and level of employment. What the Fed hopes to achieve by all this control activity is the promotion of the economy's stability and growth. Look at Exhibit 7. It depicts the way the Fed can influence real GDP, that is, engage in countercyclical policy.

Look at the sequence of events that occurs when money supply increases. First, an increase in the money supply from $M_1$ to $M_2$ causes the interest rate to fall from $i_1$ to $i_2$. That fall in the interest rate causes the quantity demanded of investment to increase from $I_1$ to $I_2$. Finally, the increase in investment spending shifts the aggregate demand curve from $AD_1$ to $AD_2$, which increases the level of real GDP in this illustration.

Of course, what goes up can come down. By reversing policy on the money supply, the Fed can engineer a decrease in the price level. How? Imagine aggregate

Browse the New York Fed's Fedpoints (http://www.ny.frb.org/pihome/fedpoint/), in particular those that address how the Federal Reserve controls the money supply: "Reserve Requirements" (http://www.ny.frb.org/pihome/fedpoint/fed45.html), "Discount Rate" (http://www.ny.frb.org/pihome/fedpoint/fed30.html), and "Open Market Operations" (http://www.ny.frb.org/pihome/fedpoint/fed32.html).

### EXHIBIT 7

### FROM CHANGES IN THE MONEY SUPPLY TO CHANGES IN REAL GDP

An increase in the money supply from $M_1$ to $M_2$ lowers the interest rate from $i_1$ to $i_2$. This fall in the interest rate raises investment spending from $I_1$ to $I_2$, which shifts the aggregate demand curve from $AD_1$ to $AD_2$. As a result, real GDP increases from $GDP_1$ to $GDP_2$.

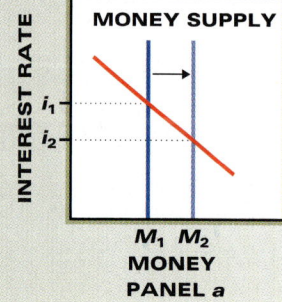

PANEL a

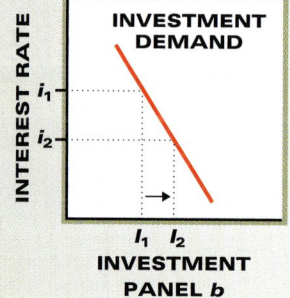

PANEL b

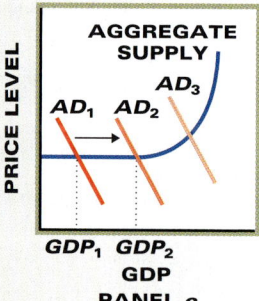

PANEL c

demand at $AD_3$. By decreasing the money supply, the interest rate rises, investment falls, and aggregate demand falls, causing the price level to fall. As you see, the Fed's key to controlling GDP and the price level—the heart and soul of **countercyclical monetary policy**—is controlling the money supply.

How does the Fed control the money supply? It relies upon three instruments: reserve requirements, the discount rate, and open market operations.

## Changing the Legal Reserve Requirement

By lowering the **reserve requirement,** the Fed can trigger a new series of additional loans and deposits throughout the banking system. For example, lowering the reserve requirement allows banks to make more loans. More borrowers mean greater real production in the economy.

If the Fed wants to curb production, it can increase the reserve requirement and restrict loans and thereby decrease the money supply. In this way, the economy's money supply can be expanded or contracted at the Fed's discretion. In times of recession, the Fed can lower the reserve requirement. In times of full employment and inflation, it can raise it. But there's a hitch to its effectiveness. Even if the Fed lowers the reserve requirement to increase the money supply, there is no guarantee that the money supply will increase. Why not? Because it depends upon whether borrowers are willing to take up the new loans that the Fed now makes available. If borrowers, for their own reasons, choose not to borrow, then the Fed can lower the legal reserve requirement all it wants without changing the money supply by one penny.

The legal reserve requirement set by the Fed applies not only to banks, but also, since the enactment of the Depository Institutions Deregulation and Monetary Control Act of 1980, to savings and loan associations and credit unions, whether or not they are state or nationally chartered or members of the Fed.

Exhibit 8 shows that the reserve requirement imposed on banks by the Fed depends on the size of a bank's total deposits.

Although the Fed's ability to change the reserve requirement would seem to be an effective tool to control money supply, it is rarely used. Why not? Because it creates uncertainty that banks prefer to avoid. For example, every time the Fed raises the requirement, it forces banks to contract outstanding loans. This can be highly disruptive to both banks and borrowers.

## Changing the Discount Rate

The Fed can change the discount rate it charges banks who borrow from the Fed. For example, if Paris First National's excess reserves are exhausted, it can approach the Dallas Fed for a loan. Suppose the Dallas Fed agrees. It charges PFN a discount rate, determined by the Fed. PFN will borrow from the Fed only if the discount rate it is obliged to pay is less than the interest rate it charges its borrowers. The spread between these two rates determines the banks' eagerness to borrow from the Fed.

If there is a recession and the Fed wants to encourage banks to provide loans in the

**Countercyclical monetary policy**
Policy directives used by the Fed to moderate swings in the business cycle.

**Reserve requirement**
The minimum amount of reserves the Fed requires a bank to hold, based on a percentage of the bank's total deposit liabilities.

The Federal Reserve maintains current and historical data on aggregate reserves for banks (http://www.federalreserve.gov/releases/H3/) and interest rates (http://www.federalreserve.gov/releases/H15/update/).

**CHECK YOUR UNDERSTANDING**
Why isn't the reserve requirement a preferred tool of monetary power?

### RESERVE REQUIREMENTS (SEPTEMBER 2000)

| BANKS WITH CHECKING ACCOUNT BALANCES | PERCENTAGE OF CHECKING ACCOUNT DEPOSITS |
|---|---|
| $0 TO $42.8 MILLION | 3 |
| MORE THAN $42.8 MILLION | 10 |

**Source:** Board of Governors of the Federal Reserve System, *Federal Reserve Bulletin* (Washington, D.C., December 2000), p. A9.

EXHIBIT 8

# APPLIED PERSPECTIVE

## HOW THE INTEREST RATE ON GOVERNMENT SECURITIES IS DETERMINED

Suppose one of your friends wanted to borrow $1,000 from you. Admittedly, that's a lot of money and you probably have dozens of other ideas concerning the disposition of the $1,000. Lending it to a friend—even a good friend—would probably not rank very high. But suppose your friend offered to pay you a 10 percent rate of interest. You quickly calculate the interest payment at $100 per year. Not bad at all. And why not help a friend. You agree. Your friend writes an IOU, stipulating the rate of interest and the date when the $1,000 loan will be repaid. It's signed and delivered. You hold the IOU (your friend's security) and he gets the $1,000.

Suppose the borrower is not a friend but the United States government. It comes to you with the following proposition: If you lend me $1,000, you will receive a 10 percent rate of interest each year. The government may not be your buddy, but its $100 interest payment each year is as good as anyone's $100.

Good idea? Many people think so, which is why many people—perhaps yourself included—hold government IOUs or securities. Have you ever wondered who in the government actually borrows the money and how the rate of interest—5 percent, 10 percent, or whatever percent—is determined?

The government borrower is the Department of the Treasury. That department actually offers a variety of federal government IOUs or securities, which include T-bills (the T stands for Treasury), which are offered with 3-, 6-, or 12-month maturities, T-notes with maturities ranging from 2 to 10 years, and T-bonds whose maturities exceed 10 years.

The interest rate? Government offers these securities hoping to pay as low an interest rate as possible. Makes sense, doesn't it? If you borrowed money by offering your own IOUs, wouldn't you want to pay as little as possible? The lenders to government (that is, the buyers of government securities), on the other hand, hope to collect as high an interest rate as possible. That makes sense too.

Well, what rate of interest does the government actually end up paying, and how is that rate determined? Here's where the securities auction comes into play. The government's T-bills, T-notes, and T-bonds are offered for sale at auctions conducted by the Federal Reserve Banks. How does that work? Consider the weekly auctions of 3- and 6-month T-bills.

Buyers of these T-bills are ordinary people like yourself, large financial institutions, and dealers who specialize in government securities. To accommodate these different types of buyers, the government permits two different kinds of bids—or offers to purchase—called competitive and noncompetitive tenders.

- *Competitive tenders:* These bidders, principally the professional dealers in government securities, will buy T-bills only if the T-bills yield an interest rate at least as attractive as a rate they can obtain elsewhere in the securities market. These dealers make their competitive bids specifying how many T-bills they want to buy and the interest rate they wish to receive. These are closed and secret bids. The government, seeking to pay the lowest possible rate, will first accept bids from those dealers willing to buy the T-bills at the lowest interest rate submitted, then the next lowest, and so on until the government has sold the amount of T-bills it wants to sell that week. Competitive bidders who tendered a bid at a comparatively too-high rate will end up with no T-bills. That's the nature of competition.
- *Noncompetitive tenders:* People who want to buy T-bills without the hassle of competitive bidding can submit noncompetitive bids, indicating how many they want to buy at the average rate of interest determined by the competitive bidders. These noncompetitive bids typically account for no more than 5 percent of the total dollar value of T-bill sales, but they make up a large majority of the buyers. They are the nonprofessional buyers, much like you.

economy, it lowers its discount rate. On the other hand, if the economy is inflationary, the Fed wants to restrict bank lending. It does so by raising the discount rate.

How are the Fed's loans to banks transacted? See, in Exhibit 9, how the accounts of both the Dallas Fed and PFN change after a $5,000 Fed loan is made to PFN.

In making the loan to PFN, the Dallas Fed simply creates a $5,000 deposit in PFN's account. That's potentially *new* money that never existed before. *The Fed brought it into being by simply changing its assets and liabilities.* The PFN, with $5,000 added to its total reserves, can now make additional loans, the amount depending upon the reserve requirement. Exhibit 10 shows how the Dallas Fed's loan affects PFN's account.

If the reserve requirement is 20 percent, then PFN's new $5,000 reserve allows PFN to loan out $4,000. That *may* trigger a series of deposits and loans throughout the banking system that could potentially raise the economy's money supply by

$$\$5,000 \times \frac{1}{.20} = \$25,000.$$

**CHANGE IN THE DALLAS FED'S ACCOUNTS AFTER PROVIDING A $5,000 LOAN TO PFN**

| ASSETS | LIABILITIES |
|---|---|
| LOAN TO PFN +$5,000 | RESERVE DEPOSIT OF PFN +$5,000 |

*EXHIBIT 9*

What do discount rates look like in the real world? How frequently do they change? Look at Exhibit 11.

As you see, the Fed is very much disposed to change its discount rate. Changes are sometimes as frequent as weekly. These changes not only affect the percentage spread that banks earn on a Fed loan, but also, no less important, reflect the Fed's thinking about the money supply. That's important information to banks, perhaps enough to make them reconsider their own loan behavior.

In practice, however, the Fed has become increasingly reluctant to provide member banks with excess reserves to expand their loans, encouraging them instead to use the **federal funds market.** What is this market?

Suppose Paris First National, at the close of a brisk banking day, discovers that it is $100,000 short of reserves the Fed requires it to hold. And suppose at the close of that same day, Paris Second National discovers that it holds $100,000 in excess reserves at the Dallas Fed.

Consider PFN's line of action. It must borrow to cover its $100,000 reserve deficit. It

**Federal funds market**
The market in which banks lend and borrow reserves from each other for very short periods of time, usually overnight.

**CHANGE IN PFN'S ACCOUNTS AFTER RECEIVING A $5,000 LOAN FROM THE DALLAS FED**

| ASSETS | LIABILITIES |
|---|---|
| RESERVES AT THE FED +$5,000 | BORROWING FROM FED +$5,000 |

*EXHIBIT 10*

## EXHIBIT 11

**FEDERAL RESERVE BANK OF NEW YORK DISCOUNT RATES: 1985–2001 (% PER YEAR)**

Rates for short-term adjustment credit. For rates applicable to other types of discount window credit, see source. See also *Historical Statistics, Colonial Times to 1970*, series X, pp. 454–455.

| EFFECTIVE DATE | RATE | EFFECTIVE DATE | RATE | EFFECTIVE DATE | RATE |
|---|---|---|---|---|---|
| 1985: MAY | 7½ | 1991: FEB. | 6 | 1995: FEB. | 5¼ |
| 1986: MARCH | 7 | APRIL | 5½ | 1996: JAN. | 5 |
| APRIL | 6½ | SEPT. | 5 | 1998: DEC. | 4½ |
| JULY | 6 | NOV. | 4½ | 1999: SEPT. | 4¾ |
| AUG. | 5½ | DEC. | 3½ | DEC. | 5 |
| 1987: SEPT. | 6 | 1992: JULY | 3 | 2000: MAY | 6 |
| 1988: AUG. | 6½ | 1994: MAY | 3 | 2001: JAN. | 5½ |
| 1989: FEB. | 7 | AUG. | 4 | | |
| 1990: DEC. | 6½ | NOV. | 4¾ | | |

**Source:** Federal Reserve Bank, St. Louis.

---

can call the Dallas Fed and borrow the $100,000 from it—paying the discount rate to the Fed. Or, it can borrow PSN's $100,000 of excess reserves at the Dallas Fed for the day—paying the **federal funds rate** to PSN. Why wouldn't Paris Second National want to make money on its excess reserves for the day?

Imagine thousands of daily transactions involving interbank loans and borrowings of excess reserves. It is a more common practice than borrowing directly from the Fed. Typically, the federal funds rate is slightly higher than the discount rate.

**Federal funds rate**
The interest rate on loans made by banks in the federal funds market.

### Engaging in Open Market Operations

*The most effective and frequently used tool the Fed has at its disposal to change the economy's money supply* is its **open market operations**—that is, its buying and selling operations in the government securities market. The Fed's operating rule is simple: It buys government securities on the open market when it wants to increase the money supply and sells some of its government securities when it wants to reduce the economy's money supply.

**Open market operations**
The buying and selling of government bonds by the Federal Open Market Committee.

The nerve center of the Fed's securities buying and selling activity is located in its Federal Open Market Committee (FOMC), which issues directives to the securities trading desk at the Federal Reserve Bank of New York. Suppose the FOMC wants to increase the money supply and decides to buy $10 million of government securities. Where would it find the security sellers? Who are they?

If you owned government securities, wouldn't you be willing to sell them if the Fed met your price? Suppose you owned a $1,000 government bond and discovered that the Fed was willing to pay $1,100 for it. Would you sell? You may not be the only one who would take the deal. Many corporations and most banks own government securities for the same reason you do; they pay interest. And like you, they will sell their interest-bearing securities if the price is right.

The market price of government securities is determined, like the price of most goods, by buyers and sellers operating in the market. The securities market is described as *open* because securities holders and would-be securities holders freely negotiate the prices of all securities.

The FOMC enters the securities market to purchase $10 million of securities. Suppose the Paris First National Bank decides to sell $10 million of the securities it owns. Exhibits 12 and 13 trace the effect of the sale on the Fed's and PFN's accounts.

PFN transfers $10 million of its securities to the Fed. The Fed now owns them. Look at the Fed's new asset position. It has increased by $10 million. However, the securities are hardly a gift. The Fed pays for the securities by adding $10 million to PFN's reserves at the Fed. This appears as a $10 million increase in the Fed's liabilities to PFN.

What about PFN? Exhibit 13 describes the change in its accounts.

Note the change in PFN's asset position. Before, it held $10 million in interest-bearing government securities. It now holds, instead, $10 million in excess reserves at the Fed. *These new excess reserves can be used by PFN to support $10 million in additional loans.*

That's precisely why the Fed went on the open market to buy the securities. It wanted to increase the economy's money supply. If sufficient numbers of borrowers can be found, the $10 million of increased reserves at PFN will trigger ($10 million × 1/0.20) = $50 million more in deposits throughout the banking system. That's a $50 million increase in the economy's money supply. And that's precisely what the Fed had in mind.

But suppose the Fed bought the $10 million of securities from individuals, not from PFN. Would it change the results? Yes, but only slightly. Let's trace the sale of these securities by supposing, for simplicity's sake, that only one person, Maria Snarski, sold the securities to the Fed.

What happens now? Maria sells her $10 million of securities on the open market. The Fed buys them. She receives a check, made out by the Fed, for $10 million. She deposits the check in her account at PFN.

What does PFN do with it? Look at Exhibit 14.

Maria's $10 million deposit increases PFN's assets and liabilities by $10 million. PFN sends the $10 million check to the Fed for collection. The Fed credits PFN's account at

**EXHIBIT 12**

**CHANGE IN THE FED'S ACCOUNTS AFTER BUYING $10 MILLION OF SECURITIES FROM PFN ($ MILLIONS)**

| ASSETS | LIABILITIES |
|---|---|
| GOVERNMENT SECURITIES +$10 | PFN'S RESERVE +$10 |

**CHECK YOUR UNDERSTANDING**

Why does the Fed buy government securities?

**EXHIBIT 13**

**CHANGE IN PFN'S ACCOUNTS AFTER SELLING $10 MILLION OF SECURITIES TO THE FED ($ MILLIONS)**

| ASSETS | LIABILITIES |
|---|---|
| GOVERNMENT SECURITIES −$10 | NO CHANGE |
| RESERVES AT FED +$10 | |

**EXHIBIT 14**

**CHANGE IN PFN'S ACCOUNTS AFTER MARIA SELLS $10 MILLION OF SECURITIES ($ MILLIONS)**

| ASSETS | LIABILITIES |
|---|---|
| CASH RESERVES +$10 | DEMAND DEPOSITS +$10 |

the Fed by $10 million. We see this recorded in Exhibit 15.

The increase of $10 million in reserves allows PFN to loan out $8 million—rather than $10 million as in the previous example—and begin the process of money creation throughout the banking system. As you see, that process occurs whether the Fed buys securities from the bank directly or from individuals like Maria.

Now suppose the economy is in an inflationary phase and the Fed decides to reduce the money supply. How would it do it? It just reverses its open market operations. It *sells* securities instead of buying them. Banks, corporations, and individuals buy them from the Fed if the price is right. Let's suppose again that PFN gets into the act. This time it decides to buy securities from the Fed. What would it do? Look at Exhibit 16.

PFN writes out a $10 million check to the Fed. PFN pays for these additional securities out of its reserves (i.e., the Fed reduces PFN's reserves by $10 million). So far, the only change has been in the composition of assets PFN holds. With $10 million fewer reserves, PFN is not in a position to loan $10 million. This eliminates a series of loans and deposits that might have taken place throughout the banking system. The reduction in credit available to consumers and businesses is likely to reduce spending. Not a bad outcome if the economy is in an inflationary phase.

The results would be the same if Maria Snarski, Merrill Lynch, or Nike Corporation did the buying.

## CONTROLLING THE INTEREST RATE: THE FED'S ALTERNATIVE TARGET OPTION

The idea of targeting the money supply to control interest rates, investment, aggregate demand, and ultimately real GDP makes sense in the simple world of Exhibit 7. That world *assumes* the Fed knows where the demand curve for money is positioned. After all, if its position weren't known, the Fed couldn't possibly associate specific changes in the money supply to specific changes in the interest rate. Without that specificity, the Fed's ability to execute policy weakens.

What, then, can it do? Look at Exhibit 17, panels *a* and *b* (a modification of Exhibit 7,

**EXHIBIT 15**

**CHANGE IN THE FED'S ACCOUNTS AFTER BUYING $10 MILLION OF SECURITIES FROM MARIA ($ MILLIONS)**

| ASSETS | LIABILITIES |
|---|---|
| GOVERNMENT SECURITIES +$10 | PFN'S RESERVES +$10 |

panel *a*). This view of the economy yields new target options for the Fed.

## Choosing the Money Supply Option

Look first at panel *a*. Suppose the Fed decides to target the money supply at $S_1$. It uses its tools—the reserve requirement, the discount rate, and open market operations—to create $S_1$. If the Fed believes that the demand curve for money is $D_1$, then it knows that the interest rate will be $i_1$. But the truth of the matter is that the Fed lives, as we all do, in a world of uncertainty. It doesn't *really* know the position of the demand curve for money, in which direction it may shift, or how often it shifts, even for the short run. For example, if after fixing the money supply at $S_1$, the money demand curve turns out to be $D_2$ or $D_3$ and not the $D_1$ curve the Fed anticipated, then the interest rate that results could vary between $i_2$ and $i_3$. That variation could create a new set of problems for the Fed. At, say, $i_2$, producers may want to invest more than the Fed anticipated or considers desirable. Simply put: *If the Fed chooses to target the money supply, it cannot at the same time control the interest rate.*

## Choosing the Interest Rate Option

The Fed, instead, can choose to target the interest rate, allowing the money supply to take its course. We see the consequences of this option in Exhibit 17, panel *b*.

Suppose the Fed, using reserve requirements, discount rates, and open market operations, wishes to fix the interest rate at $i_1$. If the demand curve for money is $D_1$, then the money supply must be set at $S_1$ (quantity of money demanded equals quantity of money supplied in equilibrium). But what if the Fed guesses incorrectly

**EXHIBIT 16**

**CHANGE IN PFN'S ACCOUNTS AFTER BUYING $10 MILLION OF SECURITIES ($ MILLIONS)**

| ASSETS | LIABILITIES |
|---|---|
| RESERVES AT FED  −$10 | NO CHANGE |
| GOVERNMENT SECURITIES  +$10 | |

**EXHIBIT 17**

**THE FED'S TARGET OPTIONS**

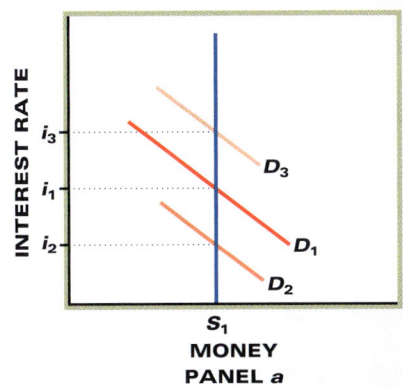

PANEL *a*

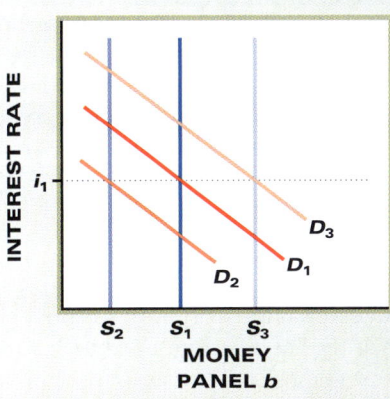

PANEL *b*

If the Fed targets the supply of money at $S_1$, as we see in panel *a*, then it cannot control the interest rate, for that depends on the positioning of the demand curve for money. If, on the other hand, it targets the interest rate at $i_1$, and if the demand curve for money is $D_1$, as we see in panel *b*, then the Fed loses control over the supply of money.

# APPLIED PERSPECTIVE

## THE U.S. BANKING SYSTEM IN A NUTSHELL

The following tables show the financial positions of all commercial banks in the United States and the Federal Reserve.

Loans represent more than 60 percent of the commercial banks' assets. Their holding of government securities adds another 13 percent, and their cash reserves of $667.3 billion are their third most important asset.

Deposits of $3,762.2 represent the single most important liabilities item. These consist of checking, savings, and large time deposits. Of the $1,220.3 billion bank borrowing, $372.5 billion are borrowings from banks in the United States.

U.S. Treasury securities represent the Fed's most important asset holding. When it engages in open market operations, it either adds to or sells off some of these securities. Loans to banks are related to its discount rate policy. Its gold holdings are holdovers from the 1930s, bought from U.S. Treasury. Gold plays no role in monetary policy, nor does it have anything to do with the money supply. The Fed's own notes—Federal Reserve Notes, that is, our dollar bills in various denominations—represent more than 85 percent of its liabilities. The commercial banks' deposits with the Fed amount to $17.6 billion.

### MORE ON THE NET

For more information about what the Fed offers to financial institutions, visit Federal Reserve Financial Services at http://www.frbservices.org/.

### CONSOLIDATED BALANCE SHEET OF U.S. COMMERCIAL BANKS: SEPTEMBER 2000 ($US BILLIONS)

| ASSETS | | LIABILITIES | |
|---|---|---|---|
| CASH | $ 667.3 | DEPOSITS | $3,762.2 |
| LOANS | 3,836.3 | BORROWING | 1,220.3 |
| GOVERNMENT SECURITIES | 807.3 | OTHER | 1,022.1 |
| OTHER SECURITIES | 518.5 | | |
| OTHER | 175.2 | | |
| TOTAL | $6,004.6 | TOTAL | $6,004.6 |

### BALANCE SHEET OF THE FEDERAL RESERVE: SEPTEMBER 2000 ($US BILLIONS)

| ASSETS | | LIABILITIES | |
|---|---|---|---|
| GOLD | $ 11,046 | FEDERAL RESERVE NOTES | $538,816 |
| COIN | 831 | BANK DEPOSITS (RESERVES) | 17,624 |
| LOANS TO BANKS | 372 | U.S. TREASURY DEPOSITS | 8,459 |
| U.S. TREASURY SECURITIES | 511,413 | OTHER LIABILITIES AND | |
| OTHER ASSETS | 61,963 | NET WORTH | 20,726 |
| TOTAL | $585,625 | TOTAL | $585,625 |

and the demand curve for money is not $D_1$, but, say, $D_2$ or $D_3$? Now the money supply, to keep the interest rate fixed at $i_1$, must be $S_2$ or $S_3$. Once again, the Fed may confront problems it didn't anticipate; that is, it may end up with a money supply it really doesn't want. But it has no alternative. *By choosing to target the interest rate, it loses control over the money supply.*

## Is There Really a Preferred Target Option?

You see the Fed's dilemma, don't you? *It faces an opportunity cost no matter which option it chooses.* But is the opportunity cost really debilitating? After all, even though the Fed loses some control over the interest rate once it targets money supply, *the interest rate still moves in the appropriate direction.* That is, any increase in the money supply, whatever the demand for money may be, lowers the interest rate. Conversely, any decrease in the target interest rate, whatever the demand for money may be, increases the money supply. *Correct directional movement counts!*

In other words, the Fed's countercyclical monetary policy works, whether it targets money supply or interest rates. And since the Fed is not entirely blind to the demand for money, the actual opportunity cost associated with either target may, except in very volatile times, be rather minimal.

## What the Fed Ended Up Choosing

Over the years, the Fed has vacillated from fixing on one target to fixing on another. Through the decades of the 1950s, 1960s, and 1970s, the Fed kept an anxious eye on both but favored the interest rate target. That is, it used its discretionary powers over reserve requirements, discount rates, and open market operations to make the money supply conform to a targeted interest rate. The linkages were understood and expected. GDP depends upon aggregate demand, which depends upon investment, which depends upon the interest rate.

But by 1980, with Paul Volcker as chairman of the Fed, the Fed's focus shifted to the money supply. Worried about persisting high inflation, the Fed's plan was to target money supply to bring inflation under control. It understood that the unavoidable consequence of lowering the money supply was rising interest rates. But in the 1980s, the Fed felt that higher interest rates were not only tolerable but desirable. After all, higher rates would reduce investment and aggregate demand, easing pressure on inflation.

The Fed's monetary target shifted once again in the 1990s. Chairman Alan Greenspan sought to bring interest rates down, ignoring the swing it might create in the money supply. The Fed hoped that lower interest rates would stimulate investment, aggregate demand, and real GDP. Inflation? It was now the lesser of the problems.

## Ancillary Tools Available to the Fed

Aside from the big three—the reserve requirement, the discount rate, and open market operations—the Fed can exercise some additional control over the money market by controlling margin requirements on the financing of stock market purchases, and by exercising moral suasion. But these are strictly the Fed's utility players in the major league game of money control.

**CONTROLLING STOCK MARKET MARGIN REQUIREMENTS** You've heard stories, haven't you, about the killings people make on the stock market? Sometimes, the lure of the market can be downright intoxicating, blurring our vision of reality. In truth, playing the stock market is about as reliable a way of getting rich quickly as playing the tables at Las Vegas or betting on the horses at Churchill Downs.

Here's how it's supposed to work. If you have real inside information (as many people suppose they do) or a strong sense of the market's moods (as many more people feel they have), then speculating on the market is a nice, clean way of making money. For example, if you believe that the price of Xerox stock, now at $50 per share on the New York Stock Exchange, will reach $60 by this time next year, it pays to buy Xerox. If you bought $50,000 worth of Xerox, you would end up netting $10,000.

# APPLIED PERSPECTIVE

## THE HONORABLE MARTHA SEGER: EX-FED GOVERNOR TELLS IT LIKE IT IS

*THE MARGIN:* You taught about the Fed in the classroom before joining it. Were there any differences between the Fed of economic textbooks and what you found when you actually became a member of the board?

SEGER: The biggest difference between the Fed as the textbook writers describe it and how it actually works is that it's just about a hundred times more tough to make the decisions. There isn't some cute little formula to use, even though the Fed has a tremendous computer system and 350 or so researchers with all sorts of Ph.D.'s in finance, economics, math, and econometrics. You can't just run some econometric model and have the policy answer pop out.

In the final analysis, the decisions have to be made by the Governors and not by the staffers. I guess the only way I can describe it is to say that it's much more difficult and involves much more judgment than the average textbook would suggest. Making monetary policy is much more an art than a science—it's not a science at all.

THE MARGIN: Could you give us a little of the flavor of an FOMC meeting? Are the discussions heated or is there an air of calm deliberation? What goes on?

SEGER: At the beginning of the meeting, you have a report from Fed staffers on what's been happening to monetary policy since the last FOMC meeting. You get a chance to compare what the FOMC had told the staff to do with the actions it actually carried out.

Then there is a staff presentation on their view of the economic outlook. Then they would go around the table and everyone who is at the meeting—the seven members of the Board of Governors plus all 12 district bank presidents—gets a chance to ask a question of the staff about their forecast. During this period some of the participants may challenge the staff forecast. It's not heated, but I would say it's an open discussion, an open exchange of views, questions, comments. Then after that's done, they go around the table and people can give a little spiel on how they see the economy. The president of the Chicago bank might say, "Well, I met some guy from Ford Motor last week and he said that they just revised downward their sales forecast for next year or they're changing their production schedules and knocking them all down." That sort of thing would be discussed.

YOU MAKE A VERY CONVINCING ARGUMENT. BUT YOU ALWAYS DO, AND YOU'RE DEAD WRONG MOST OF THE TIME!

In addition to the discussions at the meeting, members are also given two books of materials, called the "Green Books," prior to the meeting with reports and analyses about the economy. They also receive the "Blue Book," which outlines monetary policy options. The "Blue Book" usually spells out three options: option A, option B, option C. Then one of the staffers in the monetary affairs section would make the presentation on those options and what you might get in terms of monetary growth and what would happen to the federal funds rate and other interest rates if you chose A, or you chose B, or C. Again, that's information, not always accurate, but still it was presented. And then there would be a discussion after that presentation by the members about the options and about the assumptions, and people would express their views about which ones they thought were most reasonable. And then we would have a break and go for coffee and doughnuts.

While we were relaxing, the chairman would go off with this staffer who was basically in charge of the "Blue Book," and they would prepare a proposed Directive for the group to consider. The Directive gives instructions to the Fed's staff for how to conduct open market operations until the next FOMC meeting. They would draft the Directive based on what they thought they were hearing from everybody. In other words, they would try to get some sense of where the bulk of the feeling is, the bulk of the sentiment. They would write something up, and then they would come back, and then this draft Directive would be distributed. Alan [Greenspan] would talk about the proposed policy for the period ahead, again until the next FOMC meeting, and what he thought would be appropriate. Then everybody else could talk about his or her views and then finally we would have an up or down vote on it. You could either vote in favor of supporting that Directive or you could vote against it—you could be a dissenter. All the votes were recorded. You could also write something up to be put in the minutes, so later on people could go back and see why you disagreed with all those wise folks. So that's basically what goes on.

**MORE ON THE NET**

Experience a Federal Open Market Committee meeting, through a simulation (http://www.ny.frb.org/pihome/educator/fomcsim.html) created by the New York Fed.

**Source:** *The Margin,* Spring 1992.

But how do you get your hands on $50,000? Here's the trick. Just go to Paris First National and borrow $40,000. Why would PFN loan you $40,000? Because you can offer the $50,000 Xerox stock as collateral on the $40,000 loan. All you have to put up of your own money, then, is $10,000.

If you have speculated correctly, you end up making $10,000 on a $10,000 personal investment. That's a cool 100 percent. Even adjusting for the interest on the $40,000 loan, that's a mighty fine percentage.

Where's the catch? Everybody in the stock market business knows that what goes up can come down. Suppose Xerox falls from $50 to $30 two months after your purchase. Your stock is now worth $30,000. Not only has your $10,000 expected profit evaporated, but PFN realizes it can recover only $30,000 of its $40,000 loan.

What does it do? PFN may choose to take the $30,000 rather than chance waiting for an upswing in prices. A speculative loss of $10,000, or even more, may not trouble a bank whose loan portfolios are basically sound. But if the bank's assets are dominated by an array of loans to stock market speculators, then even moderate downward movements in stock prices can do the bank in.

And if the banking system itself is heavily into loans supported by stock market collateral, then any downward movement in stock prices that frightens banks enough to sell off their stock collateral will drive stock prices down even further. It may not take much to trigger a stock market panic.

That's precisely what happened in the stock market crash of 1929. When the dust clouds of that infamous October cleared, it was obvious that loans made on stock market collateral were as uncontrollable as a runaway locomotive on the downside of a mountain. As J. M. Keynes so aptly noted just a few years after the crash:

> Speculators may do no harm as bubbles on a steady stream of enterprise. But the position is serious when enterprise becomes the bubble on a whirlpool of speculation.

If it didn't make sense before, it certainly made sense after the crash that some control over the banking system's holding of stock market collateral was required. The Federal Reserve seemed to be the logical choice.

The Fed was called upon to establish stock market **margin requirements,** the fraction of the stock's price that must be put up by the person buying the stock. In the Xerox-PFN example, the margin was ($50,000 × $40,000)/$50,000 = 20 percent.

**Margin requirement**
The maximum percentage of the cost of a stock that can be borrowed from a bank or any other financial institution, with the stock offered as collateral.

## EXHIBIT 18

**FEDERAL RESERVE'S MARGIN REQUIREMENTS: 1940–94 (PERCENTAGE)**

| DATE | MARGIN | DATE | MARGIN |
|------|--------|------|--------|
| 1940 | 50  | 1960 | 70 |
| 1942 | 75  | 1962 | 50 |
| 1945 | 100 | 1963 | 70 |
| 1947 | 75  | 1970 | 65 |
| 1953 | 50  | 1972 | 65 |
| 1955 | 50  | 1974 | 50 |
| 1958 | 90  | 1994 | 50 |

**Source:** *Banking and Monetary Statistics, 1940–1970* (Washington, D.C.: Board of Governors of the Federal Reserve System, 1975), p. 799; and *Federal Reserve Bulletin,* July 1994, p. A27.

How has the Fed used this margin requirement as a selective control device? Look at Exhibit 18.

During the war years 1940–45, inflationary pressures built up in the economy. How did the Fed respond? By raising margins from 50 to 100 percent to discourage speculative bank loans. After all, the more loans, the more the banking system would fuel the inflation.

At other times—for example, during the recessions of 1949 and 1953—the Fed cut the margins back to 50 percent to help bolster a lackluster economy. The reduced margins gave banks the green light to grant stock-supported loans. The Fed hoped that by this action such loans would create new deposits, new money, and new jobs.

**MORAL SUASION** We have all used some form of moral suasion on friends and foes to promote a particular idea. How many times have you heard your high school teacher say before an exam: "No copying from your neighbor." Sometimes, this admonition would be followed by a threat: "Those found cheating will be suspended from school."

Did it work? Sometimes, on some people. The problem with relying on moral suasion is that in the final analysis it relies entirely on morality and persuasion. But that's what the Fed sometimes uses to encourage or discourage bank loans.

For example, the chairman of the Board of Governors may explain in a television interview that the Fed hopes banks show more restraint in providing consumer credit, because inflation is a problem. Sometimes these expressions of concern take the form of official Fed policy statements or direct appeals by way of letters to thousands of bank presidents.

Whatever its form, these pronouncements rely on voluntary compliance. They may seem weak as instruments of policy, but they are always supported by the unspoken threat that if moral suasion doesn't work, the Fed can always resort to more reliable instruments. Moral suasion, then, can be viewed as an omen of things to come. And banks take note.

## THE FED'S COUNTERCYCLICAL MONETARY POLICY

Let's put the analysis of the Fed's operating tools into the context of the Fed's countercyclical monetary policy. When you think about it, the Fed and the government can be described as partners in a shock-absorbing business, protecting us against the bumps of unemployment and inflation. The government manages its activity through its budget, adding or cutting taxes and spending as the occasion warrants. The Fed works either directly through the banking system or indirectly through its open market operations.

# INTERDISCIPLINARY PERSPECTIVE

## POLITICS AT THE FED?

How political is an interest rate? Several key Democrats, upset over Al Gore's defeat in the November 2000 presidential elections, charged that the Fed's chairman, Alan Greenspan, slashed the interest rate in early January 2001 only to bolster the economy for incoming president and fellow Republican George W. Bush. The cut, they thought, had politics written all over it. Greenspan, they argued, had never before reacted so quickly and boldly to such an insignificant turn in the economy. Caution has been his signature. The ½-point cut in the interest rate that he personally engineered—a break from the Fed's ¼-point tradition—was, they insisted, an action inspired more by the GOP than the GDP.

Is the criticism valid? Damien Cave posed the question to Bob Woodward, longtime Washington journalist and author of the bestseller *Maestro: Greenspan's Fed and the American Boom*. While rejecting the view that the January 2001 rate hike was politically inspired, Woodward's commentary on the issue still threw some interesting light on the political impact of Fed economics.

*Cave:* Was Greenspan's ½-point rate cut on January 3, 2001, a gift to the incoming Bush Administration? That is, was it an attempt to prop up the economy for the new president?

*Woodward:* That just doesn't make sense. If you recall the Fed's raising and lowering of rates during the 1994–95 period, you'll see that the recent rate increase fits the model. Greenspan was just trying to execute a soft landing. The timing and degree of the rate cut is basically an economic decision, not a political one. Greenspan is certainly aware of politics and apparently wanted to avoid cutting rates early in the George W. Bush administration.

*Cave:* There's an interesting subtext, though, with Bush. Greenspan and Bush's circle of advisors—particularly Dick Cheney [Bush's vice president] and Donald Rumsfeld [Bush's secretary of defense] are old friends. Yet George Sr. [U.S. president 1988–1992] blamed Greenspan for his loss to Bill Clinton. How do you think this conflict will play out?

*Woodward:* Well, it's a classic question of does the enemy of your father—allegedly Greenspan—become your enemy or your friend? Enemy is too strong a word, but father Bush has been public and direct in blaming Greenspan for his defeat—which I don't think is correct. During that period, Greenspan and the Fed had to worry about inflation and if you lower the rates too fast, too much, you can still get inflation. That's the problem right now; the Fed is still basically an inflation-fighting institution. If it didn't have to worry about inflation, it would lower rates more quickly and dramatically. So it's my sense that the way George W. Bush embraced Greenspan—talking about the high regard he held for Greenspan's skills—he was clearly reaching for the Clinton model of "let's work together." And Greenspan realizes that it's to everyone's advantage to have a good working relationship with the White House, as he had with Robert Rubin [President Clinton's secretary of the Treasury].

**ALAN GREENSPAN TESTIFYING BEFORE THE SENATE BUDGET COMMITTEE, 2001.**

### MORE ON THE NET

For more information on Alan Greenspan, visit http://www.thetopnotch.com/greenspan/.

**Source:** From a Damien Cave interview with Bob Woodward, "How Alan Greenspan Runs the World," January 10, 2001. This article first appeared in Salon.com at http://www.salon.com. An online version remains in the Salon archives. Reprinted with permission.

---

Typically, the Fed and government work in unison, pursuing common goals. For example, when a recession hits, we would expect the government to run a budget deficit by raising the level of its spending or by cutting taxes, or perhaps both. At the same time and for the same reason, we would expect the Fed to reduce the reserve requirements, reduce the discount rate, and buy securities on the open market. All three activities are engineered to promote bank loans. After all, loans create jobs.

What about Fed and government policies during periods of full employment and inflation? Both have the tools to reverse their lines of attack. We would now expect government to create a surplus budget by cutting its own spending and raising taxes. At the same time and for the same reason, we would expect the Fed to raise the reserve requirements, raise the discount rate, and sell securities on the open market. In this way, banks would find it more difficult to loan, easing the inflationary pressures on the economy.

Exhibit 19 depicts the Fed's countercyclical monetary operations. Although there appears to be symmetry in the Fed's policies during the upswing and downswing phases of the cycle, in fact, there isn't. The Fed is more effective in curbing inflation in periods of prosperity than it is in promoting employment during a recession. Why? Because the Fed can prevent banks from loaning, but it can't force people to borrow.

**CHECK YOUR UNDERSTANDING**

Why is the Fed more effective controlling inflation than stimulating the economy?

Does it make sense? Imagine a college without a library. Wouldn't that make it difficult for students to learn? Suppose a library is built. Does access to a library guarantee that students will learn? The facilities may be there, but there is no way to ensure that students will use them. In the same way, the Fed can prevent the creation of loans, but it can't force loan creation.

## The Fed and the Government Don't Always Agree

Government budgets are typically financed by taxes. When government decides to spend more, it can simply tax more. It enjoys that as a constitutional right. Yet, interestingly enough, it doesn't always exercise it. Instead, government sometimes finds it more convenient to finance its spending by creating and selling new government securities.

In the past decade, government has financed its $200 billion annual budget deficits principally by creating government securities and selling them, that is, by

**EXHIBIT 19**

**THE FED'S COUNTERCYCLICAL OPERATIONS**

In the recovery and prosperity phases of the cycle, the Fed can contain the money supply by raising the reserve requirement, raising the discount rate, or selling bonds on the open market. In the downturn and recession phases of the cycle, the Fed can lower the reserve requirement, lower the discount rate, or buy bonds on the open market to increase the supply of money.

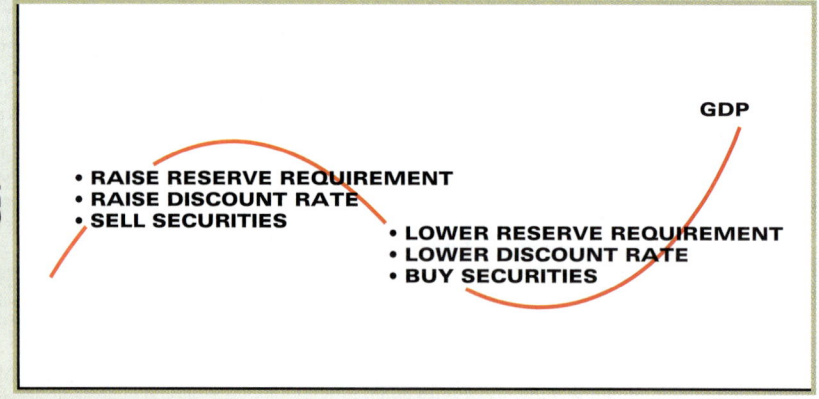

borrowing. The interest rate it must offer to attract securities buyers is no minor issue. As you would suspect, the government would much rather pay lower than higher interest rates.

But that's not how the Fed views ideal interest rates. It supports high interest rates when it wants to curb inflation, and it switches to supporting lower interest rates when it promotes employment.

There are times, then, when the Fed's interest rate policy clashes with the government's. During recession, the Fed may be working to lower interest rates so that borrowers will find it more attractive to take up bank loans, while the government, financing a deficit, may find it necessary to offer higher interest rates to sell its securities. Sometimes, their conflicting interests require a series of summit meetings to negotiate an acceptable interest rate strategy. In such cases, it is generally the pressing needs of government that win out.

**on the net**

To ensure that Congress knows what the Federal Reserve is doing, the chairman of the Federal Reserve must make a semiannual report on economic conditions and the conduct of monetary policy (http://www.federalreserve.gov/boarddocs/hh/). This report is commonly known as the Humphrey-Hawkins testimony, named for the federal statute that requires it.

# CHAPTER REVIEW

1. Colonial America's money was a mixed bag of foreign currencies. The Continental Note—the first authentic U.S. currency—was introduced during the American Revolution and, tied to the silver standard, become quickly devalued by overprinting. The first banks in the post-independence United States were state chartered, and their bank notes—serving as our new currencies—were also plagued by overprinting. The First Bank of the United States was established to overcome the chronic instability in the supply and value of U.S. money.

2. Bowing to opposition from southern and western states, Congress did not renew the First Bank's charter even though the bank was relatively successful in stabilizing the economy's monetary system. Its demise was followed by the rapid growth in state banks and a return to the undisciplined growth in the money supply. As a result of the ensuing monetary instability, the Second Bank of the United States was established. Like the First Bank, the Second Bank successfully promoted a stable financial environment and, again like the First Bank, was short-lived. The third attempt at bringing some form of control over the economy's monetary system came during the Civil War with the National Bank Act. This act was in place until the eve of World War I. The history of banking in the United States up to that time was marked by growing economic power without the direction of a central bank.

3. The Federal Reserve Act of 1913 created the Federal Reserve System, a decentralized central bank. It is composed of 12 district Federal Reserve banks, each owned by member banks in the district. Its main purpose is to provide the economy with an appropriate money supply consistent with a stable price level. It also issues the nation's currency and serves as the banker's bank.

4. To achieve its goals, the Fed uses 3 principal tools: the reserve requirement, the discount rate, and open market operations. To stimulate the economy, it can lower the reserve requirement, lower the discount rate, buy government securities on the open market, or use some combination of these actions. To check inflation, it can reduce the nation's money supply by raising the reserve requirement, raising the discount rate, selling government securities on the open market, or combining these actions in some way. By manipulating these money-supply-affecting tools, it can engage in countercyclical monetary policy during the different phases of a business cycle. The Fed also uses 2 minor tools to promote its monetary policy: stock market margin requirements and moral suasion.

5. The Fed recognizes that changes in the money supply affect the interest rate and, through the interest rate, the level of investment and the level of real GDP. If the Fed chooses to target money supply, it cannot, at the same time, target an interest rate, because it has no control

over the demand for money. For the same reason, if it chooses to target an interest rate, it cannot, at the same time, target the money supply. At times, the Fed has focused on money supply targets, allowing the interest rate to vary according to its market-determined level, and at other times, it has focused on interest rate targets, allowing the money supply to vary.

6. The Fed tends to be more effective in controlling inflation during periods of inflation than in combating unemployment during periods of recession. On occasion, the Fed's monetary policy to control inflation has conflicted with the government's fiscal policy to combat unemployment.

# KEY TERMS

Bank note
State-chartered bank
Nationally chartered bank
Federal Reserve System (the Fed)
Federal Open Market Committee
Discount rate
Countercyclical monetary policy
Reserve requirement
Federal funds market
Federal funds rate
Open market operations
Margin requirement

# QUESTIONS

1. We believe in economic freedom and yet we deny banks the right to make whatever loans they wish to make. Why? What has been our experience with unregulated banking?
2. The *Bank* of England is the central bank of England. The *Bank* of Canada is the central bank of Canada. Why did the Federal Reserve Act of 1913 create the Federal Reserve *System* instead of the Federal Reserve *Bank*?
3. When the Fed sells government bonds, the nation's money supply decreases. Explain how this works. To illustrate, you can construct your own bank transactions and changes in the assets and liabilities of the Fed and of banks.
4. What is the discount rate, and how can the Fed use it to control the nation's supply of money?
5. One way the Fed can increase the nation's money supply is by reducing the reserve requirement. Explain how this works. To illustrate, you can construct your own bank transactions and changes in the assets and liabilities of banks.
6. Why is the Fed more effective in preventing the money supply from increasing than in increasing the money supply?
7. Suppose your bill for a seafood dinner in San Francisco came to $100 and you paid it with a check drawn on your bank, the First National Bank of Boston. Describe the circuit the check would take through banks and district Feds.
8. Who prints currency for whom? How does the currency finally make its way to the thousands of banks operating in the economy?
9. How does a bank's borrowing reserves on the federal funds market differ from borrowing from the Fed? Which interest rates are typically higher?
10. Draw a sequence of figures detailing how an increase in the money supply eventually results in an increase in real GDP.

# ECONOMIC CONSULTANTS

## ECONOMIC RESEARCH AND ANALYSIS BY STUDENTS FOR PROFESSIONALS

Hans Gienepp runs one of the largest real estate agencies in Los Angeles, California. He recognizes, from his own practical experience, that changes in the interest rate and in the rate of inflation have affected his agency's sales. He also knows that the Federal Reserve is a major player in controlling interest rates and the price level, and even though he took a course in economics at college, he doesn't really understand how the Fed can exercise such influence.

He has decided that knowledge is money and has hired Economic Consultants to counsel him and his agents about the economics of the real estate industry. As a new member of the Economic Consultants team, you are assigned the task of preparing the report on the relationship between the Fed, the money system, and the real estate market. Hans specifically asked that your report include the following issues:

**1.** What is the Federal Reserve System, and what is its relationship to the commercial banking system? Is it a government agency?

**2.** How does the Fed influence interest rates and the economy's price level? Can Hans use this information to predict how interest rates and prices will behave in the short run? What kind of data would he need, and how accessible is it?

**3.** What kinds of materials are published by the Fed to address these issues, and how can Hans learn more about them?

You may find the following resources helpful as you prepare your report for Hans:

- ***U.S. Monetary Policy: An Introduction*** (http://www.frbsf.org/publications/federal reserve/monetary/index.html)—The San Francisco Fed publishes this online booklet on how the Federal Reserve conducts monetary policy.
- ***The Structure of the Federal Reserve System*** (http://www.federalreserve.gov/pubs/frseries/frseri.htm)—This online pamphlet, created by the Federal Reserve, provides an introduction to the workings of the Board of Governors, the Federal Open Market Committee, district Federal Reserve banks, and the Board of Directors of the Federal Reserve.
- ***The Federal Reserve System: Purposes and Functions*** (http://www.federalreserve.gov/pf/pf.htm)—The Federal Reserve publishes this detailed description of what the Fed is and how it operates.
- ***The Fed: Our Central Bank*** (http://www.chicagofed.org/publications/index.cfm)—The Chicago Fed publishes this online pamphlet on how the Federal Reserve operates.
- **Fedpoints** (http://www.ny.frb.org/pihome/fedpoint/)—Fedpoints, published by the New York Fed, provides discussion for over 40 aspects of the Fed's operations.
- **Federal Reserve Statistical Releases** (http://www.federalreserve.gov/releases/)—The Federal Reserve releases daily economic statistics on interest rates, among others.
- **Fed Ed on the Web** (http://www.minneapolisfed.org/econed/curric/fededweb.html)—Fed Ed is a directory of educational resources provided by the various district Federal Reserve banks.

# PRACTICE TEST

1. The first true form of money used in the United States was known as
   a. greenbacks.
   b. bank notes.
   c. Continental notes.
   d. Colonial notes.
   e. dollars.

2. When state-chartered banks first came into being, they
   a. all issued the same Continental notes.
   b. were designed to coordinate and control the nation's money supply.
   c. were not permitted to earn profits.
   d. were originally backed by the Federal Reserve System.
   e. issued their own bank notes.

3. The most effective and frequently used tool the Fed has at its disposal is
   a. open market operations.
   b. the discount rate.
   c. the federal funds rate.
   d. the money supply.
   e. the legal reserve requirement.

4. The federal funds market is the market in which
   a. the government can finance its deficit budgets.
   b. banks can borrow from the Fed by paying the discount rate.
   c. district Federal Reserve banks can borrow from the central Federal Reserve bank.
   d. banks lend and borrow from each other for short periods of time.
   e. open market operations occur.

5. All of the following are district banks of the Federal Reserve System except one. Which one?
   a. Dallas
   b. Los Angeles
   c. Richmond
   d. Philadelphia
   e. Kansas City

6. The membership of the Federal Open Market Committee consists of
   a. only the Board of Governors.
   b. only the 12 presidents of the Federal Reserve banks.
   c. the Board of Governors and five Federal Reserve bank presidents.
   d. the chairman of the Federal Reserve System and the 12 Federal Reserve bank presidents.
   e. five members of the Board of Governors and five presidents of Federal Reserve banks.

7. Responsibility for proposing discount rates
   a. does not fall under the jurisdiction of the Federal Reserve System.
   b. rests with the Board of Governors.
   c. rests with the Federal Advisory Committee.
   d. rests with the Federal Reserve banks.
   e. rests with the Federal Open Market Committee.

8. Which of the following actions by the Federal Reserve would lead to an increase in the money supply?
   a. Raising the legal reserve requirement
   b. Raising the discount rate
   c. Selling government securities on the open market
   d. Reducing the number of loans made to member banks
   e. Lowering the legal reserve requirement

9. When there is an increase in the discount rate,
   a. banks have less incentive to borrow from the Fed.
   b. the legal reserve requirement rises by the same percentage.
   c. the money supply increases.
   d. banks must keep on hand a greater percentage of their assets.
   e. interest rates fall.

10. If the Fed's policy is to target the money supply, then
    a. it cannot also control the rate of interest.
    b. the rate of interest is also held constant.
    c. it cannot do so through engaging in open market operations.
    d. it cannot do so through changing the legal reserve requirement.
    e. it cannot do so through changing the discount rate.

# PART 4

## GOVERNMENT AND THE MACROECONOMY

## CHAT ECONOMICS

**T**une into the conversation. It's about *your* course. Just change the names, and it's *your* campus, *your* classroom, *your* professor, *your* classmates, and *you*.

Carrying his lunch tray into the cafeteria dining area, Professor Gottheil spies a number of his students at a table, among them Claudia Preparata, Kim Deal, Charlie Dold, and Jon Kaufman, engaged in what seems to be a rather heated discussion. He joins them and listens.

**CLAUDIA:** So you think the government has no right to raise the tax on cigarettes?
**CHARLIE:** That's right. Why should smokers pay such an exorbitant tax on cigarettes? If they want to smoke, that's their business. If they want to eat candy, that's their business as well. But along comes government, poking its nose into our business. It interferes with our choices. It taxes us only a little on candy, but a heck of a lot on cigarettes. Why? I mean, why should government dictate what we do?
**CLAUDIA:** Are you saying that there are no occasions whatsoever in which society's choices should dominate the individual's?
**CHARLIE:** Stick to the issue of cigarettes. And I say: Yes, keep government out of my business.
**CLAUDIA:** What about speed limits? Should government not impose them? If I choose to drive 100 miles per hour through my neighborhood, should I have the right to do so?
**CHARLIE:** Now that's stupid! Who in their right mind would do that?
**CLAUDIA:** You're quibbling about numbers. Okay, let's try 50 miles per hour. If you think I'm so stupid, ask the police how many tickets they write for over-50-miles-per-hour speeding violations in 30-miles-per-hour zones. And remember, every speed zone and every ticket is government's way of controlling behavior. If you think police should write those tickets, I don't see how you could object to an exorbitant cigarette tax.
**KIM:** Look, you guys are arguing about whether the government has the right to discriminate when taxing. That's only one side of the government-interfering-in-my-life coin. How about its spending? Why should government provide billions in welfare?

**CLAUDIA:** Are you against space exploration?
**KIM:** No, I think it's legitimate. I just don't want government passing my money around to other people. Let them work for it like I do.
**CLAUDIA:** Well, some people don't want government passing their money around for space shots. Heck, I'm one of them!
**KIM:** It's not the same.
**JON:** I think she has a point. It *is* the same. Look, I happen to be in favor of space exploration and unhappy about welfare payments, but that's just my tastes. Different people want different things from government, and they also want government to tax in different ways. I don't think there's anything *intrinsically* right about anyone's taste. I bet we all agree, though, that we want government to do *some* things and want it to tax in *some* way. True, some want government to do more, and some less. But, let's face it, it's not an all-or-nothing proposition, right?
**GOTTHEIL:** I don't think I could have said it better. Almost all of this interesting discussion is normative economics. You've been talking about what government should or shouldn't do. Now, that's OK, as long as we understand that it reflects our own personal judgments and biases. We'll soon get around to discussing what government actually does. That's positive economics. It describes *what is* as distinct from *what ought to be*. Okay, finish up and get ready for class.

Consider the difference between what you think government should do—normative economics—and what government actually does—positive economics. This will help you as you read the next few chapters.

# CHAPTER 13

## CAN GOVERNMENT REALLY STABILIZE THE ECONOMY?

Most physicians will tell you that in cases they consider life threatening, they will advise the patient as a matter of course to get a second opinion. They do so not because they feel uncomfortable with their own diagnosis, but rather because they know we all live in a world of imperfect information. They realize that their understanding of the human body, however expert, is still subject to error.

A second opinion may confirm the first. But not always. If the first physician consulted advises radical surgery and the second suggests that the medical problem will correct itself, what should the patient do? Consult a third? What if the third physician prescribes a different remedy altogether? Should the patient seek a fourth opinion? How many are enough? Do additional opinions really add to the patient's stock of knowledge? Sometimes, the opinion offered reflects the temperament or set of values of the attending physician. Some physicians are known to be aggressive, immediately recommending a maximalist approach, such as strong drugs or surgery. Other physicians belong to a more conservative school and typically advise a number of approaches, from the least interfering to more interventionist treatments, before even thinking about surgery.

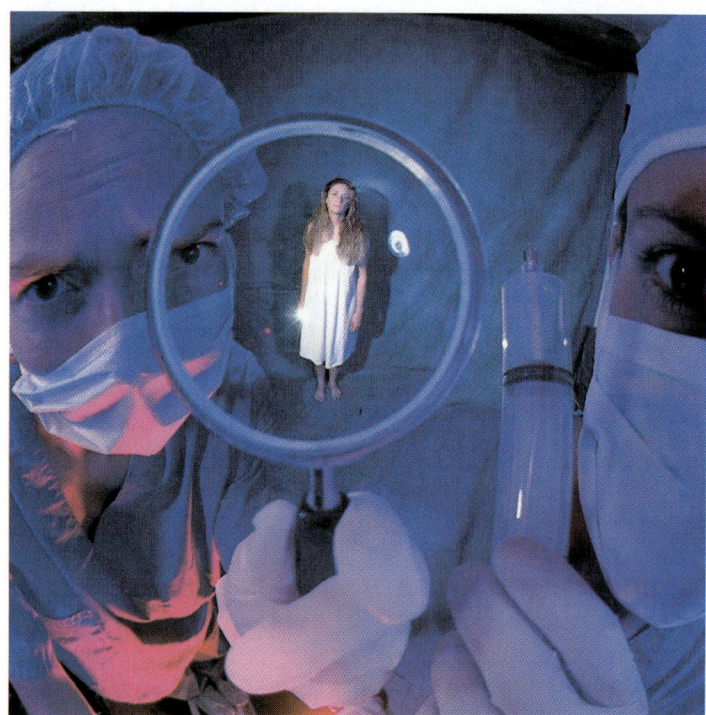

### THIS CHAPTER INTRODUCES YOU TO THE ECONOMIC PRINCIPLES ASSOCIATED WITH:

- THE CLASSICAL SCHOOL OF EMPLOYMENT AND INFLATION
- THE KEYNESIAN SCHOOL OF EMPLOYMENT AND INFLATION
- THE NEO-KEYNESIAN SCHOOL OF EMPLOYMENT AND INFLATION
- THE RATIONAL EXPECTATIONS SCHOOL OF EMPLOYMENT AND INFLATION
- THE SUPPLY-SIDE SCHOOL OF EMPLOYMENT AND INFLATION
- PHILLIPS CURVE ANALYSIS
- AUTOMATIC STABILIZERS

## THE NATURE OF ECONOMIC ADVICE

Economists, too, live in a world of limited information and have a less than perfect understanding of how the economy they study really works. They will readily confess that even after centuries of systematic observation of their subject matter, of data collecting, theory building, empirical testing, and amassing historically relevant material, they still arrive at different and sometimes even highly conflicting conclusions and recommendations.

Their opinions reflect a wide array of temperaments and ideologies. Some schools of economic thinking are interventionist by design. These economists are quick to advocate that government and the Fed, sometimes in massive doses, correct what they believe ails the economy. Other economists, looking at the same situation and reflecting a more conservative ideology, advocate much less interference in the private sector.

It is reasonable to ask whether ideology dictates economic policy, or whether economic policy is the logical derivative of an ideology-free understanding of how the system works. For example, do conservative economists advocate conservative policy because they are ideologically conservative, or do they become ideologically conservative because they see and accept a particular understanding of how the economy behaves? The same question, of course, is asked of interventionist economists. Do their liberal policies simply reflect a preconceived ideology, or is their ideology spun out of a particular understanding of the economy's behavior?

How should we view appointments to the president's Council of Economic Advisers? Economists picked by the more conservative presidents have been known advocates of conservative economic policy. For example, it was not surprising that President George H. W. Bush would choose Stanford's Michael Boskin to head his council, or that President Reagan would choose Harvard's Martin Feldstein and, later, Washington University's Murray Weidenbaum, both known and respected conservatives. Nor was it surprising that President Carter picked the Brookings Institution's Charles Schultze to head his council, and President Clinton picked Berkeley's Laura Tyson and, later, Janet Yellen. The latter economists are known and respected liberals. Isn't that precisely why they were chosen? But how should we read their appointments? Is the expert economic advice that presidents receive from the council, then, rigged from the start?

## WHY DOES THE ECONOMY GENERATE INFLATION AND UNEMPLOYMENT?

Some people, listening to expert opinion on economic policy over the years, are convinced there are more views held by economists than there are economists. Admittedly, there's some truth to that conviction, particularly when the focus of discussion is macroeconomic policy. After all, every macroeconomist sees the economic world through a unique lens. Some views are similar to others, but even among these there are important shades of differences.

Yet just as we have come to know schools of painters—French impressionists, surrealists, cubists, postmodernists—so too do we find schools of thinking on matters of economic policy. Most economists agree that the most demanding macroeconomic issue is, *Why do unemployment and inflation exist, and what should be done about them?*

Over the last century, the ideas on issues such as inflation and unemployment could be classified according to economic schools of thought. Some of these ideas might be considered a radical departure from the mainstream, such as Marxian economics, while others share many things in common.

Classical economics was the dominant school of thought until midway through the Depression of the 1930s, when Keynesian economics became conventional wisdom. Monetarism has been around for quite some time, and although its ideas have had some impact on many economists, it has never succeeded in becoming a leading school of thought. In addition to monetarism, some of the schools that might loosely be viewed as contemporary are the neo-Keynesian, supply-side, and rational expectations schools.

In each school of thought there are ideas that have shortcomings, especially in some of the older theories. Sometimes a particular economic theory does not offer an adequate explanation for a situation. In other cases, there are more fundamental difficulties. As we explore these different schools, it is important to follow the thought process involved and also understand where it tends to break down. You may find some appealing ideas in each school. In fact, many economists find considerable value in at least some ideas from each school of thought.

## THE CLASSICAL SCHOOL

**Classical economics**
The school of thought that emphasizes the natural tendency for an economy to move toward equilibrium at full employment without inflation. It argues against government intervention.

The **classical economics** view of how our economy behaves is this: *If the economy were left on its own—without the interference of government or the Fed—it would move toward an equilibrium rate of growth that would produce, with only minor interruptions, full employment without inflation.*

There's something refreshing about this approach to handling inflation and unemployment, isn't there? After all, what it really argues is that the problems of inflation and unemployment disappear by just doing nothing! That's as simple a policy as you could find.

Moreover, it doesn't make too many demands on our limited skills. Doing nothing is what most of us do well! Or do we? For if it's that simple a matter, why then do we find ourselves continually plagued by inflation and unemployment? Because, the classical economists argue, in spite of all the advice to the contrary, we still insist upon tampering with the machinery.

This hands-off view rests upon two simple propositions about markets: (1) all markets are basically competitive, and (2) as a result, all prices are flexible upward and downward, approaching equilibrium, if they are not already there.

### Why Unemployment?

How do classical economists, then, explain unemployment? In their view, unemployment is only a temporary condition, caused by wage rates climbing above the equilibrium rate. In the long run, however, these above-equilibrium wage rates cannot last. The excess labor supply, the unemployed, competes with those who have jobs, driving the wage rates down to equilibrium and employment levels to full employment. The graphics of the classical view are shown in Exhibit 1.

Suppose the wage rate lies above the $6 equilibrium, say at $10. The supply curve shows that at $10, 16,000 people are willing to work but only 12,000 people actually find employment. The 4,000 who would be willing to work are out of luck. What happens? The 4,000 compete with those already working, driving the wage rate down. As the wage rate falls toward $6, more people get hired.

How many more? At the $6 equilibrium wage rate, 14,000 people are willing to work and 14,000 are hired. That is, *everyone who is willing to work at the equilibrium wage rate will eventually find employment.* Unemployment disappears.

For each of the last several months, review the level of unemployment in the United States and the current consumer price index and employment cost index, which both measure inflation (http://stats.bls.gov/). Next, review interest rates over the same months, as published by the Federal Reserve (http://www.federalreserve.gov/releases/h15/data/m/prime.txt). Does the natural-rate-of-employment hypothesis seem to hold? Has the Federal Reserve raised or lowered interest rates in line with this hypothesis?

If classical economists insist that unemployment is only temporary, why do we find unemployment stubbornly persisting in the real world? Because, they argue, people interfere with the competitive process, preventing wage rates from reaching equilibrium. The interference creates the unemployment.

Who interferes? Labor unions, for example, might use their market power to push wage rates above equilibrium levels, but they can do so only at the expense of employment. In other words, unions might end up being their own worst enemy.

Congress, too, gets into the act. It creates unemployment by imposing minimum wage laws that necessarily cut people out of jobs they otherwise would have taken at less than the minimum wage. The unintended result is painfully clear. The unskilled, teenagers, minorities, and women are big losers. What, then, should government do? The most appropriate countercyclical policy, or **stabilization policy**, in times of unemployment, according to classical economists, is for the *government to do nothing*. The competitive market should be allowed to work its way to equilibrium.

**EXHIBIT 1**

**CLASSICAL DETERMINATION OF UNEMPLOYMENT**

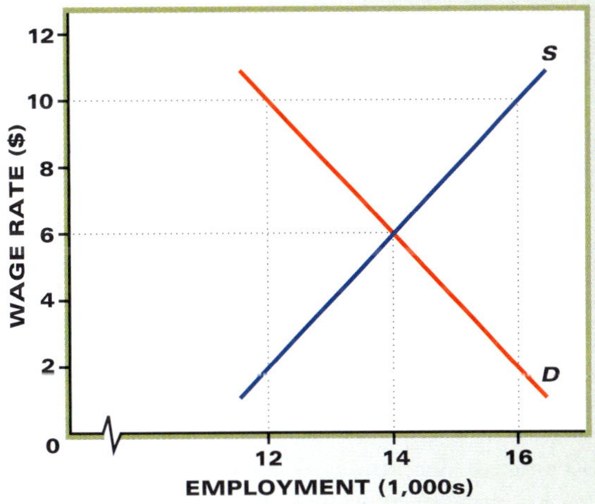

The demand curve for labor and the supply curve of labor create employment for 14,000 workers at a wage rate of $6. If the wage rate is above $6, say at $10, the quantity of labor supplied is 16,000 while the quantity of labor demanded is 12,000, creating an excess labor supply (or unemployment) of 4,000. Competition among the employed and unemployed will force the wage rate to $6, erasing the unemployment.

**Stabilization policy**
The use of countercyclical monetary and fiscal policy by the government and the Fed to stabilize the economy.

## Why Inflation?

How do classical economists explain inflation? Just as unfettered competition in the labor market will always generate full employment, unfettered competition in the market for capital generates the full employment of capital.

With labor and capital busy at work, the economy produces full-employment real GDP, or $Q$, as shown in the quantity theory of money equation:

$$P = \frac{MV}{Q}$$

Recall that $P$ is the price level, $M$ is money supply, $V$ is money velocity, and $Q$ is the quantity of goods and services produced. If resources are fully employed and if money velocity is constant, then the price level, $P$, depends on the quantity of money, $M$.

According to classical economists—in a view shared by monetarists—if the growth rate of $M$ equals the $Q$ growth rate, the price level remains unchanged. *Inflation occurs when the annual rate of growth in the money supply exceeds the annual rate of growth of full-employment real GDP.*

But the growth rate of our money supply, they remind us, is not a matter of chance. The Fed controls the money supply, they argue. The Fed is typically busy with countercyclical monetary policy, which more often than not ends up causing more damage to price-level stability than ensuring that stability. Attempting to curb the growth of money in periods of economic expansion and stimulate monetary growth during periods of recession, the Fed often worsens the problem of inflation.

After all, the Fed can only estimate how much money is needed. These estimates could overshoot or undershoot the appropriate money supply. Inflation is likely to be a serious problem if the Fed has increased the money supply so that the impact of the monetary expansion coincides with an economic climate already near full employment. If the Fed has restricted the money supply so that the impact of the monetary contraction happens when the economy is entering a recession, the downturn is likely to be more intense.

What would classical economists or the modern-day monetarists suggest? The Fed should set the rate of increase in the money supply to be approximately equal to the economy's long-run full-employment rate of growth (i.e., about 3 percent). They would contend that this noninterventionist policy would tend to reduce the intensity of recessions and promote greater price stability. In other words, *the best countercyclical policy is no countercyclical policy.*

## THE KEYNESIAN SCHOOL

**Keynesian economics** rejects the classical economists' basic premise concerning competitive markets and flexible prices and, therefore, rejects the stream of classical policy implications that follow from it. To Keynesians, monopolies and unions tend to be permanent fixtures in our economy, and the prices they create tend to be inflexible, at least downwardly. The classical idea of flexible prices, they argue, is a figment of the imagination.

Exhibit 2 depicts the Keynesian view of how changes in demand for goods affect production.

Note that prices are inflexible at $30. What *is* flexible is the firm's production level. If the demand curve for swimsuits is $D$ in Exhibit 2, the quantity produced is 100,000. If demand falls to $D'$, production falls to 80,000. Price remains fixed at $30, whether production is 100,000 or 80,000. What happens to employment in the swimsuit industry? It depends on production levels. The firms employ more workers at 100,000 than at 80,000.

### Why Unemployment?

This downward inflexibility of price in individual markets is built into any Keynesian macroeconomic analysis. Aggregate demand determines the level of GDP and therefore the level of employment in the economy.

**Keynesian economics**
The school of thought that emphasizes the possibility that an economy can be in equilibrium at less than full employment (or with inflation). It argues that with government intervention, equilibrium at full employment without inflation can be achieved by managing aggregate demand.

**EXHIBIT 2**

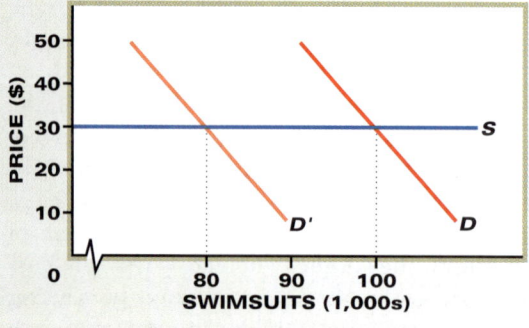

**KEYNESIAN VIEW OF DEMAND AND PRICES IN THE SWIMSUIT MARKET**

The $30 price curve for swimsuits remains unchanged over the firm's production range. If the demand curve the firm faces is $D$, it produces 100,000 swimsuits. If the demand curve falls to $D'$, price remains at $30, but production falls to 80,000.

**THE KEYNESIAN VIEW OF AGGREGATE DEMAND AND AGGREGATE SUPPLY** Panels *a* and *b* in Exhibit 3 summarize the Keynesian view.

Aggregate demand in panel *a* is *AD*. The right-angled aggregate supply depicted by *AS* reflects the early Keynesian

## AGGREGATE DEMAND, GDP, AND EMPLOYMENT

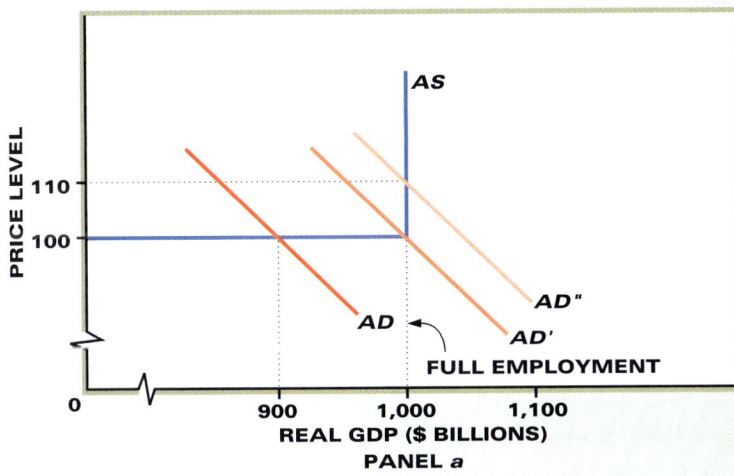

Given the right-angled aggregate supply, AS, if aggregate demand is AD, the economy in panel a is in equilibrium at $900 billion real GDP and price level P = 100. This equilibrium condition is depicted also in panel b. Aggregate expenditure AE = C + I intersects aggregate supply, C + S, at $900 billion *nominal* GDP.

If full-employment real GDP is $1,000 billion, then in both panel a and panel b the economy is in equilibrium at less than full employment. To achieve full employment without inflation, aggregate demand in panel a must shift to the right to AD', and aggregate expenditure in panel b must shift to AE' = (C + I)'.

If aggregate demand instead shifts to AD", real GDP stays at $1,000 billion full-employment level, but the price level rises to P = 110. In panel b, if C + I shifts to (C + I)", an inflationary gap of ab emerges at nominal GDP equilibrium of $1,100 billion, which is equivalent to panel a's $1,000 real GDP at a price level of 110.

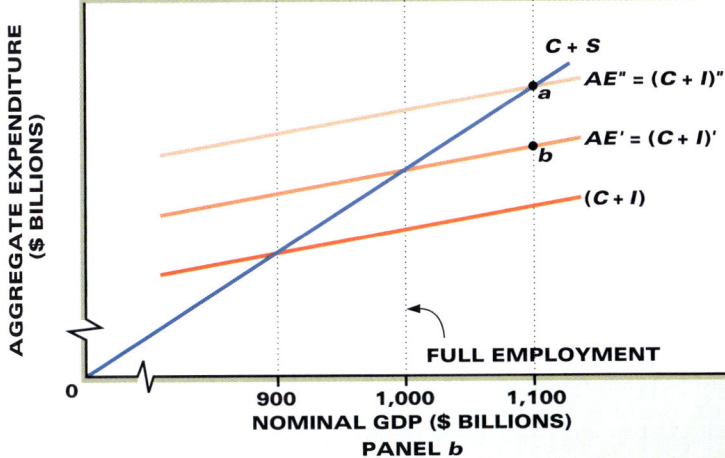

view that the price level does not rise as long as there is any unemployment. Equilibrium real GDP is $900 billion, and the price level is P = 100.

The same equilibrium condition results in the more familiar Keynesian model of panel b. Aggregate demand, AD, in panel a is depicted as aggregate expenditure AE = C + I, and aggregate supply, AS, is depicted as C + S. The economy is at equilibrium where the C + I curve intersects the C + S curve, that is, at $900 billion. In panel b, the price level, which is not explicitly shown, is assumed to be fixed.

Note that in both versions of the Keynesian model, with aggregate demand drawn as AD in panel a and aggregate expenditure as AE in panel b, equilibrium occurs at less than full-employment GDP. If aggregate demand doesn't change, unemployment is chronic.

That's why Keynesians reject the classical view that competitive markets ultimately drive the economy to full-employment equilibrium and dismiss the countercyclical policy of doing nothing—that is, allowing market forces to work—as totally inappropriate.

An economy bogged down at equilibrium with less than full employment is what Keynesians saw in the 1930s, and they believed that depressing condition could recur. Why? To Keynesians, the level of aggregate demand in the 1930s was insufficient to generate full employment. It could happen again.

What, then, should the government do? As we have already shown in earlier chapters dealing with Keynesian fiscal policy, the Keynesians focus on aggregate demand. In the model of Exhibit 3, aggregate demand should be made to shift from $AD$ to $AD'$ (which is the equivalent shift of aggregate expenditure from $AE$ to $AE'$).

**THE FULL EMPLOYMENT ACT OF 1946** In the midst of the 1930s Depression, Keynes was invited to the White House to explain his theory of employment to President Franklin D. Roosevelt. After the meeting, Keynes was asked by fellow economists whether Roosevelt understood the theory. Keynes replied that although the president didn't understand it, the president would "do the right thing" because he seemed ideologically prepared to accept its policy prescriptions.

Keynes was right about Roosevelt's willingness to use the government as a vehicle to shift aggregate demand. The president seemed undisturbed about the new and expanded role that government would play in our economic lives. Although it is unclear whether Roosevelt believed that government spending to create jobs should be a permanent feature in stabilizing the economy, it was clear that he was prepared to create deficit budgets for that purpose. The president called this commitment to full employment a New Deal for the nation.

The economic pain caused by the Depression made the New Deal ideology more digestible for many people. In 1946, Congress officially recognized its role as the economy's stabilizer by enacting the epoch-making Full Employment Act:

> The Congress hereby declares that it is the continuing policy and responsibility of the Federal Government to use all practical means . . . to foster . . . conditions under which there will be afforded useful employment for those able, willing, and seeking to work, and to promote maximum employment, production, and purchasing power.

This act, a somewhat milder version of an earlier bill that had referred to the people's "right" to employment, indicates the extent to which government had become legitimized as an agency of economic stabilization.

## Why Inflation?

What about inflation? When a house is burning, do you suppose firefighters are bothered by a little rainfall? In the 1930s, when unemployment rates climbed as high as 25 percent of the labor force, Keynesians were little troubled by the prospects of inflation.

Look at Exhibit 3, panel $a$, again. Inflation doesn't occur until aggregate demand shifts to the right, beyond $AD'$, say to $AD''$. The economy's real GDP cannot increase beyond \$1,000 billion, but the price level rises from $P = 100$ to $P = 110$. That is, a shift in aggregate demand to the right of $AD'$ causes inflation. The same phenomenon is shown in panel $b$. If aggregate expenditures shift to $AE''$, an inflationary gap, $ab$, results.

In other words, as long as aggregate demand is less than $AD'$ or $AE'$, equilibrium GDP falls short of full employment, and inflation is of no concern. In fact, fiscal policy can push the economy to full-employment real GDP—where the actual unemployment rate equals the natural rate—without worrying at all about inflation. That is to say, *it never occurred to Keynesians that they would ever have to choose between policies to control unemployment and policies to control inflation.*

## The Economics of Fine-Tuning

Countercyclical policy is rather uncomplicated for Keynesian economists. In periods of recession, government creates deficit budgets, and the Fed expands the money supply to increase economic activity and decrease the rate of unemployment. In periods of prosperity, government works with surplus budgets, and the Fed contracts the money supply to slow the economy and decrease the rate of inflation.

During the Kennedy and Johnson administrations in the 1960s, there was broad consensus among members of the Council of Economic Advisers with respect to which stabilization policy to pursue. It was mostly a matter of how well the policy could be pursued. Keynesian economists such as Arthur Okun and Nobel laureates Robert Solow, Paul Samuelson, James Tobin, and Lawrence Klein worked at perfecting techniques of economic stabilization. It was, they insisted, a matter of *fine-tuning* the economy.

But these fine-tuners, and the entire school of Keynesian fine-tuning economists, were ill-prepared for the events that beset the U.S. economy in the 1970s and 1980s: high rates of unemployment concurrent with high rates of inflation.

# THE NEO-KEYNESIAN SCHOOL

That had to be a puzzlement for Keynesian economists. After all, they see unemployment and inflation as either/or problems, not as concurrent ones. Keynesian countercyclical policy is a one-problem-at-a-time policy. How do you manage two at a time when each problem requires diametrically opposite prescriptions? Wouldn't you think the presence of high rates of unemployment *and* high rates of inflation would have undermined the confidence Keynesians placed in their understanding of how the economy works?

A new term, stagflation, came into vogue in the early 1970s to describe this unusual combination of inflation and unemployment. It was an uncomfortable mix of low rates of economic growth, high rates of unemployment, and high inflation.

What had Keynesians gotten wrong in their view of the economy? Why had inflation become a problem long before the economy approached full employment? Was stagflation an exception to the rule, or was the Keynesian view of the economy simply dead wrong?

In retrospect, it appears that the coexistence of inflation and unemployment never was a secret, not even to Keynesians. It was perhaps a situation that caused the Keynesians, still traumatized by the extraordinary unemployment of the Great Depression, to push the issue into the background.

But in 1958, New Zealand economist A. W. Phillips, after studying employment and inflation data for 1861–1957 in Britain, published his findings, which showed the inverse relationship between inflation and unemployment. Historically, inflation rose when unemployment fell. The graphic expression of this inverse relationship became quickly accepted and is known as the **Phillips curve.**

Phillips's findings, illustrated in Exhibit 4, forced Keynesians to modify their Exhibit 3 view of the economy.

**Phillips curve**
A graph showing the inverse relationship between the economy's rate of unemployment and rate of inflation.

## Phillips Curve Trade-Offs

Keynesians began to see the world in terms of Exhibit 4 and faced a dilemma they had not before considered. If government and the Fed succeed in reducing

## EXHIBIT 4

### THE PHILLIPS CURVE

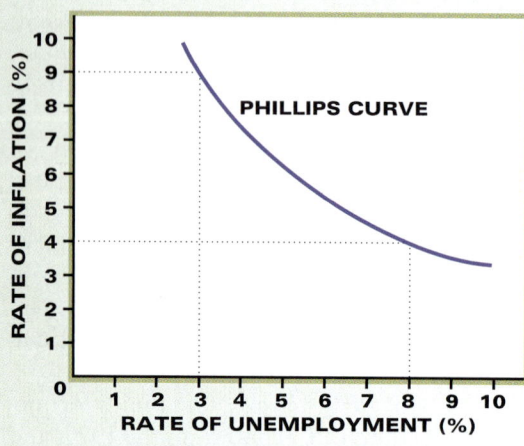

The Phillips curve traces a set of combinations of rates of unemployment and inflation. Because these rates are inversely related, the government cannot use fiscal policy to reduce both at the same time. If government chooses to cut the rate of unemployment, it must accept higher inflation. If it chooses to cut inflation, it must accept higher rates of unemployment.

unemployment, they exacerbate the problem of inflation. One cure creates the other disease. In Exhibit 4, you accept either 8 percent unemployment with 4 percent inflation, or 3 percent unemployment with 9 percent inflation. There is no option of 0 percent unemployment (that is, 0 percent cyclical unemployment) and 0 percent inflation, as the Keynesians had believed.

Incorporating the Phillips curve into the Keynesian aggregate supply curve of Exhibit 3 produces the neo-Keynesian aggregate supply curve of Exhibit 5. This is the aggregate supply curve we have been using throughout most of our study of macroeconomics.

The horizontal and vertical segments of the aggregate supply curve, shown also in Exhibit 3, are separated by an intermediate segment that represents the Phillips curve trade-offs. For example, the actual rate of unemployment at $1,000 billion real GDP is higher than the natural rate. At $1,500 billion, the actual rate equals the natural rate. If fiscal policy is designed to lower the actual rate of unemployment, real GDP increases, but only at higher price levels. If fiscal policy is designed to lower the price level, then if GDP is within the $1,000 billion to $1,500 billion range, it comes at the expense of GDP and employment.

As the Phillips curve of Exhibit 6 shows, the inflation and unemployment rates experienced during the decade of the 1960s seemed to indicate that the economy was operating on the intermediate segment of the aggregate supply curve.

**Neo-Keynesian economics**
The school of thought that emphasizes the possibility that an economy can be in equilibrium at less than full employment with inflation. It argues that by managing aggregate demand, government can achieve the most acceptable combination of unemployment and inflation.

Note the year-to-year changes in rates of unemployment and inflation. The fall in inflation from 1960 to 1961 was matched with a rise in unemployment. The fall in unemployment from 1965 to 1966 was matched with a rise in inflation. As you see, the 1960s made up a well-defined Phillips curve.

But putting the statistical evidence aside, how do proponents of **neo-Keynesian economics** explain the Phillips curve? Why should the econ-

## EXHIBIT 5

### THE NEO-KEYNESIAN AGGREGATE SUPPLY CURVE

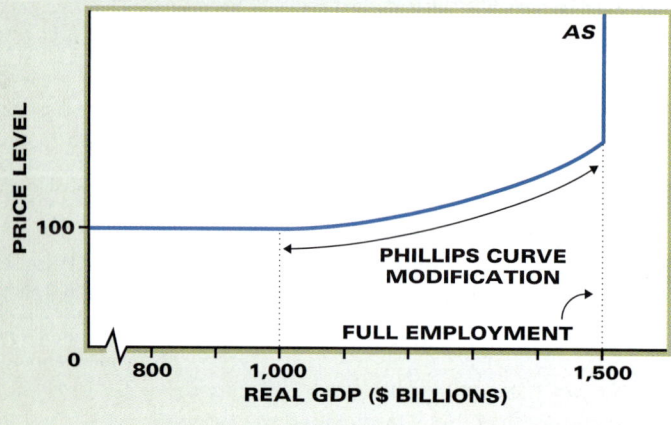

The Phillips curve reflects the intermediate, upward-sloping segment of the Keynesian aggregate supply curve of Exhibit 3. It shows that increases in real GDP create pressures on the price level before reaching full-employment real GDP.

omy behave this way? Is the inverse relationship between rates of unemployment and rates of inflation *causal*? That is to say, does a fall in the unemployment rate *cause* the rate of inflation to increase? Does a rise in the rate of inflation *cause* the rate of unemployment to decrease?

The neo-Keynesian answer is yes. The market power that unions, monopolies, and particular resource suppliers exercise in their respective markets creates the Phillips curve.

**CHECK YOUR UNDERSTANDING**

What factors create the Phillips curve?

**THE INFLUENCE OF UNIONS** Consider first the behavior of workers, particularly those organized in unions. Let's suppose the growth rate of real GDP increases from 1.5 to 3.7 percent, but the economy is still short of full employment. How do firms and workers in that economic growth environment react?

With the economy growing faster, firms attempt to increase production by hiring more workers. Unemployment rates fall. How do workers react to falling unemployment rates? Feeling somewhat more secure about their jobs, they shift their focus away from job protection, which made sense when unemployment was high, to wage demands. The firms respond positively to their higher wage demands. Why not? With the economy growing more rapidly, their main concern is retaining their workers. After all, other firms are expanding production as well and are competing aggressively for more workers by raising wage rates.

**CHECK YOUR UNDERSTANDING**

Why does a fall in the rate of unemployment cause the rate of inflation to rise?

Firms' resistance to strong wage pressure weakens for still another reason. During periods of rapid economic growth, they find it easier to pass along higher wage rates in the form of higher prices without having to worry about losing markets. In other words, a decline in the rate of unemployment *causes* higher rates of inflation.

What happens during a recession? When growth rates of GDP fall, say, from 3.7 percent to −1.5 percent, the rate of unemployment rises. Many workers are now more concerned about protecting their jobs than protecting their wage rates, so they accept smaller wage increases.

They're no dummies. They know that when the economy is sluggish, many firms have difficulty keeping production going at the same levels. If workers insist on high wage increases, then the high-wage-paying firms become disadvantaged in competition. Everybody loses. Workers must choose, then, between jobs and wage rates.

When workers accept smaller wage rate increases, they may make it possible for firms to moderate price increases. That is, higher rates of unemployment that accompany declining GDP may slow the economy's rate of inflation.

**THE INFLUENCE OF SUPPLY SHOCKS** Unusual events may sometimes trigger a resource supply shock that jolts the economy from one position on the Phillips curve to another. For example, in October 1973 OPEC—the petroleum exporting countries—drastically cut the supply of oil to the rest of the world. The result was a tripling of oil prices by January 1974. (The tight control

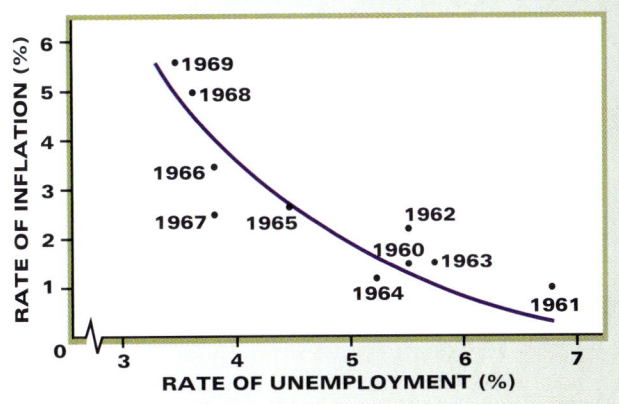

**THE PHILLIPS CURVE DURING THE 1960s**

The rates of unemployment and inflation in the 1960s map out a well-behaved Phillips curve. Stabilization policy during the 1960s centered on the trade-offs reflected in the Phillips curve.

on supply by OPEC continued throughout the 1970s, tripling the price from $6 a barrel to $18 a barrel by 1979, and almost doubling it again to $34 a barrel in 1982.) The effect on the economic performance of the rest of the world from this oil price increase was immediate and devastating. Many economists attribute the prolonged worldwide stagflation of the 1970s to the supply shock caused by OPEC. The cost of producing and delivering almost all goods and services in the oil-importing economies soared, shifting their aggregate supply curves to the left. The outcome: Price levels increased and real GDP decreased.

## The Phillips Curve and Countercyclical Policy

What do Keynesians do now? Is it back to the drawing board? The countercyclical monetary and fiscal policies that were supposed to produce full employment without inflation don't work in economies characterized by the Phillips curve. How do you avoid raising the rate of inflation when pursuing a countercyclical policy aimed at reducing the rate of unemployment during recession?

**WAGE AND PRICE CONTROL** One solution is to combine wage and price controls with a Keynesian-style job-creating policy. Something like muzzling a barking dog—the dog *wants* to bark, but can't.

That's what President Nixon tried in 1971. Facing high rates of inflation caused by the Vietnam War, he imposed wage and price controls. By prohibiting any increase in either prices or wages for 90 days, he hoped that workers and industry would come to accept more stable prices. At the same time, along with Congress and the Fed, he used monetary and fiscal policies to reduce the economy's unemployment rate.

Many economists were surprised by President Nixon's wage and price controls. Why was a conservative Republican adopting this market-interventionist stabilization policy? After all, controls distort free market signals and create market inefficiencies. Perhaps the president saw the issue as a trade-off between efficiency and stabilization, and chose stabilization.

Did Nixon's wage and price controls work? Not really. They seemed to work during the control period. But when the controls were finally lifted, inflation reappeared. That is to say, the hiatus had no impact on changing the behavior of workers or businesses. President Carter's flirtation with wage and price controls in the late 1970s was far less serious. He asked only for voluntary compliance with wage and price guidelines. His strategy was to slow inflation by recommending that firms cap their price increases to 0.5 percent below the inflation rate of the previous year. Workers were asked to limit wage demands to 7 percent. Such a stabilization policy relies heavily on worker and industry goodwill and common sense. Neither are very powerful weapons. In fact, both inflation and unemployment rates remained relatively high during most of President Carter's years in the White House.

## The Humphrey-Hawkins Act of 1978

Many neo-Keynesian economists saw the futility of trying to hammer both inflation and unemployment to zero. If we can't engineer full employment without inflation, then we must learn to live with *some* inflation and *some* unemployment (unemployment above the natural rate). That is, reality forced economists to accept the new stabilization policy of choosing the *most livable point on the Phillips curve*.

To Congress, the most livable point on the Phillips curve was spelled out in its 1978 enactment of the Full Employment and Balanced Growth Act, commonly referred to as the Humphrey-Hawkins Act. This act, a modified version of Congress's 1946 Full Employment Act, initially identified a 4 percent rate of unemployment and a 3 percent rate of inflation as acceptable and reasonable targets. But few economists took it seriously. Why? Because, for the decades of the 1970s and 1980s, these target rates proved to be hopelessly unrealistic.

Almost as soon as neo-Keynesians accepted the Phillips curve as the starting point of stabilization policy, they confronted a new problem. They discovered that the rates of inflation and unemployment in the 1970s and early 1980s seemed to have run completely amok. By no stretch of the imagination could the 1970s and early 1980s data be fitted into the Phillips curve of Exhibit 6, or into any downward-sloping Phillips curve for that matter. Look at Exhibit 7.

How do you draw a Phillips curve in Exhibit 7? It seems at first glance that the scatter of annual inflation and unemployment rates for the 1970s and 1980s has little in common with the well-behaved Phillips curve of the 1960s. What's left, then, of neo-Keynesian Phillips curve analysis if the data contradict the Phillips curve? Was the 1960s fit simply an accident?

## Long-Run Phillips Curves

Neo-Keynesians took a hard look at the 1970s and 1980s scatter of inflation and unemployment rates and found a Phillips curve hidden among them. Only what they discovered was not a single Phillips curve, but *a set of Phillips curves*. The neo-Keynesian idea that an economy can choose only between a limited set of inflation and unemployment options still holds, except that the set of options shifts over time. Exhibit 8 illustrates the point.

What had been a set of scatter points in Exhibit 7 is now points in a set of Phillips curves. What explains the shift from one Phillips curve to another? The principal cause of the shift is the follow-up reaction of workers and firms to the price increases they initially triggered.

**CHECK YOUR UNDERSTANDING**

What causes the Phillips curve to shift?

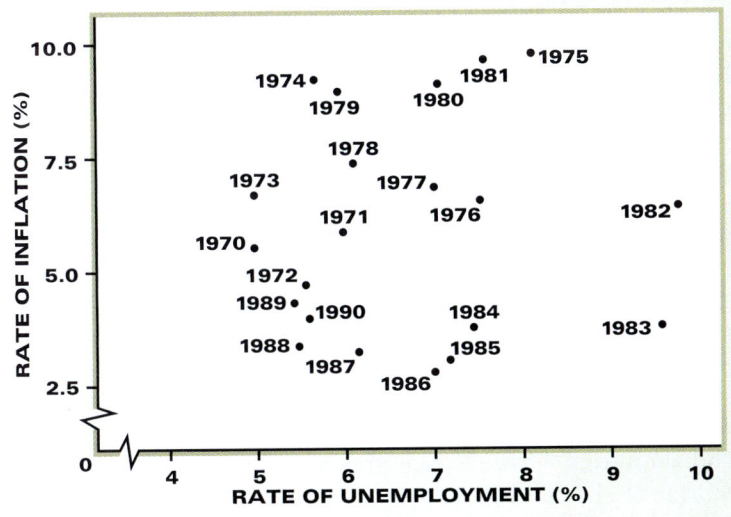

**RATES OF INFLATION AND UNEMPLOYMENT: 1970–90**

During the 1970s and 1980s, the scatter of points depicting combinations of inflation and unemployment rates seems to bear no resemblance to the well-defined Phillips curve of the 1960s, shown in Exhibit 6.

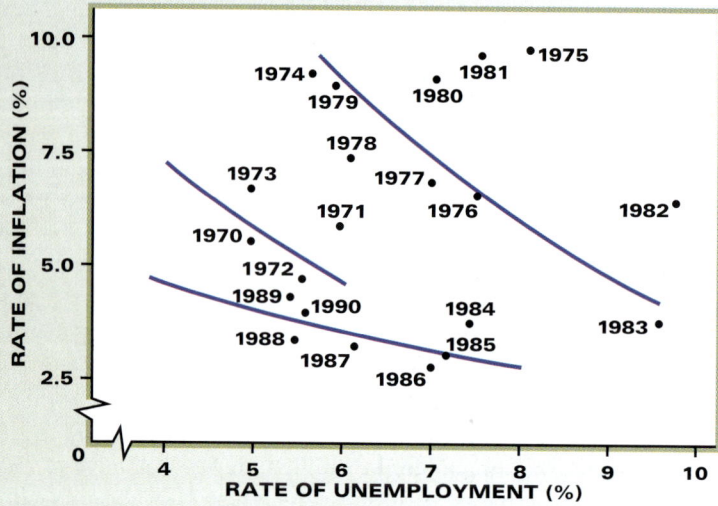

**SHIFTING PHILLIPS CURVES**

Neo-Keynesians revised their understanding of how people react to government policy to explain why the data of the 1970s and 1980s can be fitted into a *set* of Phillips curves.

The effect of the follow-up reaction is illustrated in Exhibit 9. Suppose the economy in Exhibit 9 is at point *A*, with an unemployment rate of 6 percent and an inflation rate of 4 percent. The government regards 6 percent unemployment as unacceptable. What can it do? If it insists on reducing the rate of unemployment to 4 percent, it must accept an increase in the rate of inflation to 6 percent, shown at point *B* on the Phillips curve *PC*.

But the economy doesn't stay at *B* for long. Why? Because workers learn that their real wages have been eroded by the higher prices they now pay for goods and services. Should they be upset? Wouldn't you be? How do they recover lost ground? By bargaining for wages high enough to make up what they lost through increased inflation.

Typically, they succeed. Why? Because firms enjoying higher prices and higher profit worry about losing workers to other firms that are also expanding production. Under these conditions, they are inclined to concede to wage demands.

But the workers' success is only short-lived. The higher wages raise production costs and lower profits. Production is cut back and workers are laid off. In other words, in the long run the higher rate of inflation causes the unemployment rate to climb again to, say, 6 percent, point *C* in Exhibit 9.

Good intentions notwithstanding, what has government accomplished by trying to lower the unemployment rate from 6 to 4 percent? The economy shifts from *A* on Phillips curve *PC* to *C* on Phillips curve *PC'*. The unemployment rate is back to 6 percent, but the rate of inflation stays at 6 percent.

Frustrated, the government may try again to cut the rate of unemployment to 4 percent by even stronger fiscal policy. Will it work? As we saw, only in the short run. Movement along Phillips curve *PC'* from 6 percent to 4 percent unemployment raises the rate of inflation from 6 to 8 percent, that is, from *C* to *D*.

But workers will not sit idly by. Having learned their painful lesson earlier, they know that the increase to 8 percent inflation reduces their real wages. They again press to recover lost ground. They succeed in raising their wages, but firms suffering the higher costs cut production. The rate of unemployment rises again, creating a new position E on Phillips curve PC″.

If the government insists on reducing the rate of unemployment to 4 percent, the rate of inflation will continue to increase while the rate of unemployment stays at 6 percent. This scenario is illustrated in the repeated shifting to the right of the Phillips curve shown in Exhibit 9. That is to say, *in the long run the rate of unemployment remains unchanged in spite of government stabilization policy, but the dynamics of the economic activity that the government sets in motion generates accelerating rates of inflation.* The long-run Phillips curve is effectively vertical.

That's pretty disheartening, isn't it? These short-run employment policy victories disappear in the long run, producing in their wake accel-

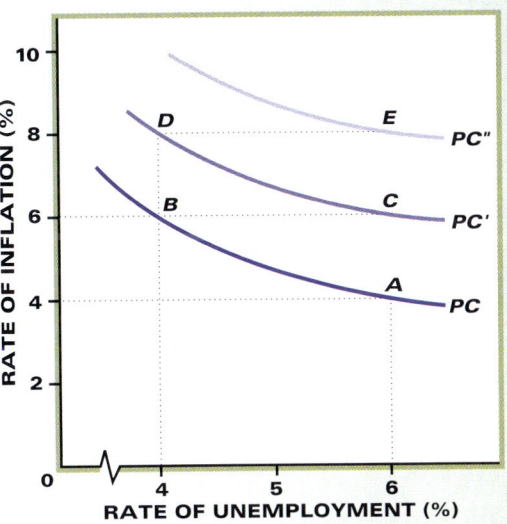

**SHIFTING PHILLIPS CURVES**

Beginning at point A on the Phillips curve PC, government policy cuts the rate of unemployment from 6 percent to 4 percent, which causes the rate of inflation to rise from 4 percent to 6 percent. This result is shown as a movement from point A to point B along the Phillips curve PC.

The inflation raises costs and lowers profit, causing firms to cut production and employment, shown as a new combination point C (the rate of unemployment is again 6 percent, while inflation remains at 6 percent). Point C lies on the new Phillips curve PC′.

Frustrated, the government tries to restore the 4 percent rate of unemployment, causing the economy to move first to point D on PC′, then to E on PC″, where the rate of unemployment is back to 6 percent but the rate of inflation has increased to 8 percent. As long as government tries to cut the rate of unemployment below 6 percent, the rate of unemployment will eventually return to 9 percent, but the rate of inflation will increase.

erating inflation. The policy implications are clear. Neo-Keynesians show the futility of trying to reduce rates of unemployment and inflation simultaneously. All that's left of stabilization policy is choosing a set of monetary and fiscal policies that achieve a desired position on the Phillips curve. Unless workers, industry, and government resist temptations to improve upon it, any attempt to manipulate a better outcome invites inflationary disaster.

## THE RATIONAL EXPECTATIONS SCHOOL

The 1970s and early 1980s world of stagflation basically broke the Keynesian consensus of the macroeconomic world. Shortly after President Nixon quipped, "We are all Keynesians," many young macroeconomists saw the hollowness of this claim when they looked at the decade of exceptionally high inflation and high unemployment.

Prior to the Nixon era, the only notable conservative voices in macroeconomics were those of the classical economists from an earlier era, and monetarists. As we noted earlier, conservatives believe that the government should abstain from activist fiscal and monetary policies. Their policy prescription is clear and simple: Set money supply growth equal to the economy's real growth rate. That's it! But classical economics and monetarism had a decidedly small presence back in the 1970s.

# THEORETICAL PERSPECTIVE

## THE POWER OF AN IDEA: THE 6 PERCENT NATURAL RATE OF UNEMPLOYMENT

**Some ideas, at least for some period of time, appear to be as indestructible as they seem to be obvious and totally defensible.** The idea that the world was flat has to be one of them. Another, perhaps, was the idea of divine monarchy. The social sciences as well as the natural sciences are replete with such "laws" or "indisputable facts of life" that were, at one time or another, beyond reasonable doubt.

Among the more recent of the economic "facts of life"—*circa* the 1980s and early 1990s—was an idea associated with the rate of unemployment. The idea that there exists in the United States a natural rate of unemployment of approximately 6 percent—give or take a half percent—was universally accepted by economists as a more or less indisputable, inarguable "fact of life." The natural rate is the lowest rate of unemployment that can be sustained in an economy without triggering inflationary pressures. To question that specific rate was to question the body of intellectual thought and research that went into the discovery of that rate, and that was a tall order!

But why 6 percent? Why not 4 or 8? After all, most economists during the 1970s accepted the idea of a natural rate, but pegged it at 4 percent. In less than a decade, that rate was considered to be as defensible as a flat earth. Among the believers in this 6 percent "fact of life" was Stanford economist Paul Krugman, a highly regarded liberal economist, who explained that the natural rate had risen during the 1980s as a result of costly government social programs that reduced incentives among the poor to get off welfare and other assistance and return to the workforce. These disincentives, he argued, coupled with the increased importance of education in getting a good job, led inevitably to the increase in long-term unemployment. The rate drift to 6 percent was the consequence.

Not only did most academic economists during the 1980s and early 1990s buy into this explanation and the 6 percent idea, but the 6 percent rate, with its academic imprimatur, also became the benchmark for both Federal Reserve and government policies. The 1978 Humphrey-Hawkins Act had mandated Congress to achieve a no-higher-than-4-percent rate of unemployment. But how could Congress be expected to act on that mandate when the academic profession—liberal and conservative wings alike—was telling Congress that such a mandated goal was impossible to achieve without creating troublesome inflation? Congress, almost without debate, accepted the 6 percent barrier and legislated employment policy accordingly. The Federal Reserve, too, accepted the rate without reservation. It based its interest rate decisions on the assumption that the nation's unemployment rate could not be reduced much below 6 percent without igniting inflation.

**ALL THE KING'S HORSES CAN'T PUT 6% TOGETHER AGAIN.**

And then it happened. During the years 1995–2000, the 6 percent natural rate "fact of life" became anything but a fact of life. The rate of unemployment in the United States fell below the once-thought-impossible 4 percent, and instead of the falling rate triggering troublesome inflation as it was supposed to do, the rate of inflation fell as well.

What about the naturalness of the 6 percent natural rate? Despite the evidence to the contrary, some economists still kept the faith. Others were less sure about it. Fed Chairman Alan Greenspan confessed at one time that he just didn't know what was going on. In economics, as in many of the other sciences, "laws" and "indisputable facts of life" may turn out to be less of a law and more disputable than we'd like to believe.

However, when the economy seemed to be stuck in the rut of stagflation and Keynesians no longer seemed to have all the answers, new and challenging conservative ideas quickly emerged. By far the most important set of conservative ideas to blossom and to draw many young adherents was **rational expectations.**

Rational-expectations economists challenge the neo-Keynesian view that stabilization policy can have some short-run success, even if it disappears in the long run. They offer a different interpretation of how workers and industry respond to government's fiscal policy. The implications of their view are striking: *There is absolutely nothing government can do, even in the short run, to reduce the economy's unemployment rate.* Compare this view of government's role in the economy to the view held by classical economists. Ends up being pretty much the same, doesn't it? Both advocate a hands-off policy. That's not quite the view held by Keynesians or even neo-Keynesians, is it? But why do rational expectations economists believe there is nothing government can do to alleviate unemployment in the short or long run?

### Anticipation of Fiscal Policy Undermines the Policy

They start with a view, quite different from the neo-Keynesian one, of how people react to the inflationary effects of government job-creating fiscal policy. Rational expectations economists believe that workers are not only rational but also smart enough to learn from experience how best to overcome the effects of the government's fiscal policy. Workers understand that a Phillips curve exists even if they don't know what a Phillips curve is. Their experience tells them that the government's attempt to lower rates of unemployment is linked to higher rates of inflation. They therefore not only respond to the past inflation that has eroded real wages, but also, expecting rates of inflation to increase again because of government policy, incorporate that expectation into their future wage demands. That is, their wage demands include anticipated inflation.

This anticipating factor transforms Exhibit 9 into Exhibit 10.

Suppose the economy is at *A,* where the unemployment rate is 6 percent and the rate of inflation is 4 percent. Workers demand a 4 percent wage increase to keep their real wages from eroding.

Suppose government tries to cut unemployment to 4 percent. The economy moves along the Phillips curve to *B.* Inflation is at 6 percent. Now trouble begins. Workers catch on quickly. They don't just try to make up for past inflation losses but try to *prevent a repeat* of the short-run erosion of real wages.

How do they do that? Because they have seen inflation increase from 4 to 6 percent, they *expect it will continue to increase at that rate.* After all, government's announced policy is to drive unemployment to 4 percent, and workers, being rational, know from

> **Rational expectations**
> The school of thought that emphasizes the impossibility of government reducing the economy's rate of unemployment by managing aggregate demand. It argues that because people anticipate the consequences of announced government policy and incorporate these anticipated consequences into their present decision making, they end up undermining the policy.

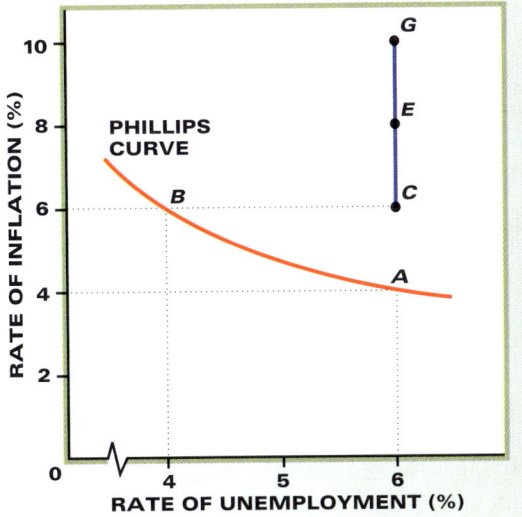

**RATIONAL EXPECTATIONS MODEL**

Correctly anticipating the increase in the rate of inflation that is generated by the government's policy to cut the rate of unemployment, workers make wage demands that cover the anticipated inflation, thereby erasing any short-run gains in profit that firms would have made. As a result, the unemployment rate remains unchanged, but the rate of inflation increases. If the government keeps trying to cut the rate of unemployment, the rate of inflation keeps increasing along the vertical path of the Phillips curve.

# APPLIED PERSPECTIVE

## DOES THE PHILLIPS CURVE *REALLY* EXIST?

**For more than 25 years, says Berkeley professor Bradford DeLong, economists' forecasts have been based on the idea that if unemployment falls below the natural rate of unemployment, inflation will start to rise.** And inflation will keep on rising until unemployment climbs back up to or above its "natural rate."

The theoretical underpinning to this idea was the Phillips curve. But since the mid-1990s, DeLong notes, economists have become a lot less certain about that Phillips curve and a lot less useful as forecasters. As well, their forecasts of economic growth, unemployment, and inflation have become less projections based on historical patterns and more pure guesses based on gut feeling about when, how, and whether the Phillips curve will return.

DeLong observes that during the 1990–92 recession, the Phillips curve looked very healthy. The unemployment rate fell to a low of 5.3 percent in 1989 and inflation, which averaged 2.4 percent per year over 1984–87, rose to 4.1 percent per year and kept rising into the early 1990s. The Phillips curve *seemed* alive and well.

That's why economists at the Federal Reserve and in the Clinton administration, watching unemployment rates drop in the early 1990s, bit their fingernails in anticipation of the return of rising inflation. Yet no inflation followed. By 1996 the unemployment rate was as low as it had ever been in the 1980s and the inflation rate fell to less than 2 percent. By 1999, unemployment was 4.2 percent—well below anyone's previous estimate of the natural rate, yet inflation was even lower and falling. So economists had to think the unthinkable. They knew the natural rate of unemployment had fallen, but how far was down?

At some primal level, all economists still believe in something like the Phillips curve. All believe that unemployment will fall and inflation will rise if demand expands faster than the economy's long-run productive capacity. It was just that the natural rate of unemployment—this signal that the long run has arrived—had fallen mysteriously far and mysteriously fast.

Perhaps the surprising thing to Professor DeLong is not that the Phillips curve–based forecasts of inflation have gone awry in the past half decade but that the complicated economic processes determining changes in inflation could have been summarized for so long by such a simple relationship as the Phillips curve. One thing seemed clear to him: The simple theory of the relation between inflation and unemployment that economists have peddled for a quarter century no longer works; if economists are to be of any use, they need to come up with a better—and in all likelihood more sophisticated—approach to understanding why inflation rises.

**WHEN UNEMPLOYMENT GOES DOWN, MUST INFLATION GO UP?**

experience that such a policy causes inflation. So, anticipating that their real wage will fall because of the government's policy, they ask not for 6 but for 8 percent. That is, they try to stay one step ahead of losing out, to preempt any short-run loss.

But firms, too, are rational and incorporate expectations into their decision making. They, too, learn to read the effects of government's fiscal policy on inflation. They also know that workers' demands will *instantaneously* eliminate the short-run price-cost gap, cutting out that source of short-run profit. Losing the incentive to expand production, they don't hire more workers. The unemployment rate, therefore, remains unchanged—frustrating the government's efforts—while the rate of inflation keeps increasing at the expected rate.

This scenario is played out in Exhibit 10. The economy moves from *B* to *C;* then from *C* directly to *E;* from *E* directly to *G;* and so on. Look at the shape of the Phillips curve these points map out. It becomes a vertical line at 6 percent unemployment.

**POLICY GOAL: NAIRU** What then becomes the policy goal of rational-expectations economists? It is to discover the **non-accelerating inflation rate of unemployment (NAIRU)** and make sure that the actual unemployment rate in the economy doesn't fall below it. As we already noted, a lower rate—say, a rate less than 6 percent in Exhibit 10—will trigger accelerating inflation. There's nothing complicated about the idea of NAIRU. It is simply the familiar natural rate of unemployment—structural and frictional unemployment—that is consistent with a non-increasing rate of inflation.

**Non-accelerating inflation rate of unemployment (NAIRU)**
Any rate equal to or higher than this rate will not cause the inflation rate to increase. Any rate lower than this rate will cause the inflation rate to increase.

## Anticipation of Monetary Policy Undermines the Policy

Suppose the Fed, worried about a prolonged recession, decides to increase GDP and employment by increasing the money supply. To do this, it announces a cut in its discount rate. How do people react? Past experience tells them that the Fed's expansionary policy typically is linked to higher rates of inflation. Incorporating that expectation into their plans, workers demand wages that will cover the anticipated inflation. Firms, expecting the rise in inflation, raise their own prices. Banks react to the expected inflation by raising interest rates. The result? Aggregate demand falls because consumer spending declines, especially for big-ticket items that normally involve some borrowing, and because business investment spending declines due to higher interest rates charged by banks.

Firms, facing decreasing aggregate demand, cut back production; anticipating inflation, they raise prices, which feeds inflation and further depresses the demand for goods and services. As a result, the rate of unemployment does not fall. This anticipation of the effects of the Fed's policy on the economy ends up undermining the Fed's ability to stabilize prices.

## A New Wrinkle to the Phillips Curve

Until at least the mid-1990s, NAIRU became an accepted fact of life for most mainstream economists, from neo-Keynesians to rational-expectations theorists. They believed that it's something we just have to live with. The only debate on the issue was the actual NAIRU rate. The consensus was that, at least for the United States, the rate approximated 6 percent, give or take a half point. The feeling was that any rate below 6 percent would generate inflationary havoc in the economy. The Fed fixed on that rate and built its monetary policy around it. Even Alan Blinder, the most liberal voice at the Fed—vice chairman from 1994–96—accepted the Fed's 6 percent position. Most policy advisers on the Clinton team bought into that rate as well.

With all this conventional wisdom shoring up the 6 percent NAIRU rate, it was more than a surprise—*shell shock* may be a better term—when empirical data on rates of inflation and unemployment for the mid- and late 1990s came in. The data not only undermined the validity of the 6 percent rate, but also seemed to undermine the idea of NAIRU itself.

What the 1990s data showed was that during that high-economic-performance decade, *both the economy's rate of unemployment and rate of inflation fell.* Look at Exhibit 11.

This was simply not supposed to happen. If the rate of unemployment falls from 5.4 percent in 1996 to 4.2 percent in 1999, how can the rate of inflation fall from

## EXHIBIT 11

### U.S. RATES OF UNEMPLOYMENT AND INFLATION: 1992–99

| YEAR | RATE OF UNEMPLOYMENT | RATE OF INFLATION |
|---|---|---|
| 1992 | 7.5 | 2.0 |
| 1993 | 6.9 | 2.5 |
| 1994 | 6.1 | 2.0 |
| 1995 | 5.6 | 2.0 |
| 1996 | 5.4 | 1.8 |
| 1997 | 4.9 | 1.7 |
| 1998 | 4.5 | 1.2 |
| 1999 | 4.2 | 1.5 |

**Source:** Council of Economic Advisers, *Economic Report of the President* (Washington, D.C.: U.S. Government Printing Office, 2000).

1.8 percent to 1.5 percent? Why didn't the cause-and-effect patterns of economic activity that the rational-expectations people predicted would develop materialize? What went wrong?

One explanation that made sense to some economists was that the world had changed rather dramatically during the decade, nullifying the expected results of the NAIRU rate. Globalization, technological innovation—especially the diffusion of computer technology—growing free international trade, growth in the use of electronic money, and the massive applications of the information-and-knowledge industries all contributed to a burst of productivity growth that absorbed inflationary pressures and allowed rates of employment to increase without fostering inflation.

But if these events could occur in the 1990s to explain why the 6 percent NAIRU was no longer applicable, what's to prevent other events in the future from making NAIRU *any* rate? If nothing, then what validity is there to NAIRU and the Phillips curve?

## SUPPLY-SIDE ECONOMICS

Keynesian countercyclical policy focused on what the government can or cannot do to change aggregate demand. Changes in aggregate demand were the principal vehicle for changing real GDP and employment. Phillips curve analysis—by neo-Keynesians and rational-expectations economists—took issue with the simplicity of the Keynesian prescriptions, but they too focused on what government spending can or cannot do.

An altogether different view on stabilization policy emerged in the early 1980s. The analytic focus of **supply-side economics** shifted from aggregate demand to aggregate supply. The idea was that changes in real GDP can best be achieved by changing the environment that suppliers live in. To supply-siders, whatever makes the suppliers happy tends to make the economy better.

What makes suppliers happy? The supply-side economists' checklist includes lower taxes, less government regulation, less government spending, and less union power in wage determination. In short, everything that promotes profit. It was this view that attracted President Reagan to supply-side economics. He believed, as supply-siders do, that not only suppliers benefit when these checklist items are addressed, but also everyone else whose job depends upon successful businesses. During the 1980s, supply-side policy became popularized as "Reaganomics." The idea was that it was possible to lower rates of inflation along with rates of unemployment— an old Keynesian idea—but by working on the supply side of the economy.

**Supply-side economics**
The school of thought that emphasizes the possibility of achieving full employment without inflation. It argues that through tax reductions, spending cuts, and deregulation, government creates the proper incentives for the private sector to increase aggregate supply.

# THEORETICAL PERSPECTIVE

## AN EXCHANGE BETWEEN A KEYNESIAN AND A RATIONAL EXPECTATIONS (NEW CLASSICAL) ECONOMIST

Professor Paul Samuelson, Nobel laureate in Economics, remains, in his words, an "eclectic Keynesian"; he thinks the government can play an important role in guiding the economy. He attacks the new breed of economic conservatives led by Robert Lucas, Thomas Sargent, and Robert Barro. Their New Classical school argues that governments can do no economic good.

Mr. Barro made his name arguing the case that bigger government deficits reduce private sector spending by an exactly offsetting amount. Why? Because people will save money in order to meet the expected increase in their descendants' tax liabilities. "I burst out laughing when one of the ablest young macroeconomists put this to me," says Mr. Samuelson. He asked whether the young conservative really believed such nonsense. "Indeed I do," was the answer, "and so do all the good economists under 40." "I felt old," says Mr. Samuelson; "The doubt kept asserting itself that maybe in this generation the loss of practical knowledge might be permanent and irreversible." Yet Mr. Samuelson does not dismiss all such theories. Take the distinction between anticipated and unanticipated changes in policy—stressed in work by Messrs. Lucas and Sargent. Modern Keynesians, including Mr. Samuelson, have embraced the idea, adapting it to their own purposes. By such means, the conservatives have pulled all of economics to the right.

PAUL SAMUELSON: THE NORTHERN STAR IN THE SKY OF STELLAR ECONOMISTS.

### MORE ON THE NET

Learn more about Paul Samuelson (http://www.nobel.se/economics/laureates/1970/index.html) and Robert Lucas (http://www.nobel.se/economics/laureates/1995/index.html), both Nobel laureates.

**Source:** Excerpted from "A New Authorised Version for Tomorrow's Policy-Makers," *The Economist*, March 14, 1987. © 1987 The Economist Newspaper Group, Inc. Further reproduction prohibited. http://www.economist.com

## Lower Tax Rates

Supply-side economists emphasize the importance of reducing tax rates. They accept the Keynesian idea that lower tax rates will increase consumer demand, but they believe a more important consequence is the added incentive it provides suppliers. For example, lower corporate tax rates increase after-tax profit, which induces suppliers to increase aggregate supply. Lower income tax rates encourage more people to work longer, adding as well to aggregate supply.

Their argument was carried a step further by economist Arthur Laffer, who insisted that high tax rates not only check the expansion of real GDP and employment, but end up producing less tax revenues. His explanation for this unusual outcome is illustrated in Exhibit 12.

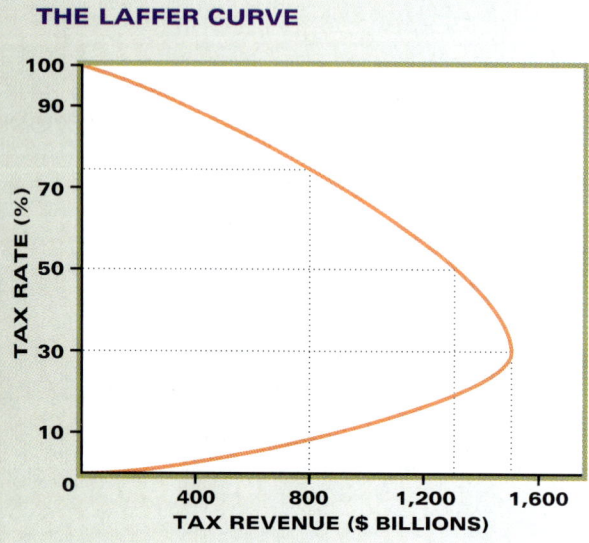

**THE LAFFER CURVE**

The Laffer curve reflects the view that when tax rates are too high, lowering them not only creates greater incentive for suppliers to increase production, but ends up generating higher tax revenues as well.

Tax revenues are measured along the horizontal axis, tax rates along the vertical axis. Consider the most extreme position first. If tax rates were 100 percent, no one would work. GDP is $0, and of course, income tax revenue is $0 as well. If the tax rate is lowered to 75 percent, some people would work, GDP grows, and the tax revenue that GDP generates is $800 billion. If the rate is reduced further, say to 50 percent, GDP increases and tax revenue is $1,300 billion. The Laffer curve shows that a tax rate of 30 percent provides suppliers with incentive to produce a GDP large enough to generate a maximum $1,500 billion tax revenue. A lower tax rate, say, at 20 percent, will increase GDP but end up lowering tax revenue.

Laffer's message was clear. Our tax rate is so high that it stifles incentive and produces less than the maximum tax revenue. By lowering the tax rate, he argued—the key factor in supply-side economics—GDP and tax revenue could grow.

Laffer's argument had considerable weight in President Reagan's decision to change the tax structure. In 1981, Congress passed the Kemp-Roth tax cut, which lowered tax rates. The highest marginal tax rate was cut from 70 to 50 percent. In 1986, the Tax Reform Act followed Kemp-Roth's lead, reducing the number of tax brackets to three and cutting the top marginal rate to 31 percent. The two other marginal tax rates were set at 28 and 15 percent.

The result? Not very positive. Tax revenues did not increase, contributing to the exceptionally large budget deficits of the 1980s.

The supply-siders' political clout ended with President Reagan. President Bush's campaign promise "Read my lips, no new taxes" was compromised early in his administration; although willing to reduce the capital gains tax, he was unable to persuade Congress to go along. President Clinton's tax policy, on the other hand, moved considerably away from supply-side economics.

## Less Government Regulation

To supply-siders, the myriad of government regulations affects almost every industry in the economy, reducing productivity and undermining industrial efficiency. Although most regulations are designed to protect consumers, workers, and the environment, they also represent a substantial added cost to suppliers. They stifle creativity and trigger higher prices.

Although supply-siders acknowledge the need for some regulation, they insist that the cure has become worse than the disease. They argue for substantial deregulation of the economy. They had some success during the Reagan years, especially in banking, energy, and transportation.

# GLOBAL PERSPECTIVE

## NAIRU ESTIMATES FOR OECD ECONOMIES

Data show that the non-accelerating inflation rate of unemployment (NAIRU) for OECD economies is considerably higher than the 6 percent rate for the United States. But why should this be so? Among the microeconomic explanations offered are greater labor market rigidities such as higher minimum wages, higher mandated vacation time, greater restrictions on dismissals, more generous unemployment benefits, and stronger unions. These rigidities are coupled with macroeconomic problems associated with the high degree of integration of Western European economies. Any countercyclical monetary or fiscal policy in one European economy affects the economic performance of other countries of the European Union. For example, if France or Germany engages in contractionary policy, Denmark, Belgium, and Italy will suffer higher unemployment without having initiated any policy of their own. These outcomes are unavoidable and affect, to some degree, the overall NAIRUs within the OECD. Look at the accompanying table.

With the exception of Japan and the Netherlands, the NAIRUs of these countries are higher, and in some cases exceptionally higher, than in the United States, and they seem to be relatively stable through the 1990–97 period. In 7 of the 10 economies shown, the 1990–97 natural rate of unemployment differential was less than 1 percent. Only in Germany was the 1990–97 NAIRU differential greater than 2 percent.

### NAIRU ESTIMATES FOR OECD IN THE 1990S

|  | 1990 | 1997 | 1990–97 DIFFERENTIAL |
|---|---|---|---|
| ITALY | 9.7 | 10.6 | 0.9 |
| FRANCE | 9.3 | 10.2 | 0.9 |
| BELGIUM | 11.0 | 11.6 | 0.6 |
| JAPAN | 2.5 | 2.8 | 0.3 |
| CANADA | 9.0 | 8.5 | 0.5 |
| DENMARK | 9.2 | 8.6 | 0.6 |
| AUSTRALIA | 8.3 | 7.5 | 0.8 |
| GERMANY | 6.9 | 9.6 | 2.8 |
| UNITED KINGDOM | 8.5 | 7.2 | 1.3 |
| NETHERLANDS | 7.0 | 5.5 | 1.5 |

## Less Government Spending

Supply-siders believe that the government's reliance on its own spending to create employment not only is not a quick fix but is a major contributor to the unemployment problem. Because government typically ends up spending more than it receives in tax revenues, budget deficits grow. These deficits are financed by the sale of government securities—that is, government borrowing—which undermines private sector investment in two ways. First, government competes in the securities market with firms trying to sell their own securities, **crowding out** these firms from the source of funds. Second, the increase in government borrowing drives up the interest rate, crowding out private investment once again. This crowding-out

**Crowding out**
A fall in private investment spending caused by an increase in government spending.

Why would less government spending result in a lower rate of unemployment?

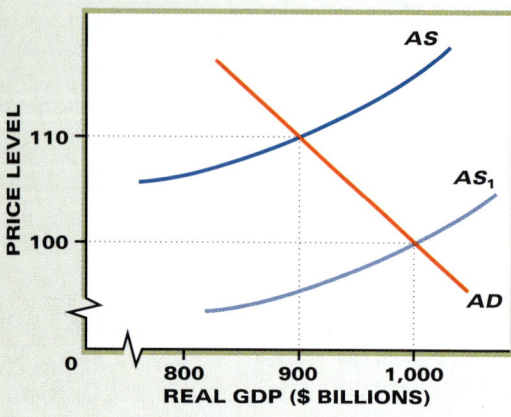

**EXHIBIT 13**

**SUPPLY-SIDE EFFECTS ON UNEMPLOYMENT AND INFLATION**

If aggregate supply shifts to the right from AS to $AS_1$, real GDP increases from $900 billion to $1,000 billion, while the price level falls from $P = 110$ to $P = 100$.

phenomenon checks the rate of economic growth.

Supply-siders argue that if the government reduces its spending, more investment capital will be made available at lower rates of interest to private sector suppliers. Combined with lower tax rates and less government regulation, lower government spending produces lower rates of inflation and unemployment. Exhibit 13 illustrates their view.

The shift in the aggregate supply curve from AS to $AS_1$ that results from supply-side stabilization policy causes a decrease in the price level, from $P = 110$ to $P = 100$, and an increase in GDP, from $900 billion to $1,000 billion, cutting the rate of unemployment.

## IS THERE A MACRO CONSENSUS?

The question of who is right on stabilization policy has as many answers as there are economists with views on stabilization. Macroeconomic models—classical, Keynesian, neo-Keynesian (the short-run and long-run Phillips curve varieties), rational expectations, and supply-side—all generate outcomes that differ and, depending on one's economic ideology, can be compelling. In other words, not everyone agrees with any one "correct" stabilization policy.

Yet real-world events of the 1970s, 1980s, and 1990s have brought macroeconomists together, notwithstanding the specific policy disagreements that make interesting bedfellows. For example, rational-expectations economists and neo-Keynesians share the same view concerning government's ability to change the economy's long-run employment position. They both demonstrate its futility. They see stabilization policy—what we can do with rates of inflation and unemployment—as constrained. Their observations are not entirely revolutionary. Classical economists came to the same conclusions, insisting that even well-intentioned government interference in the economy was not only futile but counterproductive.

Note what supply-siders and Keynesians agree and disagree on. They agree that with the correct approach to stabilization policy, it is possible to reduce both the rate of unemployment and the rate of inflation. But supply-siders and Keynesians disagree on the correct approach to stabilization. The Keynesians focus on changing aggregate demand; supply-siders focus on changing aggregate supply.

Even among Keynesians, there is disagreement about what government can and cannot do to promote employment, although they all share the belief that government has a positive role. Some Keynesians are convinced that government can create policy to increase employment without causing inflation. Others take a different view. They accept the validity of the Phillips curve, which requires us to make choices between employment and inflation. And among those economists, what policies the government should pursue is still a matter of some disagreement.

## AUTOMATIC STABILIZERS

Wouldn't it be wonderful if we had an economic stabilization thermostat built into our economy that would *automatically* create employment when the economy's rate of unemployment grew to unacceptable levels and *automatically* cut inflation when the rate of inflation became too high? It would mute much of the activist-nonactivist debate and would set aside many of the ideological differences and much of the controversial, discretionary decision making by government and the Fed that stabilization policy demands. But is it possible? Can anyone really design automatic economic stabilizers?

To some extent, that's what our economy already has. We have built into our system **automatic stabilizers** that kick in at the right times to moderate the ups and downs of business cycles. One of the principal stabilizers is the unemployment insurance system. The other is our income and corporate tax structure. How do they work?

**Automatic stabilizers**
Structures in the economy that tend to add to aggregate demand when the economy is in recession, and subtract from aggregate demand when the economy is inflationary. Unemployment insurance payments and benefits and the progressive income tax are two such automatic stabilizers.

### Unemployment Insurance

When people work, they contribute part of their earnings *indirectly* to an unemployment insurance program. Although employers, not workers, actually pay the insurance, employers are reimbursed, at least in part, by paying workers lower wages. That is, workers would probably earn higher wage rates if employers were not obligated to pay the insurance. The point is that while workers are working at jobs, part of their income is siphoned off by employer-employee contributions to the unemployment insurance program.

On the other hand, when workers are unemployed, they receive income payments in the form of unemployment insurance benefits from that program. This simple and practical spreading of workers' incomes more evenly over the business cycle not only makes life more tolerable for affected workers but acts as an automatic stabilizer in the economy.

Consider the prosperity phase of a business cycle. With unemployment approaching the natural rate and wage rates rising along with the price level, the one thing you don't want to encourage is more consumer spending. But that's just what happens when wages increase. Unemployment insurance payments (which leave less take-home dollars in paychecks than would otherwise be the case) come to the rescue. With less income, people spend less, which modifies somewhat the upward pressure on prices.

**CHECK YOUR UNDERSTANDING**

How does unemployment insurance work to moderate the ups and downs of the business cycle?

On the other hand, in the recession phase of the cycle, the unemployment insurance program automatically pumps more spending into the economy. People out of work find their earning power considerably diminished, but those who are eligible for unemployment benefits now have some spending power. In this respect, spending does not decrease as much as it would without the unemployment insurance benefits. This ultimately means fewer workers lose their jobs, which translates into less unemployment than would otherwise have occurred.

### Personal and Corporate Income Taxes

Our personal income tax structure has a built-in stabilizing feature as well. The tax structure is progressive, meaning that as income increases, the percentage of income paid to taxes increases. How does it work? When incomes and real GDP increase during a prosperity phase, taxes increase at an even higher rate, leaving less disposable income in the hands of people. With less income, people spend less. That's good news because less spending dampens the inflationary pressure on the economy.

Visit the Internal Revenue Service (http://www.irs.gov/) to learn more about the federal tax system.

During a recession, when income and real GDP are falling, less is collected in taxes. Disposable income and spending do not fall as fast. That's good news as well, because the less spending falls, the less real GDP will fall, and, consequently, fewer workers will lose their jobs. This means unemployment will not increase as much as it would in the absence of these automatic stabilizers.

Our corporate income tax structure operates the same way. In fact, economists consider the corporate profit tax to be the most countercyclical of all automatic stabilizers. In the prosperity phases of the cycle, corporate profits tend to increase faster than any other income form. In recessions, they tend to decrease faster. As a result, corporations pay considerably more taxes in inflationary periods than in recessions.

# CHAPTER REVIEW

1. Since economists have different temperaments and ideologies and work with imperfect information, they don't always agree on how an economy behaves or what appropriate policy should be. Liberal economists tend to advocate greater government intervention in the economy, while conservative economists are more disposed to advocate a laissez-faire approach.

2. The five schools of macroeconomic thought related to the analysis of employment and inflation are the classical, Keynesian, neo-Keynesian, rational expectations, and supply-side.

3. Classical economists believe that because markets are basically competitive and prices flexible, unemployment exists only in the short run. In the long run, all prices, including the price of labor, will adjust to equilibrium, eliminating unemployment. Their policy is to wait out the adjustment, that is, to do nothing. Inflation simply represents too much money chasing too few goods. Classical policy is to fix the rate of growth in the money supply to the rate of growth of real GDP.

4. Keynesian economists argue that markets are not competitive and prices are downward inflexible. Under these conditions, a fall in aggregate demand leads to lower real GDP, not a lower price level. Unemployment, then, can persist—in the short and long run—as long as aggregate demand is insufficient to absorb everyone willing and able to work. This idea supports the view that government should fine-tune the economy, creating an aggregate demand sufficient to generate full employment. Inflation becomes a problem only when aggregate demand creates a macroequilibrium level beyond full-employment real GDP. The solution: reduce government spending to reduce aggregate demand. The Full Employment Act of 1946 reflects the thinking of the Keynesian school.

5. The coexistence of inflation and unemployment—referred to as stagflation—in the 1970s led to the creation of the neo-Keynesian school. Its principal tool of analysis was the Phillips curve, which showed the inverse relationship between rates of inflation and unemployment. Unions' market power and strategic resource supply shocks explain how the Phillips curve works. For example, if government policy reduces unemployment, it relaxes the unions' concerns about jobs and allows them to focus on wage increases. If successful, these wage increases, which result in inflation, cut into firms' profits, so the firms cut back on production and, consequently, employment. The result: Government's effort to decrease unemployment succeeds in the short run but not in the long run. In the process, inflation occurs.

6. Rational-expectations economists believe that government cannot even succeed in reducing unemployment in the short run. They reason that unions learn that wages are eroded by inflation and bargain not just to make up for lost real wages but for anticipated losses that will occur if government tries to reduce unemployment. The result: Firms suffer wage increases (which raises prices in general) that include accounting for future inflation so that

firms do not increase production or employment at all. In the process, inflation occurs.
7. Supply-side economists believe that economic policy should focus on the supply side—that is, on ways of shifting the aggregate supply curve to the right. Lower taxes, less government spending, and less government regulation, they argue, are the appropriate policies to deal with issues of economic growth, unemployment, and inflation.
8. Is there a macro consensus? Not really, even though areas of agreement among economists associated with the different schools do exist. Keynesians and supply-siders agree that some form of stabilization policy can reduce unemployment and inflation, but they disagree on what that policy ought to be. Rational-expectations economists and neo-Keynesians are far less willing to accept the view that, in the long run, any stabilization policy works.
9. To some extent, the economy has automatic stabilizers built into the system. They are the unemployment insurance and progressive income tax systems. During periods of prosperity, people's after-tax incomes are reduced by the contributions they make to the unemployment insurance program and by the progressiveness of the income tax. These reductions tend to dampen the upward momentum of the prosperity phase of the business cycle. During periods of recession, people receive unemployment insurance payments and pay taxes on a lower percentage of their income, both of which tend to counteract the downward momentum of the recessionary phase of the cycle.

# KEY TERMS

Classical economics
Stabilization policy
Keynesian economics
Phillips curve

Neo-Keynesian economics
Rational expectations
Non-accelerating inflation rate of unemployment (NAIRU)

Supply-side economics
Crowding out
Automatic stabilizers

# QUESTIONS

1. Imagine yourself at dinner with a Keynesian and a classical economist. The conversation turns to why the economy is experiencing high unemployment and what the government ought to do about it. How would the Keynesian explain the unemployment, and what policies would she advocate? The classical economist would no doubt disagree with both the explanation and the policy prescription. What would he argue, and why?
2. Professor Martin Feldstein chaired President Reagan's first Council of Economic Advisers. He was never a serious consideration when President Clinton picked his council. Why?
3. Keynesian economists were fine-tuning the economy during the 1960s but found their policies ineffectual in the 1970s. Why?
4. "The key to any economic stabilization is managing aggregate demand." Keynesians and neo-Keynesians would agree with that statement, even though they see quite different outcomes stemming from such management. Discuss.
5. To supply-siders, the key to any economic stabilization is managing aggregate supply. What kinds of policy do they advocate, and what outcomes do they expect to achieve?
6. In 1958, A. W. Phillips published his celebrated article introducing the Phillips curve. It changed the way economists think about stabilization policy. Why?
7. "Unions make it difficult for government to reduce the rate of unemployment." Discuss the logic underscoring this view and show how it relates to the Phillips curve.

8. "In periods of inflation, any attempt by the Fed to increase real GDP through increases in the money supply ends up increasing only the rate of inflation." What school of economists makes this point? How do they make their argument?

9. "To rational-expectations economists, it makes no difference whether we think in terms of the short run or the long run: Government cannot reduce the rate of unemployment, period." Explain.

10. "Government may *try* to increase employment and output by increasing its spending, but it just crowds out private investment and ends up reducing employment and output." Discuss.

11. "To *some* extent, automatic stabilizers work." What are they supposed to do, and why do they work?

12. What is the Laffer curve? What impact did it have on government policy?

13. Explain why unemployment insurance is a good example of an automatic stabilizer.

14. "The Fed should just increase the money supply at the same rate that the full-employment economy grows, and the government should desist from any stabilizing urges." What school of thought would make such a suggestion, and how do economists of that school justify that prescription?

# WHAT'S WRONG WITH THIS GRAPH?

**THE PHILLIPS CURVE**

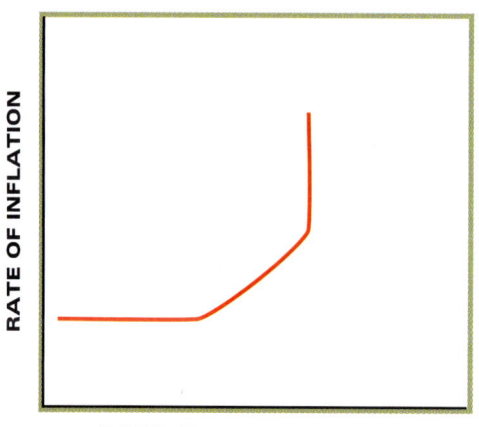

# ECONOMIC CONSULTANTS

### ECONOMIC RESEARCH AND ANALYSIS BY STUDENTS FOR PROFESSIONALS

Mindy Manolakes worked in a North Carolina textile factory before she became president of the Union of Needletrades, Industrial and Textile Employees' (UNITE) Southern District. She and other key people in UNITE's national office have been debating whether to propose a 10 percent wage increase for all unionized garment workers. Mindy supports the increase, justifying it by arguing that years of inflation have eroded the real incomes of workers. Other union leaders are hesitant because they fear that the wage demand may induce textile firms to leave the country. They cite the recent migrations of textile factories to Lima, Peru. Mindy suggests that UNITE hire Economic Consultants to evaluate the effects of a 10 percent wage increase. You are asked to prepare a report for UNITE that addresses the following issues:

1. What effects might the 10 percent increase in wages have on textile prices and the competitiveness of the American textile industry worldwide?
2. What effect might the 10 percent increase in wages have on textile employment in the United States and on inducing the migration of textile plants out of the United States?
3. What kind of support can UNITE expect from federal and state governments?

You may find the following resources helpful as you prepare your report for Mindy and UNITE:

- **Union of Needletrades, Industrial and Textile Employees (UNITE)** (http://www.unite union.org/)—UNITE provides news and information about union activities.
- **LabourStart** (http://www.labourstart.org/)—LabourStart is a collection of labor and union news from around the world.
- **UnionWeb** (http://www.unionweb.org/)—UnionWeb provides links to resources by and about unions.
- **Thomas: Legislative Information on the Internet** (http://thomas.loc.gov/)—Thomas, named after Thomas Jefferson, is a service of the Library of Congress that provides news and information about congressional activities.
- **Bureau of Labor Statistics** (http://www.bls.gov/)—The Bureau of Labor Statistics provides data and information about employment and inflation.

# PRACTICE TEST

1. According to classical economists, the best way for the government to eliminate unemployment in the economy is for government to
   a. increase spending.
   b. allow the multiplier effect to raise income and employment.
   c. pass legislation outlawing unemployment.
   d. strengthen unions.
   e. do nothing.

2. Classical economists attribute inflation to which of the following?
   a. Growth in the money supply
   b. Low levels of unemployment
   c. Money supply growth that exceeds the growth in real output
   d. Shocks to aggregate supply in the economy
   e. Shifts in the economy's aggregate demand curve

3. Keynesian economists reject many of the solutions to problems presented by classical economists because
   a. they believe that prices are not flexible.
   b. classical economists rely too heavily on expectations to derive useful policies.
   c. inflation is a worse problem than unemployment.
   d. they believe that the long-run Phillips curve is vertical.
   e. they believe that tax reductions and spending cuts are the most efficient way to achieve macroeconomic goals.

4. Inflation was not viewed as a serious problem by Keynesians in the 1930s because
   a. government intervention could easily reduce inflation.
   b. they believed that the market forces would eventually lower inflation.
   c. real GDP was above the full-employment level.
   d. when the aggregate demand curve shifts to the right, inflation decreases.
   e. proposed increases in aggregate demand would be insufficient to cause inflation.

5. The Phillips curve illustrates that
   a. as inflation rises, the rate of unemployment falls.
   b. as inflation rises, the rate of unemployment rises.
   c. as real GDP rises, the price level in the economy falls.
   d. as wages rise, real GDP rises.
   e. as real GDP rises, the rate of unemployment falls.

6. Unlike the Keynesian school, the neo-Keynesian school explains
   a. why inflation is not a problem.
   b. why markets do not automatically adjust to equilibrium.
   c. why inflation and unemployment coexist.
   d. why prices tend to be inflexible downward.
   e. how expectations affect individual behavior.

7. Rational-expectations economists argue that
   a. inflation and unemployment are avoidable.
   b. if policies are anticipated, they magnify the impact on the economy.
   c. people typically do not understand how policy affects them.
   d. government can do nothing to reduce unemployment.
   e. government can control either inflation or unemployment, but not both at the same time.

8. Which school of economics advocates spending cuts and lower tax rates as a means of achieving macroeconomic goals?
   a. Keynesian economists
   b. Classical economists
   c. Rational-expectations economists
   d. Neo-Keynesian economists
   e. Supply-side economists

9. Which of the following groups of economists are the strongest advocates for government intervention to reduce unemployment?
   a. Classical economists
   b. Keynesian economists
   c. Supply-side economists
   d. Neo-Keynesian economists
   e. Rational-expectations economists

10. The progressive income tax structure is considered an automatic stabilizer because as income increases, taxes
    a. increase by a smaller amount, which promotes spending.
    b. increase by a larger amount, which restrains spending.
    c. increase by a lower rate, which promotes spending.
    d. increase by a higher rate, which restrains spending.
    e. decrease, which restrains spending.

# GOVERNMENT SPENDING

## CHAPTER 14

There will *always* be public debate about whether government spends too much or too little, about whether it taxes too much or too little, and about whether the kinds of things it does and the way it goes about collecting revenues to pay for what it does represent the best that government can or should do.

Perhaps the first question we should ask is, *Why is government spending at all?* Why, for example, is government in the business of providing interstate roads, street lights, education, national defense, and public parks? We have already seen in our analysis of countercyclical fiscal policy the usefulness of government spending to achieve target employment and GDP levels. Government spending is a vital part of aggre-

**THIS CHAPTER INTRODUCES YOU TO THE ECONOMIC PRINCIPLES ASSOCIATED WITH:**

- PUBLIC GOODS
- MERIT GOODS
- TRANSFER PAYMENTS

gate demand. But is government spending strictly a matter of countercyclical fiscal policy?

It would seem unreasonable to argue that the only reason government builds city streets is because the dollars spent on street construction generate—through the income multiplier—desired levels of GDP and employment. Think about it. Wouldn't we need city streets even if the economy were at full-employment GDP? But why rely on government to provide the streets? Why don't we rely on the market to produce the city streets, just as we rely on it to produce automobiles?

# GOVERNMENT SPENDING AND PUBLIC GOODS

Automakers produce automobiles because people demand them. People demand them because the personal benefits they derive from an automobile are greater than the personal costs they incur buying it. That's also why raincoats, strawberries, and CDs are produced. In each case, people compare the benefits they derive against the costs they incur. Look at your own collection of household items. Didn't you calculate, perhaps subconsciously, benefits and costs before making each purchase? Why, then, can't you make the same kind of personal cost-benefit calculation for city street lights?

Hard to even imagine such a calculation, isn't it? After all, no matter how much you may personally benefit from a city street lighting system, the cost is far beyond your personal means. If each of us relied exclusively on the market to determine what to buy, we would all end up with lots of strawberries and no city street lights.

How, then, do we get city street lights, sewage systems, and police protection? By replacing the market with government. How does it work?

Consider the small community of Logan Square, with a population of 20,000. Suppose that a network of street lighting would cost the community $40 million. And suppose that the personal benefit each of the 20,000 people derives from the network is $5,000. The community's total benefit, then, is $100 million, or 2½ times its cost of production. In other words, the street lighting project is economically sound. But how do you get it built?

Suppose Doug Dubson, the mayor of Logan Square, calls a town meeting to discuss the economic costs and benefits of the project. He asks each resident to contribute $2,000. The community accepts the mayor's estimate of a $5,000 personal benefit. But Denise Miller, a Logan Square psychiatrist, has another idea. She figures that if everyone *except her* contributes $2,000, the street lights will be built anyway and she will still be able to use them. She doesn't feel too guilty about not contributing because she reasons that even if she uses the street lights, it's not at her neighbors' expense. They each still end up deriving a $5,000 benefit. What Denise doesn't count on, however, is that everyone has the same idea. The result is that nobody makes a $2,000 contribution, and, consequently, no street lights are built.

Frustrated, the mayor calls a second meeting. This time, he brings along Paul Budin, an economic consultant, who explains the difference between a **public good,** such as a city street light, and a private good, such as an automobile. Public goods, he points out, have two distinct features: nonexclusiveness and nonrivalry.

When you buy an automobile, he explains, the benefits it provides are exclusively yours, if you wish. You can prevent others from gaining any benefit simply by denying them access to the automobile. It's the same with your raincoat. When you wear it, others can't. You're dry, they're wet.

This exclusive character of a good is absent in public goods. Once the city street lights are installed and the current turned on, you cannot deny anyone on the street the benefits of the lighting. The exclusiveness of the good—the lighting—is lacking. It makes no difference who owns the good or who actually paid for it; once it is provided, no one can be excluded from deriving benefit.

Private goods are also rival goods. As you eat through a banana, there's less and less of it left. If others were expecting to eat it too, they're out of luck. In this sense, your consumption of the banana rivals theirs.

Not so with public goods. Consider the city street lights again. You can use the lighting as much as you want without others being denied its use. If others crowd the street to enjoy a late evening stroll, you won't notice the lights dimming. In other words, their benefit doesn't rival yours.

**Public good**
A good whose benefits are not diminished even when additional people consume it and whose benefits cannot be withheld from anyone.

The nonexclusivity and nonrival properties of public goods, Paul Budin explains, mean that Logan Square will never get city street lights if people rely on markets, because there is no way to exclude anyone who has not paid for the lighting from deriving equal benefits. Each individual therefore waits for everybody else to pay for them. If Logan Square wants city street lights, it must bypass the market. That bypass is government spending. We rely on government to provide the street lights and to tax the community accordingly.

## GOVERNMENT SPENDING AND MERIT GOODS

Don't you wish there was more goodwill among people? After all, goodwill is good! The truth is that we can actually generate more goodwill among ourselves if we behave more kindly to one another. But we don't.

Some goods are like goodwill. We would be much better off—at least some people think so—if we had more of them, but we don't. Economists call them **merit goods.** The reason we don't have as much of them as some people think we ought to is that market demand and supply generate less. How, then, do we get more? If the market doesn't produce the quantities some people think we should have, in many instances, government comes to the rescue.

Consider higher education. The private market is quite capable of generating the quantity of colleges and universities to educate students at demand-and-supply-determined prices. So what's the problem? It's simply this: *The government doesn't like the quantities and the prices that the market generates for higher education*. It places higher value or merit on higher education than people's individual choices declare in the private market. The result: Government produces higher education in the form of state universities and community colleges and sells the higher education at below-market prices *even though there's a flourishing private market for the good*.

What other merit goods does government produce or subsidize? You're probably familiar with many of them. For example, the government's National Endowment for the Arts subsidizes experimental film, art, and music that would otherwise never see the light of day. The National Institutes of Health produce merit goods in the form of research in medicine and medicine-related fields. Public libraries, art galleries, symphony orchestras, and museums are typically merit goods subsidized by government. In radio and television, the government's NPR and PBS networks provide programming that would otherwise not be aired by competing private networks, such as CBS and NBC.

How many private goods individuals buy on the market and how many public and merit goods they buy through the system of government spending and taxation are a matter of individual choice. That's what the ballot box allows each person in Logan Square to do: elect a mayor to represent the levels and character of government spending he or she wants.

**Merit good**
A good that market demand and supply do not produce enough of, in some people's opinion.

**CHECK YOUR UNDERSTANDING**

Why does government produce merit goods?

**on the net**

The National Endowment for the Arts (http://arts.endow.gov/), the National Institutes of Health (http://www.nih.gov/), National Public Radio (http://www.npr.org/), and the Public Broadcasting Service (http://www.pbs.org/) all produce merit goods.

## GOVERNMENT SPENDING AND TRANSFER PAYMENTS

Not all government spending is designed to satisfy our need for public and merit goods or to be used as a tool of countercyclical fiscal policy. Some government spending simply transfers income from some people—government taxes them—to other people—government pays them. These transfer payments are typically in the form of government services, price subsidies, and cash payments. They are intended to moderate the harshness of poverty among low-income people and, in some cases,

# GLOBAL PERSPECTIVE

## GOVERNMENT SPENDING ON THE ARTS

Just as there is no universal agreement about what goods should be counted among merit goods, so too are there a variety of views concerning what goods properly belong to the arts. You can draw up your own list. A 2000 National Endowment for the Arts study* identified the following: museums and galleries, music, opera, dance, drama, visual arts, community arts, festivals, literature, and film.

The 2000 NEA study compared government funding of the arts in ten OECD economies, using data that ranged from 1993 to 1995. The results are shown in the accompanying table.

Germany's $6,886 million is more than twice the government spending in France and 4½ times larger than total government spending in the United States. In terms of per capita spending, the United States was last ($6) among the OECD economies shown, while Finland topped the list ($91). Government per capita spending on the arts in Germany was 14 times larger than spending in the United States. Although the United Kingdom was second to last, its spending was still more than four times the spending in the United States.

Measured as a percent of GDP, U.S. government spending on the arts was a lowly 0.13 percent. Canada's 0.93 was more than seven times higher.

Why the peculiar positioning of the United States? Two explanations make sense: Americans are more inclined than their OECD partners to use private markets to fund the arts, and the ratio of government spending to GDP is lower in the United Sates than in all OECD economies, save Japan.

*International Data on Government Spending on the Arts, Research Note #74, National Endowment for the Arts, 2000.

### GOVERNMENT SPENDING ON THE ARTS: 10 OECD ECONOMIES

|  | TOTAL (MILLIONS $US) | PER CAPITA | PERCENT OF GDP |
|---|---|---|---|
| AUSTRALIA | $ 438 | $25 | 0.82 |
| CANADA | 1,272 | 46 | 0.93 |
| FINLAND | 460 | 91 | 2.10 |
| FRANCE | 3,275 | 57 | 1.31 |
| GERMANY | 6,886 | 85 | 1.79 |
| IRELAND | 533 | 59 | 0.43 |
| NETHERLANDS | 714 | 46 | 1.47 |
| SWEDEN | 496 | 57 | 1.02 |
| UNITED KINGDOM | 1,518 | 26 | 0.65 |
| UNITED STATES | 1,530 | 6 | 0.13 |

Social Security contributions and benefits (http://www.ssa.gov/) are examples of government transfer payments.

to moderate the economic distress suffered by groups, such as farmers, whose income source has been undermined by adverse changes in market conditions.

Government is also in the business of administering Social Security, an obligatory social insurance program. The program provides benefits to retired people, spouses of people in the program who have died, and disabled people. Every working person who contributes to Social Security—contributions are matched by employers—receives Social Security benefits.

The contributions are held in a specifically earmarked trust fund. Social Security contributions and benefits are transfer payments. Income is transferred from the young (who typically pay into the trust fund more than they receive from it) to the elderly (who typically receive more from the trust fund than they pay into it), even though the payers themselves regard their own contributions to the trust fund more as personal savings than as part of a transfer payment system.

## GOVERNMENT SPENDING AND THE PUBLIC DEBT

Each year, government makes interest payments to people who own the public debt. The debt is in the form of Treasury bills, notes, and bonds and is held not only by individuals, but by banks, corporations, the Federal Reserve, other government agencies, and foreigners. A more detailed analysis of the government's debt is offered in the next chapter.

Government helps provide for national security through the National Guard (http://www.ngb.dtic.mil/).

## HOW MUCH DOES GOVERNMENT SPEND?

Exhibit 1 shows total government spending for 2000.

Slightly less than half of total government spending is in the form of purchases of goods and services. At the federal level, purchases made up only 26.9 percent of spending, while transfer payments and interest accounted for 57.8 percent. The federal government also provided state and local governments with $229.3 billion of grants. As much as 74 percent of state and local spending is for purchases of goods and services. What do federal, state, and local governments buy? Exhibit 2 details government spending by function.

### Security

Some public and merit goods that government provides seem to be almost beyond public controversy. One of these is national security. How many people do you know who contest our need for a reliable national defense? How many people advocate leaving defense preparedness to individual purchases in the marketplace? There appears to be a wide consensus that national security properly belongs in the federal government's domain.

Some of our security is managed by other levels of government. Local governments, for example, provide police protection to safeguard our communities. State police cast a wider security net. Our National Guard is administered by state governments and is sometimes called upon to assist local police.

**HOW MUCH SECURITY IS ENOUGH?** But how much security is enough? Can we ever be *too* well protected? How many times have you heard someone say about our police, "They're always around except when you need them!" If there's any substance to the charge, it may signal a need for more police. But how many more? Do you want them around everywhere, all the time?

**FEDERAL, STATE, AND LOCAL GOVERNMENT SPENDING: 2000 ($ BILLIONS)**

|  | FEDERAL | STATE AND LOCAL | TOTAL |
| --- | --- | --- | --- |
| PURCHASES | $ 470.8 | $808.4 | $1,279.2 |
| TRANSFER PAYMENTS | 746.1 | 234.1 | 980.2 |
| NET INTEREST | 264.7 | -0.6 | 264.1 |
| GRANTS-IN-AID | 229.3 | – | 229.3 |
| OTHER | 39.3 | 50.8 | 90.1 |
| TOTAL | 1,520.9 | $1,092.7 | 2,613.6 |

**Source:** *Survey of Current Business* (Washington, D.C.: U.S. Department of Commerce, October 2000).

EXHIBIT 1

## EXHIBIT 2

### GOVERNMENT SPENDING IN 1999, BY FUNCTION ($ BILLIONS)

| | FEDERAL | STATE AND LOCAL |
|---|---|---|
| SECURITY, NATIONAL DEFENSE | $ 314.1 | $ — |
| SECURITY, CIVILIAN PROTECTION | 21.1 | 156.5 |
| EDUCATION | 41.2 | 418.4 |
| TRANSPORTATION | 15.3 | 79.9 |
| NATURAL RESOURCES | 11.4 | 9.0 |
| ENERGY | 4.0 | −7.0* |
| SPACE | 12.5 | — |
| AGRICULTURE | 32.4 | 4.8 |
| INCOME SUPPORT, SOCIAL SECURITY, AND WELFARE | 571.5 | 97.2 |
| HEALTH AND HOSPITALS | 376.4 | 211.2 |
| HOUSING AND COMMUNITY SERVICES | 30.1 | 5.3 |
| NET INTEREST | 264.7 | −3.3** |
| CENTRAL EXECUTIVE, LEGISLATIVE, AND JUDICIAL ACTIVITIES | 37.1 | 105.8 |
| OTHERS | 18.4 | 14.9 |
| **TOTAL** | **$1,750.2** | **$1,092.7** |

*The minus figure represents subsidies less current surplus of government enterprises.
**Interest paid less interest received by government.

Source: *Survey of Current Business* (Washington, D.C.: U.S. Department of Commerce, October 2000).

Doesn't our personal security also depend upon what we do with security offenders? What kinds of correction facilities—local jails, state prisons, federal penitentiaries—should we build? What should we do with offenders once they are incarcerated? Should we try to rehabilitate them? That could be expensive. Perhaps the least-expensive policy is to hang them immediately after sentencing! Ridiculous? Society has done it for centuries. Many countries still do it. Remember: *Whatever form and level of security we choose, determined by whatever sets of values we hold, carries a price tag that can be compared with those for alternative security systems.*

How would *you* go about deciding how much to spend on what? That's what Congress and the White House must do. That's also what state and local governments must do.

**HOW MUCH SECURITY DO WE BUY?** Exhibit 3 details the $491.6 billion spent in 1999 on security by federal, state, and local governments. As you see, our $314.1 billion national defense spending is our major security item, although its share of total federal spending has declined steadily and significantly over the past quarter century. (In 1970, that share was 41.8 percent; in 1999, it was 18 percent.) Not surprisingly, 85 percent of all 1999 government spending on police, fire, and corrections was done at the state and local levels.

*Suppose you are the president of the United States and must present your budget to Congress tomorrow. How would you redesign Exhibit 2? Go to the Interactive Study Center at http://gottheil.swcollege.com and click on the "Your Turn" button to submit your example. Student submissions will be posted to the Web site, and perhaps we will use some in future editions of the book!*

The $314.1 billion national defense expenditure may not be an accurate reflection of what the federal government actually spent for our 1999 national security. Left out of the defense accounting are the $43.2 billion expenditure on veterans' benefits and services and the $15.2 billion expenditure on international affairs. While these items show up as part of other federal expenditures—eduction, health, and general public service—there is reason to regard them as properly belonging to national security.

After all, veterans are men and women who have served in our armed forces. When they retire from active duty, they take with them entitlements—benefits and services—

that Congress has granted. These entitlements represent payment now for past security provided. What do the entitlements include? The major item is disability and survivor compensation. But they also provide for education and medical care.

What about international aid? Many people in government believe that providing our allies with economic and military aid is as much a security item as the purchase of a Bradley tank. As well, most of the economic aid is used to purchase our own agricultural and manufacturing output.

**GOVERNMENT SPENDING ($ BILLIONS) ON SECURITY: 1999**

|  | FEDERAL | STATE AND LOCAL | TOTAL |
|---|---|---|---|
| NATIONAL DEFENSE | $314.1 | $ — | $314.1 |
| POLICE | 11.4 | 61.2 | 72.9 |
| PRISONS | 2.9 | 46.3 | 49.2 |
| LAW COURTS | 6.5 | 27.2 | 33.7 |
| FIRE | — | 21.7 | 21.7 |
| TOTAL | $335.2 | $156.4 | $491.6 |

Source: *Survey of Current Business* (Washington, D.C.: U.S. Department of Commerce, October 2000).

## Education

Government funding of elementary and high school education has deep roots in our society. It is one of Thomas Jefferson's cherished legacies.

How much government spends each year on education is partly determined by school enrollments and the quality of education we demand. The costs associated with a quality education depend on teacher training, the length of the school term, class size, and physical facilities, such as space and classroom equipment. Think back to your own elementary and high school days. If you were on the school board then, what changes would you have made? How would those changes have affected government spending?

What's our track record on funding public education? Over the period 1980–96, the annual rate of increase in government spending on elementary, secondary, and higher education, measured in constant dollars, was 2.8 percent, slightly above the 2.6 percent rate of increase in real GDP.

As we see in Exhibit 4, the lion's share of the 1999 government spending on education—95.3 percent—was done by state and local governments.

## Transportation, Natural Resources, and Space

Interstate highways, county roads, city streets, canals, bridges, sewage systems, street lighting, city playgrounds, national parks, and zoos are just a few in a long list of public goods that government has assumed responsibility for over the years. Some are traditional public goods, with long

**FEDERAL, STATE, AND LOCAL GOVERNMENT SPENDING ON EDUCATION: 1999 ($ BILLIONS)**

|  | FEDERAL | STATE AND LOCAL | TOTAL |
|---|---|---|---|
| ELEMENTARY AND SECONDARY | $15.9 | $323.1 | $339.0 |
| COLLEGES AND UNIVERSITIES | 14.8 | 67.7 | 82.5 |
| OTHER | 10.6 | 27.5 | 38.1 |
| TOTAL | $41.2 | $418.4 | $459.6 |

Source: *Survey of Current Business* (Washington, D.C.: U.S. Department of Commerce, October 2000).

histories; others are of more recent vintage, such as space exploration and securing strategic reserves of crude oil.

**TRANSPORTATION** It's probably just as hard to imagine a highway that is privately owned as it is to imagine an economy without the highway. But like government spending on security and education, the question with highways and streets always is, How much spending is appropriate?

The answer is never without controversy. As small communities grow into large metropolitan suburbs, and as our incomes permit us to become increasingly mobile, we need to build and maintain more city streets, more bridges, more expressways, more bypasses, and more county, state, and interstate highways.

Approximately $100 billion was spent on transportation in 1999, with the lion's share being handled by state and local governments. The highway system alone accounted for 70 percent of transportation spending. No surprise, is it? Is there a road you travel on that isn't under repair or doesn't need repair?

**NATURAL RESOURCES** And what about government spending on conservation and natural resources? Although such spending is minor—$20 billion—compared to that on security, education, and transportation, the same question confronts us concerning natural resources: How much is appropriate?

How much should we spend caring for our national, state, and county parks; wildlife preserves; and government forests, minerals, and agriculture lands? How much for promoting such projects as land reclamation, irrigation, drainage, and flood control?

There are competing interests that press for different levels of spending on our environment. Environmental groups such as the Sierra Club are actively engaged in promoting greater public concern and raising money to preserve our natural resources. They are opposed by people who are more interested in committing our resources to economic development. The issue, in the short run, is whether we can afford not to develop these resources. The long-run issue, according to conservation groups, is whether we might not all lose out if we allow them to be developed.

**SPACE** If 500 years ago government spending had not included exploration, Christopher Columbus might never have ventured beyond the coastal waters of southern Europe. But King Ferdinand and Queen Isabella did finance Columbus's expedition, and the rest, as they say, is history.

Perhaps some tax-paying Spaniards then complained that such spending was a poor investment and that there were countless competitive demands being made on the Crown that were more productive. It would be hard to discredit their claims even today.

Twentieth-century space exploration faces the same kinds of charges, and those supporting our space shots and moon landings rely on the same spirit of adventure that put Columbus on our shores. But whether the opportunity costs associated with space exploration make it a worthwhile investment or not, it is clear to both advocates and opponents of space exploration that if we are to have a space program, government is the appropriate provider. Once again, the question is how much spending. In 1999, it was $12.5 billion.

## Agriculture and Public Assistance

What common denominator is there for government spending on security, education, transportation, natural resources, energy, and space? For each, the target population is everyone. Government does not intentionally target its spending on these items to satisfy any one segment of the population. National defense is intended

The Sierra Club (http://www.sierraclub.org/) promotes greater public spending on our natural resources.

to defend everyone. Interstate highways are built and maintained for everyone. Elementary and high school education is free and open, and even our community colleges and land-grant universities are open to those who meet the requirements.

Of course, not everyone takes advantage of these public and merit goods to the same degree. Families without children, for example, do not benefit from elementary education in the same way that families with children do. And some people benefit more from an interstate highway than do others. There are people who feel more secure with more people in jail. But no one is intentionally shortchanged.

But not all government spending is so universal. Some spending is exclusive and targeted to specific segments of the population and takes the form of goods and services or direct cash payments.

What's the rationale underlying such exclusion? Why is government in the transfer payment business, providing some people with goods, services, and cash, and not others? Perhaps the two most important principles governing such targeted spending are equity and stability.

**CHECK YOUR UNDERSTANDING**
Why is some government spending targeted to specific populations?

What should we do about people who simply can't afford the bare necessities of life? Economic equity has always been a concern. Private philanthropy, which at one time was the only institution to address the problems of the destitute, now shares that responsibility with government.

What should we do about people who are not destitute but are adversely affected by technological change? In some cases, the economic stability of a community or of an entire region is significantly shaken. In many of these cases, government has chosen to supplement the incomes of the people who are adversely affected.

**AGRICULTURE** Consider, for example, the government's $18.4 billion spending on agriculture. It's essentially a transfer payment. Money is taken from the general population in the form of taxes and transferred to the farm population in the form of subsidies. But why should the government transfer your money to farmers? Why not simply allow the market to solve the problem of chronic farm surpluses the way excess supplies are reduced or eliminated in other markets? Aside from the obvious—the political muscle of the farm population—the government also worries that the market consequences would undermine the stability of not only the farm economy, but the national economy as well.

**PUBLIC ASSISTANCE** The transfer payment that seems to be the lightning rod for media attention and political controversy is public assistance—the government's **welfare** program. The raison d'être of welfare is to moderate the economic hardships facing the poor, the elderly, and the disabled. This is accomplished by supplementing their incomes with government-provided goods and services, direct cash payments, or both.

In 1999, the federal government spent $130.7 billion on welfare and related social services, while state and local governments added another $83.5 billion.

Who is eligible for cash-payment welfare? Until recently, eligibility was linked to single-parent families (the Aid to Families with Dependent Children program, AFDC) and to the sick or disabled (the Supplemental Security Income program, SSI). Eligibility to either one meant entitlement, with no time limit specified. Opponents of public assistance argued that cash payments and welfare programs such as food stamps and Medicaid undermined the recipients' motivation to become independent and responsible. Advocates for welfare dismissed as nonsense the idea that people prefer to live on welfare rather than work to earn a living wage.

The mid-1990s political debate on welfare resulted in Congress legislating the Personal Responsibility and Work Opportunity Reconciliation Act of 1996. This act

**Welfare**
Government-provided assistance—cash payments and goods and services—to the poor, the elderly, and the disabled. Eligibility is based principally on income and size of family.

# APPLIED PERSPECTIVE

## WELFARE REFORM AND LOW-SKILLED EMPLOYMENT

**The motivation for "ending welfare as we know it" is rooted in the belief that most current welfare recipients are capable of finding "suitable" employment.** According to this view, welfare recipients choose not to work because benefits with no time limits provide a disincentive to find work and leave welfare. Cutting off welfare after a fixed length of time is supposed to serve as the much needed "kick in the pants" to get easily employable people into the pool of readily available jobs.

There is a problem with this perspective: The typical welfare recipient lacks the skills to find economically viable employment. Those AFDC recipients who succeed in finding employment will end up in low-wage, low-skilled jobs that will not pay enough to lift them and their children out of poverty.

Women on AFDC have significantly lower levels of formal schooling than women not on AFDC. Using a nationally representative data set from 1992, we find that 44 percent of AFDC mothers have not completed high school, while only 25 percent of nonrecipients do not have high school diplomas. Just 19 percent of adult female AFDC recipients have some schooling beyond high school, while 43 percent of other women have such education. According to the National Adult Literacy Survey (NALS), most AFDC recipients are at the lowest two levels of literacy: 35 percent are at level 1, and 37 percent are at level 2.

There is a huge gap between the skills that most AFDC recipients have and the skills that most employers require. We find that over two-thirds of all employed adults have literacy levels 3 and higher. Even service-sector jobs, reputed to be low-skilled, often require more language and math skills than AFDC recipients possess.

I'M HAPPY TO BE WORKING AND I'M HAPPY TO SERVE YOU, BUT I SURE AM WORRIED THIS JOB DOESN'T PAY ENOUGH TO SUPPORT MY FAMILY.

The national statistics on the differences between the skills employers demand and the skills of AFDC recipients do not reflect the fact that AFDC families are not evenly spread across the country. More than half of welfare beneficiaries live in just a handful of states: California, Illinois, Michigan, New York, Ohio, Pennsylvania, and Texas. The geographic concentration of AFDC recipients means that there may be a fierce competition for unskilled jobs in some cities once the federal work requirements go into effect. For example, one in fifteen U.S. recipients lives in Los Angeles County, where AFDC recipients make up 10 percent of the population.

We found that, in order to provide employment for all current AFDC recipients, Los Angeles County's economy would have to create 28 percent more level 1 and nearly 10 percent more level 2 jobs. Clearly, such a huge expansion in the number of unskilled jobs in Los Angeles would require an economic miracle.

Consequently, if the goal is to keep working families out of poverty, simply forcing AFDC recipients to find jobs in the current environment will not achieve that goal. Additional public policies will be required.

### MORE ON THE NET

A number of organizations, including the Electronic Policy Network (http://www.epn.org/), the Urban Institute (http://www.urban.org/welfare/overview.htm), and the Welfare Information Network (http://www.welfareinfo.org/), provide news and commentary on welfare reform.

**Source:** Adapted from Alec R. Levenson, Elaine Reardon, and Stefanie R. Schmidt, "Welfare Reform and the Employment Prospects of AFDC Recipients," in *Jobs and Capital* (Milken Institute, Summer 1997).

created Temporary Assistance for Needy Families, which effectively abolished what had been the two principal components of our cash-aid welfare system: AFDC and Emergency Assistance to Families with Children. This major change was followed by the Balanced Budget Act of 1997, which added a welfare-to-work grant program to assist families moving from welfare to work.

The basic idea behind these welfare changes was to eliminate entitlement. No individual or family is entitled to receive welfare. Under this new welfare scheme, the federal government provides state governments with capped block grants to administer state-run welfare programs, but welfare recipients must participate in work activities within two years of receiving welfare or risk losing it. The government also imposed a time limit on welfare. Although families may be eligible for welfare on more than one occasion, eligibility per family runs out after five years of benefits.

The government's new welfare package still contains two critical carryovers from the old system: the food stamp program and Medicaid.

What are food stamps? Welfare recipients receive **food stamps** that are accepted as money at most retail stores and supermarkets. Because these stamps are earmarked for the purchase of only some goods (and not others), the government influences, at least minimally, the welfare recipients' diets. The criteria for food stamp eligibility remain as they were before: income (or lack of it) and size of family. In 1996, the food stamp program amounted to $35.2 billion.

The single most significant service item in the welfare package—$175 billion in 1999—is still **Medicaid,** a federally subsidized, state-administered program that pays the medical and hospital costs of welfare recipients and other low-income people. Medicaid covers fee-for-service payments to private physicians as well as hospitalization, nursing-home expenses, and skilled nursing care at home.

## Social Insurance

Since the 1930s, the government has taken on the functions of an insurance agent, collecting premiums from those who participate in its insurance program and paying out benefits to claimants. These premiums and benefits appear as government taxes and spending—in fact, that's what they are commonly called—but the truth of the matter is that government is principally the agency handling the insurance dollars.

Why is government in the insurance business, and what does it insure? Government is in the business because it is responding to an insurance need that, it feels, has not being adequately served by private insurance. What does it insure? In a nutshell, government insures families against incurring sizable income reductions when they retire or when they are disabled or unemployed during their working life. As you can imagine, most people who pay into the government-managed insurance program hope that they do not have to make claims for disability or unemployment.

**SOCIAL SECURITY** The core of the government-managed insurance program was established in 1935 when Congress passed the Social Security Act. **Social Security** provides old age and survivor insurance. Payments to the insured or to their surviving dependents were originally intended to supplement incomes, not to be the major source of income. Disability insurance was added to Social Security in 1956, and health insurance—Medicare—was added in 1965.

Social Security is first and foremost a pension system. There are a host of private pension systems in the marketplace, but none compares with the size and inclusiveness of Social Security. It was designed to provide income security upon retirement to people who would not otherwise have that form of security. Social Security differs from private pension systems in a number of respects.

**on the net**

The Social Security Administration (http://www.ssa.gov/) provides information on recent federal public assistance legislation (http://www.ssa.gov/legislation/legis_intro.html). For one perspective on the Personal Responsibility and Work Opportunity Reconciliation Act, review "How Congress Reformed the Welfare System" (http://www.heritage.org/heritage/congress/chapt5.html) by Robert Rector.

**Food stamp program**
An aid program that provides low-income people with stamps that can be redeemed for food and related items.

**Medicaid**
A health care program administered through Social Security that is applicable to low-income and disabled people.

**Social Security**
A social insurance program that provides benefits, subject to eligibility, to the elderly, the disabled, and their dependents.

# APPLIED PERSPECTIVE

## ARE THE SOCIAL SECURITY AND MEDICARE SYSTEMS IN JEOPARDY?

There are about as many opinions among economists concerning the viability of Social Security and Medicare as there are economists willing to talk about it.

The overriding issue is whether the aging of our population will eventually place on those taxpayers who finance Social Security and Medicare a burden so intolerable that the modus operandi of these entitlement programs will simply become unworkable.

Consider the problem. Just a few generations ago, the ratio of working people to retirees was sufficiently high to support what was then a not-too-demanding standard of living for those in retirement. That has changed. The ratio has fallen considerably, and the standard of living of those in retirement and enjoying the fruits of Social Security and Medicare has risen dramatically. If the ratio of working people to retirees keeps falling—and it will with the baby boomers soon reaching retirement age—who's left in the workplace to pay the needed Social Security taxes?

That's what unnerves a lot of economists who look at the accompanying exhibit. It shows the projected increases in the claims on the economy by the entitlement programs between 1996 and 2035. As you can see, the projected growth of Medicare claims far outstrips that of Social Security. Not really surprising. After all, there is a direct and positive relationship between age and health care demands, and with new and more life-securing technologies available in medicine, the sky seems the limit on how much a society can invest in caring for the health needs of its senior population.

How do you deal with the implications of the exhibit? Are the Social Security and Medicare systems in jeopardy? If reform is inevitable, what kind of reform will be both politically and economically sound?

Social Security is financed largely by taxes on workers' income, and promised Social Security benefits are legislated by Congress. The problem of insufficient future tax revenues to cover promised benefits can be handled in a number of ways.

First, simply raise the Social Security tax by an amount necessary to meet the promised benefits. But legislating tax increases in this political climate is politically unhealthy, and there appears to be very little support for this option. Second, reduce future benefits by a sufficient amount so that future retirees will not exhaust the projected Social Security tax revenues. This option, too, invites strong political backlash and has few staunch supporters. Third, increase the number of years of earnings used to determine benefits. This is a disguised way of reducing benefits. Fourth, change the law to allow the Social Security system to invest some of

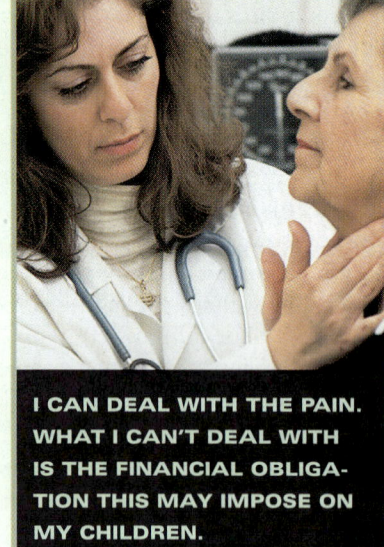

I CAN DEAL WITH THE PAIN. WHAT I CAN'T DEAL WITH IS THE FINANCIAL OBLIGATION THIS MAY IMPOSE ON MY CHILDREN.

**CURRENT AND PROJECTED LEVELS OF ENTITLEMENT PROGRAM OPERATIONS AS A PERCENTAGE OF GDP**

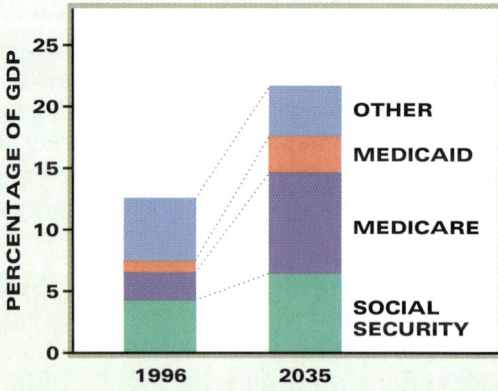

**Source:** Congressional Budget Office, *Long-Term Budgetary Pressures and Policy Options* (Washington, D.C.: Congress of the United States, March 1997), Executive Summary, Table 2.

the trust funds in the private sector, where the rates of return on investment are considerably higher than the rates currently earned by the fund's investment in long-term government bonds.

While each of these reform options will work, each is perceived by some economists as a decisive backward step in providing an acceptable standard of living for our senior citizens.

> **MORE ON THE NET**
>
> For different perspectives on Social Security reform, review the Cato Institute Project on Social Security Privatization (http://www.socialsecurity.org/) and the National Committee to Preserve Social Security and Medicare (http://www.ncpssm.org/).

First, it is compulsory. Wage earners must belong whether they like it or not. Second, Social Security transfers income across income and age groups. How so? Premiums, paid in the form of Social Security taxes, are based on ability to pay. That is, high-wage earners pay more into the system than low-wage earners. But benefits received depend not only on how much a person has paid into the system but also on the number of surviving dependents. As a result, low-wage earners tend to receive more retirement benefits, relative to their contributions, than do high-wage workers. Age is also a factor. Most people today retire with more benefits than Social Security offered, say, a generation ago. But what they paid into the system years ago was determined by what benefits were provided then. In other words, in each year younger workers paying Social Security taxes subsidize those in retirement.

Third, Social Security is a pay-as-you-go system that is financed through a payroll tax, half of which is paid by the worker and the other half by the employer. The revenues from this Social Security tax go into a trust fund from which benefits are paid out. In some years government receives less in Social Security taxes than it pays out in Social Security benefits, in which case it makes up the difference by drawing from its trust fund. In other years, more money comes in than goes out, allowing government to build up the fund.

**UNEMPLOYMENT INSURANCE** **Unemployment insurance** was introduced as a provision of the Social Security Act in 1935. Its main purpose is to provide temporary income support for unemployed workers. How much the unemployed worker receives each week and the number of weeks the unemployed worker is allowed to receive benefits varies from state to state.

**Unemployment insurance**
A program of income support for eligible workers who are temporarily unemployed.

**MEDICARE** In 1965, the government added a health care insurance program, **Medicare,** to the Social Security system. Its purpose is to reduce the financial burden of illness on the elderly. The criterion for eligibility is uncomplicated: Medicare covers everyone 65 years of age or older.

Like Social Security's pension program, Medicare's funding is anchored in a trust fund. In any year, workers pay into the Medical Insurance Trust Fund through a payroll tax system that provides the money needed to cover payments to Medicare recipients in that year.

What does Medicare provide? Subject to deductibles and caps, Medicare covers hospitalization, skilled nursing care at home, outpatient care, and physician fees.

Because Medicare is focused primarily on the elderly, who continue to be a growing percentage of our population, and because new, expensive, state-of-the-art technologies are increasingly becoming part of health care, Medicare's trust fund may soon be added to the list of endangered species. How long Medicare can continue to function as a health insurance program without radically changing its

**Medicare**
A health care program administered through Social Security that is applicable to everyone over 65 years old.

The Health Care Financing Administration, a federal agency within the Department of Health and Human Services, provides information on Medicare and Medicaid (http://www.hcfa.gov/medicaid/medicaid.htm).

## EXHIBIT 5

**SOCIAL SECURITY EXPENDITURES AS A PERCENTAGE OF GDP FOR SELECTED ECONOMIES: 1996**

| COUNTRY | PERCENTAGE OF GDP |
|---|---|
| JAPAN | 14.1 |
| UNITED STATES | 16.5 |
| CANADA | 17.7 |
| ITALY | 23.7 |
| THE NETHERLANDS | 26.7 |
| GERMANY | 29.7 |
| FRANCE | 30.1 |

**Source:** World Labour Report 2000 (Geneva: ILO, 2000), p. 313.

The Bureau of the Public Debt (http://www.publicdebt.treas.gov/), among other services, provides the amount of the federal government's debt, to the penny.

structure of revenues and benefits is a problem that ranks among the most critical government faces today.

**HOW DO OUR SOCIAL SECURITY PAYMENTS COMPARE TO THOSE ELSEWHERE?** Are our Social Security payments out of line? That is to say, is our commitment to Social Security in 1996 frightfully expensive or pitifully low? Or is it just about right? How can we assess the role of Social Security in our economy? Perhaps one way is to compare what we do to what other democratic market economies do. Exhibit 5 does just that.

What do you make of this exhibit? Whatever else can be said about our commitment to Social Security, it does not appear to be too large. The 16.5 percent of GDP is below the percentages for most similar democratic market economies. Perhaps it should give us some comfort to know we're not off the deep end.

## Interest

The government borrows, accumulates debt, and each year pays interest on that debt. In 1999 the public debt reached $5.6 trillion, and $264.7 billion was spent by government on interest payments. Both the size of the debt and the annual interest payments it creates grew considerably in the 1980s.

## IS THE LEVEL OF GOVERNMENT SPENDING TOO HIGH?

Looking back over each of these government spending items, it becomes difficult to advocate wholesale cuts in government spending. Just where would you start? What parts of what programs are expendable?

Every government dollar spent has a purpose. Moreover, every government program has a strong support system buttressed by a determined constituency. It is always possible for government to spend money foolishly, and sometimes that seems to be what it does, but what indicators should we use to gauge whether government spending—federal and state and local—is too big or too small?

### The Growth of Government Spending

Government spending in 1999 was $2,842.9 billion (or $2,500.1 in 1992 dollars), 62 percent of which was handled in Washington, D.C. How has it grown? Exhibit 6 traces the historical record of total government spending from 1970 to 1999, adjusted for inflation.

GOVERNMENT SPENDING

If your impression is that government spending just keeps going up and up, you're absolutely right! Total government spending, measured in 1992 dollars, more than doubled over the 29-year period. But that's only part of the picture. After all, our GDP was going up and up as well. Looking at the government's slice of the increasing GDP pie, then, may give us an entirely different perspective on government spending. Throughout the 1970–99 period, government's slice was no more than a few percent away from a third of the GDP pie.

**GOVERNMENT SPENDING: 1970–99 ($ BILLIONS, 1992)**

|      | TOTAL    | FEDERAL  | STATE AND LOCAL | TOTAL/GDP |
|------|----------|----------|-----------------|-----------|
| 1970 | $ 957.2  | $ 683.3  | $273.9          | 28.3      |
| 1980 | 1,392.0  | 1,030.6  | 361.4           | 30.1      |
| 1990 | 1,923.6  | 1,372.3  | 551.3           | 31.3      |
| 1999 | 2,500.1  | 1,542.5  | 957.6           | 28.3      |

Source: *Economic Report of the President, 1997* (Washington, D.C.: U.S. Department of Commerce, 2000).

## Government Spending in Other Economies

Is a third of the GDP pie too big a slice? After all, we do need our police protection, schools, and highways. How much is enough? While we are all entitled to our own opinion, it may still be worthwhile to compare our slice to those in other economies. That's what we see in Exhibit 7. We allocate a smaller portion of our GDP to government than any other nation shown, except Japan.

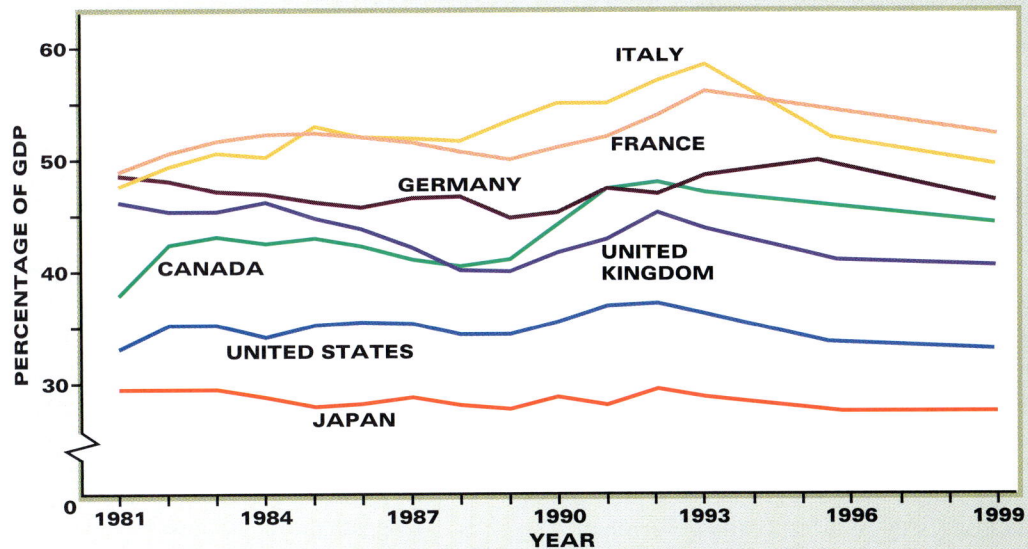

**GOVERNMENT SPENDING AS A PERCENTAGE OF GDP: 1981–99**

Source: Organisation for Economic Co-operation and Development, calendar year data.

## GOVERNMENT SPENDING AND RESOURCE ALLOCATION

As we showed in Exhibit 1, some of government spending takes the form of public and merit goods—government purchases of goods and services—and some takes the form of transfer payments.

The distinction is important. When government provides a highway, it takes steel, concrete, heavy equipment, labor, and other resources away from the production of private goods. That is, a reallocation of the economy's resources occurs. Assuming full employment, the highway we enjoy comes at the expense of private goods consumption.

What about the government's transfer payments? Do they involve the same kind of opportunity cost? Not exactly. Consider the government's welfare programs. Government spending on food stamps, for example, does not represent government purchases of goods and services. Government simply engineers a transfer of private goods and services from one group in the economy, the taxpayers, to another, the welfare recipients.

What do welfare recipients do with the transfer payments? They don't buy highways. Their purchases of private goods and services substitute for the taxpayers' purchase of private goods and services. Although these two different groups of people may buy different private goods, the allocation of GDP between private and public goods and services is unaffected.

In other words, the character of government's intervention in the allocation process depends on the character of government spending. How significant a share of GDP is in the form of government purchases? In 2000 government purchases of goods and services—putting transfer payments and interest aside—amounted to $1,279.2 billion. Big? Bigness lies in the eyes of the beholder. The $1,279.2 billion is 12.7 percent of $10,052.2 billion GDP.

# CHAPTER REVIEW

1. Government spending serves multiple purposes. On occasion, spending is used as an instrument of countercyclical policy. Government spending also provides public and merit goods as well as transfer payments.

2. Public goods are nonexclusive and nonrival. *Nonexclusive* means that once the good is provided, no one can be excluded from deriving its benefits. *Nonrival* means that one person's use of the good does not diminish the good for other people's use.

3. Merit goods are goods provided by the market, although not in quantities or at prices that government prefers. As a result, the government produces the goods and sells them at subsidized prices.

4. Transfer payments represent a redistribution of income from taxpayers to specific groups, such as welfare recipients (receiving public assistance), the unemployed (receiving unemployment insurance payments), people in retirement (receiving Social Security payments), and farm producers (receiving government subsidies).

5. Approximately 50 percent of all government spending is in the form of government purchases of public and merit goods. Another 37 percent is in the form of transfer payments. The remaining 13 percent of spending is for interest, federal grants-in-aid, and other items.

6. Approximately 60 percent of all government spending is done by the federal government. The remaining 40 percent represents state and local government spending.

7. Security, education, and transportation are the principal public and merit good items that government buys, accounting for 37 percent of total government spending.

8. The 1996 Personal Responsibility and Work Opportunity Reconciliation Act reformed our public assistance program. Welfare recipients no longer have a right to welfare and must work to receive welfare aid. Also, the government put a limit on the number of years a family can receive welfare benefits. Food stamps and Medicaid are carryovers from the old welfare program.
9. Social Security is the government's social insurance program. It takes the form of a trust fund. Contributions by both employees and employers are made to the fund, and payments are drawn from it to provide for retirement, disability, and unemployment benefits. The fund also pays for Medicare, which provides health care for the elderly.
10. Government spending during the period 1970–99 was relatively stable at 30 percent of GDP.
11. Consumer sovereignty is affected by government spending. Excluding transfer payments—since they still end up as purchasing power dictated by consumer sovereignty—government decides what goods and services will be produced for approximately 13 percent of GDP.

# KEY TERMS

Public good
Merit good
Welfare
Food stamp program
Medicaid
Social Security
Unemployment insurance
Medicare

# QUESTIONS

1. What are the principal purposes of government spending?
2. Distinguish between a public good and a merit good.
3. What are the most important spending items of the federal government? Of state and local governments?
4. Explain why each of the following is either a private good or a public good: traffic lights, in-line skates, a city park, a chicken salad sandwich, a tennis racket, national defense, a coastal lighthouse.
5. What is a transfer payment? Why does the government engage in such transfers?
6. Why is some of the federal government's spending on agriculture considered a transfer payment?
7. What are the principal 1996 changes made to our welfare program?
8. What is the principal difference between Medicare and Medicaid?
9. If government decides, it can reduce defense spending and even spending on education to a penny, but it can't do that with Social Security. Why not? (*Hint:* Distinguish between a trust fund and discretionary government spending.)
10. Is the level of government spending too high? How has it grown? How does it compare to government spending in other industrial economies?
11. Explain how government spending on transfer payments and on the purchase of public goods and services generates different patterns of resource allocations between public and private goods and services.

# ECONOMIC CONSULTANTS

## ECONOMIC RESEARCH AND ANALYSIS BY STUDENTS FOR PROFESSIONALS

The National Education Association (NEA) is an organization with over 2 million members who work at every level of education. JoAnn Weber, a high school teacher and local volunteer for the NEA, often meets with parents and school officials to discuss education funding in the United States. Recently, a group of parents expressed concerns that, first, federal government spending on education was too low, and, second, that recent political efforts to cut federal spending have had an adverse impact on education funding.

JoAnn is unsure how to answer these concerns, and she has asked Economic Consultants to provide her with information. Prepare a report for JoAnn that addresses the following issues:

1. How much does the federal government spend on education?
2. In recent years, has federal spending on education increased or decreased? By how much?
3. Does U.S. education spending, as a percentage of GDP, compare favorably or unfavorably with that of other nations?

You may find the following resources helpful as you prepare this report for JoAnn:

- **National Education Association (NEA)** (http://www.nea.org/)—The NEA provides information about its programs and activities.
- **Organisation for Economic Co-Operation and Development (OECD)** (http://www.oecd.org/els/)—The Education, Employment, Labor and Social Affairs Department of the OECD provides international data and information on education spending.
- **National Center for Education Statistics (NCES)** (http://nces.ed.gov/)—The NCES is the primary federal entity for collecting and analyzing data related to education in the United States and other nations.
- *Education Indicators: An International Perspective* (http://nces.ed.gov/pubs/eiip/index.html)—*Education Indicators: An International Perspective*, an NCES report, provides comparative data and analysis on education spending by the United States and other nations.
- **U.S. Department of Education** (http://www.ed.gov/)—The U.S. Department of Education provides information on its offices and programs, education initiatives, and reports and publications.

# PRACTICE TEST

1. The principal reasons for government spending are
   a. the funding of countercyclical policy, public goods, merit goods, and transfer payments.
   b. provisions for special interest groups.
   c. to satisfy the specific economic and political pressures placed on government.
   d. welfare and defense.
   e. education and defense.

2. Which of the following is an example of a merit good?
   a. National defense
   b. Private education
   c. Public education
   d. Professional sports
   e. Amateur sports

3. What are the properties of a public good?
   a. Government spending and government use
   b. Rivalry and exclusivity
   c. Nonrivalry and nonexclusivity
   d. Merit and security of the population
   e. Merit and government use

4. When the government receives income from one group and gives it to another group, it engages in an activity associated with
   a. countercyclical fiscal policy.
   b. transfer payments.
   c. the transformation of public into merit goods.
   d. public goods equality.
   e. merit distribution of income.

5. The largest share of state and local spending is for
   a. transfer payments.
   b. purchases.
   c. countercyclical policy.
   d. civilian protection.
   e. interest on the state and local debt.

6. Spending on public education
   a. is the largest single use of federal spending.
   b. is the largest single use of state and local spending.
   c. is divided equally among federal and state and local governments.
   d. is exclusively the responsibility of state and local governments.
   e. is exclusively the responsibility of the federal government.

7. As a percentage of GDP, spending on national defense
   a. has remained relatively constant since 1970.
   b. has risen dramatically since 1970.
   c. has fallen since 1970.
   d. is approximately 75 percent of federal spending.
   e. is approximately 75 percent of all government spending.

8. The major change in welfare legislation in the mid-1990s concerned
   a. the decrease in eligibility among welfare recipients.
   b. the elimination of entitlement to welfare.
   c. the exclusion of undocumented immigrants.
   d. the shift from cash to in-kind assistance.
   e. the shift from in-kind to cash assistance.

9. Social Security includes
   a. Medicaid.
   b. Medicare.
   c. Aid to Families with Dependent Children.
   d. public assistance.
   e. all of the above.

10. Government spending as a percentage of GDP in the United States
    a. has fallen considerably since 1970.
    b. has risen considerably since 1970.
    c. is higher than the percentages for European economies.
    d. is lower than the percentages for European economies.
    e. is similar to the average percentage for European economies.

# CHAPTER 15

# FINANCING GOVERNMENT: TAXES AND DEBT

Many years ago, one of our nation's most beloved comedians, Jack Benny, used to entertain millions on Sunday night prime-time radio. He always played the penny-pincher, obsessed with the fear of parting with money. In one of his celebrated skits, a holdup man approaches him and says, "Your money or your life." There is a long pause. The holdup man says, "Well?" And Benny replies, "Wait a minute, I'm thinking."

Change the scene and the question slightly. Ask, "Your taxes or your life," and many Americans, it seems, would be hard-pressed to decide. Exaggeration? Of course. But taxes are about as unpleasant a thought as any. We are repelled by the idea of increasing taxes, and we typically vote accordingly. As any politician who has gone through the campaign mill will tell you, the one thing you must promise never, never to do is raise taxes.

And that's strange indeed. After all, few people question our need for national defense or for most of the items that have become an integral part of our government sector. We are an intelligent people, yet we often seem to forget the obvious: There's no such thing as a free lunch.

It doesn't take much thinking, even for the village idiot, to figure out that if we demand a penny's worth of public goods, then we're going to have to tax ourselves a penny. If we raise the demand to $100 billion of public goods, then our taxes increase accordingly.

### THIS CHAPTER INTRODUCES YOU TO THE ECONOMIC PRINCIPLES ASSOCIATED WITH:

- COMMANDEERING RESOURCES
- COMMANDEERING MONEY (TAXES)
- REGRESSIVE, PROPORTIONAL, AND PROGRESSIVE TAX STRUCTURES
- SOCIAL SECURITY TAXES
- GOVERNMENT SECURITIES AND PUBLIC DEBT
- INTERNALLY AND EXTERNALLY FINANCING THE PUBLIC DEBT

## OPPORTUNITY COSTS AND TAXES

Put this one-to-one relationship between public goods and taxes in real terms. Consider a public goods demand in the form of a fighter aircraft. How do we go about getting it, and what must we give up to get it? To produce a fighter aircraft, we are obliged to give up something else that could have been produced with the resources used to produce the aircraft. That is to say, to produce a public good, *we tax our ability to produce other goods.* The opportunity cost of providing the aircraft is illustrated in the production possibilities curve of Exhibit 1.

Producing the first airplane means giving up 500 houses. The economy's output shifts from point *a* to point *b* on the production possibilities curve. Simple enough? But how do you get people to give up 500 houses? That is, how is it physically done? Even if people are willing to sacrifice houses for the airplane, how does government go about designing a mechanism that shifts resources from home building to aircraft making?

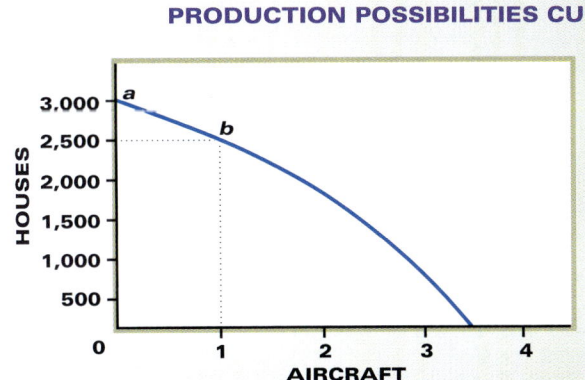

**PRODUCTION POSSIBILITIES CURVE**

The 500 houses, which are the opportunity cost of producing one aircraft, are depicted in the movement along the production possibilities curve from *a* to *b*.

EXHIBIT | 1

## COMMANDEERING RESOURCES

The most direct method a government can use to acquire resources is simply to commandeer them. In fact, that's precisely the way governments for centuries have acquired resources. That's how pharaohs built their pyramids. That's how armies have often been recruited.

In the economy of Exhibit 1, the government can just go out to the construction sites, round up a number of construction workers, transport them to the aircraft factories, and set them to work. The result is fewer houses and more airplanes.

Exaggeration? It was customary throughout the Middle Ages for governments to construct road systems by just that kind of commandeering. During our Civil War, draft animals, wagons, and food were sometimes commandeered by both southern and northern armies from unlucky farmsteads that happened to be located close to a war zone.

Even modern democratic governments haven't completely abandoned this practice of commandeering resources. After all, isn't the military draft simply another form of commandeering labor? Army wage rates are not related to the draftees' opportunity costs. Although we recently switched from the draft system to an all-volunteer army, some European armies are still recruited through a draft.

Military service aside, there are good reasons why the practice of commandeering has been virtually forsaken by democratic governments as a method of procuring resources. It can be capricious and unpopular, but above all else, it is terribly inefficient. Suppose government decides to produce that aircraft. Should it really draft construction workers to make it? Do they have the skills? Would *you* fly it?

# THE TAX SYSTEM

The tax system is an alternative way of shifting resources from the private sector to government. In this system, *government commandeers money, not resources.* Government uses the money in the marketplace to buy what it needs.

There's no need now for the government to run after construction workers or aeronautical engineers. It taxes money away from the general population and *buys* fighter aircraft. Who produces it? An aircraft company, of course. Why shouldn't it? It gets paid by government. The aeronautical engineers, along with everyone else associated with building the airplane, are hired by the company at wage rates that match or better their opportunity costs.

Since people end up—after taxes are imposed—with smaller after-tax incomes, their demand curves for private goods, such as houses, decrease. This is how resources used in the production of private goods are transferred through the government to the aircraft company.

How much money should government tax away from the people? You might suppose that it depends upon how many airplanes or other public goods and services it intends to buy. But sometimes, cause and effect get reversed. Government buys only what its tax revenues allow.

# THERE'S MORE THAN ONE WAY TO LEVY TAXES

Suppose the government decides to spend $100 billion and plans to finance the $100 billion expenditure by taxation. How does it go about taxing? Taxes are not voluntary contributions. The government has to be particularly careful about the method it uses to raise the $100 billion. It has several options.

## The Poll (or Head) Tax

**Poll tax**
A tax of a specific absolute sum levied on every person or every household.

The government can levy a fixed tax, sometimes called a **poll tax,** on every adult in the population. If tax equity—the fairness of the tax—is an issue, the poll tax presents a serious problem. If everyone is taxed the same absolute amount, say, $500, then poorer people end up paying a higher percentage of their income. Economists describe such a tax as **regressive.** The poor pay proportionally more.

**Regressive income tax**
A tax whose impact varies inversely with the income of the person taxed. Poor people have a higher percentage of their income taxed than do rich people.

But who are the poor? If the government had little or no information about people's personal incomes, then the poll tax might be the most equitable way of distributing the tax burden. You can see why a poll tax would be an attractive option in some less-developed economies where income data are virtually unknown.

## The Income Tax

In most modern economies, however, governments have access to income data. They can tax these incomes in as many ways as their imagination allows, but two options stand out as the most used.

**Proportional income tax**
A tax that is a fixed percentage of income, regardless of the level of income.

**THE PROPORTIONAL INCOME TAX SYSTEM** The government can levy a flat-rate tax on personal income, that is, tax a fixed percentage of all incomes. Unlike a poll tax, the rich and poor don't end up paying the same amount. Now the rich obviously pay more. In the **proportional income tax** system, equity is described as paying the *same proportion* of income to taxes.

Consider, for example, two people who work but earn very different incomes. Sandy Roos, an oncology nurse, earns $25,000. Her next-door neighbor, Gary

Behrman, is a psychologist earning $50,000. If the flat-tax rate is 20 percent, then the government collects a total of $15,000. Gary, who ends up paying twice the tax Sandy pays, would probably prefer the poll tax. If you were in his shoes, wouldn't you? What about Sandy?

The Internal Revenue Service (http://www.irs.gov/) provides information and statistics (http://www.irs.ustreas.gov/prod/tax_stats/) on federal individual income taxes, corporate income taxes, and excise taxes.

|  | Income | Tax Rate | Tax Bill |
|---|---|---|---|
| Gary | $50,000 | 20% | $10,000 |
| Sandy | $25,000 | 20% | $ 5,000 |

**THE PROGRESSIVE INCOME TAX SYSTEM** Sandy would probably complain about the flat-tax rate. She would argue that a flat-tax rate, although better than a poll tax, is unfair because the tax burden still falls more heavily upon the poor than upon the rich.

She believes that she suffers a greater loss in giving up 20 percent of her income than Gary does in giving up 20 percent of his. After all, he makes twice her income. She thinks that the enjoyment she derives from the $5,000 she gives up is greater than the enjoyment Gary gives up paying his $10,000 tax.

Of course, it is impossible to make interpersonal comparisons of enjoyment. How can she possibly know how he feels about giving up $10,000? But her reasoning is entirely plausible, isn't it?

At least some governments think so. Instead of taxing a flat rate across incomes, they design a **progressive income tax** structure in which the tax rate on higher incomes increases progressively. For example, the government could tax everyone's first $25,000 at 20 percent, everyone's second $25,000 at 40 percent, everyone's third $25,000 at 50 percent, and all income beyond $75,000 at 60 percent. As you see, the marginal tax rate is steeper in the higher income brackets.

What does Gary Behrman pay under such a progressive tax system? He pays 20 percent on his first $25,000, or $5,000, plus 40 percent, or $10,000, on his second $25,000. His total tax is now $15,000, $5,000 more than he paid before. Sandy's tax remains unchanged at $5,000.

**Progressive income tax**
A tax whose rate varies directly with the income of the person taxed. Rich people pay a higher tax rate—a larger percentage of their income is taxed—than do poor people.

|  | Income |  | Tax Rate | Tax Bill |
|---|---|---|---|---|
| Gary | 1st | $25,000 | 20% | $ 5,000 |
|  | 2nd | $25,000 | 40% | $10,000 |
|  |  |  |  | $15,000 |
| Sandy | 1st | $25,000 | 20% | $ 5,000 |

Gary now ends up paying three times the tax Sandy pays. Through this progressive tax system, based on ability to pay, the government hopes to achieve a more equitable sharing of the tax burden. It calculates that Gary's loss of enjoyment in giving up $15,000 now approximates the enjoyment loss incurred by Sandy.

Of course, the government can introduce exemptions and allow deductions from all sorts of taxable income. But as you would guess, there will always be some grumbling among some people no matter what exemptions and deductions are allowed and no matter what the tax rates are at various income brackets.

## The Corporate Income Tax

In most modern democratic economies, governments also tax the income of corporations. They could levy a progressive **corporate income tax,** using the same rationale that justifies imposing a progressive income tax, but there's a complicating factor here. Shareholders of corporations receive income in the form of dividends

**Corporate income tax**
A tax levied on a corporation's income before dividends are distributed to stockholders.

# APPLIED PERSPECTIVE

## ARE WE REALLY PAYING HIGH TAXES?

**N**obody likes to pay taxes, although we grudgingly accept the idea that we have to (just as we have to go to the dentist). But it's one thing to be taxed, and quite another to be weighted down with taxes. And that's the complaint we commonly hear. Don't we? In fact, it would be difficult to find anybody in the United States who would not buy into the proposition that we are, as a nation, heavily overtaxed and that this taxation will yet be the ruin of us all.

Even a comparative analysis with economies similar to our own of tax revenue share of GDP—which shows us as a relatively lightly taxed people—would not really matter. Aversion to taxes is, in many cases, visceral. Still, it may be worthwhile to make comparisons, because they are so striking. Look at the accompanying table.

Look at taxation as a percentage of GDP. Whereas taxes represent 34.3 percent of GDP in the United States, it is over 50 percent in Sweden and Denmark and over 40 percent in most other Western European economies. While the high percentages in Scandinavia might be attributed to the social democratic governments there, the same cannot be argued for the United Kingdom and Germany. The data are unambiguous. Comparatively speaking, we simply do not pay high taxes.

**TAX REVENUES, BY COUNTRY (PERCENTAGE OF GDP)**

|  | PERCENTAGE OF GDP |
|---|---|
| JAPAN | 30.5 |
| AUSTRALIA | 33.6 |
| UNITED STATES | 34.3 |
| UNITED KINGDOM | 40.6 |
| CANADA | 43.4 |
| GERMANY | 45.1 |
| THE NETHERLANDS | 46.4 |
| ITALY | 46.7 |
| BELGIUM | 49.5 |
| NORWAY | 50.0 |
| FRANCE | 51.1 |
| DENMARK | 56.8 |
| SWEDEN | 62.7 |

**Source:** OECD.

### MORE ON THE NET

Visit a few organizations that advocate tax reform, such as Americans for Tax Reform (http://www.atr.org/) and Citizens for Tax Justice (http://www.ctj.org/). Do these organizations believe U.S. citizens are taxed too heavily? Too lightly? Why?

---

and since their personal incomes are certainly not identical, the burden of the corporate income tax—whatever its progressivity—would fall unevenly among corporate shareholders.

## The Property Tax

Why limit taxes to income and profit? Why not tax wealth? Why shouldn't the government also impose a tax on part or all of a person's wealth?

Taxing wealth could involve the government in the rather messy business of taxing personal belongings, such as furniture, carpets, and household appliances. Or the government could tax financial assets, such as savings deposits, bonds, stocks, and certificates of deposit, which would be much easier to evaluate. The government could also tax real estate.

The most commonly taxed wealth holdings are residential, commercial, and industrial properties. Typically, the **property tax** is a flat-rate tax applied to the property's assessed value. In this sense it becomes a proportional wealth tax. That is, people who live in mansions on hilltops pay more than people who live in mobile homes. But how much more? The proportionality of the tax depends on accurate assessments of property values.

What about financial wealth? Don't we pay taxes on our savings accounts? No! The government typically taxes the *income earned* on savings, which is taxed as personal income, but not the accounts themselves.

## Excise Taxes

Aside from taxing personal income, corporate profits, and physical and financial property, the government can levy taxes on specific goods and services that people consume. It has several options.

It can levy (1) a **unit tax**—an amount of money per item; (2) a **sales tax**—a percentage of the sales price on every item sold; or (3) a **customs duty**—a sales tax applied to foreign goods imported into the economy. All of these are different kinds of **excise tax.**

In any form, an excise tax is regressive. For example, if you fill up your gas tank in New Hampshire, the 24-cents-per-gallon unit tax on the 20 gallons purchased yields the government $4.80. Dorothy Shelly-Vickers's Porsche at the next pump takes 20 gallons as well, and Dorothy pays the same $4.80 tax. But the $4.80 tax Dorothy pays probably represents a smaller percentage of her income than it does of yours.

If you are impressed with the $60,000 Porsche and decide to buy one yourself, the 20 percent customs duty paid by the Porsche dealer and passed on to you plus the 10 percent sales tax you pay on the $60,000 purchase nets the government $18,000. The tax is regressive, unrelated to income, but the government probably figures that a new Porsche owner can afford that level of taxation.

The equity issue may not be very disturbing in the matter of Porsches—after all, few of the poor own one—but sales taxes on bread, milk, medicine, and other basics of life do add up, and their burden tends to fall more heavily upon the poor. Governments typically exercise moral judgment in levying excise taxes. Some exclude from taxation such items as milk, medicine, and books and place a relatively high rate on items such as cigarettes and alcohol. Discriminatory? Of course.

*In many societies, governments exclude books from sales tax. What socially desirable items would you choose to exclude from sales tax? Go to the Interactive Study Center at http://gottheil.swcollege.com and click on the "Your Turn" button to submit your example. Student submissions will be posted to the Web site, and perhaps we will use some in future editions of the book!*

Like a poll tax, an excise tax is relatively easy to impose. It doesn't require the government to know much about your income, your corporation's profit, or your property assets. When you buy milk, you pay a tax. When you smoke, you pay a tax. It's as simple as that. For some governments in some economies, it's about the only tax they can administer.

## THE SOCIAL SECURITY TAX

How your $1,000 of income tax or your $10 sales tax on shoes is used by the government is left to government discretion. It can use these taxes to purchase an aircraft or an interstate highway. It can use them to retire the national debt. There is no connection between the source of the tax and the purpose it's applied to.

**Property tax**
A tax levied on the value of physical assets such as land, or financial assets such as stock and bonds.

**Unit tax**
A fixed tax in the form of cents or dollars per unit, levied on a good or service.

**Sales tax**
A tax levied in the form of a specific percentage of the value of the good or service.

**Customs duty**
A sales tax applied to a foreign good or service.

**Excise tax**
Any tax levied on a good or service, such as a unit tax, a sales tax, or a customs duty.

Why are excise taxes regressive?

However, unlike corporate and personal income taxes as well as property, estate, gift, and excise taxes, Social Security contributions, commonly referred to as Social Security taxes, are earmarked funds. That is, they are used specifically to finance the benefits that the Social Security system is obligated to pay. The system provides retirement income, survivors' income, income to the disabled, and hospital insurance.

The government is simply the Social Security system's collection and disbursement agency. Funds are collected by the government from workers and businesses, and government pays out the benefits.

In any one year, the Social Security taxes collected by the government do not necessarily equal the Social Security payments that the government makes. What happens when there is a surplus? The funds are invested in government bonds, which pay interest to the Social Security system.

Although the government acts as the system's agency, it is not simply a conduit of funds. It decides not only on the amount and quality of benefits paid out, but on the form of revenues collected.

## ACTUALLY, EVERYTHING IS TAXABLE!

When you think about it, there is probably nothing that can't be taxed. Even love and marriage. Don't we pay marriage license fees? Of course, not everything is. In fact, what gets taxed is surprisingly limited and varies among the forms of government doing the taxing. The federal government, for example, relies almost exclusively on personal income, corporate income, and excise taxes. It collects revenue from its estate and gift taxes, but these are rather minor sums.

Even among the sources it taxes, the federal government is still selective. Not all personal income or corporate income is subject to taxation. The government allows deductions, exemptions, credits, and write-offs that reduce the tax base. Matters of fairness, incentives to work, incentives to save, and incentives to invest influence what government decides.

Some state governments, too, tax personal and corporate income. Among those that do, the variations in rates, progressivity, and what actually gets taxed are great. States also levy their own excise taxes. Local governments rely heavily on property taxes.

Because the federal government taxes two of the most productive revenue sources—personal and corporate income—it shares some of its tax revenues with both state and local governments. Local governments also receive some funding from their state governments.

## THE U.S. TAX STRUCTURE

What does the U.S. tax structure look like? Exhibit 2 describes the federal income tax structure.

Note how the marginal tax rate increases from bracket to bracket, from 15 percent at the lower end to 39.6 percent at the upper end. Progressive? This five-bracket structure, legislated in the 1986 tax reform, replaced a tax structure that had more brackets and higher rates. This 2000 structure represents a remarkable change, particularly when compared to the 1959 structure for joint incomes, which had seven income brackets and an upper marginal tax rate of 91 percent.

**2000 TAX RATE SCHEDULE FOR MARRIED PERSONS FILING JOINTLY**

| INCOME BRACKET | PERCENTAGE OF INCOME TAXED | OF THE AMOUNT OVER |
|---|---|---|
| $0 TO $43,850 | 15 | |
| $43,851 TO $105,950 | 28 | $43,850 |
| $105,951 TO $161,450 | 31 | $105,950 |
| $161,451 TO $288,350 | 36 | $161,450 |
| $288,351 AND OVER | 39.6 | $288,350 |

**Source:** Internal Revenue Service, *Instructions for Form 1040* (Washington, D.C.: Department of the Treasury, 2000), p. 71.

EXHIBIT 2

# FEDERAL, STATE, AND LOCAL TAX REVENUES

The revenues generated by taxes for federal, state, and local governments are shown in Exhibit 3.

As you can see and perhaps could have guessed, the single most important tax is the income tax. The lion's share of the income tax goes to the federal government and accounts for almost half of the federal tax revenues. The income tax is also an important source of revenue for state governments. Local governments rely almost exclusively upon the property tax for their self-generating revenues. The state and local governments also receive revenues in the form of grants-in-aid from the federal government.

**FEDERAL, STATE, AND LOCAL GOVERNMENT REVENUES: 2000 ($ BILLIONS)**

| | FEDERAL | STATE AND LOCAL |
|---|---|---|
| **TAX REVENUES** | $2,090.4 | $1,243.8 |
| INCOME TAX | 1030.7 | 277.4 |
| CORPORATE INCOME | 250.5 | 41.4 |
| SALES, EXCISE, CUSTOMS | 109.1 | 413.5 |
| PROPERTY | — | 250.2 |
| FEDERAL REVENUE SHARING | — | 251.2 |
| SOCIAL SECURITY CONTRIBUTIONS | 700.1 | 10.0 |

**Source:** *Survey of Current Business* (Washington, D.C.: U.S. Department of Commerce, December 2000).

EXHIBIT 3

# INTERDISCIPLINARY PERSPECTIVE

## DON'T MESS WITH THE IRS: AL CAPONE'S ULTIMATE MISTAKE

**C**rime doesn't pay? If the crime is racketeering, intimidation, brutality, or execution-style murder, it may pay. But it probably doesn't if the crime is tax evasion. In the one case, you're only up against the FBI, the police, and the courts. In the other, you're up against the Internal Revenue Service (IRS). Forget it! It's no contest.

Al Capone, the most notorious mobster of the 1920s and 1930s, figured that out only too late. He got away with multiple murders, high-stakes bootlegging, and wholesale racketeering. But his *real* troubles began when the IRS went after him.

The key to Capone's eventual demise was a 1927 Supreme Court decision against a small-time bootlegger named Manny Sullivan. The court ruled that although reporting and paying income tax on illegally derived revenues was self-incriminating, that did not make it unconstitutional. That ruling sent the tax-evading Manny Sullivan to prison. It also gave IRS's Elmer Ivey the idea. He put together a special intelligence unit of the IRS to nail Al Capone for tax evasion.

Capone's "activities" were legendary and engaged in with virtual impunity. He had a highly disciplined and corporate-styled criminal enterprise. He bought enough of the Chicago police force and the Chicago mayor to assure himself minimal harassment, if any at all. *But he didn't pay his full share of income tax.*

HERE'S AN OFFER *YOU* CAN'T REFUSE: ELEVEN YEARS!

The IRS went to work. It knew this: When Capone wanted to be conspicuously absent from an impending Chicago crime or when he simply wanted to relax with his family—wife Mea and son Sonny—he would retreat to his palatial estate in Palm Island, Florida. That estate, to the IRS, was evidence that Capone had "earned" considerably more income than he admitted to. As well, the IRS came into possession of several of Capone's financial ledgers that detailed his enormous unreported incomes.

The accumulated evidence of Capone's unreported income was overwhelming. In October 1931, he was convicted of tax evasion and sentenced to serve 11 years at Alcatraz, a federal prison. There, his health declined rapidly. He suffered dementia, a characteristic of late-stage syphilis.

Not all tax evaders are as notorious as Al Capone. Although there are many who had some celebrity status—such as Vice-President Spiro Agnew, who was convicted of tax evasion in the 1970s—most are folks like you and me. But we are many! Some evasions are relatively large, while others are small-time, but the unreported incomes year after year add up to considerable losses of government revenue. Punishments are typically fines, although many tax evaders do end up in prison.

The accompanying table details the tax loss for the end years 1981 and 1992.

### RELATIVE MAGNITUDE OF TAX EVASION: 1981–92 ($ BILLIONS, 1992)

|  | 1981 | 1992 |
|---|---|---|
| TOTAL TAX LOSS | $76 | $127 |
| AS PERCENT OF INCOME TAX COLLECTED | 23.3 | 22.0 |
| AS PERCENT OF GDP | 1.6 | 2.0 |
| ANNUAL GROWTH RATE OF TAX LOSS |  | 6.1 |

According to the IRS, individuals account for $94 billion of the $127 billion tax loss in 1992 while corporations account for the remaining $33 billion. Approximately half of the $127 billion represents unreported income. The other half of the tax loss results from less offensive taxpayer behavior, such as errors in calculation and overstated deductions.

**MORE ON THE NET**
Review other IRS statistics at http://www.irs.gov/. Click on "Tax Stats" at the bottom of the page.

## TAXES, SPENDING, AND DEFICITS

The $253.3 billion in federal budget surplus in 2000—$2,089.4 billion in tax receipts and $1,836 billion in spending—came as a welcome relief from the long years of federal budget deficits. In the 31-year period 1970–2000, only the last three were budget surplus years. Many of the deficit years generated deficits in excess of $100 billion. The 1992 deficit, the largest in the period, was $297.5 billion. How has the government managed to stay solvent while incurring the prolonged and sizable deficits of Exhibit 4 year after year? *By borrowing*.

## FINANCING GOVERNMENT SPENDING THROUGH DEBT

When the federal government discovers that its revenues fall short of its planned spending, it instructs the Treasury Department to do precisely what private companies do when they need funds beyond their own resources to finance investment projects—print up interest-bearing IOUs and peddle them on the market.

Every $100 IOU that the Treasury sells transfers $100 to the government from the person who buys it. Why would anyone want to hold the Treasury's IOU? Because it yields interest. Besides, buying a Treasury IOU is not risky business. The U.S. government has never welshed on its IOUs.

Who buys them? Individuals like you, commercial banks—actually anyone interested in a secure, interest-bearing investment—and even the Federal Reserve. Look at Exhibit 5.

The Bureau of the Public Debt (http://www.publicdebt.treas.gov/) provides the latest statistics on the public debt, as well as information on Treasury bonds and notes.

**THE FEDERAL GOVERNMENT'S SURPLUSES AND DEFICITS: 1970–2000 ($ BILLIONS)**

| | SURPLUS/DEFICIT | | SURPLUS/DEFICIT | | SURPLUS/DEFICIT |
|---|---|---|---|---|---|
| 1970 | –14.4 | 1981 | –53.7 | 1992 | –297.5 |
| 1971 | –26.8 | 1982 | –132.6 | 1993 | –274.1 |
| 1972 | –22.5 | 1983 | –173.9 | 1994 | –212.3 |
| 1973 | –11.2 | 1984 | –168.1 | 1995 | –192.0 |
| 1974 | –13.9 | 1985 | –177.1 | 1996 | –136.8 |
| 1975 | –69.3 | 1986 | –192.1 | 1997 | –48.8 |
| 1976 | –53.0 | 1987 | –147.9 | 1998 | –46.9 |
| 1977 | –45.2 | 1988 | –137.4 | 1999 | 124.4 |
| 1978 | –26.9 | 1989 | –130.0 | 2000 | 253.3 |
| 1979 | –11.4 | 1990 | –173.0 | | |
| 1980 | –53.8 | 1991 | –215.3 | | |

Source: *Economic Report of the President, 1997* (Washington, D.C.: U.S. Government Printing Office, 1997), p. 394, and Bureau of Economic Analysis, "Overview of the Economy," 2000.

## EXHIBIT 5

### OWNERSHIP OF THE U.S. PUBLIC DEBT: 2000
### (PERCENTAGE OF TOTAL)

| OWNER | PERCENTAGE OF TOTAL |
|---|---|
| FEDERAL AGENCIES AND TRUST FUNDS | 38.5 |
| FEDERAL RESERVE | 8.9 |
| COMMERCIAL BANKS | 3.9 |
| MONEY MARKET FUNDS | 5.6 |
| INSURANCE COMPANIES | 2.1 |
| STATE AND LOCAL GOVERNMENTS, INDIVIDUALS | 4.5 |
| PENSION FUNDS | 6.8 |
| FOREIGNERS | 22.0 |
| OTHERS* | 7.7 |

*Savings and loan associations, nonprofit institutions, credit unions, mutual savings banks, corporate pension trust funds, certain U.S. Treasury deposit accounts, and federally sponsored agencies.
Source: *Federal Reserve Bulletin* (Washington, D.C., January 2001), p. A27.

Wouldn't you think that foreigners, looking for a good way to earn interest, would also consider buying the Treasury IOUs? If enough IOUs are sold, the Treasury covers the deficit created by the difference between government's spending and taxes.

But solving one problem creates another. Now the government is involved in **public debt**. After all, Treasury IOUs in the hands of others are financial claims against the government. How can the government pay these claims? One way is to raise taxes and use the revenues to redeem the IOUs. But it was insufficient taxes to cover spending that caused the deficit in the first place. The other way is to sell new IOUs to pay off the old ones.

### Treasury Bonds, Bills, and Notes

**Public debt**
The total value of government securities—Treasury bills, notes, and bonds—held by individuals, businesses, other government agencies, and the Federal Reserve.

Government sells a variety of debt forms, principally to satisfy the tastes of debt holders. People who prefer not to tie up their money in long-term debt holdings can buy Treasury bills that mature in 3 months, 6 months, or 12 months. These bills are offered in minimum amounts of $10,000 and in multiples of $5,000 above the minimum, which makes them inaccessible to some people.

Longer-term debt is available in the form of Treasury notes and bonds. Because they are sold in denominations as low as $1,000, they are more accessible than Treasury bills. Notes carry maturities of 2 to 10 years. Treasury bonds have a maturity of 30 years.

All Treasury securities (bonds, notes, and bills) are marketable debt. That is, anyone holding a Treasury security who decides to sell it before maturity can offer it for sale on the market.

## TRACKING GOVERNMENT DEBT

The federal government has been in the business of supplementing tax revenues with sales of Treasury securities for many, many years. Federal debt more than doubled during the 1930s, reflecting the extraordinarily large deficits incurred during the Great Depression. It increased fivefold during the 1940s, largely due to expenditures associated with World War II. It took a long hard climb thereafter. Exhibit 6 records a half-century of federal indebtedness, from 1945 to 1996.

In panel *a*, the sharp rise in the 1970s mirrors the sharp rise in annual federal deficits, which occurred largely because the OPEC-induced recession took its toll on tax revenues. Federal debt more than doubled. The combination of the tax reforms of 1981 and 1986 (which reduced tax rates) and the recessions of the early 1980s and early 1990s doubled the debt once again.

## THE FEDERAL DEBT

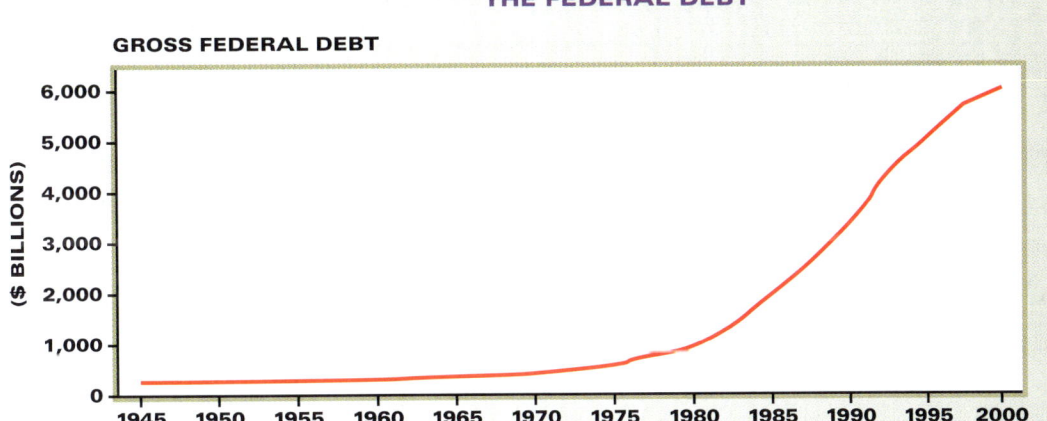

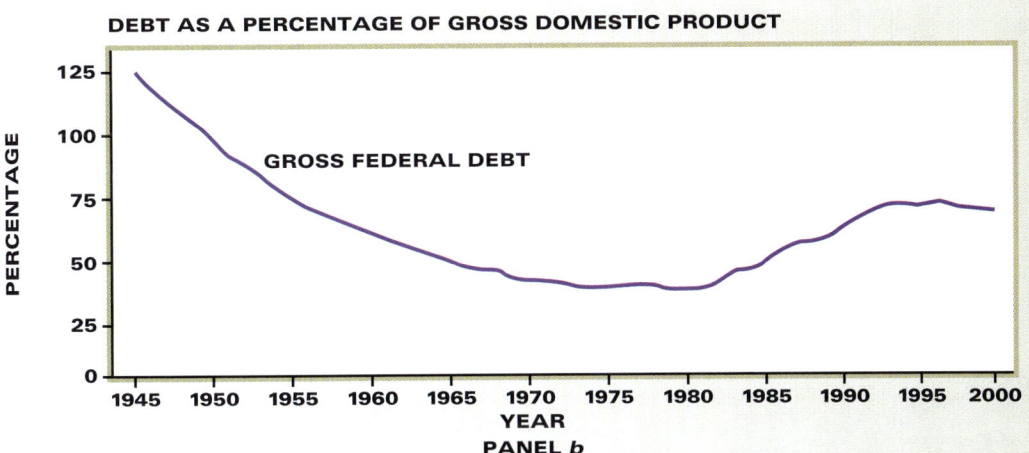

Panel *a* depicts the 1945–2000 growth of the public debt. Panel *b* depicts the ratio of the public debt to GDP. If the economy's growth rate is greater than the growth rate of public debt, the debt-to-GDP ratio falls, even though the absolute level of the public debt may increase.

Source: *Statistical Abstract of the United States, 2000* (Washington, D.C.: U.S. Department of Commerce, 2000).

### Looking at Ratios, Not Dollars

But how horrendous is the debt? It is frightening when looked at in terms of absolute dollars, but perhaps less frightening when viewed as a percentage of GDP. Look at Exhibit 6, panel *b*.

During the first half of the 1940s, the ratio rocketed above 100 percent and then drifted steadily downward to approximately 40 percent in the 1980s, before climbing again during the 1980s to reach 57 percent in 2000.

Is $5,686.0 billion too large? Is 57 percent of GDP worrisome? Exhibit 7 records the debt ratios for other democratic market economies.

Just because other economies' debt ratios are similar to our own does not necessarily mean our debt ratio or theirs isn't a problem. But it is perhaps noteworthy that our ratios are not out of line. In Italy, the ratio of public sector debt to GDP is 119.9.

## EXHIBIT 7

**GROSS PUBLIC DEBT AS A PERCENT OF GDP FOR SELECTED ECONOMIES: 1998**

Most OECD economies have debt-GDP ratios similar to or greater than the ratio for the United States.

| Country | % | Country | % |
|---|---|---|---|
| AUSTRALIA | 33.6 | ITALY | 119.9 |
| BELGIUM | 115.9 | NETHERLANDS | 67.4 |
| CANADA | 89.9 | SWEDEN | 75.5 |
| FRANCE | 66.5 | JAPAN | 97.3 |
| GERMANY | 63.1 | UNITED KINGDOM | 56.6 |

**Source:** *Statistical Abstract of the United States, 2000* (Washington, D.C.: U.S. Department of Commerce, 2000), p. 847.

Canada's ratio of net public debt to GDP in 1998 was 89.6 percent. As you can see in Exhibit 7, the ratios for France, Germany, and the Netherlands match fairly closely the ratio in the United States.

## DOES DEBT ENDANGER FUTURE GENERATIONS?

One of the most commonly held views about government debt is that "we can live in debt today, but only at tomorrow's expense." That is, by incurring debt now, we bequeath a debt problem to our children. That's a tough charge to make. And it seems to make a certain amount of sense. After all, *someone* has to pay! If the debtors don't, won't their children have to?

Let's pursue the debt burden argument by examining what happens to debt and the debt burden when a government finances a one-year war by selling bonds. We'll simplify the argument by supposing that prior to the war, GDP was $1,000. Let's assume also an economy initially with no taxes, no government spending, and no private savings. People simply consumed all of the $1,000 GDP.

Now, responding to external aggression, the government chooses not to tax but instead to finance the defense of the nation by selling Treasury bonds totaling $100 at 10 percent interest. In other words, it chooses to incur public debt.

Let's compare the prewar and wartime conditions:

| Prewar | | Wartime | |
|---|---|---|---|
| GDP = | $1,000 | GDP = | $1,000 |
| Consumption = | 1,000 | Consumption = | 900 |
| Government = | 0 | Government = | 100 |

Before the war, the people produced and consumed the $1,000 GDP. Things change when the war comes. During the war year, the government sells $100 worth of bonds to *its people*. Now the people, exchanging $100 for the bonds, can consume only $900. What did government do with the $100? It spent it on the purchase of ships, tanks, aircraft, and armed forces.

# GLOBAL PERSPECTIVE

## HATRED OF TAX COLLECTION IS THE WAY OF THE WORLD

**In Russia, tax collectors now wear commando uniforms and carry weapons. In China, only suckers pay taxes. In Sweden, the government and your employer do your taxes for you.** Perhaps the only thing universal about taxes is that no one likes to pay them.

"We are too heavily taxed," gripes securities industry executive Peter Walker in London. "People who have more money have more places to hide it," grumbles Harry Brum, a 36-year-old elevator repairman in Stuttgart, Germany. "They pay less in taxes than those of us who earn an average income."

For all its faults, the U.S. tax system is one of the world's most efficient. About 83 percent of taxes owed come into the U.S. Internal Revenue Service voluntarily, a figure that is the envy of most other nations. IRS audits and investigations bring in an additional 3 percent, leaving 14 percent of U.S. taxes owed uncollected every year. The IRS spends 50 cents to collect $100 in taxes. British tax collectors spend $1.72 to collect $100; Japanese, $1.00; Canadians, $1.13.

**FRANCE:** Everyone pays a 20.6 percent value-added tax on most goods and services; food and other essentials are taxed at 5.5 percent. Then the government takes money out of paychecks to cover the state health service and social security. The French also pay income taxes ranging from 10.5 percent to 54 percent, but there are so many deductions that half of France's households pay no income tax at all.

French tax collectors also are more sympathetic than their IRS counterparts: They'll negotiate lower tax payments and waive penalties for taxpayers who lose their jobs or face other hardships.

**RUSSIA:** Collecting taxes is a dangerous business. Hundreds of Russian tax collectors have been assaulted; some have been murdered. Tax cheating is widespread, as is corruption among the tax cops.

YOU WANT TAXES? FOR WHOSE POCKETS? THE GOVERNMENT'S OR YOURS? I WORK HARD, I KEEP MY MONEY. GO AHEAD, SHOOT ME.

In a desperate effort to bolster its finances, the Russian government launched a major effort to encourage taxpayers to file their income taxes by the spring deadline. It also tried to frighten evaders by parading a recently established tax police brigade, decked out in commando uniforms and heavily armed.

Meanwhile, Russian politicians are squabbling over a plan to overhaul the nation's antiquated tax system, trimming five income tax brackets (ranging from 12 percent to 35 percent) to two (12 percent and 30 percent). The Yeltsin administration figures tax reform is needed to ensure the continued flow of Western aid and investment.

**CHINA:** Virtually no one pays income tax voluntarily. Those who do almost always understate their earnings. Chinese citizens are supposed to go to the local tax bureau by the 7th of each month to pay taxes for the previous month. Only income over 800 yuan a month, slightly less than $100, is taxable. There is a graduated scale starting at 5 percent of income and rising to 45 percent.

The government newspapers are always extolling the virtues of model citizens who pay their taxes voluntarily, but any individual or business owner who does so is viewed as a fool. The few peasants who earn enough to pay taxes are in a tougher situation. In some places, they must pay their taxes in grain.

Until about five years ago, the government didn't view individual incomes as a significant source of revenue because incomes were so low. The government has begun to get more zealous about collecting taxes, but it still generally targets state companies, private businesses, and joint ventures. Chinese business owners typically evade taxes by keeping only a token amount of money in their "principal bank account." By law, they are not allowed to have more than one account for their businesses, but that law is widely ignored.

*continued on next page*

**GERMANY:** The federal government has been tied up all year trying to reform the tax system and cut the income tax. The reform effort has failed for now, except for a cut in the so-called "solidarity tax" on income paid by all taxpayers to help bring eastern Germany's infrastructure and economy up to par with the western part of the country.

Meanwhile, German taxpayers complain that their tax system unfairly favors the wealthy. "People who earn a lot of money should be sharing the burden," says Erika Geldner, 63, a retired secretary who lives in Esslingen, near Stuttgart.

**SWEDEN:** Most citizens don't have to worry about filing their taxes. Businesses deduct the tax from the employees' wages and send it into the government. Banks send the government information about citizens' accounts. The government calculates citizens' tax bills. Once a year, in the spring, it sends a notice saying whether money is owed or a refund is due. If citizens accept it, the form is signed and sent back. Or they can try to claim some special deductions (for job-related expenses, for instance). But they had better be ready to document them with receipts.

The new system had a rocky start. The government made some well-publicized gaffes, miscalculating some people's taxes. But now it seems to be working well. "The reform has been very popular," says Lars Mathlein, an official who specializes in finance and economics at the Swedish embassy in Washington, D.C. In fact, a congressional commission in the United States, looking for ways to improve the IRS, suggested that the Swedish system, and a similar one in Denmark, might be worth a look.

### MORE ON THE NET

Tax World (http://www.taxworld.org/) provides links and information about local, federal, and international taxes.

**Source:** Adapted from Paul Wiseman, "Hatred of Tax Collection Is the Way of the World," *USA Today*, November 5, 1997, p. 18A. Copyright 1997, USA TODAY. Reprinted with permission.

---

Now let's compare the postwar condition to the blissful prewar status:

| Prewar | | Postwar | |
|---|---|---|---|
| GDP = | $1,000 | GDP = | $1,000 |
| Consumption = | 1,000 | Tax = | −10 |
| Government = | 0 | GDP − Tax = | $ 990 |
| | | Interest = | +10 |
| | | Consumption = | $1,000 |
| | | Government = | 0 |

It's really not terribly complicated. After the war, GDP remains at $1,000—the quantity of resources remains the same—and the government no longer sells Treasury bonds. But there is $100 worth of bonds *already sold,* and the government is obligated to pay the promised 10 percent interest on its $100 debt. That is, government's postwar annual interest payments are $10.

Where does it get the revenue to pay the interest? Suppose it chooses to tax. Now the people, producing and earning $1,000 GDP, can't keep it all. Every year, they pay a $10 tax to government, leaving them with $990. Government now has the money to pay its $10 interest obligation. People who hold the bonds receive the $10 as interest payments; that $10, coupled with the $990, ends up as $1,000 available to the people for consumption.

What about production? Government spending returns to $0—no need for ships, tanks, or aircraft—so that the economy is producing precisely what it did before the war.

Let's suppose 25 years pass. The government still taxes and pays $10 annually. Suppose also that the people who bought the $100 worth of Treasury bonds 25 years ago have died and bequeathed the bonds to their children. Should the children be thankful? *For what?*

Although their parents left them bonds that yield $10 each year, they left them also the obligation to pay taxes. After all, dead people cannot pay taxes. Are the children any poorer because they must assume the tax obligation? No. What they pay in taxes, they receive in interest payments. Perhaps they are richer on one account: Their parents were wise enough to secure their future by choosing to produce less consumption and more defense back in the war years.

**CHECK YOUR UNDERSTANDING**

Why is an internally financed public debt not a burden to future generations?

## Are There No Problems with Incurring Debt?

Do you feel as if you've been had? That somehow a sleight of hand has taken place? First you see it, then you don't. Not at all. There's no magic, no tricks, no illusions. The debt, held by the people themselves, neither adds to nor subtracts from national production or consumption. But that neutrality doesn't rule out complications.

**NOT EVERYONE HOLDS THE DEBT** Although the nation neither gains nor loses, individuals may. For example, not everyone holds the debt. If the bondholders are only the rich, then they alone receive the interest payments. Depending on how many bonds they hold, they may end up receiving more in interest than they pay in taxes. On the other hand, because they hold fewer bonds, poorer people may end up paying more in taxes than they receive in interest. Under these conditions, the debt can indeed be a burden to some. The progressiveness of the income tax and the presence of the corporate income tax might mitigate somewhat the inequity of the burden.

Government is particularly conscious of this burden effect and has kept a watchful eye on who holds what bonds. For example, it has at times instructed commercial banks to reduce their total debt by divesting some of their bond holdings. That's also why the Treasury created the relatively low-priced **savings bond**. It allows more people to buy and hold government debt.

**Savings bond**
A nonmarketable Treasury bond that is the most commonly held form of public debt.

**DEBT PROMOTES OVERCONSUMPTION** The debt can also distort our choices of consumption and saving. How? Many people who hold bonds tend to consume more out of their income than they should because they *think* they are wealthier than they really are. They mistakenly view the bonds as their personal assets and as the government's liabilities, without realizing that in the end the government's liabilities are actually their own. They don't realize that the source of the interest they receive is the taxes they must pay. By regarding their bond holdings as part of their savings, they feel they can afford to spend more on consumption. That is, by holding bonds, they end up undersaving and overconsuming.

**CHECK YOUR UNDERSTANDING**

How does debt promote consumption?

**DEBT CAN CREATE INFLATION** Debt complications can develop if government chooses to finance its debt interest obligations not by taxing people or by issuing and selling more bonds directly to people, but by issuing bonds that are purchased by the Federal Reserve. Since the Fed pays for the bonds by creating an equivalent deposit in the Treasury's account at the Fed, the economy's money supply increases, which may cause prices to rise.

**CROWDING OUT PRIVATE INVESTMENT** If, to sell its bonds, the government raises the interest rate on the bonds it offers, it forces private businesses, who must stay competitive as suppliers of bonds in the bond market, to raise the

**CHECK YOUR UNDERSTANDING**

How does crowding out slow the growth process in the private sector?

rates they offer on their corporate bonds. That is, financing government spending by government debt makes it more costly for private industry to finance its own investment. As a result, government debt may end up crowding out private investment and slowing economic growth in the private sector.

Some economists who acknowledge this crowding-out phenomenon do not necessarily subscribe to the idea that crowding out undermines overall economic growth. After all—to exaggerate their point—is it really detrimental to economic growth if private investments in gambling casinos are crowded out by debt-financed government spending on public schools? The effects of crowding out, then, aren't so much a matter of who crowds out whom as they are of measuring the relative contributions to economic growth made by the specific private and public investments.

## External Debt Is a Different Matter

Suppose that foreigners, not the people living and working in the economy, buy the government bonds. For example, suppose that Saudi Arabians, attracted by the Treasury's high interest rates, buy a large share of the bonds issued by the U.S. government.

To simplify, we assume GDP = $1,000 for both the U.S. and the Saudi economies, and that the $100 U.S. government bond issue is bought entirely by the Saudis.

**Year of Bond Purchase**

| United States | Saudi Arabia |
|---|---|
| GDP = $1,000 | GDP = $1,000 |
| Government = +100 | Bond = −100 |
| Consumption = $1,100 | Consumption = $ 900 |

**Thereafter**

| United States | Saudi Arabia |
|---|---|
| GDP = $1,000 | GDP = $1,000 |
| Tax = −10 | Interest = +10 |
| Consumption = $ 990 | Consumption = $1,010 |

What happens to national consumption in each country during the year of the bond purchase? Suppose that the U.S. war effort involves the purchase of $100 of Saudi oil, which is financed by selling $100 worth of bonds to Saudi Arabia. During the war period, U.S. civilian and war consumption increases to $1,100. Americans consume their own $1,000 GDP and the additional $100 Saudi oil, which is recorded as government spending, G = $100. The Saudis, now holding the U.S. debt, consume $100 less. Their consumption falls to $900 in the year that they buy the U.S. bonds.

Thereafter, the burdens shift. In subsequent years GDP remains $1,000 in each country, but the U.S. government taxes its people $10 to make its annual debt payments to the Saudis. That reduces American consumption to $990. On the other hand, the $10 interest paid to the Saudis allows them to claim $10 of U.S. production, increasing their consumption to $1,010.

What happens after 25 years? The new generation is still debt-obligated. American children grow up and are taxed to pay the grown-up Saudi children who inherited the $100 worth of bonds. In other words, if government debt is an **external debt,**

**External debt**
Public debt held by foreigners.

that is, held outside the country, the debt burden can be passed on to future generations. Of course, the U.S. government can always buy back its own bonds.

## ARE DEFICITS AND DEBT INEVITABLE?

Aside from whether or not budget deficits and the public debt burden are really troublesome, what can the government do to reduce deficit and debt levels? Basically, there are only two ways for the government to tackle the problem. It can increase taxes or reduce spending. Everyone in government is aware of these options. But knowing isn't doing. Putting either of these alternatives into action is the difficult part.

### The Tax Reforms of 1981 and 1986

Let's look at the tax-design efforts associated with deficit and debt reduction. In 1981 President Ronald Reagan came to the White House with a tax-cutting agenda in mind. He was intent on revising the basic income tax structure by reducing tax brackets and marginal tax rates and by eliminating tax loopholes. This, he hoped, would be coupled with a cut in government spending. He expected the combination to reduce the government's deficit and debt.

Congress responded positively, at least with respect to taxes, by legislating the Economic Recovery Tax Act of 1981 (often called the Kemp-Roth Act), which cut marginal tax rates. It was less forthcoming on government spending. At the time, the economy was in recession, and the idea of leaving more money in the hands of people by cutting tax rates was not only politically popular but made good sense as countercyclical fiscal policy.

President Reagan was convinced that the tax reform would not only stimulate the economy through the demand side—raise aggregate demand—but also stimulate the economy through the supply side—encourage investments and production. He believed the tax rates in the United States were too high and acted as a disincentive to production. Supply-side advocates, delighted with the 1981 tax reform, pushed the argument for tax reduction further, asserting that such a tax move would end up creating more tax revenues. Their arithmetic was elementary. Lower tax rates mean expanded production, employment, and income. More income adds up to more tax revenues.

The Tax Reform Act of 1986 completed the Reagan tax agenda. It lowered the marginal tax rates further, reduced the number of tax brackets, eliminated many tax loopholes, and instituted changes in deductions, exemptions, and capital gains.

Both the 1981 and 1986 tax reforms were integral parts of the president's political agenda, which was to disengage the government from the economic life of the nation. In a sense, the reduction in tax rates was compensation for the elimination of the myriad of specific tax-incentive schemes—deductions, exemptions, allowances, and loopholes—that government discretion allowed. The tax reform not only simplified the tax structure but reduced the government's ability to discriminate with respect to who pays what taxes.

Supply-side expectations notwithstanding, the tax reforms did not do much to increase tax revenues during the 1980s. At the same time, government spending continued to grow. That combination of tax cuts and government spending growth produced in the 1980s the largest annual deficits in the history of the republic. As a result, the public debt increased dramatically.

Visit the House (http://www.house.gov/) and the Senate (http://www.senate.gov/). What initiatives do you see Congress promoting to reduce the federal deficit?

# Congressional Attempts to Reduce the Deficit

Most members of Congress were convinced that it was absolutely necessary to cut government spending to reduce deficits and debt. The question that paralyzed Congress on spending was, What gets cut? Everyone seemed to be willing to cut spending, as long as the spending cuts were not made in areas that served their own special interests. The results were obvious. Spending continued to grow.

Senators Phil Gramm, Warren Rudman, and Ernest Hollings hit on a scheme. If Congress was incapable of cutting through the normal process of discretionary budget making, then the Gramm-Rudman-Hollings Act of 1985 would go to work. The act requires that every budgetary item be automatically cut by the same percentage, according to a timetable that eventually reduces the deficit to zero.

No sooner had Congress voted for the GRH idea than it tried to change the ground rules. Many members of Congress tried to exclude defense from the chopping block, while others sought preferential treatment for social welfare items. The deficit-reduction targets of GRH were revised in 1987 and again in 1991. In the end, it didn't work.

Another stab at deficit-limiting legislation came with the Budget Deficit Reduction Act of 1993. It structured a one-quarter reduction in real discretionary spending over the period 1993–98. To achieve this outcome, Congress was required to implement a pay-as-you-go plan, meaning that it must find the means to pay for any new spending by either cutting equivalent old spending or raising taxes.

Some members of Congress, frustrated by the failed attempts to reduce the deficit, argued for a constitutional amendment that would prohibit government, year-to-year, from spending more than it collects in tax dollars. Since tax revenues in any year depend on the level of national income, the amendment may end up requiring spending cuts regardless of the nation's needs. This would-be constitutional demand of unhitching needs and spending worried many in Congress and undermined support for the amendment.

# The Clinton Era

Try your hand at balancing the federal budget (http://garnet.berkeley.edu:3333/budget/budget.html). Did you finish with a surplus or a deficit?

The combination of the Clinton presidency and the Republican Congresses in the latter part of the 1990s, along with the unprecedented sustained economic growth in the United States, did what some had thought was undoable: Deficits actually shrunk. Tax revenues increased because national income increased, and the government's spending appetite was curbed by welfare reform, defense cuts (made possible by the collapse of the Soviet Union), and a growing conservative view in government, academia, and society in general that government is not the answer to all social and economic ills.

While President Clinton championed these spending cuts, he still played an activist role in promoting, with minimal success, national health care, infrastructure investment, and education. By choosing these selective and limited targets, he was able to influence not only the size of the deficit and debt, but the role the government would play in the economy as well.

# CHAPTER REVIEW

1. In pre-modern economies, when government required resources to create public goods such as a road or an army, it commandeered them. In modern economies, when government requires resources to create public goods such as a road or an army, it commandeers money through taxes and uses the money to buy the required resources.

2. Taxes are either regressive, progressive, or proportional. A regressive tax is one in which the poor pay a higher tax rate, that is, a higher percentage of their income to taxes. A poll tax and a sales tax are examples of regressive taxes. A progressive tax is one in which the poor pay a lower tax rate, that is, a lower percentage of their income to taxes. An income tax is an example of a progressive tax. A proportional tax is one in which everyone, rich and poor, pays the same tax rate, that is, the same percentage of his or her income to taxes. A property tax is an example of a proportional tax.

3. Social Security contributions (taxes) are levied on employees and their employers and are earmarked to finance the benefits that the Social Security system is obligated to provide.

4. The federal income tax structure is progressive. The marginal rates in its five tax brackets range from 15 to 39.6 percent. It is the largest source of revenue for the federal government.

5. Deficits arise when tax revenues are insufficient to finance government spending. The government creates and sells Treasury securities to finance its deficits. The securities are attractive to buyers because they are relatively secure and bear a competitive rate of interest.

6. The federal debt, representing the accumulation of federal deficits, has risen steadily since the 1930s and quite sharply since the 1970s. While debt rose through the four decades preceding the 1980s, the corresponding debt-to-GDP ratio actually fell. It rose with the debt during the 1980s and 1990s.

7. An internally financed debt does not necessarily burden future generations. It can, however, create problems of inequity, overconsumption, and crowding out of private investment. An externally financed debt, on the other hand, can burden future generations.

8. The tax reform acts of 1981 and 1986 reduced tax revenues. Government spending, however, continued to rise. The Gramm-Rudman-Hollings Act of 1985 and the Budget Deficit Reduction Act of 1993 attempted to curb the soaring deficits created in the 1980s. Deficit levels began to fall in the 1990s, and the prolonged prosperity, which provided higher tax revenues, combined with more conservative government spending appetites (led by cuts in defense and welfare) cut the deficit to zero in 1997.

# KEY TERMS

Poll tax
Regressive income tax
Proportional income tax
Progressive income tax
Corporate income tax

Property tax
Unit tax
Sales tax
Customs duty

Excise tax
Public debt
Savings bond
External debt

# QUESTIONS

1. If the government wants to build a highway, why doesn't it just commandeer the necessary land, labor, and capital to build the highway?
2. What is a poll tax? Why would governments sometimes favor such a tax? Does the tax affect rich people and poor people alike?
3. What is the fundamental difference between regressive, proportional, and progressive tax structures?
4. How does an excise tax differ from an income tax?
5. What is the federal government's most important source of tax revenue? What are the state and local governments' most important sources of tax revenue?
6. What are Treasury securities? Who owns them?
7. What is the relationship between Treasury securities and the public debt?
8. What is the relationship between the public debt and the debt-to-GDP ratio? How does the U.S. debt ratio compare to the ratios in other democratic market economies?
9. Explain why some economists believe the burden of a public debt cannot be shifted onto future generations.
10. Some economists believe that the public debt may be detrimental to the economy's growth. Explain.
11. How does an externally held public debt differ from an internally held public debt?

# ECONOMIC CONSULTANTS

**ECONOMIC RESEARCH AND ANALYSIS BY STUDENTS FOR PROFESSIONALS**

Kristen Hersh plans to run in 2004 for the presidency of the United States. Kristen, a successful businesswoman, worked as a campaign strategist for Steve Forbes's failed run for president in 1996. During the 1996 campaign, Kristen observed that Forbes's primary message, to simplify the federal tax structure, was well received, and his primary initiative, the flat tax, was popular with some voters. As a result, Kristen intends to establish a political platform around tax reform.

Kristen has hired Economic Consultants to explain to her the economic issues surrounding the tax reform debate. Prepare a report for Kristen that addresses the following issues:

**1.** What are the major positions in the debate over tax reform?
**2.** What is a flat tax, and what are the pros and cons of this system of taxation?
**3.** What initiatives are underway in government to reform the tax system?

You may find the following resources helpful as you prepare this report for Kristen:

- **Internal Revenue Service (IRS)** (http://www.irs.gov/)—The IRS provides news and information about federal taxes.
- **EconDebate Online: Tax Reform** (http://www.swcollege.com/bef/policy_debates/tax_reform.html)—EconDebate Online provides links to and commentary on primary and secondary resources addressing the tax reform debate.
- **Americans for Tax Reform (ATR)** (http://www.atr.org/)—The ATR works with hundreds of organizations active at the federal, state, and local levels on issues that pertain to taxes.
- **Citizens for Tax Justice** (http://www.ctj.org/)—Citizens for Tax Justice is a research and advocacy organization addressing taxation at the federal, state, and local levels.
- **Citizens for an Alternative Tax System (CATS)** (http://www.cats.org/)—CATS is a national grassroots public interest group established to abolish the federal income tax system and replace it with a national retail sales tax.
- **Joint Economic Committee Taxation Page** (http://www.house.gov/jcc/tax.htm)—The U.S. Congress's Joint Economic Committee maintains a page addressing issues of taxation.
- **1040.com** (http://www.1040.com/)—1040.com provides tax information and resources.

# PRACTICE TEST

1. Referring to a two-goods—public and private—production possibilities curve, the tax that society pays to produce a unit of public goods is
   a. the amount of goods each person pays to government.
   b. the quantity of goods government receives from the population.
   c. the opportunity cost of producing a unit of public goods.
   d. the opportunity cost of producing a unit of private goods.
   e. the shift of resources from public to private goods production.

2. A poll tax is a
   a. tax on those exercising their voting privileges.
   b. fixed tax levied equally on all taxpayers.
   c. fixed rate of taxation on all taxpayers.
   d. fixed tax on all taxpayers, but the amount of tax varies with the taxpayer's income.
   e. prepaid tax, that is, a tax paid before income is received.

3. The federal government's most important source of tax revenue is
   a. sales tax.
   b. property tax.
   c. corporate tax.
   d. custom duties.
   e. income tax.

4. The federal government's tax revenue for 2000 amounted to approximately
   a. $2,000 billion.
   b. $5,000 billion.
   c. $500 billion.
   d. $50 billion.
   e. $5 billion.

5. A proportional tax means that each taxpayer pays
   a. the same amount of tax.
   b. the same percentage of his or her income to taxes.
   c. a tax rate proportional to his or her income; that is, the higher the income, the higher the tax rate.
   d. a tax rate proportional to his or her income; that is, the higher the income, the lower the tax rate on the higher income.
   e. a tax proportional to his or her share of the public goods provided.

6. The 1980 and 1986 tax reforms
   a. reduced the number of tax brackets but increased the percentage of income taxed.
   b. increased the number of tax brackets and increased the percentage of income taxed.
   c. increased the number of tax brackets, which increased the tax revenues in subsequent years.
   d. reduced the number of tax brackets and reduced the percentage of income taxed.
   e. reduced the number of tax brackets, which increased the tax revenues in subsequent years.

7. An income tax structure is progressive when
   a. the average tax rate increases as income increases.
   b. the tax rate on each tax bracket is the same.
   c. the amount of tax paid by the rich is greater than the amount paid by the poor.
   d. the tax base is not reduced by exemptions and deductions.
   e. taxpayers earning the same income pay the same income tax.

8. The Social Security tax is
   a. a regressive tax.
   b. a proportional tax.
   c. the largest source of state and local tax revenues.
   d. an earmarked tax.
   e. a poll tax.

9. An alternative way government can finance its spending, aside from taxing, is by
   a. selling government securities, which creates public debt.
   b. selling government securities, which reduces the government's deficit.
   c. creating surplus budgets.
   d. reducing its public debt.
   e. invoking the Gramm-Rudman-Hollings Act.

10. Does an internally financed public debt endanger future generations?
    a. Yes, because someone has to pay it off at some future time.
    b. Yes, because the interest will eventually overtake the debt, and the interest is what future generations will have to pay.
    c. Yes, because inflation increases the debt, making it impossible for one generation to pay it off.
    d. No, because future generations not only pay interest on the debt, but also receive an equivalent value in interest payments.
    e. No, because inflation erodes the value of the debt, which means that future generations are not endangered.

# PART 5

## THE WORLD ECONOMY

**Tune into the conversation.** It's about *your* course. Just change the names, and it's *your* campus, *your* classroom, *your* professor, *your* classmates, and *you*.

Professor Gottheil and his student, Chris Stefan, a senior majoring in international economics, meet up with each other walking across campus. Gottheil had just assigned the chapters on international trade and exchange rates for next week's discussion. Chris opens the conversation.

**CHRIS:** Professor Gottheil, I don't know if you recognize me, but I'm in your 10 o'clock class.
**GOTTHEIL:** You're Chris Stefan, and you sit in the second row.
**CHRIS:** That's right! If it's not too much of an imposition, could I chat with you while we're walking?
**GOTTHEIL:** No imposition at all. What's on your mind?
**CHRIS:** I've already read the chapters on international trade and exchange rates, and I'm really confused. I mean . . . really confused. Mainly about exchange rates. But I'm also sort of puzzled about the way you arranged the chapters in the text.
**GOTTHEIL:** You mean the chapter organization? What's wrong?
**CHRIS:** Well, throughout the semester you kept mentioning that we live in a global economy. You kept stressing the term *global*, and how important international trade is in our lives. Many of the examples you use in the text are international, yet we don't really get to international trade and exchange rates until now, toward the end of the course! Why did we wait so long? I mean, don't these chapters belong up front in the textbook because they're so important?
**GOTTHEIL:** OK, I see your point. You're right about how important these chapters are. But what we really have to understand before we can appreciate the value of international economics are the basic principles of economics, which are what you've been reading about up to now. Once you know the principles, you can apply them everywhere and to all things. Look, we buy bananas from Honduras, and that's called international trade. But is there something special about this trade? Not really. In terms of understanding how economics works, buying bananas from Honduras is no different than buying oranges from California. If you understand how supply and demand for oranges determines the prices of oranges, you really understand all there is to know about international trade and international prices. It's the exact same economics, just carried across international borders. That's why we can leave international trade and exchange rates until now.
**CHRIS:** You say understanding the market for oranges is the same as understanding the market for bananas, but is it? It doesn't seem that simple to me. Where do exchange rates fit in? I can understand buying oranges for dollars, but what baffles me is the market for other people's money, like buying so many pesos for a dollar or so many dollars for a peso. That's a different kind of thing, isn't it?
**GOTTHEIL:** Not really. Let me try to unconfuse you by explaining exchange rates in a very different context. Just forget all about oranges, bananas, dollars, and pesos for now.
**CHRIS:** OK.
**GOTTHEIL:** Suppose there are two night spots on campus featuring live entertainment. Let's call them Mabel's and the Blind Pig. And suppose both Mabel's and the Blind Pig sell sets of tickets—say, 10 tickets to a set. Students buy these packets of tickets—let's pick an easy number, say, 100 Mabel's sets and 100 Blind Pig. Are you with me so far?
**CHRIS:** Sure. There are 200 sets of tickets sold to students and these tickets—2,000 of them—buy admission to live entertainment events. Right?
**GOTTHEIL:** Right. You can't get in without a ticket. Well, suppose the Breeders are booked to play at Mabel's, and a lot of people holding tickets to the Blind Pig want to see the Breeders. And suppose the Flaming Lips are booked to play at the Blind Pig, and a lot of other students holding Mabel's tickets want to see the Flaming Lips. What do you think would happen?
**CHRIS:** Well, if I had a Blind Pig ticket but wanted to go to the Breeders concert at Mabel's, I would try to trade my Blind Pig ticket to someone who had Mabel's

*continued on next page*

# CHAT ECONOMICS

tickets but wanted to see the Flaming Lips concert at the Blind Pig.

**GOTTHEIL:** That makes good sense. And suppose there were 10 like you who wanted to trade Blind Pig tickets for Mabel's tickets, and 10 others who had Mabel's tickets looking for Blind Pig tickets. You would be able to exchange 1 for 1 and satisfy all 20 students. Right?

**CHRIS:** That's right.

**GOTTHEIL:** But let's suppose there were 10 like you looking for Mabel's tickets, but only 5 like the other students looking for Blind Pig tickets. Then what? How would you get a Mabel's ticket?

**CHRIS:** If I really wanted to see the Breeders at Mabel's, I would offer 2, maybe even 3 of my Blind Pig tickets for a single Mabel's.

**GOTTHEIL:** What if others like you offered 3 Blind Pig tickets, too. You may still not get 1.

**CHRIS:** That's right. But if I offered 4, maybe someone who had a Mabel's ticket would say, "Hey, I could get to see 4 Blind Pig concerts if I give up the Breeders concert at Mabel's. That's a good deal—I'll do it."

**GOTTHEIL:** Well that's right, Chris. And that's all there is to exchange rates. Nothing more complicated, and you already understand how it works. Just substitute the United States and Mexico for the two night spots, and substitute U.S. dollars and Mexican pesos for the two kinds of tickets. If you're in the United States and you want to buy something from Mexico, you have to first get Mexican "tickets." We call their tickets Mexico's currency, which is the peso. What we have to give up to get those pesos depends on how many of our own "tickets"—called dollars—Mexicans want, and that depends on how much they want to buy from us. If we want to buy more from Mexicans than they want to buy from us, just like you had to give up more Blind Pig tickets for the Mabel's ticket, we will have to give up more dollars for pesos. These dollars for pesos determine the exchange rate, and the reason why there's a market for other people's money is because we want things from each other.

**CHRIS:** You know, I think I actually have a better feel for international trade and exchange rates now. I'll try to keep Mabel's and the Blind Pig in mind when I read the chapters again.

To understand how the world economy works, keep in mind the principles you have learned so far. You can apply these principles everywhere and to all things, including the next few chapters.

# INTERNATIONAL TRADE

# 16

Imagine yourself driving in late August along Trans-Canada Highway 401 through the Canadian farmlands of southern Ontario. Suppose you cross the border at Port Huron, Michigan, and continue south along Interstate 69 to Interstate 74, then turn west through central Indiana and Illinois. If you're interested in corn farms, you'll be impressed by the changing heights of the corn stalks you see along the route. They stand under 5 feet in Ontario but reach well over 8 feet in Illinois. That's why so many farmers grow corn in Illinois.

If you later connect with Interstate 57 and drive south to St. Louis, you will see, just off the highway, a profusion of oil wells scattered among the corn fields. Their pumps keep churning away, but the wells don't really produce much oil. At least not nearly the barrels that oil wells in Oklahoma produce.

**THIS CHAPTER INTRODUCES YOU TO THE ECONOMIC PRINCIPLES ASSOCIATED WITH:**

- ABSOLUTE ADVANTAGE
- COMPARATIVE ADVANTAGE
- FREE TRADE
- TARIFFS
- QUOTAS
- CUSTOMS UNIONS
- FREE TRADE AREAS

If you think about it for a while, you may come to the conclusion that folks in Illinois would be much better off if they just produced corn and left the oil producing to folks in Oklahoma. And you'd be right. Not only would they be better off, but so would folks in Oklahoma. Economic specialization always creates a win-win outcome.

To explain why it's win-win, let's analyze the Illinois economy and compare what people there end up producing and consuming before and after economic specialization. We'll also show that what works for Illinois works as well for Oklahoma, for Mexico, and for the rest of the world.

## INTRASTATE TRADE
### Illinois Corn for Illinois Oil

Imagine the Illinois economy sealed off from the rest of the world. And suppose that working people in Illinois are either corn farmers or oil producers. In other words, Illinois is a two-goods economy. Let's also suppose that labor is the only resource used to produce goods and that it takes 1 hour of labor to produce either a bushel of corn or a barrel of oil. And to round out the supposes, let's suppose that there are 200 labor hours.

Exhibit 1 portrays Illinois's production possibilities. If the straight-line curve looks unfamiliar to you—a production possibilities curve typically balloons out from the origin—it is because we assume away the law of increasing costs.

How many barrels and bushels does Illinois produce? Look at point *a*. It shows that if Illinois devotes all of its 200 hours of labor to corn production, it produces 200 bushels of corn and 0 barrels of oil. On the other hand, if it puts its 200 hours to oil production, it produces 200 barrels of oil and 0 bushels of corn, point *b*. It can also choose any combination of corn and oil, such as 100 bushels of corn and 100 barrels of oil, point *c*. Let's suppose the choice is point *c*.

If corn farmers want to trade corn for oil, or oil producers want to trade oil for corn, how do they do it? How do they arrive at mutually acceptable prices? For example, how many bushels of corn would an Illinois oil producer expect to get trading a barrel of oil? What about the corn farmer? How many barrels of oil would he get for his bushel? If they produce and sell in competitive markets, the relative prices of oil and corn reflect the relative costs of producing oil and corn.

Given their cost equivalents, a bushel trades for a barrel. That is, if a corn farmer is willing to trade 10 bushels of corn, she can expect to get 10 barrels of oil for them.

EXHIBIT 1

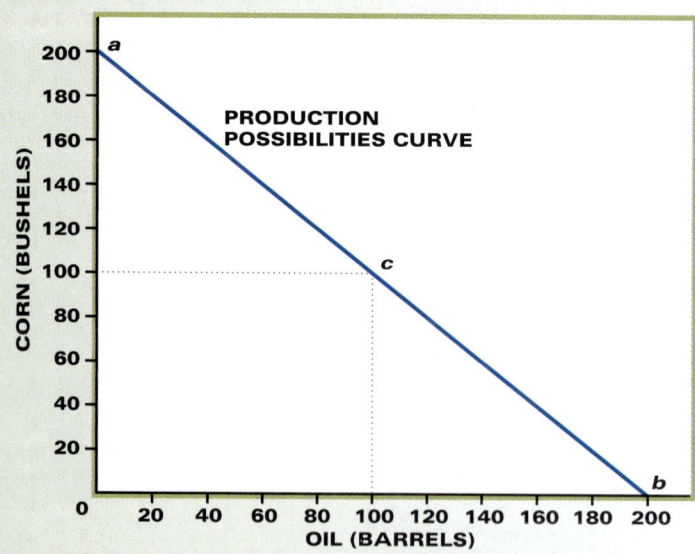

**ILLINOIS PRODUCTION POSSIBILITIES CURVE**

The production possibilities curve is drawn as a straight line, reflecting the fact that the opportunity cost is one barrel per bushel regardless of the number of bushels or barrels produced. The economy can use its 200 hours of labor to produce any combination of oil and corn, such as 100 bushels of corn and 100 barrels of oil, shown at point *c*.

## Oklahoma Corn for Oklahoma Oil

Let's now look at Oklahoma and suppose, as we did for Illinois, that the Oklahoma economy has 200 hours of labor and is sealed off from the rest of the world. Let's also suppose that Oklahomans, like the folks in Illinois, produce corn and oil, but the labor costs involved in producing corn and oil are different. It takes not 1, but 4 hours of Oklahoma labor to produce a bushel of corn. Their oil fields, however, are another matter. They are gushers. It takes only 20 minutes of labor to fill up a barrel.

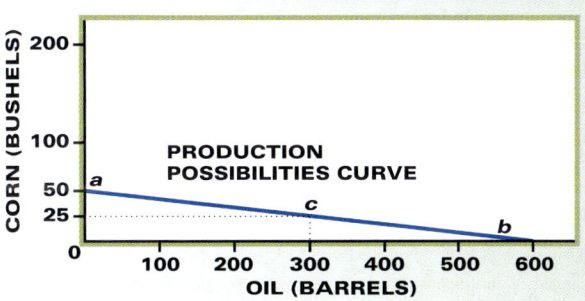

**OKLAHOMA PRODUCTION POSSIBILITIES CURVE**

The opportunity cost of producing a bushel of corn is 12 barrels of oil. The economy can use its 200 hours of labor to produce any combination of the two, such as 300 barrels of oil and 25 bushels of corn, shown at point *c*.

EXHIBIT 2

Exhibit 2 represents Oklahoma's production possibilities. Look at point *a*. If Oklahoma devotes its 200 labor hours to corn, it gets 50 bushels of corn and 0 barrels of oil. If it devotes the 200 labor hours to oil, it gets 600 barrels of oil and 0 bushels of corn, point *b*. Suppose it chooses point *c*, 100 labor-hours producing 25 bushels of corn and 100 labor-hours producing 300 barrels of oil. Since corn and oil exchange according to their relative costs, 1 bushel of corn trades for 12 barrels of oil.

## INTERSTATE TRADE

Let's now relax the assumption of sealed-off economies and suppose that people in Illinois can trade with people in Oklahoma, and vice-versa. Imagine yourself as an Illinois corn farmer looking for oil. Here are your options. You can stay in Illinois and trade—at Illinois prices—your bushel of corn for a barrel of oil, or you can take your bushel of corn to Oklahoma and there—at Oklahoma prices—get 12 barrels of oil. No difficulty deciding what to do, right?

For the same reason, an Oklahoma oil producer prefers to buy corn in Illinois. Instead of getting 1/12 of a bushel of corn for his barrel in Oklahoma, he gets an entire bushel of corn trading in Illinois.

It's no secret what would happen if Illinois and Oklahoma engage in **free trade**. Oklahoma oil producers would quickly drive Illinois oilers out of business. Think about it. How can any Illinois oiler who has to pay 1 hour of labor for each barrel compete against a producer who can fill a barrel in 20 minutes?

**Free trade**
International trade that is not encumbered by protectionist government policies such as tariffs and quotas.

What about corn producers? Here, the tables are turned. Oklahoma farmers wouldn't stand a chance. By the time they could put a bushel of corn together, the Illinois farmer would have 4 in the bin.

### The Case for Geographic Specialization

The case for geographic specialization, producing corn in Illinois and oil in Oklahoma, is simple enough: Everybody benefits. We all end up with more corn *and* more oil.

### EXHIBIT 3

**PRODUCTION OF CORN AND OIL IN ILLINOIS AND OKLAHOMA, BEFORE AND AFTER FREE TRADE (BUSHELS AND BARRELS)**

|  | NO TRADE | | FREE TRADE | |
|---|---|---|---|---|
|  | CORN | OIL | CORN | OIL |
| ILLINOIS | 100 | 100 | 200 | 0 |
| OKLAHOMA | 25 | 300 | 0 | 600 |
| TOTAL | 125 | 400 | 200 | 600 |

How can we show the benefits? Suppose people in Illinois use their 200 labor-hours to produce corn exclusively, and people in Oklahoma use their 200 labor-hours to produce oil exclusively. How much better off would they be with this kind of geographic specialization? Exhibit 3 compares their combined productions before and after specialization and free trade.

The results of specialization are dramatic. Illinois workers now produce 200 bushels of corn, or 60 percent more than the amount that two states, with the same number of labor-hours expended, had produced before free trade.

The oil yields are also impressive. The 200 hours of labor expended in Oklahoma produce 600 barrels, or 50 percent more than the amount the two states, with the same number of labor-hours expended, had produced before free trade.

What set of relative prices—barrels in terms of bushels—would they end up with? The price should fall somewhere between 1 barrel per bushel prevailing in Illinois and 12 barrels per bushel prevailing in Oklahoma.

Let's suppose the price is 3 barrels per bushel. Exhibit 4 shows the gains that trade offers to both Illinois and Oklahoma.

Look at Oklahoma's consumption. People there produce 600 barrels of oil, keep 300 barrels for themselves, and sell the remaining 300 barrels to Illinois for 100 bushels of corn. They now have four times their pre-trade corn consumption.

What about people in Illinois? Having bought 300 barrels of oil from Oklahoma with 100 of their 200 bushels of corn, they have 100 bushels of corn left. Look at their improved condition. They have 200 more barrels than their pre-trade consumption. In other words, everybody gains!

Impressive? That's why we consume Oklahoma oil, Illinois corn, Washington apples, Michigan automobiles, Georgia peaches, Idaho potatoes, Florida grapefruit, Hawaii pineapples, Ohio steel, Pennsylvania coal, Oregon lumber, New York banking, North Carolina furniture, Iowa hogs, Louisiana sugar, Wyoming cattle, Vermont maple syrup, and California wine.

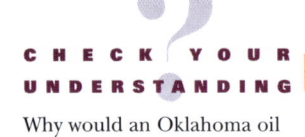

**CHECK YOUR UNDERSTANDING**

Why would an Oklahoma oil producer buy Illinois corn?

### EXHIBIT 4

**CORN AND OIL CONSUMPTION IN ILLINOIS AND OKLAHOMA, BEFORE AND AFTER FREE TRADE (BUSHELS AND BARRELS)**

|  | NO TRADE (PRODUCTION = CONSUMPTION) | | FREE TRADE (PRODUCTION) | | FREE TRADE (CONSUMPTION) | |
|---|---|---|---|---|---|---|
|  | CORN | OIL | CORN | OIL | CORN | OIL |
| ILLINOIS | 100 | 100 | 200 | 0 | 100 | 300 |
| OKLAHOMA | 25 | 300 | 0 | 600 | 100 | 300 |

## Nobody Loses?

Are we all always winners? Does nobody lose? Why, then, do we find some people objecting vigorously to free trade? Well, imagine how you would feel if, as an Illinois oil producer, you suddenly discovered an Oklahoma oil producer selling oil in your backyard.

You wouldn't be overjoyed, would you? In fact, you probably couldn't survive the competition. Of course, there's always a place for you farming corn. Still, it isn't entirely painless to give up doing what you know best, oil rigs, and turn to corn farming.

You can count on some oilers trying to prevent Oklahoma oil from coming into Illinois. How could they do that? By exercising political muscle on their Illinois legislators. Nothing really new, is it? That's the primary reason we have protective tariffs.

Of course, if everything else fails, you could always get on a Greyhound bus bound for Tulsa. That's assuming Oklahoma places no restrictions on interstate immigration.

# INTERNATIONAL TRADE

The same economic argument that promotes interstate free trade should promote international free trade. After all, why should national boundaries have any bearing on the economic benefits that people derive from free trade?

Suppose, for example, that it takes only 10 minutes to produce a barrel of oil in Mexico. That's half the labor cost of an Oklahoma barrel. Suppose also that it takes Mexican farmers one hour to produce a bushel of corn.

The conditions are ripe, now, for exploiting the full benefits of **international specialization** and trade. United States corn for Mexican oil. Why not? *Everybody ends up with more corn and more oil.*

Let's pursue the argument. Exhibit 5 details the before-and-after conditions of international free trade. Before free trade, the United States split its 400 labor-hours evenly, with 200 hours devoted to oil and 200 to corn production. Mexico did the same with its 400 labor-hours.

U.S. oilers now face the same problem Illinois oilers did before interstate trade. How can U.S. oilers survive against a more efficient Mexican competitor?

Look at the relative prices of corn and oil in the United States and Mexico. U.S. farmers could get 3 barrels of oil for their bushel of corn. However, if they sold their bushel of corn on the Mexican market at Mexican prices, they could take home 6 barrels of oil!

Mexican oilers will immediately discover the advantages of international free trade as well. Why should they sell their oil for Mexican corn? The relative prices in Mexico—6 barrels to 1 bushel—will give the Mexican oiler only ⅙ bushel of corn for his barrel. By selling the Mexican barrel north of the border at U.S. prices, the Mexican takes home ⅓ bushel of corn. That's twice the quantity of corn that could be obtained in Mexico.

**International specialization**
The use of a country's resources to produce specific goods and services, allowing other countries to focus on the production of other goods and services.

**PRODUCTION OF CORN AND OIL IN THE UNITED STATES AND MEXICO, BEFORE AND AFTER FREE TRADE (BUSHELS AND BARRELS)**

|  | NO TRADE | | FREE TRADE | |
| --- | --- | --- | --- | --- |
|  | CORN | OIL | CORN | OIL |
| UNITED STATES | 200 | 600 | 400 | 0 |
| MEXICO | 200 | 1,200 | 0 | 2,400 |
| TOTAL | 400 | 1,800 | 400 | 2,400 |

EXHIBIT 5

International competition will drive both the United States and Mexico to specialize. The United States becomes the corn producer; Mexico becomes the oil producer.

As we see in Exhibit 5, total production increases from 400 bushels of corn and 1,800 barrels of oil to 400 bushels of corn and 2,400 barrels of oil. That's a net gain of 600 barrels of oil.

What set of prices—barrels in terms of bushels—would prevail on the international market? Clearly, it has to be at least 3 barrels per bushel, otherwise U.S. farmers would do better buying oil at home. It also has to be no more than 6 barrels per bushel, because Mexican oilers can purchase a bushel of corn in Mexico for 6 barrels.

Exhibit 6 shows what happens to the consumption of corn and oil in the United States and Mexico before and after free trade when price is 4 barrels per bushel.

The United States produces 400 bushels of corn, keeps half, and exports the remaining 200 bushels to Mexico in exchange for 800 barrels of oil. Free trade has increased U.S. oil consumption by $800 - 600 = 200$ barrels.

What about Mexico? Having bought 200 bushels of corn from the United States with 800 barrels of oil, it is left with $2,400 - 800 = 1,600$ barrels, which is 400 barrels more than it had before. Both the United States and Mexico have gained.

## ABSOLUTE AND COMPARATIVE ADVANTAGE

Some trading economies are considered perfect trading partners because each can produce one of the goods with fewer resources than the other, that is, using less labor.

Economists describe each economy engaged in such trade as having an **absolute advantage.** In our illustration of interstate trade, Illinois has an absolute advantage in growing corn, and Oklahoma has an absolute advantage in producing oil. It's easy to think of real-world absolute advantage cases. What about trade of Japan's automobiles for Egypt's cotton? Do you suppose each country has an absolute advantage? Or Colombian coffee for U.S. steel? Or Czech glass for Russian caviar? Or Israeli oranges for Icelandic fish? Or Dutch tulips for Danish furniture?

**Absolute advantage**
A country's ability to produce a good using fewer resources than the country it trades with.

### Comparative Advantage

Absolute advantage, however, is not always the condition under which nations trade. In fact, absolute advantage is not present when the United States trades corn for Mexican oil (see Exhibit 5 again).

**EXHIBIT 6**

**CORN AND OIL CONSUMPTION IN THE UNITED STATES AND MEXICO, BEFORE AND AFTER FREE TRADE (BUSHELS AND BARRELS)**

|  | NO TRADE (PRODUCTION = CONSUMPTION) | | FREE TRADE (PRODUCTION) | | FREE TRADE (CONSUMPTION) | |
|---|---|---|---|---|---|---|
|  | CORN | OIL | CORN | OIL | CORN | OIL |
| UNITED STATES | 200 | 600 | 400 | 0 | 200 | 800 |
| MEXICO | 200 | 1,200 | 0 | 2,400 | 200 | 1,600 |

There, Mexico uses fewer resources than the United States to produce oil—10 minutes per barrel versus 20 minutes per barrel—but the same quantity of resources as the United States to produce corn—both one hour per bushel. The United States had no absolute advantage in trading with Mexico. Yet Mexico still gains by specializing in oil.

Why? Why should Mexico bother importing corn from the United States when it can grow its own corn at home using the same quantity of labor that Americans use? The reason is that even though the absolute cost of producing corn in Mexico is the same as it is in the United States, the *opportunity cost of producing corn in Mexico is higher.* Consider this: The one hour of labor used to produce corn in Mexico could be used to produce 12 barrels of oil. That is, Mexico gives up 12 barrels of oil to get that 1 bushel of corn. In the United States, Americans give up only 3 barrels of oil to produce a bushel of corn. In other words, the opportunity cost of producing corn in the United States is considerably lower. This lower opportunity cost is defined by economists as a **comparative advantage** for the United States.

The United States has a comparative advantage—a lower opportunity cost—in producing corn, and Mexico has a comparative advantage—a lower opportunity cost—in producing oil. Both countries gain if each specializes in producing the good that affords it a comparative advantage. Even if Mexico had an absolute advantage over the United States in both corn and oil production, it would still benefit Mexico to abandon producing the good that has the higher opportunity cost.

**CHECK YOUR UNDERSTANDING**
Why would Mexico import U.S. corn when it can produce the corn using the same labor-hours?

**Comparative advantage**
A country's ability to produce a good at a lower opportunity cost than the country with which it trades.

## How Much Is Gained from Free Trade Depends on Price

Look at Exhibit 7. Suppose price is 4 barrels per bushel. Look at Mexico's consumption of oil and corn before and after trade. Mexico, specializing in oil, keeps 1,600 of the 2,400 barrels it produces and trades the remaining 800 barrels to the United States for corn. It ends up, then, with 200 bushels of corn. This 1,600 barrels and 200 bushels compares favorably to the 1,200 barrels and 200 bushels Mexico would have consumed if it did not trade with the United States.

Suppose, however, that the price is set at 5 barrels per bushel instead of 4. The gains from trade are now distributed somewhat differently. At 5 barrels per bushel, the United States, still producing 400 bushels of corn, keeps half and exports the remaining 200 bushels to Mexico for 1,000 barrels of oil. That's 1,000 − 800 = 200 barrels more than it got from Mexico when the price was 4 barrels per bushel.

**CORN AND OIL CONSUMPTION IN THE UNITED STATES AND MEXICO, UNDER CONDITIONS OF NO TRADE AND FREE TRADE**

|  | NO TRADE | | FREE TRADE | | | |
|---|---|---|---|---|---|---|
|  | | | 4 BARRELS/BUSHEL | | 5 BARRELS/BUSHEL | |
|  | CORN | OIL | CORN | OIL | CORN | OIL |
| UNITED STATES | 200 | 600 | 200 | 800 | 200 | 1,000 |
| MEXICO | 200 | 1,200 | 200 | 1,600 | 200 | 1,400 |

EXHIBIT 7

What about Mexico? Having bought 200 bushels of corn from the United States with 1,000 barrels of oil, it is left with 1,400 barrels, which is still more oil than it consumed before free trade. That is, the shift in price from 4 to 5 barrels per bushel shifts the gains from free trade to the United States. If the price increases to 6 barrels per bushel, the gains from trade would shift *completely* to the United States.

Political power sometimes influences international prices and therefore the distribution of gains among the trading nations. During the era of European colonialism in the 17th through 19th centuries, lopsided gains were commonplace. Trade between the colonies and the European colonial powers was often politically engineered, giving the Europeans exclusive rights to markets and at prices designed to shift most of the gains to them.

Today, it's not so much political power as the market power of supply and demand that determines international prices. An increase in world demand for corn, for example, will have more influence in shifting prices from $2 to $3 per bushel than all the speeches in the Mexican Assembly or the U.S. Congress.

## CALCULATING TERMS OF TRADE

Many of the less-developed countries (LDCs) of Asia, Africa, and Latin America are behind the proverbial eight ball when it comes to international prices and gains from trade. Why? LDC exports, which are typically agricultural, trade on highly competitive markets. Their principal **imports** from the industrially advanced economies, on the other hand, are manufactured goods traded in markets that tend to be far less competitive. As a result, new technologies in agriculture and shifts in demand for agricultural exports over the years have depressed the LDCs' **export** prices, while new technologies in manufacturing and changing demands for manufacturing imports have raised the LDCs' import prices.

### The Dilemma of the Less-Developed Countries

Exhibit 8 illustrates the problem facing the less-developed economies. It shows what happens to the prices of Japanese motorcycles and Bolivian tin when demands and supplies for these goods change over time. Let's look at 1995 and 2001.

In panel *a*, a strong increase in demand combines with a moderate increase in supply to raise the price of motorcycles from $6,000 to $7,500. (These are hypothetical numbers, of course.) In panel *b*, a moderate increase in demand combines with a strong increase in supply to decrease the price of tin from $6,000 to $5,000 a ton. Back in 1995, Bolivians bought a motorcycle with a ton of tin. Not so in 2001. Now, it takes 1½ tons of tin to buy that same motorcycle.

Economists express Bolivia's deteriorating international trade position with Japan in the **terms of trade** equation:

$$\frac{\text{index of export prices}}{\text{index of import prices}} \times 100$$

Using Bolivia's tin export prices to represent the index of its export prices in general, and using Japan's motorcycle prices to represent the index of the price of goods Bolivia imports, then the terms of trade for Bolivia in 1995 was

$$\frac{\$6,000}{\$6,000} \times 100 = 100.$$

**Imports**
Goods and services bought by people in one country that are produced in other countries.

**Exports**
Goods and services produced by people in one country that are sold in other countries.

**Terms of trade**
The amount of a good or service (export) that must be given up to buy a unit of another good or service (import). A country's terms of trade are measured by the ratio of the country's export prices to its import prices.

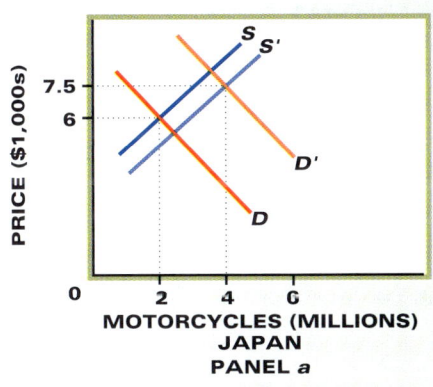
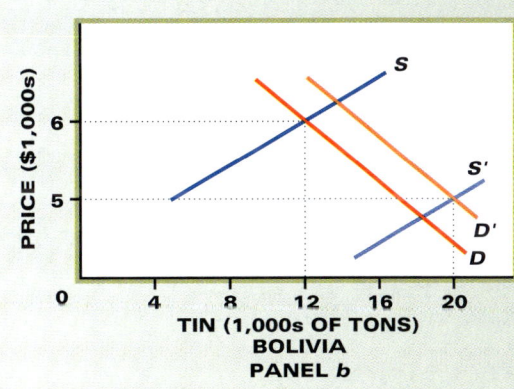

**JAPANESE MOTORCYCLE AND BOLIVIAN TIN EXPORTS**

Panel *a* depicts the shifts in the demand for and supply of Japanese motorcycles. The robust demand shift, from *D* to *D'*, combines with the moderate supply shift, from *S* to *S'*, to raise the price of motorcycles from $6,000 to $7,500. Panel *b* depicts the shifts in the demand for and supply of Bolivian tin. The moderate demand shift, from *D* to *D'*, combines with the robust supply shift, from *S* to *S'*, to reduce price from $6,000 to $5,000 per ton.

Look what happens in 2001. Bolivia's terms of trade deteriorates to

$$\frac{\$5{,}000}{\$7{,}500} \times 100 = 66.7.$$

Bolivia's exports end up with only 67 percent of their former purchasing power. Of course, the Japanese are delighted. The gains from international trade move in their favor. And there isn't much Bolivia can do about it. It simply obeys the dictates of the markets. Should Bolivia give up trading with Japan? Certainly not! Bolivia is still better off trading than not trading. After all, the opportunity cost of producing a motorcycle in Bolivia is, more likely than not, greater than the 1½ tons of tin it must now pay for the Japanese motorcycle.

**CHECK YOUR UNDERSTANDING**

Why shouldn't Bolivia stop trading when its terms of trade worsens?

## Looking at Real-World Numbers

What do real-world LDC terms of trade look like? Two features seem to dominate: year-to-year volatility and for many LDCs, steadily worsening terms of trade. The data in Exhibit 9 show a worsening condition for ten LDCs over the period 1995–98. In the Central African Republic, for example, a unit of exports in 1998 buys less than two-thirds of the imports it was able to buy in 1995. For Pakistan, a unit of its exports in 1998 buys a little less than 90 percent of what that unit bought in 1995.

As you see in Exhibit 10, most of the data for the six LDCs show evidence of high

**LDC TERMS OF TRADE FOR 1998 (1995 = 100)**

| | | | |
|---|---|---|---|
| PAKISTAN | 88.9 | COLOMBIA | 84.6 |
| NIGERIA | 86.8 | REPUBLIC OF CONGO | 82.3 |
| UGANDA | 78.2 | ETHIOPIA | 89.1 |
| ZAMBIA | 83.7 | JAMAICA | 77.3 |
| CENTRAL AFRICAN REP. | 64.3 | BURUNDI | 76.2 |

**Source:** *World Development Indicators, 2000,* The World Bank.

## EXHIBIT 10

### TERMS OF TRADE VOLATILITY FOR LDCS: 1990–98 (1995 = 100)

|  | 1990 | 1992 | 1994 | 1996 | 1998 |
|---|---|---|---|---|---|
| BURUNDI | 74.6 | 56.7 | 102.8 | 74.1 | 76.2 |
| ETHIOPIA | 89.6 | 139.0 | 83.7 | 89.0 | 89.0 |
| GUATEMALA | 83.4 | 91.9 | 97.3 | 89.2 | 100.0 |
| NIGERIA | 161.0 | 117.0 | 102.2 | 163.2 | 86.8 |
| UGANDA | 74.1 | 61.5 | 66.9 | 80.1 | 78.2 |
| BANGLADESH | 92.9 | 82.9 | 93.6 | 102.5 | 98.8 |

**Source:** *World Development Indicators, 2000,* The World Bank.

volatility during the 1990–98 period. Burundi's terms of trade, for example, bounced from 56.7 in 1992 to 102.8 in 1994 to 74.1 in 1996.

## WHO TRADES WITH WHOM? TRACKING INTERNATIONAL TRADE

Small wonder that the world's economies are engaged in massive exchanges of almost every kind of familiar and exotic good. We find food processors from France, television sets from Japan, wool sweaters from Scotland, processed meat from Australia, microchips from Israel, cheese from Switzerland, coffee from Brazil, tin from Bolivia, anchovies from Portugal, shirts from China, and shoes from Italy in almost every one of our metropolitan and small-town markets.

They are found as well in markets all over the world. No surprise also that the United States is a major world trading partner. Our imports provide vital markets to many exporting countries. Our exports rank among the highly competitive goods and services sold on international markets.

More and more, the world's economies are becoming linked into one unified market network. In 1999, more than 15 percent of the world's GDP made its way onto the international market in the form of exports. That compares to less than 3 percent of the world's GDP in 1970. As communications and transportation technologies become even more advanced and accessible, we should expect that exports and imports in the 21st century will account for even higher percentages of the world's production.

The one striking observation we can draw from international trade statistics is that the big ones play with the big ones and even the little ones want to play with the big ones. Look at Exhibit 11.

**on the net**

The World Trade Organization (WTO) (http://www.wto.org/), an international body addressing trade among nations, provides data and analysis on international trade.

## EXHIBIT 11

### PERCENTAGE DISTRIBUTION OF EXPORTS TO DEVELOPED, LDCs, AND OTHER ECONOMIES: 1999

| EXPORTER | EXPORTS TO | |
|---|---|---|
|  | DEVELOPED | LDCs |
| DEVELOPED | 72.9 | 26.4 |
| LDCs | 58.4 | 34.7 |
| WORLD | 68.0 | 30.9 |

**Source:** *Direction of Trade Statistics, Yearbook 2000* (Washington, D.C.: International Monetary Fund, 2000).

**1999 EXPORTS AND IMPORTS OF THE MAJOR DEVELOPED ECONOMIES ($ BILLIONS)**

|  | EXPORTS | IMPORTS |  | EXPORTS | IMPORTS |
|---|---|---|---|---|---|
| UNITED STATES | $702.1 | $1,059.4 | CANADA | $238.5 | $214.8 |
| GERMANY | 541.1 | 472.2 | ITALY | 230.2 | 216.6 |
| JAPAN | 419.4 | 311.3 | THE NETHERLANDS | 200.3 | 187.5 |
| FRANCE | 300.9 | 291.3 | BELGIUM | 178.9 | 163.9 |
| BRITAIN | 268.2 | 317.9 | KOREA | 144.8 | 119.8 |

Source: *Direction of Trade Statistics, Yearbook 2000* (Washington, D.C.: International Monetary Fund, 2000).

Approximately two-thirds of world exports in 1999 were exported to the industrially developed countries. The less-developed countries accounted for the remaining one-third. The major markets for the exports of the developed economies were themselves. They absorbed 72.9 percent of their own exports. They also absorbed 58.4 percent of LDC exports.

## The Major Leagues

There's no doubt which of the developed economies play in the major leagues. Exhibit 12 lists them in order of their 1999 trade volumes.

The United States dominates the list. Its $1,761.5 billion trade volume is followed by Germany's $1,013.3 billion. But, as you see, all 10 countries have annual trade volumes in excess of $250 billion. That puts them in a league by themselves.

*The World Factbook* (http://www.cia.gov/cia/publications/factbook/), compiled by the U.S. Central Intelligence Agency, provides detailed economic information, including exports and imports, on all of the nations of the world.

## WHO DOES THE UNITED STATES TRADE WITH?

There is so much heated discussion over our trade relations with Japan that sometimes we tend to forget that Japan comes in third to our primary trading partners, Canada and Mexico.

Proximity is important. Look at Exhibit 13. Trade between Canada and the United States represents the largest trade flow between any two countries in the

The U.S. Department of Commerce, International Trade Administration (http://www.ita.doc.gov/), provides foreign trade data by country and trade sector.

**1999 U.S. TRADE WITH ITS MAJOR TRADING PARTNERS ($ BILLIONS)**

|  | U.S. EXPORTS TO | U.S. IMPORTS FROM |  | U.S. EXPORTS TO | U.S. IMPORTS FROM |
|---|---|---|---|---|---|
| CANADA | $162.9 | $198.8 | CHINA | $25.6 | $97.4 |
| MEXICO | 86.4 | 109.5 | KOREA | 22.2 | 31.8 |
| JAPAN | 57.7 | 134.0 | THE NETHERLANDS | 19.3 | 8.9 |
| BRITAIN | 38.5 | 39.9 | FRANCE | 18.8 | 26.7 |
| GERMANY | 27.0 | 55.8 | ITALY | 10.1 | 23.2 |

Source: *Direction of Trade Statistics, Yearbook 2000* (Washington, D.C.: International Monetary Fund, 2000).

# INTERDISCIPLINARY PERSPECTIVE

## TRADE AND CULTURE

**Disneyland Paris is the number one tourist destination in Europe! Does that surprise you?** The United States's own Disneyland and Disney World are tourist magnets attracting millions of Americans and foreign visitors year after year. But that's understandable. Disney is as American as apple pie and has come to symbolize, both here and abroad, what American culture is, circa 2000.

But *Europe?* While the changing of the guards at Buckingham Palace makes a lovely Kodak moment and strolling the Champs-Elysées or climbing the Eiffel Tower are activities that European tourists—and the French, in particular—love to do on vacation, none of them can exert the pull on European hearts and wallets that Mickey Mouse can.

And wouldn't you think that would annoy the French? In fact, they're almost schizophrenic about it! On the one hand, the French are frightfully proud of their culture—their food and drink, their music, their cinema, their fine arts and entertainment—but on the other hand, they seem to be more and more willing to trade in their baguette for the Big Mac, their wine for Coke, and their cinema for Hollywood.

What had been uniquely French about the French is becoming less and less so and what is American about the French is becoming more and more so. And it's not because U.S. marines are imposing an unwanted American culture on the defenseless French. It is, instead, the French going into the marketplace with their hard-earned francs and with much eagerness to buy that American culture. The lesson is learned everywhere: In an open and free market economy, consumer sovereignty dictates.

What annoys the French annoys others as well. The Canadians, sharing a 3,000-mile open border with the United States, are particularly anxious about the Canadian infatuation with American culture. They fear that in the free exchange of goods, services, ideas, and culture, the cherished differences—real and imagined—between Canadian and American life will all but disappear.

Whether there's any legitimacy to the French or Canadian or any other national concern about erosion of culture, the question arises about trade and culture in the 21st century: Can *any* national culture survive the global market?

That's what was at the heart of the matter when in June 1998, culture ministers from 23 countries met in Canada at the invitation of the Canadian government to discuss their shared fear that the United States routinely and aggressively sacrifices culture for free trade.

VIVA MICKEY MOUSE.

The immediate provocation for the Canadians was their loss to the United States at the World Trade Organization (WTO) of a vital cultural matter. The WTO struck down Canada's 80 percent excise tax on split-run editions of foreign (mainly U.S.) magazines. The WTO insisted that America's *Newsweek, Time, U.S. News & World Report,* and others should be able to compete on equal terms with Canadian magazines, such as *Maclean's*. The Canadian fear is that in an open and competitive marketplace, Canadian-owned and Canadian-focused *Maclean's* would not survive. That is, Canadian readers would prefer the American choices just as many Canadian television viewers prefer America's CNN to its Canadian equivalents.

Another incendiary issue to Canadians is the fate of hockey in Canada. To many sports-minded Canadians, Canadian culture is hockey. But that, too, is changing. In the mid-1990s, two of the seven Canadian teams in the National Hockey League (NHL) left Canada for the green pastures (read: money) to the south: the Winnipeg Jets to Phoenix and the Quebec Nordiques to Colorado. No less upsetting to Canadian hockey fans was the sale of the Montreal Canadiens in 2001 to an American multimillionaire, the Canadiens' only non-Canadian owner in its 91-year history. While the nationality of buyers and sellers is of little consequence in the U.S. marketplace, it is a matter of much concern in Canada.

But what are the Canadian—and French, and Spanish, and British, *and American*—alternatives to the global marketplace? Is national culture destined to be a casualty of modern technology, as were the stagecoach, the steam locomotive, and first-class mail? The marketplace, it appears, takes no prisoners.

> **MORE ON THE NET**
>
> Visit the International Network on Cultural Policy (http://www.pch.gc.ca/network-reseau/eng.htm), which grew out of the cultural meeting that took place in Ottawa in 1998. What is the goal of this network? How does it intend to achieve this goal?

world. Mexico ranks as our second largest trading partner. U.S. exports to Canada and Mexico were greater than the combined U.S. exports to all the other countries shown in Exhibit 13.

No wonder many Canadians are upset about our benign neglect of them. Important as they are to us, however, we are much more important to them. The United States alone bought 83.2 percent of Canada's 1999 exports to the world. U.S. markets also bought as much as 89.6 percent of Mexico's exports.

Their import packages, too, carry a clear U.S. stamp. U.S. exports to Canada added up to 87.2 percent of their total 1999 imports, and U.S. exports to Mexico accounted for 88.1 percent of its 1999 total imports. For both neighboring economies, that's an enormous one-country dependence.

The singular importance of the United States to Canada and Mexico is striking when compared to their next-best markets. For example, Canada's 208 billion in exports to the United States was followed by its $5.3 billion exports to Japan. Mexico's $120.4 billion exports to the United States towered over its $1.2 billion exports to Canada.

## DO WE NEED PROTECTION AGAINST FREE TRADE?

No one, not even those who lobby Congress for protection against free trade, deny the economic benefits that free trade offers. The evidence is overwhelming. The arguments against free trade, then, are made strictly as *exceptions to the rule*. They address particular circumstances.

Ask U.S. oil producers how much they benefit when we allow Mexican oil into U.S. markets. The economic pain *they* suffer is, unquestionably, real. Although in general the nation gains from free trade—tens of millions of U.S. oil consumers now pay less for oil—some individuals do get hurt.

How do we weigh the widespread general gains against the particular losses? Should we simply ignore the downside of free trade, or is that pushing a good thing too far? For example, should we sacrifice gains to protect injured parties? *All* injured parties?

A number of classic arguments have been made against *indiscriminate* free trade. These have had considerable effect not only in persuading Congress to limit trade in specific industries of our economy, but also in persuading other governments to do precisely the same in their economies, and for the same reasons.

## The National Security Argument

Suppose France's Mirage is a less costly, more effective fighter aircraft than our own F-16. Should we close down our F-16 factories and import Mirages? Although this move might create gains from trade for both the United States and France, we do not want to rely on France for our national survival. Most of the major industrial economies of the world produce their own security systems, even though most understand that they forfeit the gains that would result from international specialization. Production of weapons, munitions, missiles, tanks, submarines, aircraft carriers, cannons, and radar equipment are obvious candidates for protection against free trade on national security grounds.

Some goods, however, are less obvious, and that's when abuse begins. It's not terribly difficult, particularly for industry lobbyists, to draw some connection between any industry and national security.

The national security argument against free trade has a long and active history. As early as 1815, the British Parliament enacted a series of corn laws that established tariffs on grain imports from Europe. Although corn law advocates insisted that England must never be beholden to Europeans for their food supply, their main objective was to protect the English landlord class (and their rents) from the cheaper European grain.

What worked then, works today. Our agricultural industries, too, have invoked the national security argument to protect markets from cheaper imports.

In fact, almost everything can be brought under the umbrella of the national security argument. In times of national crisis, can we really rely on foreign supplies of sheet metal? What about photographic equipment, surveying instruments, lumber, pharmaceuticals, steel fabrication, optical equipment, orthopedic equipment, radio communication systems, and petrochemicals? Shouldn't they, too, qualify for protection on national security grounds?

*If you had to make the case in Congress for widening protection on grounds of national security, what other industries would you suggest protecting? Go to the Interactive Study Center at http://gottheil.swcollege.com and click on the "Your Turn" button to submit your example. Student submissions will be posted to the Web site, and perhaps we will use some in future editions of the book!*

## The Infant Industries Argument

Learning curves—time required to gain expertise—apply to new industries just as they do to people. Because of that, it's sometimes unfair to expect a fledgling industry at home to survive free trade competition from its older, more-experienced foreign competitors. It needs more time.

Protecting infant industries from foreign competition, then, has some validity, because without such protection, many promising industries just wouldn't get started. It's perhaps worthwhile for a country to suffer the higher prices of its own less-efficient new industries in the short run because it expects to gain from greater efficiency and lower prices in the long run.

But how long is the long run? When is an industry's infancy period over? There's the problem. The comforts of protection, once experienced by the infant industry, are difficult to forgo. Many, having run the learning curve many times over, are still as inefficient as they were the day protection was granted. Others remain protected under new guises. Our steel industry, for example, was protected as an infant industry over a century ago and is still protected today. It's an argument that can too easily be abused.

## The Cheap Foreign Labor Argument

Perhaps the most frequently invoked battle cry against indiscriminate free trade is the injustice of having to compete in markets against foreign firms that employ cheap labor. How can the U.S. textile industry, for example, employing highly paid unionized labor, compete against textiles imported from Jamaica, China, Brazil, Mexico, the Philippines, and Malaysia? Those countries, even if unions exist at all, still pay wage rates considerably below U.S. levels. Some argue that the U.S. textile industry can't compete, and the consequences are declining wages rates, real incomes, employment, and standards of living at home.

You may wonder if that is really so. The cheap foreign labor argument ignores the fact that higher levels of productivity (output per hour) typically accompany the higher wage rates in the United States, so that the wage cost per unit of U.S. manufactured goods is not necessarily higher than the wage cost associated with the foreign good.

**CHECK YOUR UNDERSTANDING**

What is the major flaw in the cheap foreign labor argument supporting protection?

If raincoats produced in China are less costly because of cheap labor than the raincoats produced in New York, shouldn't we take advantage of the lower price? After all, isn't that precisely why we engage in specialization? Rather than lowering our standard of living, trade with low-wage economies increases the real goods we are able to purchase, so that our living standards should actually improve.

Of course, the widespread gains consumers enjoy from such trade are not universally shared. Some people end up losing. Some firms, for example, cannot survive the competition. People lose jobs and don't always find new ones. Entrepreneurs fail, and many never recover. Stockholders lose their investment, and many never invest again.

## The Diversity-of-Industry Argument

Some economies have become so highly specialized in one or two production activities that these alone account for a major share of national product and, typically, an even greater share of exports. Think, for example, of Saudi Arabia and oil, or Honduras and bananas. When the prices of their few specialized exports are relatively high, their economies perform well. When prices fall, however, their economies suffer.

Since these prices reflect the swings of demand and supply in the international market, in many cases the fate of highly specialized economies is out of their hands. Moreover, if the swings are erratic, these economies also tend to become unpredictable and unstable.

No one wants to live in an unstable world. Good enough reason to diversify industrial production, isn't it? That's where protection comes in.

Many less-developed countries argue for such protection. They understand the costs involved in abandoning specialization but still prefer the greater economic stability that the protection affords. In their case, it may make sense. However, it is hardly the argument that industries in the United States can make for protection. The United States and Western European economies are already sufficiently diversified.

## The Antidumping Argument

Some industries seeking protection insist that it is not lack of absolute or comparative advantage on the international market that does them in, but rather the sinister strategies of their foreign competition. Why sinister? Because their foreign competitors dump goods on the market, *priced below cost,* to knock them out of the game. Once the competition is eliminated, these sinister producers—now monopolists—

**Dumping**
Exporting a good or service at a price below its cost of production.

will use their monopoly power to raise prices to levels even higher than they were before. That's pretty cheeky, isn't it?

Our Congress thought so, and made **dumping** on our markets illegal. The problem is, how do we go about proving that low-cost foreign goods are priced below cost? One way is to compare the export prices of the foreign producer to the prices it charges in its own domestic market. That's not always easy to do, and sometimes the comparisons are rigged to support inefficient producers in the United States.

## The Retaliation Argument

Should we allow other countries free access to our markets if they restrict our exports in theirs? That's rather unfair, isn't it? Yet that's precisely the trading conditions we confront with many of our trading partners. Perhaps the most glaring case of such lopsided access is our trading experience with Japan. Our complaints to them about their restrictive practices seem to fall on deaf ears.

Many U.S. producers, frustrated by Japanese protection of their own domestic markets, call for retaliation. If the Japanese won't allow us free entry into their markets, they argue, we should simply deny them free entry into ours. Since we are a major market for their exports, the retaliation may "encourage" them to rethink their protection strategies.

It may in fact work. With greater access to their markets, our own export and even import volumes would most likely increase, benefiting both us and the Japanese. It may make sense, then, to threaten retaliation—and even in some cases to carry out the threat.

But suppose retaliation doesn't work. If it leaves us with less, not greater trade, it makes no sense at all. After all, even with restricted access to their markets, we still benefit by importing Japanese goods. Otherwise, we wouldn't import them.

# THE ECONOMICS OF TRADE PROTECTION

How do we restrict imports? Basically, with tariffs and quotas. What are they, and how do they work?

## Tariffs

**Tariff**
A tax on an imported good.

A **tariff** is a government-imposed tax on imports. It can be levied as a percentage of the import's value or as a specific tax per unit of import. Like any other tax, it becomes government revenue. Although U.S. importers pay the tariff to U.S. customs when importing foreign goods, they typically shift at least part of it onto the consumer by raising prices. To the consumer, the tariff is invisible. After all, do you really know what percentage of the price you pay for an Italian bike is the tariff on the bike and what percentage represents the price the Italian bike producer actually receives?

The U.S. International Trade Commission (http://www.usitc.gov/), the Office of the U.S. Trade Representative (http://www.ustr.gov/), and the U.S. Department of State (http://www.state.gov/www/issues/economic/trade_reports/) issue reports on foreign trade barriers and unfair practices.

How can a U.S. tariff on bikes protect U.S. producers? Let's suppose that bike manufacturers in the United States cannot produce a bike as inexpensively as manufacturers in Italy. Suppose the Italians price their bikes in U.S. markets at $200, which is $250 less than the $450 price for U.S. bikes on the U.S. market.

Without a tariff, the U.S. manufacturers are in serious trouble. How can they compete with the cheaper Italian bike? But suppose Congress, persuaded by any one of the protectionist arguments, imposes a 100 percent tariff, that is, a $200 add-on to the price of Italian bikes. Exhibit 14 shows what happens to the price and quantity of bikes bought and sold under conditions of no foreign trade, unrestricted foreign trade, and tariff-restricted foreign trade.

INTERNATIONAL TRADE

## TARIFF-RESTRICTED TRADE

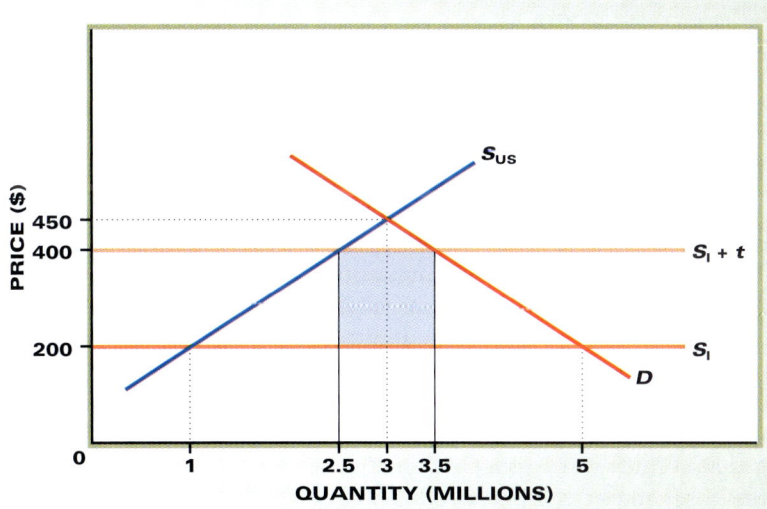

The supply curve, $S_{US}$, records the quantity of bikes U.S. producers are willing to supply at varying prices. The demand curve records the quantity of bikes Americans are willing to buy at varying prices. With no foreign suppliers, 3 million would be bought and sold at an equilibrium price of $450.

$S_I$ records the willingness of Italian bike producers to supply any quantity at $200. When Italian suppliers are allowed to enter the U.S. market, equilibrium price and the quantities of bikes demanded and supplied in the United States change dramatically. Price falls from $450 to $200 and the quantity demanded increases to 5 million; 1 million supplied by U.S. producers and 4 million imported from Italy.

If the U.S. government imposes a 100 percent tariff on bikes, the Italian supply curve in the United States becomes $S_I + t$. At a price of $400, 3.5 million bikes are demanded: 2.5 million supplied by U.S. producers and 1 million imported from Italy. The shaded area shows the U.S. government's tariff revenue.

The supply curve, $S_{US}$, represents the quantities of bikes that U.S. producers are willing to supply at various prices. The demand curve represents U.S. demand for bikes. If the market were completely insulated from foreign competition, U.S. manufacturers would be busy producing 3 million bikes and selling them at a price of $450.

Let's now introduce free trade. Suppose Italian producers are willing to supply any quantity of bikes at a $200 price. The Italian supply curve on the U.S. market is shown as $S_I$. How does that supply affect U.S. manufacturers?

At a $200 price, U.S. consumers increase their quantity demanded from 3 to 5 million bikes. Only 1 million of the 5 million, however, would be supplied by U.S. manufacturers. That is, the U.S. firms lose 2 million of their former sales to Italian competitors and now have only 20 percent of this new, flourishing market. We now import 4 million Italian bikes. You can imagine how the U.S. bike manufacturers would react.

Suppose a 100 percent tariff, $t$, is applied to bikes. The Italian supply curve shifts to $S_I + t$, and the price of Italian bikes in the U.S. market increases to $400. At this higher price, the quantity demanded by U.S. consumers falls from 5 to 3.5 million. U.S. firms produce 2.5 million, and importers of Italian bikes provide the other million.

In other words, the tariff gives the U.S. bike industry a new lease on life, but only at the expense of the U.S. consumer. What about government? It ends up with a revenue of $200 × 1 million = $200 million, the shaded rectangle in Exhibit 14.

## Quotas

Sometimes governments prefer to restrict imports by imposing a **quota** instead of a tariff. What's the difference? Tariffs are import taxes added to prices; quotas limit the amount of a good that is allowed into the country at any price.

**Quota**
A limit on the quantity of a specific good that can be imported.

The outcomes are different. Let's suppose that instead of placing a 100 percent tariff on Italian bike imports, the government limits the number of imports to 500,000 units. Picture the scene. U.S. importers would be busy making long-distance calls to Rome to buy up the 500,000 Italian bikes. These are brought into the U.S. market at the free trade price of $200 each. What happens now? Look at Exhibit 15.

The supply curve is horizontal until we reach 1.5 million bikes, reflecting 500,000 supplied by Italian producers and 1 million that U.S. producers are willing to supply at $200. At higher prices, the supply curve becomes $S'$, the horizontal sum of the U.S. supply curve, $S$, and the 500,000 quota.

There we have it. The U.S. producers suffer a slight fall from the quantities they would sell if there were no Italian competitors in the market, from 3 million to 2.75 million. Quota protection raises the price from $200 to $420, although it is still less than the $450 that would prevail without competition from Italy.

What about the Italian bike producers? They sell their 500,000 quota to importers at $200 per bike. The importers, then, end up with a $420 − $200 = $220 windfall on each bike.

The protection options with the quota are almost countless. Each specific quota yields a unique U.S. production and market price. As with the tariff, there's no magic number that defines every quota. It could be any number, depending on the objectives of the government and U.S. producers.

## Other Nontariff Barriers

Tariffs and quotas are not the only mechanisms that can be used by domestic producers and by government to reduce imports. The government can also pass a law that specifies highly restrictive health and safety standards that imports must meet. For example, the government can insist that all Italian bikes be dismantled and reassembled by U.S. bike inspectors—at a cost, say, of $75 per bike—to guarantee safety.

**EXHIBIT 15**

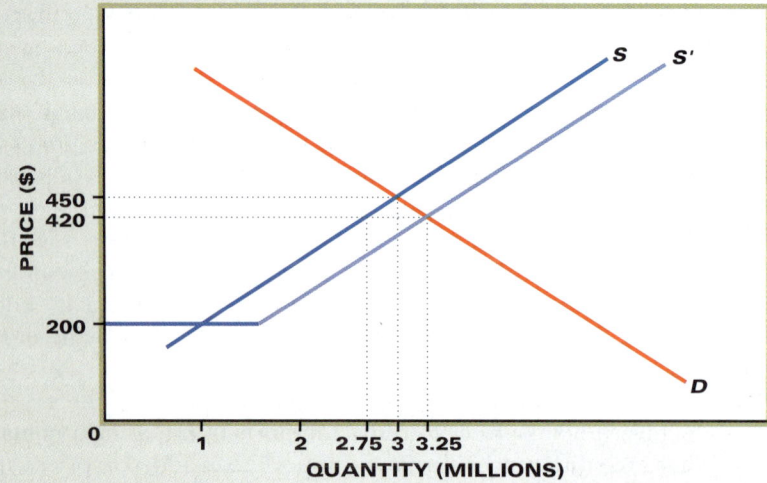

**QUOTA-RESTRICTED TRADE**

With no free trade, 3 million bikes are bought and sold in the United States at an equilibrium price of $450. If the U.S. government sets an import quota of 500,000 bikes, the relevant supply curve becomes $S'$ (which is $S$ + 500,000). The equilibrium price falls to $420, and 3.25 million bikes are bought and sold, of which 2.75 million are produced by U.S. suppliers.

That's not a particularly creative idea. The Japanese once prohibited ski imports because, they maintained, only Japanese skis were suitable for Japanese snow. The Germans disallowed foreign-brewed beer on grounds of health and safety. U.S. beef imports were shut out of European markets because U.S. cattle were fed with government-approved hormones.

In some cases, import barriers are self-imposed by foreign exporters who agree to "voluntarily" limit the quantity of their exports. For example, Japanese automakers voluntarily agreed to limit auto exports to the United States. They understood the alternatives: Volunteer or face higher tariffs or lower quotas.

# NEGOTIATING TARIFF STRUCTURES

Whatever tariff structure a nation chooses, it would seem only fair that the structure, once established between two trading partners, should apply to all other countries as well. For example, if the United States and France agree to a mutual reduction, from 40 to 25 percent, in their tariffs on imported wine, then a third country, say Portugal, should be allowed to sell its wine in the United States and France at the same 25 percent tariff rate. Otherwise, international trade would be marked by country-to-country discrimination.

This idea of tariff **reciprocity** became the guiding principle industrial nations adopted after World War II in establishing rules of international trade. The aim was to increase the free movement of goods across national boundaries, and to do so nondiscriminately.

**Reciprocity**
An agreement between countries in which trading privileges granted by one to the others are the same as those granted to it by the others.

## GATT

The **General Agreement on Tariffs and Trade (GATT)** served as the framework for this multilateral trade objective. Nations came together under GATT rules to negotiate trade policies. Organized in the aftermath of World War II with 22 nations participating, GATT has grown to 97 member nations plus 9 observer nations. It includes all industrial market economies, several from Eastern Europe, and more than 50 economies from the less-developed countries. Together, these GATT members represent over 80 percent of all international trade.

GATT's principal objective is to reduce the level of all tariffs. The nondiscriminating provision of GATT is called the *most-favored nation clause*. The clause applies to all member nations. What is offered to one member as a tariff concession is offered to all.

As you might expect, the United States's role in GATT, which is critical to GATT's functioning, reflects Congress's own interest in promoting free trade. In 1962, Congress legislated the Trade Expansion Act, which led to the Kennedy rounds of tariff cuts. Later, the Tokyo round, which cut tariffs further, was negotiated under the authority of the 1974 Trade Reform Act. The most recent GATT round of negotiations—the Uruguay round—tackled the issue of reducing nontariff protective barriers to trade.

**GATT (General Agreement on Tariffs and Trade)**
A trade agreement to negotiate reductions in tariffs and other trade barriers and to provide equal and nondiscriminating treatment among members of the agreement. Around 100 countries are members of GATT.

Review GATT (http://trading.wmw.com/gatt/) in its entirety.

## GATT Concessions to Less-Developed Countries

The less-developed countries were never really happy with GATT. In fact, they were downright annoyed. With good reason. They saw it as strictly a rich nation's club. How could they be excited about lowering their own tariffs when their principal concern was economic development? After all, if the infant-industry argument against free trade had meaning anywhere, didn't it make most sense for them?

# GLOBAL PERSPECTIVE

## HOW MUCH DO BARRIERS TO IMPORTS COST JAPANESE CONSUMERS?

**M**ention Japan's trade barriers to its trading partners, and they will leave you in no doubt about their effects. They will point to firms in their countries that cannot price their way into Japanese markets, and lament the profits and jobs that are lost to protectionism.

Such moans are understandable. And yet a hefty chunk of the cost of Japanese protection is paid not by foreigners, but by the Japanese themselves. Trade barriers, which raise the price of foreign goods or keep them out altogether, force consumers to buy more costly domestic alternatives. They also distort firms' inputs, pushing them toward expensive local sources and raising the prices of goods made at home. Indeed, the most persuasive argument for scrapping trade barriers, in Japan or anywhere else, ought to be that they damage protected economies.

DID YOU SEE THE MANIFEST? THIS IS ALL GOING TO JAPAN. MOST UNUSUAL. THEY TYPICALLY DON'T IMPORT MUCH.

So much for the theory. But how much does Japan really pay for its own protection? In a new book (*Measuring the Costs of Protection in Japan,* Institute for International Economics, 1995), three Japanese economists, Yoko Sazanami, Shujiro Urata, and Hiroki Kawai, provide an answer. They compare the price of imports on the dockside (i.e., before tariffs and wholesalers' markups have been added) with the price of Japanese goods at the factory gate. They use the difference to estimate the cost of trade barriers to Japanese consumers.

They conclude that Japanese protection is limited to agricultural products and a few manufacturing industries. Where protection exists, though, it is heavy (see table). They estimate that in 1989 the prices of some foods were several hundred percent higher than import prices. Japanese-made radios and televisions were over 600 percent more expensive than imports. Clothing was marked up by nearly 300 percent; petrol by more than 200 percent.

**DIFFERENCE BETWEEN PRICE OF DOMESTIC GOODS AND IMPORTS: 1989 (AS A PERCENTAGE OF IMPORT PRICE)**

|  | PRICE DIFFERENCE | TARIFF RATE | IMPLIED NONTARIFF BARRIER RATE |
|---|---|---|---|
| **MILLED RICE** | 737.1 | 0.0 | 737.1 |
| **TEA AND COFFEE** | 718.4 | 11.9 | 706.5 |
| **COSMETICS** | 661.6 | 2.0 | 659.6 |
| **RADIOS AND TVs** | 607.0 | 0.0 | 607.0 |
| **WHEAT** | 477.8 | 0.0 | 477.8 |
| **SOYBEANS** | 423.6 | 0.0 | 423.6 |
| **CLOTHING** | 292.6 | 10.4 | 282.2 |
| **PETROL** | 229.0 | 5.5 | 223.5 |

**Source:** Y. Sazanami, S. Urata, and H. Kawai, Datastream.

The cost to Japanese consumers totals around 15 trillion yen a year ($110 billion at 1989 exchange rates), or 3.8 percent of GDP. The cost to the Japanese economy as a whole is a good deal smaller, because protection earns profits for domestic producers and tariff revenues for the government. But the estimated damage is still hefty, at about 0.6 percent of Japanese national income. Moreover, say the three economists, these numbers may understate the costs of protection. More foreign competition would force Japanese industry to become more efficient: costs and prices would fall.

In addition, the prices of imports are affected by trade restraints. By making imports scarcer, they create monopoly power for foreign suppliers (as long as imports and domestic goods are not perfect substitutes). This enables them to charge higher prices for their wares in countries that protect local producers.

The conclusion for Japanese consumers (and policy makers) is a sobering one: Trade barriers not only push up the price of Japanese goods, they probably make imports dearer as well.

**MORE ON THE NET**

The Japanese Ministry of Economy, Trade and Industry (http://www.meti.go.jp/english/index.html), the Japan External Trade Organization (http://www.jetro.go.jp/top/index.html), and the Japan Economic Foundation (http://www.jef.or.jp/) provide news and information on Japanese trade.

**Source:** "Japan's Protection Racket," *The Economist,* January 7, 1995. © 1995 The Economist Newspaper Group, Inc. Reprinted with permission. Further reproduction prohibited. http://www.economist.com

---

GATT got the message. The less-developed countries are exceptions to the GATT rules. Although enjoying most-favored nation status, their exports typically face lower tariffs than industrial nations grant to each other. Moreover, reciprocity rights do not apply to the less-developed countries. They can enjoy the industrial economies' tariff concessions without having to reciprocate.

## Customs Unions

In 1958, the six West European economies of France, Germany, Italy, Holland, Belgium, and Luxembourg established a **customs union**—the **European Economic Community (EEC)**—whose special trade arrangements allowed for complete free trade within the union and a common tariff schedule against the rest of the world. That's precisely the economic arrangement that exists between Vermont and California, isn't it? In the 1970s, Denmark, England, and Ireland joined the community. In the 1980s the EEC expanded again to include Greece, Spain, and Portugal. In the 1990s, Iceland, Finland, Sweden, and Austria joined. Hungary, Poland, the Czech Republic, Estonia, and Slovenia are next in line.

The objectives of the EEC raise fundamental questions that concern the reciprocity principle underlying the GATT agreements. For example, if the United States lowers its tariff against French wine, according to GATT instruction it must also lower its tariff against wine imported from other countries.

The United States is disadvantaged, however, when it comes to competing with French wine in Britain. While French wine comes into Britain tariff-free, California wine faces a common EEC tariff. That's not fair, say California wineries. The French respond that California wine comes in tariff-free to Vermont; French wine doesn't. It's the same, *n'est-ce pas?* Not exactly. California trade with Vermont is strictly domestic; trade between France and England is still international. *GATT's rules apply only to international trade.*

**Customs union**
A set of countries that agree to free trade among themselves and a common trade policy with all other countries.

**European Economic Community (EEC)**
A customs union consisting of France, Italy, Belgium, Holland, Luxembourg, Germany, Britain, Ireland, Denmark, Greece, Spain, Portugal, Iceland, Finland, Sweden, and Austria.

## Free Trade Areas

A variant of the customs union is the **free trade area.** The single difference between it and the customs union, such as the EEC, is that the free trade area permits free trade among members, but each is allowed to establish its own tariff policy with respect to nonmembers. In other words, the free trade area permits each member greater independence in trade policy making.

## The North American Free Trade Agreement

By far the most significant trade agreement concluded by the United States is with Canada and Mexico. In 1989 both the U.S. Congress and the Canadian House of Commons enacted the **North American Free Trade Agreement (NAFTA).** Mexico joined NAFTA in 1993, making it the largest free trade area in the world, matching the total production of goods and services of the EEC.

NAFTA calls for the elimination of all tariffs, quotas, and other trade barriers within 10 years. Although over 75 percent of Canadian-U.S. trade was tariff-free even before NAFTA, the expansions in both U.S. and Canadian markets that NAFTA is expected to create makes the agreement a very significant economic event for both countries. Canadians gain a considerable advantage vis-à-vis other exporting countries in a market ten times the size of its own. On the other hand, the United States, having faced tariff rates in Canada higher than those Canadians faced in the United States prior to NAFTA, gains more when both cut their rates to zero.

Still, NAFTA was not engineered without some political controversy. Although some debate concerning its merits took place in the United States, NAFTA was a major political issue in Canada. The U.S. economy has always been regarded by Canadians as a potentially threatening colossus. Some Canadians feared that free access to each other's markets would result in U.S. production overwhelming their own. But their voices were muted by the logic of comparative advantage. It proved too much for Canadians to ignore.

Mexico's entry into NAFTA generated a somewhat more unsettling promise for the future. Although the expansion of all three markets—Canada, Mexico, and the United States—is seen by all three as an outcome of Mexico's membership in NAFTA, a disquieting note is voiced in the United States and Canada. The issue is low-wage Mexican labor. With tariffs completely eliminated, many worry that low-wage Mexican labor will lure firms, particularly labor-intensive ones, out of Canada and the United States to Mexico. Polluting firms that are forced to adhere to tough Canadian and U.S. environmental regulations will also be attracted to Mexico, where pollution regulations are fewer and poorly enforced.

Advocates of NAFTA respond with compelling arguments of their own. The economic development of Mexico, which NAFTA will assist, provides not only markets for Canadians and Americans, but employment opportunities for Mexicans. In other words, NAFTA can help reduce the illegal immigration flow across the Rio Grande. And the low-wage jobs that Americans and Canadians will lose are precisely the jobs that should be lost in the United States and Canada. The greater production in Canada and the United States that Mexico-included NAFTA generates should be able to reemploy those Canadian and American job-losers in higher-paying jobs.

## TRACKING TARIFFS SINCE 1860

Some people see a half glass of water as being half empty, while others view the same glass as half filled. It's just a matter of how you look at things. The same idea applies when we assess tariffs and trade performance. Look at Exhibit 16.

---

**Free trade area**
A set of countries that agree to free trade among themselves but are free to pursue independent trade policies with other countries.

**North American Free Trade Agreement (NAFTA)**
A free trade area consisting of Canada, the United States, and Mexico.

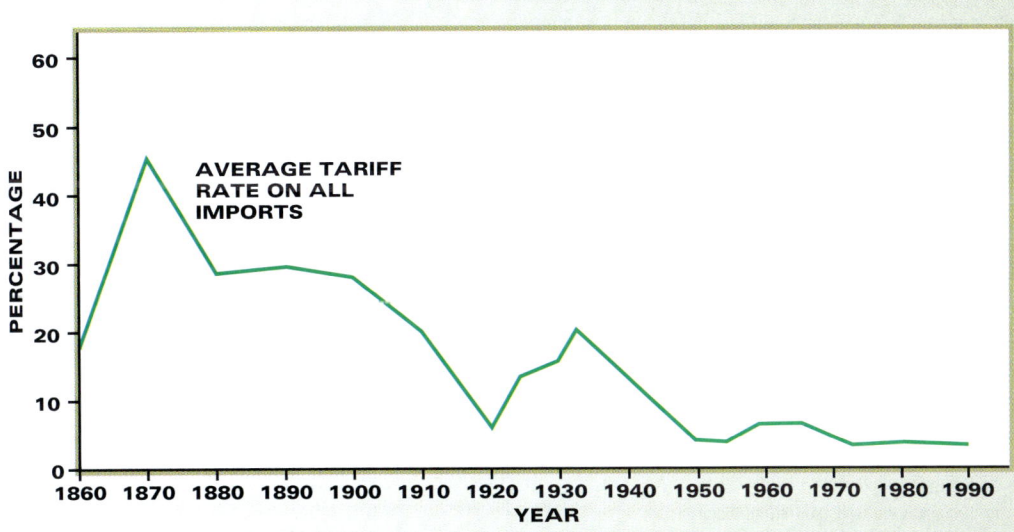

**AVERAGE U.S. TARIFF RATES ON IMPORTS**

The dramatic increase in the rates during the 1920s and early 1930s evaporated by 1950. Thereafter, the rates steadily declined and by 1970 were less than 10 percent.

Source: *Economic Report of the President,* January 1989 (Washington, D.C.: U.S. Government Printing Office, 1989), p. 152.

Just a cursory glance shows that whatever our view about whether tariffs are too high or too low, they have clearly dropped dramatically during the past 50 years.

As you can see, our tariff history shows some erratic behavior. In earlier years, our international trade policy was clearly protectionist. During the period 1870 to 1900, the average tariff rate on imports was over 25 percent. But note how the average tariff rate on all imports steadily declined during the next two decades.

The skyrocketing of rates during the 1920s and early 1930s appears as an exception, the direct result of the highly protectionist Fordney-McCumber Tariff Act of 1922 and the Smoot-Hawley Tariff Act of 1930. The Reciprocal Trade Agreement Act of 1934 reversed the upward movement in rates, and by 1950, rates were back to pre-1920 levels. Since 1970, the rates have fallen below 10 percent and continue to decline.

Are our tariff rates still too high? The average U.S. tariff, 1990–93, was 5.9 percent, which compares to Canada's 10.5 percent, Australia's 9.8 percent, Japan's 6.3 percent, and the EEC's 6.7 percent.

# APPLIED PERSPECTIVE

## IS NAFTA WORKER FRIENDLY?

The heated discussion in the United States that preceded the passage in 1993 of the North American Free Trade Agreement (NAFTA) continues unabated almost a decade later. The mountains of research on NAFTA's impact on real GDP, trade, and employment in the United States have resolved very little. Economists, typically in agreement on matters of free trade, line up on both sides of the NAFTA issue. Their central concern—although by no means the only one—is jobs: job creation and job losses.

Jobs, it appears, was also the principal reason some members of Congress voted in favor of NAFTA. They believed that NAFTA would promote economic growth and that the growth would increase jobs and wages in their districts. Others in Congress voted against the legislation because they feared NAFTA would result in fewer jobs and lower wages in their districts. Many of them saw the logic in 1992 presidential candidate Ross Perot's argument that "If you're paying $12, $13, $14 an hour for factory workers and you can move your factory south of the border, pay a dollar an hour for labor, have no health care . . . have no environmental controls, and no retirement and you don't care about anything but making money, there will be a giant sucking sound going south . . . ."

But has there really been a sucking sound? Among the many studies that estimate the impact of NAFTA on job creation or job losses are Robert Scott's (1999) and Mary Bolle's (2000). Scott focused on documenting state-by-state job losses. According to him, NAFTA was responsible for destroying 440,172 U.S. jobs over the period 1994–98. The big losers were California with approximately 45,000 job losses, Michigan, with over 30,000, and New York, with over 25,000. Others that registered losses greater than 15,000 were Georgia, Illinois, North Carolina, Ohio, Pennsylvania, Tennessee, and Texas. What Scott didn't estimate, however, were NAFTA-created jobs.

Mary Bolle's research, on the other hand, addressed both state-by-state job creations and losses for the same period, 1994–98. In her account, Texas led with a net job creation (job creation minus job loss) of 116,816. California followed with a net gain of 101,406 jobs. Michigan gained 79,304, Illinois gained 37,389, and New York gained 28,387. Only Vermont and New Mexico ended up with negative numbers, but their combined losses were less than 2,000 jobs.

What's the significance of Scott's NAFTA-induced loss-only estimates when Bolle's research included both state losses and gains? Aside from the methodological differences associated with their acquiring and applying relevant data, Bolle's net gain estimates tend to paint a rosier picture of NAFTA's job impact than they perhaps deserve.

If 100 jobs are lost and at the same time another 100 jobs are created, the benefits associated with the jobs gained don't necessarily cancel out the negatives associated with the losses. After all, the 100 workers who lost their jobs may have been relatively well paid, experienced, and older. Finding new and comparable jobs for them may be difficult. On the other hand, the majority of the 100 jobs gained may have gone to less experienced, younger, and perhaps lower-wage workers. That is to say, even though the job numbers net to zero, the impact on workers may not be zero. For this reason, Scott's job-loss data is significant and points to a probable source of real NAFTA-generated problems in the U.S. economy. It may also explain why some economists and members of Congress continue to be less excited about the net gains in jobs than others.

The importance of the job loss data imports as well on the peripheral issue of workers' wage bargaining ability when jobs are threatened by the potential exodus of U.S. companies to Mexico and Canada. Professor Kate Bronfenbrenner, NAFTA's Labor Secretariat, reported that U.S. companies often exercise the threat option when confronted with union efforts to organize U.S. workers.

The argument isn't that NAFTA's impact on U.S. jobs is "worker unfriendly." It is instead that the job creations NAFTA induced—as valuable as they are to U.S. workers and to the U.S. economy in general—still must be measured against the not inconsiderable job losses and economic distress that fall disproportionately on some U.S. workers.

# CHAPTER REVIEW

1. The prices of goods in competitive markets reflect their costs of production. Any differences in the costs of producing a specific good in any two countries—or within regions of a country—present opportunities for geographic specialization that, when taken, result in more total goods produced.
2. If the United States can produce a good using fewer resources than, say, Canada, then the United States is said to have an absolute advantage over Canada in producing that good.
3. If the United States can produce a good whose opportunity cost is lower than the opportunity cost of producing the good in, say, Canada, then the United States is said to have a comparative advantage over Canada in producing that good.
4. In a two-country, two-goods world, specialization will create absolute, comparative, or both types of advantages for both countries, and goods will exchange at prices that fall within the relative price range—or relative labor costs—in each of the countries. The gains each country derives from international trade depend upon the prices at which the two goods trade for each other.
5. While both countries gain from specialization and free trade, people in each country who produce goods that have been displaced by the more efficient producer in the other country end up losing, at least in the short run.
6. The quantity of Canadian goods the United States gets trading a unit of its own goods with Canada depends on the prices of the goods it exports and imports. The terms of trade for the United States measures the ratio of its export prices to its import prices and reflects the purchasing power of a U.S. unit of goods.
7. Because the less-developed economies specialize and trade in agricultural goods while industrially advanced economies specialize and trade in manufactured goods, and because changes in relative prices tend to favor manufactured goods, changes in terms of trade typically work to the disadvantage of less-developed economies.
8. The industrially advanced economies do most of the world's trading, and their trading is mostly with each other.
9. The United States's major trading partners are Canada, Japan, and Mexico, and the United States is even more important to them as a trading partner than they are to us.
10. Advocates of limitations to free trade cite the following reasons for exceptions to free trade: national security, infant industries, cheap foreign labor, diversity of industry, antidumping, and retaliation against countries limiting our exports to them.
11. Tariffs and quotas are used to limit free trade. A tariff is a tax on imported goods that, by raising its price, makes domestic goods more competitive. A quota, by limiting the quantity of imported goods, creates a larger market share for domestic goods than tariffs do.
12. The General Agreement on Tariffs and Trade (GATT) seeks to lower tariffs. A tariff concession offered to one member of GATT must be offered to all. GATT members offer LDCs lower tariffs than are granted to industrial countries, without demanding reciprocity.
13. A customs union, such as the European Economic Community, allows free trade among member countries and a common trade policy with all other countries. A free trade area allows free trade among member countries but grants each member country the right to pursue independent trade policies with other countries.

## KEY TERMS

Free trade
International specialization
Absolute advantage
Comparative advantage
Imports
Exports
Terms of trade

Dumping
Tariff
Quota
Reciprocity
GATT (General Agreement on Tariffs and Trade)

Customs union
European Economic Community (EEC)
Free trade area
North American Free Trade Agreement (NAFTA)

## QUESTIONS

1. Why do nations trade?
2. Georgia exports its peaches to Maine, and Maine exports its lobsters to Georgia. Considering this trade alone, do you suppose Georgia and Maine are trading under conditions of absolute or comparative advantage? Make an educated guess about resource use and opportunity cost in producing those goods in Georgia and Maine.
3. Suppose Canadians can produce a bushel of wheat for half the cost it takes to produce a bushel in Belgium. And they can produce a ton of fish for only one-quarter the Belgium cost. Should Canadians bother trading with Belgium? If not, why not? If they do trade, what should each end up producing?
4. Suppose the cost of producing a bushel of wheat in Canada is $2 and the cost of producing a ton of fish is $20. If Canada and Belgium do decide to trade, what range of international prices—bushels of wheat per ton of fish—would be acceptable to both?
5. Lower tariffs create greater international specialization. Explain.
6. Many Detroit autoworkers do not buy the argument that everybody gains in international trade. What's their point?
7. Suppose Iraq can produce surface-to-surface missiles more efficiently than we can, while we are able to produce artichokes more efficiently than they can. Should we specialize in artichokes, trading them for Iraqi missiles? Make the pro and con arguments.
8. The Irish complain that they never got a chance to make automobiles because the English, their major trading partner, are more experienced and therefore more efficient at it. Would-be Irish automakers ask their government to impose a tariff on foreign automobiles to help them get started. Can you make the case supporting their complaint and request?
9. American sport-fishing equipment producers argue that Japanese manufacturers are selling rods, reels, and tackle below Japanese cost in American markets to drive out American competitors. The American producers ask for quotas on such imports. They argue that, without government-imposed quotas on the Japanese sport-fishing equipment, American sportfishermen will ultimately pay more. Can you make the case supporting the American producers' complaint and request?
10. What is reciprocity?
11. What economic arguments can be made to support the idea of the European Economic Community?
12. Canada, Mexico, and the United States have negotiated a free trade agreement. Many Canadians, Mexicans, and Americans opposed the agreement, but even more supported it. Why would anyone oppose it? Or support it?

# PRACTICE PROBLEMS

1. The U.S. demand for, U.S. supply of, and Japanese supply of VCRs are shown in the following schedule.

| | UNITED STATES | | JAPAN |
|---|---|---|---|
| PRICE | QUANTITY DEMANDED | QUANTITY SUPPLIED | QUANTITY SUPPLIED |
| $100 | 500 | 100 | 100 |
| 200 | 400 | 200 | 200 |
| 300 | 300 | 300 | 300 |
| 400 | 200 | 400 | 400 |
| 500 | 100 | 500 | 500 |

   If Japanese VCRs are prohibited from entering the United States, what will be the equilibrium price and quantity bought and sold by Americans in the VCR market in the United States?

2. Suppose the United States allowed Japan free trade privileges in the U.S. market. What would happen to the equilibrium price and total quantity of VCRs bought and sold in the U.S. market?

3. Suppose the United States imposed a $100 tariff on each Japanese VCR imported. What would happen to the equilibrium price and total quantity bought and sold in the United States?

4. Graph the situations described in practice problems 1 to 3.

5. England and France can produce both wine and cloth. The English use 80 labor-hours to produce a unit of cloth and 40 labor-hours to produce a unit of wine. The French use 100 labor-hours to produce a unit of cloth.

| | CLOTH | WINE |
|---|---|---|
| ENGLAND | 80 | 40 |
| FRANCE | 100 | |

   Fill in the blank cell—labor-hours to produce a unit of French wine—to show France's absolute advantage in producing wine. Explain.

6. Fill in the blank cell—labor-hours to produce a unit of French wine—to show France's comparative advantage in producing cloth. Explain.

7. Fill in the blank cell—labor-hours to produce a unit of French wine—to show no advantage to either France or England in trading with each other. Explain.

# WHAT'S WRONG WITH THIS GRAPH?

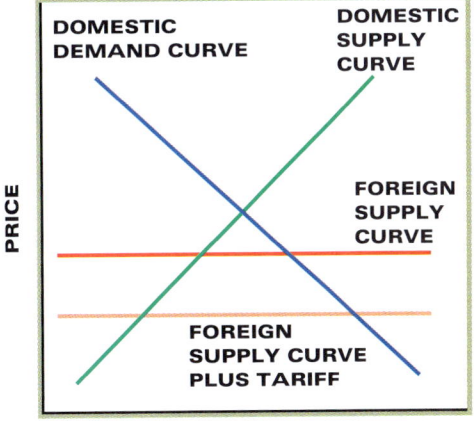

TARIFF-RESTRICTED TRADE

# ECONOMIC CONSULTANTS

## ECONOMIC RESEARCH AND ANALYSIS BY STUDENTS FOR PROFESSIONALS

Viva, a U.S. bicycle firm, designs and manufactures racing bicycles, favorites of world-class riders in the United States. Given the increased success of bicycle racing in the United States, many European riders have expressed interest in buying Viva bikes. However, Viva bikes currently are sold only in the United States, although Viva's owners want to expand their distribution into Europe, particularly into France, Italy, and Germany.

Viva's owners have hired Economic Consultants to examine what barriers exist to selling Viva bikes in France, Italy, and Germany. Prepare a report for Viva that addresses the following issues:

1. What barriers, if any, exist to exporting bikes into France, Italy, and Germany?
2. What government agencies exist to assist firms in exporting their products?

You may find the following resources helpful as you prepare this report for Viva:

- ***The World Factbook*** (http://www.cia.gov/cia/publications/factbook/)—*The World Factbook* provides information on trade with France, Italy, and Germany.
- **U.S. International Trade Commission (ITC)** (http://www.usitc.gov/)—The ITC issues reports on foreign trade barriers and unfair practices.
- **U.S. Department of State** (http://www.state.gov/www/issues/economic/trade_reports/)—The U.S. State Department publishes *Country Reports on Economic Policy and Trade Practices*, which is based on information supplied by U.S. embassies and analyzed and reviewed by the Department of State in consultation with other U.S. government agencies.
- **Bureau of Export Administration** (http://www.bxa.doc.gov/)—The Bureau of Export Administration administers export control policies, issues export licenses, and prosecutes violators.
- **International Trade Administration (ITA)** (http://www.ita.doc.gov/) The ITA provides export assistance and information by country and by industry. Of note is the Trade Information Center (http://www.ita.doc.gov/tic/).
- **Export-Import Bank of the United States (Ex-Im Bank)** (http://www.exim.gov/)—The Ex-Im Bank is an independent U.S. government agency that helps finance the overseas sales of U.S. goods and services.

# PRACTICE TEST

1. If Canada has an absolute advantage over Cuba in the production of wheat, it means that
   a. Canada can produce more wheat than Cuba.
   b. the price of wheat is higher in Canada than it is in Cuba.
   c. the price of wheat is higher in Cuba than it is in Canada.
   d. fewer resources are used to produce wheat in Canada than in Cuba.
   e. the opportunity cost of producing wheat in Canada is lower than in Cuba.

2. If Cuba has a comparative advantage over Canada in the production of sugar, it means that
   a. Cuba can produce more sugar than Canada.
   b. the price of sugar is higher in Cuba than it is in Canada.
   c. the price of sugar is higher in Canada than it is in Cuba.
   d. fewer resources are used to produce sugar in Cuba than in Canada.
   e. the opportunity cost of producing sugar is lower in Cuba than in Canada.

|  | WHEAT (BUSHELS) | SUGAR (SACKS) |
|---|---|---|
| CANADA | 200 | 600 |
| CUBA | 200 | 1,200 |

3. The table shows the production and consumption of wheat and sugar in Canada and Cuba under conditions of no trade. When free trade occurs, the entire gains from such trade shift completely to Canada when the price of sacks per bushel is
   a. 3 sacks per bushel.
   b. 4 sacks per bushel.
   c. 5 sacks per bushel.
   d. 6 sacks per bushel.
   e. 7 sacks per bushel.

4. The terms of trade is said to worsen for Cuba when
   a. its volume of exports increases more than its volume of imports.
   b. its volume of imports increases more than its volume of exports.
   c. its export prices increase more than its import prices.
   d. its import prices increase more than its export prices.
   e. it minimizes its gains from trade.

5. The United States's most important trading partner is
   a. Germany.
   b. United Kingdom.
   c. Japan.
   d. Mexico.
   e. Canada.

6. Which of the following arguments against free trade is based on the idea that industries should be protected through their learning-curve stage of development?
   a. Cheap foreign labor
   b. Diversity of industry
   c. Infant industry
   d. Antidumping
   e. Retaliation

7. When the United States imposes a tariff against Canadian leather goods, it
   a. limits its imports of Canadian leather goods to a specific quantity.
   b. fixes a percentage rate on the price of the imported goods, which creates a revenue that becomes a subsidy for domestic leather producers.
   c. fixes a percentage rate on the price of the imported goods, which creates a revenue for the U.S. government.
   d. disallows the importation of Canadian leather goods unless Canadians allow an equal value of U.S. leather goods into Canada.
   e. disallows the importation of Canadian leather goods.

8. The nondiscriminatory provision of GATT is called the
   a. most-favored nation clause.
   b. free trade clause.
   c. limited reciprocity clause.
   d. affirmative-action-in-trade clause.
   e. nontariff barrier clause.

9. The members of the North American Free Trade Agreement (NAFTA) are
   a. Canada and the United States.
   b. Canada, Mexico, and the United States.
   c. Japan and the United States.
   d. the European Community, Canada, Mexico, and the United States.
   e. Canada, Mexico, North West Territories (NWT), Greenland, and the United States.

10. A customs union is several countries that agree to free trade
    a. among themselves and a common trade policy with other countries.
    b. among themselves and allow each to determine its own policy with other countries.
    c. among themselves and with every other country.
    d. with other countries, fixing common tariffs among themselves.
    e. with other countries, fixing common quotas among themselves.

# CHAPTER 17

# EXCHANGE RATES, BALANCE OF PAYMENTS, AND INTERNATIONAL DEBT

Suppose you were on vacation on an exotic South Pacific island and chanced upon a native craftsman finishing off a beautiful teakwood carving of a swordfish. Just the thing you were hoping to find. Suppose you offered to buy it for $10, but the craftsman insisted on 4 yaps. After all, it's the only money he knows. He can buy anything he wants with it. The U.S. dollar? It's as unfamiliar to him as the yap is to you. It's not accepted on the island. You raise the offer to $20, but he won't budge. It's yaps or nothing.

Frustrating, isn't it? But, really, if the craftsman can't use the dollar in his everyday business of life, what good is it to him?

Let's change the scene. Suppose the craftsman was on vacation in Boston and noticed streams of cars heading toward Fenway Park. Upon inquiring, he discovers that they are all going to a Red Sox baseball game. Suppose he joins the crowd just to see how U.S. natives play.

He offers 4 yaps, but the ticket vendor insists on $10. He raises the offer to 6 yaps, but nobody at Fenway Park will take the yaps. They politely explain to him that Bostonians haven't heard of the yap and that it simply won't pass as currency in Boston. He goes away disappointed, never to see Nomar Garciaparra belt one out of the park.

**THIS CHAPTER INTRODUCES YOU TO THE ECONOMIC PRINCIPLES ASSOCIATED WITH:**

- EXCHANGE RATES
- FOREIGN EXCHANGE MARKETS
- APPRECIATION AND DEPRECIATION OF CURRENCIES
- FLOATING AND FIXED EXCHANGE RATES
- ARBITRAGE
- DEVALUATION
- BALANCE OF PAYMENTS
- INTERNATIONAL DEBT AND DEBT SERVICE

# THE MONEY TOWER OF BABEL

It would be convenient if everyone in the world used one currency, but, alas, we don't. The French use French francs. The Swiss use their own francs, the British use the pound, Italians use the lira, Jordanians use the dinar, Israelis use the shekel, Mexicans use the peso, Brazilians use the cruzado, Japanese use the yen, Chinese use the yuan, Spaniards use the peseta, Canadians use the Canadian dollar, and we, of course, use the U.S. dollar. And there are many more economies, each with its own specific currency.

How then do we trade? How do we buy each other's goods? We know why some French fishermen may want to buy Greek boats, but how do they actually go about paying for them? With French francs? Why would Greeks take the francs? Nobody uses francs in Athens. How do the Japanese buy Brazilian coffee? What would a Brazilian want with yen? What would the South Pacific island craftsman do with U.S. dollars?

# THE FOREIGN EXCHANGE MARKET: THE BUYING AND SELLING OF CURRENCIES

Perhaps the only way we could persuade the South Pacific craftsman to accept U.S. dollars is to find someone on his island who wants U.S. goods and needs U.S. dollars to buy them. Then we could just swap dollars for yaps. It would work. But finding each other—that is, people with dollars looking for yaps meeting people with yaps looking for dollars—is too accidental. Yet if there were enough such people looking for each other's currencies, we could establish a currency market, or **foreign exchange market,** where people could easily buy dollars with yaps and yaps with dollars.

That's what the foreign exchange market is all about. Suppose we still want to buy that teakwood swordfish. The islander wants 4 yaps for it. We can now exchange our dollars for yaps on the foreign exchange market. With the purchased yaps, we buy the teakwood carving. But is 4 yaps a reasonable price for the carving? How can we measure its worth in dollars? It would depend on how many dollars it takes to buy a yap.

The price of the yap in terms of dollars depends, like other prices, on market demand and supply. Look at Exhibit 1.

The foreign exchange market determines how many dollars it takes to buy a yap just as the umbrella market determines how many dollars it takes to buy an umbrella. The equilibrium price of a yap, shown in Exhibit 1, is $3. If the islander asks 4 yaps for the teakwood swordfish, its price in dollars is $12. Economists define the price of one country's currency, such as the dollar, in terms of another country's currency, such as the yap, as the **exchange rate.**

## The Demand Curve for Yaps

If the exchange rate was not $3 but, say, only $1 per yap, then the 4 yap teakwood carving would be considerably less expensive *in terms of dollars*. And because it's cheaper, we would buy more carvings. That's simply the law of demand, isn't it? But to buy more carvings, we would need more yaps. In Exhibit 1, the quantity demanded of yaps increases from 30,000 to 50,000 when the exchange rate drops from $3 to $1 per yap. That's why the demand curve for yaps is downward sloping.

What about the craftsman? Whether the exchange rate is $3 or $1 per yap, that is, whether we end up paying $12 or $4 for the carving, he still ends up with 4 yaps.

**Foreign exchange market**
A market in which currencies of different nations are bought and sold.

**Exchange rate**
The number of units of foreign currency that can be purchased with one unit of domestic currency.

**CHECK YOUR UNDERSTANDING**

Why do we buy more foreign goods when the exchange rate—dollars for yaps—decreases?

## EXHIBIT 1

### FOREIGN EXCHANGE MARKET

Keep this in mind when you think about exchange rates: Americans demand yaps to buy South Pacific goods, and South Pacific islanders supply yaps to buy U.S. goods.

The demand curve for yaps, D, depicts the demand for yaps at varying rates of exchange, that is, number of dollars required to buy a yap. At $2 per yap, the quantity of yaps demanded is 40,000. At $3 per yap—the yap is now more expensive, that is, people have to give more dollars to buy a yap—the quantity of yaps demanded falls to 30,000.

The supply curve of yaps, S, depicts the supply of yaps at varying rates of exchange, dollars for yaps. At $6 per yap—1 yap buys a $6 U.S. good—the quantity of yaps supplied by people holding yaps and wanting to buy dollars is 60,000. At $1 per yap—1 yap now buys only a $1 U.S. good—the quantity of yaps supplied by people holding yaps and wanting to buy dollars is 10,000.

At $1 per yap, a 50,000 − 10,000 = 40,000 excess demand for yaps emerges, driving up the exchange rate. The market reaches equilibrium at $3 per yap, where the quantity of yaps demanded and supplied is 30,000.

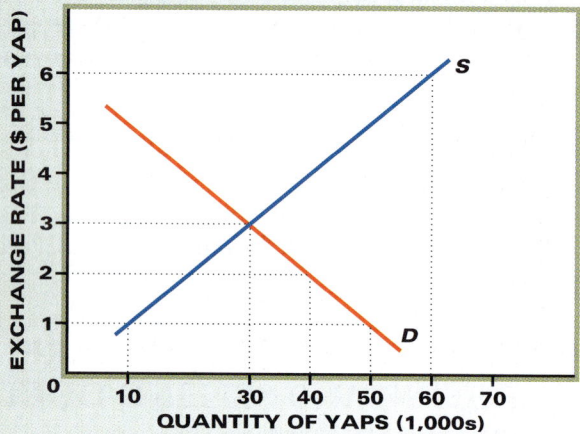

How does he feel about the exchange rate? If he had any say in the matter, he would probably prefer the $1 per yap. Why? Because at $1 per yap, we buy more of his carvings.

### The Supply Curve of Yaps

What about the supply curve of yaps in Exhibit 1? The South Pacific islanders supply yaps—exchange them for dollars—to buy our goods. Suppose a South Pacific islander on vacation in New York spots a graphite fishing rod in a window at Macy's. It sells for $60. He immediately translates the price into yaps. After all, that's the currency he's familiar with. At $3 per yap, that rod costs him 20 yaps. Not a bad buy. But at $1 per yap, the rod's price jumps to 60 yaps. It makes a difference.

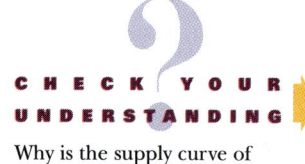

Why is the supply curve of a foreign currency upward sloping?

That's why the supply curve of yaps is upward sloping. At $3 per yap, South Pacific island people find U.S. goods relatively inexpensive *in terms of yaps* and end up buying more goods. To buy more, they supply yaps for dollars. That's what we see in Exhibit 1. The quantity supplied of yaps increases from 30,000 to 60,000 as the exchange rate increases from $3 to $6 per yap.

### Shifts in the Demand Curve for Yaps

Changes in the dollars-for-yaps exchange rate cause people demanding yaps to change the quantity of yaps demanded, which is shown as a movement along the demand curve for yaps in the foreign exchange market. But what causes the demand curve itself to shift?

**CHANGES IN INCOME** Imagine what would happen to our demand for yaps if our incomes increased by, say, 20 percent. With more dollars in our pockets, we end up buying more goods. Suppose among the more goods we buy are teakwood carvings from the South Pacific islands. To buy more teakwood imports, we need more yaps. Look at Exhibit 2.

Our demand curve for yaps shifts to the right. As a result, the equilibrium exchange rate increases from $3 to $5 per yap, and the quantity of yaps demanded and supplied on the foreign exchange market increases from 30,000 to 50,000.

## CHANGES IN TASTE

What about changes in taste? If teakwood carvings catch on, the increased demand for the carvings creates an increase in the demand for yaps as well.

On the other hand, suppose our tastes change from wood carvings to Irish cut glass. What happens to our demand for yaps? The fall in demand for teakwood carvings shifts our demand for yaps to the left, depressing the exchange rate to below $3 per yap.

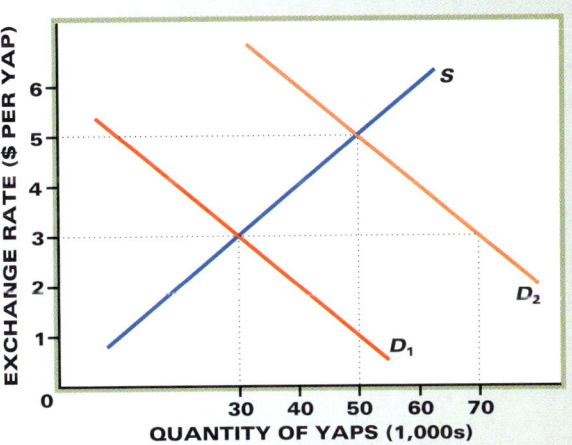

**EFFECT OF AN INCREASE IN THE DEMAND FOR YAPS ON THE DOLLARS-FOR-YAPS RATE OF EXCHANGE**

The demand curve for yaps shifts from $D_1$ to $D_2$, reflecting an increase in demand for yap-priced imports. At the old equilibrium exchange rate of $3 per yap, a new 70,000 − 30,000 = 40,000 excess demand for yaps emerges, driving the equilibrium exchange rate from $3 to $5 per yap, where the quantity of yaps demanded and supplied is 50,000.

**CHANGES IN INTEREST RATES** A fall in the interest rate in the United States or a rise in the interest rate in the South Pacific island will affect the demand for yaps as well. For example, suppose you were looking through the pages of the *Wall Street Journal* and came upon an announcement that the Teakwood Carvings Company, a South Pacific island firm, wants to expand its plant capacity and expects to finance the expansion by offering bonds, in denominations of 10,000 and 20,000 yaps, at a 10 percent rate of interest. If the rate of interest offered by U.S. companies on their corporate bonds is 6 percent, the 4 percent rate spread makes the South Pacific bond rather attractive. Wouldn't you be tempted to buy a 10,000-yap bond?

But how do you go about buying the bond? You first must exchange your dollars for 10,000 yaps and with the purchased yaps, buy the 10,000-yap bond. That shifts the demand curve for yaps to the right, as in Exhibit 2.

## Shifts in the Supply Curve of Yaps

Just as changes in U.S. incomes, tastes, and interest rates shift the demand curve for yaps, changes in South Pacific incomes, tastes, and interest rates shift the supply curve of yaps. After all, South Pacific islanders are very much like us.

If their incomes increase, wouldn't you expect that they, too, would buy more goods, which might include imports from the United States? Their increase in demand for U.S. goods results in an increase in their demand for U.S. dollars. They buy dollars by supplying yaps; that is, the supply curve for yaps shifts to the right. The effect of this supply shift on the dollars-for-yaps rate of exchange is depicted in Exhibit 3.

The equilibrium exchange rate decreases from $3 to $2 per yap, and the quantity of yaps demanded and supplied on the foreign exchange market increases from 30,000 to 40,000. And if the interest rate on the island falls, wouldn't that fall

## EXHIBIT 3

### EFFECT OF AN INCREASE IN THE SUPPLY OF YAPS ON THE DOLLARS-FOR-YAPS RATE OF EXCHANGE

The supply curve of yaps shifts from $S_1$ to $S_2$, reflecting an increase in demand for dollar-priced imports. At the old equilibrium exchange rate of $3 per yap, a new 50,000 − 30,000 = 20,000 excess supply of yaps emerges, driving the equilibrium exchange rate from $3 to $2 per yap, where the quantity of yaps demanded and supplied is 40,000.

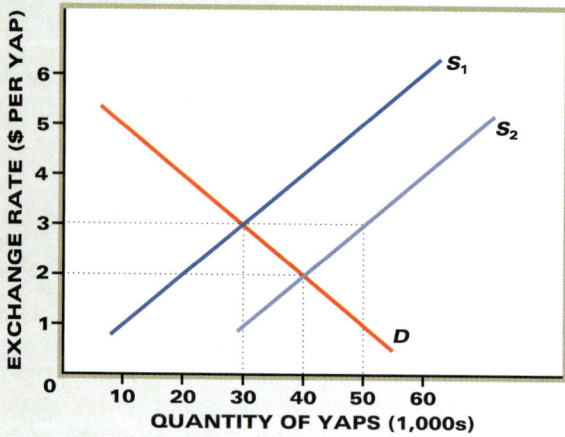

encourage islanders to look elsewhere for possible investments? They may end up buying U.S. bonds, which creates a demand for U.S. dollars and a supply of yaps.

## FLOATING EXCHANGE RATES

Imagine a world of economies, all importing and exporting goods from each other, investing in each other's capital markets, and demanding and supplying each other's currencies to carry out these many international transactions. That would create a multiplicity of exchange rates, each one reflecting the specific demand and supply condition for its own national currency.

Such an array of exchange rates would be **floating,** that is, in a continuous state of flux, adjusting always to the changing demand and supply conditions in the international market for goods and capital.

**Floating exchange rate**
An exchange rate determined strictly by the demands and supplies for a nation's currency.

### Depreciation and Appreciation

The market forces that determine floating exchange rates are really no different from the market forces that determine the prices of goods such as umbrellas, microwave popcorn, and houses. Yet, curiously, many people seem to be more than just a little confused about the significance of a change in exchange rates.

*CBS Evening News's* Dan Rather and his media friends report regularly on how the U.S. dollar has fared against other currencies during the week. For example, in reporting the dollar's **appreciation,** meaning we pay fewer dollars for a yap, or the dollar's **depreciation,** meaning we pay more dollars for a yap, they typically go one step further by referring to the appreciation as a *strengthening* of the dollar and to the depreciation as a *weakening* of the dollar.

In other contexts, the words *strength* and *weakness* convey moral attributes. Do they convey the same in foreign exchange markets? Is a weak dollar bad? Not if we're interested in exporting U.S. goods. After all, Italians, who are getting more

**Appreciation**
A rise in the price of a nation's currency relative to foreign currencies.

**Depreciation**
A fall in the price of a nation's currency relative to foreign currencies.

# APPLIED PERSPECTIVE

## TOURISTS AT THE MALL

Imagine having a cousin George from Calgary in Alberta, Canada, who came to visit you in the summer of 2001, bringing with him 302 Canadian dollars that his mother gave him to buy gifts for the Calgary family.

Suppose he shopped in your neighborhood mall and the gift shops there were willing to exchange his Canadian dollars for U.S. dollars at the 2001 exchange rate. He would end up buying gifts worth 200 U.S. dollars. Not knowing much about free-floating exchange rates, he would be a little disappointed. Why? Because his mother told him that when she visited your folks back in 1960, she was able to use her 302 Canadian dollars to buy as much as 302 U.S. dollars' worth of gifts. What could possibly explain the difference?

Suppose also that at the mall, George and you met a Japanese tourist from Tokyo who also was gift shopping for family back home. You notice that she exchanges 2,350 Japanese yen for 200 U.S. dollars and makes the same purchases your cousin does. While you are all waiting for gift wrapping, she tells you a surprising story. Her mother was here back in 1960 and she, too, bought 200 U.S. dollars' worth of gifts. But her mother had to exchange 7,160 Japanese yen for those gifts! What could possibly explain the difference?

If tourists from Italy, Britain, and Germany were at the mall, what stories would they tell about buying U.S. gifts with lire, pounds, and marks in 1960 and 2001?

**FANTASTIC BUY! I WOULD SPEND TWICE AS MANY YEN IN JAPAN TO BUY SOMETHING NOT HALF AS NICE.**

### MORE ON THE NET

The Board of Governors of the Federal Reserve Board publishes current and historical exchange rates (http://www.federalreserve.gov/releases/H10/).

**Source:** End-of-year exchange rates from International Monetary Fund, *International Financial Statistics* (Washington, D.C.: IMF, 1997).

### EXCHANGE RATES OF SELECTED COUNTRIES (CURRENCY UNITS PER U.S. DOLLAR)

| YEAR | CANADIAN DOLLAR | JAPANESE YEN | FRENCH FRANC | GERMAN MARK | ITALIAN LIRA | BRITISH POUND |
|------|-----------------|--------------|--------------|-------------|--------------|---------------|
| 1960 | 1.00 | 358 | 4.90 | 4.17 | 621 | .36 |
| 1970 | 1.01 | 358 | 5.52 | 3.65 | 623 | .42 |
| 1980 | 1.19 | 203 | 4.52 | 1.96 | 931 | .42 |
| 1990 | 1.16 | 134 | 5.13 | 1.49 | 1,130 | .52 |
| 2001 | 1.51 | 117.5 | 7.10 | 2.11 | 2,094 | .69 |

dollars for their lire, buy more U.S. goods. That makes our exporters happy. It also contributes to employment in the United States.

On the other hand, if we're interested in consuming imports, then a strong dollar isn't bad. Why? We can buy Italian imports more cheaply.

### Arbitrage Creates Mutually Consistent Exchange Rates

Suppose you pick up a copy of *USA Today* and read the following set of exchange rates: (1) 2 U.S. dollars per British pound, (2) 2,000 Italian lire per British pound, and (3) 1,500 lire per U.S. dollar. You go over it again to make sure you have read it correctly. No mistake. What would you do?

Wouldn't it be profitable for you to take $100 to the foreign exchange market and buy 150,000 lire? With those 150,000 lire, you could then buy 75 British pounds. You take the 75 British pounds and buy 150 U.S. dollars. Look what you've done. You started with $100 and ended up with $150. That's **arbitrage.**

Can you do this forever? Not really. Because others, too, will probably have noticed the chance for arbitrage; together the total buying and selling of currencies will change the demand and supply curves in the foreign exchange market, making all exchange rates mutually consistent with each other.

**Arbitrage**
The practice of buying a foreign currency in one market at a low price and selling it in another at a higher price.

### Problems with Floating Exchange Rates

Sometimes free-floating exchange rates are not desirable. Suppose we are importers of wood carvings and strike a deal with a South Pacific island producer to buy 1,000 pieces at 4 yaps each, with the exchange rate at $3 per yap. We expect, then, to pay $12,000. Six months later when the 1,000 wood carvings are delivered, we send a check for $12,000 only to be told that it is now insufficient. Why? Because in the six months between the contract agreement and the delivery, the exchange rate changed from $3 to $5 per yap. The 4,000 yaps we promised to pay, expecting that they would cost $12,000, now cost $20,000. There goes our profit and more.

Of course, the exchange rate could have gone the other way. For example, it could have fallen to $2 per yap. We would then end up with a windfall. Instead of paying $12,000 for the 1,000 carvings, we would have to pay only $8,000.

But our business is importing, not gambling. Floating exchange rates add an element of uncertainty to international trade, making it a less reliable venture than simple domestic trade.

**CHECK YOUR UNDERSTANDING**

What disadvantage can a free-floating exchange rate create?

### Fixing Exchange Rates

Can we avoid that kind of uncertainty? After all, shifts in demand and supply curves that change equilibrium levels of exchange rates simply reflect our changing preferences. Do we really want to interfere with these preferences?

Perhaps the way out of the dilemma is to *fix* exchange rates—to no longer allow them to float—in such a way that uncertainty is reduced to zero, but at the same time allow demand and supply conditions on the market to dictate the quantities of imports and exports.

How can this be done? Look at Exhibit 4. Panel *a* depicts what happens to the exchange rate over three years of changing demands for island goods when the rate is allowed to float. Look at the first year. Demand, $D$, and supply, $S$, generate an exchange rate of $3 per yap. The quantity demanded and supplied is 30,000 yaps.

Suppose in the second year an increase in demand for South Pacific island goods shifts the demand for yaps to the right, to $D_1$. The exchange rate increases to $4 per yap, and the quantity demanded and supplied increases to 40,000 yaps.

Now suppose in the third year the demand for island goods decreases. This time, the demand curve for yaps shifts to the left, to $D_2$. The exchange rate falls to $2 per yap, and the quantity demanded and supplied decreases to 20,000 yaps.

These roller-coaster exchange rates are precisely what we want to avoid. If the rate can drop from $4 to $2 per yap in one year, what's in store for us next year?

# EXCHANGE RATES, BALANCE OF PAYMENTS, AND INTERNATIONAL DEBT

Not a very comfortable world if you're an importer or exporter calculating profits and losses on constantly fluctuating exchange rates. But what can we do?

Let's bring government into the market. The government announces that it is replacing the floating exchange rate system with a **fixed exchange rate.** All trade will take place at the government's fixed rate of exchange. Follow the effects of government intervention in Exhibit 4, panel b. Suppose the government fixes the exchange rate at $3 per yap. How can it keep it fixed when our demand for imports from the South Pacific island changes?

The first year is no problem. The economy's exports and imports themselves create a set of demand and supply conditions on the exchange rate market that, by chance, drives the rate precisely to the government's fixed rate. The quantity demanded and supplied is 30,000 yaps, and the market clears.

In the second year, demand for South Pacific island goods increases, raising our demand for yaps to $D_1$. Look what happens. At that rate, the quantity demanded becomes 50,000 yaps. However, only 30,000 are supplied. The market now generates an excess demand of 20,000.

How can the government handle the 20,000-yap excess demand pressure on the foreign exchange market? It does so *by coming up with its own supply of yaps*. It goes into the foreign exchange market to exchange its own 20,000 yaps for $60,000. It absorbs the entire excess demand for yaps, relieving pressure on the exchange rate. Of course, to play such a role, the government must have sufficient **foreign exchange reserves.**

Look at panel b's third year. A fall in demand for South Pacific island goods shifts the demand curve for yaps to the left, to $D_2$. At $3 per yap, only 10,000 yaps are demanded but 30,000 are supplied, creating now an excess supply of 20,000 yaps. This time, the government intervenes by supplying $60,000 of its own dollar reserves to buy up the 20,000 excess supply of yaps. We're back where we started. The government has replenished its foreign exchange reserves.

## EXHIBIT 4

### TRADE UNDER FREE AND FIXED EXCHANGE RATES

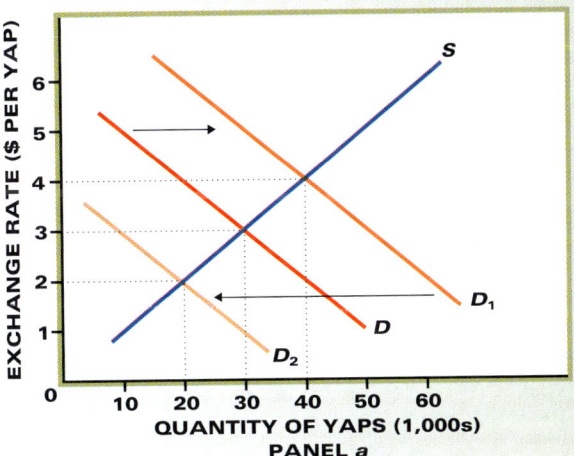

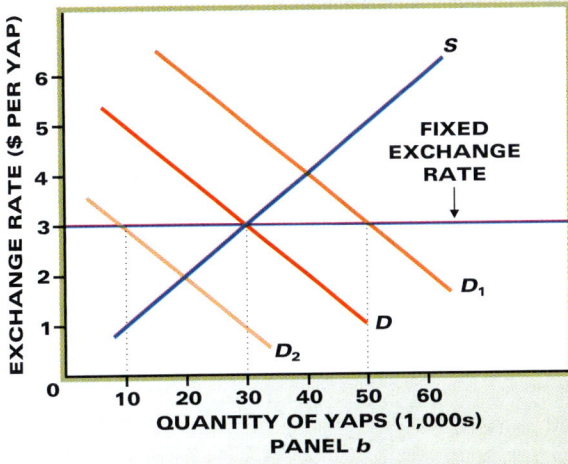

Panel *a* depicts changes in the equilibrium exchange rate—dollars per yap—caused by shifts in the demand curve. In panel *b*, the U.S. government fixes the exchange rate at $3 per yap and supports that rate regardless of changes in the U.S. demand for yaps.

**Fixed exchange rate**
A rate determined by government and then maintained through the process of buying and selling quantities of its own currency on the foreign exchange market.

**Foreign exchange reserves**
The stock of foreign currencies a government holds.

# GLOBAL PERSPECTIVE

## BRAZIL AND THE IMF

What happens to the price of imports when a country devalues its currency? Well, imagine Brazil devaluing its currency, the real, by, say, 50 percent—from two reals per U.S. dollar to 3 reals per dollar. If you lived and worked in Brazil, earning 500 reals per week you might be justifiably upset. Why? Because the Maytag dishwasher you were planning to buy at the appliance store down the street has just increased in price from 2,000 reals to 3,000 reals. That's a smack in your pocketbook! The appliance store is not at fault. After all, the dishwasher, produced in New Jersey, is priced at $1,000. To import it, the store must buy the $1,000, and at the devalued real, that's 3,000 reals. Even prices of locally produced goods will inflate with devaluation, at least those made with imported materials. Devaluation creates inflation.

Is devaluation, then, such a great idea? It may be if Brazil is experiencing chronic unfavorable balances of trade and wants to bring exports and imports more in balance—which is what the International Monetary Fund (IMF) advises Brazil to do—but be careful! The inflationary consequences can be so destabilizing and demoralizing that the cure may be worse than the disease.

That's what worried Brazil's president, Fernando Henrique Cardoso, who faced such a problem and much pressure from the IMF. As a defender of Brazil's poor, he knows that in spite of the fact that IMF economists called the 1994 Mexican peso devaluation—which it helped engineer—a success, the devaluation created an inflationary whirlwind that pushed as many as 20 million Mexicans below the poverty line. He also knows about the IMF's "success" in getting Thailand to float its exchange rate for the baht, which many believe sparked an Asian monetary crisis.

What's wrong with the IMF? It's not that the IMF misdiagnoses the economic problems plaguing many of the less-developed economies or prescribes inappropriate medicine. It's just that, at times, the doses prescribed are so strong—according to some economists—that they end up killing the patient. The IMF, of course, dismisses this view as the apologetics of those who refuse to bite the bullet. It sees itself as trustworthy and straightforward: If there's an economic problem, such as undisciplined fiscal policies or persistent trade imbalances, the country should take corrective action. To the IMF, the aggressive manipulation of exchange rates is both appropriate and effective.

Some economists believe that instead of the IMF coaxing Brazil into a devaluation, it should have used its power to support currency stability. This would have entailed letting the government and the economy adapt to a sound currency rather than having Brazil adapt the currency to the vagaries of its budgetary policy.

THE SCENE: A RIO DE JANEIRO MARKETPLACE TEEMING WITH GOODS. BUT THERE ARE FEWER AND FEWER AMERICAN IMPORTS. THEY'VE BECOME TOO EXPENSIVE.

### MORE ON THE NET

For current information on the Brazilian economy, visit the Brazilian embassy in London (http://www.brazil.org.uk/) or review *Gazeta Mercantil*, a Brazilian newspaper covering economics, business, political, and financial news. Also review current news at the IMF (http://www.imf.org/external/news.htm).

# EXCHANGE RATES, BALANCE OF PAYMENTS, AND INTERNATIONAL DEBT

## What If the Government Runs Out of Foreign Exchange Reserves?

Exhibit 4, panel *b*, is carefully drawn to allow the third year's excess supply of yaps to replenish the shortage created by the excess demand for yaps in the second year. Unfortunately, life isn't always that convenient. The economy's foreign exchange reserves can build up far beyond sufficient levels or can be drawn down to dangerously low levels.

Suppose the excess demand for yaps, shown for only panel *b*'s second year, persists year after year. How long can the government keep digging into its foreign exchange reserves before it comes up empty? And what can it do if it confronts that predicament?

**ADJUSTING THE EXCHANGE RATE** Perhaps the simplest remedy is **devaluation** to adjust the fixed exchange rate at a higher level. For example, if the government fixed the exchange rate at $5 instead of $3 per yap, our exports would rise, our imports would fall, and excess demand for yaps would disappear. The drain on the government's foreign exchange reserves would cease.

**IMPOSING IMPORT CONTROLS** A second option is to impose **import controls** by tariff and quota adjustments. By either raising tariffs or lowering quotas, the government can limit imports. Either way, it can shift the economy's demand curve for yaps as far to the left as it needs to bring the quantity of yaps demanded and supplied into line at $3 per yap.

**IMPOSING EXCHANGE CONTROLS** Another way of accomplishing the same goal is for the government to introduce **exchange controls.** It can require exporters earning yaps to turn them over to the government in exchange for dollars at the $3 per yap rate. In this way, government ends up with all the yaps in the economy. It then rations them out among importers, keeping the quantity of yaps demanded and supplied in balance.

**BORROWING FOREIGN CURRENCIES** Finally, the government can go to the **International Monetary Fund (IMF)** or into the foreign exchange market and borrow yaps to cover the country's excess demand for yaps. Sometimes borrowing is the most reasonable option. In periods of crisis, such as wars or famines, the government cannot afford to cut basic imports, nor can it easily increase exports. To stabilize the economy, its best option may be borrowing. The IMF was created in 1944 to provide temporary loans of foreign currencies to countries that borrow to stabilize their own currency. The loan is actually a purchase-and-resale agreement in which the borrowing country sells its own currency to the IMF for the foreign currencies, agreeing to reverse the transaction at a later date.

But if not held in check, borrowing can lead to problems. Just as doctors who prescribe narcotics to overcome postoperative pain always worry about addiction, so must governments who borrow foreign currencies to overcome economic crises worry about becoming addicted to the habit. Borrowing, and the interest payments that accompany it, can too quickly lock an economy into unmanageable international debt.

## BALANCE OF PAYMENTS

An economy's **balance of payments** account provides a statement of the economy's financial transactions with the rest of the world. For example, the U.S. balance of payments account for 1999, shown in Exhibit 5, records the dollars that flowed into

---

**Devaluation**
Government policy that lowers the nation's exchange rate; its currency instantly is worth less in the foreign exchange market.

**Import controls**
Tariffs and quotas used by government to limit a nation's imports.

**Exchange controls**
A system in which government, as the sole depository of foreign currencies, exercises complete control over how these currencies can be used.

**CHECK YOUR UNDERSTANDING**
What does the IMF do?

**International Monetary Fund (IMF)**
An international organization formed to make loans of foreign currencies to countries facing balance of payments problems.

Visit the International Monetary Fund (http://www.imf.org/).

**Balance of payments**
An itemized account of a nation's foreign economic transactions.

## EXHIBIT 5

### THE U.S. BALANCE OF PAYMENTS ACCOUNT: 1999 ($ BILLIONS)

| CURRENT ACCOUNT | |
|---|---|
| 1. MERCHANDISE EXPORTS | 684.4 |
| 2. MERCHANDISE IMPORTS | –1,030 |
| 3. BALANCE OF TRADE | –345.6 |
| 4. EXPORT OF SERVICES | 271.9 |
| 5. IMPORT OF SERVICES | –191.3 |
| 6. INCOME RECEIPTS ON INVESTMENTS | 276.2 |
| 7. INCOME PAYMENTS ON INVESTMENTS | –294.7 |
| 8. UNILATERAL TRANSFERS | –48.0 |
| 9. BALANCE ON CURRENT ACCOUNT | –331.5 |
| **CAPITAL ACCOUNT** | |
| 10. CHANGE IN U.S. ASSETS ABROAD | –430.2 |
| 11. CHANGE IN FOREIGN ASSETS IN U.S. | 753.6 |
| 12. STATISTICAL DISCREPANCY | 8.1 |
| 13. BALANCE ON CAPITAL ACCOUNT | 331.5 |

**Source:** *Survey of Current Business* (Washington, D.C.: U.S. Department of Commerce, January 2001), p. 56.

the U.S. economy in 1999 from the rest of the world and the dollars that flowed out of the United States to the rest of the world. These flows influence the demand and supply for foreign exchange.

## Balance on Current Account

The **balance on current account** summarizes U.S. trade in goods and services, net investment income, and unilateral transfers that occur during the current year. Exports of goods and services and income receipts on investments abroad represent dollar inflows (+) from the rest of the world. Imports of goods and services and income payments to the rest of the world represent dollar outflows (–).

**Balance on current account**
A category that itemizes a nation's imports and exports of goods and services, income receipts and payments on investment, and unilateral transfers.

The Bureau of Economic Analysis publishes U.S. balance of payments data (http://www.bea.doc.gov/bea/bpatbl-d.html).

**Balance of trade**
The difference between the value of a nation's merchandise exports and its merchandise imports.

**MERCHANDISE EXPORTS** Look at line 1. The single most important source of dollar inflow was the $612.1 billion that foreigners paid for our merchandise exports. How do exports contribute to the dollar inflow?

Suppose Dennis Wiziecki, a British engineer from Liverpool, wants to buy a $30,000 Buick LeSabre manufactured in Detroit. He first needs to get his hands on $30,000. After all, that's the currency General Motors wants. How does he get the dollars? By trading his own British pounds for U.S. dollars in the foreign exchange market. That is, the Buick export from the United States creates the demand for U.S. dollars. Dennis buys the $30,000 with his British pounds, then transfers the $30,000 to General Motors in Detroit. That's a $30,000 inflow into the U.S. balance of current account.

**MERCHANDISE IMPORTS** Line 2 records the $1,030 billion outflow from the United States to the rest of the world. That's a lot of dollars going out. Of course, it represents a lot of imports coming in.

How do imports translate into dollar outflow? Well, suppose Carolyn Hatch, a New York tea importer, decides to buy 500 pounds of Darjeeling tea from India. She learns that the Indian tea exporter wants 50 rupees per pound. That adds up to 25,000 rupees. Carolyn obtains 25,000 rupees by going into the foreign exchange market. There, she supplies U.S. dollars in exchange for Indian rupees. This simple transaction represents a U.S. dollar outflow.

**BALANCE OF TRADE** The focus of much discussion and debate on the balance of payments is fixed on the **balance of trade** account, that is, the value of exports minus the value of imports, shown in line 3. The terms we use to describe the balance reveal how we view it. For example, when exports are greater than

EXCHANGE RATES, BALANCE OF PAYMENTS, AND INTERNATIONAL DEBT

imports, we describe the balance as *favorable*. When imports are greater than exports, the balance is described as *unfavorable*.

In 1999, the value of the goods we exported was $345.6 billion less than the value of the imports of foreign goods we bought. As Exhibit 6 shows, the United States has been running negative balances of trade since 1975.

Negative balances are seen by American industrial workers as a factor that undermines their economic well-being. If the bumper-to-bumper traffic in Cleveland is a stream of imported Toyotas and Hondas, Detroit becomes a wasteland.

How do you switch from an unfavorable to a favorable balance of trade? Depreciate the exchange rate? Impose import quotas? Increase tariffs? Considerable pressure from American exporters and labor unions is continually being brought to bear on the Congress and the administration.

**EXPORT OF SERVICES** Another source of U.S. dollar inflow into the current account was the $271.9 billion export of services, shown in line 4 of Exhibit 5. When Mary Constantine, an account executive in one of Italy's leading advertising agencies, flew from Rome to New York on TWA, she had to purchase the $900 ticket with U.S. dollars. After all, that's the currency TWA demands. To make life more convenient for its passengers, TWA may accept her Italian lire and itself go into the foreign exchange market, exchanging lire for $900.

What about exports carried out of the United States by foreigners? For example, when Ryan Walter, a Dubliner, spends his vacation in Cincinnati, that vacation is equivalent to our exporting goods and services to Ireland. If he stays at the Cincinnati Hyatt Hotel, isn't that equivalent to an export of our services? He supplies Irish pounds and demands U.S. dollars for the hotel service.

The *United States Foreign Trade Data* (http://www.ita.doc.gov/industry/otea/usftd/), published by the International Trade Administration, includes monthly analysis of U.S. trade balances.

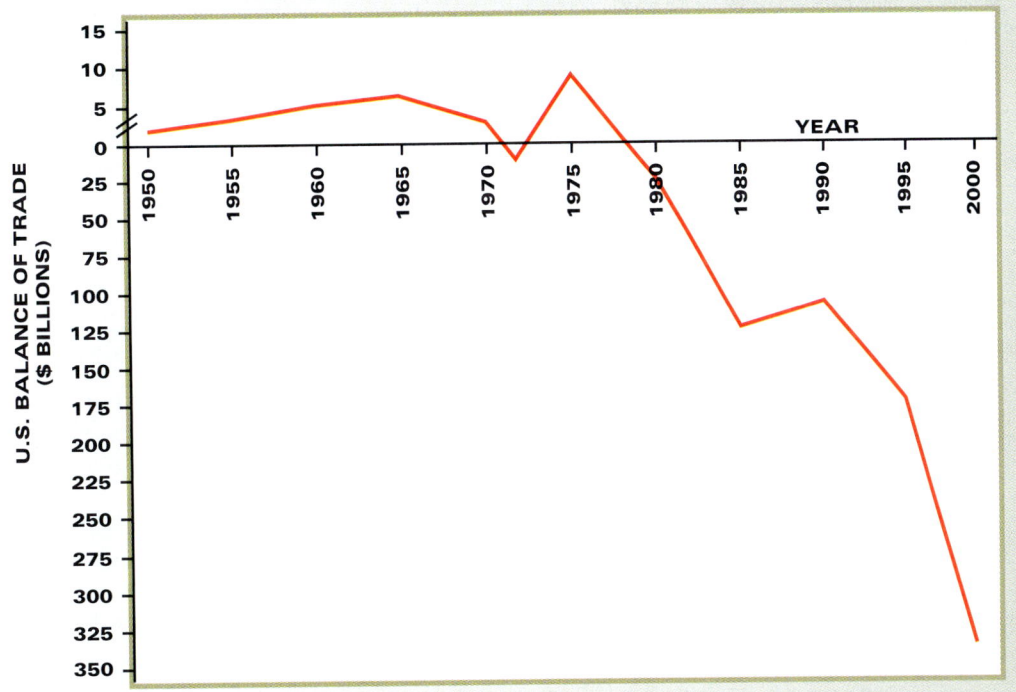

EXHIBIT 6

The year 1975 marks a watershed in the U.S. balance of trade accounts. It turned from moderate surpluses for most years prior to 1975 to deficits. Note the sharp plunge in the U.S. balance of trade (increases in the annual deficit) from 1983 to 1987, with a slight improvement (more moderate deficits, but deficits nonetheless) thereafter.

**IMPORT OF SERVICES** What about the $191.3 billion of imported services, shown in line 5? Remember Mary Constantine's flight to New York on TWA? Now suppose, at the same time, Jonathan Richman, a welder from Kenosha, Wisconsin, decides to visit Canada. He buys a deluxe package tour that includes round-trip fares, hotels, and sightseeing trips to Montreal. Just as TWA demanded U.S. currency, Air Canada and Canadian hotels demand Canadian dollars. The travel agent handling the tour takes Jonathan's U.S. dollars to the foreign exchange market and there trades them for the needed Canadian dollars. Jonathan's trip, then, represents an outflow of U.S. dollars.

**INCOME RECEIPTS ON INVESTMENTS** Many U.S. companies have investments abroad that earn income. For example, United Fruit, a U.S. food conglomerate with investments in Honduran banana plantations, earns income each year selling bananas to the rest of the world. Part of the income earned remains in Honduras as additional investment, and part ends up in the United States as income receipts. The $276.2 billion, shown in line 6, is the sum of the income receipts of U.S. investments in the rest of the world.

**INCOME PAYMENTS ON INVESTMENTS** In the same way that U.S. investments abroad create annual income that flows into the United States, so do foreign investments in the United States generate income that flows out of our economy. The Japanese investment in an Ohio Honda plant, for example, generates income that is repatriated to Japan. In 1999, such income payments, or outflows, amounted to $294.7 billion.

**Unilateral transfers**
Transfers of currency made by individuals, businesses, or government of one nation to individuals, businesses, or governments in other nations, with no designated return.

**UNILATERAL TRANSFERS** The final item in the current account is **unilateral transfers.** These are both private and government income transfers that we make to governments or to people abroad—typically family members living there—or receive from people living abroad. In 1999, net outflow of unilateral transfers amounted to $48 billion.

What are private transfers? Suppose you decide to study at Oxford, England, and your parents send you $100 monthly. That represents a unilateral transfer of dollars. It's described as unilateral because it flows in only one direction—in this case, out of the United States. What do you do with $100? March right down to an Oxford bank to exchange it for British pounds. After all, the local restaurant takes British pounds, not U.S. dollars.

*Can you think of other activities that involve unilateral transfers? Go to the Interactive Study Center at http://gottheil.swcollege.com and click on the "Your Turn" button to submit your example. Student submissions will be posted to the Web site, and perhaps we will use some in future editions of the book!*

Foreign students studying in the United States create private unilateral dollar transfers that flow in the opposite direction, that is, into the United States. There are thousands of students from the rest of the world on U.S. campuses who exchange their own currencies for U.S. dollars.

The economic and military aid that the U.S. government provides other governments is an example of a government unilateral transfer. Although such aid represents a dollar outflow, the recipient countries typically use the aid to purchase U.S. goods (adding to our exports).

**BALANCE ON CURRENT ACCOUNT** Line 9 sums up the inflows (+) and outflows (−) on the U.S. current account, which in 1999 amounted to −$331.5 billion.

## Balance on Capital Account

What about capital account entries? These entries refer to the flow of capital into and out of the United States that takes place when people buy and sell real and financial assets across borders.

### CHANGES IN U.S. ASSETS ABROAD

When a U.S. natural-fiber broom company decides to take advantage of the low labor costs in Mexico to build a factory on the outskirts of Mexico City, it needs pesos to construct the plant, buy and install the machinery, and hire workers. How does the company get the pesos? By supplying dollars on the foreign exchange market (an outflow of dollars). In the end, U.S. assets abroad, in the form of a new broom factory in Mexico, increase.

You don't have to be a broom company to own assets abroad. Individuals can buy assets abroad as well. For example, suppose Gary Adelman, a university professor, chanced upon a prospectus at his broker's office describing a new stock issue by an Israeli medical equipment company and bought 50,000 shekels worth of the stock. His assets now include a piece of the Israeli company. But to get that asset, he created an outflow of dollars.

In 1999 the outflow of dollars from the United States that ended up as changes in U.S. assets abroad amounted to $430.2 billion, shown in line 10 of Exhibit 5.

### CHANGES IN FOREIGN ASSETS IN THE UNITED STATES

Just as Gary Adelman can buy assets abroad, so can foreigners buy U.S. assets. Imagine a Saudi sheik, sitting in his living room in Mecca reading *The Wall Street Journal*. He reads that the U.S. government has put a new issue of its bonds on the market at a 6 percent rate of interest. He decides to buy $10 million of them. But how? He needs U.S. dollars to make the purchase. His broker goes into the foreign exchange market, supplying the sheik's Saudi riyals and demanding 10 million U.S. dollars. The bond is a U.S. asset.

Foreigners buying any U.S. asset—such as Japanese automakers building an Ohio automobile factory—provide an inflow of dollars. In 1999 changes in foreign assets in the United States amounted to $753.6 billion (line 11). As you see, changes in foreign assets in the United States in 1999 were higher than changes in U.S. assets abroad.

### BALANCE ON CAPITAL ACCOUNT

Subtracting capital inflows from capital outflows and introducing an 8.1 billion statistical discrepancy produces a $331.5 billion **balance on capital account**, shown in line 12. As you see, it equals the negative $331.5 billion in the current account.

**Balance on capital account**
A category that itemizes changes in the foreign asset holdings of a nation and that nation's asset holdings abroad.

## WHAT IS A BALANCE OF PAYMENTS PROBLEM?

Do U.S. dollar inflows and outflows always cancel each other out? Is it by chance or is there some kind of magic at work bringing these dollar flows into balance? And if current and capital accounts always balance, how can we possibly end up with a balance of payments problem?

*The problem associated with the balance of payments is how the balance is obtained.* Consider, for example, what happens when the outflow of dollars to pay for our imports exceeds the inflow of dollars earned by our exports. Some source of financing has to be found to cover the difference. Foreigners don't export for the love of it. And currencies don't just materialize out of thin air.

How, then, do we cover? There are three alternatives. First, we can dip into our foreign currency reserves. For example, if we import more from Japan than we

# GLOBAL PERSPECTIVE

## THE EURO

Look at the exchange rates listed in *The Wall Street Journal*. One U.S. dollar buys 2094 Italian lire. One U.S. dollar buys 0.69 British pound sterling. One U.S. dollar buys 2.11 German marks. These exchange rates—U.S. dollars for specific European currencies—will all but disappear in July 2002 when 11 of the 15 countries of the European Union discard their national currencies in favor of a common currency, the euro.

Making the shift to the euro are Austria, Belgium, Finland, France, Germany, Ireland, Italy, Luxembourg, the Netherlands, Portugal, and Spain. Not participating in the first round of this monetary union—but likely to join anyway—are the United Kingdom, Greece, Denmark, and Sweden.

Why the shift? The euro represents a major commitment to the idea of a "State of Europe." It virtually undermines the ability of any one country within the European Union to pursue independently its own national economic interests. By giving up the French franc, for example, France cannot control the money supply in France. Nor is it able to control its exchange rate—to devalue or appreciate—to promote French trade. While the French no doubt will continue to celebrate Bastille Day, its adoption of the euro necessarily alters for the French the meaning of French political independence.

Replacing the central bank of France, the central bank of Italy, the central bank of the Netherlands, and so on is a new European central bank. The advantage: People, trade, and investment will be able to move throughout the European Union as easily as people, trade, and investment move through the 50 states of the United States. And just as the economic strength of the United States is greater than the sum of its parts, so it is expected that the economic strength of Europe will be greater than the sum of its parts. The euro is indispensable in putting the European parts together. Global economic power—vis-à-vis other national or regional economies, and the United States in particular—is the sought-after European Union goal.

Will the euro successfully challenge the U.S. dollar as *the* international currency? Not likely, at least not in the foreseeable future. Even though the combined countries of the European Union rival the United States in population, GDP, volume of trade, and banking, most of the people and institutions involved in global economic activity—importers, exporters, international lenders, international borrowers, commercial and central banks—rely on and use the currency that other global participants are using. That currency is the U.S. dollar and is likely to remain the dollar for a long time. Like the English language, people use the dollar internationally because, at this time and in this world, everyone else is using it.

A NEW GIANT IN THE WORLD OF CURRENCY.

### MORE ON THE NET

Find out more about the euro, including what the banknotes and coins will look like, at http://www.euro.ecb.int/.

---

export to Japan, we can use our yen reserves to cover the difference. Second, the Japanese may decide to buy some of our assets, such as the Sears Tower in Chicago. Their supply of yen to buy the dollars needed for the Sears Tower purchase may be just the yen we need to cover the difference between our imports from and exports to them. Third, we can go into the foreign exchange market or to the IMF to borrow the needed yen. Each alternative serves to bring dollar inflows and outflows into balance.

But that's also how we get into trouble! How deep are our currency reserves? How many assets do we really want to sell off? How many foreign currency loans can we take out before foreigners close the door?

## Do Trade Imbalances Always Create Problems?

Governments are not always concerned about trade imbalances even when their economies import considerably more than they export. Why not? Because if an economy's principal imports are in the form of industrial and agricultural machinery, the government may expect that by building up the economy with these imports, the economy will *eventually* expand its export markets. That is, the government believes that imports, properly selected, can contribute to future exports and, therefore, *future* dollar inflows.

Foolhardy? Not really. No one would call a farmer foolhardy for scattering seed during spring sowing. The late summer harvest is expected to more than make up for the cost of seed. If imports modernize the economy's productive capacity and improve its competitiveness in world markets, then greater export sales would make the earlier balance of payments problem a gamble well worth taking.

The problem with such a strategy is that it doesn't always work. There is simply no way of guaranteeing that imports intended to develop the productive base of the economy today translate into exports tomorrow. Too often, governments are too optimistic about their export prospects. They view the future through rose-colored glasses. In the end, what was thought to be a calculated risk becomes a real problem.

In many cases, an economy's deficit on current account may not reflect any government strategy at all, not even a failed one. It may simply record the economy's lackluster export performance, at least compared to its import appetites. But why lackluster, and why the appetite?

# HOW DEFICITS ON CURRENT ACCOUNT DEVELOP

## The Trouble with Being Popular

It's sometimes hard to stay out of trouble when you're too popular. That may be precisely why the United States sometimes gets into balance of payment difficulties. Paradoxically, it is the strength and stability of the U.S. economy compared to other economies that creates the problem. That's the way many economists explain the sharp reversal from favorable balances on current account to deficit ones during the mid-1980s.

Foreigners shopping around the world for attractive investment opportunities found them right here in the United States. In very few other economies did they find such inviting combinations of investment security and reasonable rates of return. Not surprisingly, then, foreigners invested in the U.S. economy, supplying their own currencies on the foreign exchange market and demanding U.S. dollars.

But consider what this popular demand for U.S. dollars does to the U.S. exchange rate. It drives it up. *We now find foreign goods relatively inexpensive in terms of dollars, while foreigners find our goods increasingly expensive in terms of their currencies.* As a result, we import more and export less. If foreigners persist in viewing our economy as a popular domicile for their investments, we may end up with chronic deficits on current account.

### The High Cost of High Interest Rates

We can arrive at the same deficit on current account when our interest rates climb above those prevailing in other economies. Canadians, for example, compare interest rates offered at home and abroad and choose those yielding the highest rates. Many individuals, regardless of nationality, invest in securities offering the highest rates. The rising U.S. interest rates in the 1980s shifted the demand curve for the U.S. dollar to the right, driving up the exchange rate on the U.S. dollar. As a result, it made imports more attractive, our exports less attractive.

In this same way, domestically driven monetary policy can inadvertently affect the balance on current account. If the Fed, fighting inflation in the economy, raises its discount rate, it may trigger an increase in interest rates. If the interest rates in the United States climb above foreign rates, the demand for U.S. dollars will increase, appreciating the U.S. dollar, and in this way contributing to the deficit on current account.

### The High Cost of Budgetary Deficits

Keeping in mind this link between exchange rates and interest rates, imagine what happens to the deficit on current account when the government, pursuing a purely domestic fiscal policy, finances its deficit budget by selling government securities. If it offers a relatively high interest rate to attract buyers, wouldn't foreigners be just as receptive to the securities offer as Americans?

Budgetary deficits can affect exchange rates and, consequently, balances on current account.

### The High Cost of Low Productivity

There's little that the government can do—even correcting for troublemaking monetary and fiscal policies—if the economy's level of productivity, compared to the levels of productivity in other economies, is low and falling. Maintaining export markets becomes increasingly difficult for industries that cannot compete with foreign prices and quality. In fact, when confronted by stiff foreign competition, domestic producers have difficulty holding on to their own domestic markets.

In an economy characterized by low productivity, there are no quick-fix solutions. Unless its industries make the effort to match foreign competition by adopting successful technologies or by creating a more productive culture within its management and labor force, the economy's balance on current account position will steadily worsen.

How serious can a trade imbalance become? How much can an economy borrow or how much of its assets can it sell to finance chronic deficits on current account before pressure builds up to force changes in its exchange rate? Ultimately, depreciation of its rate must occur, making its exports cheaper and its imports more expensive. But unless a low-productivity economy confronts the problem of its low-level productivity, even exchange rate adjustments won't work in the long run.

## INTERNATIONAL DEBT

It isn't only the very low-income, low-productivity, less-developed economies that make their way to lending institutions. In many cases, it is economies with higher incomes, among them relatively high performers that still find themselves strapped to substantial **international debt**. It doesn't matter whether an economy is borrow-

**International debt**
The total amount of outstanding IOUs a nation is obligated to repay other nations and international organizations.

ing to survive or borrowing to sustain high-gear development—both are still borrowing. If the high-gear economy jams, it can create international debt havoc.

A large volume of international debt in economies, such as Argentina's $144 billion, is not the only, or even the best, measure of the debt's burden on an economy. A small or moderate amount of international debt can become a very heavy burden on a developing economy if the interest payments on the debt account for a large percentage of the economy's export revenues.

Exhibit 7 records the **debt service** (the ratio of interest payments on the debt to the economy's exports) for 10 less-developed debtor economies.

Once debt accumulates, it is sometimes difficult to pay off, or even keep under control. Imagine yourself in debt to a credit agency, with the interest payments you make each month on the debt eating up as much as 30 percent of your monthly take-home pay. Not much room to maneuver, is there? Look at Argentina's debt service in 1998. It represents 58.2 percent of Argentina's 1998 exports. Unless Argentina changes the character of its balance of payments, that debt service may become increasingly unmanageable.

**Debt service**
Interest payments on international debt as a percentage of a nation's merchandise exports.

## WILL IT ALL WORK OUT RIGHT IN THE LONG RUN?

David Hume, an 18th-century political philosopher, explained why Spain's demise as an economic superpower was inevitable. Hume argued that Spain lost its ability to compete successfully in world markets because it was so successful in amassing great quantities of gold, then the international currency, from the New World. The more gold Spain acquired, the less able it was to maintain its export markets.

Hume understood why. He saw the relationship between money, prices, exchange rates, and exports. As money, in the form of gold, flowed into Spain, it drove up Spanish prices, making foreign imports less expensive in Spain and Spanish exports more expensive abroad. As a result, Spain's balance on current account became negative, with gold now flowing out of the country. It was as unavoidable as the common cold.

We can apply that same logic to our modern economies. In spite of what they try to do, economies with negative balances on current account will find their exchange rates falling. And unless these rates are propped up by government intervention, they will fall to stem the currency outflows. As long as a negative balance

The World Bank (http://www.worldbank.org/) maintains data on international debt.

**EXHIBIT 7**

**DEBT SERVICE OF SELECTED COUNTRIES, AS A PERCENTAGE OF EXPORTS: 1998**

| ZIMBABWE | 38.2 | BRAZIL | 74.1 |
| --- | --- | --- | --- |
| BANGLADESH | 91.1 | ARGENTINA | 58.2 |
| HAITI | 81.6 | SUDAN | 97.9 |
| EGYPT | 94.9 | MYANMAR | 53.3 |
| GHANA | 28.4 | PARAGUAY | 52.5 |

**Source:** The World Bank, *World Development Indicators, 2000* (Washington, D.C.: World Bank, 2000).

# APPLIED PERSPECTIVE

## FORGIVING THE INTERNATIONAL DEBT OF LDCs

**Some people with limited incomes and unlimited appetites borrow to satisfy their insatiable appetites. Too often, the borrowing becomes habitual.** And that can be very dangerous business. The borrowing, of course, is not interest-free; very quickly, the interest payments the borrowers are obliged to make get to be as burdensome as, if not more burdensome than, the debt repayment itself. So they borrow again to cover their interest and debt obligations and the debt numbers spiral upward. How long does it take before their debt situation becomes utterly hopeless?

What would you do if you were one of these people? Work harder to increase your income? Curb your appetite? How about going to your creditors on bended knees to ask for debt forgiveness. After all, they may know, as you do, that forgiveness or not, you're not going to repay the debt *ever* because you simply can't.

Many developing (or not so developing) countries are in precisely that situation. With limited GDPs and unlimited appetites, they plunge into international borrowing that eventually puts them in that hopeless situation. What can they do about it? What can their creditors—commercial banks, Western governments, the World Bank, and the International Monetary Fund (IMF)—do about it?

Can these developing countries really "work harder" to increase their GDPs? Not if, as it is for many, their resources and energies are diverted to war activity or to curbing internal conflicts. And even if they were to "work harder" on their economies, most are agriculturally based and because agricultural prices are typically weak on world markets, their GDP growth performance can't be anything but unimpressive. Adding to their woes is the fact that industrial world economies, receptive to special interests at home, are reluctant to open their markets to LDC agricultural exports.

COME, LET US REASON TOGETHER.

What about curbing their appetites? Theoretically, LDC borrowing was designed to develop productive capacity. But in fact, too much of their debt was siphoned off by corrupt government leaders—in many cases, nonelected, military dictatorships (Suharto, Marcos, Samoza, Noriega, and Banzer, to name a few)—and stored away in Swiss, Bahamian, and Cyprus banks. Debt that did find its way into development projects was often mismanaged or used to support politically showcased, grandiose development schemes that had minimal if any impact on the economies of these nations. The development success stories were simply too few.

The result was that for most of the debtor nations, the debt created more problems than it solved.

Most of the $2 trillion of LDC debt is owed by 33 countries, 90 percent of them African. None of them are able to repay. What's left to do?

The issue of forgiveness is on the table. Creditor nations and institutions, such as the United States and the IMF, are disposed to forgive many for much of their debt, *but with strings attached*. The IMF wants assurances that the debtor nations "get their houses in order." By that it means cutting spending to stabilize their currencies; slashing social spending on education, health, and social services; cutting government employment and payrolls; converting inefficient small-scale farming to large-scale export crop farming; and privatizing public industries. The IMF formula is traumatic: Living standards must get worse for many in the indebted world—particularly the middle class and poor—before they can bet better.

The IMF positions has been challenged not only by the indebted countries, but also by the World Bank and creditor governments such as the United States. The United States favors debt relief only if the debtor countries apply the savings toward primary health and education. Non-governmental organizations (NGOs) such as Oxfam America support that position and emphasize poverty reduction as well.

There appears to be little disagreement among the debtor and creditor nations concerning the basic problem and solution: The major percentage of the debt is beyond repayment, and creditor forgiveness of the debt is the only viable policy option.

> **MORE ON THE NET**
> Find out about the International Monetary Fund at http://www.imf.org/. The World Bank Group's home page is at http://www.worldbank.org/, and Oxfam America is at http://www.oxfamamerica.org/.

exists, the exchange rate will keep on falling. Eventually, the rate will reach the level appropriate to a zero balance on current account. It takes only time.

This automatic correction mechanism, however, may also push the economy into lower living standards. Some people may be pleased when the economy's exchange rate generates a zero trade balance, but it is somewhat less pleasing if the economy cannot afford to provide the majority of its population with the necessities of life.

In many cases, that is indeed what results. If the Zambian kwacha, for example, is driven so low relative to the U.S. dollar that its people lose the ability to import needed food, then whatever the equilibrium level of its exchange rate, Zambia's standard of living falls. Equilibrium levels of exchange rates, perhaps inevitable, do not guarantee a desirable outcome.

But what's to be done? Is there anything the less-developed economies like Zambia can do to correct their international trade and debt problems? Perhaps the starting point is first to understand why their economies look the way they do. That's the task we set for ourselves in the next chapter.

# CHAPTER REVIEW

1. The U.S. demand curve for French francs is downward sloping. When the price of the franc—dollars for francs—is relatively high, a 10-franc bottle of French wine for an American is relatively expensive in terms of the dollars needed to pay for the wine. When the dollars-for-francs exchange rate falls, that same 10-franc bottle of wine for the American is now less expensive in terms of dollars. Because wine now costs fewer dollars, the quantity demanded by the American increases. This increase in quantity demanded of wine creates the increase in quantity demanded of francs.

2. The French supply curve of francs is upward sloping. When the price of the franc—dollars for francs—is relatively high, a $10 CD for the French is relatively inexpensive in terms of the francs needed to pay for the CD. When the dollars-for-francs exchange rate falls, that same $10 CD for the French is now more expensive in terms of francs. Because the CD now costs more francs, the quantity demanded by the French decreases. This fall in quantity demanded of CDs creates the decrease in quantity supplied of francs.

3. The demand curve for French francs—reflecting U.S. demand for French goods—and the supply curve of French francs—reflecting French demand for U.S. goods—create on the foreign exchange market the equilibrium exchange rate of dollars for francs (or francs for dollars).

4. Shifts in the demand and supply curves for francs—occasioned by changes in income,

tastes, and interest rates—change the equilibrium exchange rate. Appreciation of the dollar means we pay fewer dollars for francs, while depreciation of the dollar means we pay more dollars for francs.

5. To decrease the volatility of its exchange rate, a government may impose a fixed exchange rate. This may require the government to intervene in the foreign exchange market, using its foreign exchange reserves to buy and sell foreign currencies in sufficient quantities to eliminate any excess demand or supply generated on the foreign exchange market.

6. When the fixed exchange rate becomes difficult to maintain, the government can resort to policies such as devaluation, import controls, exchange controls, or borrowing foreign currencies.

7. An economy's balance of payments account describes its financial transactions with the rest of the world. The current account adds up exports and imports of merchandise and services, income payments and receipts on investments, and unilateral transfers. The capital account shows the sum of changes in the value of overseas assets and the value of foreign assets in the economy. The difference between merchandise exports and merchandise imports is the balance of trade. When imports exceed exports, there is an unfavorable balance of trade.

8. Exports of services occur when foreigners purchase U.S. services. When Americans travel overseas they create service imports. When we earn income on our investments overseas, an inflow of dollars from the rest of the world is created. Similarly, when foreign companies operating in the United States earn profits, dollars flow abroad. Unilateral transfers are payments by individuals that are sent abroad and exchanged for a foreign currency.

9. The capital account line for changes in U.S. assets abroad shows the extent to which firms in the United States have invested overseas. These investments create an outflow of dollars. Foreign firms' investments in the United States show up as changes in foreign assets in the United States. Such investments create an inflow of dollars.

10. If the outflow of dollars to pay for imports exceeds the inflow of dollars to pay for exports, then the difference must be financed. Four financing options exist. Reserves of foreign currency can be drawn down. Domestic assets can be sold. Government securities can be sold. Or a country can go into foreign exchange markets and borrow the difference.

11. It may make sense for a country to import more than it exports if the kinds of goods being imported contribute to future gains in productivity.

12. International debt can become a problem for a developing country if interest payments on the debt take a large percentage of export revenues. The debt service is the percentage of a country's exports that interest payments on the debt represent.

# KEY TERMS

Foreign exchange market
Exchange rate
Floating exchange rate
Appreciation
Depreciation
Arbitrage
Fixed exchange rate

Foreign exchange reserves
Devaluation
Import controls
Exchange controls
International Monetary Fund (IMF)
Balance of payments

Balance on current account
Balance of trade
Unilateral transfers
Balance on capital account
International debt
Debt service

# QUESTIONS

1. Why would anyone in Butte, Montana, or Lyons, France, want yaps?
2. How could people get the yaps they want?
3. Suppose the equilibrium exchange rate is $3 per yap. Explain what that rate signifies in terms of quantities of goods imported and exported.
4. What does *arbitrage* mean, and how does it work?
5. How can the government fix an exchange rate? Can the government fix it at any level, for any length of time? Discuss the limitations that a government faces in maintaining a fixed rate.
6. What control mechanisms can a government introduce to support its exchange rate policy?
7. What are the major categories and items in a balance of payments account?
8. How would each of the following affect the U.S. balance of payments account?
   a. Every month, a Bangladeshi professor at the University of Utah sends $200 to his family living in Bangladesh.
   b. A Japanese businessperson in Nagasaki buys 100 shares of General Motors stock.
   c. The U.S. government sells 20 Patriot missiles to the Israeli government.
   d. The U.S. government gives the Russian government 50 million tons of wheat, priced at $3 per ton, in the form of a unilateral transfer.
9. In some cases, a balance of payments problem really isn't a problem at all. Yet in other cases, it could signal a fundamental problem in the economy. Explain.
10. Some economists argue that our budgetary deficits contribute to our balance of payments problems. How do they make their case?
11. Balance of payments problems and long-term international debt plague the less-developed economies. The two issues are related. Explain.

# PRACTICE PROBLEMS

1. The only information given for the following table is that the equilibrium exchange rate is 4 Israeli shekels per U.S. dollar.

   | SHEKELS PER U.S. DOLLAR | QUANTITY DEMANDED (SHEKELS) | QUANTITY SUPPLIED (SHEKELS) |
   |---|---|---|
   | 6 | | |
   | 5 | | |
   | 4 | | |
   | 3 | | |
   | 2 | | |

   Fill in the blank cells, constructing quantity demanded and quantity supplied schedules so that the equilibrium exchange rate occurs at 4 shekels per dollar.

2. Change the numbers in the table in practice problem 1 so that the equilibrium exchange rate is 5 shekels per U.S. dollar. What explanation can you offer for such changes?

3. Suppose the following data represent Israel's international transactions (in shekels). What is Israel's balance of trade? What is its balance on current account? What is its balance on capital account?

   | ITEM | SHEKELS |
   |---|---|
   | MERCHANDISE EXPORTS | 10 |
   | CHANGE IN FOREIGN ASSETS IN ISRAEL | 2 |
   | EXPORTS OF SERVICES | 5 |
   | INCOME RECEIPTS ON INVESTMENT | 3 |
   
   | ITEM | SHEKELS |
   |---|---|
   | MERCHANDISE IMPORTS | −8 |
   | CHANGE IN ASSETS ABROAD | −5 |
   | IMPORT OF SERVICES | −4 |
   | INCOME PAYMENTS ON INVESTMENT | −2 |
   | UNILATERAL TRANSFERS | −1 |

4. How would each of the following events affect the quantity demanded and quantity supplied

schedules in practice problem 1? Indicate whether the numbers in the schedules would increase or decrease and the resulting increase or decrease in the equilibrium exchange rate. Then show how each event would affect the numbers in each of the categories in practice problem 3.

a. A U.S. manufacturer moves a factory from New Jersey to Israel.

b. Hilton builds a new 150-room hotel in Jerusalem.

c. The United States removes its tariff on oranges from Israel.

d. Israeli citizens working in the United States send part of their income back to Israel.

# WHAT'S WRONG WITH THIS GRAPH?

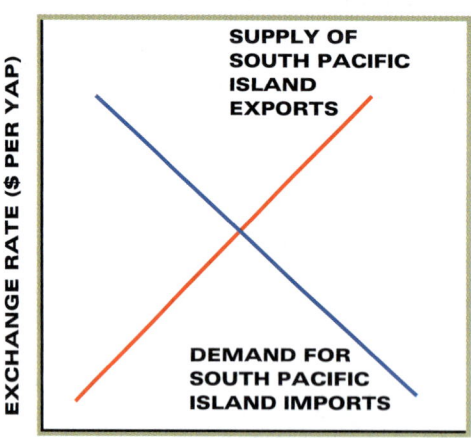

# ECONOMIC CONSULTANTS

## ECONOMIC RESEARCH AND ANALYSIS BY STUDENTS FOR PROFESSIONALS

David Tietlebaum recently opened Excursions Around the World, a travel agency that conducts tours in over 50 countries. Before opening Excursions Around the World, David worked as a tour guide in Europe and, in this role, had experience with different currencies and exchange rates. However, as owner of Excursions Around the World, David must be able to explain to customers how exchange rates work and, in particular, what the value of their own currency is in relation to the currency of the country, or countries, these customers want to visit.

David has hired Economic Consultants to prepare a brochure that customers may read to familiarize themselves with foreign currencies and the dynamics of exchange rates. Prepare a brochure for Excursions Around the World that addresses the following issues:

**1.** What information is available about foreign currencies?

**2.** In basic terms, how do exchange rates work? What do customers traveling in foreign countries need to consider about exchanging currencies?

**3.** Where can customers find current information about exchange rates?

You may find the following resources helpful as you prepare this brochure for Excursions Around the World:

- **Currency News** (http://biz.yahoo.com/reports/currency.html)—Yahoo! Finance provides the latest news, taken from Reuters, concerning currencies.
- **The Interactive Currency Table** (http://www.xe.com/ict/) and **Universal Currency Converter** (http://www.xe.com/ucc/)—The Interactive Currency Table and the Universal Currency Converter, maintained by Xenon Laboratories, automatically provide exchange rate values and foreign exchange rate conversions.
- **Pacific Exchange Rate Service** (http://pacific.commerce.ubc.ca/xr/)—This service provides access to current and historic daily exchange rates. Also provided is a list of all the currencies of the world and the countries' exchange rate arrangements.
- **Federal Reserve Statistical Release, Foreign Exchange Rates** (http://www.federalreserve.gov/releases/H10/)—The Federal Reserve releases, every Monday, official foreign exchange rates.

# PRACTICE TEST

1. Which of the following would cause the demand curve for the French franc to shift to the right?
   a. A decrease in the exchange rate of francs for dollars
   b. An increase in the exchange rate of francs for dollars
   c. A decrease in foreigners' tastes for French goods and services
   d. A decrease in French interest rates
   e. A decrease in foreigners' incomes

2. If the supply curve for German marks shifts to the left, then
   a. the demand curve for German marks will shift to the right.
   b. the equilibrium exchange rate of German marks for other currencies will rise.
   c. there will be more marks in equilibrium held in world markets.
   d. the equilibrium exchange rate of German marks for other currencies will fall.
   e. the demand curve for German marks will shift to the left.

3. If the United States fixes its exchange rates, such as four Belgian francs per dollar, then to keep it fixed at the four-francs-per-dollar rate,
   a. Belgian and American exporters and importers must agree to keep their mutual trade in balance.
   b. Belgian and American exporters and importers must agree not to trade at any other exchange rate.
   c. The U.S. government must do the exporting and importing for the United States.
   d. both the U.S. and Belgian governments must do the exporting and importing for their respective countries.
   e. the U.S. government must buy and sell U.S. dollars on the foreign exchange market.

4. If there is an appreciation in the dollar relative to the Japanese yen, then
   a. more dollars are needed for Americans to buy Japanese goods.
   b. Americans get fewer yen per dollar on the foreign exchange market.
   c. American goods become cheaper for the Japanese to buy than before.
   d. American goods become more expensive for the Japanese to buy than before.
   e. the supply curve of the yen will shift to the right.

5. Which of the following groups would benefit from a depreciation in the German mark relative to the Canadian dollar?
   a. Exporters of Canadian goods
   b. Exporters of German goods
   c. Consumers of Canadian goods in Germany
   d. Consumers of German goods in Germany
   e. Importers of Canadian goods

6. One problem with floating exchange rates is that they
   a. do not take into account shifts in the demand for a nation's currency.
   b. do not take into account shifts in the supply of a nation's currency.
   c. add uncertainty to international trade.
   d. decrease price variability in world markets.
   e. eliminate the possibility of arbitrage in foreign exchange markets.

7. If Costa Rica uses import controls to maintain its foreign exchange reserves, it means that the Costa Rican government
   a. uses international borrowing to finance its imports.
   b. sells foreign exchange reserves to finance its imports.
   c. imposes tariffs and quotas to limit its imports.
   d. devalues the Costa Rican peso to limit its imports.
   e. appreciates the Costa Rican peso to limit its imports.

8. All of the following except one are included in a nation's balance on current account. Which one?
   a. Foreign exchange reserves
   b. Unilateral transfers
   c. Export of services
   d. Income receipts on investments
   e. Income payments on investments

9. Which of the following is an example of a unilateral transfer?
   a. The United States borrows dollars from Italy in the foreign exchange market.
   b. Spain purchases oil from Venezuela.
   c. Norway pays dividends on bonds issued to Chinese citizens.
   d. A French citizen working in the United States sends money home to her family.
   e. Colombia imports shoes from Italy.

10. Interest payments on a country's international debt are referred to as
    a. debt service.
    b. loan payments.
    c. currency devaluation.
    d. trade imbalances.
    e. income payments on investments.

# CHAPTER 18
## THE ECONOMIC PROBLEMS OF LESS-DEVELOPED ECONOMIES

Imagine two infants born at the same instant, one in the delivery room of the maternity ward at Barnes Hospital in St. Louis, Missouri, the other in a one-room, earthen-floored, mud brick home in El Fashn, a small village along the Nile river in Egypt, about 150 miles south of Cairo.

Like all newborns, these are two beautiful human beings. But, tragically, they face very different futures. The Missouri baby will probably survive her early years and just as probably live to the ripe old age of 85. The El Fashn baby, on the other hand, will have a much less certain chance of surviving to her first birthday and, according to life tables for Egypt, has a life expectancy at birth of only 62 years.

The Missouri baby, like most in the United States, can expect to attend a day-care center and then at age five join the neighborhood kids in kindergarten. Her education is compulsory; she will attend elementary and high school. Moreover, the probability is quite high that she will graduate from some college or university with a degree that prepares her for an intellectually and financially rewarding, productive life.

What about her counterpart in Egypt? The El Fashn infant may learn how to read and write, but the chances of her acquiring an advanced degree are rather remote. She will probably marry at an early age, have more than seven children, and work long, hard hours on a few nonirrigated cultivated acres surrounding the village.

**THIS CHAPTER INTRODUCES YOU TO THE ECONOMIC PRINCIPLES ASSOCIATED WITH:**

- POVERTY IN THE LESS-DEVELOPED COUNTRIES (LDCs)
- ECONOMIC DUALISM
- THE BIG-PUSH STRATEGY FOR ECONOMIC DEVELOPMENT
- THE UNBALANCED GROWTH STRATEGY FOR ECONOMIC DEVELOPMENT
- FOREIGN INVESTMENT IN THE LDCs
- ECONOMIC AID TO THE LDCs

Perhaps the most disheartening part of this tale of two cities, at least for the Egyptian baby, is that the story repeats. Her children will probably face similar prospects. The unfairness—isn't it unfair?—continues.

## CONFRONTING NATIONAL POVERTY

Being poor is certainly no crime. But *accepting* poverty and allowing it to continue unchecked seem to be, perhaps, crimes not only against the population's impoverished victims, but against those generations of impoverished yet to come. Who's to blame? Obviously, people whose standards of living are not much above physical subsistence don't *choose* to remain poor. The world they inhabit affords them little choice. Is their national poverty, then, inevitable? Is there nothing anyone can do?

Economists, at least since the early 1950s, focused some attention on the issue of persisting national poverty in the economies of Asia, Africa, and Latin America. It was clear in 1950, and even clearer now, that the kinds of problems confronting these economies in their attempt to achieve higher standards of living differ fundamentally from those faced by the industrial economies of the West.

### The Language of National Poverty

The language used by economists to describe these economies has changed over time. In the 1950s, economists began to take a hard, close look at the economies of Asia, Africa, and Latin America. For the first time they were seen as something more than trading posts for our raw materials. During that period, economists were quick to identify their national poverty as endemic, the consequence of economic *backwardness* or *underdevelopment*.

The terms seemed appropriate. The differences between Canada and Egypt, for example, cannot be measured in terms of higher or lower GDP. The real differences are not quantitative, but qualitative. Egypt's inability to raise its standard of living has more to do with its social, political, and economic institutions and with its perceptions of past, present, and future than with any lack of effort or personal talents.

Economies that have yet to invest in basic energy, housing, education, or transportation systems or that have yet to develop legal, financial, and communication systems to support modern ways of producing goods and services simply cannot compete in the same economic world as the industrial economies of the West. In this sense, the terms *backwardness* and *underdevelopment* conveyed that idea.

But in the 1960s, economists dropped the terms *backwardness* and *underdevelopment* in favor of *newly developing countries,* or **less-developed countries (LDCs)**. The change reflected the view that the terms *backwardness* and *underdevelopment* were much too prejudicial. After all, many Asian, African, and Latin American societies, although poor and lacking the prerequisites of development, were in other respects the equals of their counterparts in the West. The United Nations, with expanding memberships from the newly independent former colonies, had much to do with promoting this language change.

### There Are Important Differences Among the Less-Developed Economies

Sometimes, labels can be misleading. Many of the less-developed economies have, indeed, made considerable progress. For example, in the past 25 years, Brazil, Korea, Singapore, Hong Kong, Israel, Taiwan, and Iran have made spectacular leaps in modernizing and developing their economies, achieving for their people substantially higher levels of per capita income. And many other developing economies have made moderate progress.

---

**Less-developed countries (LDCs)**
The economies of Asia, Africa, and Latin America.

*But many others haven't.* Some LDCs still seem to be stalled in a mode that keeps yielding, decade after decade, the same kinds of subsistence-level incomes and the same employment opportunities and investment patterns that inhibit them from making even very modest transitions to modernization.

## LDC PER CAPITA INCOMES

While there is no consensus among economists concerning just what specific level of per capita income or what specific rate of output growth would allow us to identify LDCs, *some* levels and *some* rates are so obviously troublesome that economists have little difficulty making the identification.

Exhibit 1 compares the income performance records of 15 LDCs of the world.

The data in Exhibit 1 are about as striking and painfully clear as any set of income numbers can possibly be. Even though you have to be on guard against translating these incomes into the purchasing power they would represent in our own economy, still, would you question the economic impoverishment they suggest?

Look at Ethiopia's $100 and Kenya's $350 per capita income for 1998. Consider the per capita income growth rates for these economies over the 1990–98 period. How can their average annual growth rates suggest anything but economic sluggishness?

Even though a dollar does not provide you with as much purchasing power in the United States as it would a person earning its equivalent in an LDC, still, the low-level per capita income data in Exhibit 1 paints a fairly accurate picture of national poverty in the LDCs. The $390 annual per capita income in Ghana, for example, is pitifully low no matter what purchasing power measure you choose to use. According to data in the 2000 *World Bank Atlas,* people in more than 40 LDCs, including India's 930 million people, have per capita incomes less than $500 a year.

Nor does the future look particularly bright for some of the LDCs of Exhibit 1. The 1990–98 per capita income growth for several was actually negative—the people became poorer. Algeria's per capita income, for example, fell 1.0 percent each year during the years of Exhibit 1.

How successful or unsuccessful an economy is in raising its per capita income depends not only on how well it generates economic growth, but also on how well it contains population growth. If

The World Bank (http://www.worldbank.org/) maintains economic data (http://www.worldbank.org/data/) on the regions and countries of the world. *The World Factbook* (http://www.cia.gov/cia/publications/factbook/) maintains region- and country-specific economic, political, and cultural profiles.

### PER CAPITA INCOME, PER CAPITA INCOME GROWTH RATE, AND POPULATION GROWTH RATE IN SELECTED LDCs: 1990–98

| | PER CAPITA INCOME $ | PER CAPITA INCOME GROWTH RATE | POPULATON GROWTH RATE |
|---|---|---|---|
| **LOW-INCOME LDCs** | | | |
| ETHIOPIA | 100 | 2.6 | 2.6 |
| DEM. REP. CONGO | 110 | –8.5 | 3.6 |
| KENYA | 350 | 0.0 | 3.1 |
| MONGOLIA | 380 | –1.5 | 2.2 |
| GHANA | 390 | 1.4 | 3.1 |
| **LOW-MIDDLE-INCOME LDCs** | | | |
| ZIMBABWE | 620 | –0.2 | 2.1 |
| CAMEROON | 610 | –2.3 | 3.2 |
| IVORY COAST | 700 | 1.4 | 3.1 |
| SRI LANKA | 810 | 3.9 | 1.4 |
| SYRIA | 1,020 | 1.3 | 3.3 |
| **UPPER-MIDDLE-INCOME LDCs** | | | |
| ALGERIA | 1,550 | –1.0 | 2.5 |
| VENEZUELA | 3,530 | –0.1 | 2.5 |
| BOTSWANA | 3,070 | 0.9 | 2.9 |
| SOUTH AFRICA | 3,310 | –0.1 | 2.3 |
| BRAZIL | 4,630 | 1.7 | 1.6 |

**Source:** The World Bank, *World Bank Atlas, 2000* (Washington, D.C.: World Bank, 2000).

EXHIBIT 1

## EXHIBIT 2

### PERCENTAGE OF POPULATION UNDER 15 YEARS OF AGE FOR SELECTED COUNTRIES: 1997

| | PERCENTAGE UNDER 15 | | PERCENTAGE UNDER 15 |
|---|---|---|---|
| ETHIOPIA | 46.3 | UNITED STATES | 21.4 |
| GHANA | 41.7 | UNITED KINGDOM | 19.1 |
| PAKISTAN | 40.9 | FRANCE | 18.5 |
| NIGERIA | 44.4 | GERMANY | 15.2 |
| KENYA | 42.1 | THE NETHERLANDS | 18.2 |
| PHILIPPINES | 37.0 | AUSTRALIA | 20.8 |

**Source:** *Statistical Abstract of the United States, 1999* (Washington, D.C.: U.S. Department of Commerce, 1999), p. 835.

**CHECK YOUR UNDERSTANDING**

What does per capita income depend on?

population grows faster than income, per capita income falls. It's simple but devastating arithmetic:

$$\text{per capita income growth} = \frac{\text{income growth}}{\text{population growth}}$$

Therein lies an LDC's double-whammy problem. While income growth has been less than impressive in some LDCs, population growth has been *too* impressive. Look at the population data in column 4 of Exhibit 1. Some of the LDCs have population growth rates greater than 2.5 percent per year. This means that their economic growth rates must be at least 2.5 percent per year just to sustain their already low-level per capita incomes.

High population growth rates also create an age distribution profile that loads the population in the under-15-years-old group. The consequences for national poverty are dire. Look at the contrast between the age distributions in the LDCs and those of the industrially advanced economies shown in Exhibit 2.

Almost half the population of Ethiopia is under 15 years old. Most of them—particularly those under 10 years of age—although consuming meagerly, still consume more than they are able to produce. Because they represent so large a proportion of Ethiopia's population, these many-mouths-to-feed Ethiopians undercut Ethiopia's ability to shift resources from the production of consumption goods to the production of capital goods. Economists refer to this condition as the vicious circle of poverty: People are poor because they can't invest in capital goods, and they can't invest in capital goods because they are poor. The problem is illustrated in the production possibilities curve of Exhibit 3.

**CHECK YOUR UNDERSTANDING**

What is meant by the vicious circle of poverty?

Point *a* signals the predicament. The demands of Ethiopia's growing population force it to devote its meager resources almost exclusively to the production of consumption goods, impeding the development of its capital goods production. Point *b* is where it prefers to be. But how do you get there with a fast-growing population? Is Ethiopia, or any of the other economically troubled LDCs, willing to adopt a population policy similar to the one initiated in China in the 1970s, which limits

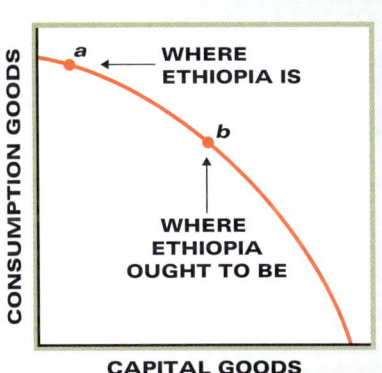

**THE VICIOUS CIRCLE OF POVERTY**

If Ethiopia is going to get onto an economic growth path, it will have to move down along its production possibilities curve from point *a* to a production possibilities position that affords it greater capital goods production, such as point *b*. That may be difficult with population growth at 2.6 percent per year.

families to one child? Unlikely. But it was effective. China's 1985–95 population growth rate was down to 1.3 percent.

## OTHER INDICATORS OF THE LDCs' LACK OF ECONOMIC WELL-BEING

When you think of investments in capital goods production, you are more likely to think about building machinery and the factories that house the machinery than anything else. These investments are very tangible and very productive. But the capital investments that yield the highest payoffs in an economy are not necessarily those made in machinery and factories. Investments in **human capital**—in the form of education and health care—rank among the most important of the capital goods contributing to national economic growth. The problem is that although their payoffs are relatively high, they require considerable time to generate. Better health and education improve a person's working efficiency, but the improvement occurs gradually and the gains in productivity resulting from it are spread over a person's lifetime.

For these and other reasons, many LDCs, anxious for quick, visible investment payoffs, are disinclined to put their very limited resources in human capital development. Exhibit 4 records the consequences.

The direct link between LDCs' poverty and life expectancy is unmistakable: Life expectancy among the poorest of the LDCs peaks at 50 years, while it reaches 80 among the industrial economies of the world. Moreover, life expectancy is predicted to increase even further in the richer countries and to actually decline in some of the poorest countries of Africa.

Almost half of the world's people suffer from diseases related to contaminated or insufficient water. While considerable progress has been made in providing safe water in many LDCs, as many as two-thirds of them still lack adequate sanitation or safe water. Africa is especially far from reaching acceptable standards. Look at Exhibit 4, column 6. More than 30 percent of the population of half the LDCs have no access to safe water.

**Human capital**
The investment in workers' health and knowledge, acquired through education, training, and/or experience that enhances their productivity.

## EXHIBIT 4

**LIFE EXPECTANCY, INFANT MORTALITY, PEOPLE PER PHYSICIAN, PERCENTAGE OF CHILDREN IN SCHOOL, AND PERCENTAGE OF PEOPLE WITH SAFE WATER FOR SELECTED COUNTRIES: 1998 OR LATEST YEAR AVAILABLE**

|  | LIFE EXPECTANCY (YEARS) | INFANT MORTALITY (PER 1,000) | PEOPLE PER PHYSICIAN | PERCENTAGE OF CHILDREN IN SCHOOL | PERCENTAGE OF PEOPLE WITH SAFE WATER |
|---|---|---|---|---|---|
| **LOW-INCOME LDCs** | | | | | |
| ETHIOPIA | 43 | 107 | 37,811 | 18 | 27 |
| DEM. REP. CONGO | 48 | 90 | 15,442 | 49 | 27 |
| KENYA | 51 | 76 | 7,751 | 73 | 53 |
| MONGOLIA | 66 | 50 | 414 | 67 | 66 |
| GHANA | 60 | 65 | 13,705 | 60 | 56 |
| **LOW-MIDDLE-INCOME LDCs** | | | | | |
| ZIMBABWE | 43 | 115 | 7,671 | 91 | 77 |
| CAMEROON | 54 | 77 | 11,594 | 64 | 41 |
| IVORY COAST | 46 | 88 | 19,023 | 49 | 72 |
| SYRIA | 69 | 28 | 1,161 | 79 | 85 |
| SRI LANKA | 73 | 16 | 2,507 | 55 | 46 |
| **UPPER-MIDDLE-INCOME LDCs** | | | | | |
| ALGERIA | 71 | 35 | 1,137 | 81 | 79 |
| VENEZUELA | 73 | 21 | 634 | 81 | 79 |
| BOTSWANA | 46 | 62 | 5,189 | 91 | 70 |
| SOUTH AFRICA | 63 | 51 | 1,875 | 97 | 70 |
| BRAZIL | 67 | 33 | 749 | 85 | 72 |

**Source:** Ruth Leger Sivard, *World Military and Social Expenditures, 1966* (Washington, D.C.: World Priorities, 1966), pp. 30–52, and The World Bank, *World Bank Atlas, 2000* (Washington, D.C.: World Bank, 2000).

What about education? Between 1960 and 1995, the proportion of LDC children attending primary school increased from less than 50 to 75 percent. Yet, lack of education remains one of the chief obstacles to social progress. In the South Asian and African countries ravaged by war and civil unrest, enrollment in the primary levels is critically low. The school-aged population in Africa, for example, is growing almost twice as fast as elsewhere, but a quarter of those of primary school age are not enrolled. Look at Ethiopia, Ivory Coast, and the Democratic Republic of the Congo in Exhibit 4, column 5.

## ECONOMIC DUALISM

Of course, not everybody in the LDCs suffers these basic deprivations. Some live as well as your neighbors. Many LDC doctors, lawyers, merchants, accountants, exporters and importers, manufacturers, hotel owners, bank managers, cosmetics salespeople, customs officials, and government clerks have access to safe water, hospitals, education, decent housing, telephones, automobiles, and a variety of imported durables that make their lives relatively comfortable.

# APPLIED PERSPECTIVE

## CHINA'S POPULATION POLICY: ONE COUPLE, ONE CHILD

**What do you know about China? Probably that it has the largest population in the world. And you're right.** China's 1.26 billion people account for as much as 21 percent of the world's total. That's very many people! In fact, to China's economic and social planners, that's simply too many! It interferes, they believe, with China's ability to create the instrumentalities for rapid economic development. China has been at war with underdevelopment since its 1949 revolution. Its fight to increase standards of living—per capita income—is waged on two fronts: the need to increase GDP and the need to curb population growth.

To deal with its critical demographic concern, the Chinese government in the 1970s introduced an uncompromising family planning policy that confronted China's reality. The policy advocates the practice of "one couple, one child," allowing "a second child only with proper spacing and in accordance with the laws and regulations."

What are these "laws and regulations?" They're excessively harsh by anyone's standards. For example, all pregnancies must be authorized by the government. Menstrual cycles are publicly monitored and pelvic examinations are performed on women suspected of being pregnant. Unauthorized pregnancies are terminated by abortion when detected regardless of the stage of pregnancy. Mandatory IUDs are inserted in women with one child. Removal is difficult and x-ray detection is capriciously applied. There is mandatory sterilization of couples with 2 or more unauthorized children. Women are required to obtain a birth coupon before conceiving a child, the coupon serving as a food rationing device. Without it, family food allotment remains unchanged so that per capita food consumption within the family falls when family size increases without authorization.

THE MESSAGE IS CLEAR IN ANY LANGUAGE.

These stringent procedures and practices have resulted in a high rate of infanticide and, in particular, the abandonment of female infants. But the cold facts are that China's population growth, since the initiation of the "one couple, one child" policy, has been brought under effective control. From 1970 to 1999, China's birth rate decreased from 3.34% to 1.53%. The total fertility rate of Chinese women fell below replacement levels.

The impact of the falling birth rates on family size is notable. Average family size fell from 4.54 members in 1980 to 3.36 members in 1999. Families with 4 or more members fell from 46.3 percent of total families to 23.3 percent. Compared to the developed countries of Europe and North America, China has accomplished these changes in a relatively short period of time.

Chinese planners translate these achievements into movements along and shifts in China's production possibilities curve. By averting the births of an estimated 250 million people and basing the per-child rearing costs from birth to 16 years at 19,000 yuan, China was able to shift resources valued at approximately 4.75 trillion yuan from consumption goods production to investment. That shift contributed to China's "second front" effort to raise standards of living: GDP growth. China's GDP quadrupled since 1980.

Have the high costs been too high? You be the judge.

### MORE ON THE NET

Visit the China Population Information and Research Center at http://www.cpirc.org.cn/eindex.htm to find articles and updates on China's population strategy.

**Economic dualism**
The coexistence of two separate and distinct economies within an LDC; one modern, primarily urban, and export-driven, the other traditional, agricultural, and self-sustaining.

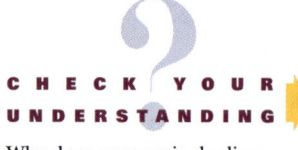

**CHECK YOUR UNDERSTANDING**

Why does economic dualism tend to persist?

The problem is that such a lifestyle is reserved for the few. Most people in LDCs live in remote villages, in overpopulated cities, or on their outskirts, in crowded, squalid shelters. Their employment, if they are employed, is typically in low-productivity agriculture or marginal service-related jobs.

These two very different worlds exist side by side without affecting each other. Exhibit 5 illustrates this **economic dualism.**

The demand curve for workers, $D$, in the traditional sector of panel $a$ is relatively low, reflecting traditional technology and weak prices. The supply curve of labor, $S$, reflects the availability of large numbers of unskilled workers with low opportunity costs willing and even eager to work at minimum wage rates.

In comparison, the modern sector of panel $b$ yields substantially higher wage rates. The demand curve, $D'$, reflects industrial technology applied to the export market, where productivity is higher and prices firmer. Its labor supply curve, $S'$, is relatively steep, reflecting the scarcity of technical skills in the LDCs.

This economic dualism tends to persist because the skills of those in the traditional sector are completely inadequate for the modern sector. They lack the education, the technological culture, and the specific talents, as well as the knowledge needed to obtain them. Although sharing the same geography, they are as far removed from that modern world as they are from the moon. The vast majority of these people are trapped in poverty conditions.

**EXHIBIT 5**

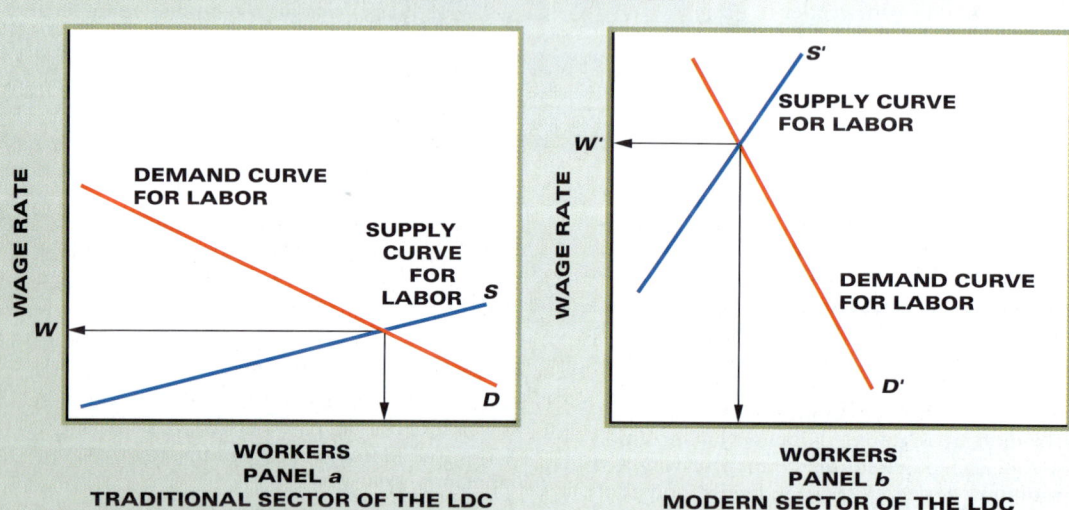

In the traditional sector of the LDC, depicted in panel $a$, the demand curve for labor, $D$, is relatively low and flat. The relatively low opportunity costs associated with traditional labor produce the relatively flat supply curve of labor at relatively low wage rates, $S$. The traditional market, then, generates the relatively low equilibrium wage rate, $W$.

The modern sector of the LDC, depicted in panel $b$, contrasts sharply with the traditional sector of panel $a$. The demand curve for labor, $D'$, is higher. The higher opportunity costs associated with the skilled workers in this sector generate a steeper supply curve of labor, $S'$. The equilibrium wage rate is $W'$, considerably higher than $W$.

# THE ABSENCE OF BASIC PREREQUISITES

Some things are so basic to the proper functioning of an economy and to economic progress in general, and so commonplace in our own economy, that we are sometimes inclined to overlook their importance.

## Political Instability

For example, can you imagine how difficult it would be to plan our economic future if we thought not only that our government could be overthrown overnight, but that the character of our political system would change radically with the overthrow?

Laws become meaningless when governments that displace each other too frequently and by force are inclined to set aside past government commitments and, at times, even basic property rights. Such political discontinuities must interfere with routine economic decision making, increasing people's uncertainty every where in the economy.

For example, how can anyone rely on a military junta or on a revolutionary party government whose political support among the people is always questionable and whose legitimacy can be contested only in disruptive ways? How can such a regime provide confidence in anyone's economic future when its own time horizon is, by past experience, short?

In many LDC economies, juntas, single-party regimes, and puppet-like monarchies are precisely the kinds of governments that hold power. Generals in government are soon deposed by their colonels, and one revolutionary party is undone by another, with each new regime always claiming power on behalf of the people. For many, secret police and political prisoners are commonplace.

While some changes in regime may represent new faces in old uniforms or new revolutionary parties replacing old ones, many incoming regimes actually do go about undoing much in the economy.

## Nonscientific Perceptions

A no-less-fundamental factor inhibiting economic development is the perceptions LDC citizens have concerning their economic status, the societal goals they consider most desirable, and the accepted ways they go about pursuing them. These perceptions reflect the psychological, religious, and cultural character of LDC economies.

**THE POWER OF TRADITIONALISM** Consider Exhibit 1 once more. The high population growth rates are no accident. Large numbers of children are highly desired, particularly sons. The opportunity cost, measured in terms of sacrificed material goods and services, of having large families is clearly understood. *These are choices people make.* They just reflect a different set of accepted values.

Just as people in some LDCs are reluctant to exchange large families for more goods, so also are they reluctant to part with known and accepted ways of producing goods for new and more productive ways. Their reliance on custom and tradition is a powerful inhibitor of development. In this respect, too, they differ substantially from the way people in industrial economies view technology. We are quick to discard the familiar when new goods or ways of producing them are offered.

That same healthy respect for custom and tradition works against willingness to apply scientific methodology to the everyday business of life. Peasants are slow to adopt modern chemistry or even mechanization, and they are disinclined to change the kinds of crops they cultivate. Even if LDC governments are eager to help the peasants increase productivity, the governments often meet resistance.

How do you overcome traditionalist perceptions of life, or how do you modify the behavior of the ruling regimes? Without applying value judgments to either, we can consider them deadweights to economic development. Unless some modification takes place, it is highly unlikely that tradition-bound LDC economies can make the transition to economic modernization.

### The Absence of Infrastructure

While overcoming noneconomic barriers is critical to any effort at development, several economic barriers pose equally insurmountable obstacles. Among them is the conspicuous absence of economic **infrastructure**.

**Infrastructure**
The basic institutions and public facilities upon which an economy's development depends.

What is infrastructure? When we think about how our own economy works, we tend to take for granted the money and banking system that provides the major investment loans to our nation's businesses; the educational system that turns out the incredible varieties of skills and basic research that actually run our nation's production lines; the extensive transportation and communications system—interstate roads, railroads, airports, canals, telephones, Internet sites, postal systems, television stations—that links almost every piece of our geography into one market; the energy system that powers our factories; and, of course, the market system itself, which brings our nation's goods and services into our households.

Although the basic systems that make up our economic infrastructure were either completely absent or underdeveloped when the United States became a republic, they are now so common to us that we tend to overlook the fact that without them our national productive capacity would suddenly and dramatically collapse.

Review *The World Factbook* profile of Chad (http://www.cia.gov/cia/publications/factbook/geos/cd.html).

Imagine transplanting a modern Detroit automobile plant to Chad, an African country southwest of Egypt. Even if U.S. technicians were sent along to put it in place, this major piece of private direct investment would probably do the Chadians little good.

Why? Because physical plants themselves cannot create output. The manufacture of automobiles requires, at the least, a variety of skilled workers, engineers, accountants, salespeople, plant managers, and maintenance crews. Just who in Chad would be qualified? But that's just the beginning.

Who would do the financing? Chadians have always financed the purchase of seed for their few acres or a new milk cow with funds drawn from their own savings or from a moneylender, but neither the moneylender nor the saver is capable of financing an automobile plant. The Chadian banking system is still embryonic.

The plant, of course, requires some energy source. What good is the plant and its state-of-the-art machinery if there is no electricity to power it? Chad simply doesn't have the megawatts. But suppose it did—what's the point of the plant if there are no decent roads in the country?

*Can you think of any other components of an infrastructure that would be needed in order to transplant an automobile plant to Chad besides the ones mentioned in the text? Go to the Interactive Study Center at http://gottheil.swcollege.com and click on the "Your Turn" button to submit your example. Student submissions will be posted to the Web site, and perhaps we will use some in future editions of the book!*

Obviously, we've only scratched the surface of the problem. Even with a road system, the plant would still require an accessible service station industry, with ready stocks of fuel, spare parts, repair equipment, and, most important, people with completely different sets of skills, to make it work. It gets rather complicated, doesn't it?

# GLOBAL PERSPECTIVE

## INTERNET AND INFRASTRUCTURE

**The unusually high rates of labor productivity growth in the United States and in many of the OECD countries during the last decade of the 20th century can be largely attributed to the coming of age of computer technology.** Just as the copper age, iron age, bronze age, and petroleum age linked new and improved labor productivity with new and improved technology, this computer age is associated with an impressive productivity lift in the 21st century.

Already, we have experienced the effects of this incredible technology. During the last few decades of the 20th century, the Internet boosted efficiency and enhanced global market integration dramatically. It raised labor productivity by increasing procurement efficiency, strengthening inventory control, lowering retail transaction costs, and eliminating layers of production intermediaries. The prices of most goods and services have fallen as a result while product quality has improved. And that's only the beginning. Our economic future looks even brighter than our recent high-performance past. The only question is: Which economies belong to the "our" of "our economic future"? Where do developing countries fit in?

The Internet represents basic infrastructure. It is as indispensable a prerequisite to economic development as are roads, electric power, housing, education, and health. The Internet provides a platform for firms in the developing world to leapfrog from the traditional to the most advanced technologies, allowing them to compete successfully with the industrial economies in producing high-value-added goods and services. It can do this by lowering costs of transportation and communication, making previously inaccessible markets of the industrial world accessible to them. It may even reverse the chronic worsening of terms of trade for the developing economies.

CAN'T WAIT FOR THAT TECH JOB.

As attractive as these prospects may seem, they remain for many countries in the developing world only tantalizing potential and for some no more than fantasies. The reality they face is an extraordinary Internet gap between themselves and the rest of the world. This gap is shown in the accompanying table.

Narrowing the Internet access gap may be exceedingly difficult for many of the developing economies. It requires considerable capital outlay and the availability of highly skilled labor, both typically in short supply. In 1966, the average cost of Internet access in Africa was over $60 per month, more than most Africans' total monthly income. That is why it may seem more reasonable for developing countries to stay focused on the lesser skill-demanding, labor-intensive technologies. But such a short-sighted view will only keep the Internet gap shown in the table wide open. A new version of the vicious circle of poverty results: the developing country can't access the Internet because it is poor, and it is poor because it cannot access the Internet.

Still, prospects may not be as bleak as they appear to be. After all, the costs of accessing the Internet continue to fall—thanks to incredible and continuing technological changes in the computer industry—and these costs may soon make access affordable for many in the developing countries. Note that the Internet access shown in the table for the developing countries, while considerably less than access for the developed countries, is still not zero. In Kenya, telecommunication microwave towers are beginning to dot the landscape. Some access is even filtering down to the education process, where it must take root: A senior school in Kampala, Uganda, has a virtual exchange program, via the Internet, with a comparable high school in Jackson Hole, Wyoming. All roads have beginnings.

*continued on next page*

**INTERNET HOSTS PER 10,000 POPULATION AND PERSONAL COMPUTERS PER 1,000 POPULATION FOR SELECTED COUNTRIES**

|  | INTERNET HOSTS | PERSONAL COMPUTERS |
|---|---|---|
| ALGERIA | 0.0 | 4.2 |
| ARGENTINA | 27.8 | 44.3 |
| BOLIVIA | 0.5 | 7.5 |
| BRAZIL | 18.5 | 30.1 |
| EGYPT | 0.3 | 9.1 |
| INDIA | 0.2 | 2.7 |
| INDONESIA | 0.7 | 8.2 |
| KENYA | 0.2 | 2.5 |
| MOROCCO | 0.3 | 2.5 |
| NICARAGUA | 2.2 | 7.8 |
| PAKISTAN | 0.2 | 3.9 |
| PERU | 3.1 | 18.1 |
| ZIMBABWE | 0.9 | 3.0 |
| UNITED STATES | 1,122.6 | 458.6 |
| CANADA | 365.7 | 330.0 |
| ISRAEL | 160.4 | 217.2 |
| FRANCE | 82.6 | 207.8 |

**Source:** The World Bank Group, 2000. "Internet hosts" refers to the number of computers with active Internet protocol (IP) addresses connected to the Internet.

Where do all these skilled people come from? Without a modern educational system, the answer is nowhere. Too few colleges in Chad graduate engineers, accountants, and doctors. Its literacy rate is critically low. Peasants farming in traditional ways rely upon experience, not education.

To educate people involves not only the monumental task of acquiring compliance—a population willing to send its children to school—but the funds needed to build the schools and to staff them. Where do these funds come from?

As you can see, the automobile plant would quickly rust unless it were accompanied by an expansive set of direct and indirect investments. That's all but impossible. Chadians have neither the material nor the human resources to undertake such a tremendous development departure. Chad's poverty trap seems rather formidable, doesn't it?

## PURSUING STRATEGIES OF DEVELOPMENT

If you were asked to map out a grand strategy for economic development in Chad, just where would you begin? Economists have struggled with this vexing challenge and have come up with essentially two competing strategies. Both focus on the task of breaking the vicious circle of underdevelopment that traps the LDCs into national poverty.

The vicious circle of underdevelopment refers to LDCs that are poor because of the underdeveloped state of their economies, a state of underdevelopment that persists because they are poor. It's both logical and frustrating. The only way to cut into that self-sustaining trap is by massive doses of infrastructure and accompanying investments. But how? Is there a particular order or sequence of investing that works? Who does what investing? What role does government play? Should the private sector do it alone?

## The Big Push

One idea that has found a receptive audience among development economists is the **big-push** strategy. It argues that because each potential investment's success depends upon there being a market for its output, none of the potential projects ever get realized because none have ready markets.

How do you create ready markets for, say, 1,000 potential investment projects when none exist? By investing in the 1,000 projects *all at once*. That's the idea behind the big push.

For example, a new rubber tire plant would have no chance of succeeding unless it had an automobile plant to serve. Investing in both tire and automobile plants provides the ready market for the tire plant. Investing in road construction provides the beginnings of a market for automobiles and trucks. After all, the tire plant needs trucks to move its raw materials in and its tires out to market—impossible without a road system, possible with one. The road construction project itself needs trucks to move its equipment and materials. That, too, becomes a market for the auto plant.

Investments in steel and concrete production now become feasible because each can see a new, ready market. Steel is the primary raw material in automobile production. It is also needed in the construction of the physical plants. Concrete's major market emerges with road construction. Both steel and concrete works, of course, need trucks and automobiles. The automobile market expands.

You can see the connections to investments in the mining industries, can't you? Iron ore, if available, is used in the production of steel. If ore is produced, it finds a ready market in steel, which in turn becomes a market for automobiles and trucks. Of course, none of this could happen without the infrastructure investment in roads.

**HOW BIG MUST A BIG PUSH BE?** The bigger the total all-at-once investment commitment, the easier it is to generate ready, attractive markets for each project. And that's the trick. But it's just the first phase. Once the big push is introduced, creating ready markets for the interlocking projects, the growing markets in the economy make many other investment projects attractive.

In other words, the big-push strategy triggers a dynamic swelling of investments in the economy that serves to break through the vicious circle of underdevelopment. There is a critical minimum level required for a big push to set the strategy in motion. The initial projects must be carefully chosen to take advantage of the economy's human and material resources and synchronized to form interlocking markets. And each of the selected projects must be large enough to absorb the other outputs.

Is there an upper bound to a big push? Is bigger always better? The problem with grandiose big-push schemes is not only their cost, but the inevitability of confronting bottlenecks that can stall an otherwise well-planned strategy. Among the first of the serious bottlenecks confronted is the shortage of technical expertise and skilled production-line workers. There are always many in the economy eager

**Big push**
The development strategy that relies on an integrated network of government-sponsored and financed investments introduced into the economy all at once.

to work, but almost as many lacking the simplest of skills required to operate modern technology.

Breakdowns in production lines are common to all economies, but if the skills and materials needed to maintain the lines are too few and spread too thinly across too many big-push projects, the big push becomes distorting and itself distorted. Like a picture puzzle, the pieces must be formed to fit and put together to make the fit; otherwise, the picture is lost.

It sometimes pays to think in more modest and reasonable terms rather than pursue a big-push strategy, and to curb an ambitious development appetite to guarantee proper digestion.

**WHO DOES THE PUSHING?** Big-push economists argue that such an interlocking, balanced set of infrastructure and development investments can be initiated, financed, and managed only by government. Why government? Because such a scheme requires long-term planning, and its rewards are forthcoming only in the long run. Who else but government has a time horizon big enough to make such investments and wait upon their results?

CHECK YOUR UNDERSTANDING

Why is government the logical choice to execute the big push?

Entrepreneurs in the private sector cannot be expected to invest long term in an economy with limited investment promise. After all, it is unreasonable to expect them to think that by the time their output is ready for market, there will be a market. What assurances do they have? How are they supposed to know that others are thinking the same thoughts? And if they wait upon others to start, nothing starts.

But once the government-sponsored big push gets underway, the private sector is indeed expected to participate. Entrepreneurs do so not because they want to develop the economy, but because they now discover a stream of new, profitable opportunities that the big-push strategy has created.

**WHO FINANCES THE BIG PUSH?** Big-push strategies, depending on their aggressiveness, require enormous national commitments that can sometimes tax an economy beyond its capabilities. Government funds the push because no one else can.

How? Primarily through taxes. But levying even more taxes on an already impoverished people not only is painful but can be destabilizing. Because government's ability to tax incomes is restricted by its lack of effective tax collecting at the source, LDC governments typically rely on sales taxes on consumer goods and on customs duties. The results tend to be regressive. Egypt's attempt in the 1970s to cut government subsidies on food led to riots in Cairo that almost brought the government down.

Less painful to LDCs in the short run, but perhaps more costly in the long run, is government's attempt to finance the big push by external borrowing from foreign private and government lending agencies. Ultimately, LDCs pay for the development they undertake.

## The Unbalanced Development Strategy

The competing strategy to the big push relies essentially upon entrepreneurs themselves doing the major part of investing and funding development once projects become potentially profitable.

How do investments, unprofitable before the strategy, suddenly become profitable? Like the big-push strategy, the profitability of private investment projects depends upon the initial undertaking of infrastructure projects. In this respect, the unbalanced development strategy still counts on government initiative. But unlike the big push, these initial government undertakings are tailored in size and scope. How does it work?

The strategy is based on the idea that every investment, however small, has its own set of **forward and backward linkages** into the economy. Once undertaken, the investment creates new demands and new supplies in the economy. That's the trick. Production projects emerge to satisfy these new demands, and their outputs make other previously unfeasible projects feasible. These new projects, now undertaken, create a succeeding round of entirely new demands and new outputs. And so on.

**LINKAGES IN SRI LANKA** Imagine the Sri Lankan government thinking about a strategy to get its development process started. Suppose Sri Lanka, a world supplier of raw tea, does not have its own tea processing plants. Its tea is shipped in bulk to the industrial economies and there gets treated.

But no longer. The Sri Lankan government decides that tea is the trigger industry in its development process. It invests in a large, modern processing plant that prepares the raw tea for the consumer market. While the plant goes into construction, a number of Sri Lankans take note.

It becomes quite clear that when the government-owned tea processing plant gets underway, it will need packaging material. A sharp Sri Lankan entrepreneur seizes the opportunity. He can now get into the container business with a ready market. Government doesn't have to worry about packaging. It created the backward linkage.

But the container factory can produce more packaging than the government-owned processing plant can absorb. Once in operation, it can diversify its packaging product to satisfy almost every packaging demand. In other words, the development process, triggered by the processing plant, created an imbalance between packaging supply capacity and the government's demand for packaging.

Such an imbalanced development process is preferred by some economists to the balanced development strategy of the big push. Why? Because not only is there a new supply source where one hadn't existed before, but the imbalance will spark new forward and backward linkages throughout the economy. How does it work?

Since it is no longer necessary for Sri Lankan businesses to import expensive packaging into the economy—domestic supply, employing Sri Lankan labor, is typically less expensive and more accessible—the availability of this domestic supply can make the difference between a profit and a loss to businesses for which packaging is a major input.

Other businesses, now confident about getting access to this new supply, expand their operations. But their expansions create new imbalances between their new supplies and the demands for their goods.

*The mutually reinforcing imbalances caused by new supplies creating new demands—forward linkages—and these new demands creating new and different supplies—backward linkages—play off against each other, forming a dynamic chain reaction of economic development.*

The attraction of such a development strategy is that it places minimal stress on government. It requires neither a grandiose design nor a grandiose taxing scheme. Again like a picture puzzle, the individual linkage pieces make up the development picture, but the actual picture isn't known beforehand.

**WHO DOES THE INVESTING?** The key to success in the unbalanced strategy is the role played by entrepreneurs. The idea is that in all societies, in whatever stage of economic development, there are always creative, energetic people who,

---

**Forward linkages**
Investments in one industry that create opportunities for profitable investments in other industries, using the goods produced in the first as inputs.

**Backward linkages**
Investments in one industry that create demands for inputs, inducing investment in other industries to produce those inputs.

# APPLIED PERSPECTIVE

## THE ROAD TO BETTER FARMING

On present trends, Africa's population will double in the next 20 years, pushing its people on to ever more marginal land. Over-grazed pastures will turn to desert. Topsoil on newly cultivated hillsides will be washed away. Exhausted soil will support fewer crops. And ever more Africans will go hungry.

Or so environmental doomsters claim. Not so, argues a new study by researchers from Britain's Overseas Development Institute and the University of Nairobi. Using colonial records, satellite images, and field research, they have looked at farming in the Machakos district of Kenya, a region of low rainfall and occasional drought, over the period 1930–90. Sixty years ago most farmers kept cattle—for milk, meat, and as a bride price—and grew some grain and pulses. The region faced periodic food shortages: during the 1940s and 1950s it needed regular famine relief. Soil erosion had deeply scarred the landscape.

By 1990 the population had swelled fivefold, to 1.4 million. Result: disaster? No. Total output had risen fifteenfold: more land was under cultivation (by 1979 there was no unclaimed land left) and yields per square kilometer were up tenfold. The "badlands" of the past had been transformed into a landscape of neatly terraced hills and fenced fields.

How did it happen? Most important, Machakos became integrated fairly early—during the 1960s—into the market economy. Farmers diversified from subsistence crops into ones they could trade: coffee, bananas, peas, pawpaws. Under British rule the region's Kamba people had not been allowed to grow coffee in competition with white farmers, or to sell grains outside the area without a permit. After independence in 1963, land reform and the lifting of some state controls encouraged smallholders to invest in higher-value crops—and to conserve soil and water so the land could support them.

Capital for investment came from new opportunities to earn money outside farming. By 1990 most farm families in Machakos had at least one son or daughter earning money from nonfarm work, such as weaving baskets or making carvings for tourists. This helped families buy better tools, fertilizer, drought-resistant strains of maize, and seed for second crops to plant among first ones to take advantage of Kenya's second seasonal rains.

Decent road links to Nairobi, dating from the 1950s, made a huge difference. It became profitable to grow fruit and vegetables as Asian traders began to travel to Machakos to buy crops—and later other goods—for city markets.

Better communications also helped government advisers spread news about new farming methods. Yet expert advice was not the key. Productivity grew fastest between 1960 and 1980, when the government, busy with more promising farming areas, was making no special effort for Machakos. Yet farmers there invested hard in better land and crops: advised or not, they had the incentives, and the means, to gain from doing it.

**WHERE THERE WAS ONCE LITTLE, THERE IS NOW PLENTY. PEOPLE EAT, BUT PEOPLE ALSO PRODUCE.**

### MORE ON THE NET

The Bureau of African Affairs (http://www.state.gov/www/regions/africa/index.html), part of the State Department, provides data and information about Africa. Africa Online (http://www.africaonline.com/) also offers news, information, and resources about Africa.

**Source:** *The Economist,* December 11, 1993. © 1993 The Economist Newspaper Group, Inc. Reprinted with permission. Further reproduction prohibited. http://www.economist.com

presented with a chance at enterprise, will take it. Personal commitment is stronger and more reliable than government commitment and reliability.

**WHO DOES THE FUNDING?** While government triggers the process by funding and putting into place some of the economy's key infrastructure investments, the primary source of development finance is the private sector. Entrepreneurs themselves are expected either to invest their own savings in their own businesses or to find the funding in the banking system.

Although for most LDCs the banking system is limited or nonexistent, it is precisely the demands for private business loans that create the *rationale* for commercial banking. If domestic banks aren't available, foreign banks, lured by the new prospects, will come in. It's just a matter of time before Sri Lankan entrepreneurs get into the banking business.

# FOREIGN DIRECT INVESTMENT

You might think that LDC governments would jump at the chance of having foreign direct investment join in their development programs. After all, foreign direct investment is about the only way an LDC economy can get into development at zero opportunity cost. Exhibit 6 illustrates its appeal.

Without foreign direct investment, the LDC economy must sacrifice 120 − 90 = 30 consumption goods to expand capital goods from 10 to 15. There is no other way. But suppose it now decides to invite foreign investment. If it attracts 5 units of foreign capital goods, it can stay at 120 consumption and still get 15 capital goods into its development process. Point *C* in Exhibit 6 is impossible without foreign investment.

Foreign direct investment typically brings in not only new capital goods but new expertise. As well, it provides the LDCs with markets in the industrial economies that otherwise would be unavailable.

As a contributor to LDC development, foreign investment just seems too good to be true. Yet almost universally, LDC governments have had serious reservations about designing their development programs with a foreign direct investment imprint. Why their reluctance?

## Images from the Colonial Past

The arguments for and against foreign investments are based as much upon emotion as upon economic logic. Many development economists argue that it was the uninvited foreign direct investment of the colonial

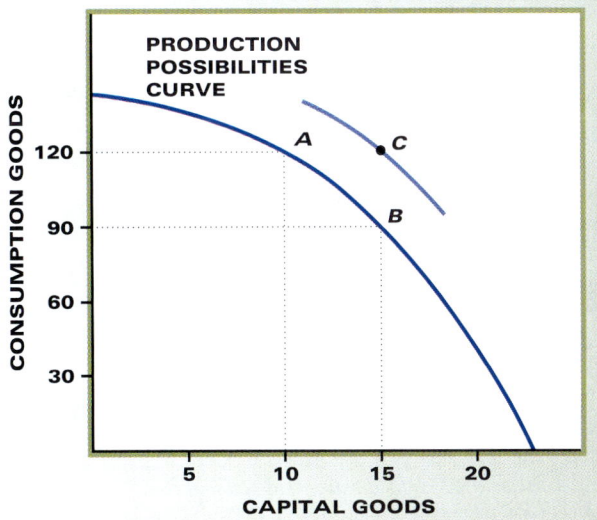

**PRODUCTION POSSIBILITIES CURVE WITH FOREIGN INVESTMENT**

Without foreign investment, the production possibilities for the LDC economy are restricted to combinations of capital goods and consumption goods along the *AB* curve. Position *C* is an impossible choice. With the added capital resources provided by foreign investments, *C* is attainable.

EXHIBIT 6

19th century that left LDC economies underdeveloped in the first place. The LDCs' inability to pursue domestic industry, they insist, was not a result of failing to provide the human and material resources required, but rather the result of coercive interference by colonial regimes in the LDCs.

By colonial design, LDC economies became economic caricatures, restructured into raw material supply bases for the West. Their entrepreneurs had no freedom to operate, except perhaps in small-scale retail trade or in traditional artisan production. The promising industries were reserved for the colonial power. Managerial skills remained underdeveloped because those employment opportunities, too, were available only to the colonial power.

To some economists, then, it would be the height of irony if after finally gaining independence—in some cases at great human sacrifice—the LDCs were to turn right around and invite back into their economies the colonial powers, even if the economic gains from foreign investments were undeniable.

Yet the contribution that foreign direct investment can make to an LDC development process is just too important to overlook, even for the most reluctant LDCs. Although worried about the consequences of inviting in foreign investment, the LDC governments worry as well about the consequences of not inviting in foreign investment!

What do they do? Most end up with a "yes, but" policy. Yes, foreign investment is wanted, but not without serving LDC designs. Typically, foreign investment in the LDCs is well harnessed. It is subject to more-stringent regulation than is domestic investment. Foreign investors are sometimes excluded from particular fields of activity. In some economies, they are obliged to hire nationals in managerial positions or are required to meet employment quotas. In most cases foreign investors must also accept profit-repatriation ceilings. That is, foreign investment is carefully monitored to suit the development objectives of the host economy.

On the other hand, foreign direct investment in some LDCs, typically the more successful ones, is as welcome as Santa Claus at Christmas. Some LDCs provide tax holidays—as long as five years free of all domestic taxes—and some have investment subsidies to encourage foreign investment. Many offer duty-free imports of capital goods as added inducements.

Visit the U.S. Agency for International Development (http://www.usaid.gov/), part of the Department of State (http://www.state.gov/).

## FOREIGN ECONOMIC AID

While foreign direct investment is essentially a private sector activity, foreign economic aid—loans and grants—is government to government. Our own aid program is housed in the Department of State and is administered by the Agency for International Development (USAID).

Exhibit 7 records the growth of our economic aid program. Aid is offered in the form of loans and grants, and the distinction is important. Loans are repayable with interest, although interest charges have typically been below market rates. In some cases, the loans

**U.S. FOREIGN ECONOMIC AID: 1970–99 ($ MILLIONS)**

|  | TOTAL | LOANS | GRANTS |
|---|---|---|---|
| 1970 | $ 3,676 | $1,389 | $ 2,288 |
| 1980 | 7,573 | 1,993 | 5,580 |
| 1990 | 10,834 | 756 | 10,078 |
| 1997 | 9,170 | 218 | 8,952 |

Source: *Statistical Abstract of the United States, 1999* (Washington, D.C.: U.S. Department of Commerce, 1999), p. 800.

# GLOBAL PERSPECTIVE

## FOOD FOR PEACE

There's a lot wrong with foreign aid, and critics of foreign aid are not at all shy about telling you. Much of our foreign aid goes to governments, not to people, and the recipient governments are about as corrupt as governments can be. Many are one-party governments (no real choice) or military juntas. In too many cases, the spoils of our foreign aid end up in their Swiss bank accounts. There is little, if any, accountability given or, perhaps more distressing, even demanded. In a real sense, the foreign aid we offer results in a twisted international welfare scheme: Dollars are taken from average income-earning Americans and given to not-so-average wealthy foreigners.

A National Bureau of Economic Research (NBER) paper by Professors Alberto Alesina and Beatrice Weder found that countries receiving more aid tend to have higher levels of corruption. They found no evidence that foreign aid reduces corruption levels in recipient countries. That's not what foreign aid was supposed to do.

Adding insult to injury, many of these nondemocratic governments are anything but the United States' allies in international diplomacy. Their voting records at the United Nations are exemplary anti-United States.

Proponents of foreign aid emphasize the positive, and there are strong positives. Among the aid programs that work and have made a difference in the lives of destitute people is the food aid program PL 480 Food for Peace.

Food for Peace was formalized in the Agricultural Trade Development and Assistance Act of 1954. Modified many times, it establishes the policy of using the United States' abundant agricultural resources and food processing capabilities to enhance food security in the developing world through the provision of culturally acceptable nutritious food. More than 800 million people today are chronically undernourished, and more than 180 million children are significantly underweight. The strategic goal of Food for Peace is to reduce those numbers. The program gives food resources to help those in need and in crisis and seeks to eliminate the food insecurity that fuels political instability and environmental degradation.

Food for Peace's FY2000 budget was $787 million. It was used to respond to both protracted emergency food aid requirements as well as the sudden emergencies caused by natural disasters and political and economic instability. Although beneficiaries include victims of natural disasters, such as droughts, typhoons, and cyclones, the majority of programs addressed complex humanitarian situations frequently caused or complicated by civil strife. Emergency food aid targets refugees or internally displaced people, particularly malnourished or unaccompanied children, women, orphans, and the elderly.

In Kenya, for example, emergency food aid reached drought-affected groups, including 452,016 school children and 443,702 food-insecure families. The provision of food to school children maintained attendance of children at the pre-primary and primary school level in the drought-affected areas.

In Angola, emergency food aid programs responded to changing situations as the country attempted to draw away from years of war but still struggled with socioeconomic problems and instability. Food-for-work activities rehabilitated rural infrastructure and revitalized agricultural production and farming systems. By 1998, 56,393 internally displaced persons were resettled.

Activities in Peru illustrate how well-designed food aid programs can contribute to improving food security of targeted groups and thus stabilize vulnerable populations during crisis periods. In the 1980s, during the height of the civil unrest and resulting economic depression in Peru, direct food distribution activities were the primary method of reaching those without food. As civil disturbances declined and economic stability has returned, aid has gradually shifted to poverty reduction and income-generating efforts.

have been forgiven. Grants, on the other hand, are outright gifts. As you can see, for 1997 almost all of the U.S. aid flow to the LDCs was in the form of grants.

How is the aid used? It depends on the LDC's priorities at the time. In the best of times, it is used for infrastructure development. In the worst of times, but for good reason, it is used to supplement the LDC's food stocks. In either case, it tends to nudge the LDC off its low-level production possibilities curve in the same way that foreign direct investment does.

How generous have we been? It depends on the measuring rod. In terms of absolute dollars, we have been, for most years, the largest aid contributor to the LDCs. But we are also the richest contributor. Measured in terms of an aid-to-GDP ratio or an aid-to-population ratio, we rank below such donors as Canada, Norway, Sweden, Japan, the Netherlands, and France.

# CHAPTER REVIEW

1. Economists have been concerned with the problem of persistent national poverty in the LDCs since the 1950s. Per capita income for most of the LDCs is not only low—under $500—but, in some cases, falling even further. Low-level economic growth combines with high-level rates of population growth to threaten already meager standards of living.

2. Many of the LDCs are caught in the vicious circle of poverty: They are poor because they don't invest in capital goods production, and the reason they don't is that they are poor. The consequences are high infant mortality rates, low life expectancy, a small percentage of people using safe water, and a small percentage of school-aged children in school. These consequences end up causing further poverty. Contributing to this poverty is the lack of political stability and a development infrastructure, and a reluctance to accept change.

3. Economic dualism refers to the condition in which a minority of the LDC population is engaged in modern technology production, earning incomes similar to those earned in industrial economies, while the rest of the population is engaged in low-level technology production earning substantially less, so that income disparity between these dual sectors of the economy is severe.

4. There are many competing development strategies for the LDCs. The big-push strategy emphasizes investment in many projects all at once to create both productive capacity and markets for the production. Government plays a dominant role as coordinator, planner, and financier of the strategy.

5. An alternative approach to development is the unbalanced strategy, which relies less heavily on government. Here, initial private sector development in key areas of the economy creates backward and forward linkages to new projects that had been unthinkable before these key investments. These linkages provide opportunities and incentives for private firms to invest, creating even more opportunities and incentives.

6. Foreign direct investment allows an LDC to create capital goods production without having to sacrifice consumption goods production. Foreign economic aid can do the same. The United States gives more economic aid, in the form of loans and grants, than any other industrial country, although it is not a relatively large donor if the aid is measured as a percentage of GDP.

## KEY TERMS

Less-developed countries (LDCs)
Human capital
Economic dualism

Infrastructure
Big push

Forward linkages
Backward linkages

## QUESTIONS

1. The historical data of falling birth rates and falling death rates in LDCs helps explain the difficulty they face in raising per capita incomes. Explain.
2. What is meant by the LDC poverty trap?
3. What is economic dualism, and why does it create a formidable obstacle to national economic development for LDCs?
4. Why is political stability vital to the economic development process?
5. What is economic traditionalism? Compare its characteristics to the modern sector of an economy.
6. Describe the components of an economy's infrastructure. What aspects are lacking in LDCs?
7. Describe the economic logic associated with the big-push development strategy. What are its pitfalls?
8. Describe the economic logic associated with the unbalanced development strategy. What are its pitfalls?
9. Why are some LDC governments reluctant to invite in foreign direct investment? What are the pros and cons of such investment?
10. Show the effect of foreign direct investment on an economy's production possibilities curve.
11. Professor Miguel Ramirez asks his students at Trinity College to respond to the following problem: Economists, notably those in the World Bank and the IMF, argue that free trade and open markets are important factors contributing to LDC economic growth. On the other hand, American policy makers in the early 19th century—when the United States was beginning to industrialize—pursued a highly protective strategy vis-à-vis England, the premier industrial power of the world. Should LDCs follow the advice of World Bank and IMF economists or take their cue from U.S. economic history?

    Make your case using economic analyses offered in the chapters on international trade; exchange rates, balance of payments, and international debt; and the economic problems of less-developed economies.

# WHAT'S WRONG WITH THIS GRAPH?

## ECONOMIC DUALISM

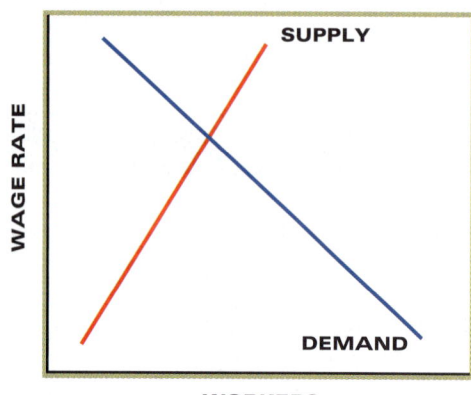

TRADITIONAL SECTOR

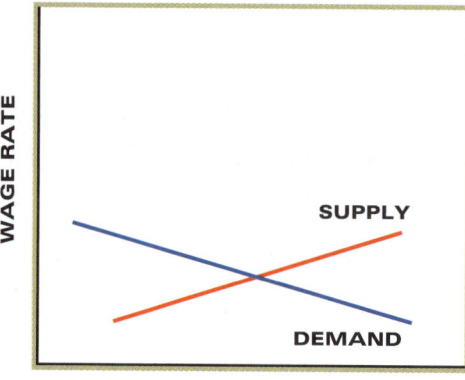

MODERN SECTOR

# ECONOMIC CONSULTANTS

### ECONOMIC RESEARCH AND ANALYSIS BY STUDENTS FOR PROFESSIONALS

South African businesspeople and government officials have formed an organization, Economic Development in South Africa (EDSA), to map a strategy for economic development in post-apartheid South Africa. EDSA understands the need for direct foreign investment and foreign aid, but individuals within EDSA are worried that such strategies may make South Africa overdependent on foreign powers. EDSA also understands the need for controlled growth and investment, but the group is unsure about the best strategy to pursue to ensure stable growth.

EDSA has hired Economic Consultants to present to its members the pros and cons of different economic development strategies. Prepare a report for EDSA that addresses the following issues:

1. What basic strategies should South Africa pursue for economic development, particularly in terms of foreign investment?
2. What problems arise with different economic development strategies? How can South Africa avoid uncontrolled growth and investment?
3. What groups and organizations specialize in direct foreign investment and foreign aid?

You may find the following resources helpful as you prepare this report for EDSA:

- **PRAXIS: Resources for Social and Economic Development** (http://caster.ssw.upenn.edu/~restes/praxis.html)—PRAXIS provides a library of links to resources on international and comparative social development.
- **World Bank** (http://www.worldbank.org/)—The World Bank provides news, publications, and country and regional economic reports.
- **World Bank Institute** (http://www.worldbank.org/wbi/home.html)—The World Bank Institute promotes awareness of development strategies through publications and educational initiatives.
- **Finance and Development** (http://www.imf.org./fandd/)—*Finance and Development* is a joint quarterly publication of the International Monetary Fund and the World Bank.

# PRACTICE TEST

1. The principal factors contributing to low per capita incomes in LCDs are
    a. high population growth and low literacy rates.
    b. traditional development and lack of infrastructure.
    c. low economic growth rates and high population growth rates.
    d. lack of foreign investment and low levels of economic aid.
    e. political instability and lack of social cohesion.

2. The vicious circle of poverty associated with LCDs refers to
    a. their ability to borrow but inability to pay their debts.
    b. their traditional sector becoming modern only to revert back to traditionalism.
    c. their misuse of capital goods over and over again.
    d. their being poor because they choose population growth over economic growth.
    e. their being poor because they cannot devote resources to capital goods production because they are poor.

3. LCDs typically end up investing relatively little in human capital because
    a. human capital is typically less productive than LCD investments in factory and equipment.
    b. human capital has a considerably longer time horizon than other types of investment.
    c. human capital has a considerably shorter time horizon than other types of investment.
    d. the investment is wasted when LCD people migrate out of the country.
    e. human capital is generally restricted to the modern sector, which does not need the capital as much as the traditional sector.

4. Economic dualism refers to
    a. the lack of integration between an LCD's traditional and modern sectors.
    b. the enormous gap between an LCD's rich and poor.
    c. the disparity between investments in consumption goods and capital goods production.
    d. the disparity between consumption and investment.
    e. the dominance of government over private citizens in an LCD's economy.

5. Among the basic prerequisites for development that are absent in LCDs are
    a. foreign investment and entrepreneurs.
    b. honest government and development strategies.
    c. human capital and market incentives.
    d. political stability and infrastructure.
    e. productive resources and technically skilled labor.

6. The big-push strategy proposes all-at-one-time multiple investments because
    a. they provide markets for each other.
    b. they create forward, rather than backward, linkages.
    c. they involve a smaller initial investment than do alternative strategies.
    d. unsuccessful projects would be canceled by successful ones.
    e. foreign governments are more inclined to finance this strategy.

7. The unbalanced development strategy
    a. relies on government to finance each stage of the strategy.
    b. creates forward, but not backward, linkages, which trigger top-down development.
    c. creates backward, but not forward, linkages, which trigger bottom-up development.
    d. creates forward and backward linkages, which play off each other to create the development.
    e. involves an imbalance between the roles played by LCD and foreign entrepreneurs.

8. Forward linkages are investments in industries that create
    a. investment opportunities for other industries using the goods produced in the first as inputs.
    b. demands for inputs, inducing investments in other industries to produce those inputs.
    c. future demands for investments in the same industries.
    d. future supplies of investment in the same industries.
    e. top-down development.

9. Some LCDs are reluctant to accept foreign investment because
    a. the LCDs fear a repeat of their colonial past.
    b. foreign firms repatriate most of the profit they earn in the LCD to the home country.
    c. foreign firms use LCD managers but pay them minimal salaries.
    d. foreign firms refuse to accept LCD government regulation.
    e. foreign firms insist on infrastructure development rather than investing in plant and equipment.

10. Economic aid from the United States to the LCDs
    a. is mainly given as loans, not grants.
    b. represents a higher percentage of its GDP compared to other donor countries.
    c. is greater than the economic aid given annually by other donor countries.
    d. is mainly for military purchases of U.S. weaponry by LCDs.
    e. is mainly allocated to sub-Saharan Africa.

# PHOTO CREDITS

*Part 1:* p. 1: Courtesy of Fred Gottheil/University of Illinois Urbana-Champaign. *Chapter 1:* p. 2: © Chip Simons/FPG International; p. 5: © Len Rue Jr./H. Armstrong Roberts; p. 11: © Richard Hamilton Smith/Corbis. *Chapter 2:* p. 24: © Chip Simons/FPG International; p. 29: © Corbis; p. 30: © FPG International; p. 35: © Nathan Benn/Stock, Boston. *Chapter 3:* p. 44: © Chip Simons/FPG International; p. 52: © Jim Sugar/Corbis; p. 55: © Bettmann/Corbis. *Part 2:* p. 73: Courtesy of Fred Gottheil/University of Illinois Urbana-Champaign. *Chapter 4:* p. 75: © Chip Simons/FPG International; p. 78: © Emanuele Taroni/PhotoDisc; p. 81: © Jose Galvez/PhotoEdit; p. 86: © Eriako Associates/Stone. *Chapter 5:* p. 100: © Chip Simons/Chip Simons Photography; p. 105: © Michael Goldman/FPG International; p. 111: © Jon Riley/Stone; p. 116: © Wayne Eastep/Stone. *Chapter 6:* p. 122: © Chip Simons/Chip Simons Photography; p. 127: © Bettmann/Corbis; p. 136: © Sean Justice/Image Bank. *Chapter 7:* p. 147: © Chip Simons/Chip Simons Photography; p. 150: © Dick Young/Unicorn Stock Photos; p. 157: © Fergus O'Brien/FPG International; p. 161: © Leslye Borden/PhotoEdit; p. 165: © Chip Henderson/Stone. *Chapter 8:* p. 171: © Chip Simons/Chip Simons Photography; p. 174: © Archive Photos; p. 179: © AP/Wide World Photos; p. 183: © AP/Wide World Photos; p. 185: © Philip Lee Harvey/Stone. *Chapter 9:* p. 196: © Chip Simons/FPG International; p. 199: © AP/Wide World Photos; p. 205: © Hulton-Deutsch Collection/Corbis; p. 208: © Paul Conklin/PhotoEdit. *Part 3:* p. 221: Courtesy of Fred Gottheil/University of Illinois Urbana-Champaign. *Chapter 10:* p. 223: © Chip Simons/Chip Simons Photography; p. 226: © Elizabeth Watt/Liaison Agency; p. 229: © Eyewire Collection; p. 236: © Tom Stewart/Stock Market. *Chapter 11:* p. 245: © Chip Simons/FPG International; p. 248: © Security First Network Bank/Feldman & Associates; p. 255: © Andy Sacks/Stone. *Chapter 12:* p. 266: © Chip Simons/Chip Simons Photography; p. 288: © Markel/Liaison Agency; p. 291: © AP/Wide World Photos. *Part 4:* p. 297: Courtesy of Fred Gottheil/University of Illinois Urbana-Champaign. *Chapter 13:* p. 298: © Chip Simons/FPG International; p. 312: © AP/Wide World Photos; p. 314: © AP/Wide World Photos; p. 317: © AP/Wide World Photos. *Chapter 14:* p. 327: © Chip Simons/Chip Simons Photography; p. 336: © AP/Wide World Photos; p. 338: © Daniel Nichols/Liaison Agency. *Chapter 15:* p. 346: © Chip Simons/Chip Simons Photography; p. 354: © Bettmann/Corbis; p. 359: © Reuters/Vladimir Voronov/Archive Photos. *Part 5:* p. 369: Courtesy of Fred Gottheil/University of Illinois Urbana-Champaign. *Chapter 16:* p. 371: © Chip Simons/Chip Simons Photography; p. 382: © AP/Wide World Photos; p. 390: © Camermann International, Ltd. *Chapter 17:* p. 400: © Chip Simons/Chip Simons Photography; p. 405: © J. Chiasson/Liaison Agency; p. 408: © Stephanie Maze/Woodfin Camp & Associates; p. 414: © AP/Wide World Photos; p. 418: © AP/Wide World Photos. *Chapter 18:* p. 425: © Chip Simons/FPG International; p. 431: © Bettmann/Corbis; p. 435: © AFP/Corbis; p. 440: © Francis Li/Liaison Agency.

*Economic Consultants* (all chapters): © PhotoDisc, Inc.

# PRACTICE TESTS
## ANSWER KEY

**CHAPTER 1**
1. e
2. d
3. e
4. b
5. c
6. a
7. c
8. d
9. b
10. b

**CHAPTER 2**
1. a
2. c
3. a
4. c
5. b
6. b
7. b
8. c
9. e

**CHAPTER 3**
1. b
2. a
3. d
4. a
5. a
6. b
7. e
8. d
9. e
10. e

**CHAPTER 4**
1. d
2. b
3. e
4. a
5. e
6. a
7. b
8. d
9. b
10. d

**CHAPTER 5**
1. b
2. d
3. e
4. d
5. a
6. c
7. e
8. a
9. c
10. c

**CHAPTER 6**
1. d
2. a
3. b
4. e
5. d
6. e
7. b
8. a
9. d
10. e

**CHAPTER 7**
1. c
2. b
3. c
4. a
5. b
6. e
7. a
8. c
9. a
10. d

**CHAPTER 8**
1. b
2. a
3. b
4. b
5. a
6. d
7. e
8. d
9. b

**CHAPTER 9**
1. d
2. c
3. e
4. b
5. a
6. b
7. a
8. c
9. a
10. b

**CHAPTER 10**
1. c
2. e
3. a
4. b
5. c
6. d
7. a
8. e
9. b
10. e

**CHAPTER 11**
1. b
2. a
3. c
4. a
5. b
6. b
7. e
8. b
9. d
10. d

**CHAPTER 12**
1. c
2. e
3. a
4. d
5. b
6. c
7. d
8. a
9. a
10. a

**CHAPTER 13**
1. e
2. c
3. a
4. e
5. a
6. c
7. d
8. b
9. b
10. d

**CHAPTER 14**
1. a
2. c
3. c
4. b
5. b
6. b
7. c
8. b
9. b
10. d

**CHAPTER 15**
1. c
2. b
3. e
4. a
5. b
6. d
7. a
8. d
9. a
10. d

# PRACTICE TESTS

**CHAPTER 16**
1. d
2. e
3. d
4. d
5. e
6. c
7. c
8. a
9. b
10. a

**CHAPTER 17**
1. b
2. b
3. e
4. d
5. b
6. c
7. c
8. a
9. a
10. a

**CHAPTER 18**
1. c
2. e
3. b
4. a
5. d
6. a
7. d
8. a
9. a
10. c

# GLOSSARY

**45° line** A line, drawn at a 45° angle, showing all points at which the distance to the horizontal axis equals the distance to the vertical axis. (Chapter 6)

## A

**Absolute advantage** A country's ability to produce a good using fewer resources than the country it trades with. (Chapters 2 and 16)

**Absolute income hypothesis** As national income increases, consumption spending increases, but by diminishing amounts. That is, as national income increases, the MPC decreases. (Chapter 6)

**Accelerator** The relationship between the level of investment and the change in the level of national income. (Chapter 9)

**Actual investment** Investment spending that producers actually make-that is, intended investment (investment spending that producers intend to undertake), plus or minus unintended changes in inventories. (Chapter 7)

**Administrative lag** The time interval between deciding on an appropriate policy and the execution of that policy. (Chapter 9)

**Aggregate demand** The total quantity of goods and services demanded by households, firms, foreigners, and government at varying price levels. (Chapter 4)

**Aggregate expenditure** Spending by consumers on consumption goods, spending by businesses on investment goods, spending by government, and spending by foreigners on net exports. (Chapter 7)

**Aggregate expenditure curve (AE)** A curve that shows the quantity of aggregate expenditures at different levels of national income or GDP. (Chapter 7)

**Aggregate supply** The total quantity of goods and services that firms in the economy are willing to supply at varying price levels. (Chapter 4)

**Appreciation** A rise in the price of a nation's currency relative to foreign currencies. (Chapter 17)

**Arbitrage** The practice of buying a foreign currency in one market at a low price and selling it in another at a higher price. (Chapter 17)

**Automatic stabilizers** Structures in the economy that tend to add to aggregate demand when the economy is in recession, and subtract from aggregate demand when the economy is inflationary. Unemployment insurance payments and benefits and the progressive income tax are two such automatic stabilizers. (Chapter 13)

**Autonomous consumption** Consumption spending that is independent of the level of income. (Chapter 6)

**Autonomous investment** Investment that is independent of the level of income. (Chapter 6)

## B

**Backward linkages** Investments in one industry that create demands for inputs, inducing investment in other industries to produce those inputs. (Chapter 18)

**Balance of payments** An itemized account of a nation's foreign economic transactions. (Chapter 17)

**Balance of trade** The difference between the value of a nation's merchandise exports and its merchandise imports. (Chapter 17)

**Balance on capital account** A category that itemizes changes in the foreign asset holdings of a nation and that nation's asset holdings abroad. (Chapter 17)

**Balance on current account** A category that itemizes a nation's imports and exports of goods and services, income receipts and payments on investment, and unilateral transfers. (Chapter 17)

**Balance sheet** The bank's statement of liabilities (what it owes) and assets (what it owns). (Chapter 11)

**Balanced budget multiplier** The effect on the equilibrium level of national income of an equal change in government spending and taxes. The balanced budget multiplier is 1. (Chapter 8)

**Balanced budget** Government spending equals tax revenues. (Chapter 8)

**Bank note** A promissory note, issued by a bank, pledging to redeem the note for a specific amount of gold or silver. The terms of redemption are specified on the note. (Chapter 12)

**Barter** The exchange of one good for another, without the use of money. (Chapter 10)

**Base year** The reference year with which prices in other years are compared in a price index. (Chapter 4)

**Big push** The development strategy that relies on an integrated network of government-sponsored and -financed investments introduced into the economy all at once. (Chapter 18)

**Budget deficit** Government spending exceeds tax revenues. (Chapter 8)

**Budget surplus** Tax revenues exceed government spending. (Chapter 8)

**Business cycle** Alternating periods of growth and decline in an economy's GDP. (Chapter 4)

## C

**Capital** Manufactured goods used to make and market other goods and services. (Chapter 2)

**Capital deepening** A rise in the ratio of capital to labor. (Chapter 9)

**Capital depreciation** The value of existing capital stock used up in the process of producing goods and services. (Chapter 5)

**Capital-labor ratio** The ratio of capital to labor, reflecting the quantity of capital used by each laborer in production. (Chapter 9)

**Capital-output ratio** The ratio of capital stock to GDP. (Chapter 9)

**Ceteris paribus** The Latin phrase meaning "everything else being equal." (Chapter 1)

**Change in demand** A change in quantity demanded of a good that is caused by factors other than a change in the price of that good. (Chapter 3)

**Change in quantity demanded** A change in the quantity demanded of a good that is caused solely by a change in the price of that good. (Chapter 3)

**Change in supply** A change in quantity supplied of a good that is caused by factors other than a change in the price of that good. (Chapter 3)

**Circular flow model** A model of how the economy's resources, money, goods, and services flow between households and firms through resource and product markets. (Chapter 1)

**Circular flow of goods, services, and resources** The movement of goods and services from firms to households, and of resources from households to firms. (Chapter 5)

**Circular flow of money** The movement of income in the form of resource payments from firms to households, and of income in the form of revenue from households to firms. (Chapter 5)

**Classical economics** The school of thought that emphasizes the natural tendency for an economy to move toward equilibrium at full employment without inflation. It argues against government intervention. (Chapter 13)

**Comparative advantage** A country's ability to produce a good at a lower opportunity cost than the country with which it trades. (Chapters 2 and 16)

**Complementary goods** Goods that are generally used together. When the price of one increases, the demand for the other decreases. (Chapter 3)

**Consumer price index (cpi)** A measure comparing the prices of consumer goods and services that a household typically purchases to the prices of those goods and services purchased in a base year. (Chapter 4)

**Consumer sovereignty** The ability of consumers to exercise complete control over what goods and services the economy produces (or doesn't produce) by choosing what goods and services to buy (or not buy). (Chapter 1)

**Consumption function** The relationship between consumption and income. (Chapter 6)

**Corporate income tax** A tax levied on a corporation's income before dividends are distributed to stockholders. (Chapter 15)

**Cost-push inflation** Inflation caused primarily by a decrease in aggregate supply. (Chapter 4)

**Countercyclical fiscal policy** Fiscal policy designed to moderate the severity of the business cycle. (Chapter 9)

**Countercyclical monetary policy** Policy directives used by the Fed to moderate swings in the business cycle. (Chapter 12)

**Crowding out** A fall in private investment spending caused by an increase in government spending. (Chapter 13)

**Currency** Coins and paper money. (Chapter 10)

**Customs duty** A sales tax applied to a foreign good or service. (Chapter 15)

**Customs union** A set of countries that agree to free trade among themselves and a common trade policy with all other countries. (Chapter 16)

**Cyclical unemployment** Unemployment associated with the downturn and recession phases of the business cycle. (Chapter 8)

## D

**Debt service** Interest payments on international debt as a percentage of a nation's merchandise exports. (Chapter 17)

**Demand curve** A curve that depicts the relationship between price and quantity demanded. (Chapter 3)

**Demand schedule** A schedule showing the specific quantity of a good or service that people are willing and able to buy at different prices. (Chapter 3)

**Demand-pull inflation** Inflation caused primarily by an increase in aggregate demand. (Chapter 4)

**Depreciation** A fall in the price of a nation's currency relative to foreign currencies. (Chapter 17)

**Depression** Severe recession. (Chapter 4)

**Devaluation** Government policy that lowers the nation's exchange rate; its currency instantly is worth less in the foreign exchange market. (Chapter 17)

**Discount rate** The interest rate the Fed charges banks that borrow reserves from it. (Chapter 12)

**Discouraged workers** Unemployed people who give up looking for work after experiencing persistent rejection in their attempts to find work. (Chapter 8)

**Disposable personal income** Personal income minus direct taxes. (Chapter 5)

**Downturn** A phase in the business cycle in which real GDP declines, inflation moderates, and unemployment emerges. (Chapter 4)

**Dumping** Exporting a good or service at a price below its cost of production. (Chapter 16)

**Durable goods** Goods expected to last at least a year. (Chapter 5)

# E

**Econometrics** The use of statistics to quantify and test economic models. (Chapter 1)

**Economic dualism** The coexistence of two separate and distinct economies within an ldc; one modern, primarily urban, and export-driven, the other traditional, agricultural, and self-sustaining. (Chapter 18)

**Economic efficiency** The maximum possible production of goods and services generated by the fullest employment of the economy's resources. (Chapter 2)

**Economic growth** An increase in real GDP, typically expressed as an annual rate of real GDP growth. (Chapter 9)

**Economic model** An abstraction of an economic reality. It can be expressed pictorially, graphically, algebraically, or in words. (Chapter 1)

**Economics** The study of how people work together to transform resources into goods and services to satisfy their most pressing wants, and how they distribute these goods and services among themselves. (Chapter 1)

**Entrepreneur** A person who alone assumes the risks and uncertainties of a business. (Chapter 2)

**Equation of exchange** $MV = PQ$. The quantity of money times its velocity equals the quantity of goods and services produced times their prices. (Chapter 10)

**Equilibrium level of national income** $C + I_i = C + S$, where saving equals intended investment. (Chapter 7)

**Equilibrium price** The price that equates quantity demanded to quantity supplied. If any disturbance from that price occurs, excess demand or excess supply emerges to drive price back to equilibrium. (Chapter 3)

**European Economic Community (EEC)** A customs union consisting of France, Italy, Belgium, Holland, Luxembourg, Germany, Britain, Ireland, Denmark, Greece, Spain, Portugal, Iceland, Finland, Sweden, and Austria. (Chapter 16)

**Excess demand** The difference, at a particular price, between quantity demanded and quantity supplied, quantity demanded being the greater. (Chapter 3)

**Excess reserves** The quantity of reserves held by a bank in excess of the legally required amount. (Chapter 11)

**Excess supply** The difference, at a particular price, between quantity supplied and quantity demanded, quantity supplied being the greater. (Chapter 3)

**Exchange controls** A system in which government, as the sole depository of foreign currencies, exercises complete control over how these currencies can be used. (Chapter 17)

**Exchange rate** The number of units of foreign currency that can be purchased with one unit of domestic currency. (Chapter 17)

**Excise tax** Any tax levied on a good or service, such as a unit tax, a sales tax, or a customs duty. (Chapter 15)

**Expenditure approach** A method of calculating GDP that adds all expenditures made for final goods and services by households, firms, and government. (Chapter 5)

**Exports** Goods and services produced by people in one country that are sold in other countries. (Chapter 16)

**External debt** Public debt held by foreigners. (Chapter 15)

# F

**Factor of production** Any resource used in a production process. Resources are grouped into labor, land, capital, and entrepreneurship. (Chapter 2)

**Federal Deposit Insurance Corporation (FDIC)** A government insurance agency that provides depositors in FDIC-participating banks 100 percent coverage on their first $100,000 of deposits. (Chapter 11)

**Federal funds market** The market in which banks lend and borrow reserves from each other for very short periods of time, usually overnight. (Chapter 12)

**Federal funds rate** The interest rate on loans made by banks in the federal funds market. (Chapter 12)

**Federal Open Market Committee** The Fed's principal decision-making body, charged with executing the Fed's open market operations. (Chapter 12)

**Federal Reserve System (the Fed)** The central bank of the United States. (Chapter 12)

**Fiat money** Paper money that is not backed by or convertible into any good. (Chapter 10)

**Final goods** Goods purchased for final use, not for resale. (Chapter 5)

**Financial intermediaries** Firms that accept deposits from savers and use those deposits to make loans to borrowers. (Chapter 11)

**Firm** An economic unit that produces goods and services in the expectation of selling them to households, other firms, or government. (Chapter 1)

**Fiscal policy** Government spending and taxation policy to achieve macroeconomic goals of full employment without inflation. (Chapter 8)

**Fixed exchange rate** A rate determined by government and then maintained through the process of buying and selling quantities of its own currency on the foreign exchange market. (Chapter 17)

**Floating exchange rate** An exchange rate determined strictly by the demands and supplies for a nation's currency. (Chapter 17)

**Food stamp program** An aid program that provides low-income people with stamps that can be redeemed for food and related items. (Chapter 14)

**Foreign exchange market** A market in which currencies of different nations are bought and sold. (Chapter 17)

**Foreign exchange reserves** The stock of foreign currencies a government holds. (Chapter 17)

**Forward linkages** Investments in one industry that create opportunities for profitable investments in other industries, using the goods produced in the first as inputs. (Chapter 18)

**Fractional reserve system** A banking system that provides people immediate access to their deposits but allows banks to hold only a fraction of those deposits in reserve. (Chapter 11)

**Free trade area** A set of countries that agree to free trade among themselves but are free to pursue independent trade policies with other countries. (Chapter 16)

**Free trade** International trade that is not encumbered by protectionist government policies such as tariffs and quotas. (Chapter 16)

**Frictional unemployment** Relatively brief periods of unemployment caused by people deciding to voluntarily quit work in order to seek more attractive employment. (Chapter 8)

**Full employment** An employment level at which the actual rate of employment in the economy is equal to the economy's natural rate of unemployment. (Chapter 8)

## G

**GATT (General Agreement on Tariffs and Trade)** A trade agreement to negotiate reductions in tariffs and other trade barriers and to provide equal and nondiscriminating treatment among members of the agreement. Around 100 countries are members of GATT. (Chapter 16)

**GDP deflator** A measure comparing the prices of all goods and services produced in the economy during a given year to the prices of those goods and services purchased in a base year. (Chapter 4)

**Government purchases** All goods and services bought by government. (Chapter 5)

**Gross domestic product (GDP)** Total value of all final goods and services, measured in current market prices, produced in the economy during a year. (Chapter 4)

**Gross national product (GNP)** The market value of all final goods and services in an economy produced by resources owned by people of that economy, regardless of where the resources are located. (Chapter 5)

**Gross private domestic investment** The purchase by firms of plant, equipment, and inventory goods. (Chapter 5)

## H

**Household** An economic unit of one or more persons, living under one roof, that has a source of income and uses it in whatever way it deems fit. (Chapter 1)

**Human capital** The investment in workers' health and knowledge, acquired through education, training, and/or experience that enhances their productivity. (Chapters 2 and 18)

# I

**Import controls** Tariffs and quotas used by government to limit a nation's imports. (Chapter 17)

**Imports** Goods and services bought by people in one country that are produced in other countries. (Chapter 16)

**Income approach** A method of calculating GDP that adds all the incomes earned in the production of final goods and services. (Chapter 5)

**Income multiplier** The multiple by which income changes as a result of a change in aggregate expenditure. (Chapter 7)

**Inflation** An increase in the price level. (Chapter 4)

**Inflationary gap** The amount by which aggregate expenditure exceeds the aggregate expenditure level needed to generate equilibrium national income at full employment without inflation. (Chapter 8)

**Infrastructure** The basic institutions and public facilities upon which an economy's development depends. (Chapter 18)

**Innovation** An idea that eventually takes the form of new, applied technology. (Chapter 2)

**Intended investment** Investment spending that producers intend to undertake. (Chapter 6)

**Intermediate goods** Goods used to produce other goods. (Chapter 5)

**International debt** The total amount of outstanding ious a nation is obligated to repay other nations and international organizations. (Chapter 17)

**International Monetary Fund (imf)** An international organization formed to make loans of foreign currencies to countries facing balance of payments problems. (Chapter 17)

**International specialization** The use of a country's resources to produce specific goods and services, allowing other countries to focus on the production of other goods and services. (Chapter 16)

**Inventory investment** Stocks of finished goods and raw materials that firms keep in reserve to facilitate production and sales. (Chapter 5)

**Invisible hand** Adam Smith's concept of the market, which, as if it were a hand, guides firms that seek only to satisfy their own self-interest to produce precisely those goods and services that consumers want. (Chapter 1)

# K

**Keynesian economics** The school of thought that emphasizes the possibility that an economy can be in equilibrium at less than full employment (or with inflation). It argues that with government intervention, equilibrium at full employment without inflation can be achieved by managing aggregate demand. (Chapter 13)

# L

**Labor force** People who are gainfully employed or actively seeking employment. (Chapter 8)

**Labor productivity** The quantity of GDP produced per worker, typically measured in quantity of GDP per hour of labor. (Chapter 9)

**Labor specialization** The division of labor into specialized activities that allow individuals to be more productive. (Chapter 2)

**Labor** The physical and intellectual effort of people engaged in producing goods and services. (Chapter 2)

**Land** A natural-state resource such as real estate, grasses and forests, and metals and minerals. (Chapter 2)

**Law of demand** The inverse relationship between price and quantity demanded of a good or service, ceteris paribus. (Chapter 3)

**Law of increasing costs** The opportunity cost of producing a good increases as more of the good is produced. The law is based on the fact that not all resources are suited to the production of all goods and that the order of use of a resource in producing a good goes from the most productive resource unit to the least. (Chapter 2)

**Legal reserve requirement** The percentage of demand deposits banks and other financial intermediaries are required to keep in cash reserves. (Chapter 11)

**Less-developed countries (ldcs)** The economies of Asia, Africa, and Latin America. (Chapter 18)

**Leveraged buyout** A primarily debt-financed purchase of all the stock or assets of a company. (Chapter 4)

**Life-cycle hypothesis** Typically, a person's mpc is relatively high during young adulthood, decreases during the middle-age years, and increases when the person is near or in retirement. (Chapter 6)

**Liquidity** The degree to which an asset can easily be exchanged for money. (Chapter 10)

**Long run** The time interval during which suppliers are able to change the quantity of all the resources they use to produce goods and services. (Chapter 3)

# M

**M1 money** The most immediate form of money. It includes currency, demand deposits, and traveler's checks. (Chapter 10)

**M2 money** M1 money plus less-immediate forms of money, such as savings accounts, money market mutual fund accounts, money market deposit accounts, repurchase agreements, and small-denomination time deposits. (Chapter 10)

**M3 money** M2 money plus large-denomination time deposits and large-denomination repurchase agreements. (Chapter 10)

**Macroeconomics** A subarea of economics that analyzes the behavior of the economy as a whole. (Chapter 1)

**Macroequilibrium** The level of real GDP and the price level that equate the aggregate quantity demanded and the aggregate quantity supplied. (Chapter 4)

**Margin requirement** The maximum percentage of the cost of a stock that can be borrowed from a bank or any other financial institution, with the stock offered as collateral. (Chapter 12)

**Marginal propensity to consume (MPC)** The ratio of the change in consumption spending to a given change in income. (Chapter 6)

**Marginal propensity to save (mps)** The change in saving induced by a change in income. (Chapter 6)

**Market demand** The sum of all individual demands in a market. (Chapter 3)

**Market-day supply** A market situation in which the quantity of a good supplied is fixed, regardless of price. (Chapter 3)

**Medicaid** A health care program administered through Social Security that is applicable to low-income and disabled people. (Chapter 14)

**Medicare** A health care program administered through Social Security that is applicable to everyone over 65 years old. (Chapter 14)

**Merit good** A good that market demand and supply do not produce enough of, in some people's opinion. (Chapter 14)

**Microeconomics** A subarea of economics that analyzes individuals as consumers and producers, and specific firms and industries. It focuses especially on the market behavior of firms and households. (Chapter 1)

**Money supply** Typically, M1 money. The supply of currency, demand deposits, and traveler's checks used in transactions. (Chapter 10)

**Money** Any commonly accepted good that acts as a medium of exchange, a measure of value, and a store of value. (Chapter 10)

# N

**National income** The sum of all payments made to resource owners for the use of their resources. (Chapter 5)

**Nationally chartered bank** A commercial bank that receives its charter from the comptroller of the currency and is subject to federal law as well as the laws of the state in which it operates. (Chapter 12)

**Natural rate of unemployment** The rate of unemployment caused by frictional plus structural unemployment in the economy. (Chapter 8)

**Natural resources** The lands, water, metals, minerals, animals, and other gifts of nature that are available for producing goods and services. (Chapter 1)

**Neo-Keynesian economics** The school of thought that emphasizes the possibility that an economy can be in equilibrium at less than full employment with inflation. It argues that by managing aggregate demand, government can achieve the most acceptable combination of unemployment and inflation. (Chapter 13)

**Net domestic product (NDP)** GDP minus capital depreciation. (Chapter 5)

**Net exports** An economy's exports to other economies, minus its imports from other economies. (Chapter 5)

**Nominal GDP** GDP measured in terms of current market prices-that is, the price level at the time of measurement. (It is not adjusted for inflation.)

**Non-accelerating inflation rate of unemployment (NAIRU)** Any rate equal to or higher than this rate will not cause the inflation rate to increase. Any rate lower than this rate will cause the inflation rate to increase. (Chapter 13)

**Nondurable goods** Goods expected to last less than a year. (Chapter 5)

**Normal good** A good whose demand increases or decreases when people's incomes increase or decrease. (Chapter 3)

**Normative economics** A subset of economics founded on value judgments and leading to assertions of what ought to be. (Chapter 1)

**North American Free Trade Agreement (NAFTA)** A free trade area consisting of Canada, the United States, and Mexico. (Chapter 16)

## O

**Open market operations** The buying and selling of government bonds by the Federal Open Market Committee. (Chapter 12)

**Opportunity cost** The quantity of other goods that must be given up to obtain a good. (Chapter 2)

## P

**Peak** The top of a business cycle. (Chapter 4)

**Permanent income** Permanent income is the regular income a person expects to earn annually. It may differ by some unexpected gain or loss from the actual income earned. (Chapter 6)

**Permanent income hypothesis** A person's consumption spending is related to his or her permanent income. (Chapter 6)

**Personal consumption expenditures** All goods and services bought by households. (Chapter 5)

**Personal income** National income, plus income received but not earned, minus income earned but not received. (Chapter 5)

**Phillips curve** A graph showing the inverse relationship between the economy's rate of unemployment and rate of inflation. (Chapter 13)

**Poll tax** A tax of a specific absolute sum levied on every person or every household. (Chapter 15)

**Positive economics** A subset of economics that analyzes the way the economy actually operates. (Chapter 1)

**Potential money multiplier** The increase in the money supply that is potentially generated by a change in demand deposits. (Chapter 11)

**Price level** A measure of prices in one year expressed in relation to prices in a base year. (Chapter 4)

**Production possibilities** The various combinations of goods that can be produced in an economy when it uses its available resources and technology efficiently. (Chapter 2)

**Progressive income tax** A tax whose rate varies directly with the income of the person taxed. Rich people pay a higher tax rate-a larger percentage of their income is taxed-than do poor people. (Chapter 15)

**Property tax** A tax levied on the value of physical assets such as land, or financial assets such as stock and bonds. (Chapter 15)

**Proportional income tax** A tax that is a fixed percentage of income, regardless of the level of income. (Chapter 15)

**Prosperity** A phase in the business cycle marked by a relatively high level of real GDP, full employment, and inflation. (Chapter 4)

**Public debt** The total value of government securities-Treasury bills, notes, and bonds-held by individuals, businesses, other government agencies, and the Federal Reserve. (Chapter 15)

**Public good** A good whose benefits are not diminished even when additional people consume it and whose benefits cannot be withheld from anyone. (Chapter 14)

## Q

**Quantity theory of money** $P = MV/Q$. The equation specifying the direct relationship between the money supply and prices. (Chapter 10)

**Quota** A limit on the quantity of a specific good that can be imported. (Chapter 16)

## R

**Rational expectations** The school of thought that emphasizes the impossibility of government reducing the economy's rate of unemployment by managing aggregate demand. It argues that because people anticipate the consequences of announced government policy and incorporate these anticipated consequences into their present decision making, they end up undermining the policy. (Chapter 13)

**Real GDP** GDP adjusted for changes in the price level. (Chapter 4)

**Recession** A phase in the business cycle in which the decline in the economy's real GDP persists for at least a half-year. A recession is marked by relatively high unemployment. (Chapter 4)

**Recessionary gap** The amount by which aggregate expenditure falls short of the level needed to generate equilibrium national income at full employment without inflation. (Chapter 8)

**Reciprocity** An agreement between countries in which trading privileges granted by one to the others are the same as those granted to it by the others. (Chapter 16)

**Recovery** A phase in the business cycle, following a recession, in which real GDP increases and unemployment declines. (Chapter 4)

**Regressive income tax** A tax whose impact varies inversely with the income of the person taxed. Poor people have a higher percentage of their income taxed than do rich people. (Chapter 15)

**Relative income hypothesis** As national income increases, consumption spending increases as well, always by the same amount. That is, as national income increases, mpc remains constant. (Chapter 6)

**Reserve requirement** The minimum amount of reserves the Fed requires a bank to hold, based on a percentage of the bank's total deposit liabilities. (Chapter 12)

# S

**Sales tax** A tax levied in the form of a specific percentage of the value of the good or service. (Chapter 15)

**Saving** That part of national income not spent on consumption. (Chapter 6)

**Savings bond** A nonmarketable Treasury bond that is the most commonly held form of public debt. (Chapter 15)

**Scarcity** The perpetual state of insufficiency of resources to satisfy people's unlimited wants. (Chapter 1)

**Services** Productive activities that are instantaneously consumed. (Chapter 5)

**Short run** The time interval during which suppliers are able to change the quantity of some but not all the resources they use to produce goods and services. (Chapter 3)

**Social Security** A social insurance program that provides benefits, subject to eligibility, to the elderly, the disabled, and their dependents. (Chapter 14)

**Stabilization policy** The use of countercyclical monetary and fiscal policy by the government and the Fed to stabilize the economy. (Chapter 13)

**Stagflation** A period of stagnating real GDP, inflation, and relatively high levels of unemployment. (Chapter 4)

**State-chartered bank** A commercial bank that receives its charter or license to function from a state government and is subject to the laws of that state. (Chapter 12)

**Structural unemployment** Unemployment that results from fundamental technological changes in production, or from the substitution of new goods for customary ones. (Chapter 8)

**Substitute goods** Goods that can replace each other. When the price of one increases, the demand for the other increases. (Chapter 3)

**Supply curve** A curve that depicts the relationship between price and quantity supplied. (Chapter 3)

**Supply schedule** A schedule showing the specific quantity of a good or service that suppliers are willing and able to provide at different prices. (Chapter 3)

**Supply-side economics** The school of thought that emphasizes the possibility of achieving full employment without inflation. It argues that through tax reductions, spending cuts, and deregulation, government creates the proper incentives for the private sector to increase aggregate supply. (Chapter 13)

# T

**Tariff** A tax on an imported good. (Chapter 16)

**Tax multiplier** The multiple by which the equilibrium level of national income changes when a dollar change in taxes occurs. The multiple depends upon the marginal propensity to consume. The equation for the tax multiplier is $-MPC/(1 - MPC)$. (Chapter 8)

**Terms of trade** The amount of a good or service (export) that must be given up to buy a unit of another good or service (import). A country's terms of trade are measured by the ratio of the country's export prices to its import prices. (Chapter 16)

**The paradox of thrift** The more people try to save, the more income falls, leaving them with no more and perhaps with even less saving. (Chapter 7)

**Transactions demand for money** The quantity of money demanded by households and businesses to transact their buying and selling of goods and services. (Chapter 10)

**Transfer payments** Income received but not earned. (Chapter 5)

**Transitory income** The unexpected gain or loss of income that a person experiences. It is the difference between a person's regular and actual income in any year. (Chapter 6)

**Trough** The bottom of a business cycle. (Chapter 4)

# U

**Underemployed resources** The less than full utilization of a resource's productive capabilities. (Chapter 2)

**Underemployed workers** Workers employed in jobs that do not utilize their productive talents or experience. (Chapter 8)

**Underground economy** The unreported or illegal production of goods and services in the economy that is not counted in GDP. (Chapter 5)

**Unemployment insurance** A program of income support for eligible workers who are temporarily unemployed. (Chapter 14)

**Unilateral transfers** Transfers of currency made by individuals, businesses, or government of one nation to individuals, businesses, or governments in other nations, with no designated return. (Chapter 17)

**Unit tax** A fixed tax in the form of cents or dollars per unit, levied on a good or service. (Chapter 15)

**Unwanted inventories** Goods produced for consumption that remain unsold. (Chapter 7)

# V

**Value added** The difference between the value of a good that a firm produces and the value of the goods the firm uses to produce it. (Chapter 5)

**Velocity of money** The average number of times per year each dollar is used to transact an exchange. (Chapter 10)

# W

**Welfare** Government-provided assistance-cash payments and goods and services-to the poor, the elderly, and the disabled. Eligibility is based principally on income and size of family. (Chapter 14)

# INDEX

## A

Absolute advantage, 38, 376–377
Accelerator, 211
Actual investment, 151
Administrative lag, 214, 215
Age
   consumption and, 130
   structural unemployment and, 173
Agency for International Development, 442–444
Aggregate demand, 83–89, 302–304
   defined, 83
   demand-pull inflation, 92–93
   depression of 1930s, 91–92
   full employment and, 94–95, 176–177
   inflation, government spending and full employment, 94–95
   interest rate, 85
   international trade effect, 87
   macroequilibrium, 89–90
   real wealth effect, 85
   recession and economic stagnation of early 1990s, 94
   shifts in, 88
   stagflation, 92, 93
Aggregate expenditure
   curve, 153, 154
   defined, 148
   income multiplier, 158–161
Aggregate supply, 83–89, 302–304
   defined, 83
   demand-pull inflation, 92–93
   depression of 1930s, 91–92
   employment, 83–85
   full employment and, 176–177
   macroequilibrium, 89–90
   shifts in, 89
   stagflation, 92, 93
Agnew, Spiro, 354
Agriculture, government spending on, 335
Aid to Families with Dependent Children (AFDC), 335, 337
Alesina, Alberto, 443
Algeria
   human capital and, 430
   income in, 427
   Internet access in, 436
Appreciation, floating exchange rate, 404–405
Arbitrage, 406
Argentina
   debt service of, 417
   hyperinflation in, 179
   Internet access in, 436
Australia
   art funding, 330
   long-run growth in real GDP, 205
   NAIRU for, 319
   public debt in, 358
   rate of taxation in, 350
Automatic stabilizers, 321–322
Autonomous consumption, 130
   in consumption equation, 133–134
   national income equilibrium calculation and, 158
Autonomous investment, 138

## B

Backward linkages, 439
Balanced budget, 186–188
   balanced budget multiplier, 188–189
   tax multiplier and, 186–187
Balanced Budget Act, 337
Balanced budget multiplier, 188–189
Balance of payments, 409–415
   balance on capital account, 413
   balance on current account, 410–412
   deficits on, 415–416
   deficits on current account, 415–416
   defined, 409
   problems of, 413–415
   trade imbalances, 415
   of U.S., in 1999, 410
Balance of trade, 410–411
   for U.S. in 1950–2000, 411
Balance on capital account, 413
Balance on current account, 410–412
   balance of trade, 410–411
   export of services, 411
   import of services, 412
   income payments on investments, 412
   income receipts on investments, 412
   merchandise exports, 410
   merchandise imports, 410
   unilateral transfers, 412
Balance sheet, 246
Bangladesh
   debt service of, 417
   terms of trade for, 380
Banking industry. *See also* Federal Reserve System
   audit and examinations, 256
   balance sheet, 246
   bank debacle of 1980s and 1990s, 256–259
   bank failures, 254, 256–259
   consolidated balance sheet of U.S. commercial bank, 286
   Continental Illinois Bank, 257, 259
   cyberbanking, 248
   deregulation, 259
   electronic, 248
   excess reserves, 251–252
   Federal Deposit Insurance Corporation, 255, 256
   Fed services for, 274–278
   financial intermediaries, 250
   First Bank of United States, 268
   fractional reserve system, 246
   growth of M2 money, 231
   inflation and, 178, 180
   Knickerbocker Trust disaster, 270
   legal reserve requirement, 247
   money creation by, 246–251
   National Bank Act, 269–270
   nationally chartered banks, 268, 271
   potential money multiplier, 251
   saving and loan debacle of 1980s and 1990s, 259–260
   Second Bank of the United States, 268–269
   state-chartered banks, 267–268, 271
Bank note, 267
Barro, Robert, 317
Barter, 223–224
Base year, 79–80
Belgium
   bank deposit insurance in, 258
   exports and imports of, 381
   long-run growth in real GDP, 205
   NAIRU for, 319
   public debt in, 358
   rate of taxation in, 350
Black market, 116
Blinder, Alan, 315
Bolivia
   hyperinflation in, 179
   Internet access in, 436
Bonds
   savings, 361
   treasury, 280, 356
Boskin, Michael, 299
Botswana
   human capital and, 430
   income in, 427
Brazil
   bank debacle of 1980s and 1990s, 256–257
   debt service of, 417
   devaluation, 408, 409
   human capital and, 430
   hyperinflation in, 179
   income in, 427
   Internet access in, 436
Budget deficit, 189, 318. *See also* Public debt
Budget Deficit Reduction Act, 364
   Clinton era, 364
   deficits on current account, 416
   Gramm-Rudman-Hollings Act, 364
   Keynesian economics, 185
   recession and economic stagnation of early 1990s, 93
   size of, in 1970–2000, 355
   tax reforms of 1981 and 1986, 363

I-1

# INDEX

Budget Deficit Reduction Act, 364
Budget surplus, 190
   size of, in 1970–2000, 355
Bureau of Labor Statistics (BLS), definition of unemployment, 175
Burns, Arthur, 273
Burundi, terms of trade for, 379, 380
Bush, George H. W., 299
Bush, George W., 272, 291
Business cycle
   accelerator-multiplier theory of, 211
   countercyclical fiscal policy, 213–215
   defined, 76
   economic growth, 77
   external theories of, 207–210
   housing cycle and, 209–210
   innovation cycle, 210
   internal theories of, 210–211
   phases of, 76–77
   in real business cycle theory, 212–213
   sunspot theory of, 207
   theories of, 207–211
   in U.S. during 1860–1990, 206
   war-induced cycle theory, 208–209

## C

Cameroon
   human capital and, 430
   income in, 427
Canada
   art funding, 330
   bank deposit insurance in, 258
   exports and imports of, 381
   GDP for, 111
   government spending in, 341
   income multiplier and, 161
   Internet access in, 436
   long-run economic growth in, 199
   long-run growth in real GDP, 205
   NAIRU for, 319
   North American Free Trade Agreement, 392
   public debt in, 358
   real GDP, 87
   Social Security expenditures in, 340
   tax rate, 350
   trade with U.S., 381–383
*Cannery Row* (Steinbeck), 174
Capacity utilization, autonomous investment and, 140
Capital
   defined, 25
   as factors of production, 26
   human capital, 26
   role in economic growth, 200–201, 203
Capital deepening, 200–201, 203
Capital depreciation, 112
Capital-labor ratio, 200
Capital-output ratio, 201
Capone, Al, 354–355
Cardoso, Fernando Henrique, 408
Carroll, Christopher, 136
Carter, Jimmy, 5, 272, 299
Cave, Damien, 291
Central African Republic, terms of trade for, 379

Ceteris paribus, 8
Change in demand, 53–57
   vs. change in quantity demanded, 56–57
   expectation of future prices, 56
   income and, 54
   population size change, 56
   substitute goods, 55–56
   taste, 54–55
Change in quantity demanded, vs. change in demand, 56–57
Change in supply
   defined, 57
   number of suppliers of, 58
   resource prices and, 58
   substitute goods and, 58
   technology and, 57–58
Checks, 228, 229
   sequence of, to clear, 275
Chenery, Hollis, 161
China
   population policy in, 431
   taxation in, 359
   trade with U.S., 381
Circular flow model, 8–11
   invisible hand, 11
Circular flow of goods, services and resources, 100–101, 106–107
Circular flow of money, 100–102
Classical economics, 300–302
   countercyclical policy, 301–302
   demand for money, 238, 240
   employment, 300–301
   Federal Reserve System, 301–302
   inflation, 301–302
   minimum wage, 301
   quantity theory of money, 235–237
   stabilization policy, 301
   unemployment, 300–301
   unions, 301
   wage rate, 300–301
Clemenceau, Georges, 260
Clinton, Bill, 299, 364
Coal, 4
*Coal Question, The* (Jevons), 4
Colombia, terms of trade for, 379
Comparative advantage, 38, 376–377
Complementary goods, 56
   change in demand and, 56
Consumer price index, 79–81
   base year in, 79–80
   calculating, 80
   defined, 79
   items in basket of goods, 79, 81
Consumer sovereignty, 6
Consumption, 122–137
   absolute income hypothesis, 123–125
   autonomous consumption spending, 130
   consumption function, 123
   induced, 133
   interaction between consumers and producers, 148
   life-cycle hypothesis of, 128, 130
   marginal propensity to consume (MPC), 124–125
   permanent income hypothesis, 128–129
   public debt and overconsumption, 361
   relative income hypothesis, 125–128

   role of, in national income equilibrium, 149–155
   shifts in consumption curve, 130–131
Consumption function, 123
Continental Illinois Bank, 257, 259
Continental notes, 267
Corporate income tax, 349–350
   as automatic stabilizer, 321–322
   revenues from, 353
Corporations, profit as income in GDP, 109
Cost
   law of increasing costs, 28–31
   opportunity, 27–28
Cost-of-living adjustment (COLA), 180
Cost-push inflation, 93
Countercyclical fiscal policy, 213–215, 307
   administrative lag, 214, 215
   classical economics, 301–302
   Keynesian economics, 305
   neo-Keynesian economics, 308
   Phillips curve, 308
   rational expectations economics, 313–316
   stabilization policy, 301
   supply-side economics, 316–320
Countercyclical monetary policy, 290–293
   controlling interest rates, 284–287
   money supply, 278–284, 287
Credit cards, 230–231
Crowding out, 319–320
   public debt, 361–362
Currency, 227. *See also* Money
Curves, 19–23
   demand, 45
   hill-shaped, 22
   horizontal, 22–23
   income, 135–137
   Laffer, 318
   Phillips curve, 315–311
   slope of, 20–22
   slope of tangent, 23
   supply, 47
   u-shaped, 22
   vertical, 22–23
Customs duty, 351
Customs unions, 391
Cyberbanking, 248
Cyclical unemployment, 173

## D

Debt. *See also* Public debt
   international, 416–419
Debt service, 417
DeLong, Bradford, 314
Demand
   aggregate, 83–89
   changes in, 45, 53–57
   complementary goods, 56
   equilibrium price, 58–60
   excess, 49
   expectations about future prices, 56
   income changes and, 54
   law of, 45
   measuring consumer demand, 45–46
   measuring individual demand, 45–46

measuring market demand, 46–47
for money, 238–240
population size change and, 56
Say's law, 183
substitute goods and price, 55–56
taste changes, 54–55
Demand curve, 45
Demand deposits, 228
Demand-pull inflation, 92–93
Demand schedule, 45
Democratic Republic of Congo
human capital and, 430
income in, 427
Denmark
GDP for, 111
long-run growth in real GDP, 205
NAIRU for, 319
rate of taxation in, 350
Dependent variable, 19
Depository Institutions Deregulation and Monetary Control Act, 279
Depreciation, floating exchange rate and, 404–405
Depression
defined, 75, 76
of 1930s, 91–92, 127, 183, 304
Devaluation, 408, 409
Discount rate, 274
money supply and, 279–282
Discouraged workers, 173
Disposable personal income, 114
Dissaving, 134
Dog market, 67–69
Downturn of business cycle, 76–77
Duesenberry, James, 125–128
Dumping, antidumping argument against free trade, 385–386
Durable goods, 104

## E

Econometrics, 13
Economic dualism, 430–432
Economic efficiency, 36
production possibilities, 36
Economic growth
business cycle and, 77
capital deepening, 200–201, 203
causes of, 200
creating environment for, 197–200
defined, 200
labor productivity, 200–201, 203
long-run, 197–206
markets and, 198–199
political uncertainty and, 197–199
saving's role in, 201–204
simple model of, 200–204
technology's role in, 204
in U.S. during 1900–2000, 197, 204, 206
Economic model
ceteris paribus, 8
circular flow model, 8–11
defined, 7–8
economic forecasting, 12–13
purpose of, 7–8
Economic Recovery Tax Act, 363

Economics. See also specific schools of economic thought
defined, 6
economic forecasting, 12–13
macroeconomics, 10
microeconomics, 10
normative, 12
as part of social sciences, 6–7
positive, 12
Education
government spending on, 333
in LDC, 430
Egypt
debt service of, 417
Internet access in, 436
Eisenhower, Dwight D., 30, 272
Employment. See also Labor; Unemployment
aggregate supply and, 83–85
classical economics, 300–301
full employment, 176–177
inflationary gap and full employment, 182
inflation, government spending and full employment, 94–95
Keynesian economics, 302–304
North American Free Trade Agreement, 394
recessionary gap and full employment, 181–182
stagflation, 305
Entrepreneurs. See also Sole proprietorship
as defined, 26
as factors of production, 26
Environment. See also Pollution
damage to, and GDP, 117
Equation of exchange, 234–238
Equilibrium level of national income. See National income equilibrium
Equilibrium price, 48–50
defined, 49
demand, 58–60
as rationing mechanism, 60–62
supply, 58–60
Ethiopia
human capital and, 430
income in, 427
terms of trade for, 379, 380
vicious circle of poverty in, 428–429
Euro, 414
European Economic Community (EEC), 391
European Union, 414
Excess demand, 49
Excess reserves, 251–252
Excess supply, 48
Exchange controls, 409
Exchange rate. See also Foreign exchange market
arbitrage, 406
defined, 401
devaluation, 409
fixed exchange rate, 406–409
floating exchange rate, 404–406
Excise tax, 351
revenues from, 353
Expenditure approach to calculating GDP, 101–108

Exports. See also International trade
balance of trade, 410–411
defined, 378
for less-developed countries (LDC), 380
of major developed economies, 381
merchandise exports, 410
net, 103, 108
of services, 411
trade imbalances, 415
External debt, 362–363

## F

Factor of production, 25–26
Federal budget. See Budget deficit; Fiscal policy; Government spending; Public debt
Federal deficit. See Budget deficit
Federal Deposit Insurance Corporation (FDIC), 255, 256
Federal funds market, 281
Federal funds rate, 282
Federal Open Market Committee (FOMC), 273
open market operations, 282–284
Federal Reserve Act, 266, 270
Federal Reserve System, 227, 261, 270–293
balance sheet of, 286
as bankers' bank, 274–278
classical economics, 301–302
controlling interest rate, 284–287
controlling money supply, 278–284, 287
controlling stock market margin requirements, 287–290
countercyclical monetary policy, 279, 290–293
defined, 270
description of, 270–271
discount rate, 274, 279–282
Federal Open Market Committee, 273
geography of, 271
historical perspective on creation of, 266–270
inflation, 281, 287, 292, 301–302
as money printer, 273
moral suasion, 290
open market operations, 282–284
purpose and organization of, 272–273
recession, 279, 292
reserve requirement, 279
Federal Savings and Loan Insurance Corporation (FSLIC), 260
Feldstein, Martin, 299
Fiat money, 227
Final goods, 103
Financial Institutions Reform, Recovery and Enforcement Act, 260
Financial intermediaries, 250
Finland
art funding, 330
bank deposit insurance in, 258
Firm
in circular flow model, 8–11
defined, 8
gross private domestic investment, 103, 107–108
invisible hand, 11

Fiscal policy, 186–191. *See also* Countercyclical fiscal policy; Government spending
  balanced budget, 186–188
  balanced budget multiplier, 188–189
  budget deficit, 189
  budget surplus, 190
  countercyclical fiscal policy, 213–215
  defined, 186
  tax multiplier, 187
Fixed exchange rate, 406–409
Floating exchange rate
  appreciation, 404–405
  depreciation, 404–405
  problems with, 406
Food for Peace, 443
Food stamps, government spending on, 337
Foreign economic aid, 442–444
Foreign exchange market, 401–409. *See also* Balance of payments
  appreciation, 404–405
  arbitrage, 406
  depreciation, 404–405
  devaluation, 408, 409
  exchange controls, 409
  fixed exchange rate, 406–409
  floating exchange rate, 404–406
  foreign exchange reserves, 407, 409
  import controls, 409
  income changes and, 402–403
  interest rate changes and, 403
  taste changes and, 403
Foreign exchange reserves, 407, 409
45° line, 135–137
Forward linkages, 439
Fractional reserve system, 246
France
  art funding, 330
  bank deposit insurance in, 258
  Disneyland Paris, 382
  exports and imports of, 381
  GDP for, 111
  government spending in, 341
  Internet access in, 436
  long-run growth in real GDP, 205
  NAIRU for, 319
  public debt in, 358
  real GDP, 87
  Social Security expenditures in, 340
  taxation in, 350, 359
  trade with U.S., 381
Franklin, Benjamin, 166
Free trade. *See also* International trade
  antidumping argument against, 385–386
  cheap foreign labor argument, 385
  customs unions, 391
  defined, 373
  diversity-of-industry argument against, 385
  effect on price, 377–378
  free trade areas, 392
  infant industries argument against, 384
  national security argument against, 384
  quotas, 387–388
  retaliation argument against, 386
  tariffs, 386–387

Free trade areas, 392
Frictional unemployment, 172
Friedman, Milton, 128–129
Full employment, 176–177
  inflationary gap, 182
  recessionary gap, 181–182
Full Employment Act, 304
Full Employment and Balanced Growth Act, 308–309

## G

GATT (General Agreement on Tariffs and Trade), 389, 391
  Less-developed countries (LCD), 389, 391
GDP. *See* Gross domestic product (GDP)
GDP deflator, 80, 82
General Motors, 165
*General Theory of Employment, Interest and Money, The* (Keynes), 123, 127
Germany
  art funding, 330
  bank deposit insurance in, 258
  exports and imports of, 381
  GDP for, 111
  government spending in, 341
  hyperinflation in, 179
  NAIRU for, 319
  public debt in, 358
  Social Security expenditures in, 340
  taxation in, 350, 360
  trade with U.S., 381
Ghana
  debt service of, 417
  human capital and, 430
  income in, 427
Gold
  gold-backed paper as money, 225–226
  as money, 225
Goods. *See also* Capital
  in circular flow of goods, services and resources, 100–101, 106–107
  complementary, 56
  durable, 104
  final, 103
  government purchases, 103, 108
  gross private domestic investment, 103, 107–108
  intermediate, 25, 103
  merit, 329
  net exports of, 103, 108
  nondurable, 105–106
  normal, 54
  personal consumption expenditures, 103–107
  public, 327–328
  substitute, 55
  value added, 103
Gottheil, Irving, 150
Government purchases, 103, 108
Government spending, 327–342. *See also* Fiscal policy
  aggregate demand, full employment, inflation, 94–95
  on agriculture, 335
  amount of, 331, 332

  on arts, 330
  balanced budget, 186–188
  balanced budget multiplier, 188–189
  budget deficit, 185, 189
  budget surplus, 190
  crowding out, 319–320
  education, 333
  financing through treasury securities, 355–356
  growth of, 340–341
  interest, 340
  Medicare, 339–340
  merit goods, 329
  on national security, 331–333
  on natural resources, 334
  public assistance, 335–337
  public good, 328–329
  recessionary gap and, 184–185
  resource allocation and, 342
  Social Security, 337–339
  on space exploration, 334
  supply-side economics, 319–320
  tax multiplier, 187
  total amount of, 340–341
  transfer payments, 329–331
  on transportation, 334
  unemployment insurance, 339
  on welfare, 335–337
Gramm, Phil, 364
Gramm-Rudman-Hollings Act, 364
Graphs
  curves in, 19–23
  graphing relationships, 18–19
  measuring distances on, 18
  origin in, 17–18
  variables, 18–19
Great Britain. *See also* United Kingdom
  exports and imports of, 381
  trade with U.S., 381
Great Depression, 91–92, 127, 183, 304
Greece, long-run growth in real GDP, 205
Greenspan, Alan, 272, 287, 291, 312
Gresham's law, 226
Gresham, Thomas, 226
Gross domestic product (GDP)
  adjusting for prices, 79–80
  aggregate demand and aggregate supply model, 82–89
  capital-output ratio, 201
  composition of U.S., in 1960–2000, 111
  cost of environmental damage, 117
  cost-push inflation, 93
  defined, 78
  demand-pull inflation, 92–93
  depression of 1930s, 91–92
  18th and 19th centuries view of, 105
  exclusions from, 114–118
  expenditure approach to calculating, 101–108
  full employment, inflation and government spending, 94–95
  GDP deflator, 80, 82
  gross national product, 110, 112
  housework, 114–115
  income approach to calculating, 108–110
  leisure, 115
  macroequilibrium, 89–90

national income, 110–113
net domestic product, 112
nominal, 79, 80, 82, 86–87
personal income and personal
    disposable income, 113–114
real, 79, 80, 82, 86–87
recession and economic stagnation of
    early 1990s, 93–94
for 2000, 113
underground economy, 115
Gross national product (GNP), 110, 112
defined, 110
for 2000, 113
Gross private domestic investment, 103, 107–108
Guatemala, terms of trade for, 380
Gutmann, Peter, 115

# H

Haiti, debt service of, 417
Hamilton, Alexander, 268
Helfer, Ricki, 255
Hill-shaped curve, 22
Hobbes, Thomas, 197
Hollings, Ernest, 364
Household
    in circular flow model, 8–11
    defined, 8
    invisible hand, 11
Housework, gross domestic product (GDP), 114–115
Housing market, business cycle and, 209–210
Hubbard, Robert, 213, 215
Human capital, 26, 429–430
Hume, David, 417
Humphrey-Hawkins Act, 308–309, 312
Hungary
    bank deposit insurance in, 258
    hyperinflation in, 179

# I

Import controls, 409
Imports. *See also* International trade
    balance of trade, 410–411
    defined, 378
    import controls, 409
    for less-developed countries (LDC), 380
    of major developed economies, 381
    merchandise imports, 410
    of services, 412
    trade imbalances, 415
Income. *See also* National income
    absolute income hypothesis, 123–125
    change in demand, 54
    consumption function, 123
    disposable personal income, 114
    inflation and fixed income, 178
    in LDC, 427–429
    national, 109–110
    permanent income hypothesis, 128–129
    personal, 113–114
    relative income hypothesis, 125–128
    transfer payments, 114

Income approach to calculating GDP, 108–110
Income curves, 135–137
Income multiplier, 158–163
    accelerator-multiplier theory of business cycle, 211
    marginal propensity to consume, 158–160
    price, 162–163
Income tax. *See also* Taxation
    corporate income tax, 349–350
    progressive income tax, 349
    proportional income tax, 348–349
    regressive income tax, 348
    revenues from, 353
    tax structure, 352–353
Independent variable, 19
India
    bank deposit insurance in, 258
    Internet access in, 436
Inflation, 177–182
    automatic stabilizers, 321–322
    banking, 178, 180
    in business cycle, 76
    classical economics, 301–302
    cost-push inflation, 93
    defined, 76
    demand-pull inflation, 92–93
    Fed policy and, 281, 287, 292, 301–302
    fixed incomes and, 178
    full employment and government spending, 94–95
    gainers from, 178–180
    hyperinflation, 179–180
    Keynesian economics, 304–305
    losers from, 178
    margin requirement, 290
    neo-Keynesian economics, 305–311
    non-accelerating inflation rate of unemployment, 315–316
    Phillips curve, 305–311
    public debt, 361
    saving, 178
    stagflation, 305
    taxation, 180
Inflationary gap
    closing, 182, 184–186
    defined, 182
Infrastructure
    absence of, in LDC, 434–436
    Internet as, 435–436
Innovation
    business cycle and, 210
    defined, 33
    product possibilities, 33–34
    in real business cycle theory, 212–213
Intended investment, 137
Interest
    government spending on, 340
    as income in GDP, 109
Interest rate
    aggregate demand, 85
    changes in, and foreign exchange market, 403
    consumption curve shifts and, 131
    deficits on current account, 416
    discount rate, 274, 279–282
    Fed controlling, 284–287

federal funds rate, 282
investment, 138–139
money supply, 284–286
Intermediate goods, 25, 103
Internal Revenue Service, 354–355
International debt, 416–419
    forgiving international debt of LDCs, 418–419
International Monetary Fund (IMF), 408
    creation of, 409
    forgiving international debt of LDCs, 418–419
    role of, 408, 409
International specialization, 375–376
International trade. *See also* Free trade
    absolute advantage, 376–377
    aggregate demand and, 87
    balance of payments, 409–415
    benefits of, 375–376
    comparative advantage, 376–377
    customs unions, 391
    effect on price, 377–378
    free trade areas, 392
    GATT (General Agreement on Tariffs and Trade), 389, 391
    international specialization, 375–376
    major trading partners with U.S., 381, 383
    need for protection against free trade, 383–386
    quotas, 387–388
    tariffs, 386–387
    terms of trade, 378–380
    tracking, 380–381
    trade barriers in Japan, 390–391
    trade imbalances, 415
Internet
    access to, in LDC, 435–436
    cyberbanking, 248
Interstate trade, 373–375
Intrastate trade, 372–373
Inventory investment, 108
Investment, 137–141. *See also* Saving
    actual, 151
    autonomous investment, 138
    determinants of, 137–140
    intended investment, 137
    interest rate, 138–139
    role of, in national income equilibrium, 149–158
    technology and, 138
    volatile nature of, 140–141
Invisible hand, 10, 11
Ireland
    art funding, 330
    bank deposit insurance in, 258
    long-run growth in real GDP, 205
Israel, Internet access in, 436
Italy
    bank deposit insurance in, 258
    exports and imports of, 381
    GDP for, 111
    government spending in, 341
    income multiplier and, 161
    long-run growth in real GDP, 205
    NAIRU for, 319
    public debt in, 358
    Social Security expenditures in, 340

I-5

Italy *(continued)*
    tax rate, 350
    trade with U.S., 381
Ivory Coast
    human capital and, 430
    income in, 427

## J

Jackson, Andrew, 269
Jamaica, terms of trade for, 379
Japan
    bank deposit insurance in, 258
    exports and imports of, 381
    GDP for, 111
    government spending in, 341
    long-run growth in real GDP, 205
    NAIRU for, 319
    public debt in, 358
    real GDP, 86
    rebuilding after WWII, 34
    Social Security expenditures in, 340
    tax rate, 350
    trade barriers in, 390–391
    trade with U.S., 381
Jefferson, Thomas, 267, 268
Jevons, William Stanley, 207
Johnson, Lyndon B., 272

## K

Kellner, Irwin, 185
Kemp-Roth Act, 363
Kemp-Roth tax cut, 318
Kennedy, J. F., 272
Kenya
    human capital and, 430
    improvements in farming, 440
    income in, 427
    Internet access in, 436
Keynesian economics, 302–305
    absolute income hypothesis, 123–125
    aggregate demand and aggregate supply, 302–304
    budget deficit, 185
    countercyclical policy, 305
    demand for money, 238
    employment, 302–304
    inflation, 304–305, 305
    quantity theory of money, 237–238
    recession, 305
    Say's law, 183
    stabilization policy, 305
    unemployment, 302–304
Keynes, John Maynard, 123–125, 127, 147, 183, 185, 289
Klein, Lawrence, 305
Knickerbocker Trust disaster, 270
Korea
    exports and imports of, 381
    trade with U.S., 381
Korean War, economic upturn and, 209
Krugman, Paul, 312
Kuznets cycle, 209–210
Kuznets, Simon, 125, 209–210

## L

Labor. *See also* Employment; Unions; Wage rate
    cheap foreign labor argument against free trade, 385
    defined, 25
    as factors of production, 25
    North American Free Trade Agreement, 394
    role in economic growth, 200–201, 203
    technology and, 200, 204
Labor productivity, 200–201, 203
Labor specialization, 36–39
    absolute advantage, 38
    benefit of, 36–37
    comparative advantage, 38
    defined, 36
Labor union. *See* Unions
Laffer curve, 318
Land
    defined, 26
    as factors of production, 26
Law of demand, 45
Law of increasing costs, 28–31
Legal reserve requirement, 247
Legislation, typical path of bill, 214
Leisure, in gross domestic product (GDP), 115
Less-developed countries (LDC)
    absence of infrastructure, 434–436
    big push strategy of development, 437–438
    defined, 426
    economic dualism, 430–432
    education, 430
    exports and imports for, 380
    Food for Peace, 443
    foreign direct investment, 441–442
    foreign economic aid, 442–444
    forgiving international debt of, 418–419
    GATT (General Agreement on Tariffs and Trade), 389, 391
    human capital and, 429–430
    Internet and, 435–436
    life expectancy in, 429, 430
    nonscientific perceptions, 433–434
    per capita incomes in, 427–429
    political instability of, 433
    population growth in, 428
    terms of trade for, 378–380
    unbalanced development strategy, 438–441
Leverage buyout, 93
Life-cycle hypothesis, 128, 130
Liquidity
    defined, 227
    money and, 227–230
Long run
    defined, 51
    supply, 50–53
Lucas, Robert, 317

## M

Macroeconomics, 10, 13
Macroequilibrium, 89–90
Madison, James, 268
Malthus, Thomas, 198
Marginal propensity to consume (MPC), 124–125
    in consumption equation, 133–134
    income multiplier, 158–160
    national income equilibrium calculation and, 158
    tax multiplier, 187
Marginal propensity to save (MPS), 134
Margin requirement
    Fed controlling, 287–290
    inflation, 290
    recession, 290
Market-day supply, 47, 53
Market demand, 46–47
Markets, economic growth and, 198–199
Marshall, Alfred, 136, 147
Martin, William McChesney, 272
Medicaid, 335
    government spending on, 337
    Medicare
    government spending, 339–340
    return options for, 338
Merchandise exports, 410
Merchandise imports, 410
Merit goods, government spending, 329
Mexico
    bank debacle of 1980s and 1990s, 256–257
    bank deposit insurance in, 258
    North American Free Trade Agreement, 392
    real GDP, 87
    trade with U.S., 381
Microeconomics, 10, 13
Military spending, production possibilities, 30, 39
Minimum wage, classical economics, 301
M1 money, 228
M2 money, 228–229
    growth of, 231
M3 money, 230
Modigliani, Franco, 130
Monetarist economics
    demand for money, 240
    quantity theory of money, 237
Money. *See also* Banking industry; Federal Reserve System; Foreign exchange market
    circular flow of, 100–102
    continental notes, 267
    credit cards, 230–231
    defined, 224
    demand for, 238–240
    early U.S., 224–225, 267
    equation of exchange, 234–238
    Fed controlling, 278–284, 287
    fiat, 227
    function of, 225
    gold as, 225
    gold-backed paper, 225–226
    Gresham's law, 226
    growth of money supply, 231, 233
    liquidity of, 227–230
    money creation by banks, 246–251
    money supply, 228–230

near money, 230
paper, 227
potential money multiplier, 251
precautionary demand motive, 239
prerequisites of, 224, 225
printing, 273
quantity theory of, 232–238
real GDP and, 239–240
speculative demand motive, 239
strength/weakness of dollar, 404–405
transactions demand for money, 238–240
U.S. supply of, 231–232
velocity of, 232–235
Money market deposit account, 231
Money market mutual funds, 231
Money supply, 228–232
   Fed controlling, 278–284, 287
   growth of, 231, 233
   interest rate, 284–286
   liquidity character of, 228
   open market operations, 282–284
   in U.S., 231–232
Mongolia
   human capital and, 430
   income in, 427
Monopoly, dumping, 385–386
Moral suasion, Federal Reserve System, 290
Morocco, Internet access in, 436
Myanmar, debt service of, 417

## N

National Bureau of Economic Research, 443
National income, 109–110. *See also* National income equilibrium
   calculating, 109–110
   in consumption equation, 133–134
   gross domestic product (GDP), 110–113
   importance of, 113
   investment level and, 137–139
   nation's marginal propensity to consume, 125, 126
   personal income and personal disposable income, 113–114
   relative income hypothesis, 125–128
   for 2000, 113
*National Income and Its Composition* (Kuznets), 125
National income equilibrium, 148–166
   aggregate expenditure curve, 153, 154
   alternative method of calculating, 158
   balanced budget multiplier, 188–189
   changes in investment and, 155–158
   examples of economy moving toward, 149–153
   full employment and, 181–186
   income multiplier, 158–163
   paradox of thrift, 164, 166
   tax multiplier, 187
Nationally chartered banks, 271
National poverty, 426–430. *See also* Less-developed countries (LDC)

National security
   arguments against free trade, 384
   government spending on, 331–333
Natural rate of unemployment, 175–176, 312
Natural resources, 3–6
   coal supply and, 4
   defined, 3
   government spending on, 334
   land, 26
   nonrenewable, 3–5
   renewable, 3–5
Near money, 230
Neo-Keynesian economics, 305–311
   countercyclical policy, 308
   inflation, 305–311
   Phillips curve, 305–311
   unemployment, 305–311
   unions, 307
   wage and price control, 308
Net domestic product (NDP), 112
Net exports of goods and services, 103, 108
Netherlands
   art funding, 330
   bank deposit insurance in, 258
   exports and imports of, 381
   GDP for, 111
   long-run growth in real GDP, 205
   NAIRU for, 319
   public debt in, 358
   real GDP, 87
   Social Security expenditures in, 340
   tax rate, 350
   trade with U.S., 381
New Deal, 304
Nicaragua, Internet access in, 436
Nigeria, terms of trade for, 379, 380
Nixon, R., 272
Nixon, Richard, 308, 311
Nominal GDP, 79, 80, 82, 86–87
Non-accelerating inflation rate of unemployment (NAIRU), 315–316, 319
Nondurable goods, 105–106
Nonrenewable natural resources, 3–5
Normal good, 54
Normative economics, 12
North American Free Trade Agreement, 392
   labor and, 394
Norway
   bank deposit insurance in, 258
   tax rate, 350

## O

Oil industry
   bank debacle of 1980s and 1990s, 256–257
   supply of oil, 5
Okun, Arthur, 305
*On the Progress of Wealth* (Malthus), 198
OPEC (Organization of Petroleum Exporting Countries)
   income multiplier and, 161
   stagflation and, 92, 93, 307–308

Open market operations, 282–284
Opportunity cost
   coin on sidewalk, 29
   comparative advantage, 376–377
   defined, 27
   law of increasing costs, 28–31
   production possibilities, 27–28
   taxes and, 347
Organ transplant market, 69–71
Origin, on graph, 17–18

## P

Pakistan
   Internet access in, 436
   terms of trade for, 379
Paradox of thrift, 164, 166
Paraguay, debt service of, 417
Peak of business cycle, 76–77
Permanent income, 128
Permanent income hypothesis, 128–129
Personal consumption expenditures, 103–107
Personal income, 113–114
Personal income tax, as automatic stabilizer, 321–322
Personal Responsibility and Work Opportunity Reconciliation Act, 335–337
Peru
   hyperinflation in, 179
   Internet access in, 436
Philippines, bank deposit insurance in, 258
Phillips, A. W., 305
Phillips curve, 305–311, 314
   countercyclical policy, 308
   long run, 309–311
   supply shocks, 307–308
   unions, 307
Poll tax, 348
Pollution
   GDP and, 117
   North American Free Trade Agreement, 392
Population
   controlling in China, 431
   growth of, in LDC, 428
Positive economics, 12
Potential money multiplier, 251
Poverty
   national, 426–430
   production possibilities, 32–33
   vicious circle of, 33, 428–429
Price
   changes in demand and, 53–57
   changes in supply and, 57–58
   consumption curve shifts and, 131
   equilibrium, 48–50, 58–60
   excess demand, 49
   excess supply, 48
   income multiplier, 162–163
   international trade and, 377–378
   long-run supply, 50–53
   market-day supply, 50–53

I-7

Price *(continued)*
  price control and inflation, 308
  as rationing mechanism, 60–62
  short-run supply, 50–53
  velocity of money and, 235–238
Price formation
  as measure of consumers' willingness, 45
  measuring consumer demand, 45–46
  measuring supply, 47
Price index
  consumer price index, 79–81
  GDP deflator, 80, 82
Price level, 80
  aggregate demand, 83, 85
  aggregate supply, 83–84
  full employment and, 176–177
  macroequilibrium, 89–90
*Principles of Economics* (Marshall), 136, 147
*Principles of Political Economy* (Malthus), 198
Production
  factors of, 25–26
  interaction between consumers and producers, 148
Production possibilities
  defined, 27
  economic efficiency, 36
  innovation and, 33–34
  labor specialization and, 36–39
  law of increasing costs, 28–31
  military spending, 30, 39
  opportunity cost, 27–28
  poverty, 32–33
  underemployed resources, 34–36
  universality of, 39
  wealth, 32
Progressive income tax, 349
Property tax, 350–351
Prosperity
  in business cycle, 76
  defined, 76
Public assistance
  government spending on, 335–337
  Personal Responsibility and Work Opportunity Reconciliation Act, 335–337
Public debt
  Budget Deficit Reduction Act, 364
  Clinton era, 364
  crowding out, 361–362
  defined, 356
  effect on future generations, 358–363
  as external debt, 362–363
  Gramm-Rudman-Hollings Act, 364
  inflation, 361
  overconsumption, 361
  ownership of U.S. debt in 2000, 356
  problems from, 361–363
  size of, in 1970–2000, 355
  tax reforms of 1981 and 1986, 363
  tracking, 356–358
Public good
  defined, 328
  government spending, 328–329

## Q

Quantity theory of money, 232–238
  classical economic view of, 235–237
  equation of exchange, 234–238
  Keynesian view of, 237–238
  monetarism view of, 237
  velocity of money, 232–235
Quotas, 387–388
  import controls, 409

## R

Rational expectations economics, 311–316
  countercyclical policy, 313–316
  non-accelerating inflation rate of unemployment, 315–316
  unemployment, 311–315
Rationing, price as rationing mechanism, 60–62
Reagan, Ronald, 272, 299, 363
Reaganomics, 316
Real business cycle theory, 212–213
Real GDP, 79, 80, 82, 86–87
  average annual percentage change in, 209
  changes in money supply and changes to, 278–279
  macroequilibrium, 89–90
  money's affect on, 239–240
  in U.S. during 1900–2000, 197
Recession
  automatic stabilizers, 321–322
  in business cycle, 76–77
  cyclical unemployment and, 173
  defined, 75, 76
  depth, duration and unemployment during, 90
  Fed policy and, 279, 292
  historical view of, since 1945, 90
  Keynesian economics, 305
  margin requirement, 290
  recession and economic stagnation of early 1990s, 93–94
Recessionary gap, 181–182
  balanced budget and, 186–189
  closing, 182, 184–185
  defined, 181
  government spending, 184–185
Reciprocity, 389
Recovery of business cycle, 76–77
Regressive income tax, 348
Regulation, supply-side economics, 318
Relative income hypothesis, 125–128
Renewable natural resources, 3–5
Rent, profit as income in GDP, 110
Republic of Congo, terms of trade for, 379
Reserve requirement, 279
Resources
  changes in price of, and change in supply, 58
  in circular flow of goods, services and resources, 100–101, 106–107
  government commandeering, 347
  land, 26
  natural, 3–6
  scarcity of, 6
  underemployed, 35–36
Rotterdam, Holland, 35
Rudman, Warren, 364
Russia, taxation in, 359

## S

Salaries, as income in GDP, 109
Sales tax, 351
  revenues from, 353
Samuelson, Paul, 305, 317
Sargent, Thomas, 317
Saving, 134–137
  dissaving, 134
  economic growth, 201–204
  gross national saving in U.S. in 1960–1999, 201–204
  inflation, 178
  marginal propensity to save, 134
  negative, 134
  paradox of thrift and national income equilibrium, 164, 166
  role of, in national income equilibrium, 149–155
Savings and loan associations, 231
  debacle of 1980s and 1990s, 259–260
Savings bond, 361
Say, Jean Baptiste, 183
Say's law, 183
Scalper's market, 71–72
Scarcity, 6
Schultze, Charles, 299
Schumpeter, Joseph, 210, 212
Security, national, 331–333
Seger, Martha, 288–289
Services
  in circular flow of goods, services and resources, 100–101, 106–107
  defined, 106
  government purchases, 103, 108
  gross private domestic investment, 103, 107–108
  net exports of, 103, 108
  personal consumption expenditures, 103–107
Short run
  defined, 51
  supply, 50–53
Slope of curve, 20–22
  measuring slope of a point, 23
  negative, 21
  positive, 21
Smith, Adam, 11, 36, 105, 200
Social Security, 330–331
  characteristics of, 339
  government spending on, 337–339
  in other countries, 340
  as pay-as-you-go system, 339
  return options for, 338
Social Security tax, 351–352
  revenues from, 353
Sole proprietorship. *See also* Entrepreneurs
  profit as income in GDP, 110
Solow, Robert, 305
South Africa
  human capital and, 430
  income in, 427
Space exploration, government spending on, 334
Spain, long-run growth in real GDP, 205
Specialization
  case for geographic, 373–375
  international specialization, 375–376

Spending. *See* Consumption; Government spending
Sri Lanka
   human capital and, 430
   income in, 427
Stabilization policy
   agreement on, 320
   classical economics, 301
   countercyclical policy, 301
   Keynesian economics, 305
   supply-side economics, 316–320
Stagflation, 92, 93, 305
   OPEC, 307–308
State-chartered bank, 267–268, 271
Steinbeck, John, 174
Stocks/Stock market
   crash of 1929, 289
   Fed controlling stock market margin requirements, 287–290
   leverage buyout, 93
Structural unemployment, 172–173
Substitute goods, 55
   change in demand, 55
   change in supply, 58
   number of suppliers, 58
Sudan, debt service of, 417
Sunspot theory of business cycle, 207
Supplemental Security Income program, 335
Supply
   aggregate, 83–89
   changes in and price, 57–58
   equilibrium price, 58–60
   excess, 48
   long run, 50–53
   market-day, 47, 53
   measuring, 47
   price of substitute goods and, 58
   resource price changes, 58
   Say's law, 183
   short run, 50–53
   technology changes and, 57–58
Supply curve, 47
Supply schedule, 47
Supply-side economics, 316–320
   countercyclical policy, 316–320
   government regulation, 318
   government spending, 319–320
   stabilization policy, 316–320
   taxation, 317–318
   tax reforms of 1981 and 1986, 363
Sweden
   art funding, 330
   long-run growth in real GDP, 205
   public debt in, 358
   taxation in, 350, 360
Syria
   human capital and, 430
   income in, 427

# T

Tangent, 23
   slope of, 23
Tariffs, 386–387
   customs unions, 391
   GATT (General Agreement on Tariffs and Trade), 389, 391
   import controls, 409
   North American Free Trade Agreement, 392
   reciprocity, 389
   tracking since 1860, 392–393
Taxation, 348–355
   as automatic stabilizer, 321–322
   consumption curve shifts and, 131
   corporate income tax, 349–350
   customs duty, 351
   Economic Recovery Tax Act, 363
   excise, 351
   federal, state, and local tax revenues, 353
   indirect taxes and national income, 113
   inflation, 180
   opportunity cost, 347
   poll tax, 348
   progressive income tax, 349
   property, 350–351
   proportional income tax, 348–349
   regressive income tax, 348
   sales, 351
   Social Security, 351–352
   supply-side economics, 317–318
   tax evasion, 354–355
   tax multiplier, 187
   Tax Reform Act, 363
   tax structure, 352–353
   underground economy and, 115, 116
   unit, 351
   U.S. compared to other countries, 350, 359–360
Tax multiplier, 187
Tax Reform Act, 318, 363
Technology
   indestructible nature of ideas, 34
   investment and, 138
   labor and, 200, 204
   productive power of advanced technology, 33–34
   in real business cycle theory, 212
   role in economic growth, 204
   structural unemployment, 172–173
   supply and changes in, 57–58
Temporary Assistance for Needy Families, 337
Terms of trade, 378–380
Thrift, paradox of, 164, 166
Tobin, James, 305
Trade. *See also* Free trade; International trade
   interstate, 373–375
   intrastate, 372–373
Trade Expansion Act, 389
Trade Reform Act, 389
Transactions demand for money, 238–240
Transfer payments, 114
   government spending on, 329–331, 335–337
Transitory income, 128
Transportation, government spending on, 334
Treasury bills, 280, 356
Treasury bonds, 280, 356
   savings, 361
Treasury notes, 280, 356
Treasury securities
   financing government spending through, 355–356
   open market operations, 282–284
   ownership of U.S. debt in 2000, 356
*Treatise on Money, A* (Keynes), 127
Trough of business cycle, 76–77
Tyson, Laura, 299

# U

Uganda, terms of trade for, 379, 380
Ukraine, hyperinflation in, 179
Underemployed resources, 35–36
Underemployed workers, 173–174
Underground economy, 115–116
   gross domestic product and, 115
Unemployment. *See also* Employment
   Bureau of Labor Statistics definition of, 175
   calculating rate of, 174–175
   classical economics, 300–301
   cyclical, 173
   depression of 1930s, 91–92
   discouraged workers, 173
   frictional, 172
   full employment, 176–177
   identifying, 172–174
   Keynesian economics, 302–304
   natural rate of, 175–176, 312
   neo-Keynesian economics, 305–311
   non-accelerating inflation rate of unemployment, 315–316
   Phillips curve, 305–311
   rate of, in recession, 90
   rational expectations economics, 311–315
   structural, 172–173
   underemployed workers, 173–174
Unemployment insurance
   as automatic stabilizer, 321
   government spending on, 339
Unilateral transfers, 412
Unions
   classical economics, 301
   neo-Keynesian economics, 307
   Phillips curve, 307
United Kingdom
   art funding, 330
   GDP for, 111
   government spending in, 341
   long-run growth in real GDP, 205
   NAIRU for, 319
   real GDP, 86
   tax rate, 350
United States
   art funding, 330
   balance of payments in 1999, 410
   balance of trade in 1950–2000, 411
   bank deposit insurance in, 258
   business cycle during 1860–1990, 206
   exports and imports of, 381
   government spending in, 341
   gross national saving in 1960–1999, 201–204
   Internet access in, 436
   long-run growth in real GDP, 205

United States *(continued)*
   major trading partners with, 381, 383
   money supply in, 231–232
   public debt in, 356–358
   Social Security expenditures in, 340
   in U.S. during 1900–2000, 197, 204, 206
Unit tax, 351
Unwanted inventories, 151
U-shaped curve, 22

# V

Value added, 103
Variables
   dependent, 19
   independent, 19
Velocity of money, 232–235
   historical record of, 237
Venezuela
   human capital and, 430
   income in, 427
Vietnam War, demand-pull inflation, 92–93
Volcker, Paul, 272, 273, 287

# W

Wage rate. *See also* Labor
   classical economics, 300–301
   full employment and, 176–177
   wage controls and inflation, 308
War-induced cycle theory of business cycle, 208–209
Wealth
   production possibility, 32
   real wealth effect and aggregate demand, 85
*Wealth of Nations, The* (Smith), 11, 36, 105, 200
Weder, Beatrice, 443
Weidenbaum, Murray, 299
Welfare
   government spending on, 335–337
   Personal Responsibility and Work Opportunity Reconciliation Act, 335–337
   welfare reform, 335–337
Wiegand, Bruce, 116
Woodward, Bob, 291

World War I, economic upturn and, 209
World War II
   aggregate demand and supply, 91–92
   economic upturn and, 209
   production possibility and, 30
   rebuilding after, 34, 35

# Y

Yellen, Janet, 299
Yugoslavia, hyperinflation in, 179

# Z

Zambia, terms of trade for, 379
Zimbabwe
   debt service of, 417
   human capital and, 430
   income in, 427
   Internet access in, 436